ACCLAIM FOR THE
HOLLANDER TRANSLATION OF
INFERNO

"A distinguished act of poetry and scholarship in one and the same breath, the Hollander Dante, among the strong translations of the poet, deserves to take its own honored place."

—Robert Fagles, translator of *The Iliad* and *The Odyssey*

"The new *Inferno*, as this is likely to be called, is both majestic and magisterial and the product of a lifelong devotion to Dante's poetry and to the staggering body of Dante scholarship. The Hollanders capture each and every accent in Dante, from the soft-spoken, effusive stilnovist poet, to the wrathful Florentine exile, to the disillusioned man who would become what many, including T. S. Eliot, consider the best poet who ever lived. The Hollanders' adaptation is not only an intelligent reader's Dante, but it is meant to enlighten and to move and ultimately to give us a Dante so versatile that he could at once soar to the hereafter and remain unflinchingly earthbound."

—André Aciman, author of *Out of Egypt: A Memoir*

"The present volume makes the poem accessible to the lay reader and appealing to the specialist: the translation is both faithful to the original and highly readable; the introduction and notes are dense without being overly scholarly; the bibliography consists predominantly of studies in English, encouraging further investigation by English-language readers. . . . A highly worthy new *Inferno* that is the mature fruit of years of scholarly, pedagogical, and creative work."

—*Choice*

ROBERT HOLLANDER has taught *The Divine Comedy* to Princeton stu-
dents for forty years. He is the author of a dozen books and some six dozen
articles on Dante, Boccaccio, and other writers. A member of Prince-
ton's Department of French and Italian and the former chairman of its
Department of Comparative Literature, he has received many awards,
including the Gold Medal of the city of Florence in recognition of his
Dante scholarship.

JEAN HOLLANDER, his wife, is a poet, teacher, and director of the Writers'
Conference at the College of New Jersey. They are at work translating
Dante's *Purgatorio* and *Paradiso*, and Doubleday will publish the first of these
in 2002.

INFERNO

Dante Alighieri
INFERNO

TRANSLATED BY ROBERT & JEAN HOLLANDER

INTRODUCTION & NOTES BY ROBERT HOLLANDER

ANCHOR BOOKS
A Division of Random House, Inc.
New York

FIRST ANCHOR BOOKS EDITION, JANUARY 2002

The Library of Congress has cataloged the Doubleday edition as follows:
Dante Aligheri, 1265–1321
[Inferno. English]
The Inferno / Dante Aligheri; translated by Robert Hollander and Jean
Hollander; introduction & notes by Robert Hollander.
p.   cm.
ISBN 0-385-49697-4
Includes bibliographical references and index.
I. Hollander, Robert. II. Hollander, Jean. III. Title.
PQ4315.2 .H65 2000
851'.1—dc21   00-034531

Anchor ISBN: 0-385-49698-2

Author photograph of Robert Hollander by Pryde Brown
Book design by Pei Loi Koay
Map design by Jeffrey L. Ward

www.anchorbooks.com

Printed in the United States of America

10   9   8

for

Francesco,

Maria Grazia,

Stefano,

Simonetta,

Enrico,

& Tommaso

"Reader, this is an honest book." Montaigne says this of his *Essays*. We would like to say the same of this translation. We have tried to bring Dante into our English without being led into the temptation of making the translation sound better than the original allows. The result may be judged by all who know him in his own idiom. This is not Dante, but an approximation of what he might authorize had he been looking over our shoulders, listening to our at times ferocious arguments. We could go on improving this effort as long as we live. We hope that as much as we have accomplished will find an understanding ear and heart among those who know the real thing. Every translation begins and ends in failure. To the degree that we have been able to preserve some of the beauty and power of the original, we have failed the less.

The accuracy of the translation from the Italian text established by Giorgio Petrocchi (1966–67) has been primarily my responsibility, its sound as English verse primarily that of the poet Jean Hollander, my wife and collaborator. As will be clear from various notes in the text, I am not always in accord with Petrocchi's readings; however, I thought it imperative to use as the base of this entire project the current standard Italian text of the work, indicating my occasional desire to diverge from it only in its margins. My original intention was to reproduce the John D. Sinclair translation (1939) of *Inferno*, cleaning up its just barely post-Victorian "thee"s and "thou"s and other such, to a twenty-first-century ear, outdated usages. However, (a) differences between the Italian in the Società Dantesca Italiana (1921) edition, from which Sinclair translated, and Petrocchi's edition, (b) later "corrections" of Sinclair's version by a later translator, Charles

Singleton, (c) further study of Dante's lines themselves, (d) a sense of ways in which a prose translation eventually fails to be "sayable"—all of these considerations led us to attempt a new verse translation of the first *cantica*, despite our original debt to Sinclair.

Those who come to our text familiar with the Singleton translation (1970) will perhaps think that it is *its* resonance that they occasionally hear; this is because a tremendous amount of Singleton's translation conforms word-for-word to Sinclair's, as anyone may see simply by opening the two volumes side by side. Thus, having decided to begin with Sinclair and to modify him, we found that Singleton had apparently done essentially the same thing. To his credit, his changes are usually for the better; to his blame is his failure to acknowledge the frequency of his exact coincidence with Sinclair. And thus, on his own advice, we have considered it "a mistake . . . not to let the efforts of one's predecessors contribute to one's own" (p. 372), and have on occasion included his divergences from Sinclair when we found them just. However, let there be no mistake: the reason our translation seems to reflect Singleton's, to the extent that it does, is that ours, on occasion, and Singleton's, almost always, are both deeply indebted to Sinclair.

In February 1997, when my wife and I decided to commit ourselves to this effort, we were able to consult the draft of a verse translation of *Inferno* composed by Patrick Creagh and me (begun in 1984 and abandoned in 1988, with some 80 percent of the work Englished). Some of its phrases have found their way to our text, and we owe a considerable debt to Patrick Creagh (and to my earlier self), which we are glad to acknowledge. We also owe a debt to the prose paraphrases of difficult Italian passages found in the still helpful English commentary by the Rev. Dr. H. F. Tozer (1901); and to glosses gleaned from various Italian commentaries (most particularly, in the early cantos, those of Francesco Mazzoni [1965–85], but also to the interpretive paraphrases found in the Bosco/Reggio commentary [1979]). We decided early on that we would not consult contemporary verse translations until after we had finished our work, so as to keep other voices out of our ears.

Several friends and colleagues have helped us in our task. Lauren Scancarelli Seem, administrative coordinator of the Princeton Dante Project, was our first reader, making a number of suggestions for changes. Margherita Frankel, a veteran Dantist as well as a good friend, gave us a close reading and made many valuable criticisms to which we have attended. The poet Frederick Tibbetts lent us his exacting ear and made dozens of helpful suggestions. Lino Pertile, the Dante scholar at Harvard University, also combed through our text and made a number of helpful suggestions. The paperback edition benefitted from the eagle eye of Peter D'Epiro, who caught a number of slips that have been corrected in this printing. Our greatest debt is to Robert Fagles, who went through this translation verse by verse and made many hundreds of comments in our margins. To have had such attentive advice from the most favored translator of Homer of our day has been our extraordinary fortune and pleasure.

Our goal has been to offer a clear translation, even of unclear passages. We have also tried to be as compact as possible—not an easy task, either. It is our hope that the reader will find this translation a helpful bridge to the untranslatable magnificence of Dante's poem.

February 1997 (Florence)–February 1998 (Tortola)

1. Dante's works:

Conv.	*Convivio*
Dve	*De vulgari eloquentia*
Egl.	*Egloghe*
Epist.	*Epistole*
Inf.	*Inferno*
Mon.	*Monarchia*
Par.	*Paradiso*
Purg.	*Purgatorio*
Quest.	*Questio de aqua et terra*
Rime	*Rime*
Rime dub.	*Rime dubbie*
VN	*Vita nuova*

Detto	*Il Detto d'Amore* ("attributable to Dante")
Fiore	*Il Fiore* ("attributable to Dante")

2. Commentators on the *Commedia* (these texts are all either currently available or, in the case of Landino, Bennassuti, and Provenzal, should one day be available, in the database known as the Dartmouth Dante Project; dates, particularly of the early commentators, are often approximate):

Jacopo Alighieri (1322) (*Inferno* only)
L'anonimo lombardo (1322) (Latin) (*Purgatorio* only)
Graziolo de' Bambaglioli (1324) (Latin) (*Inferno* only)

Jacopo della Lana (1324)
Guido da Pisa (1327) (Latin) (*Inferno* only)
L'Ottimo (1333)
L'anonimo selmiano (1337) (*Inferno* only)
Pietro di Dante (1340) (Latin) [also *Inferno* of 2nd & 3rd redactions]
Il codice cassinese (1350?) (Latin)
Giovanni Boccaccio (1373) (*Inferno* I–XVII only)
Benvenuto da Imola (1380) (Latin)
Francesco da Buti (1385)
L'anonimo fiorentino (1400)
Giovanni da Serravalle (1416) (Latin)
Guiniforto Barzizza (1440) (*Inferno* only)
★Cristoforo Landino (1481)
Alessandro Vellutello (1544)
Bernardino Daniello (1568)
Lodovico Castelvetro (1570) (*Inferno* I–XXIX only)
Pompeo Venturi (1732)
Baldassare Lombardi (1791)
Luigi Portirelli (1804)
Paolo Costa (1819)
Gabriele Rossetti (1826–40) (*Inferno* & *Purgatorio* only)
Niccolò Tommaseo (1837)
Raffaello Andreoli (1856)
★Luigi Bennassuti (1864)
Henry W. Longfellow (1867) (English)
Gregorio Di Siena (1867) (*Inferno* only)
Brunone Bianchi (1868)
G. A. Scartazzini (1874; but the 2nd ed. of 1900 is used)
Giuseppe Campi (1888)
Gioachino Berthier (1892)
Giacomo Poletto (1894)
H. Oelsner (1899) (English)
H. F. Tozer (1901) (English)
John Ruskin (1903) (English; not in fact a "commentary")
John S. Carroll (1904) (English)
Francesco Torraca (1905)
C. H. Grandgent (1909) (English)
Enrico Mestica (1921)
Casini-Barbi (1921)
Carlo Steiner (1921)

Isidoro Del Lungo (1926)
Scartazzini-Vandelli (1929)
Carlo Grabher (1934)
Ernesto Trucchi (1936)
★Dino Provenzal (1938)
Luigi Pietrobono (1946)
Attilio Momigliano (1946)
Manfredi Porena (1946)
Natalino Sapegno (1955)
Daniele Mattalia (1960)
Siro A. Chimenz (1962)
Giovanni Fallani (1965)
Giorgio Padoan (1967) (*Inferno* I–VIII only)
Giuseppe Giacalone (1968)
Charles Singleton (1970) (English)
Bosco-Reggio (1979)
Pasquini-Quaglio (1982)

★Not yet available

NB: All references to other works (e.g., Mazz.1967.1) are keyed to the List of Works Cited at the back of this volume, with the exception of references to commentaries contained in the Dartmouth Dante Project database, accessible online (telnet library.dartmouth.edu; at the prompt type: connect dante). Informational notes derived from Paget Toynbee's *Concise Dante Dictionary of Proper Names and Notable Matters in the Works of Dante* (Oxford: Clarendon, 1914) are followed by the siglum **(T)**. References to the *Enciclopedia dantesca*, 6 vols. (Rome: Istituto della Enciclopedia Italiana, 1970–78) are indicated by the abbreviation *ED*. Commentaries by Robert Hollander are (at times) shorter versions of materials found in the Princeton Dante Project, a multimedia edition of the *Commedia* currently including most materials relevant to *Inferno* (the last two *cantiche* are under development). Subscription (without charge to the user) is possible at www.princeton.edu/dante.

MAP OF DANTE'S HELL

The Ten Malebolge

The Frozen Floor of Hell

River Cocytus

River Phlegethon

Violence

Heresy

GATE OF DIS

River Styx

Anger & Sullenness

Avarice & Prodigality

Gluttony

Lust

Limbo

© 2000 Jeffrey L. Ward

River Acheron

The Dark Wood

SIN	CANTO	RIVERS	Monsters
	I–II	Prologue: somewhere in Italy (?)	
	III	ACHERON (marks the confine of the netherworld)	
	III	**Circle 0:** THE NEUTRALS	*Charon*
	IV	**Circle 1:** LIMBO	
I		(virtuous heathens & unbaptized babes)	
N	V	**Circle 2:** LUST	*Minos*
C			
O	VI	**Circle 3:** GLUTTONY	*Cerberus*
N			
T	VII	**Circle 4:** AVARICE & PRODIGALITY	*Plutus*
I			
N	VIII	STYX (muddy river of fleshly sins)	
E	VIII	**Circle 5:** ANGER & SULLENNESS	*Phlegyas*
N			
C	IX	Gate of Dis (lower Hell)	*Furies, Medusa*
E			
	X–XI	**Circle 6:** HERESY	
V		**Circle 7:** VIOLENCE	
I	XII	PHLEGETHON (river of blood)	
O	XII	[i] against others	*Minotaur*
L	XIII	[ii] against self	*Harpies*
E	XIV	[iii] against God: 1. blasphemy	
N	XV–XVI	2. homosexuality	
C	XVII	3. usury	
E	XVII	Descent to Malebolge	*Geryon*
S		**Circle 8:** THE TEN MALEBOLGE	
I	XVIII	[i] panders and seducers	*horned demons*
M	XVIII	[ii] flatterers	
P	XIX	[iii] simoniacs	
L	XX	[iv] diviners	
E	XXI–XXII	[v] barrators	*winged demons*
F	XXIII	[vi] hypocrites	
R	XXIV–XXV	[vii] thieves	*serpents & Cacus*
A	XXVI–XXVII	[viii] false counsellors	
U	XVIII	[ix] schismatics	*devil with a sword*
D	XXIX–XXX	[x] counterfeiters	
T		**Circle 9:** THE FROZEN FLOOR OF HELL	
R	XXXI	COCYTUS (river of ice)	
E	XXXI	Descent to Cocytus	*giants*
A	XXXII	[i] Caïna (against relatives)	
C	XXXII	[ii] Antenora (against party or homeland)	
H	XXXIII	[iii] Ptolomea (against guests)	
E	XXXIV	[iv] Judecca (against rightful lords)	
R	XXXIV		*Satan*
Y			

What is a "great book"? It is probably impossible to define the concept analytically to anyone's satisfaction, but it may be described pragmatically: a work that is loved, over time, by millions of more-or-less ordinary readers *and* by thousands of scholars. Dante, by the time he was writing the fourth canto of *Inferno*, had already decided he was writing such a book. He sets his name down as one of the six all-time great writers: only Homer, Virgil, Ovid, Horace, and Lucan have preceded him (he will later add Statius). Unspeakably self-assured as this poet may seem, many today would now shorten that list, perhaps even to two: Homer and Dante. His self-confidence may seem overweening, but he was even more of a prophet than he realized.

In about 1306, having entered his forties, he set about work on his *Comedy*. By 1295 he had written a "little book" (the nomenclature is his own), *The New Life,* thirty-one of his lyric poems surrounded by a governing prose commentary that almost explains the eventual meaning of his love for a young woman of Florence named Beatrice, who had died in 1290 at the age of twenty-five. We know nothing absolutely certain about her, whether she was an actual woman (if so, probably a member of the Portinari family, and then almost certainly married) or whether she is a fictitious lady of the sort that love-poets invented in order to have a subject to write about. The text, on the other hand, makes it clear that we are to treat her as historical, and also suggests that we are to understand that she means more than she seems, for she is ineluctably joined with the Trinity, and in particular with the life of Christ. Dante seems completely aware of the radical newness of a lady loaded with such lofty theological meaning in the tradition of vernacular poetry of love. That is, he knows that what he is proposing is out of bounds. And this is why he is usually so very diffident in his remarks, forcing us to draw some rather disquieting conclusions about the nature of the very special kind of love that eventually informs his praise of Beatrice.

Before he began work on his "theological epic," the *Comedy*, he had also written major parts of two other works, one a presentation of his ideas about eloquence in the vernacular, *De vulgari eloquentia,* the second, *Convivio,* a lengthy study of moral philosophy (in the form of commentary to his own odes), of which he had completed four of the projected fifteen "treatises." He had been actively involved in the often bitterly contested political life of Florence, at that time one of the most important European cities, swollen with new wealth and consequent political power. At a time when that city had only six of them, he served the customary two-month term as one of its priors, the highest political office in the city. By 1302, having inherited the wrong political identity, he lost practically everything when his party, the White Guelph faction, was outfoxed by the Black Guelphs, supported by the allied forces of Pope Boniface VIII and the French king. He was exiled in 1302 and never returned home again. He then lived a mainly itinerant life in northern Italy, with two longish stays in Verona and a final one in Ravenna, where he died of malarial fever in September 1321 at the age of fifty-six.

The political situation of northern Italy during his lifetime was distinguished by factionalism and chaos. The emperors who were supposed to govern all of Europe had, for centuries, mainly avoided their Italian responsibilities. The last of them to rule in Italy was Frederick II (we hear of him in *Inferno* X and XIII), and he, while one of the greatest figures in Europe, was not a leader to Dante's liking. Dead in 1250, Frederick was the last emperor to govern from Italy. Dante hoped for an imperial restoration of the proper kind, and, to everyone's amazement, including his own, had his hopes rewarded when the newly crowned Henry VII, a compromise candidate from Luxembourg, allowed to become emperor primarily because of the machinations of Pope Clement V, descended into the peninsula to rule Europe from Italy in 1310. When his military expedition eventually failed because of his death in 1313, Dante's imperial hopes were dealt a terrible blow, but not finally dashed. To the end of his days (and in the text of *Paradiso* XXVII and XXX) he insisted on believing that a new "Augustus" would fulfill God's design for Italy and Europe.

On the local level, late-thirteenth-century northern Italy (Milano, to the north, and Rome, to the south, are barely on Dante's personal political map; rather we hear, in addition to Florence, of such cities as Genoa, Pisa, Pistoia, Siena, etc.) was in constant turmoil. The two main "parties" were the Guelphs (those essentially allied with the papacy) and the Ghibellines (aligned with the emperor—when there was one to be aligned with—or at least with imperial hopes). But most politics, as they are in our own time, were local. And there, labels did not count so much as family. In Florence the Ghibellines had been defeated and banished in 1266, a year after Dante's birth, leaving the city entirely Guelph. But that did not betoken an era of unity. The Guelphs themselves were already divided (as they were in many northern cities) in two factions, the "Blacks," led by the Donati family (into a less powerful branch of which Dante married), and the "Whites," led by the Cerchi. (It is probably correct to say that the Whites were more devoted to a republican notion of governance, while the Blacks were more authoritarian.) The first impetus toward political division had occurred early in the century, when a young man, member of a Ghibelline family, broke off his engagement and married a Guelph Donati (in Pistoia, not entirely dissimilarly, the roots of division supposedly began in a snowball fight). A member of a White Guelph family, and having married into the most important Black family, Dante was therefore tied to Guelph interests. How then, do we explain his patent allegiance, in the *Comedy*, to the imperial cause? In 1306 or so he seems to have, rereading the Latin classics, reformulated his own political vision (as is first evident in the fourth and fifth chapters of the last treatise of the *Convivio*, before which there is not a clear imperialist sentiment to be found in his writing). And so, nominally a Guelph, Dante was far more in accord with Ghibelline ideas, except that, in practice, he found Ghibellines lacking in the religious vision that he personally saw as the foundation of any imperialist program. Politics are everywhere in the poem, which is far from being the purely religious text that some of its readers take it for.

In his exile, the *Commedia* (first called the *Divina Commedia* only in 1555 by a Venetian publisher) became his obsession. For about fifteen years, with few exceptions (a notable one being his treatise,

Monarchia, concerning the divine prerogatives of the empire, perhaps composed in 1317), the poem absorbed almost all of his time and energy. Its "motivating idea" is a simple one, outrageously so. In the Easter period of 1300 a thirty-five-year-old Florentine, struggling with failure and apparently spiritual death, is rescued by the shade of the Roman poet Virgil. He, won to the project by the living soul of Beatrice, who descends to hell from her seat in heaven in order to enlist his aid, agrees to lead Dante on a journey through hell and purgatory. Beatrice herself will again descend from heaven to take Dante the rest of the way, through the nine heavenly spheres and into paradise, where angels and souls in bliss gaze, in endless rapture, on God. The entire journey takes nearly precisely one week, Thursday evening to Thursday evening. It begins in fear and trembling on this earth and ends with a joyous vision of the trinitarian God. It is perhaps difficult to imagine how even a Dante could have managed to build so magnificent an edifice out of so improbable a literary idea. The result was a book that began to be talked about, known from parts that seem to have circulated before the whole, even before it was finished (first citations begin to be noted around 1315). By the time he had completed it, shortly before his death, people were eagerly awaiting the publication of *Paradiso*. And within months of his death (or even before) commentaries upon it began to be produced. It was, in short, an instant "great book," probably the first of its kind since the last century of the pagan era, when Romans (no less of them than Augustus himself) awaited eagerly the finished text of Virgil's *Aeneid*.

One of the most striking things about the *Comedy* is the enormous apparatus that has attached itself to it. No secular work in the western tradition has so developed a heritage of line-by-line commentary, one that began in Latin and Italian and that has now entered any number of languages, European, Slavic, and Asian. It is clear that Dante's work convinced the scholars of his time that this was a poem worthy of the most serious attention, both as a purveyor of the most important ideas of Christianity (e.g., sin, grace, redemption, transcendence) and as a response to the greatest of the Latin poets (Virgil foremost, but also Ovid, Statius, Lucan, and others) and philosophers (Aristotle [in his Arabic/Latin form] and Cicero, primarily). Knowledge of Greek had essentially disappeared from the time of the establishment of Latin Christianity as the dominant religion and culture of the West in the fifth and sixth centuries. The study of the language would only gradually begin again some fifty years after Dante's death. And thus while Dante knows about Greek philosophy, all he has experienced of it comes from the works (most of Aristotle) and bits and pieces (only one work of Plato's, the *Timaeus*, and excerpts of some of the pre-Socratics) that had been translated into Latin. Strangely, for a modern reader, his first commentators pay little or no attention to his close and fairly extensive dealings with the poems of his vernacular predecessors and co-practitioners (Guido Guinizzelli, Arnaut Daniel, Brunetto Latini, Guido Cavalcanti, Cino da Pistoia, and others). Perhaps the most impressive aspect of these commentaries (and we are speaking of line-by-line analyses, on the model of commentary to the Bible or to a handful of especially respected classical authors, a form essentially denied to modern writers before 1300) is the vast number of them. From the first twenty years after Dante's death at least ten have survived; by our own time there are hundreds.

Along with conquering the allegiance of scholars, Dante won the hearts of less-erudite Italians (or, at first, Tuscans) who found in his vast poem the first use of Italian as a literary language in an indisputably major work. Italian poetry, beginning at the time of St. Francis in the early twelfth century, had performed wonders, but it had rarely found a subject that seemed serious enough. Here was a poem that tackled everything: theology, religion, philosophy, politics, the sciences of heaven (astronomy/astrology) and of earth (biology, geology), and, perhaps most of all, the study of human behavior. And it did all these things in a language that everyone could understand, or at least thought he could. It is probably not true to suggest that Dante "invented modern Italian." What he did do was to deploy Italian as a literary language on a major scale, incorporating the "serious" subjects that had hitherto been reserved to Latin. If the Italian language had been waiting for a voice, Dante gave it that voice. Before him it did not exist in a global form, a complete language fit for all subjects; after him it did. It is probably not because of him that Italian has changed no more between his time and today than English has since Shakespeare's day. It is, nonetheless, a continuing surprise and reward for contemporary Italians to have so ancient and yet so approachable a father, speaking, at least most of the time, words that they themselves use (and sometimes that he had invented).

Is Dante an "easy" poet? That depends on what passages we happen to be reading. He can be as simple and straightforward as one's country neighbor, or as convoluted as the most arcane professor. (Boccaccio, one of his greatest advocates, also shows both proclivities in the prose of the *Decameron*.) Yet he has always found a welcome from the least schooled of readers, and even from those who could not read at all, but learned the poem by rote. A living Tuscan farmer/poet, Mauro Punzecchi, years ago memorized the poem while he worked his fields and is today able to recite all of it. Who does not envy him his gift?

Each of us reads his own *Commedia*, which makes perfect sense, most of the time. It is only when we try to explain "our" poem to someone else that the trouble starts.

The commentary that accompanies this new translation is, like every one that has preceded it, except the first few, indebted to earlier discussions of this text. And what of that text, as Dante left it? No one has ever seen his autograph version. As a result, the manuscript tradition of the poem is vast and complicated. Nonetheless, and despite all the difficulties presented by particular textual problems, the result of variant readings in various manuscripts, it must be acknowledged that in the *Comedy* we have a remarkably stable text, given the facts that we do not possess an autograph and that the condition of the manuscripts is so unyieldingly problematic. However, we do know that Dante left us precisely 14,233 verses arranged in one hundred cantos, all of which contained precisely the number of verses we find in them today in every modern edition. And that is no small thing.

And so each reader comes to a text that offers some problems of the textual variety; these pale beside problems of interpretation. What we can all agree on is that the work is a wonder to behold. Reading Dante is like listening to Bach. It is unimaginable to think that a human being, so many years ago (or indeed ever), could make such superhuman magic. Yet there it is, beckoning, but also refusing to yield some of its secrets.

When I considered how I might present this poem in a brief introduction, after years of thinking about it and teaching it and writing about it, I thought of what I myself missed when I started reading Dante. The first was a sense of Dante's intellectual biography; the second was a set of answers to a series of questions: how does allegory work (i.e., how does this poem "mean")? What does Virgil represent and why is he the first guide in the poem? How am I supposed to react to the sinners of *Inferno*, especially those that seem so sympathetic to me? The first subject is too vast for treatment here. My own attempt at an intellectual biography of the poet is available in Italian (*Dante Alighieri,* Rome, Editalia, 2000; an English version was published by Yale University Press in 2001). The three questions I have tried to answer, both in the "Lectures" found currently in the Princeton Dante Project, and, in shorter form, in an essay I wrote a year ago ("Dante: A Party of One," *First Things* 92 [April 1999]: 30–35; the essay on Virgil also has some points in common with my article, "Virgil," in the *Dante Encyclopedia,* ed. Richard Lansing, New York, Garland, 2000). What follows is another attempt to deal with three important matters facing any first-time reader of the poem, or any reader at all.

(1) *Allegory.*
When I was young I was taught that Dante's poem was the very essence of allegorical writing. What exactly is allegory? Simply put, it is the interpretive strategy of understanding one thing as meaning not itself but something other. A lady, blindfolded, holding a pair of scales in one hand, is not to be understood as a being with a particular history, but as a timeless entity, an abstraction: justice. If we understand just this much, we are prepared to comprehend how we might read—and how many of his first readers did understand—Dante's poem as an "allegory." Virgil is not the Roman poet so much as he is human reason unenlightened by faith; when he acts or speaks in the poem he does so without the historical context supplied by his life or works. And what of the second guide in the poem, Beatrice? She, too, is removed from her historical role in Dante's life, and is treated as an abstraction, in her case the truths discovered through faith, or perhaps revelation, or theology. And what of the protagonist, Dante himself? That he has a very personal history, of which we hear a good deal, matters not. He is a sort of "Everyman," and represents the ordinarily appetitive human soul. Please let me explain that I myself think very little of such formulations, but they are found in almost all the early commentators. In a term derived from Cicero, these interpreters thought of allegory as a "continuous metaphor." The most significant actions performed in the poem, they thought, could best be understood as part of this single, developing metaphor, in which the flawed human soul called "Dante" is gradually educated, first by reason (referred to as "Virgil"), and then by theological certainty (code name "Beatrice").

Since something like this does seem to occur in the course of the poem, we can sense why the formulation has its appeal. The problem is that it shortchanges the entire historical referentiality of the poem. Dante's life disappears as a subject worthy of attention; Virgil's texts need not be read or understood as ways to find out what the poem means when it refers to them; Beatrice's earthly existence as a young woman becomes utterly superfluous, as does her "relationship" (a curiously and precisely wrong word, given its contemporary usage) with Dante. Fourteen centuries ago Isidore of Seville defined allegory as "otherspeech," in which a speaker or writer said one thing but meant something else by it. Without exploring the limitations that he himself imposed upon that formula, we can merely note that it is frequently used in modern days to explain allegory simply and quickly. If I say "Beatrice" I do not mean her, but what she means. We are back to the lady holding the scales. To use a medieval example, St. Thomas explains (*Summa* I.i.9) that when the Bible refers to the arm of God (Isaiah 51:9) it does not mean that God has an arm, but that He has operative power. That is, we can discard the literal for its significance, or, in more modern terms, the signifier for the signified. Does this way of reading Dante utterly denature the text we have before us? Perhaps not utterly, but enough so that we should avoid it as much as we can.

The matter gets more interesting and more complicated because Dante himself wrote about the question of allegory. In his *Convivio* he distinguishes between allegory as it is understood and practiced by poets (along the lines we have been discussing) and as it is used by theologians in order to understand certain passages in the Bible (a very different procedure that we will examine in a moment). And in *Convivio* (II.i) he says the "correct" thing: it is his intention, in the explication of his odes, to follow the allegorical procedures of the poets ("since it is my intention here to follow the method of the poets, I shall take the allegorical sense according to the usage of the poets"). There are those who put this remark to the service of the claim that the "allegory of the theologians" thus has nothing to do with Dante's procedures in the *Comedy*, either. However, that is exactly what he claims in the letter he wrote to his patron, Cangrande della Scala of Verona. The authenticity of his *Epistle to Cangrande*, written sometime after Dante had begun writing the *Paradiso*, and thus probably no earlier than 1316, is one of the most debated of Dantean questions. It is difficult for this writer to be fair to the negative argument, which is so obviously based in a desire to cancel what the epistle says. Whether or not Dante wrote it (and current scholarly opinion is, once again, decidedly in favor), this remarkable document puts forward the disturbing (to use a mild word) idea that Dante's poem was written with the same keys to meaning as was the Bible. No one had ever said as much about his own work before, and it must be made clear that it is anathema to any sensible person of Dante's (or any) time. If this were the only occasion on which this most venturesome of writers had said something outrageous, one might want to pay more heed to those who try to remove the text from his canon on the ground that he had no business making such a claim.

The principal tenet of theological allegory is that it holds certain (but not all) historical events in the Bible as a privileged and limited class of texts. Some historical passages in the Bible possessed four senses. The four senses of the Bible are generally put forth, and especially in the wake of Thomas Aquinas (*Summa theologiae* I.i.10), as follows: (1) historical/literal, (2) allegorical, (3) moral or tropological, (4) anagogical. It is helpful to understand that these senses unfurl in a historical continuum. For instance, the *historical* Moses, leading the Israelites out of captivity, gains his *allegorical* meaning in Christ, leading humankind out of bondage to the freedom of salvation. His *moral* (or *tropological*—these words are used synonymously) sense is present now—whenever "now" occurs—in the soul of the believer who chooses to make his or her "exodus" from sin; while the *anagogical* sense is found only after the end of time, when those who are saved are understood as having arrived in the New Jerusalem, eternal joy in heaven. To offer a second example, one favored by Dante's early commentators: Jerusalem was the *historical* city of Old Testament time; it points to the *allegorical* Jerusalem in which Jesus was crucified; it is the *moral* or *tropological* "city" (whether within a single believer or as the entity formed by the Church Militant now) at any present moment; it is, *anagogically,* the New Jerusalem, which will exist only at the end of time. As opposed to the literal sense of poet's allegory, the literal sense of theological allegory is historically true, found only in events narrated in the Bible (e.g., the fall of Adam and Eve, Moses leading the Israelites in the Exodus, the birth of Jesus, the Crucifixion). According to the *Epistle to Cangrande* and, more importantly, as found in the treatment of subjects in his poem itself (most of which was written before he wrote the epistle, it is important to remember), Dante has adapted the techniques of theological allegory to the making of his poem. Characters and events in it are portrayed in a historical mode and as part of a historical continuum. Adam, Moses, Icarus, Aeneas, Paul, Augustus, Virgil, and Dante are all portrayed as having said things or accomplished deeds that are seen in a historical and meaningful pattern that gives shape to this poem. Their actual historical status does not matter. Dante surely did not believe that Icarus had enjoyed a life on earth beyond that conferred by poets and mythographers. But he treats him, in *Inferno* XVII, as a possible precursor to himself, should Dante, a latter-day flyer through space, have had a bad end and fallen from the back of Geryon.

If we have been able to rid ourselves of the interpretive problems engendered by the "allegory of the poets," here we have a still larger problem. How can Dante have written the *Comedy* in the same way that God wrote the Bible through his inspired human agents? Obviously he could not have. Then why does he make so outrageous a claim? Because what he is most concerned with is establishing the "right" of poetry to truth. This is a complex argument, and needs to be undertaken with a sense of the standing of poetry in a theological age. Let us say that it was not propitious. St. Thomas Aquinas had been clear about the issue. Poetry was the least of the human sciences, was basically devoid of cognitive value, and its practitioners were liars. In an intellectual climate of that kind, Dante was forced into making a choice. Either he did what all others who defended poetry had done (and as he himself had done in *Convivio*), admit that poets are literally liars who nonetheless tell moral and philosophical truths through (poets') allegory, or he had to find a new answer to the attacks on poetry by friars like Thomas. Typically, he went his own way. If religious detractors of poetry say it lacks truth, he will give them truth. The *Comedy* is presented, from end to end (no reader can possibly miss this fact), as a record of an actual experience. Let us be honest with one another. You do not believe, and I do not believe, that Dante took a seven-day trip to the otherworld. But we can agree that his claims for total veracity are in the poem. Why? Because Dante took Thomas seriously. It is a wonderful game that he plays, daring and at times very funny, and surely he enjoyed playing it. Let me offer a single example, drawn from a pretty "serious" setting, the Earthly Paradise. Describing the six wings adorning each of the four biblical beasts that represent the authors of the Gospels in *Purgatorio* XXIX, Dante assures us that their wings were six in number (Ezechiel's cherubic creatures had only four), that is, as many as are found in John's description of the same cherubs (Revelation 4:8). The text puts this in an arresting way: "John sides with me, departing from him [Ezechiel]." No one but Dante would have said this in this way. "Here I follow John" would have been the proper way for a poet to guarantee the truthfulness of his narrative. Not for Dante. Since the pretext of the poem is that he indeed saw all that he recounts as having seen, his own experience, in completely Thomistic spirit, comes first—he knows this by his senses. And so John is *his* witness, and not he John's.

The whole question of exactly how and how much the "allegory of the theologians" permeates the *Comedy* is not to be rehashed here. It is the subject of a number of books, including two by this writer. It is important to grasp that, by breaking out of the lockstep of other poets, who give us narratives that are utterly and only fabulous, i.e., patently untrue in their literal sense, Dante wanted to take poetry somewhere new. The greatest French medieval poem, the *Romance of the Rose*, is built around the presentation of a series of abstractions speaking to one another in a garden. Marianne Moore, borrowing from another writer, once referred to poems as "imaginary gardens with real toads in them." The *Romance of the Rose* is an imaginary garden filled with imaginary toads; the *Comedy* presents itself as a real garden containing real toads. If the student (or teacher) who is wrestling with this difficult matter for the first time takes only this much away from this discussion, it should be of considerable aid. The reader is not asked by the poem to see Virgil as Reason, Beatrice as Faith (or Theology or Revelation), Francesca as Lust, Farinata as Heresy, etc. We may banish such abstractions from mind, unless Dante himself insists on them. On occasion he does—e.g., the Lady Poverty, beloved of St. Francis [*Paradiso* XI.74], who is not to be confused with any historical earthly woman, but is to be regarded as the ideal of Christ's and the Apostles' renunciation of the things of this world. It is a useful and pleasing freedom that, in consequence, we may enjoy: "The allegory of the *Comedy* is not allegory as the commentators urge me to apply it. I may read this poem as history, and understand it better." That, at least provisionally, is a good way to begin reading this poem.

(2) *Virgil.*

We should be aware that Virgil was not always Dante's guide in poetry. The *Vita nuova* is essentially without major reference to him;

De vulgari and the first three treatises of *Convivio* are similar in this respect. It is only in the fourth and last treatise of the latter that we can begin to see how the *Comedy* could make Virgil so essential a presence, for there Virgil's texts are present in important ways, as Dante begins to think of moral philosophy, Roman polity, and the jettisoning of allegorical procedures in the same breath. As the world of political reality, of human choices made in time and with real consequence, for the first time becomes a stage for Dante's thought, Virgil becomes his most important resource. As is widely understood, Dante's recovery of Virgilian text is the most noteworthy example of this phenomenon that we find in the Middle Ages. We have not yet entered the world of the Renaissance, but we are getting close.

There are few surprises awaiting the reader of the *Comedy* as unsettling as to find a pagan poet serving as guide in a Christian poem. We have perhaps gotten so used to the idea of Dante's Virgil that we forget to be surprised by it. For reasons that we find it difficult to fathom, Dante needed Virgil in order to make this poem; and he wanted him to serve as a central character in it. Lesser minds would have made a less provocative choice: an anonymous friar, a learned Christian theologian, anyone less troubling than Virgil. One tradition of Christian reception of Virgil, which is at least as old as the emperor Constantine, held that his much-discussed fourth *Eclogue* actually foretold the coming of Christ. Had Dante so believed, his choice of guide might have been less burdensome. However, we may be certain from *Monarchia* (I.xi.1) that Dante knew that Virgil's "virgin" was not the blessèd Mary but Astraea, or "justice." Any number of passages within the *Comedy* make it plain that Dante did not consider the Roman poet a Christian *avant-la-lettre*. We must conclude that he willfully chose a pagan as his guide, leaving us to fathom his reasons for doing so.

In recent years a growing number of Dante's interpreters have been arguing for the view that Dante deliberately undercuts the Latin poet, showing that both in some of his decisions as guide and in some of his own actual texts he is, from Dante's later and Christian vantage point, prone to error. If this is the case, we must not forget that Dante at the same time is intent upon glorifying Virgil. And then we might consider the proposition that Dante's love for him, genuine and heartfelt, needed to be held at arm's length and chastised, perhaps revealing to a pagan-hating reader that Dante knew full well the limitations of his Virgil. Yet he could not do without him. Virgil is the guide in Dante's poem because he served in that role in Dante's life. It was Virgil's *Aeneid* and not the works of Aristotle or of Aquinas which served as model for the poem; it was Virgil who, more than any other author, helped to make Dante Dante.

It may take readers years of rereading before they discover an extraordinary fact about Dante's Virgil. For all the excitement, even exhilaration, brought forth by Virgil's mere presence in this poem (a text that would seem to need to exclude him on theological grounds), sooner or later the fact that he is treated, on occasion, rather shabbily begins to impress us. This is so obvious, once it is pointed out, that one can begin to understand how thoroughly trained we have all been to look with pleased eyes upon a Dantean love for Virgil that heralds Renaissance humanism. To take only a few examples from the goodly supply presented in the text of *Inferno* (and *Purgatorio* will add many another), we witness Virgil embarrassed by the recalcitrant fallen angels who deny him entrance to the City of Dis (*Inf.* VIII and IX); later teased by his pupil for that momentary failure (XIV); being careful to get Dante out of observing distance lest Geryon prove as difficult as the rebel angels had been and thus embarrass him again (XVI); completely fooled by the demons of the pitch, who cause him acute discomfort over three cantos (XXI–XXIII). If such scenes make it seem more than unlikely that Virgil could possibly represent Reason (and commentators who think so grow silent at the margins of these scenes, only occasionally being honest enough even to say, "here the allegory is intermittent"), they also make us wonder about Dante's motives in treating his "master and author" so disrespectfully. It is perhaps only because he loved Virgil so deeply that he feels the need to remind himself and his reader that the pagan was, in the end, a failure, capable of causing another Roman poet, Statius, to convert to Christianity, but not of taking that step himself. All of that seems wrong to us. There is perhaps no doctrine in the entire *Comedy* so hateful to modern readers as that which makes pagans—and others outside the Christian dispensation—responsible for knowing Christ. When we consider Dante's situation, however, his motives may seem more understandable to us. Having fought off the temptation to make Virgil a Christian, Dante must now show himself and his reader that he has not gone overboard in his affections.

There is another disturbing element to Dante's Virgilianism.

Not only is Virgil the character forced to undergo some seriously humiliating moments, but his texts are also on the receiving end of Dante's playful mockery. Perhaps the most evident moment of this occurs in the twentieth canto, where Virgil is made to revise an episode in the tenth book of the *Aeneid* so that it accords better with Christian ideas about divination. It is a richly woven scene, and is extremely funny (Dante is a much funnier poet than we like to acknowledge), once we begin to understand the literary game that is being played under our eyes. And this is not the only time that Virgil's texts receive such treatment. We will even find the *Aeneid* remembered in the very last canto of *Paradiso*, with its reminder of what the Sibyl told of Christian truth to an ear that could understand her utterance—if not Virgil's.

It is simply impossible to imagine the *Comedy* without Virgil. And no one before Dante, and perhaps very few after, ever loved Virgil as he did. At the same time there is a hard-edged sense of Virgil's crucial failure as poet of Rome, the city Dante celebrates for its two suns, church and empire, but which Virgil saw only in the light of the one. For Dante, that is his great failure. As unfair as it seems to us, so much so that we frequently fail to note how often Virgil is criticized by the later poet who so loved him, it is the price that Dante forces him to pay when he enters this Christian precinct. And it may have been the price that he exerted from himself, lest he seem too available to the beautiful voices from the pagan past, seem less firm as the poet of both Romes. The Virgilian voice of the poem is the voice that brings us, more often and more touchingly than any other, the sense of tragedy that lies beneath the text of the *Comedy*.

(3) *The Moral Situation of the Reader.*
How are we meant to respond to the sinners in hell? That seems an easy question to resolve. In the *Inferno* we see the justice of God proclaimed in the inscription over the gate of hell (III.4): "Justice moved my maker on high." If God is just, it follows logically that there can be no question concerning the justness of His judgments. All who are condemned to hell are justly condemned. Thus, when we observe that the protagonist feels pity for some of the damned, we are probably meant to realize that he is at fault for doing so. Dante, not without risk, decided to entrust to us, his readers, the responsibility for seizing upon the details in the narratives told by sinners, no matter how appealing their words might be, in order to condemn them on the

evidence that issues from their own mouths. It was indeed, as we can see from the many readers who fail to take note of this evidence, a perilous decision for him to have made. Yet we are given at least two clear indicators of the attitude that should be ours. Twice in *Inferno* figures from heaven descend to hell to further God's purpose in sending Dante on his mission. Virgil relates the coming of Beatrice to Limbo. She tells him, in no uncertain terms, that she feels nothing for the tribulations of the damned and cannot be harmed in any way by them or by the destructive agents of the place that contains them (*Inf.* II.88-93). All she longs to do is to return to her seat in Paradise (*Inf.* II.71). And when the angelic intercessor arrives to open the gates of Dis, slammed shut against Virgil, we are told that this benign presence has absolutely no interest in the situation of the damned or even of the living Dante. All he desires is to complete his mission and be done with such things (*Inf.* IX.88; 100-103), reminding us of Beatrice's similar lack of interest in the damned.

The complex mechanism that Dante has developed to establish what we today, after Henry James, call "point of view" has perhaps not been examined as closely as it should be. If we consider it, we realize how "modern" it is. The essential staging of any scene in *Inferno* involving a confrontation with a sinner potentially contains some or all of the following voices: (1) the all-knowing narrator, who has been through the known universe (and beyond!) and knows and understands everything a mortal being can understand; (2) Virgil, the wise guide who understands (most of the time) all that an extremely intelligent pagan can understand (which is considerable, if at some times more limited than at others); (3) the gradually more-and-more-informed protagonist, who moves from alarming cowardice and ignorance to relatively sound moral competence and judgment before the *Inferno* ends; (4) a sinner (sometimes more than one) who may or may not be trying to tell his or her story in a distorted, self-serving way, seeking a better reputation, whether in Dante's eyes or in the view of posterity. That is a brief morphology of the possible combination of speakers in any given scene. We all should be able to agree that such an arrangement is, if nothing else, complex. If the only speaker were Dante the narrator, we would always know where he (and we) stood. When we reflect that he hardly ever intervenes with moral glosses within scenes, we learn something important about this poem: it will not do our work for us. Most of the speakers are, thus, at best usually reliable, at worst completely unreliable. The gradations of their qualifications may change with every scene. And we are left with the problem of evaluating the result. Let us examine only a single scene to see how this grid of potential understanding functions.

In one of the most celebrated passages in all of literature, Francesca da Rimini tells the protagonist her story (*Inf.* V.72–142). As is usual, the omniscient narrator tells us nothing but the facts. From him we learn that the protagonist was overcome by pity (72—is this a good or bad thing?); that the sinners look like doves (82–84—what is the "iconography" of these doves, birds of Venus or signs of the Holy Spirit [the two most usual medieval associations for these birds]?); that Francesca and Paolo come from a line of sinners that includes Dido (85—Dido has a pretty rocky medieval reputation as adulteress; does Francesca suffer from guilt by association?); that the protagonist's summoning call was full of affection and was effective (87—is this to be applauded?). Later, he will tell us that Dante was greatly stirred by Francesca's first speech (109–111—again, what moral view should we take of his behavior?). And he concludes the canto with the information that Paolo was weeping all through Francesca's second speech (139–140—what do we make of these tears?) and that the protagonist, filled with pity, collapsed in a faint (141–142—what moral view should we take of that?). The omniscient narrator could have given us answers to all these questions; he is content to raise them (intrinsically, he rarely asks questions outright) and leave them in our minds. Often, and surely in the Romantic era, many readers have thought that we are meant to identify with the protagonist's view of the scene. And that view, at least, is unambiguous. He is intrigued by the sight of these two handsome shades (73–75), cries out to them with courteous regard for their prerogatives (80–81), bursts into a passionately-felt sense of identification with them (112–114), tells Francesca as much (116–117), and then asks her to spell out exactly how she was overcome by love (118–120). And that is all he *says.* Of course the narrator tells us that, at the conclusion of Francesca's words, he faints from pity, perhaps his single most eloquent response. We at least know where he stands.

What of Virgil, Dante's guide? He only speaks twice, first to assure Dante that these lovers will come if he but summon them in the name of love (77–78—his laconic remark may be read either as a mere statement of fact or as the world-weary remark of the poet who knows all too much about what my friend John Fleming calls

"Carthaginian love," i.e., the passion that undermines reason, exemplified in Dido, as Virgil himself has told the tale in *Aeneid* IV). And then he has only one more two-word utterance (in Italian it is the laconic "che pense"): "What are your thoughts?" (111—is he merely asking, seeing Dante so deep in reverie about the lovers, or is he delicately reminding Dante that he should be thinking, rather than feeling, since we have already been told by the narrator [at verse 39] both that the sin of lust makes "reason subject to desire" and that the protagonist has understood this?). Virgil has fewer than three verses of the seventy-one dedicated to the scene. What would he have said if the poet had allotted him more? It is interesting to speculate.

What about Francesca herself, the most loquacious of the four? She has thirty-eight verses to tell her story, well over half of the scene (88–107; 121–138). What she tells is moving and beautiful, like the woman herself, we imagine. In this reader's view, one common element in both her speeches is that someone or something else is always being blamed for her unhappiness: the God who will not hear her prayers, the god of Love who made Paolo fall in love with her beautiful physical being and made her respond similarly to his, her husband for killing them, the book that, describing an adulterous kiss, encouraged them to engage in an adulterous embrace, and the man who wrote that book. I admit that I am here taking a dour view. Are we meant to read the scene this way? Most people do not. (A. B. Giamatti, with whom I used to converse endlessly about Dante, loved the Romantic reading of this canto. He once cursed me, complaining, "Are you going to try to ruin this scene for me too, Hollander?") I hope it is clear that we all need to watch more carefully the actual exchanges among the various characters that might help establish a point of view from which we can study the events brought forward in the poem. Whatever else we can say, we should all be ready to admit that this is complicated business. Dante is beautiful, yes, but he is complicated.

It is important to acknowledge that Romantic readers have a point. Had Dante thought that all those in hell deserved as little attention as the saved afford them, in other words, if he felt about them as do Beatrice and the descended angel, he could have begun the poem in purgatory, offering a brief notice of the pains of the damned, of which it is better, he might have had the guardian of purgatory say, not to speak. But he was interested in them, and not only as negative exemplars for those Christians who need to reaffirm their faith and will. The saints may have no interest in the damned, but neither we nor Dante are saints. And thus, one might argue, *Inferno,* the most effective part of the poem, in human terms, deals with the problem (sin) and not its solution (faith and good works). Do we have sympathy for the damned, at least those of them that reveal traits that we admire (effective rhetoric, strong feeling, a sense of their personal wrongness, even, at times, courtesy)? Of course we do. Yet we should be aware that there is a trap for us if we go too far. We need to learn to read ironically (a word that is only used once in all Dante's works, in the incomplete thought that ends what we have of *De vulgari eloquentia* [II.xiv]), finding an angle of vision that corresponds to the author's, who expresses thoughts through his characters that need to be examined with care. That is a difficult goal.

Nonetheless, it is noteworthy (though rarely, if ever, noted) that the "best" people in hell are not necessarily those whom we tend to admire most. They include those who were involved in Florentine public affairs, always championing the cause of good governance: Ciacco (*Inf.* VI), Farinata degli Uberti (X), Brunetto Latini (XV), Jacopo Rusticucci and his mates (XVI), even Mosca dei Lamberti (XXVIII). All of these are unusual among the denizens of hell in that they either own up to their sins (not making an effort to persuade Dante of their innocence or simply to avoid his questions about their guilt) or want to be remembered for their good deeds on earth. That the "standard list" of sympathetic sinners only mentions two of them (Farinata and Brunetto) is informative: Francesca da Rimini (canto V), Farinata, Pier delle Vigne (XIII), Brunetto, Ulysses (XXVI), and Ugolino della Gherardesca (XXXIII). Francesca, Pier, Ulysses, and Ugolino all try to convince Dante of their worthiness, avoiding the subject of their sins. Their behavior in this regard might serve as a clue to an attentive reader. On this score, Ciacco is a good deal more reliable a witness than is Francesca.

There is more to say about many things. The text of the poem awaits, with annotations that will address many of these. Your translators wish you an invigorated journey through hell (not a bad place once you get used to it) and your commentator hopes that you will find his remarks helpful.

Robert Hollander
Tortola, 23 February 2000

INFERNO I

Nel mezzo del cammin di nostra vita
mi ritrovai per una selva oscura,
3   ché la diritta via era smarrita.

Ahi quanto a dir qual era è cosa dura
esta selva selvaggia e aspra e forte
6   che nel pensier rinova la paura!

Tant' è amara che poco è più morte;
ma per trattar del ben ch'i' vi trovai,
9   dirò de l'altre cose ch'i' v'ho scorte.

Io non so ben ridir com' i' v'intrai,
tant' era pien di sonno a quel punto
12   che la verace via abbandonai.

Ma poi ch'i' fui al piè d'un colle giunto,
là dove terminava quella valle
15   che m'avea di paura il cor compunto,

guardai in alto e vidi le sue spalle
vestite già de' raggi del pianeta
18   che mena dritto altrui per ogne calle.

Allor fu la paura un poco queta,
che nel lago del cor m'era durata
21   la notte ch'i' passai con tanta pieta.

E come quei che con lena affannata,
uscito fuor del pelago a la riva,
24   si volge a l'acqua perigliosa e guata,

così l'animo mio, ch'ancor fuggiva,
si volse a retro a rimirar lo passo
27   che non lasciò già mai persona viva.

Midway in the journey of our life
I came to myself in a dark wood,
for the straight way was lost.

Ah, how hard it is to tell
the nature of that wood, savage, dense and harsh—
the very thought of it renews my fear!

It is so bitter death is hardly more so.
But to set forth the good I found
I will recount the other things I saw.

How I came there I cannot really tell,
I was so full of sleep
when I forsook the one true way.

But when I reached the foot of a hill,
there where the valley ended
that had pierced my heart with fear,

looking up, I saw its shoulders
arrayed in the first light of the planet
that leads men straight, no matter what their road.

Then the fear that had endured
in the lake of my heart, all the night
I spent in such distress, was calmed.

And as one who, with laboring breath,
has escaped from the deep to the shore
turns and looks back at the perilous waters,

so my mind, still in flight,
turned back to look once more upon the pass
no mortal being ever left alive.

Poi ch'èi posato un poco il corpo lasso,
ripresi via per la piaggia diserta,
30   sì che 'l piè fermo sempre era 'l più basso.

Ed ecco, quasi al cominciar de l'erta,
una lonza leggiera e presta molto,
33   che di pel macolato era coverta;

e non mi si partia dinanzi al volto,
anzi 'mpediva tanto il mio cammino,
36   ch'i' fui per ritornar più volte vòlto.

Temp' era dal principio del mattino,
e 'l sol montava 'n sù con quelle stelle
39   ch'eran con lui quando l'amor divino

mosse di prima quelle cose belle;
sì ch'a bene sperar m'era cagione
42   di quella fiera a la gaetta pelle

l'ora del tempo e la dolce stagione;
ma non sì che paura non mi desse
45   la vista che m'apparve d'un leone.

Questi parea che contra me venisse
con la test' alta e con rabbiosa fame,
48   sì che parea che l'aere ne tremesse.

Ed una lupa, che di tutte brame
sembiava carca ne la sua magrezza,
51   e molte genti fé già viver grame,

questa mi porse tanto di gravezza
con la paura ch'uscia di sua vista,
54   ch'io perdei la speranza de l'altezza.

E qual è quei che volontieri acquista,
e giugne 'l tempo che perder lo face,
57   che 'n tutti suoi pensier piange e s'attrista;

After I rested my wearied flesh a while,
I took my way again along the desert slope,
30   my firm foot always lower than the other.

But now, near the beginning of the steep,
a leopard light and swift
33   and covered with a spotted pelt

refused to back away from me
but so impeded, barred the way,
36   that many times I turned to go back down.

It was the hour of morning,
when the sun mounts with those stars
39   that shone with it when God's own love

first set in motion those fair things,
so that, despite that beast with gaudy fur,
42   I still could hope for good, encouraged

by the hour of the day and the sweet season,
only to be struck by fear
45   when I beheld a lion in my way.

He seemed about to pounce —
his head held high and furious with hunger—
48   so that the air appeared to tremble at him.

And then a she-wolf who, all hide and bones,
seemed charged with all the appetites
51   that have made many live in wretchedness

so weighed my spirits down with terror,
which welled up at the sight of her,
54   that I lost hope of making the ascent.

And like one who rejoices in his gains
but when the time comes and he loses,
57   turns all his thought to sadness and lament,

tal mi fece la bestia sanza pace,
che, venendomi 'ncontro, a poco a poco
60   mi ripigneva là dove 'l sol tace.

Mentre ch'i' rovinava in basso loco,
dinanzi a li occhi mi si fu offerto
63   chi per lungo silenzio parea fioco.

Quando vidi costui nel gran diserto,
"*Miserere* di me," gridai a lui,
66   "qual che tu sii, od ombra od omo certo!"

Rispuosemi: "Non omo, omo già fui,
e li parenti miei furon lombardi,
69   mantoani per patrïa ambedui.

Nacqui *sub Iulio*, ancor che fosse tardi,
e vissi a Roma sotto 'l buono Augusto
72   nel tempo de li dèi falsi e bugiardi.

Poeta fui, e cantai di quel giusto
figliuol d'Anchise che venne di Troia,
75   poi che 'l superbo Ilïón fu combusto.

Ma tu perché ritorni a tanta noia?
perché non sali il dilettoso monte
78   ch'è principio e cagion di tutta goia?"

"Or se' tu quel Virgilio e quella fonte
che spandi di parlar sì largo fiume?"
81   rispuos' io lui con vergognosa fronte.

"O de li altri poeti onore e lume,
vagliami 'l lungo studio e 'l grande amore
84   che m'ha fatto cercar lo tuo volume.

Tu se' lo mio maestro e 'l mio autore,
tu se' solo colui da cu' io tolsi
87   lo bello stilo che m'ha fatto onore.

such did the restless beast make me—
coming against me, step by step,
60   it drove me down to where the sun is silent.

While I was fleeing to a lower place,
before my eyes a figure showed,
63   faint, in the wide silence.

When I saw him in that vast desert,
'Have mercy on me, whatever you are,'
66   I cried, 'whether shade or living man!'

He answered: 'Not a man, though once I was.
My parents were from Lombardy—
69   Mantua was their homeland.

'I was born *sub Julio*, though late in his time,
and lived at Rome, under good Augustus
72   in an age of false and lying gods.

'I was a poet and I sang
the just son of Anchises come from Troy
75   after proud Ilium was put to flame.

'But you, why are you turning back to misery?
Why do you not climb the peak that gives delight,
78   origin and cause of every joy?'

'Are you then Virgil, the fountainhead
that pours so full a stream of speech?'
81   I answered him, my head bent low in shame.

'O glory and light of all other poets,
let my long study and great love avail
84   that made me delve so deep into your volume.

'You are my teacher and my author.
You are the one from whom alone I took
87   the noble style that has brought me honor.

Vedi la bestia per cu' io mi volsi;
aiutami da lei, famoso saggio,
90   ch'ella mi fa tremar le vene e i polsi."

"A te convien tenere altro vïaggio,"
rispuose, poi che lagrimar mi vide,
93   "se vuo' campar d'esto loco selvaggio;

ché questa bestia, per la qual tu gride,
non lascia altrui passar per la sua via,
96   ma tanto lo 'mpedisce che l'uccide;

e ha natura sì malvagia e ria,
che mai non empie la bramosa voglia,
99   e dopo 'l pasto ha più fame che pria.

Molti son li animali a cui s'ammoglia,
e più saranno ancora, infin che 'l veltro
102   verrà, che la farà morir con doglia.

Questi non ciberà terra né peltro,
ma sapïenza, amore e virtute,
105   e sua nazion sarà tra feltro e feltro.

Di quella umile Italia fia salute
per cui morì la vergine Cammilla,
108   Eurialo e Turno e Niso di ferute.

Questi la caccerà per ogne villa,
fin che l'avrà rimessa ne lo 'nferno,
111   là onde 'nvidia prima dipartilla.

Ond' io per lo tuo me' penso e discerno
che tu mi segui, e io sarò tua guida,
114   e trarrotti di qui per loco etterno;

ove udirai le disperate strida,
vedrai li antichi spiriti dolenti,
117   ch'a la seconda morte ciascun grida;

'See the beast that forced me to turn back.
Save me from her, famous sage—
90   she makes my veins and pulses tremble.'

'It is another path that you must follow,'
he answered, when he saw me weeping,
93   'if you would flee this wild and savage place.

'For the beast that moves you to cry out
lets no man pass her way,
96   but so besets him that she slays him.

'Her nature is so vicious and malign
her greedy appetite is never sated—
99   after she feeds she is hungrier than ever.

'Many are the creatures that she mates with,
and there will yet be more, until the hound
102   shall come who'll make her die in pain.

'He shall not feed on lands or lucre
but on wisdom, love, and power.
105   Between felt and felt shall be his birth.

'He shall be the salvation of low-lying Italy,
for which maiden Camilla, Euryalus,
108   Turnus, and Nisus died of their wounds.

'He shall hunt the beast through every town
till he has sent her back to Hell
111   whence primal envy set her loose.

'Therefore, for your sake, I think it wise
you follow me: I will be your guide,
114   leading you, from here, through an eternal place

'where you shall hear despairing cries
and see those ancient souls in pain
117   as they bewail their second death.

e vederai color che son contenti
nel foco, perché speran di venire
120   quando che sia a le beate genti.

A le quai poi se tu vorrai salire,
anima fia a ciò più di me degna:
123   con lei ti lascerò nel mio partire;

ché quello imperador che là sù regna,
perch' i' fu' ribellante a la sua legge,
126   non vuol che 'n sua città per me si vegna.

In tutte parti impera e quivi regge;
quivi è la sua città e l'alto seggio:
129   oh felice colui cu' ivi elegge!"

E io a lui: "Poeta, io ti richeggio
per quello Dio che tu non conoscesti,
132   a ciò ch'io fugga questo male e peggio,

che tu mi meni là dov' or dicesti,
sì ch'io veggia la porta di san Pietro
e color cui tu fai cotanto mesti."
136   Allor si mosse, e io li tenni dietro.

'Then you will see the ones who are content
to burn because they hope to come,
120   whenever it may be, among the blessed.

'Should you desire to ascend to these,
you'll find a soul more fit to lead than I:
123   I'll leave you in her care when I depart.

'For the Emperor who has his seat on high
wills not, because I was a rebel to His law,
126   that I should make my way into His city.

'In every part He reigns and there He rules.
There is His city and His lofty seat.
129   Happy the one whom He elects to be there!'

And I answered: 'Poet, I entreat you
by the God you did not know,
132   so that I may escape this harm and worse,

'lead me to the realms you've just described
that I may see Saint Peter's gate
and those you tell me are so sorrowful.'
136   Then he set out and I came on behind him.

1.   The first of the 14,233 lines that constitute the *Comedy* immediately establishes a context for the poem that is both universal and particular. It also immediately compels a reader to realize that this is a difficult work, one that may not be read passively, but calls for the reader's active engagement.

Many commentators have pointed out that this opening verse echoes a biblical text, Isaiah's account of the words of Hezekiah, afflicted by the "sickness unto death" (Isaiah 38:10): "in dimidio dierum meorum vadam ad portas inferi" (in the midst of my days, I shall go to the gates of the nether region). Many another potential "source" has found proponents, but this one is so apposite that it has probably received more attention than any other. One other should also be mentioned here, the *Tesoretto* of Brunetto Latini (see note to *Inf.* XV.50). Another tradition holds that the reference is to the age of Dante when he made his voyage (he was thirty-five years old in 1300, half of the biblical "three score and ten"—Psalms 89:10). In addition, some commentators have noted the resonance of the epic tradition in Dante's opening phrase, since epics were seen as beginning, like this poem, *in medias res*, "in the midst of the action," not at its inception.

Related issues are also debated by the earliest commentators, in particular the date of the vision. While there has been disagreement even about the year of the journey to the otherworld, indicated at various points as being 1300 (e.g., *Inf.* X.79–80, XXI.113, *Purg.* II.98, XXXII.2), it is clear that Dante has set his work in the Jubilee Year, proclaimed by Pope Boniface VIII in February of 1300. Far more uncertainty attends the question of the actual days indicated. Dante's descent into hell is begun either on Friday, 25 March or on Friday, 8 April, with the conclusion of the journey occurring almost exactly one week later. In favor of the March date, one can argue that Dante could hardly have chosen a more propitious date for a beginning: March 25 was the anniversary of the creation of Adam, of the conception and of the Crucifixion of Christ, and also marked the Florentine "New Year," since that city measured the year from the Annunciation.

2.   *mi ritrovai* (I came to myself) has the sense of a sudden shocked discovery. "It is the pained amazement of one who has only now, for the first time, become aware that he is in peril" (Padoan, comm. to *Inf.* I.2).

The grammatical solecism ("Nel mezzo del cammin di *nostra* vita / *mi* ritrovai". [Midway in the journey of our life I came to myself . . .]), mixing plural and singular first-persons, is another sign of the poet's desire to make his reader grasp the relation between the individual and the universal, between Dante and all humankind. His voyage is meant to be understood as ours as well.

The *selva oscura* is one of the governing images of this canto and of the poem. Many commentators point to the previous metaphorical statement found in the Dantean work that is probably nearest in time to it, the fourth treatise of his *Convivio* (*Conv.* IV.xxiv.12), where the author refers to "la selva erronea di questa vita" (the error-filled wood of this life). But here the wood is to be taken "historically" in at least a certain sense, and seems to reflect, to some readers, the condition of Eden after the Fall. In such a reading, Dante's sinful life is as though lived in the ruins of Eden, the place to which he has let himself be led, away from the light of God. In any case, the wood indicates not sin itself, but human life lived in the condition of sin.

3. See Wisdom 5:7: "Lassati sumus in via iniquitate et perditionis, et ambulavimus vias difficiles; viam autem Domini ignoravimus" (We grew weary in the way of iniquity and perdition, and we walked difficult pathways; to the way of the Lord, however, we paid no attention)—perhaps first noted in Padoan's commentary to this verse.

7. Perhaps the first serious interpretive tangle for readers of the poem. The problem is a simple one to describe: what is the antecedent of the implicit subject of the verb *è* ("*It* is so bitter . . .")? There are three feminine nouns that may have that role, since the predicate adjective, *amara* (bitter), is also in the feminine: *cosa dura* (hard thing, v. 4), *selva* (wood, v. 5), *paura* (fear, v. 6). Several current commentators are convinced that *selva* is the antecedent. On the other hand, it seems likely that the antecedent is the phrase *cosa dura* (as in Castelvetro's commentary). The entire passage makes good sense when read this way. To tell of his experience in the dark and savage wood is difficult (vv. 4–6) and so bitter that only dying seems more bitter; *but*, in order to treat of the better things he found in the wood, he *will* speak.

8–9. These innocent-sounding lines have been the cause of considerable puzzlement. What is "the good" that Dante found? What are the "other things"? It may be that these terms are in antithetic relation. Over five hundred years ago Filippo Villani (Bell.1989.1, p. 93) offered this gloss: "de bonis et malis in silva repertis" (of the good and the bad found in the forest). Following this line of interpretation yields the following general sense of the passage: "Even in the depths of my sin I found God in terrible things." And thus the *ben* is not here Virgil (as many commentators suggest despite the fact that Virgil does not appear to Dante *in* the forest), but God's grace in allowing Dante to learn of His goodness even in his worst experiences.

11. *pien di sonno.* The date is Thursday, 24 March (or 7 April?) 1300. As the text will later make clear (*Inf.* XXI.112–114), we are observing the 1266th anniversary of Good Friday (which fell on 8 April in 1300 [but see note to v. 1, above]). This would indicate that the poem actually begins on Thursday evening, the 1266th anniversary of Maundy Thursday, when the Apostles slept while Christ watched in the garden, and continued to sleep even as He called to them to rise. That this moment is recalled here seems likely: Dante, too, is "asleep" to Christ in his descent into sin. See Matth. 26:40–46.

13. The *colle* (hill) is generally interpreted as signifying the good life attainable by humankind under its own powers; some, however, believe it has a higher and spiritual meaning, involving salvation. For discussion and strong support for the first reading, based in texts of Aristotle, Brunetto Latini, and Dante himself (esp. *Mon.* III.xvi.7: *beatitudo huius vitae* [the blessedness of this life]), see Mazz.1967.1, pp. 58–60.

14. *valle* (valley): another key word in this landscape. Dante's descent into the valley where the *selva* is located marks a major moral failure and brings him close to death.

15. *paura* (fear), as many have pointed out, is perhaps the key word, in the beginning of the poem, that describes Dante's perilous inner condition. It occurs five times in the canto: at vv. 6; here; 19; 44; 53.

17. *pianeta:* the rays of the sun are meant.

18. *altrui* (others): all those who walk in the ways of the Lord.

20. For Boccaccio, this "lake" or "concavity" in the heart is the place to which our emotions flow; he goes on to mention fear as the exemplary emotion, thus giving Dante's verse a "medical" explanation.

22–27.   This is the first simile in a poem filled with similes, as many as four hundred of them. Here, in response to the first of these, it is perhaps helpful to observe that "similes" in Dante are varied, and possibly fall into three rough categories: "classical" similes, like this one, perfectly balanced and grammatically correct; "improper classical" similes, which are similarly balanced but not expressed with grammatical precision; and simple comparisons, brief and unembellished. For a study in English of the Dantean simile see Lans.1977.1; for bibliography see Sowe.1983.1.

This simile probably takes its setting from the *Aeneid* (I.180–181), the scene of Aeneas's shipwreck on the coast of Carthage, and begins a series of linking allusions to the narrative of the first book of that poem that run through *Inferno* I and II. Dante begins his role as protagonist in this "epic" as the "new Aeneas"; his first words as speaker will later suggest that he is the "new David" as well (v. 65).

26–27.   A much-disputed passage. Almost all commentators equate the *passo* with the *selva* (see note to v. 2, above). The debate centers on whether the relative pronoun *che* is objective or subjective, i.e., do we say "the pass that never let a mortal being go alive" or "the pass no mortal being ever left behind"? Mazzoni (Mazz.1967.1, pp. 79–86) offers convincing evidence for the second reading, on the basis of Dante's elsewise constant use of the verb *lasciare* in this way (to mean "abandon," "leave behind"). We have followed Mazzoni in our translation.

Dante's verse may reflect one of the first vernacular poems in Italian, the "Laudes creaturarum" of St. Francis, vv. 27–28: "Laudato si', mi' Signore, per sora nostra morte corporale, / de la quale nullu homo vivente pò skappare" (Blessed be thou, my Lord, for our sister mortal death, from whom no living man can escape). Whether or not this is the case (and we might consider a second possible citation of Francis's poem in v. 117—see note to that verse, below), the meaning would seem to be that Dante's extraordinary voyage into the afterworld will uniquely separate him, if only temporarily, from the world of the living while he is still alive.

30.   It seems likely that the words are meant both literally and figuratively: Dante, sorely beset by his fatigue and probably by his fear as well, is inching up the slope toward the hill by planting his bottom foot firm and pushing off it to advance the higher one. As Filippo Villani was first to note, there is a Christian tradition for such a difficult progress toward one's goal, found precisely in St. Augustine, who for a long time remained a catechumen before he chose his life in Christ (Bell.1989.1, p. 109). John Frec-

cero formed a similar opinion. According to his article "Dante's Firm Foot and the Journey without a Guide" (1959, reprinted in Frec.1986.1), Dante moves forward with the right foot, representing intellect, supported by the left foot, representing will. Freccero goes on to show that the resultant figuration is one of *homo claudus*, a limping man, wounded in both his feet by Adam's sin.

32–54.   The *lonza* (a hybrid born of leopard and lion) is the first of the three beasts to move against Dante as he attempts to mount the hill. Commentators frequently point to a biblical source for Dante's three beasts, the passage in Jeremiah (5:6) that describes three wild animals (lion, wolf, and "pard" [a leopard or panther]) that will fall upon Jerusalemites because of their transgressions and backsliding. For an extensive review of the problem see Gaetano Ragonese, "fiera," *ED* (vol. 2, 1970, with bibliography through 1969).

The early commentators are strikingly in accord; for them the beasts signify **(1) three of the seven mortal sins: lust, pride, and avarice.** Modern interpreters mainly—but not entirely, as we shall see—reject this formulation. One of these interpretations is based on *Inferno* VI. 75, the three "sparks" that have lit evil fires in the hearts of contemporary Florentines, according to Ciacco, who is seconded by Brunetto Latini [*Inf.* XV. 68]): **(2) envy, pride, and avarice.** Others suggest that the key is found at *Inferno* XI. 81–82, where, describing the organization of the punishment of sin, Virgil speaks of **(3) "the three dispositions Heaven opposes, incontinence, malice, and mad brutishness."** Even within this approach there are strong disagreements as to which beast represents which Aristotelian/Ciceronian category of sin: is the leopard fraud or incontinence? is the she-wolf incontinence or fraud? (the lion is seen by all those of this "school" as violence). For instance, some have asked, if the leopard is fraud, the worst of the three dispositions to sin, why is it the beast that troubles Dante the least? A possible answer is that fraud is the disposition least present in Dante.

Perhaps the single passage in the text of *Inferno* that identifies one of the three beasts in such a way as to leave little doubt about its referentiality occurs in XVI. 106–108, where Dante tells us that he was wearing a cord that he once used in his attempt to capture the beast with "the painted pelt." That this cord is used as a challenge to Geryon, the guardian of the pit of Fraud, makes it seem nearly necessary that in this passage the leopard is meant to signify Fraud. If that is true, it would seem also necessary that the lion would stand for Violence and the she-wolf for Incontinence. The last formulation is the trickiest to support. The she-wolf is mainly associated, in the poem, not so much with Incontinence as with avarice (e.g., *Purg.* XX. 10–15). Thus Dante presents himself as most firm against Fraud, less firm against Violence, and weak when confronted by Incontinence. In his case the sin of Incontinence that afflicts him most is lust, not avarice.

There are few passages in the poem that have generated as much discussion and as little common understanding. Now see Gorni's extended discussion (Gorn. 1995.1, pp. 23–55).

The formulation of the early commentators (**[1] lust, pride, and avarice**) has had a resurgence in our time. It would certainly be pleasing to have reason to assent to their nearly unanimous understanding. Mazzoni (Mazz. 1967.1. pp. 99–102) has given, basing his argument on texts found in the Bible and in the writings of the Fathers and Doctors of the Church, good reason for returning to this view. If it were not for *Inferno* XVI. 106–108, it would be a fairly convincing argument. However, that passage seems unalterably to associate Geryon with the *lonza*.

It should also be noted that a number of still other modern interpreters have proposed various political identities for the three beasts, perhaps the most popular being **(4) the leopard as Dante's Florentine enemies, the lion as the royal house of France, the she-wolf as the forces of the papacy.** It is difficult to align such a view with the details in the text, which seem surely to be pointing to a moral rather than a political view of the situation of the protagonist as the poem begins.

For an extended discussion of the problem in English see Cassell (Cass. 1989.2), pp. 45–76.

33. *di pel macolato . . . coverta* (covered with a spotted pelt). For the resonance of the *Aeneid* (*Aen.* I.323), see the phrase *maculosae tegmine lyncis* (the spotted hide of the lynx), first noted by Pietro Alighieri (first redaction of commentary to *Inf.* I.33).

38. Dante and others in his time believed that the sun was in the constellation of Aries at the creation, which supposedly occurred on 25 March, the date of the Annunciation and of the Crucifixion as well.

55–60. Dante's second simile in the canto turns from the semantic field of epic and perilous adventure to the more mundane but not much less perilous activity of the merchant or the gambler, his financial life hanging in the balance as he awaits news of an arriving ship or the throw of the dice—just at that moment at which his stomach sinks in the sudden awareness that he has in fact, and unthinkably, lost. See the simile involving gambling and gamblers that opens *Purgatorio* VI.

61. For Dante's verb *rovinare* see Mazzoni (Mazz.1967.1, p. 114), citing *Conv*. IV.vii.9: "La via . . . de li malvagi è oscura. Elli non sanno dove rovinano" (The path of the wicked is a dark one. They do not know where they are rushing). Mazzoni points out that Dante is translating Proverbs 4:19, substituting *ruinare* for the biblical *correre*.

62. Dante's phrasing that describes Virgil's appearance to the protagonist ("dinanzi a li occhi mi si fu offerto") reminded Tommaseo (commentary to *Inf*. I.62) of the phrasing that describes Venus's appearance to her son, Aeneas, when the latter is intent on killing Helen in order to avenge the harm done to Troy by the Greek surprise attack within the walls of the city: "mihi se . . . ante ocul[o]s . . . obtulit" (she offered herself to my eyes).

63. Both Brugnoli (Brug.1981.1) and Hollander (Holl.1983.1, pp. 23–79) independently agree on most of the key elements in this puzzling verse: *fioco* is to be taken as visual rather than aural; *silenzio* is understood as deriving from the Virgilian sense of the silence of the dead shades (e.g., *Aen*. VI.264: *umbrae silentes*). It is fair also to say that neither deals convincingly with the adjective *lungo*. How can one *see* that a "silence" is of long duration? A recent intervention by Casagrande (Casa.1997.1, pp. 246–48) makes a strong case for interpreting the adjective *lungo* as here meaning "vast, extensive," having a spatial reference. In his reading the verse would mean "who appeared indistinct in the vast silence"; our translation reflects Casagrande's view.

64. Virgil appears to Dante *nel gran diserto*. The adjective is probably meant to recall the first description of the place, *la piaggia diserta* (the desert slope—v. 29).

65–66. Dante's first spoken word as character in his own poem is Latin (*Miserere*, "Have mercy"). This is the language of the Church, the first word of the fiftieth Psalm (50:1). Thus our hero is identified as a son of the Church—albeit a currently failing one—at the outset of the work. It has also been pointed out that, typically enough, this first utterance made by the protagonist involves a double citation, the first biblical, the second classical, Aeneas's speech to his mother, Venus (*Aen*. I.327–330).

That Dante is trying to ascertain whether Virgil is a shade or a living soul helps interpret v. 63, i.e., he looks as though he is alive, and yet some-how not.

67–87.   Alessio and Villa (Ales.1993.1) offer an important consideration of Dante's debt to the traditional classical and medieval "lives of the poets" in formulating his own brief *vita Virgilii* in this passage. Among other things, such a view undercuts the argument of those interpreters who try to make Virgil an "allegory" of reason. He is presented as a real person with a real history and is thoroughly individuated. No one could mistake the details of this life for that of another, and no one has.

70.   This much-debated verse has left many in perplexity. In what sense are we to take the phrase *sub Iulio*? What is the implicit subject of the verb *fosse*? What is the precise meaning of *tardi* ("late")? Virgil was born in 70 B.C., Julius died in 44 B.C., and Virgil died in 19 B.C. Hardly any two early commentators have the same opinion about this verse. Has Dante made a mistake about the date of Julius's governance? Or does *sub Iulio* only mean "in the days of Julius"? Was Virgil's birth too late for him to be honored by Julius? Or does the clause indicate that, although he was born late in pagan times, it was still too early for him to have heard of Christianity? The most usual contemporary reading is perhaps well stated in Padoan's commentary to this verse: the Latin phrase is only meant to indicate roughly the time of Julius, and nothing more specific than that; when Julius died, Virgil was only twenty-six and had not begun his poetic career, which was thus to be identified with Augustus, rather than with Julius.

73.   The word *poeta* is one of the most potent words in Dante's personal vocabulary of honor and esteem. It is used thirty times in all throughout the poem in this form, seven more times in others. In its first use, here, it constitutes Virgil's main claim as Dante's guide.

74.   Anchises was the father of Aeneas.

75.   The phrase *superbo Ilïón* clearly mirrors *Aen*. III.2–3, "superbum / Ilium." It almost certainly has a moralizing overtone here (see also the note to v. 106, below), while in Virgil it probably only indicates the "topless towers of Troy"; in Dante it gives us some sense that Troy may have fallen because of its *superbia*, or pride.

77.   *dilettoso monte*: in no ways different from the *colle* of verse 13.

79. At this first appearance of Virgil's name in Dante's text (it will appear thirty times more) it is probably worth noting that Dante's spelling of the name is not only his, but a widespread medieval idiosyncrasy. Translating "Vergilius" with "Virgilio" was intended to lend the Latin poet a certain dignity (by associating him with the noun *vir*, man) and/or a certain mysterious power (by associating him with the word *virga*, or "rod" with magical power).

81. Why is Dante's head "bent low in shame"? The immediate context is that of Virgil's rebuke to Dante for his failure to climb the hill and consequent ruinous flight. It is for this reason—or so one might understand—that he feels ashamed.

84. For the lofty resonance of the word *volume* in the *Comedy* (as compared with *libro*, another and lesser word for "book") see Holl.1969.1, pp. 78–79. The Bible is the only other book so referred to. Two other words that usually refer to God's divine authority are also each used once to refer to Virgil or his writing: *autore* (*Inf.* I.85) and *scrittura* (*Purg.* VI.34).

86–87. There has been much discussion of exactly what the "noble style" is and where it is to be found in Dante's work. The style is the "high style" or "tragic style" found in Virgil and other classical poets and was achieved by Dante in his odes (three of which are collected in *Convivio*), as he himself indicated in *De vulgari eloquentia* (see *Dve* II.vi.7).

Dante's formulation here goes further, making Virgil his sole source. His later interactions with other poets in hell (e.g., Pier delle Vigne [*Inf.* XIII], Brunetto Latini [*Inf.* XV]) or relatives of poets (Cavalcante [*Inf.* X]) show that not one of them is interested in the identity of Dante's guide, a fact that reflects directly on the poems left by these three practitioners, which are markedly without sign of Virgilian influence. Thus, not only is Virgil Dante's sole source for the "noble style," but Dante portrays himself as Virgil's sole follower among the recent and current poets of Italy. Perhaps more than any other claim for a literary identity, this sets him apart from them. For Dante's complicated relationship with his poetic precursors see Barolini (Baro.1984.1).

100–105. In a canto filled with passages that have called forth rivers of commentators' ink, perhaps none has resulted in so much interpretive excitement as this one. While our commentary always follows Petrocchi's text of the poem, even when we are in disagreement, we should say that here we are in disagreement. We would capitalize the two nouns "Feltro" and "Feltro," so that they would indicate place names in northern Italy. The person in Dante's mind would then be Cangrande della Scala, the youthful general of the armies of Verona when Dante first visited that city ca. 1304. In that case, what we would deal with here is the first of three (see also *Purg.* XXXIII.37–45, *Par.* XXVII.142–148) "world-historical" prophecies of the coming of a political figure (in the last two surely an emperor) who, in his advent, also looks forward to the Second Coming of Christ. For an excellent review of the entire problem see C. T. Davis, "veltro," *ED* (vol. 5, 1976). For the notion that there is indeed a Virgilian (and imperial) source for Dante's prophecy in the prediction of Augustan rule in *Aeneid* I.286–296 see Holl.1969.1, pp. 90–91.

106.   The phrase *umile Italia* surely recalls Virgil's *humilem . . . Italiam* (*Aen.* III.522–523), as has been frequently noted. Some have argued that, in Dante, the words have a moral tint, mainly contending that the reference is to Italy's current lowly political condition.

107–108.   The curious intermingling of enemies (Camilla and Turnus fought *against* the Trojan invaders, Euryalus and Nisus *with* them) helps establish Dante's sense that Aeneas's Italian war was a necessary and just one, its victims as though sacrificed for the cause of establishing Rome, the "new Troy." For the centrality of Rome in Dante's thought see the volume of the late Charles Till Davis (Davi.1957.1), still the essential study of this important subject.

109–111.   Mazzoni (Mazz.1967.1, pp. 137–38) argues strongly for the interpretation of *prima* as an adjective modifying *invidia*, and thus for a phrase meaning "primal envy," when death entered the created world precisely because of Satan's envy (see Wisdom 2:24: "Through envy of the devil came death into the world."). He notes the resulting parallel between this line and *Inf.* III.6, where God is, in His third person, "Primo Amore" (Primal Love).

117.   The possibilities for interpreting this verse are various. The "second death" may refer to what the sinners are suffering now (in which case they cry out either for a cessation in their pain—a "death" of it—or against their condition) or it may refer to the "death" they will suffer at the end of time in Christ's final Judgment (in which case they may either be crying out *for* that finality or *against* that horrifying prospect). Mazzoni

(Mazz.1967.1, p. 143) was perhaps the first to hear an echo here (now heard by several others) of v. 31 of St. Francis's "Laudes creaturarum" (for an earlier possible citation of that poem see note to v. 27): "ka la morte secunda no 'l farrà male" (the good soul, liberated by death, hopes that it will not suffer eternal damnation at the Last Judgment). Thus, while the question remains a difficult one, the best hypothesis probably remains Mazzoni's (Mazz.1967.1, pp. 139–45): the sinners are crying out in fear of the punishments to come after the Last Judgment.

122.   Virgil's self-description as unworthy may reflect a similar self-description, that of John the Baptist. See John 1:27 and related discussion in Holl.1983.1, pp. 63, 71–73. In this formulation Virgil is to Beatrice as John was to Christ. For an earlier moment in Dante's writing that is based on exactly such a typological construction, one in which Guido Cavalcanti's Giovanna/John the Baptist is portrayed as the "forerunner" to Dante's Beatrice/Christ, see VN XXIV.3–4.

125.   It is fair to say that most commentators dodge this troublesome word. How could Virgil have been a "rebel" against a God he did not know? We should remember that this formulation is Virgil's own and may simply reflect his present sense of what he should have known when he was alive. That is, Virgil may be exaggerating his culpability.

132.   "This harm" is Dante's present situation in the world; "and worse" would be his damnation.

134–135.   Dante has apparently understood clearly enough that Virgil will lead him through hell and purgatory, but not paradise. Having read the poem, we know that Beatrice will assume the role of guide for the first nine heavens. Virgil seems to know this (see vv. 122–123), but not Dante, who seems to be aware only that some soul will take up the role of Virgil when his first guide leaves him.

INFERNO II

Lo giorno se n'andava, e l'aere bruno
toglieva li animai che sono in terra
da le fatiche loro; e io sol uno

3

m'apparecchiava a sostener la guerra
sì del cammino e sì de la pietate,
che ritrarrà la mente che non erra.

6

O Muse, o alto ingegno, or m'aiutate;
o mente che scrivesti ciò ch'io vidi,
qui si parrà la tua nobilitate.

9

Io cominciai: "Poeta che mi guidi,
guarda la mia virtù s'ell' è possente,
prima ch'a l'alto passo tu mi fidi.

12

Tu dici che di Silvïo il parente,
corruttibile ancora, ad immortale
secolo andò, e fu sensibilmente.

15

Però, se l'avversario d'ogne male
cortese i fu, pensando l'alto effetto
ch'uscir dovea di lui, e 'l chi e 'l quale

18

non pare indegno ad omo d'intelletto;
ch'e' fu de l'alma Roma e di suo impero
ne l'empireo ciel per padre eletto:

21

la quale e 'l quale, a voler dir lo vero,
fu stabilita per lo loco santo
u' siede il successor del maggior Piero.

24

Per quest' andata onde li dai tu vanto,
intese cose che furon cagione
di sua vittoria e del papale ammanto.

27

Day was departing and the darkened air
released the creatures of the earth
3   from their labor, and I, alone,

prepared to face the struggle—
of the way and of the pity of it—
6   which memory, unerring, shall retrace.

O Muses, O lofty genius, aid me now!
O memory, that set down what I saw,
9   here shall your worth be shown.

I began: 'Poet, you who guide me,
consider if my powers will suffice
12   before you trust me to this arduous passage.

'You tell of the father of Sylvius
that he, still subject to corruption, went
15   to the eternal world while in the flesh.

'But that the adversary of all evil showed
such favor to him, considering who and what he was,
18   and the high sequel that would spring from him,

'seems not unfitting to a man who understands.
For in the Empyrean he was chosen
21   to father holy Rome and her dominion,

'both of these established—if we would speak
the truth—to be the sacred precinct where
24   successors of great Peter have their throne.

'On this journey, for which you grant him glory,
he heard the words that prompted him
27   to victory and prepared the Papal mantle.

Andovvi poi lo Vas d'elezïone,
per recarne conforto a quella fede
30   ch'è principio a la via di salvazione.

Ma io, perché venirvi? o chi 'l concede?
Io non Enëa, io non Paulo sono;
33   me degno a ciò né io né altri 'l crede.

Per che, se del venire io m'abbandono,
temo che la venuta non sia folle.
36   Se' savio; intendi me' ch'i' non ragiono."

E qual è quei che disvuol ciò che volle
e per novi pensier cangia proposta,
39   sì che dal cominciar tutto si tolle,

tal mi fec' ïo 'n quella oscura costa,
perché, pensando, consumai la 'mpresa
42   che fu nel cominciar cotanto tosta.

"S'i' ho ben la parola tua intesa,"
rispuose del magnanimo quell' ombra,
45   "l'anima tua è da viltade offesa;

la qual molte fïate l'omo ingombra
sì che d'onrata impresa lo rivolve,
48   come falso veder bestia quand' ombra.

Da questa tema a ciò che tu ti solve,
dirotti perch' io venni e quel ch'io 'ntesi
51   nel primo punto che di te mi dolve.

Io era tra color che son sospesi,
e donna mi chiamò beata e bella,
54   tal che di comandare io la richiesi.

Lucevan li occhi suoi più che la stella;
e cominciommi a dir soave e piana,
57   con angelica voce, in sua favella:

'Later, the Chosen Vessel went there
to bring back confirmation of our faith,
the first step in our journey to salvation.

30

'But why should I go there? who allows it?
I am not Aeneas, nor am I Paul.
Neither I nor any think me fit for this.

33

'And so, if I commit myself to come,
I fear it may be madness. You are wise,
you understand what I cannot express.'

36

And as one who unwills what he has willed,
changing his intent on second thought
so that he quite gives over what he has begun,

39

such a man was I on that dark slope.
With too much thinking I had undone
the enterprise so quick in its inception.

42

'If I have rightly understood your words,'
replied the shade of that great soul,
'your spirit is assailed by cowardice,

45

'which many a time so weighs upon a man
it turns him back from noble enterprise,
the way a beast shies from a shadow.

48

'To free you from this fear
I'll tell you why I came and what I heard
when first I felt compassion for you.

51

'I was among the ones who are suspended
when a lady called me, so blessèd and so fair
that I implored her to command me.

54

'Her eyes shone brighter than the stars.
Gentle and clear, the words she spoke to me—
an angel's voice was in her speech:

57

'O anima cortese mantoana,
di cui la fama ancor nel mondo dura,
60   e durerà quanto 'l mondo lontana,

l'amico mio, e non de la ventura,
ne la diserta piaggia è impedito
63   sì nel cammin, che vòlt' è per paura;

e temo che non sia già sì smarrito,
ch'io mi sia tardi al soccorso levata,
66   per quel ch'i' ho di lui nel cielo udito.

Or movi, e con la tua parola ornata
e con ciò c'ha mestieri al suo campare,
69   l'aiuta sì ch'i' ne sia consolata.

I' son Beatrice che ti faccio andare;
vegno del loco ove tornar disio;
72   amor mi mosse, che mi fa parlare.

Quando sarò dinanzi al segnor mio,
di te mi loderò sovente a lui.'
75   Tacette allora, e poi comincia' io:

'O donna di virtù sola per cui
l'umana spezie eccede ogne contento
78   di quel ciel c'ha minor li cerchi sui,

tanto m'aggrada il tuo comandamento,
che l'ubidir, se già fosse, m'è tardi;
81   più non t'è uo' ch'aprirmi il tuo talento.

Ma dimmi la cagion che non ti guardi
de lo scender qua giuso in questo centro
84   de l'ampio loco ove tornar tu ardi.'

'Da che tu vuo' saver cotanto a dentro,
dirotti brievemente,' mi rispuose,
87   'perch'i' non temo di venir qua entro.

' "O courteous Mantuan spirit,
whose fame continues in the world
60   and shall continue while the world endures,

' "my friend, who is no friend of Fortune,
is so hindered on his way upon the desert slope
63   that, in his terror, he has turned back,

' "and, from what I hear of him in Heaven,
I fear he has gone so far astray
66   that I arose too late to help him.

' "Set out, and with your polished words
and whatever else is needed for his safety,
69   go to his aid, that I may be consoled.

' "I who bid you go am Beatrice.
I come from where I most desire to return.
72   The love that moved me makes me speak.

' "And when I am before my Lord
often will I offer praise of you to Him."
75   Then she fell silent. And I began:

' "O lady of such virtue that by it alone
the human race surpasses all that lies
78   within the smallest compass of the heavens,

' "so pleased am I at your command that my consent,
were it already given, would be given late.
81   You have but to make your desire known.

' "But tell me why you do not hesitate
to descend into the center of the earth
84   from the unbounded space you long for."

' "Since you are so eager to know more,"
she answered, "I shall be brief in telling you
87   why I am not afraid to enter here.

Temer si dee di sole quelle cose
c'hanno potenza di fare altrui male;
90   de l'altre no, ché non son paurose.

I' son fatta da Dio, sua mercé, tale,
che la vostra miseria non mi tange,
93   né fiamma d'esto 'ncendio non m'assale.

Donna è gentil nel ciel che si compiange
di questo 'mpedimento ov' io ti mando,
96   sì che duro giudicio là sù frange.

Questa chiese Lucia in suo dimando
e disse: "Or ha bisogno il tuo fedele
99   di te, e io a te lo raccomando."

Lucia, nimica di ciascun crudele,
si mosse, e venne al loco dov' i' era,
102   che mi sedea con l'antica Rachele.

Disse: "Beatrice, loda di Dio vera,
ché non soccorri quei che t'amò tanto,
105   ch'uscì per te de la volgare schiera?

Non odi tu la pieta del suo pianto,
non vedi tu la morte che 'l combatte
108   su la fiumana ove 'l mar non ha vanto?"

Al mondo non fur mai persone ratte
a far lor pro o a fuggir lor danno,
111   com' io, dopo cotai parole fatte,

venni qua giù del mio beato scanno,
fidandomi del tuo parlare onesto,
114   ch'onora te e quei ch'udito l'hanno.'

Poscia che m'ebbe ragionato questo,
li occhi lucenti lagrimando volse,
117   per che mi fece del venir più presto.

' "We should fear those things alone
that have the power to harm.
90   Nothing else is frightening.

' "I am made such by God's grace
that your affliction does not touch,
93   nor can these fires assail me.

' "There is a gracious lady in Heaven so moved
by pity at his peril, she breaks stern judgment
96   there above and lets me send you to him.

' "She summoned Lucy and made this request:
«Your faithful one is now in need of you
99   and I commend him to your care.»

' "Lucy, the enemy of every cruelty,
arose and came to where I sat
102   at venerable Rachel's side,

' "and said: «Beatrice, true praise of God,
why do you not help the one who loved you so
105   that for your sake he left the vulgar herd?

' "«Do you not hear the anguish in his tears?
Do you not see the death besetting him
108   on the swollen river where the sea cannot prevail?»

' "Never were men on earth so swift to seek
their good or to escape their harm as I,
111   after these words were spoken,

' "to descend here from my blessèd seat,
trusting to the noble speech that honors you
114   and those who have paid it heed."

'After she had said these things to me,
she turned away her eyes, now bright with tears,
117   making me more eager to set out.

E venni a te così com' ella volse:
d'inanzi a quella fiera ti levai
120   che del bel monte il corto andar ti tolse.

Dunque: che è? perché, perché restai,
perché tanta viltà nel core allette,
123   perché ardire e franchezza non hai,

poscia che tai tre donne benedette
curan di te ne la corte del cielo,
126   e 'l mio parlar tanto ben ti promette?"

Quali fioretti dal notturno gelo
chinati e chiusi, poi che 'l sol li 'mbianca,
129   si drizzan tutti aperti in loro stelo,

tal mi fec' io di mia virtude stanca,
e tanto buono ardire al cor mi corse,
132   ch'i' cominciai come persona franca:

"Oh pietosa colei che mi soccorse!
e te cortese ch'ubidisti tosto
135   a le vere parole che ti porse!

Tu m'hai con disiderio il cor disposto
sì al venir con le parole tue,
138   ch'i' son tornato nel primo proposto.

Or va, ch'un sol volere è d'ambedue:
tu duca, tu segnore e tu maestro."
Così li dissi; e poi che mosso fue,
142   intrai per lo cammino alto e silvestro.

'And so I came to you just as she wished.
I saved you from the beast denying you
120   the short way to the mountain of delight.

'What then? Why, why do you delay?
Why do you let such cowardice rule your heart?
123   Why are you not more spirited and sure,

'when three such blessèd ladies
care for you in Heaven's court
126   and my words promise so much good?'

As little flowers, bent and closed
with chill of night, when the sun
129   lights them, stand all open on their stems,

such, in my failing strength, did I become.
And so much courage poured into my heart
132   that I began, as one made resolute:

'O how compassionate was she to help me,
how courteous were you, so ready to obey
135   the truthful words she spoke to you!

'Your words have made my heart
so eager for the journey
138   that I've returned to my first intent.

'Set out then, for one will prompts us both.
You are my leader, you my lord and master,'
I said to him, and when he moved ahead
142   I entered on the deep and savage way.

1–6.   Against the common opinion (as it exists even today, most recently exhibited by Merc.1998.1) that the first two cantos perform separate functions (e.g., I = prologue to the poem as a whole, II = prologue to the first *cantica*), Wilkins (Wilk.1926.1) argues, on the basis of discussion of the defining characteristics of prologues found in the *Epistle to Cangrande* (*Epist.* XIII.43–48), that Cantos I and II form a unitary prologue to the entire poem as well as to its first *cantica* (or "canticle"). This reader finds his comments just and convincing. In actuality, all three *cantiche* begin with two-canto-long prologues containing an invocation, some narrated action, and presentation of details that prepare the reader for what is to follow further along in the poem.

For the structural parallels that also tend to merge the two cantos into a single entity see Holl.1990.2, p. 97:

Inferno I	*Inferno* II
1–27 Dante's peril	1–42 Dante's uncertainty
simile (22–27)	*simile* (37–40)
28–60 three beasts	43–126 three blessed ladies
simile (55–58)	*simile* (127–130)
61–136 Virgil's assurances	127–142 Dante's will firmed

1–3.   The precise Virgilian text that lies behind Dante's generically "Virgilian" opening flourish is debated. (Major candidates include *Aen.* III.147, *Aen.* IV.522–528, *Aen.* VIII.26–27, *Aen.* IX.224–225, *Georg.* I.427–428. See discussion in Mazz.1967.1, pp. 165–66.) These three lines, as has often been noted, have a sad eloquence that establishes a mode of writing to which the poet will return when he considers the Virgilian "tears of things" in the lives of some of his characters.

3.   The protagonist, about to descend into hell, is described, perhaps surprisingly, since he is in the company of Virgil, as being alone ("sol uno"). But see *Conv.* IV.xxvi.9, where Dante describes Aeneas, about to begin his descent *ad inferos*, similarly as being "alone": ". . . when Aeneas prepared, *alone* with the Sibyl [*solo con Sibilla*], to enter the underworld." In Dante's view, it would seem that the condition of a mortal soul, about to enter the underworld, is one of loneliness, even though it is accompanied by a shade. See Holl.1993.1, p. 256.

4–5.   This formulation perhaps refers to the struggle of the protagonist
with the difficulties of proceeding (his struggles with fearsome exterior
forces ranged against him, from the previously-encountered three beasts in
the first canto to Satan in the last) and with his own interior weakness,
demonstrated by his occasional surrender to the emotion of pity (begin-
ning with Francesca in the fifth canto and ending when he does not yield
to Ugolino's entreaties for his pity in the thirty-third). For a possible five-
part program that marks the development of the protagonist's strength, as
he moves through five cycles of pity and fear in hell, see Holl.1969.1,
pp. 301–7.

6.   In the words of Singleton's gloss, "Memory will now faithfully retrace
the real event of the journey, exactly as it took place. This most extraordi-
nary journey through the three realms of the afterlife is represented, never
as dreamed or experienced in vision, but as a real happening. . . . Here,
then, and in the following invocation, the poet's voice is heard for the first
time as it speaks of his task as poet."

7–9.   The passage including the poem's first invocation is challenging and
has caused serious interpretive difficulty. Why does Dante invoke the
Muses in a Christian work? What does *alto ingegno* (lofty genius) refer to? Is
the invocation of two powers ("Muses" and "lofty genius") or of three
(the *mente*, or "memory," of verse 8)? For a discussion of these points see
Holl.1990.2, pp. 98–100, arguing that the "muses" are the devices of poetic
making that the individual poet may master, that the "lofty genius" is not
Dante's, but God's, and that only these two elements are invoked, while
"mente" is merely put forward as having been effective in recording the
facts of the journey (and is surely not "invoked," as the very language of
the passage makes plain). In this formulation, here and in some of his later
invocations Dante is asking for divine assistance in conceptualizing the
matter of his poem so that it may resemble his Creator, its source, while
also asking for the help of the "muses" in finding the most appropriate
expressive techniques for that conceptualization. As for the raw content,
that he has through his own experience; he requires no external aid for it.
What he does need is conceptual and expressive power, *alto ingegno* and the
poetic craft represented by the "muses."

   It is, given Dante's fondness for the number of Beatrice, nine, difficult
to believe that the fact that there are nine invocations in the poem may
be accidental (see Holl.1976.2). For perhaps the first reckoning that
accounts for all nine invocations see Fabb.1910.1. It is curious that few

commentators have noted the fact that there are, in fact, nine invocations (and only nine) in the poem. They are as follows: *Inf.* II.7, XXXII.10–12; *Purg.* I.7–12, XXIX.37–42; *Par.* I.13–21, XVIII.83–88, XXII.112–123, XXX.97–99, XXXIII.67–75.

10.   This verse begins a series of conversations that give the canto its shape. With the exception of the eleventh Canto, 92 percent of which is devoted to dialogue (mainly Virgil's explanations of the circles of hell, joined by Dante's responses and questions), no other Infernal canto contains so much dialogue, with 118 of its 142 verses being spoken (83 percent). These conversations form a chiasmus (from the Greek *chi*, our letter 'x'), the device of shaping the parts of a text into a perfectly balanced pattern (see Holl.1990.2, p. 100):

> 1. Dante (10–36)
>   2. Virgil (43–57)
>   3. Beatrice (58–74)
>   4. Virgil (75–84)
>   5. Beatrice (85–114)
>   6. Virgil (115–126)
> 7. Dante (133–140)

12.   The meaning of the phrase *alto passo* is debated. See Mazz.1967.1, pp. 180–84, for documentation. Mazzoni gives good reasons for accepting a literal reading, one that makes the *passo* correspond to the journey, rather than, as some have proposed, a metaphorical one, in which it signifies the poem. Mazzoni paraphrases these words with the phrase "impresa eccezionale" (extraordinary undertaking), while also stressing the difficulty of that adventure. Our translation seeks a similar solution.

13.   Aeneas was the father of Silvius (Ascanius).

15.   In his commentary Padoan points out that the insistence on the physicality of Aeneas's descent effectively undercuts that tradition of medieval allegorized Virgil which asserts that the "descent" is to be taken as a "philosophical," rather than as a literal, journey. Aeneas's journey, like Dante's own, is to be dealt with as actually having occurred in space and time.

16–19.   For the commentators, the most troubling aspect of a difficult tercet is found in the phrase "e 'l chi e 'l quale" ("considering who and what he was," v. 18—see Mazzoni, pp. 192–96). The sense, however, may be fairly straightforward: it is not surprising that God should have chosen Aeneas to found Rome, with its profound impact on human history, both imperial and ecclesiastical, since Aeneas (the "who" of the verse) was both the founder of a royal line (ancestor of Julius Caesar through Ascanius) and "divine" (the "what," since he was the son of a goddess, Venus).

Dante uses the word "cortese" (courteous, i.e., as in the favoring generosity of a lord or lady) in v. 17 in a way that theologizes its usual courtly context. For the tradition of the concept as it comes into Dante see Crim.1993.1.

20–21. The adjective *alma* (here translated as "holy") has had various interpretations in the commentary tradition, e.g., "exalted" (*eccelsa:* Boccaccio), "lofty" (*alta:* Buti), "nurturing" (*alma:* Landino), "holy" (*sancta:* Benvenuto). Citing Paget Toynbee, Mazzoni (Mazz.1967.1), p. 198, makes a strong argument for the last of these. Our translation reflects his view. And this formulation knits up these two tercets into a single meaning: Aeneas was chosen by God to be the founder of imperial *and* ecclesiastical Rome. Such a view disturbs those who believe that Dante, when he began the *Comedy*, was still a Guelph (i.e., a supporter of the papacy) in his political attitudes and not a Ghibelline (a supporter of the empire). A reading of the fourth book of *Convivio* (Mazzoni [Mazz.1967.1], pp. 216–20), demonstrates the close correspondence between what Dante says here and what he had said in *Convivio* IV, iv-v. There he had already made a decisive shift toward recognizing the importance of what we would call "secular Rome." Dante, as the prophecy of the *veltro* (depending on one's interpretation of it) may already have demonstrated, now believes in the divine origin and mission of the empire. See note to *Inf.* I.100–105.

22–24. See Mazzoni (Mazz.1967.1), pp. 198–220, for a thorough review of this tercet, made problematic not because its words or the sense of these words is difficult, but because what it says is assumed by many commentators to be premature in its championing of the empire, a position Dante is supposed to have embraced only later. See the preceding note. For a recent attempt to describe the political aspect of the poem see Hollander (Holl.2000.1), the section, in the discussion devoted to the *Commedia*, entitled "La politica."

26. Aeneas understood things from what was revealed to him in the underworld, most notably by his father, Anchises (see Mazz.1967.1, p. 222).

27.   This verse concludes the "imperial theme" of this canto, initiated in v. 13. These five tercets continually break Aeneas's identity or task into two aspects ("e 'l chi e 'l quale" [who and what he was—v. 18], "de l'alma Roma e di suo impero" [holy Rome and her dominion—v. 20], "la quale e 'l quale" [both of these established—v. 22], "di sua vittoria e del papale ammanto" [to victory and . . . the papal mantle—v. 27]). This speech is not in the mouth of Virgil, but of Dante, and for a reason. It purveys, with some heated enthusiasm, the view of Roman imperial excellence that Dante had only recently developed. He cannot allow its religious dimension authoritative utterance by Virgil, whose credentials as "Christian" are not exactly imposing. And so the otherwise not-very-mature protagonist is here given the author's voice to say what that author wants most definitely to set down before us.

28.   For Paul as the *Vas d'elezïone* (Chosen Vessel) see Acts 9:15. For his ascent to heaven while still alive see II Cor. 12:4.

This flat statement that Paul's journey actually occurred contrasts with the less forthright claim made for Aeneas's in verse 13: "Tu dici che" (You tell that). This and the subsequent phrasing, in which that same journey is referred to as the "andata onde li dai tu vanto" (journey for which you grant him glory) at v. 25, both imbue the speaker's acceptance of the veracity of Virgil's account of that journey with a certain sense of dubiety (see Holl.1990.2, p. 103), at least when compared with the biblical authority enjoyed by Paul's.

With regard to the question of whether or not Dante believed Paul had been to hell (as recounted in the *Visio Pauli*) see Padoan's comment, with bibliography (to which now should be added Silv.1997.1). Most commentators would seem to believe that Dante is here alluding only to Paul's heavenly journey, not to his apocryphal descent.

32.   It has frequently been remarked that Dante's denial must be taken ironically. What the protagonist says is not what his author thinks: Dante *is* to be understood as both the "new Aeneas" and the "new Paul." Jacoff and Stephany offer an ample deliberation on this subject (Jaco.1989.1), pp. 57–72. For a recent study of Paul's presence in Dante's works see DiSc.1995.1.

33–36.   Dante's apparent modesty is obviously meant to be taken rather as cowardice, as Virgil's response at v. 45 ("your spirit is assailed by cowardice") makes pellucidly clear.

37–40. A type of simile Dante enjoys deploying, one in which both elements ("tenor" and "vehicle") are eventually seen to involve the same agent: "and as a man . . . so was I." See note to *Inferno* XXX.136–141.

41. For the importance of the word *impresa* (enterprise) in the overall economy of the poem see Holl.1969.1, p. 230. It occurs twice in this canto (next at v. 47), where it refers to Dante's journey, then in *Inf.* XXXII.7, where it refers to the poem that Dante is writing, and finally in *Par.* XXXIII.95, where it surely refers to the voyage, and perhaps to the poem as well. See note to *Inferno* XXXII.1–9.

43. This is the first occurrence of the word "word" (*parola*) in the poem and in this canto. It will reappear four more times in the canto at vv. 67, 111, 135, and 137. If, as several commentators have urged (see Holl.1990.2, p. 96), the first Canto of the poem is the "canto della paura" (canto of fear—the word *paura* appears five times [see note to canto I.15], as does *parola* in this one, and neither appears so many times in any other canto), then *Inferno* II perhaps should be construed as the 'canto della parola' (canto of the word). See Holl.1990.2, *passim*.

48. For a possible source for this verse, not hitherto cited, see *Aeneid* X.592–593, where Aeneas scornfully addresses Lucagus, whom he has just mortally wounded, and tells his fallen enemy that he cannot blame his plight on the shying of his horses: "Lucagus, the cowardly flight of your horses has not betrayed your chariot, nor has the empty shadow [*vanae . . . umbrae*] of an enemy turned them away." See Holl.1993.1, p. 256.

52. The verbal adjective *sospesi* (suspended), that is, in a position between the presence of God and actual punishment, is a technical term for the virtuous heathen who dwell in Limbo. See Mazzoni's note (Mazz.1967.1), pp. 239–47.

53–54. Beatrice's anonymous first appearance and Virgil's instinctive obeisance might easily lead a reader to assume that this lady has primarily an "allegorical" meaning. For a recent study of the roots of the problematic allegorical interpretation of Beatrice see Porc.1997.2. We will in time be told who she is (*Inf.* II.70). Dante's first extended work, *Vita nuova* (ca. 1293), celebrated his lady, Beatrice, as a mortal woman unlike any other, her meaning indissolubly linked with the Trinity, and in particular with the Second Person, Christ.

56–57.   Virgil describes Beatrice's speech as being *soave e piana* (gentle and clear). She will, in turn, describe his speech as *parola ornata* (polished words—at v. 67). The two adjectives, *piana* and *ornata*, may remind us of a major distinction, found in medieval categorizations of rhetorical styles, between the plain, or low, style, and the ornate, or high. Benvenuto, commenting on this passage, was the first to point this out, glossing "soave e piana" as follows: "divine speech is sweet and humble, not elevated and proud, as is that of Virgil and the poets." Thus Virgil's description of Beatrice's words corresponds antithetically to hers of his; her speech represents the sublimely humble style valorized by the *Comedy*, while his recalls the high style that marked pagan eloquence (the observation is drawn from Holl.1990.2, p. 107, where there are references to previous discussions in Auer.1958.1, pp. 65–66; Mazz.1979.1, pp. 157–58).

58.   Beatrice's first words, which Daniello (commentary to this verse) compared to Juno's attempt to win over Aeolus at *Aeneid* I.66–67, offer a striking example of *captatio benevolentiae*, the rhetorical device of gaining favor with one's audience. They will be effective enough in gaining Virgil's goodwill. And, despite Virgil's characterization of her speech, in v. 56, as being "gentle and clear," it is also unmistakably lofty in its rhetorical reach.

61.   For a consideration of the fullest implications of this verse see Mazzoni (Mazz.1967.1), pp. 256–68. According to him, the literal sense is that Dante is not a friend to Fortune, not that Fortune has forsaken *him*. The upshot of these readings is that Beatrice makes Dante her friend in true spiritual friendship, denying that he is "friendly" to Fortune.

62–64.   Words familiar from the first canto come back into play here: *diserta piaggia* (I.29), *cammin* (I.1), *paura* (I.53), *smarrito* (I.3). This is not the last time we will look back to the protagonist's desperate condition evident at the beginning of the poem.

67.   See Holl.1990.2, p. 118, for discussion of the undercutting of Virgil's "ornate speech" (*parola ornata*) when it is seen as linked to Jason's *parole ornate* (*Inf.* XVIII.91), the deceptive rhetoric by which he seduces women.

74.   Beatrice's promise to speak well of Virgil to God has drawn some skeptical response, e.g., Castelvetro on this verse: "Questo che monta a

Virgilio che è dannato?" (What good is this to Virgil, who is damned?). We are probably meant to be more impressed than that.

76–78.   The meaning of this much-disputed tercet would seem to be: "O lady of virtuous disposition which alone, shared by others, may bring them, too, to salvation out of the sublunar world of sin . . ." This is to rely on Mazzoni's affirmation (Mazz.1967.1, pp. 276–77) of Barbi's reading of the verse (Barb.1934.2, p. 22), which continues to find detractors.

83.   *in questo centro*. Singleton, in his comment on this verse, speaks of the "strong pejorative connotation" of Dante's phrase, stemming from "the well-established view that the earth's position at the center of the universe is the most ignoble—because it is farthest from God and His angels." Singleton goes on to cite from a sermon of Fra Giordano da Rivalto, characterizing the true center of the earth as "that point within the earth which is in its midst, as the core is in the midst of an apple. We believe that hell is located there, at the true center."

85–93.   Beatrice's insistence that she is not "touchable" by the grim powers of the pains of hell underlines the marginality of sin for the saved. Hell is simply not of concern to them. It is important to know, as one begins reading the poem, what one can only know once one has finished it: no soul in purgation or in grace in heaven has a thought for the condition of the damned (only the damned themselves do). Their concern for those who do not share their redeeming penitence or bliss is reserved for those still alive on earth, who have at least the hope of salvation. Hell, for the saved, is a sordid reality of which it is better not to speak.

94.   While every modern commentator recognizes (quite rightly) Mary in this lady, none of the early interpreters do, a fact that may seem astonishing (Castelvetro, in 1570, may have been the first to do so).

97.   Lucy, the martyred Syracusan virgin (fourth century), whose name itself associates her with light, obviously played a special role in Dante's devotional life. She will reappear in *Purg.* IX.52–63, where she indeed carries Dante from the valley in which he sleeps in the ante-purgatory to the gate of purgatory itself; and then she is seen seated in blessedness (*Par.* XXXII.137–138). See the discussion in Jacoff and Stephany (Jaco.1989.1), pp. 29–38.

102.   Rachel, the fourth lady indicated as dwelling in heaven, presented here as Beatice's "neighbor," is traditionally interpreted (as she is by Dante himself—see *Purg.* XXVII.94–108) as the contemplative life, as her sister Leah represents the active one. Since the fourteenth century there have been frequent (and widely varying) attempts to "allegorize" the Virgin, Lucy, and Beatrice, most often as various varieties of grace (see Padoan's commentary to v. 97 for a brief summary). There is no textual basis for such efforts, as appealing as many readers apparently find them.

105.   What exactly does it mean, Lucy's insistence to Beatrice that, for her sake, Dante "left the vulgar herd" (*la volgare schiera*)? Guido da Pisa interprets the phrase to mean Dante turned from the study of the liberal arts to theology. Without debating such a judgment, one might add a poetic dimension to it, as has Francesco Mazzoni (Mazz.1967.1, pp. 289–93). According to him, the most important meaning of the verse is to reflect Dante's turning from a "conventional" amorous poetic subject matter to what he will later call the "dolce stil novo" (*Purg.* XXIV.57), a poetry that presents, in a new "style," the higher meaning of Beatrice. (Some would go further, still, and suggest that this meaning is essentially Christological— see Holl.1999.1.) Mazzoni's view is seconded by the importance of the word *volgare* to Dante. While it is surely at times limited to the negative sense of the Latin *vulgus*, pertaining to the common people, the "mob," it is also the word that he uses to describe his own vernacular speech, as in the title of his treatise *De vulgari eloquentia* ("On Eloquence in the Vernacular").

The view that Dante's sense of his own poetic vocation is central to the meaning of this verse is supported by the text at *Inf.* IV.101, where the group of classical poets, who so graciously include Dante in their number, is also described as a *schiera* (company).

107–108.   As tormented a passage as may be found in this canto, and one of the most difficult in the entire work, whether for its literal sense (what "death"? what "river"? what "sea"?) or its possibly only metaphorical meaning. See Mazzoni's summary of the centuries-long debate over the passage (Mazz.1967.1), pp. 294–303, as well as Freccero's essay (Frec.1986.1 [1966]), pp. 55–69. For discussion of a "typological" reading of the passage see Holl.1990.2, pp. 110–11, associating the narrated action with a temporarily halted attempt to enter the River Jordan.

For the literal sense in which the Dead Sea is not a "sea," but a "lake" that receives the waters of Jordan see Filippo Villani (Bell. 1989.1, p. 109): "And, in the literal sense, the river Jordan does not flow into a sea, but ends in a lake that is bright and clear, even pleasant."

109–114. Beatrice concludes her speech by expressing the efficacy of Lucy's words on Dante's behalf, which won her over to interceding with Virgil in order to give her beloved a second chance. (*Purgatorio* XXX and XXXI will reveal that she had grounds for being less charitable to her backsliding lover.) Her speech concludes with the same sort of *captatio benevolentiae* that marked its inception at v. 58, now couched in terms that praise Virgil's *parlare onesto*. The phrase means more than "honest speech," as is made clear by its etymological propinquity to the verb *onora* (honors) in the next line. "Noble" (found also in Sinclair's translation) seemed to the translators a reasonable way to attempt to bridge the gap between "honest" and "decorous," retaining a sense of moral and stylistic gravity for the words of the greatest poet of pagan antiquity—which Virgil was for Dante.

116. Beatrice's tears remind us of Venus's when the goddess weeps for her burdened son in *Aeneid* I.228, as was perhaps first suggested by Holl. 1969.1, pp. 91–92. See also Jaco. 1982.1, p. 3, showing that the verse probably reflects Rachel's tears for her lost children (Jeremiah 31:15)— who are eventually restored to her (as will Dante be to Beatrice).

118–126. Virgil offers a summation, as might a modern lawyer concluding his charge to a jury or a classical or medieval orator convincing his learned auditors as he concludes his argument. Virgil has saved Dante from the she-wolf; why has his pupil not been more ready to follow him? And now there is the further evidence of the three heavenly ladies who have also interceded on Dante's behalf, thus giving confirmation of the justness of what Virgil had sketched as a plan for Dante's journey (*Inf.* I.112–123).

133–135. For the resonance of I Kings 17:22–24, especially the phrase "the word of the Lord in your mouth is truth," see Ferr. 1995.1, p. 114. And for the *vere parole* of Beatrice, see also the "veras . . . voces" that Aeneas would like to exchange with mother Venus, *Aeneid* I.409, as noted by Jaco. 1989.1, pp. 21–22.

140. For the words *duca, segnore,* and *maestro,* as well as others, terms used by Dante for his guide, see Gmel. 1966.1, pp. 59–60, offering the following

enumeration of these: *duca* is used 19 times in *Inferno* and 17 times in *Purgatorio*; *maestro,* 34 times in *Inferno*, 17 in *Purgatorio*; *signore,* 8 times; *poeta,* 8 times in *Inferno*, 7 times in *Purgatorio*; *savio,* 6 times; *padre,* 10 times.

142.   Knitting together the two proemial cantos, the word *cammino* occupies their first and final verses.

INFERNO III

"Per me si va ne la città dolente,
per me si va ne l'etterno dolore,
3   per me si va tra la perduta gente.

Giustizia mosse il mio alto fattore;
fecemi la divina podestate,
6   la somma sapïenza e 'l primo amore.

Dinanzi a me non fuor cose create
se non etterne, e io etterno duro.
9   Lasciate ogne speranza, voi ch'intrate."

Queste parole di colore oscuro
vid' ïo scritte al sommo d'una porta;
12   per ch'io: "Maestro, il senso lor m'è duro."

Ed elli a me, come persona accorta:
"Qui si convien lasciare ogne sospetto;
15   ogne viltà convien che qui sia morta.

Noi siam venuti al loco ov' i' t'ho detto
che tu vedrai le genti dolorose
18   c'hanno perduto il ben de l'intelletto."

E poi che la sua mano a la mia puose
con lieto volto, ond' io mi confortai,
21   mi mise dentro a le segrete cose.

Quivi sospiri, pianti e alti guai
risonavan per l'aere sanza stelle,
24   per ch'io al cominciar ne lagrimai.

Diverse lingue, orribili favelle,
parole di dolore, accenti d'ira,
27   voci alte e fioche, e suon di man con elle

THROUGH ME THE WAY TO THE CITY OF WOE,
THROUGH ME THE WAY TO ETERNAL PAIN,
3   THROUGH ME THE WAY AMONG THE LOST.

JUSTICE MOVED MY MAKER ON HIGH.
DIVINE POWER MADE ME,
6   WISDOM SUPREME, AND PRIMAL LOVE.

BEFORE ME NOTHING WAS BUT THINGS ETERNAL,
AND I ENDURE ETERNALLY.
9   ABANDON ALL HOPE, YOU WHO ENTER HERE.

These words, dark in hue, I saw inscribed
over an archway. And then I said:
12   'Master, for me their meaning is hard.'

And he, as one who understood:
'Here you must banish all distrust,
15   here must all cowardice be slain.

'We have come to where I said
you would see the miserable sinners
18   who have lost the good of the intellect.'

And after he had put his hand on mine
with a reassuring look that gave me comfort,
21   he led me toward things unknown to man.

Now sighs, loud wailing, lamentation
resounded through the starless air,
24   so that I too began to weep.

Unfamiliar tongues, horrendous accents,
words of suffering, cries of rage, voices
27   loud and faint, the sound of slapping hands—

facevano un tumulto, il qual s'aggira
sempre in quell' aura sanza tempo tinta,
30   come la rena quando turbo spira.

E io ch'avea d'error la testa cinta,
dissi: "Maestro, che è quel ch'i' odo?
33   e che gent' è che par nel duol sì vinta?"

Ed elli a me: "Questo misero modo
tegnon l'anime triste di coloro
36   che visser sanza 'nfamia e sanza lodo.

Mischiate sono a quel cattivo coro
de li angeli che non furon ribelli
39   né fur fedeli a Dio, ma per sé fuoro.

Caccianli i ciel per non esser men belli,
né lo profondo inferno li riceve,
42   ch'alcuna gloria i rei avrebber d'elli."

E io: "Maestro, che è tanto greve
a lor che lamentar li fa sì forte?"
45   Rispuose: "Dicerolti molto breve.

Questi non hanno speranza di morte,
e la lor cieca vita è tanto bassa,
48   che 'nvidïosi son d'ogne altra sorte.

Fama di loro il mondo esser non lassa;
misericordia e giustizia li sdegna:
51   non ragioniam di lor, ma guarda e passa."

E io, che riguardai, vidi una 'nsegna
che girando correva tanto ratta,
54   che d'ogne posa mi parea indegna;

e dietro le venìa sì lunga tratta
di gente, ch'i' non averei creduto
57   che morte tanta n'avesse disfatta.

all these made a tumult, always whirling
in that black and timeless air,
30   as sand is swirled in a whirlwind.

And I, my head encircled by error, said:
'Master, what is this I hear, and what people
33   are these so overcome by pain?'

And he to me: 'This miserable state is borne
by the wretched souls of those who lived
36   without disgrace yet without praise.

'They intermingle with that wicked band
of angels, not rebellious and not faithful
39   to God, who held themselves apart.

'Loath to impair its beauty, Heaven casts them out,
and depth of Hell does not receive them
42   lest on their account the evil angels gloat.'

And I: 'Master, what is so grievous to them,
that they lament so bitterly?'
45   He replied: 'I can tell you in few words.

'They have no hope of death,
and their blind life is so abject
48   that they are envious of every other lot.

'The world does not permit report of them.
Mercy and justice hold them in contempt.
51   Let us not speak of them—look and pass by.'

And I, all eyes, saw a whirling banner
that ran so fast it seemed as though
54   it never could find rest.

Behind it came so long a file of people
that I could not believe
57   death had undone so many.

Poscia ch'io v'ebbi alcun riconosciuto,
vidi e conobbi l'ombra di colui
60   che fece per viltade il gran rifiuto.

Incontanente intesi e certo fui
che questa era la setta d'i cattivi,
63   a Dio spiacenti e a' nemici sui.

Questi sciaurati, che mai non fur vivi,
erano ignudi e stimolati molto
66   da mosconi e da vespe ch'eran ivi.

Elle rigavan lor di sangue il volto,
che, mischiato di lagrime, a' lor piedi
69   da fastidiosi vermi era ricolto.

E poi ch'a riguardar oltre mi diedi,
vidi genti a la riva d'un gran fiume;
72   per ch'io dissi: "Maestro, or mi concedi

ch'i' sappia quali sono, e qual costume
le fa di trapassar parer sì pronte,
75   com' i' discerno per lo fioco lume."

Ed elli a me: "Le cose ti fier conte
quando noi fermerem li nostri passi
78   su la trista riviera d'Acheronte."

Allor con li occhi vergognosi e bassi,
temendo no 'l mio dir li fosse grave,
81   infino al fiume del parlar mi trassi.

Ed ecco verso noi venir per nave
un vecchio, bianco per antico pelo,
84   gridando: "Guai a voi, anime prave!

Non isperate mai veder lo cielo:
i' vegno per menarvi a l'altra riva
87   ne le tenebre etterne, in caldo e 'n gelo.

After I recognized a few of these,
I saw and knew the shade of him
60   who, through cowardice, made the great refusal.

At once with certainty I understood
this was that worthless crew
63   hateful alike to God and to His foes.

These wretches, who never were alive,
were naked and beset
66   by stinging flies and wasps

that made their faces stream with blood,
which, mingled with their tears,
69   was gathered at their feet by loathsome worms.

And then, fixing my gaze farther on,
I saw souls standing on the shore of a wide river,
72   and so I said: 'Master, permit me first

'to know who they are and then what inner law
makes them so eager for the crossing,
75   or so it seems in this dim light.'

And he to me: 'You shall know these things,
but not before we stay our steps
78   on the mournful shore of Acheron.'

Then, my eyes cast down with shame,
fearing my words displeased him,
81   I did not speak until we reached that stream.

And now, coming toward us in a boat,
an old man, his hair white with age, cried out:
84   'Woe unto you, you wicked souls,

'give up all hope of ever seeing heaven.
I come to take you to the other shore,
87   into eternal darkness, into heat and chill.

E tu che se' costì, anima viva,
pàrtiti da cotesti che son morti."
90   Ma poi che vide ch'io non mi partiva,

disse: "Per altra via, per altri porti
verrai a piaggia, non qui, per passare:
93   più lieve legno convien che ti porti."

E 'l duca lui: "Caron, non ti crucciare:
vuolsi così colà dove si puote
96   ciò che si vuole, e più non dimandare."

Quinci fuor quete le lanose gote
al nocchier de la livida palude,
99   che 'ntorno a li occhi avea di fiamme rote.

Ma quell' anime, ch'eran lasse e nude,
cangiar colore e dibattero i denti,
102   ratto che 'nteser le parole crude.

Bestemmiavano Dio e lor parenti,
l'umana spezie e 'l loco e 'l tempo e 'l seme
105   di lor semenza e di lor nascimenti.

Poi si ritrasser tutte quante insieme,
forte piangendo, a la riva malvagia
108   ch'attende ciascun uom che Dio non teme.

Caron dimonio, con occhi di bragia
loro accennando, tutte le raccoglie;
111   batte col remo qualunque s'adagia.

Come d'autunno si levan le foglie
l'una appresso de l'altra, fin che 'l ramo
114   vede a la terra tutte le sue spoglie,

similemente il mal seme d'Adamo
gittansi di quel lito ad una ad una,
117   per cenni come augel per suo richiamo.

'And you there, you living soul,
move aside from these now dead.'
90   But when he saw I did not move,

he said: 'By another way, another port,
not here, you'll come to shore and cross.
93   A lighter ship must carry you.'

And my leader: 'Charon, do not torment yourself.
It is so willed where will and power are one,
96   and ask no more.'

That stilled the shaggy jowls
of the pilot of the livid marsh,
99   about whose eyes burned wheels of flame.

But those souls, naked and desolate,
lost their color. With chattering teeth
102   they heard his brutal words.

They blasphemed God, their parents,
the human race, the place, the time, the seed
105   of their begetting and their birth.

Then, weeping bitterly, they drew together
to the accursèd shore that waits
108   for every man who fears not God.

Charon the demon, with eyes of glowing coals,
beckons to them, herds them all aboard,
111   striking anyone who slackens with his oar.

Just as in autumn the leaves fall away,
one, and then another, until the bough
114   sees all its spoil upon the ground,

so the wicked seed of Adam fling themselves
one by one from shore, at his signal,
117   as does a falcon at its summons.

Così sen vanno su per l'onda bruna,
e avanti che sien di là discese,
120   anche di qua nuova schiera s'auna.

"Figliuol mio," disse 'l maestro cortese,
"quelli che muoion ne l'ira di Dio
123   tutti convegnon qui d'ogne paese;

e pronti sono a trapassar lo rio,
ché la divina giustizia li sprona,
126   sì che la tema si volve in disio.

Quinci non passa mai anima buona;
e però, se Caron di te si lagna,
129   ben puoi sapere omai che 'l suo dir suona."

Finito questo, la buia campagna
tremò sì forte, che de lo spavento
132   la mente di sudore ancor mi bagna.

La terra lagrimosa diede vento,
che balenò una luce vermiglia
la qual mi vinse ciascun sentimento;
136   e caddi come l'uom cui sonno piglia.

Thus they depart over dark water,
and before they have landed on the other side
120   another crowd has gathered on this shore.

'My son,' said the courteous master,
'all those who die in the wrath of God
123   assemble here from every land.

'And they are eager to cross the river,
for the justice of God so spurs them on
126   their very fear is turned to longing.

'No good soul ever crosses at this place.
Thus, if Charon complains on your account,
129   now you can grasp the meaning of his words.'

When he had ended, the gloomy plain shook
with such force, the memory of my terror
132   makes me again break out in sweat.

From the weeping ground there sprang a wind,
flaming with vermilion light,
which overmastered all my senses,
136   and I dropped like a man pulled down by sleep.

1–9.   Modern editions vary in using capital or lower-case letters for this inscription over the gate of hell. Lacking Dante's autograph MS, we can only conjecture. For the view that the model for these words is found in the victorious inscriptions found on Roman triumphal arches, sculpted in capital letters in stone, see Holl.1969.1, p. 300. In this view every condemned sinner is being led back captive to "that Rome of which Christ is Roman" (*Purg.* XXXII.102), "under the yoke" into God's holy kingdom, where he or she will be eternally a prisoner.

1–3.   For the city as the poem's centering image of political life, the hellish earthly city, resembling Florence, "which stands for the self and against the common good," and the heavenly city, an idealized view of imperial Rome, see Ferrante (Ferr.1984.1), pp. 41–42. The anaphora, or repetition, of the phrase *per me si va,* as it comes "uttered" by the gate of hell itself in the first three verses, has a ring of inevitable doom about it.

4.   "Justice moved my maker on high." Dante's verse may seem to violate the Aristotelian/Thomist definition of God as the "unmoved mover." Strictly speaking, *nothing* can "move" God, who Himself moves all things (even if He can be described in the Bible as feeling anger at humankind, etc.). Dante's apparently theologically incorrect statement shows the importance of his sense of justice as the central force in the universe, so encompassing that it may be seen as, in a sense, God's "muse," as well as the primary subject of the poem. The word in its noun form appears fully thirty-five times in the poem (see Holl.1992.1, pp. 40–41).

5–6.   The three attributes of the Trinity—Power, Wisdom, and Love—are nearly universally recognized as informing these two verses. Hell is of God's making, not an independent "city" of rebels, but a totally dependent *polis* of those who had rebelled against their maker. For the postbiblical concept of the Trinity, especially as it was advanced in St. Augustine's *De Trinitate,* where Father, Son, and Holy Spirit is each identified by one of these attributes, respectively, see G. Fallani, "Trinità" (*ED,* vol. 5, 1976, pp. 718–21).

7–8.   The apparent difficulty of these verses (perhaps reflected in Dante's difficulty in understanding the writing over the gate, *Inf.* III.12) is resolved once we understand that here "eternal" is used to mean "sempiternal," that is, as having had a beginning in time but lasting ever after. Only God, who is not created but all-creating, may be considered eternal. See Mazz.1967.1, pp. 331–36. Mazzoni, in agreement with B. Nardi (Nard.1959.1), p. 17, allows this status to three classes of being: angels, prime matter (that is, the potential form of the as yet uncreated world), and the heavenly spheres. For Matthew's description of Christ's Judgment of the damned see Matth. 25:41, 46: "Then shall he say also unto them on the left hand, Depart from me, ye cursed, into everlasting fire, prepared for the devil and his angels . . . And these shall go away into everlasting punishment: but the righteous into life eternal."

10. Are the letters of these words "dark in hue," as are the inset carvings over actual gates, begrimed by time (or, as some early commentators urged, because they are hellishly menacing)? Or are they rhetorically difficult, and "dark" in that respect? The phrase "rhetorical colors" to indicate the rhetor's stylistic techniques is familiar from classical rhetoric and is found in Dante's *Vita nuova*, e.g., *VN* XXV.7; XXV.10. Whichever understanding one chooses, one will have to make a decision consonant with an interpretation of verse 12, below.

12. There is a fairly serious disagreement over the most probable interpretation of the words "for me their meaning is hard." Our translation tries to reflect both possibilities, suggesting that one is clearly present, while the second may be only latent. Are the words over the gate of hell (1) threatening to Dante? Or (2) are they hard for him to understand? It seems clear that the traveler is frightened by the dire advice tendered in verse 9, which would have him abandon all hope. Mazzoni (Mazz.1967.1), pp. 337–42, offers a lengthy gloss to this tercet. It seems impossible not to accept his basic premise, namely that the context of the scene makes the meaning immediate and moral: the traveler is afraid, and Virgil reproves him for his fear (vv. 14–15).

13–15. The phrase "as one who understood" lends Virgil authority in two regards: he is aware of Dante's moral shortcomings and he understands the underworld, since he has descended once before (see *Inf.* IX.22–27, XXI.63).

18. The "good of the intellect" has long been understood as God. See Mazz. 1967.1, p. 343, citing *Paradiso* IV.116, where God is the "fonte ond' ogne ver deriva" (the source from which all truth derives).

21. The translation "things unknown [*segrete*] to man" avoids the rendering of *segrete* by the English cognate "secret." The word here does not mean "secret" so much as "cut off from."

22–30. This first sense impression of the underworld is exclusively aural. We are probably meant to understand that Dante's eyes are not yet accustomed to the darkness of hell. Cf. *Inferno* IV.25–27 and XI.11—where his olfactory capacity must become used to the stench of nether hell.

24. This first instance of Dante's weeping is part of a program of the protagonist's development in hell, in which he (very) gradually overcomes the twin temptations to weep for or feel fear at the situation of the sinners in Inferno. See Holl.1969.1, pp. 301–7.

25. The adjective *diverse* here means either "different the one from the other" (on the model of the confused languages spoken after the construction of the Tower of Babel) or "strange," a meaning for the adjective frequently found in Dante. In our translation we have tried to allow for both meanings. Mazzoni (Mazz.1967.1), p. 348, cites v. 123 as further evidence for the first interpretation; there those who die in the wrath of God "assemble here from every land," a phrasing that calls attention to differing nationalities and thus suggests a plurality of tongues.

27. *E suon di man con elle* (the sound of slapping hands): Boccaccio's gloss to *Inferno* IX.49–51, "battiensi a palme" (strike themselves with the palms of their hands), which describes the Furies beating their breasts "as here on earth do women who feel great sadness, or who behave as though they did," may help unravel this verse as well: the sound is that of hands striking the sinners' own bodies as they beat their breasts, as Boccaccio had already suggested in his gloss to this verse; "as women do when they strike themselves with their open palms."

34–36. For the history of the interpretation of this tercet, now generally understood to indicate the presence in the "ante-inferno," or vestibule of hell, of the neutrals, those who never took a side, see Mazzoni (Mazz.1967.1), pp. 355–67. And, for the existence of exactly such a "vestibule" in hell in the apocryphal *Visio Pauli*, describing St. Paul's descent to the netherworld, see Silverstein (Silv.1937.1). In Paul's vision (for the most recent text see Silv.1997.1) there is a river of flame separating "those who were neither hot nor cold" (Revelation 3:15–16) from the other sinners.

37–39.   There has been a lengthy dispute in the commentary tradition as to whether or not Dante has invented the neutral angels or is reflecting a medieval tradition that had itself "invented" them (since they are not, properly speaking, biblical in origin). This is presented at length by Mazzoni (Mazz.1967.1), pp. 368–76, who shows that such a tradition did exist and probably helped to shape Dante's conceptualization. On this problem see Nardi (Nard.1960.1), pp. 331–50. See also Freccero's 1960 essay "The Neutral Angels" (Frec.1986.1), pp. 110–18.

40–42.   To what does the adjective *rei* ("evil") refer, the neutral angels or *all* of the damned? The neutral angels (v. 38) are the antecedent of the pronoun *li* in vv. 40 and 41. It seems clear that this is also true with respect to the adjective in v. 42, and thus our translation, "lest on their account the evil angels gloat." That the adjective is to be treated as an adjectival noun for "the wicked," i.e., the damned in general, is an idea that has only entered commentaries in our own century.

46–48.   Paraphrased: "Like all the rest, these sinners have no hope of improving their posthumous lot; but their foul condition is such that they are envious of every other class of sinners."

50.   *Misericordia e giustizia* ("Mercy and justice") are here to be understood as heaven and hell, neither of which will entertain any report of such vile creatures.

52–57.   Dante's essential technique for indicating the crucial moral failures of his various groups of sinners is here before us for the first time. The neutrals, who never took a side, are portrayed as an organized crowd following a banner: exactly what they were not in life (e.g., the neutral angels who neither rebelled directly against God nor stood with Him, but who kept to one side). And in this respect the neutrals are punished by being forced to assume a pose antithetic to that which they struck in life. At the same time, the banner that they follow is the very essence of indeterminacy. Not only is there no identifying sign on it, it is not held in the anchoring hand of any standard-bearer; it is a parody of the standard raised before a body of men who follow a leader. Elsewhere we will encounter other such symbolic artifacts. In Dante's hell the punishment of sin involves the application of opposites and similarities. This form of just retribution is what Dante will later refer to as the *contrapasso* (*Inf.* XXVIII.142).

58–60.   The most-debated passage of this canto, at least in the modern
era. Many of the early commentators were convinced that it clearly
intended a biting reference to Pope Celestine V (Pier da Morrone), who
abdicated the papacy in 1294 after having held the office for less than four
months. He was followed into it by Dante's great ecclesiastical enemy,
Pope Boniface VIII, and colorful contemporary accounts would have it
that Boniface mimicked the voice of the Holy Spirit in the air passages
leading to Celestine's bedchamber, counseling his abdication. Mazzoni
(Mazz.1967.1), pp. 390–415, offers a thorough history of the interpretation
of the verse. Two factors led to growing uneasiness with the identification
of Celestine: (1) in 1313 he had been canonized, (2) ca. 1346 Francesco
Petrarca, in his *De vita solitaria*, had defended the motives for his abdica-
tion. Thus, beginning with the second redaction of the commentary of
Pietro di Dante, certainty that the vile self-recuser was Celestine began to
waver. The names of many others have been proposed, including those of
Esau and Pontius Pilate. It seems fair to say that there are fatal objections to
all of these other candidacies. For strong, even convincing, support for that
of Celestine see Padoan (Pado.1961.1) and Simonelli (Simo.1993.1), pp.
41–58. Telling objections to Petrocchi's denial that Dante would have put
the canonized (in 1313) Celestine in hell (Petr.1969.1 [1955], pp. 41–59) are
found in Nardi (Nard.1960.1).

   The word *viltà* (cowardice) is the very opposite of nobility of charac-
ter. See *Convivio* IV.xvi.6 for Dante's own statement of this commonplace:
" 'nobile' [. . .] viene da 'non vile' " ["noble" derives from "not vile"]. And
we should remember that Dante himself has twice been accused by Virgil
of *viltà* because of his cowardice in not immediately accepting his Heaven-
ordained mission (*Inf.* II.45, II.122).

64–69.   The second descriptive passage that indicates the condition of
these sinners continues the *contrapasso*. Now we see that these beings, who
lacked all inner stimulation, are stung (*stimolati*) by noxious insects. Their
tears mix with the blood drawn by these wounds only to serve as food for
worms. Dante's personal hatred for those who, unlike him, never made
their true feelings or opinions known irradiates this canto. There is not a
single detail that falls short of the condition of eternal insult.

64.   M. Barbi (Barb.1934.1), p. 261: *sciaurati* must be understood as "vile,
abject, worthless," as a bitterly negative term with no softness in it. Simi-
larly, the phrase *che mai non fur vivi* (who never were alive) is darkened by

its probable source, cited by several modern commentators (perhaps first by Sapegno) in Rev. 3:1: "Nomen habes quod vivas, et mortuus es" (you have a name that you are alive, and are dead), a fitting castigation for Dante to have had in mind for the neutrals.

70–71. These verses mark a split between the second and third scenes of the canto, the neutrals and those other sinners, of all kinds, who are destined to begin their travel to their final destinations in Charon's bark. From this point on the action of the canto moves to the near bank of the Acheron. The next canto will begin on the other side of the river.

75. The "dim light": Dante's first experience of hell proper was one of utter darkness. Indeed, his first sense impressions of the neutrals are entirely auditory (vv. 22–33). Now the character himself assures us that he has begun to see at least a little (starting at v. 52).

76–78. Virgil's rather clipped response, in marked contrast with his ready response to Dante's question about the identity of the neutrals (vv. 34–42), causes Dante to feel ashamed (vv. 79–81). The exact reason for Virgil's reproof is a matter of some debate. One might argue that his point is that Dante has gotten ahead of himself. In the first instance, he asked about the nature of those he saw displayed just before him. Now he is anticipating, literally looking ahead, and Virgil warns him against such behavior.

88. Charon's insistence on Dante's difference—he is alive, the others dead—will find frequent repetition as the protagonist's extraordinary presence in hell is noted by various guardians and damned souls.

91–93. Most today take Charon's formulation to refer to Dante's eventual passage to purgatory aboard the angel-guided ship that we see in *Purgatorio* II.41.

94. Charon, introduced first (vv. 82–83) only by his characteristics (in a typical Dantean gesture, making us wonder who this imposing figure might be), is now named, and will be twice more (vv. 109, 128). This highly insistent naming should make it plain that Dante is serious about proposing the notion that the guardian of hell is derived from the Sixth Book of Virgil's poem. It is fascinating, however, to watch the early commentators, so used to reading any fiction as though it were "allegorical,"

"dehistoricizing" Charon. Among the early commentators Charon is variously understood as "fleshly desire," "disordered love," "ancient sinfulness," "vice," "time," etc. It is surely better to understand him first and foremost as himself.

95–96.   These two verses are repeated, word for word, at *Inferno* V.23–24. This is the longest example of a word-for-word repetition that we find in the entire poem.

104–105.   Our translation is in accord with the literal interpretation of Padoan's comment to this verse, against those who understand *seme* to refer to their ancestors, *semenza* to their parents. For an apposite citation of Job 3:3 ("Let the day perish wherein I was born, and the night in which it was said: A man child is conceived") see Fron.1998.1, p. 47.

109.   For Dante's possible reliance, in his description of Charon's eyes, on the *Roman d'Enéas*, v. 2449 ("roges les oitz come charbons" [his eyes were red as coals]), see Spag.1997.1, pp. 120–22; 134–35.

111.   The verb *s'adagia* has been variously interpreted, either to mean that the souls delay entering Charon's skiff, or that, once in it, they seat themselves in so self-indulgent a manner as to draw Charon's wrath.

112–120.   Where each of the first two cantos has had two major similes (*Inf.* I.22–27; I.55–60; II.37–42; II.127–132), the third canto has only this double simile that describes the final action of the canto, the departure of the sinners in Charon's skiff. It is a commonplace that the third canto is the most "Virgilian" canto of the *Commedia*. In fact, study has shown that it has more than twice as many Virgilian citations than any other canto in the poem (see Holl.1993.1, pp. 250–51). This double simile has long been recognized as involving an amalgam of two Virgilian passages (*Aen.* VI.309–312 and *Georg.* II.82). It has also been understood as comprising the "controlling simile" for the entire poem, combining pagan and Christian elements: see the article by M. Frankel (Fran.1982.1).

125–126.   Virgil now is willing to answer the question that Dante posed earlier (vv. 73–74): divine justice spurs these sinners so that they are eager to cross the river and find their perdition.

130–134.   For the Aristotelian/Thomist sources of Dante's meteorology, the subterranean winds that cause earthquakes, see Mazzoni (Mazz.1967.1), pp. 446–52.

136.   Dante's falling into unconsciousness indicates his inability to deal with the overwhelming experience of his crossing into the realm of hell proper, an "inability" apparently shared by the poet, who simply does not tell us how he crossed the river. The protagonist will suffer a similar lapse at the conclusion of the fifth canto (*Inf.* V.142).

The question of how Dante crosses Acheron is much debated. The pointed lack of concrete reference to how he is transported is a sign either of the poet's reticence or confusion or of his having set a little problem for his readers. It has become acceptable, on the heels of the lengthy gloss offered by Mazzoni (Mazz.1967.1), pp. 452–55, to suggest that the poet has deliberately left the issue unresolved. Yet that does not seem a likely hypothesis. The moment is too important, supported by too many details, to be dealt with as anything less than a problematic mystery that the poet asks us to solve. Mazzoni registers the various theories that account for his transporter (Charon, an angel, Virgil, Beatrice, Lucia, some unnamed supernatural force.) But see the countering argument of Hollander (Holl.1984.1), p. 292: We are in fact meant to understand that it is Charon who takes Dante across and that this *crux* is entirely the result of interpretive overexertion that has made the self-evident confusing. Charon indeed does wish to refuse Dante passage in his skiff (vv. 88–93); to his protestations Virgil responds as follows (vv. 94–96): "Charon, do not torment yourself. It is so willed where will and power are one, and ask no more." Daniello, commenting on these verses, says that Virgil's words have the same effect on Charon that the Sibyl's display of the golden bough had on him. For Charon to be able to resist such a command would involve Dante in a theological or at least a poetic absurdity. Cf. the similar moment at *Inferno* V.16–24, where Minos likewise would resist Dante's passage through his realm and where Virgil employs the same incantatory phrase that he had uttered in Canto III to achieve the same result. Would Virgil have uttered the spell again had it not previously proved efficacious? That seems a most doubtful proposition. It seems likely that Dante's reason for not permitting us to witness the first scene being played out (we are given another version of the scene upon which it is modeled a bit later at *Inf.* VIII.25–27) is that he found that poetic choice an excessive one, too self-consciously reminiscent of Aeneas's fanciful entrance into the underworld for him to make evident reference to it at this important moment, the threshold of his Christian afterworld. If this argument has merit, it accounts for the poet's reticence on poetic grounds. Dante easily could have told us what he wants us to make ourselves responsible for; but that is not his way. Rather, he makes us his partners in taking responsibility for such incredible details as these all through this incredible poem.

INFERNO IV

Ruppemi l'alto sonno ne la testa
un greve truono, sì ch'io mi riscossi
3   come persona ch'è per forza desta;

e l'occhio riposato intorno mossi,
dritto levato, e fiso riguardai
6   per conoscer lo loco dov' io fossi.

Vero è che 'n su la proda mi trovai
de la valle d'abisso dolorosa
9   che 'ntrono accoglie d'infiniti guai.

Oscura e profonda era e nebulosa
tanto che, per ficcar lo viso a fondo,
12   io non vi discernea alcuna cosa.

"Or discendiam qua giù nel cieco mondo,"
cominciò il poeta tutto smorto.
15   "Io sarò primo, e tu sarai secondo."

E io, che del color mi fui accorto,
dissi: "Come verrò, se tu paventi
18   che suoli al mio dubbiare esser conforto?"

Ed elli a me: "L'angoscia de le genti
che son qua giù, nel viso mi dipigne
21   quella pietà che tu per tema senti.

Andiam, ché la via lunga ne sospigne."
Così si mise e così mi fé intrare
24   nel primo cerchio che l'abisso cigne.

Quivi, secondo che per ascoltare,
non avea pianto mai che di sospiri
27   che l'aura etterna facevan tremare;

A heavy thunderclap broke my deep sleep
so that I started up like one
3   shaken awake by force.

With rested eyes, I stood
and looked about me, then fixed my gaze
6   to make out where I was.

I found myself upon the brink
of an abyss of suffering
9   filled with the roar of endless woe.

It was full of vapor, dark and deep.
Straining my eyes toward the bottom,
12   I could see nothing.

'Now let us descend into the blind world
down there,' began the poet, gone pale.
15   'I will be first and you come after.'

And I, noting his pallor, said:
'How shall I come if you're afraid,
18   you, who give me comfort when I falter?'

And he to me: 'The anguish of the souls
below us paints my face
21   with pity you mistake for fear.

'Let us go, for the long road calls us.'
Thus he went first and had me enter
24   the first circle girding the abyss.

Here, as far as I could tell by listening,
was no lamentation other than the sighs
27   that kept the air forever trembling.

ciò avvenia di duol sanza martìri,
ch'avean le turbe, ch'eran molte e grandi,
30   d'infanti e di femmine e di viri.

Lo buon maestro a me: "Tu non dimandi
che spiriti son questi che tu vedi?
33   Or vo' che sappi, innanzi che più andi,

ch'ei non peccaro; e s'elli hanno mercedi,
non basta, perché non ebber battesmo,
36   ch'è porta de la fede che tu credi;

e s' e' furon dinanzi al cristianesmo,
non adorar debitamente a Dio:
39   e di questi cotai son io medesmo.

Per tai difetti, non per altro rio,
semo perduti, e sol di tanto offesi
42   che sanza speme vivemo in disio."

Gran duol mi prese al cor quando lo 'ntesi,
però che gente di molto valore
45   conobbi che 'n quel limbo eran sospesi.

"Dimmi, maestro mio, dimmi, segnore,"
comincia' io per volere esser certo
48   di quella fede che vince ogne errore:

"uscicci mai alcuno, o per suo merto
o per altrui, che poi fosse beato?"
51   E quei che 'ntese il mio parlar coverto,

rispuose: "Io era nuovo in questo stato,
quando ci vidi venire un possente,
54   con segno di vittoria coronato.

Trasseci l'ombra del primo parente,
d'Abèl suo figlio e quella di Noè,
57   di Moïsè legista e ubidente;

These came from grief without torment
borne by vast crowds
30   of men, and women, and little children.

My master began: 'You do not ask about
the souls you see? I want you to know,
33   before you venture farther,

'they did not sin. Though they have merit,
that is not enough, for they were unbaptized,
36   denied the gateway to the faith that you profess.

'And if they lived before the Christians lived,
they did not worship God aright.
39   And among these I am one.

'For such defects, and for no other fault,
we are lost, and afflicted but in this,
42   that without hope we live in longing.'

When I understood, great sadness seized my heart,
for then I knew that beings of great worth
45   were here suspended in this Limbo.

'Tell me, master, tell me, sir,' I began,
seeking assurance in the faith
48   that conquers every doubt,

'did ever anyone, either by his own
or by another's merit, go forth from here
51   and rise to blessedness?'

And he, who understood my covert speech:
'I was new to this condition when I saw
54   a mighty one descend, crowned, with the sign of victory.

'Out of our midst he plucked the shade
of our first parent, of Abel his son, of Noah,
57   and of Moses, obedient in giving laws,

Abraàm patrïarca e Davìd re,
Israèl con lo padre e co' suoi nati
60   e con Rachele, per cui tanto fé,

e altri molti, e feceli beati.
E vo' che sappi che, dinanzi ad essi,
63   spiriti umani non eran salvati."

Non lasciavam l'andar perch' ei dicessi,
ma passavam la selva tuttavia,
66   la selva, dico, di spiriti spessi.

Non era lunga ancor la nostra via
di qua dal sonno, quand' io vidi un foco
69   ch'emisperio di tenebre vincia.

Di lungi n'eravamo ancora un poco,
ma non sì ch'io non discernessi in parte
72   ch'orrevol gente possedea quel loco.

"O tu ch'onori scïenzïa e arte,
questi chi son c'hanno cotanta onranza,
75   che dal modo de li altri li diparte?"

E quelli a me: "L'onrata nominanza
che di lor suona sù ne la tua vita,
78   grazïa acquista in ciel che sì li avanza."

Intanto voce fu per me udita:
"Onorate l'altissimo poeta;
81   l'ombra sua torna, ch'era dipartita."

Poi che la voce fu restata e queta,
vidi quattro grand' ombre a noi venire:
84   sembianz' avevan né trista né lieta.

Lo buon maestro cominciò a dire:
"Mira colui con quella spada in mano,
87   che vien dinanzi ai tre sì come sire:

'the patriarch Abraham, and King David,
Israel with his father and his sons,
60   and with Rachel, for whom he served so long,

'as well as many others, and he made them blessed.
And, I would have you know, before these
63   no human souls were saved.'

We did not halt our movement as he spoke,
but all the while were passing through a wood—
66   I mean a wood of thronging spirits.

We had not yet gone far from where I'd slept
when I beheld a blaze of light
69   that overcame a hemisphere of darkness,

though still a good way from it,
yet not so far but I discerned
72   an honorable company was gathered there.

'O you who honor art and knowledge,
why are these so honored they are set
75   apart from the condition of the rest?'

And he answered: 'Their honorable fame,
which echoes in your life above,
78   gains favor in Heaven, which thus advances them.'

Just then I heard a voice that said:
'Honor the loftiest of poets!
81   His shade returns that had gone forth.'

When the voice had paused and there was silence,
I saw four worthy shades approach,
84   their countenances neither sad nor joyful.

The good master spoke: 'Take note
of him who holds that sword in hand
87   and comes as lord before the three:

quelli è Omero poeta sovrano;
l'altro è Orazio satiro che vene;
90 Ovidio è 'l terzo, e l'ultimo Lucano.

Però che ciascun meco si convene
nel nome che sonò la voce sola,
93 fannomi onore, e di ciò fanno bene."

Così vid' i' adunar la bella scola
di quel segnor de l'altissimo canto
96 che sovra li altri com' aquila vola.

Da ch'ebber ragionato insieme alquanto,
volsersi a me con salutevol cenno,
99 e 'l mio maestro sorrise di tanto;

e più d'onore ancora assai mi fenno,
ch'e' sì mi fecer de la loro schiera,
102 sì ch'io fui sesto tra cotanto senno.

Così andammo infino a la lumera,
parlando cose che 'l tacere è bello,
105 sì com' era 'l parlar colà dov' era.

Venimmo al piè d'un nobile castello,
sette volte cerchiato d'alte mura,
108 difeso intorno d'un bel fiumicello.

Questo passammo come terra dura;
per sette porte intrai con questi savi:
111 giugnemmo in prato di fresca verdura.

Genti v'eran con occhi tardi e gravi,
di grande autorità ne' lor sembianti:
114 parlavan rado, con voci soavi.

Traemmoci così da l'un de' canti,
in loco aperto, luminoso e alto,
117 sì che veder si potien tutti quanti.

'He is Homer, sovereign poet.
Next comes Horace the satirist,
90   Ovid is third, the last is Lucan.

'Since each is joined to me
in the name the one voice uttered,
93   they do me honor and, doing so, do well.'

There I saw assembled the fair school
of the lord of loftiest song,
96   soaring like an eagle far above the rest.

After they conversed a while,
they turned to me with signs of greeting,
99   and my master smiled at this.

And then they showed me greater honor still,
for they made me one of their company,
102   so that I became the sixth amidst such wisdom.

Thus we went onward to the light,
speaking of things that here are best unsaid,
105   just as there it was fitting to express them.

We came to the foot of a noble castle,
encircled seven times by towering walls,
108   defended round about by a fair stream.

Over this stream we moved as on dry land.
Through seven gates I entered with these sages
111   until we came to a fresh, green meadow.

People were there with grave, slow-moving eyes
and visages of great authority.
114   They seldom spoke, and then in gentle tones.

When we withdrew over to one side
into an open space, high in the light,
117   we could observe them all.

Colà diritto, sovra 'l verde smalto,
mi fuor mostrati li spiriti magni,
120   che del vedere in me stesso m'essalto.

I' vidi Eletra con molti compagni,
tra 'quai conobbi Ettòr ed Enea,
123   Cesare armato con li occhi grifagni.

Vidi Cammilla e la Pantasilea;
da l'altra parte vidi 'l re Latino
126   che con Lavina sua figlia sedea.

Vidi quel Bruto che cacciò Tarquino,
Lucrezia, Iulia, Marzïa e Corniglia;
129   e solo, in parte, vidi 'l Saladino.

Poi ch'innalzai un poco più le ciglia,
vidi 'l maestro di color che sanno
132   seder tra filosofica famiglia.

Tutti lo miran, tutti onor li fanno:
quivi vid'ïo Socrate e Platone,
135   che 'nnanzi a li altri più presso li stanno;

Democrito che 'l mondo a caso pone,
Dïogenès, Anassagora e Tale,
138   Empedoclès, Eraclito e Zenone;

e vidi il buono accoglitor del quale,
Dïascoride dico; e vidi Orfeo,
141   Tulïo e Lino e Seneca morale;

Euclide geomètra e Tolomeo,
Ipocràte, Avicenna e Galïeno,
144   Averoìs che 'l gran comento feo.

Io non posso ritrar di tutti a pieno,
però che sì mi caccia il lungo tema,
147   che molte volte al fatto il dir vien meno.

There before me on the enameled green
the great spirits were revealed.
120 In my heart I exult at what I saw.

I saw Electra with many of her line,
of whom I recognized Hector, Aeneas,
123 and Caesar, in arms, with his falcon eyes.

I saw Camilla and Penthesilea.
Seated apart I saw King Latinus,
126 and next to him Lavinia, his daughter.

I saw that Brutus who drove out Tarquinius,
Lucretia, Julia, Marcia, and Cornelia.
129 And Saladin I saw, alone, apart.

When I raised my eyes a little higher,
I saw the master of those who know,
132 sitting among his philosophic kindred.

Eyes trained on him, all show him honor.
In front of all the rest and nearest him
135 I saw Socrates and Plato.

I saw Democritus, who ascribes the world
to chance, Diogenes, Anaxagoras, and Thales,
138 Empedocles, Heraclitus, and Zeno.

I saw the skilled collector of the qualities
of things—I mean Dioscorides—and I saw
141 Orpheus, Cicero, Linus, and moral Seneca,

Euclid the geometer, and Ptolemy,
Hippocrates, Avicenna, Galen,
144 and Averroes, who wrote the weighty glosses.

I cannot give account of all of them,
for the length of my theme so drives me on
147 that often the telling comes short of the fact.

La sesta compagnia in due si scema:
per altra via mi mena il savio duca,
fuor de la queta, ne l'aura che trema.

151   E vegno in parte ove non è che luca.

The company of six falls off to two
and my wise leader brings me by another way
out of the still, into the trembling, air.
151   And I come to a place where nothing shines.

1–9.   The last canto had come to its dramatic conclusion with a shaking of the earth accompanied—indeed perhaps caused by—a supernatural lightning bolt that made Dante fall into a fainting "sleep." In medieval opinion such earthquakes were caused by winds imprisoned in the earth. Now he is awakened by the following thunder. As the last verse of *Inferno* III has him overcome by sleep ("sonno"), so in the first line of this canto that sleep is broken, overriding the sharp line of demarcation that a canto ending or beginning seems to imply, as at the boundary between *Inferno* II and III.

There has been a centuries-long debate over the question of whether *this* "thunder" (*truono*), the noise made by the sorrowing damned (v. 9), is the same as the thunderclap of v. 2 (*truono* [the reading in most MSS and editions]). Mazzoni (Mazz.1965.1), pp. 45–49, summarizes that debate. It seems best to understand that *this* noise is not the one that awakens Dante, but the one that he first hears from the inhabitants of Limbo, i.e., that the two identical words indicate diverse phenomena.

13.   That, even according to Virgil, who dwells in it, the world of Limbo is "blind" might have helped hold in check some of the more enthusiastic readings of this canto as exemplary of Dante's "humanistic" inclinations. For important discussions along these lines see Mazzoni, *Introduzione* (Mazz.1965.1), pp. 29–35; Padoan (Pado.1965.1). And see Virgil's own later "gloss" to Limbo (*Purg.* VII.25–30), where he describes his punishment for not believing in Christ-to-come as consisting in his being denied the sight of the Sun. Dante describes Limbo as being without other punishment than its darkness (and indeed here it is described as a "blind world" [*cieco mondo*]), its inhabitants as sighing rather than crying out in pain (v. 26). Had he wanted to make Limbo as positive a place as some of his commentators do, he surely would have avoided, in this verse, the reference to the *descent* that is necessary to reach it. Such was not the case for the neutrals in the previous circle, who apparently dwell at approximately the same level as the floor of the entrance through the gate of hell. This is the first downward movement within the Inferno.

16–17.   Virgil's sudden pallor (v. 14) causes Dante to believe that his guide is fearful, as he himself had been at the end of the previous canto (III.131).

18.   Virgil has given comfort to Dante when the latter has succumbed to doubt in each of the first two cantos.

19–21.   Virgil makes plain the reason for his pallor: he is feeling pity for those who dwell in Limbo (and thus himself as well), not fear. That much seems plain enough. But there has been controversy over the centuries as to whether Virgil refers only to the inhabitants of Limbo or to *all* the damned. Mazzoni (Mazz.1965.1), pp. 58–65, offers a careful review of the problem and concludes that the better reading is the former, demonstrating that Dante has, in five passages in earlier works, made sighs *(sospiri)* the result of feeling anguish *(angoscia)*—as they are here (v. 26).

25–27.   As was true in the last Circle (where the neutrals were punished) the darkness is at first so great that Dante apparently cannot see; his first impressions are only auditory. Compare *Inferno* III.21–30.

30.   This line, seemingly innocent of polemical intent, is in fact in pronounced and deliberate disagreement with St. Thomas (though in accord with Virgil's description of the crowds along the bank of Acheron [*Aen.* VI.306–307]). For Thomas, the inhabitants of Limbo were in one of two classes: the Hebrew saints, harrowed by Christ and taken to heaven, and all unbaptized infants. They are now of that second group alone. Dante's addition of the virtuous pagans is put forward on his own authority. This is perhaps the first of many instances in which Dante chooses to differ with Thomas. For a helpful analysis of the ways in which Dante both follows and separates himself from "authoritative" accounts of the Limbus, see Mazzoni (Mazz.1965.1), pp. 70–80. Mazzoni shows that Dante is in total agreement with Thomas about the presence of the unbaptized infants in Limbo, but disagrees with him (following Bonaventure instead) about whether these infants suffer the pain that comes from knowing of their inability to see God—which Thomas allows himself to doubt. Dante (as does Bonaventure) holds a harsher view on this point. His view of the unbaptized pagans, however, is as mild as his view of the pain of the infants is severe. It is in sharp disagreement with the views of most Christians on this issue. Padoan (Pado.1969.1), p. 371, cites Guido da Pisa's commentary to this verse as exemplary of early puzzled or hostile responses to Dante's inclusion of the virtuous pagans in Limbo: "The Christian faith, however, does not hold that there are any here other than the innocent babes. Here, and in certain other passages, this poet speaks not as a theologian but as a poet."

42.   Virgil's insistence that the inhabitants of Limbo "without hope live in longing" does not as greatly reduce the sense of punishment suffered here, as some argue. See St. Thomas, *De malo*, q. 5, art. 2 (cited by Mazzoni [Mazz.1965.1], p. 69): "Original sin is not fitly punished by sensation, but only by damnation itself, that is, the absence of the sight of God." If their only punishment is that absence, it is nonetheless total.

44.   In at least one respect *Inferno* I and II are cantos paired in opposition, the first rooted in Dante's fear *(paura)*, the second in the reassurance granted by the word *(parola)*, as spoken by Virgil and Beatrice. The same may be said for Cantos III and IV. Mazzoni, following the lead of Forti (Fort.1961.1), identifies the central subject of the first of this pair as "pusillanimità" (cowardice), of the second as "magnanimità" (greatness of soul— Mazz.1965.1, pp. 34–35). See note to Canto III.58–60.

45.   The word *sospesi* ("suspended") has caused great dispute. Are the *limbicoli* "hanging" between heaven and hell? between salvation and damnation? Is there some potential better state awaiting them? Mazzoni's note (Mazz.1965.1), pp. 89–93, leaves little doubt, and resolves their situation as follows: they are punished eternally for their original sin, but are aware (as are none of the other damned souls) of the better life that is denied them. They are "suspended," in other words, between their punishment and their impossible desire.

46–51.   Dante's question has caused discomfort. Why should he seek confirmation of Christ's ascent to heaven from a pagan? Why should he need to confirm his Christian faith on this indisputable point of credence, without which there is no Christian faith? Neither Dante's question nor Virgil's answer concerns itself primarily with Christ's descent to Limbo and ascent to heaven, but rather with the more nebulous facts regarding those who went up *with Him* after the harrowing of hell. See, for a modern recovery of the importance of the harrowing as a concern in Limbo, the work of Iannucci (Iann.1979.2; Iann.1992.1). "Did ever anyone, either by his own or by another's merit, go forth from here and rise to blessedness?" Dante's question refers, first, to the Hebrew patriarchs and matriarchs, second, to unbaptized infants and to all those who were later taken up from Limbo and whose ascent Virgil might have witnessed. Indeed, Virgil's answer will identify more than twenty of those harrowed by Christ; thus we know how he understood Dante's first concern. Dante was interested in confirming what he had heard about the harrowing. But his question does have a second point. Virgil has himself been elevated from hell, if but for a moment. Dante's question alludes, tacitly, to him as well: "Are you one of the saved?" Dante's "covert speech," as the phrase intimates, is focused on the salvation of pagans, and on Virgil in particular. In his gloss to v. 51 Benvenuto da Imola characterizes Dante's view of his own "covert speech" as follows: ". . . as though my words had hidden the thought, 'you great philosophers and poets, your great wisdom, what did it, without faith, accomplish for your salvation? Certainly nothing at all, for even the ancient patriarchs, in their simple, faithful credence, were drawn up out of this prison, in which place you are to remain for ever and ever.' "

52–54.   Virgil tells Dante what he witnessed in 34 A.D., when he was "new" to his condition, some fifty-three years after his death in 19 B.C. He saw a "mighty one" (Christ recognized by Virgil only for his power, an anonymous harrower to the pagan observer). He is either crowned with the sign of victory or crowned and holding the sign of victory, a scepter representing the Cross.

55–61.   Virgil's list of the patriarchs and matriarchs, beginning with "our first parent," Adam (Eve, similarly harrowed, will be seen in the Empyrean [Par. XXXII.5]), Abel, Noah, Moses, Abraham, David, Jacob, Isaac, the (twelve) sons of Jacob (and his daughter, Dinah? [but it seems unlikely that Dante was considering her]), and Rachel. The twenty-one (or twenty-two—if Dante counted Jacob's progeny as we do) Hebrew elders will be added to in Par. XXXII.4–12: Eve, Sarah, Rebecca, Judith, and Ruth, thus accounting for some of the "many others" whom Virgil does not name here, twenty-five men and seven women in all, when we include the others added along the way: Samuel (Par. IV.29), Rahab (Par. IX.116), Solomon (Par. X.109), Joshua (Par. XVIII.38), Judas Maccabeus (Par. XVIII.49), and Ezechiel (Par. XX.49).

62–63.   Virgil's conclusion effectively voids the second part of Dante's question. He has told only of those who were taken by Christ for their own merits.

72.   This new place, the only place in hell in which light is said to overcome darkness (vv. 68–69), is immediately linked to the "key word" of this section of the canto, "honor." This is the densest repetition of a single word and its derivates in the Comedy: seven times in 29 lines (72–100: at

vv. 72, 73, 74, 76, 80, 93, 100), with a "coda" tacked on at v. 133. Can there be any doubt that honor and poetry are indissolubly linked in Dante's view of his own status? As lofty as noble actions and great philosophy may be for him (but that part of the canto, vv. 106–147, has only a single occurrence of the word "honor"), it is poetry that, for Dante, is the great calling.

73.   Padoan's gloss on Dante's phrase is worth noting: *scïenzïa* ("knowledge") is represented by philosophy and the seven liberal arts, while *arte* ("art" in a more restricted sense than is found in the modern term) has to do with the means of expressing knowledge.

78.   Dante's enthusiasm for the power of great poetry is such that he claims that God, in recognition of its greatness, mitigates the punishment of these citizens of Limbo with respect to that of the others there who dwell in darkness (and who were not, we thus conclude, great poets—or doers of great deeds or accomplishers of philosophic wisdom, for these, too, dwell in this lightest part of hell [vv. 106–147]).

79.   There has been debate over the identity of the speaker of the following two lines. Since Dante does not say, specifically, that Homer speaks them, we cannot know that it was he who spoke. Dante steps back and lets us make the ascription. Who else would have spoken? Horace? Perhaps. Certainly not Ovid, not exactly Virgil's greatest supporter. And even less Lucan, whose work rather pointedly attacks what Virgil champions. But the scene makes its inner logic clear: the leader of the group is Homer, who "comes as lord before the three" (v. 87). He speaks first, and Virgil responds.

80–81.   Homer's great compliment to Virgil has so claimed our affectionate attention, resonating in its grave "o" and "a" sounds, that we have not seen the drama in the following verse: "his shade returns that had gone forth." What did Homer and Virgil's other companions think when Beatrice came to Limbo to draw Virgil up to the world of the living? They have witnessed this sort of event before, at least once (the harrowing), and perhaps at least once more (Trajan's latter-day resurrection). A student, Elizabeth Statmore (Princeton '82), in a seminar in February 1982 offered an interesting hypothesis (see Holl.1984.2, p. 219): Virgil's companions thought that he, too, had now been harrowed. But no, here he is again, right back where he belongs.

86.   The sword in Homer's hand indicates not only that he was an epic poet, not only that he is the first among poets, but that, as a result, epic poetry is to be taken as the foremost poetic genre. See note to vv. 95–96.

88–90.   Alessio and Villa argue that the Latin poets in Dante's *bella scola* are divided into generic categories as follows: Virgil: tragedy; Ovid: elegy; Horace: satire; Lucan: history. Missing from such a list is a representative of comedy. They argue that almost any reader would have expected to find Terence's name here, and go on to surmise that Dante has deliberately excluded Terence as the representative of comedy because he has taken that role unto himself (Ales.1993.1, pp. 56–58). For Dante's knowledge of Terence see Vill.1984.1.

For all these authors consult the entries found in the *Enciclopedia dantesca*: Guido Martellotti, "Omero" (*ED*, vol. 4, 1973), pp. 145a–48a; Ettore Paratore, "Ovidio" (*ED*, vol. 4, 1973), pp. 225b–36b; Giorgio Brugnoli and Roberto Mercuri, "Orazio" (*ED*, vol. 4, 1973), pp. 173b–80b; Ettore Paratore, "Lucano" (*ED*, vol. 3, 1971), pp. 697b–702b.

88.   See Mazzoni's discussion of what Dante who, not having Greek, could not and did not read Homer's texts, could in fact know about him (Mazz.1965.1), pp. 137–39. And see Brugnoli (Brug.1993.1).

89.   For Horace's medieval reputation as a satirist see Mazzoni (Mazz. 1965.1), pp. 139–40, Villa (Vill.1993.1), and Reynolds (Reyn.1995.1).

90.   In recent years there has been a growing amount of concerted attention finally being paid to Dante's enormous debt to Ovid, historically overshadowed by the at least apparently even greater one to Virgil. E.g., Jaco.1991.1, containing seven essays on Dante's responses to Ovid, and Pico.1991.1, Pico.1993.1, Pico.1994.1. And see the lengthy treatment by Marthe Dozon (Dozo.1991.1).

Lucan, not studied enough as source for so many of Dante's verses, is also beginning to receive more attention. For a recent study arguing for Dante's close and highly nuanced reading of Lucan, one that helps to account for much of the portrait of his Ulysses, see Stull and Hollander (Stul.1991.1).

93.   Virgil is not suggesting that his fellow ancient poets do well to praise him, but that in praising him they honor their shared profession. If there is

a "humanistic" gesture in this canto, we find it here, "a solemn celebration of the worth of poetry" (Padoan's comment).

95–96.   Two problems of interpretation continue to assault these lines. (1) Is the "lord of loftiest song" Homer or Virgil? Most today agree that Homer is meant. (2) Does the relative pronoun *che* in v. 96 refer to the singer or the song? That is, is it Homer (or Virgil) who soars above all other poets, or is it the lofty style of epic that flies higher than all other forms of poetic expression? Most today prefer the second reading. This argument depends heavily upon the reference of the adjective *altri*. Those who think that the second meaning is most likely point out that the adjective seems to refer to *canto* in the preceding line, while a reference to the "other poets" can only be assumed, since there is no noun to attach to them. Our translation leaves the meaning ambivalent, as Dante seems to do.

99.   The poets' greeting of Dante is the occasion for the only smile found in *Inferno*.

101.   In *Inferno* II.105 Lucy tells Beatrice that Dante, for her sake, had left "the vulgar herd" *(la volgare schiera)*. Exactly what this means is a matter of some dispute, yet some believe that it refers to his distancing himself from the rest of contemporary vernacular poets in his quite different championing of his own and most special lady. (See note to *Inf.* II.105.) Such an interpretation is lent support by the fact that here the word *(schiera)* returns to designate a quite different group of poets, the great *auctores*. (Of the nineteen uses of the noun in the poem, only these two make it refer to a group that Dante either leaves or joins.) In this interpretation Dante makes himself unique among contemporary poets in part because of his adherence to Beatrice, in part because of his involvement with Virgil and the other great poets of antiquity.

102.   For a review of the various sorts of discomfort among the commentators occasioned by Dante's promotion of his own poetic career in this verse (some going so far as to insist that he displays humility here rather than pride) see Mazzoni (Mazz.1965.1), pp. 147–54. It is clear that Dante is putting himself in very good company on the basis of very little accomplishment: a series of lyrics, the *Vita nuova*, two unfinished treatises, and three cantos of the *Comedy*. His daring is amazing. However, we ought to consider that most of his readers today will readily agree that he is not

only justly included in this company of the great poets of all time between Homer and Dante, but is one of its foremost members. It was a dangerous gesture for him to make. It is redeemed by his genius.

For a possible source for this verse see Gmel.1966.1, p. 91: Ovid's *Tristia*, IX.x.54, where that poet makes himself fourth in the line of poets after Tibullus, Gallus, and Propertius. And we should look ahead to *Purg.* XXI.91 when the inclusion of Statius will make Dante not the sixth but the seventh in this group.

That there are forty named or otherwise identified inhabitants in Limbo is probably not accidental (the five poets and the thirty-five souls later observed in the precincts of the noble castle). In one tradition of medieval numerology the "number" of man is four (of God, three). In a widely practiced mode of medieval "counting," $40 = 4 + 0 = 4$.

104–105.   What was the subject under discussion that is now not reported? Mazzoni (Mazz.1965.1, pp. 154–56), following an early indication of D'Ovidio's, argues that the subject is poetry, or the secrets of those involved in this sacred art, adducing as evidence two passages in *Purg.* XXII (104–105; 127–129). In the first of these Virgil tells Statius that he and his poetic companions in Limbo often speak of the Muses; then Dante is allowed to overhear Statius and Virgil speaking of the art of poetic making. To be sure, the poet deliberately refuses (and this will not be the last time) to tell us what was said. Yet it is clear that we are meant to wonder what it was, and to come up with some sort of reasonable hypothesis in explanation. No writer would otherwise include such a provocative detail.

106–111.   The noble castle with its seven walls and surrounding stream that Dante and the poets walk over as though it were dry land in order then to pass through the seven gates and into a green meadow: what do these things signify? It is clear that here we are dealing with the conventional kind of allegory, in which poetic objects stand for abstract ideas. But which ones? As is often the case, allegories (here, a brief extended metaphor) of this kind have proven to be extremely difficult for Dante's readers, and not only for his modern readers. Mazzoni (Mazz.1965.1) presents the history of the question (pp. 156–68); yet it cannot be said that he has resolved it. Is the castle the good life of the human being without Grace, all that can be done with the moral and speculative virtues that pagans could perfect despite their lack of faith (Mazzoni)? Or does the castle represent philosophy, with its seven disciplines (physics, metaphysics, ethics, politics, economics, mathematics, and dialectic [Padoan's comment])? Or something else? And what does it mean that the pagan poets and Dante all can cross the stream as though it were not water? Surely that stands for some impediment that keeps the rest of the inhabitants of Limbo out, since apparently only those worthy of entrance can move over it. There are thirty-five designated inhabitants within the walls and fully two-fifths of these are "actives" (and the majority of these are women: eight of the fourteen). The more numerous "contemplatives"—had they been the only inhabitants discussed—might indicate that the castle stands for "philosophy." But what have Caesar, Camilla, Latinus, or Lavinia got to do with philosophy? What, then, do the castle and its surroundings stand for? The best that human beings can be without God, in whatever precise further formulation: that seems a plausible, if not satisfying, response to Dante's riddle.

115–117.   The resemblance to the vision of the Elysian fields, the best place in the pagan underworld, in *Aen.* VI.752–755 was not lost on Boccaccio—nor on Pietro di Dante before him, in the third redaction of his commentary, as discussed by Mazz.1965.1, p. 172.

121–122.   The first group is Trojan: Electra, mother of Dardanus, founder of Troy; Hector; Aeneas. The line becomes Roman with Aeneas.

123.   For Caesar as the first emperor of Rome see *Convivio* IV.v.12. For the source in Suetonius of his falcon-like eyes see Campi's comment to this verse. That Caesar is here in armor may well be a reminder of his crossing of the Rubicon in arms to attack Rome (see Stul.1991.1, p. 36).

124–126.   The next group is Latian, those who fought and lost against Aeneas; first named are two warrior maidens, then Latinus, king of Latium, and his daughter, Lavinia. Aeneas won the right to marry her by his victory over the forces led by Turnus.

127–128.   This group is associated with the Roman Republic, first its founder, Lucius Brutus, and then four of its matronly heroines.

129.   That Saladin, for all the good report that he enjoyed, is included by Dante in Limbo (along with two other "infidels," Avicenna and Averroes, at vv. 143–144) is nonetheless extraordinary. They are the only three "moderns" in Limbo, all representatives of that Islamic culture which Dante usually saw in negative terms and only as the enemy of Christendom.

131.   This "master" of knowledge, the teacher of philosophy for nearly every major thinker in the Middle Ages, is, of course, Aristotle. For two important studies in English of the Aristotelian basis of Dante's thought see Boyde (Boyd.1981.1 and Boyd.1993.1).

134–140.   Socrates and Plato lead the listing of other Greek philosophers. Dante's knowledge of the pre-Socratics is, of course, limited; but his interest in them was great.

140–141.   The group of four combines poets (Orpheus, Linus) and moral philosophers (Cicero, Seneca).

142–144.   The last grouping combines classical mathematicians and doctors of medicine with two "moderns," both Muslims, Avicenna (eleventh-century philosopher) and Averroes (twelfth-century commentator of Aristotle). For Dante's surprising "liberality" in including Avicenna and Averroes in Limbo see note to v. 129.

145–147.   Dante's abrupt switch to the role of author from that of narrator is noteworthy. With the exception of the invocation in *Inferno* II.7, this is the first time he has assumed that role, this time addressing remarks *about* the poem to us, his readers: "I cannot give account of all of them, for the length of my theme so drives me on, the telling often comes short of the fact." The effect is, as we have observed before (note to vv. 64–66, above), to put together an appeal to his experience as voyager, returned from a veracious visit to the otherworld, and insistence on his absolute control over what he has in fact invented. As readers we are aware that it is he who has created the inhabitants of Limbo; his remark both insists that he is only recording what he observed and simultaneously allows a shared understanding of his contrivance. What is genial in it is that it turns his reader into a collaborator. The use of the word *tema* (here "poetic subject") underlines the literary nature of the enterprise.

INFERNO V

Così discesi del cerchio primaio
giù nel secondo, che men loco cinghia
3   e tanto più dolor, che punge a guaio.

Stavvi Minòs orribilmente, e ringhia:
essamina le colpe ne l'intrata;
6   giudica e manda secondo ch'avvinghia.

Dico che quando l'anima mal nata
li vien dinanzi, tutta si confessa;
9   e quel conoscitor de le peccata

vede qual loco d'inferno è da essa;
cignesi con la coda tante volte
12   quantunque gradi vuol che giù sia messa.

Sempre dinanzi a lui ne stanno molte:
vanno a vicenda ciascuna al giudizio,
15   dicono e odono e poi son giù volte.

"O tu che vieni al doloroso ospizio,"
disse Minòs a me quando mi vide,
18   lasciando l'atto di cotanto offizio,

"guarda com' entri e di cui tu ti fide;
non t'inganni l'ampiezza de l'intrare!"
21   E 'l duca mio a lui: "Perché pur gride?

Non impedir lo suo fatale andare:
vuolsi così colà dove si puote
24   ciò che si vuole, e più non dimandare."

Or incincian le dolenti note
a farmisi sentire; or son venuto
27   là dove molto pianto mi percuote.

Thus I descended from the first circle
down into the second, which girds a smaller space
but greater agony to goad lament.

There stands Minos, snarling, terrible.
He examines each offender at the entrance,
judges and dispatches as he encoils himself.

I mean that when the ill-begotten soul
stands there before him it confesses all,
and that accomplished judge of sins

decides what place in Hell is fit for it,
then coils his tail around himself to count
how many circles down the soul must go.

Always before him stands a crowd of them,
going to judgment each in turn.
They tell, they hear, and then are hurled down.

'O you who come to this abode of pain,'
said Minos when he saw me, pausing
in the exercise of his high office,

'beware how you come in and whom you trust.
Don't let the easy entrance fool you.'
And my leader to him: 'Why all this shouting?

'Hinder not his destined journey.
It is so willed where will and power are one,
and ask no more.'

Now I can hear the screams
of agony. Now I have come
where a great wailing beats upon me.

3

6

9

12

15

18

21

24

27

Io venni in loco d'ogne luce muto,
che mugghia come fa mar per tempesta,
30   se da contrari venti è combattuto.

La bufera infernal, che mai non resta,
mena li spirti con la sua rapina;
33   voltando e percotendo li molesta.

Quando giungon davanti a la ruina,
quivi le strida, il compianto, il lamento;
36   bestemmian quivi la virtù divina.

Intesi ch'a così fatto tormento
enno dannati i peccator carnali,
39   che la ragion sommettono al talento.

E come li stornei ne portan l'ali
nel freddo tempo, a schiera larga e piena,
42   così quel fiato li spiriti mali

di qua, di là, di giù, di sù li mena;
nulla speranza li conforta mai,
45   non che di posa, ma di minor pena.

E come i gru van cantando lor lai,
faccendo in aere di sé lunga riga,
48   così vid'io venir, traendo guai,

ombre portate da la detta briga;
per ch'i' dissi: "Maestro, chi son quelle
51   genti che l'aura nera sì gastiga?"

"La prima di color di cui novelle
tu vuo' saper," mi disse quelli allotta,
54   "fu imperadrice di molte favelle.

A vizio di lussuria fu sì rotta,
che libito fé licito in sua legge,
57   per tòrre il biasmo in che era condotta.

I reached a place mute of all light,
which bellows as the sea in tempest
30   tossed by conflicting winds.

The hellish squall, which never rests,
sweeps spirits in its headlong rush,
33   tormenting, whirls and strikes them.

Caught in that path of violence,
they shriek, weep, and lament.
36   Then how they curse the power of God!

I understood that to such torment
the carnal sinners are condemned,
39   they who make reason subject to desire.

As, in cold weather, the wings of starlings
bear them up in wide, dense flocks,
42   so does that blast propel the wicked spirits.

Here and there, down and up, it drives them.
Never are they comforted by hope
45   of rest or even lesser punishment.

Just as cranes chant their mournful songs,
making a long line in the air,
48   thus I saw approach, heaving plaintive sighs,

shades lifted on that turbulence,
so that I said: 'Master, who are these
51   whom the black air lashes?'

'The first of them about whom
you would hear,' he then replied,
54   'was empress over many tongues.

'She was so given to the vice of lechery
she made lust licit in her law
57   to take away the blame she had incurred.

Ell' è Semiramìs, di cui si legge
che succedette a Nino e fu sua sposa:
60   tenne la terra che 'l Soldan corregge.

L'altra è colei che s'ancise amorosa,
e ruppe fede al cener di Sicheo;
63   poi è Cleopatràs lussurïosa.

Elena vedi, per cui tanto reo
tempo si volse, e vedi 'l grande Achille,
66   che con amore al fine combatteo.

Vedi Parìs, Tristano"; e più di mille
ombre mostrommi e nominommi a dito,
69   ch'amor di nostra vita dipartille.

Poscia ch'io ebbi 'l mio dottore udito
nomar le donne antiche e ' cavalieri,
72   pietà mi giunse, e fui quasi smarrito.

I' cominciai: "Poeta, volontieri
parlerei a que' due che 'nsieme vanno,
75   e paion sì al vento esser leggieri."

Ed elli a me: "Vedrai quando saranno
più presso a noi; e tu allor li priega
78   per quello amor che i mena, ed ei verranno."

Sì tosto come il vento a noi li piega,
mossi la voce: "O anime affannate,
81   venite a noi parlar, s'altri nol niega!"

Quali colombe dal disio chiamate
con l'ali alzate e ferme al dolce nido
84   vegnon per l'aere, dal voler portate;

cotali uscir de la schiera ov' è Dido,
a noi venendo per l'aere maligno,
87   sì forte fu l'affettüoso grido.

'She is Semiramis, of whom we read
that she, once Ninus' wife, succeeded him.
60   She held sway in the land the Sultan rules.

'Here is she who broke faith with the ashes
of Sichaeus and slew herself for love.
63   The next is wanton Cleopatra.

'See Helen, for whose sake so many years
of ill rolled past. And see the great Achilles,
66   who battled, at the last, with love.

'See Paris, Tristan,' and he showed me more
than a thousand shades, naming as he pointed,
69   whom love had parted from our life.

When I heard my teacher name the ladies
and the knights of old, pity overcame me
72   and I almost lost my senses.

I began: 'Poet, gladly would I speak
with these two that move together
75   and seem to be so light upon the wind.'

And he: 'Once they are nearer, you will see:
if you entreat them by the love
78   that leads them, they will come.'

As soon as the wind had bent them to us,
I raised my voice: 'O wearied souls,
81   if it is not forbidden, come speak with us.'

As doves, summoned by desire, their wings
outstretched and motionless, move on the air,
84   borne by their will to the sweet nest,

so did these leave the troop where Dido is,
coming to us through the malignant air,
87   such force had my affectionate call.

"O animal grazïoso e benigno
che visitando vai per l'aere perso
90   noi che tignemmo il mondo di sanguigno,

se fosse amico il re de l'universo,
noi pregheremmo lui de la tua pace,
93   poi c'hai pietà del nostro mal perverso.

Di quel che udire e che parlar vi piace,
noi udiremo e parleremo a voi,
96   mentre che 'l vento, come fa, ci tace.

Siede la terra dove nata fui
su la marina dove 'l Po discende
99   per aver pace co' seguaci sui.

Amor, ch'al cor gentil ratto s'apprende,
prese costui de la bella persona
102   che mi fu tolta; e 'l modo ancor m'offende.

Amor, ch'a nullo amato amar perdona,
mi prese del costui piacer sì forte,
105   che, come vedi, ancor non m'abbandona.

Amor condusse noi ad una morte.
Caina attende chi a vita ci spense."
108   Queste parole da lor ci fuor porte.

Quand'io intesi quell'anime offense,
china' il viso, e tanto il tenni basso,
111   fin che 'l poeta mi disse: "Che pense?"

Quando rispuosi, cominciai: "Oh lasso,
quanti dolci pensier, quanto disio
114   menò costoro al doloroso passo!"

Poi mi rivolsi a loro e parla' io,
e cominciai: "Francesca, i tuoi martìri
117   a lagrimar mi fanno tristo e pio.

'O living creature, gracious and kind,
that come through somber air to visit us
90   who stained the world with blood,

'if the King of the universe were our friend
we would pray that He might give you peace,
93   since you show pity for our grievous plight.

'We long to hear and speak of that
which you desire to speak and know,
96   here, while the wind has calmed.

'On that shore where the river Po
with all its tributaries slows
99   to peaceful flow, there I was born.

'Love, quick to kindle in the gentle heart,
seized this man with the fair form taken from me.
102   The way of it afflicts me still.

'Love, which absolves no one beloved from loving,
seized me so strongly with his charm that,
105   as you see, it has not left me yet.

'Love brought us to one death.
Caïna waits for him who quenched our lives.'
108   These words were borne from them to us.

And when I'd heard those two afflicted souls
I bowed my head and held it low until at last
111   the poet said: 'What are your thoughts?'

In answer I replied: 'Oh,
how many sweet thoughts, what great desire,
114   have brought them to this woeful pass!'

Then I turned to them again to speak
and I began: 'Francesca, your torments
117   make me weep for grief and pity,

Ma dimmi: al tempo d'i dolci sospiri,
a che e come concedette amore
120   che conosceste i dubbiosi disiri?"

E quella a me: "Nessun maggior dolore
che ricordarsi del tempo felice
123   ne la miseria; e ciò sa 'l tuo dottore.

Ma s'a conoscer la prima radice
del nostro amor tu hai cotanto affetto,
126   dirò come colui che piange e dice.

Noi leggiavamo un giorno per diletto
di Lancialotto come amor lo strinse;
129   soli eravamo e sanza alcun sospetto.

Per più fïate li occhi ci sospinse
quella lettura, e scolorocci il viso;
132   ma solo un punto fu quel che ci vinse.

Quando leggemmo il disïato riso
esser basciato da cotanto amante,
135   questi, che mai da me non fia diviso,

la bocca mi basciò tutto tremante.
Galeotto fu 'l libro e chi lo scrisse:
138   quel giorno più non vi leggemmo avante."

Mentre che l'uno spirto questo disse,
l'altro piangëa; sì che di pietade
io venni men così com' io morisse.
142   E caddi come corpo morto cade.

'but tell me, in that season of sweet sighs,
how and by what signs did Love
120   acquaint you with your hesitant desires?'

And she to me: 'There is no greater sorrow
than to recall our time of joy
123   in wretchedness—and this your teacher knows.

'But if you feel such longing
to know the first root of our love,
126   I shall tell as one who weeps in telling.

'One day, to pass the time in pleasure,
we read of Lancelot, how love enthralled him.
129   We were alone, without the least misgiving.

'More than once that reading made our eyes meet
and drained the color from our faces.
132   Still, it was a single instant overcame us:

'When we read how the longed-for smile
was kissed by so renowned a lover, this man,
135   who never shall be parted from me,

'all trembling, kissed me on my mouth.
A Galeotto was the book and he that wrote it.
138   That day we read in it no further.'

While the one spirit said this
the other wept, so that for pity
I swooned as if in death.
142   And down I fell as a dead body falls.

1–3.   A descent again marks a border, this time between the Limbus and the second Circle. Singleton's gloss argues that the presence here of Minos in judgment indicates that "real hell" begins only now, that Limbo is "marginal." It is true, however, that the Limbus is inside the gate of hell. Not only does "real hell" begin there, it in a sense begins with those who are barely inside the gate, the neutrals. They are so pusillanimous that they are not even allowed "a proper burial," as it were. One may not even say, as some have, that only with the second Circle do we begin to witness actual punishment being meted out for past sins, since the neutrals are indeed tormented by stinging insects as a fit punishment for their feckless conduct (*Inf.* III.65–66).

4–5.   Padoan, in his gloss, argues that the present tense of the verbs in this tercet *(sta, ringhia, essamina, giudica, manda, avvinghia)* reflects the continuous condition of Minos's behavior. In fact *all* the verbs in the passage describing Minos's judgment, vv. 4–15, are in the present, as Dante leaves little doubt but that he wants his readers to imagine themselves—unless a life of good conduct and God's grace combine to gain a better end—coming before that judgment in the future. This is the everlasting present of the moment of damnation, occurring, the text would make us feel, even as we read. For a study of the historical present in the *Commedia*, with attention (pp. 266–68) to this passage, see Sanguineti (Sang.1958.1).

Dante fairly often portrays infernal monsters and characters as having bestial traits. For this particular one, canine vociferation, see also Cerberus (*Inf.* VI.43), Plutus (*Inf.* VII.43), Hecuba (*Inf.* XXX.20), Bocca degli Abati (*Inf.* XXXII.105; *Inf.* XXXII.108); Brutus and Cassius in *Inferno* XXXIV (described as "barking" retrospectively at *Par.* VI.74). See discussion in Spag.1997.1, p. 112.

For the conflation here in the figure of Minos of the roles of Minos and of Rhadamanthus in Virgil's underworld, see Moor.1896.1, pp. 183–84; the texts are found at *Aeneid* VI.432–433 and 566–569.

6.   The precise way that Minos winds his tail about himself is a subject in dispute. Does he flap it back and forth as many times as he wishes to indicate the appropriate Circle? Or does he wind it like a vine around a tree? See Mazz.1977.1, pp. 104–5, for a brief summary of the debate and reasons to prefer the second hypothesis.

7.   Sinners are "ill-begotten" in that their end is this, eternal damnation, because of their sins (and not because their procreation in itself so fated them). Padoan, commenting on this verse, points out that Dante himself is later described as "bene nato" (wellborn)—*Par.* V.115.

8.   Dante presents Minos as a parody of a confessor meting out penance to a sinner (see Beno.1983.1). The word *confessa* marks the beginning of this canto's concern with confession, which will be parodied again when Dante "confesses" Francesca (vv. 118–120). For now we are perhaps meant to ruminate on the perversity of sinners. In the world above they were offered, through this office of the Church, the possibility of confession and remission of sins. We may infer that those sinners whom we find in hell probably did not avail themselves of their great opportunity. (We never hear the word "confession" on the lips of any of them except for Guido da Montefeltro [*Inf.* XXVII.83]. And he, having confessed and become a friar, then sins again and is condemned. His second [and vain] confession is made, too late, in hell and only to Dante.) This moment offers a brief but cogent vision of human perversity: in their lives all those whom we see in hell had the opportunity to be rid of their sins by owning up to them in confession. They apparently did not do so. Here, in hell, what is the very first thing that they do? They make full disclosure of their sins . . . to Minos.

9–12.   The mechanical nature of Minos's judgment—he is a judge who renders judgment with his tail, not his head—underlines the lack of authority of the demons in hell: Minos is merely doing God's work. Hell is presented as a perfectly functioning bureaucracy. If some of Satan's minions are at times rebellious (e.g., the rebel angels in *Inf.* IX, the winged demons in XXI–XXIII), they are so in vain. Hell, too, is a part of God's kingdom.

17.   Once the narrated action of Dante's descent continues (it had been suspended at v. 3), the tense moves back to the past definite: "Minos *said*."

18–19.   Minos, seeing a rarity, to say the least—a living man before him at the entrance—steals a moment from his incessant judgment to offer this warning. How kindly are his intentions? Most commentators seem to think he is the most "humane" of the infernal demons, and even courteous to Dante. However, and as Padoan points out (in his commentary), his calling into question, albeit indirectly, the competence of Virgil as guide ("beware . . . whom you trust"), is evidently meant to unsettle Dante. He would obviously prefer not to have such visitors.

20.   Commentators customarily note that here Dante builds his line out of two sources: *Aeneid* VI.126: "Facilis descensus Averno" (the *descent* to the underworld is easy [but not the return from there]); Matth. 7:13: "spatiosa via est, quae ducit ad perditionem" (broad is the way that leads to perdition).

22–24.   Virgil obviously understands that Minos's words were meant to scare Dante off (and perhaps he also understands the implicit insult to himself contained in them). For the repetition here of the identical verses (23 and 24) used to quell Charon's rebellious desires see *Inf.* III.95–96 and note. It seems clear that Virgil would not have used them again had they not been efficacious the first time, that is, had Charon not relented and rowed Dante across (see note to *Inf.* III.136).

25.   Here the present tense is an example of the "historical" (or "vivid") present.

26–33.   The "hellscape" that is established by the sounds in the darkness (once again Dante's eyes need to adjust to the deepening shadows) mates well with the sin of lust: darkness, passionate winds in conflict that bear their victims in unceasing agitation in their storm of passion. For a passage that might have had some effect on Dante's shaping of this scene, see II Peter 2:10–22, the Apostle Peter's denunciation of the lustful.

34.   One of the most debated verses in this canto because of the word *ruina* (literally, "ruin"). What precisely does it mean? Two discussions of the commentary tradition are available, the first by Letterio Cassata (Cass.1971.1), the second, still more complete, by Nicolò Mineo (*ED*, vol. 4, 1973), pp. 1056–57. Mineo points out that there have been six identifiable schools of interpretation for the meaning of *la ruinà*. Unfortunately, there are severe problems associated with all of them. Many American and some Italian students of the problem have been drawn to Singleton's solution (commentary to *Inf.* XII.32 and XII.36–45): Dante suppresses the meaning of the noun here only to reveal it at *Inferno* XII.32–41, where *questa ruina* (v. 32) refers to the crack in the wall of hell made by the earthquake that accompanied Christ's crucifixion. However, it does remain

extremely dubious, as many rightly point out, that Dante would, for the only time in his poem, hold back the reference necessary to a word's clear literal sense for seven cantos. We agree with Mazzoni's tentative judgment (Mazz. 1977.1, pp. 106–8) that the meaning of *ruina* here is not "ruin," but "fury, violence," as in the impetus of the wind that drives these sinners.

40–49.   The first two similes of the canto (and see the third one, vv. 82–85) associate the lustful with birds, a natural association given their condition, driven by the wind, and one in accord with the medieval view that lust is the property of beings less than human, and indeed frequently of birds.

40–43.   The first vast group of the "ordinary" lovers is compared to a flock of starlings, with their ragged, darting, sky-covering flight on a winter's day. (T. S. Eliot's typist and house agent's clerk in *The Waste Land*, vv. 222–248, would eventually be assigned here, one imagines.)

46–49.   The group in the second simile of the canto is more select, the "stars" of lustful living. Where the starlings are as though without individual identities, the "masses" of the lustful, as it were, each of these has a particularity and a certain fame, and is thus worthy of being treated as exemplary. (For a discussion of exemplary literature in the middle ages see Delc.1989.1, with special attention to Dante, pp. 195–227.) Padoan (commentary), on the other hand, suggests that this second group is distinguished from the first on moral grounds, since they all died by their own hand or at the hand of others, and are as a result more heavily punished. The evidence for such a view does not seem present in the text.

For the cranes see *Aeneid* X.264–266 as well as Statius, *Thebaid* V.11–16.

58–67.   This is the second important "catalogue" that we find in *Inferno*. The first named the forty identified inhabitants of Limbo (see note to *Inf.* IV.102—at the end of that note). In the Circle of lust we find these seven identified sinners and two more: Francesca and Paolo, who bring the total to nine. As Curtius argued quite some time ago, given the importance for Dante of the number nine (the "number" of his beloved Beatrice), it seems likely that these nine souls who died for love are associated with her by opposition (Curt.1948.1, p. 369).

It is also notable that Dante's catalogues are unlike (and pronouncedly so in this case) later humanist catalogues of the famous, which thrive on additions, in display of "erudition": *the more the better* seems to be the motto of such writers. Dante, on the other hand, frequently sculpts his groupings to a purpose.

One of the insistent poetic *topoi* that we find in medieval writers—and certainly in Dante—is that of *translatio*. This is the notion that certain ideas or institutions have their major manifestations in movement through historical time and space. The two most usually deployed examples of this *topos* are *translatio imperii* (the movement of imperial greatness from Troy to Rome to "new Rome"—wherever that may be in a given patriotic writer's imagination [in Dante's case the empireless Rome of his own day]) and *translatio studii* (the development of serious intellectual pursuit from its birth in Athens, to its rebirth in Rome, to its new home [Paris, according to some, in Dante's day]). It is perhaps useful to think of Dante's catalogues as reflecting a similar sense of history, of movement through time and space. In this one, a sort of *translatio amoris*, we have three triads: Semiramis (incestuous paramour of her own son), Dido (partner of Aeneas, abandoned by him), Cleopatra (lover of Julius Caesar and of Mark Antony), all three lustful queens of the African coast; Helen and Paris (Greek and Trojan lovers whose lusts brought down a kingdom) with Achilles (Greek lover of the Trojan woman Polyxena); Tristan (a man caught up in destructive passion for King Mark's wife, Isolde, in the court of Cornwall, as we move into Europe and toward the present); Francesca and Paolo (lovers from the recent past [ca. 1285] in Rimini, here in Italy).

58. Semiramis was the legendary queen of Assyria (Dante has confused the name of her capital, Babylon, for that of the Egyptian city, and thus misplaced her realm). She was supposed to have legalized incest in order to carry out her sexual liaison with her son. For more about her see Samu.1944.1 and Shap.1975.1.

61–62. Dante's use of periphrasis (circumlocution) represents one of his favored "teaching techniques," in which he (generally, but certainly not always) offers his readers fairly easy problems to solve. Use of periphrasis has a second effect: it tends to emphasize the importance of the person or thing so presented. The "Dido" that we scribble in our margins, remembering that her husband's name was Sichaeus, stands out from the page, partly because it is we who have supplied the name. That Dido is the quintessential presence in this "flock" is underlined by v. 85, where she is the *only* named presence in it, having previously been alluded to only indirectly.

61.   Dido's presence here frequently upsets readers who think that she ought to be found in Canto XIII, since she committed suicide. It is clear that Dante thinks of the psychology of sin with a certain sophistication, isolating the impulse, the deeper motive, that drives our actions from the actions themselves. In Dido's case this is her uncontrolled desire for Aeneas. She does not kill herself from despair (as do the suicides in the thirteenth canto), but rather to give expression to her need for her lover— or so Dante would seem to have believed.

62.   Virgil's similar one-line description of Dido's "infidelity" occurs at *Aeneid* IV.552, where she admits that she had not "kept the faith promised to the ashes of Sichaeus."

63.   For Dante's knowledge that Cleopatra committed suicide by having an asp bite her, see *Paradiso* VI.76–78.

65.   It is important to remember that Dante, Greekless, had not read Homer, who only became available in Latin translation much later in the fourteenth century. His Achilles is not the hero of the *Iliad* known to some of us, but the warrior-lover portrayed by Statius and others.

69–72.   *di nostra vita*. The echo of the first line of the poem is probably not coincidental. Dante was lost "midway in the journey of our life" and, we will later learn, some of his most besetting problems arose from misplaced affection. He was, indeed, near death as a result of his transgressions. The repetition of the word *smarrito* to describe Dante's distraught condition also recalls the first tercet of the poem. Here we can see an emerging pattern in his reuse of key words from previous contexts in order to enhance the significance of a current situation in the poem.

71.   Dante refers to the great figures of the olden days with strikingly anachronistic terms, the medieval "ladies and knights" emphasizing the continuity of the historical record. No "humanist" writer would be likely to use such a locution that so dramatically erases the gap between classical antiquity and the present age.

74.   To be "light upon the wind" is, to some readers, a sign of Francesca's and Paolo's noble ability to triumph over their dismal surroundings; to others, it indicates that they are driven even more wildly than some other shades by the winds of passion. This first detail begins a series of

challenging phrasings that invite the reader to consider closely the ambiguities of the entire episode. For a summary of the issues at stake here, see Mazz.1977.1, pp. 124–28. And for a thorough consideration of the history of interpretation of the episode of Francesca see A. E. Quaglio, "Francesca" (*ED*, vol. 3, 1971, pp. 1–13).

76–78.   Virgil's only complete tercet in the second half of the canto (see note to vv. 109–117) is laconic, as though he were aware of the emotions felt by Dante (which he himself had so devastatingly presented in *Aeneid* IV, the story of love's destructive power over Dido) and realized there was nothing he had said or could say that might rein in his excited pupil.

80.   The protagonist's adjective for the two sinners (they are "anime *affannate*") may well be meant to remind us of the only other time we find that adjective in *Inferno* (*Inf.* I.22), when Dante is described as being like a man who has escaped from the sea "with laboring breath" (*con lena affannata*). If that is true, it further binds the character's sense of identity with these sinners.

82–84.   The third simile involving birds in this canto (and there are only three similes in it) compares the two lovers to doves. As Shoaf (Shoa.1975.1) has demonstrated, there is a "dove program" in the *Comedy*, beginning with the Venereal doves reflected here, passing through the doves at their feeding in *Purgatorio* II.124–129, and finishing in the reference to James and Peter as "doves" of the Holy Spirit in *Paradiso* XXV.119–121. Dante's doves here seem to reflect both *Aeneid* V.213–217 and *Georgics* I.414.

88.   Francesca da Polenta of Ravenna was affianced to Giovanni Malatesta of Rimini, who was crippled. History or legend has it that the marriage was arranged when his younger brother, Paolo, was sent to make the pledge of betrothal. Francesca, seeing him, was under the impression that it was this handsome man who was to be her husband. Her delusion on her wedding day is not difficult to imagine. Commentators point out that her adulterous conduct was a lot more calculated than Dante presents it (she and Paolo, also married, both had children and she had then been married for ten years). The fact is, however, that Dante's version of the story makes her conduct seem about as understandable as possible, an effort on which the character herself spends her considerable resources of persuasion.

The beginning of her highly rhetorical speech reflects the tradition of classical rhetoric that would have a speaker first seek to gain the sympathy of the audience, a device referred to as *captatio benevolentiae*, the capturing of the goodwill of one's auditors. For noteworthy earlier examples of *captatio* see Beatrice's first words to Virgil (*Inf.* II.58–60) and Virgil's first words to her (*Inf.* II.76–81).

91–93. Francesca's locutions are revealing and instructive: God is portrayed as having turned away from the two lovers, while Dante is welcomed for not having done so, for feeling *pietà* for them. This canto has one of its "key words" in *amore*, which occurs fully eleven times in it (vv. 61, 66, 69, 78, 100, 103, 106, 119, 125, 128, 134). But this word, "pity," is crucial as well (vv. 72, 93, 117, 140, and, in the continuing narrative of the next canto, VI.2). Dante is filled with pity for lost lovers. Should he be? That may be the central question facing a reader of *Inferno* V (see further discussion, below [note to v. 142]).

91. For the source of this verse in Cavalcanti's line "Se Mercé fosse amica a' miei disiri" (Were Mercy friendly to my desires) see Contini (Cont.1976.1), p. 155.

100–106. The use of anaphora (repetition) here at the beginning of each tercet, "Amor . . . Amor . . . Amor . . . ," underlines the rhetorical skill of Francesca, who presses her case with listening Dante: it was Love's fault that she and Paolo fell into carnal passion. "Amor" appears three times as the first word in a tercet after an end-stopped line and thus must be capitalized. It seems also reasonable to believe that Francesca is here referring to her "god," the Lord of Love, Cupid, whose name is "Amor." He is the only god she seems to own, since, by her account (v. 91), the "King of the universe" is not her friend.

102. Against Pagliaro (Pagl.1967.1), pp. 136–49, who argues that Francesca is referring to the way in which she was made to fall in love, Padoan (commentary and Pado.1993.1, pp. 189–200) argues persuasively that she refers in fact to the brutal manner of her death. This verse is much debated. The wording of the text allows, in itself, either interpretation. Our translation therefore leaves the meaning ambiguous, as does, indeed, the original, whatever Dante's intentions.

103. The *dicta* of Andreas Capellanus are often cited as lying behind Francesca's speech (e.g., *De amore* II, 8): "Amor nil posset amori denegare"

(Love can deny love nothing at all). A closer parallel exists between a line in a love poem by Cino da Pistoia and this one: "A nullo amato amar perdona amore" ("Love allows no one beloved not to love," cited by Enrico Mestica [commentary]). But we do not know if Dante is echoing Cino or Cino, Dante.

107.   Francesca, whose chief rhetorical strategy is to remove as much blame from herself as she is able, finding other forces at fault wherever possible (e.g., Paolo's physical beauty, her despicable husband, the allure of a French romance), here tries to even the score with her husband. She may be damned, but he, as the killer of his wife and brother, will be much lower down, in the ninth Circle. Since Gianciotto, who killed them in 1283–84, lived until 1304, his shade could not be seen by Dante in Caïna. We have, as a result, no basis on which to question her opinion. However, had Dante wanted to guarantee it, it would have taken a line or so to do just that—and he does several times have sinners tell of the impending arrival of still others in a given Circle in ways that clearly call for acceptance (see note to *Inf.* XXXII.54–69). And so we are left wondering at Francesca's remark, and should at least keep this question open. It seems better to view her prediction as a wish stated as a fact than as a fact. However, for an example of the view that accepts Francesca's predictive placement of her husband in hell see Bald.1988.1, p. 1070.

        Iannucci suggests that Gianciotto may have been conceived by Dante as being misshapen and lame like Vulcan, the cuckolded husband of Venus (Iann.1980.1, p. 345).

109–117.   These nine verses contain the "drama" of the canto *in nuce.* Dante's pensive condition in the first tercet reflects his being moved deeply by Francesca's beautiful speech; Virgil attempts to spur him to thoughtful appreciation of what he has seen and heard; the second tercet records his more emotional than rational outburst: he is totally sympathetic to the lovers, and now, in the third, he turns to tell Francesca that he is filled with pity for her. She has won him over.

        Some twenty years ago Dante's tearful state (v. 117) reminded Elizabeth Raymond and Susan Saltrick (both Princeton '78) of the tears Augustine shed for Dido—see Pine.1961.1, p. 34 (*Confessions* I.13).

118–120.   In 1972, Georgia Nugent, then a student at Princeton, pointed out that Dante's question mimics the questions used by confessors to ascertain the nature of a penitent's sins. Here, we may reflect, Dante is behaving more like a priest in the so-called "religion of Love" than a Christian confessor. See the earlier discussion of confession in this canto, note to v. 8.

121–126.   "This [the first tercet] imitates Virgil . . . but literally translates Boëtius" (Taaf.1822.1, p. 326). See the *Consolation of Philosophy* II, pr. 4: "in omni adversitate fortunae infelicissimum est genus infortunii fuisse felicem" (among fortune's many adversities the most unhappy kind is once to have been happy).

For the Virgilian resonances (*Aen.* II.3–13), see the fairly detailed account in Holl.1969.1, pp. 110–11.

123.   There is debate as to whether the word *dottore* (here "teacher") refers to Boethius or Virgil. Most prefer the second hypothesis. We should realize that either choice forces upon us a somewhat ungainly hypothesis, the first that Francesca knows Boethius well (it is only several years since Dante had characterized the *Consolation of Philosophy* as a work known only to few [*Conv.* II.xii.2]), the second that she recognizes the Roman poet Virgil without having had him identified by Dante. Since Virgil is referred to by Dante as "il mio dottore" in this very canto (v. 70), it seems the wiser choice to accept the notion that Dante, taking advantage of poetic license, allows Francesca to recognize Virgil.

127–128.   In the Old French *Lancelot of the Lake*, King Arthur's queen, Guinevere, betrayed her husband with the knight Lancelot. Much has been written on the sources of this scene. Work in English includes articles by Carozza (Caro.1967.1) and Maddox (Madd.1996.1). And for a possible link to the love story of Eloise and Abelard see Dronke (Dron.1975.1).

132.   Francesca's account of her and Paolo's conquest by Amor is "corrected" by a later text, Dante's reference to God as the "punto che mi vinse" (*Par.* XXX.11), where Dante is, like Paolo, "constrained" by love (*strinse* [v. 128]; *Paradiso* XXX, 15: *amor mi costrinse*)—but his desire is for Beatrice, not for a fleshly liaison. The passage in *Paradiso* is clearly meant to reflect negatively, not only on the amorous activity of Francesca and Paolo, but on the protagonist's reactions to it. The god of Love and Francesca are being played against God and Beatrice—or so we will understand once we reach the last *cantica*. For the resonance of this self-

citation see Holl.1988.1, pp. 7–8, discussing the contributions of Contini (Cont.1976.1), p. 206; Hollander (Holl.1983.1), pp. 139–40; and Dronke (Dron.1989.1), p. 30.

137.   Once again Francesca blames another for their predicament, this time the go-between, Gallehault, in the tale of Lancelot and Guinevere as well as its author. By now we have come to see—or should have—how often she lays her problems at the doors of others. At least in part because of Dante's reference to him here, Gallehault became synonymous with "pander."

138.   Francesca, reading a book that leads to her "conversion" to sin and death in the company of a man named Paul, is the "negative antitype" of St. Augustine, reading a book by Paul that leads to his conversion (*Confessions* VIII.xii [Pine.1961.1, p. 178]—see Swing for what seems to be the first observation of this striking connection [Swin.1962.1], p. 299, and further discussion by Hollander [Holl.1969.1], pp. 112–13). Augustine is converted by reading a passage in St. Paul (Romans 13:13–14): "Let us walk honestly as in the day; not in rioting and drunkenness, not in chambering and wantonness, not in strife and envying. But put you on the Lord Jesus Christ, and make not provision for the flesh, to fulfill the lusts thereof." Here, we may reflect, Francesca reads a book and is "converted," by doing so, to the lust that leads to death. And if Augustine was converted by reading a man named Paul, Francesca gives herself to adultery with a man bearing the same name. As Swing has pointed out, Francesca's last words, *quel giorno più non vi leggemmo avante* (that day we read in it no further), seem more than coincidentally close to Augustine's *nec ultra volui legere* (and I did not wish to read any further). For support of the idea that Dante is here thinking of this pivotal moment in Augustine's spiritual autobiography, see Scot.1979.1, p. 14. If we are meant to think of Augustine's *Confessiones* here, that would round off this canto's concern with confession (see discussion, above, in notes to vv. 8 and 118–120).

140.   We now realize that during the entire episode we have not heard a word from Paolo. Dante will return to this strategy when he twice again involves pairs of sinners in suffering together, Diomedes with Ulysses in *Inferno* XXVI, Ruggieri with Ugolino in *Inferno* XXXIII. In each case one of the two is a silent partner. We can try to imagine what an eternity of silence in the company of the voluble being who shares the culpability for one's damnation might be like.

141. Dante's death-like swoon has him experiencing something akin to the death in sensuality experienced by Francesca and Paolo. This is to be at odds with the view of Pietrobono (commentary), who argues that Dante's death-like collapse mirrors his attaining of the state urged by Paul in his Epistle to the Romans, chapter 6, wherein the Christian "dies" to sin in imitation of Christ (e.g., "For he that is dead is freed from sin"—Romans 6:7). It would rather seem that this is exactly *not* the state attained by the protagonist at this point in the poem.

Maddox (Madd.1996.1), pp. 119–22, draws a parallel between Dante's fainting spell and that suffered by Galehot in the prose *Lancelot*.

142. Torraca, commenting on this verse, was perhaps the first commentator to note the Arthurian material that lies behind Dante's famous line: the Italian prose version of the stories of Arthur's court, *La tavola ritonda*, XLVII, where Tristan's response to Isolde's death is described as follows: "e cadde sì come corpo morto." The protagonist is thus compared to the victim of overwhelming passion. His fainting marks him here as unable to control his pity, as it had had the same effect with respect to fear two cantos earlier (*Inf.* III.136).

The fifth Canto of *Inferno* is the cause of continuing debate. Where are we to locate ourselves as witnesses to these scenes? Romantic readers understandably tend to align themselves with the love that Francesca emblematizes and/or the pity that Dante exhibits; moralizing ones with the firmness that an Augustinian reader would feel. Virgil perhaps, given his silence through most of the second half of the canto (once Francesca appears on the scene he speaks only two words: "che pense?" [what are your thoughts?—v. 111]), would then seem to be trying to rein in Dante's enthusiastic involvement with this enticing shade. Yet even as theologically-oriented a reader as Mazzoni (Mazz.1977.1, pp. 125–26) finds it important to distance himself from such "rigid moralizing" as is found in Busn.1922.1 and Mont.1962.1. A view similar to Mazzoni's is found in a much-cited essay by Renato Poggioli: "The 'romance' of Paolo and Francesca becomes in Dante's hands an 'antiromance,' or rather, both things at once. As such, it is able to express and to judge romantic love at the same time" (Pogg.1957.1, p. 358). In America, the role of the "rigid moralizer" has been played, in recent times, most notably by Cassell (Cass.1984.1), with similar responses from most of his reviewers. For Mazzoni and many, perhaps most, contemporary readers, the canto needs to be responded to more generously than the "moralizers" would like. And, to be sure, there is at times a certain perhaps unfortunately zealous tone in the words of such critics. On the other hand, their views seem only to accord with the overall aims of the poet and his poem. Francesca is, after all, in hell. The love she shares with Paolo was and is a "mad love" (for this concept see Aval.1975.1). The text clearly maintains that the lustful punished here "make reason subject to desire" (v. 39). And so, where some would find pity the middle ground for the reader to occupy, between the sinful lust of Francesca and Paolo and the "rigid moralizers," others, including this commentator, argue that it is pity itself that is here at fault. *Amore* and *pietà* are no doubt among the "key words" of the canto (see above, note to vv. 91–93); that does not mean that they must function in opposition to one another; they may be versions of the same emotion. Indeed, if we see that Francesca's aim is precisely to gain Dante's pity, and that she is successful in doing so, we perhaps ought to question his offering of it. Sympathy for the damned, in the *Inferno*, is nearly always and nearly certainly the sign of a wavering moral disposition.

INFERNO VI

Al tornar de la mente, che si chiuse
dinanzi a la pietà d'i due cognati,
3   che di trestizia tutto mi confuse,

novi tormenti e novi tormentati
mi veggio intorno, come ch'io mi mova
6   e ch'io mi volga, e come che io guati.

Io sono al terzo cerchio, de la piova
etterna, maladetta, fredda e greve;
9   regola e qualità mai non l' è nova.

Grandine grossa, acqua tinta e neve
per l'aere tenebroso si riversa;
12   pute la terra che questo riceve.

Cerbero, fiera crudele e diversa,
con tre gole caninamente latra
15   sovra la gente che quivi è sommersa.

Li occhi ha vermigli, la barba unta e atra,
e 'l ventre largo, e unghiate le mani;
18   graffia li spirti ed iscoia ed isquatra.

Urlar li fa la pioggia come cani;
de l'un de' lati fanno a l'altro schermo;
21   volgonsi spesso i miseri profani.

Quando ci scorse Cerbero, il gran vermo,
le bocche aperse e mostrocci le sanne;
24   non avea membro che tenesse fermo.

E 'l duca mio distese le sue spanne,
prese la terra, e con piene le pugna
27   la gittò dentro a le bramose canne.

With my returning senses that had failed
at the piteous state of those two kindred,
3   which had confounded me with grief,

new torments and new souls in torment
I see about me, wherever I may move,
6   or turn, or set my gaze.

I am in the third circle, of eternal,
hateful rain, cold and leaden,
9   changeless in its monotony.

Heavy hailstones, filthy water, and snow
pour down through gloomy air.
12   The ground it falls on reeks.

Cerberus, fierce and monstrous beast,
barks from three gullets like a dog
15   over the people underneath that muck.

His eyes are red, his beard a greasy black,
his belly swollen. With his taloned hands
18   he claws the spirits, flays and quarters them.

The rain makes them howl like dogs.
The unholy wretches often turn their bodies,
21   making of one side a shield for the other.

When Cerberus—that huge worm—noticed us,
he opened up his jaws and showed his fangs.
24   There was no part of him he held in check.

But then my leader spread his hands,
picked up some earth, and with full fists
27   tossed soil into the ravenous gullets.

Qual è quel cane ch'abbaiando agogna,
e si racqueta poi che 'l pasto morde,
30   ché solo a divorarlo intende e pugna,

cotai si fecer quelle facce lorde
de lo demonio Cerbero, che 'ntrona
33   l'anime sì, ch'esser vorrebber sorde.

Noi passavam su per l'ombre che adona
la greve pioggia, e ponavam le piante
36   sovra lor vanità che par persona.

Elle giacean per terra tutte quante,
fuor d'una ch'a seder si levò, ratto
39   ch'ella ci vide passarsi davante.

"O tu che se' per questo 'nferno tratto,"
mi disse, "riconoscimi, se sai:
42   tu fosti, prima ch'io disfatto, fatto."

E io a lui: "L'angoscia che tu hai
forse ti tira fuor de la mia mente,
45   sì che non par ch'i' ti vedessi mai.

Ma dimmi chi tu se' che 'n sì dolente
loco se' messo, e hai sì fatta pena,
48   che, s'altra è maggio, nulla è sì spiacente."

Ed elli a me: "La tua città, ch'è piena
d'invidia sì che già trabocca il sacco,
51   seco mi tenne in la vita serena.

Voi cittadini mi chiamaste Ciacco:
per la dannosa colpa de la gola,
54   come tu vedi, a la pioggia mi fiacco.

E io anima trista non son sola,
ché tutte queste a simil pena stanno
57   per simil colpa." E più non fé parola.

As the dog that yelps with craving
grows quiet while it chews its food,
30   absorbed in trying to devour it,

the foul heads of that demon Cerberus were stilled,
who otherwise so thunders on the souls
33   they would as soon be deaf.

We were passing over shades sprawled
under heavy rain, setting our feet
36   upon their emptiness, which seems real bodies.

All of them were lying on the ground,
except for one who sat bolt upright
39   when he saw us pass before him.

'O you who come escorted through this Hell,'
he said, 'if you can, bring me back to mind.
42   You were made before I was undone.'

And I to him: 'The punishment you suffer
may be blotting you from memory:
45   it doesn't seem to me I've ever seen you.

'But tell me who you are to have been put
into this misery with such a penalty
48   that none, though harsher, is more loathsome.'

And he to me: 'Your city, so full of envy
that now the sack spills over,
51   · held me in its confines in the sunlit life.

'You and my townsmen called me Ciacco.
For the pernicious fault of gluttony,
54   as you can see, I'm prostrate in this rain.

'And in my misery I am not alone.
All those here share a single penalty
57   for the same fault.' He said no more.

Io li rispuosi: "Ciacco, il tuo affanno
mi pesa sì, ch'a lagrimar mi 'nvita;
60 ma dimmi, se tu sai, a che verranno

li cittadin de la città partita;
s'alcun v'è giusto; e dimmi la cagione
63 per che l'ha tanta discordia assalita."

E quelli a me: "Dopo lunga tencione
verranno al sangue, e la parte selvaggia
66 caccerà l'altra con molta offensione.

Poi appresso convien che questa caggia
infra tre soli, e che l'altra sormonti
69 con la forza di tal che testé piaggia.

Alte terrà lungo tempo le fronti,
tenendo l'altra sotto gravi pesi,
72 come che di ciò pianga o che n'aonti.

Giusti son due, e non vi sono intesi;
superbia, invidia e avarizia sono
75 le tre faville c'hanno i cuori accesi."

Qui puose fine al lagrimabil suono.
E io a lui: "Ancor vo' che mi 'nsegni
78 e che di più parlar mi facci dono.

Farinata e 'l Tegghiaio, che fuor sì degni,
Iacopo Rusticucci, Arrigo e 'l Mosca
81 e li altri ch'a ben far puoser li 'ngegni,

dimmi ove sono e fa ch'io li conosca;
ché gran disio mi stringe di savere
84 se 'l ciel li addolcia o lo 'nferno li attosca."

E quelli: "Ei son tra l'anime più nere;
diverse colpe giù li grava al fondo:
87 se tanto scendi, là i potrai vedere.

I answered him: 'Ciacco, your distress so weighs
on me it bids me weep. But tell me,
60   if you can, what shall be the fate

'of the citizens within the riven city?
Are any in it just? And tell me why
63   such discord has assailed it.'

And he to me: 'After long feuding
they shall come to blood. The rustic faction,
66   having done great harm, will drive the others out.

'But it in turn shall fall to them,
within three years, by power of him
69   who now just bides his time.

'These in their arrogance will long subject
the other faction to their heavy yoke,
72   despite its weeping and its shame.

'Two men are just and are not heeded there.
Pride, envy, and avarice are the sparks
75   that have set the hearts of all on fire.'

With that he ended his distressing words.
And I to him: 'I wish you would instruct me more,
78   granting me the gift of further speech.

'Farinata and Tegghiaio, who were so worthy,
Jacopo Rusticucci, Arrigo, and Mosca,
81   and the rest whose minds were bent on doing good,

'tell me where they are and how they fare.
For great desire presses me to learn
84   whether Heaven sweetens or Hell embitters them.'

And he: 'They are among the blacker souls.
Different vices weigh them toward the bottom,
87   as you shall see if you descend that far.

Ma quando tu sarai nel dolce mondo,
priegoti ch'a la mente altrui mi rechi:
90   più non ti dico e più non ti rispondo."

Li diritti occhi torse allora in biechi;
guardommi un poco e poi chinò la testa:
93   cadde con essa a par de li altri ciechi.

E 'l duca disse a me: "Più non si desta
di qua dal suon de l'angelica tromba,
96   quando verrà la nimica podesta:

ciascun rivederà la trista tomba,
ripiglierà sua carne e sua figura,
99   udirà quel ch'in etterno rimbomba."

Sì trapassammo per sozza mistura
de l'ombre e de la pioggia, a passi lenti,
102   toccando un poco la vita futura;

per ch'io dissi: "Maestro, esti tormenti
crescerann' ei dopo la gran sentenza,
105   o fier minori, o saran sì cocenti?"

Ed elli a me: "Ritorna a tua scïenza,
che vuol, quanto la cosa è più perfetta,
108   più senta il bene, e così la doglienza.

Tutto che questa gente maladetta
in vera perfezion già mai non vada,
111   di là più che di qua essere aspetta."

Noi aggirammo a tondo quella strada,
parlando più assai ch'i' non ridico;
venimmo al punto dove si digrada:
115   quivi trovammo Pluto, il gran nemico.

'But when you have returned to the sweet world
I pray you bring me to men's memory.
90   I say no more nor answer you again.'

With that his clear eyes lost their focus.
He gazed at me until his head drooped down.
93   Then he fell back among his blind companions.

And my leader said: 'He wakes no more
until angelic trumpets sound
96   the advent of the hostile Power.

'Then each shall find again his miserable tomb,
shall take again his flesh and form,
99   and hear the judgment that eternally resounds.'

So we passed on through the foul mix
of shades and rain with lagging steps,
102   touching a little on the life to come.

'Master,' I asked, 'after the great Judgment
will these torments be greater, less,
105   or will they stay as harsh as they are now?'

And he replied: 'Return to your science,
which has it that, in measure of a thing's perfection,
108   it feels both more of pleasure and of pain.

'Although these accursèd people
will never come to true perfection,
111   they will be nearer it than they are now.'

We went along that curving road,
with much more talk than I repeat,
and reached the point of our descent.
115   And there we came on Plutus, our great foe.

1.   His consciousness returned after his swoon, Dante begins to investi-
gate his new surroundings. Once again we are not told how he moved (or
was moved) from one Circle to the next, from Lust to Gluttony.

2.   As many commentators now point out, the technical word for "in-
laws" *(cognati)* used here reminds the reader who has become caught up in
Francesca's words (as was the protagonist) that her adultery was particu-
larly sinful, since she engaged in it with her brother-in-law.

7.   See Domb.1970.1 for the notion that the hellish downpour takes its
central and antithetic model from the manna promised by God to Moses
in the Bible (Exod. 16:4): "Ecce ego pluam vobis panes de caelo" (Behold,
I will rain bread from heaven for you).

13–14.   For Virgil's description of Cerberus, the three-headed dog guard-
ing the entrance to the underworld in classical mythology, see *Aen.*
VI.417–418. Dante's version of the creature is unique in its inclusion of
human attributes.

25–27.   The "sop" to Cerberus, in Virgil a honeyed cake (*Aen.*
VI.419–422), here becomes mere earth (*terra*). Kleinhenz (Klei.1975.1,
p. 190) has pointed out that Dante's strategic redoing of Virgil has its bibli-
cal resonance, as God's malediction of the serpent (Gen. 3:14) concludes
". . . *terram* comedes cunctis diebus vitae tuae" (and dust shall you eat all the
days of your life). The serpent's punishment for having urged Eve to eat
the fruit of the tree is himself to eat the dead earth; his punishment is
shared now by Cerberus.

28–32.   This is the only simile found in this, the shortest canto we have
yet read (only *Inferno* XI will have so few verses—115). It is as though
Dante had begun paring his art, striving for succinctness more than he had
before.
     The distribution of canto lengths throughout the poem would seem
to indicate that Dante originally was limiting himself to composing in
shorter units than he would generally employ later in his text. If we exam-
ine the first twenty cantos we find that fourteen, or 70% of them, are 136
lines long or fewer (115 to 136), while 9 (or 11%) of the final eighty are in

this group (and all of these between 130 and 136 lines). Confining ourselves to the very shortest cantos (those from 115 to 130 verses), we find that these occur six times in the first twenty cantos, with only one (of 130 lines) in this shorter group occurring after *Inferno* XX. Of the eighty final cantos, 88.75% (71 of them) are between 139 and 160 lines long; only 11.25% (9 cantos) of the final eighty are 136 lines or fewer. See Ferrante (Ferr.1993.1), pp. 154–55, for the distribution of Dante's canto lengths. Such data surely make it seem that Dante was experimenting with this distribution as he progressed, a tentative conclusion that would cast some doubt on the position of Thomas Hart, who has argued, carefully and well, that it seems plausible that Dante may have planned even these details from the very beginning. For a summary of his copious and interesting work, affording an overview of it, see Hart.1995.1.

34–36. In hell, we are given to understand, matter and bodies can interact, but not matter and shades. Accordingly, we might expect Dante to be soaked and chilled by the awful rain, while the shades of the gluttons feel nothing. Instead, in a single *terzina*, the poet forces us to make two allowances: Dante, walking through the rain that strikes the sinners, apparently feels nothing of it. The sinners, of course, feel it all too well. We are reminded again that the physical laws of the afterworld are immutable— except when the writer chooses to break them in order to make the details of his poetry work better.

37–39. For the first (but not the last) time in the poem Dante is recognized by one of the dead souls. This moment introduces the Florentine "subtext" of the *Comedy*. Ciacco (as we shall learn to call this figure at v. 52) is the first of some three dozen Florentine characters found in the poem, the vast majority of them in hell.

43–45. As Padoan (commentary) points out, even those purging their former gluttony on their way to salvation are so changed in their facial expressions that Dante cannot recognize an old friend: Forese Donati in *Purg.* XXIII.43.

49–51. The metaphor of a sack out of which the contents spill introduces the main theme of the canto, not gluttony, but political rivalry (even if the image itself relates to the overabundant storage of food). Many commentators try to find reasons to explain Dante's having related the two, but none has found a genuinely convincing link. Until now, each group of sinners, the neutrals, the virtuous pagans, the lustful, has been portrayed as expressing their most pertinent activities on earth in everything that they do or say. Dante, however, chose not to keep to such a scheme on a regular basis and obviously decided to introduce "subcategories," as it were, in certain Circles (e.g., politics [again] in the Circle of heresy). The fact is, Dante wants to address certain concerns and brings them to his text when he wants to.

The envy that Dante sees as the source of the terrible political rivalries in Florence in 1300 is traditionally understood as that felt by the nobler but poorer Donati (Black) faction of the Guelphs against the richer Cerchi (White) faction. Yet, and given both the political situation and the main meaning of envy in Dante's understanding (e.g., the desire to see one's opponents suffer loss), it seems clear that *all* Florentines are marked by this sin in Dante's eyes. Envy, seen in *Inf.* I.111 as the motive force behind Satan's seduction of Eve, is the second worst (after pride) of the seven mortal sins. In our time we tend not to understand either its gravity nor its widespread hold on human hearts. An envious person does not want another's wealth or happiness so much as he wishes his neighbor to be deprived of wealth or happiness.

52.   One of the most debated questions of this canto has to do with the identity and the name of this character. Was his name actually "Ciacco"? If it was, an enduring supposition is that of Isidoro Del Lungo (commentary): he is the thirteenth-century Florentine poet Ciacco dell'Anguillaia. While such a solution is attractive, there is as yet not a shred of evidence to support it. A more likely hypothesis is that his name was a nickname, granted him either because of his gluttonous habits ("ciacco" was a noun that in Tuscany meant "pig," or "hog," according to some fourteenth-century commentators, most notably Francesco da Buti, but none of the earliest report that this was the case and there is no other confirming record) or because his physiognomy was such as to call for such a name (i.e., his nose was flattened on his face [Pézard, *ED,* vol. 1, 1970, p. 983b]). And there is the further possibility that the nickname suggested no reference to offensive traits (Mazzoni points out that there are many examples in public documents of the time in which such names are used as Christian names [Mazz.1967.2, p. 36]). The fourteenth-century commentator published as the *Chiose selmiani* states that Ciacco was a Florentine banker who ate and drank so much that his eyesight went bad—as a result he could not count money and people made fun of him; he knew Dante, and

died before Dante turned fourteen. That is the most detailed and specific account we find in any early commentator. Boccaccio's reference to Ciacco (*Decameron* IX.viii.4) would suggest that he read Dante's phrasing ("Voi cittadini mi chiamaste Ciacco") as indicating that this man had a different name but was called by the Florentines by his nickname: "essendo in Firenze uno da tutti chiamato Ciacco" (there being in Florence a man who was called "Ciacco" by everyone). For a recent review of the entire problem, opting for the porcine nickname on the basis of Isidore of Seville's discussion of Epicureans as hogs, see Simone Marchesi's article (Marc.1999.1).

64–66. This is the first prophecy about events that will have importance in Dante's own life (as opposed to the "world-historical" prophecies that concern Dante as part of the human family) in a poem that is studded with them. For the "personal prophecies" in the poem see Pasq.1996.1, p. 419: Ciacco's, Farinata's (*Inf.* X.79–81); Brunetto's (*Inf.* XV.55–57); Vanni Fucci's (*Inf.* XXIV.143–150); Currado Malaspina's (*Purg.* VIII.133–139); Oderisi's (*Purg.* XI.139–141); Bonagiunta's (*Purg.* XXIV.37–38); Forese's (*Purg.* XXIV.82–90); and, ninth and last, Cacciaguida's (*Par.* XVII.46–93). Ciacco's prophecy concerns the events of May 1300, three or five weeks after the date of the journey, and thus events genuinely near at hand. The White faction, led by the Cerchi family, *selvaggia* in the sense of "rustic" (in that its members come from the wooded outskirts of the city), will drive out the Black faction in 1300.

67–69. Within three years (in fact in 1302) the White faction will fall as the Blacks return to the city through the treachery of Pope Boniface VIII, who currently takes no action to help the city.

73. "Two men are just . . ." For a brief but strong reading of the *due giusti* as referring to Dante and another Florentine, identity not knowable, see Barb.1934.1, p. 266. Currently a great debate rages over this verse, fanned by the exertions of Mazzoni. Following the gloss of Pietro di Dante, who argues that the phrase refers not to two human beings, but to two *laws*, natural and posited, (i.e., made by man), Mazzoni argues that the source for such an interpretation exists in St. Thomas's commentary on a passage in Aristotle's *Ethics* (VIII, c. xv, 1243): "Duplex est iustum" (Justice is twofold), that is, natural and posited. Perhaps even more helpful to Mazzoni's case is Dante's own phrasing in his epistle against his fellow towns-

men (*Epist.* VI.5), whom he accuses of transgressing laws both divine and man-made ("Vos autem *divina iura et humana* transgredientes"). The traditional reading of the verse, which has gathered massive support, is as we have translated it: "Two men are just and are not heeded there." Mazzoni's "translation" would read, in English, "the two kinds of justice are not followed there." One can see both the force and the charm of his argument. It is a possible line of interpretation. But it has to date failed to convince most who address the problem. They continue to find the traditional reading a much more likely one (e.g., Bara.1981.1).

74–75.   See the similar remark offered by Brunetto Latini, *Inf.* XV.68. For Florence to be afflicted by pride, envy, and avarice is for her to be afflicted by the worst of the seven mortal sins.

79–81.   The identity of Arrigo remains a puzzle. If there are only two just Florentines in the city in 1300, in "the good old days" there seem to have been at least five, men who made great effort to offer sustenance to goodness. The meaning of the tercet is clear enough. The problem arises because one of the five, Arrigo, is never mentioned again—or surely does not seem to be. The other four are seen in hell, Farinata in Canto X, among the heretics, Tegghiaio and Iacopo in XVI, among the Florentine homosexual politicians (the most positively presented sinners since those we met in Limbo), and Mosca, in a sense the only "surprise" here, since he is punished in Canto XXVIII for his treachery on the battlefield, but, in Dante's mind, is praiseworthy for his efforts to bring peace to the city before that. See the study of Pietro Santini (Sant.1923.1) for this argument. Of course, it is the puzzle created by Arrigo's not being further referred to in hell that has drawn commentators' fullest attention. For a review of the many competing "Harrys" who began to populate the margins of Dante's poem in the fourteenth century and have continued to do so into our own, see Vincenzo Presta, "Arrigo" (*ED,* vol. 1, 1970, pp. 391–92). It is strange that Dante picked the names of five men, four of whom he goes on to include prominently in his poem, and one that he does not mention again—especially since he has Ciacco say explicitly that the protagonist will see all of them in his descent (v. 87). This is a mystery that will probably forever remain a mystery.

88.   The world of the living is almost always characterized as being filled with the light of the sun, as "sweet," when it is remembered by the damned in their bitter darkness.

90.   A sixteenth-century commentator, Castelvetro, paraphrases this line as follows: "it has been conceded me by God to make clear to you what I have revealed, at your insistence, but, as for the future, I say no more either to you or to anyone else until the Day of Judgment."

91–93.   Ciacco's last "gesture," his glance moving from Dante's face and going vacant, has been a puzzle to many readers. The commentary of Bosco/Reggio is clear and to the point: "Ciacco passes from his temporarily fully-human phase to one of nearly pure animality; first he looks askance; then he continues to fix Dante with a stunned gaze in which, bit by bit, any last trace of humanity is extinguished; then his head droops, deprived of any human vitality; finally he falls headfirst into the muck, unfeeling and inert."

99.   In the opinion of Benvenuto da Imola (commentary) "the judgment that eternally resounds" has a biblical source, the words of Christ: "Depart from me, you cursed ones, into everlasting fire" (Matth. 25:41). For the resonance here of the angelic trumpet blast that will herald the Last Judgment see Singleton (commentary), citing I Cor. 15:51–53.

102.   For all the interest shown in the present situation of Florence in this canto, it is clear that the future of the damned is to be understood as having greater eventual importance. This, at least, is Dante's "official" position.

106–108.   Mazzoni (Mazz. 1967.2, p. 50) shows that this tercet derives from a passage in St. Thomas's commentary to Aristotle's *De anima*: "quanto anima est perfectior, tanto exercet plures perfectas operationes et diversas" (as the soul becomes more perfect, so it is more perfect in its several operations). *La tua scïenza* is thus Aristotle's *De anima*, and not the *Physics* or the *Ethics*, as some have variously argued.

109–111.   Thoroughly in accord with the penal code of hell, this "improvement" in the condition of the damned will only result in their ability to feel more pain.

INFERNO VII

"*Pape Satàn, pape Satàn aleppe!*"
cominciò Pluto con la voce chioccia;
3   e quel savio gentil, che tutto seppe,

disse per confortarmi: "Non ti noccia
la tua paura; ché, poder ch'elli abbia,
6   non ci torrà lo scender questa roccia."

Poi si rivolse a quella 'nfiata labbia,
e disse: "Taci, maladetto lupo!
9   consuma dentro te con la tua rabbia.

Non è sanza cagion l'andare al cupo:
vuolsi ne l'alto, là dove Michele
12   fé la vendetta del superbo strupo."

Quali dal vento le gonfiate vele
caggiono avvolte, poi che l'alber fiacca,
15   tal caddé a terra la fiera crudele.

Così scendemmo ne la quarta lacca,
pigliando più de la dolente ripa
18   che 'l mal de l'universo tutto insacca.

Ahi giustizia di Dio! tante chi stipa
nove travaglie e pene quant' io viddi?
21   e perché nostra colpa sì ne scipa?

Come fa l'onda là sovra Cariddi,
che si frange con quella in cui s'intoppa,
24   così convien che qui la gente riddi.

Qui vid' i' gente più ch'altrove troppa,
e d'una parte e d'altra, con grand' urli,
27   voltando pesi per forza di poppa.

'*Pape Satàn, Pape Satàn, aleppe!*'
burst out Plutus in his raucous voice.
And the courteous, all-discerning sage,

3

to comfort me, said: 'Do not be overcome
by fear. However powerful he may be,
he'll not prevent our climbing down this cliff.'

6

Then he turned to that bloated face
and said: 'Silence, accursèd wolf!
Let your fury feed itself inside you.

9

'Not without sanction is this journey down the pit.
It is willed on high, where Michael
did avenge the proud rebellion.'

12

As sails, swollen by the wind,
fall in a tangle when the mainmast snaps,
so fell that cruel beast to the ground.

15

Into the fourth hollow we made our way,
descending the dismal slope
that crams in all the evil of the universe.

18

Ah, Justice of God, who heaps up
such strange punishment and pain as I saw there?
And why do our sins so waste us?

21

Just as the waves clash above Charybdis,
one breaking on the other when they meet,
so here the souls move in their necessary dance.

24

Here the sinners were more numerous than elsewhere,
and they, with great shouts, from opposite sides
were shoving burdens forward with their chests.

27

Percotëansi 'ncontro; e poscia pur lì
si rivolgea ciascun, voltando a retro,
30   gridando: "Perché tieni?" e "Perché burli?"

Così tornavan per lo cerchio tetro
da ogne mano a l'opposito punto,
33   gridandosi anche loro ontoso metro;

poi si volgea ciascun, quand' era giunto,
per lo suo mezzo cerchio a l'altra giostra.
36   E io, ch'avea lo cor quasi compunto,

dissi: "Maestro mio, or mi dimostra
che gente è questa, e se tutti fuor cherci
39   questi chercuti a la sinistra nostra."

Ed elli a me: "Tutti quanti fuor guerci
sì de la mente in la vita primaia,
42   che con misura nullo spendio ferci.

Assai la voce lor chiaro l'abbaia,
quando vegnono a' due punti del cerchio
45   dove colpa contraria li dispaia.

Questi fuor cherci, che non han coperchio
piloso al capo, e papi e cardinali,
48   in cui usa avarizia il suo soperchio."

E io: "Maestro, tra questi cotali
dovre' io ben riconoscere alcuni
51   che furo immondi di cotesti mali."

Ed elli a me: "Vano pensiero aduni:
la sconoscente vita che i fé sozzi,
54   ad ogne conoscenza or li fa bruni.

In etterno verranno a li due cozzi:
questi resurgeranno del sepulcro
57   col pugno chiuso, e questi coi crin mozzi.

They crashed into each other, turned
and beat retreat, shoving their loads and shouting:
30   'Why do you hoard?' or 'Why do you squander?'

Thus they proceeded in their dismal round
on both sides toward the opposite point,
33   taunting each other with the same refrain.

Once at that point, each group turned back
along its semi-circle to the next encounter.
36   And I, my heart pierced almost through,

said: 'Master, now explain to me
who these people are. Were those with tonsured heads,
39   the ones there to our left, all clerics?'

'All of them had such squinting minds
in their first lives,' he said,
42   'they kept no measure in their spending.

'Their voices howl this clear enough
just as they reach the twin points on the circle
45   where opposing sins divide them.

'These were clerics who have no lid of hair
upon their heads, and popes and cardinals,
48   in whom avarice achieves its excess.'

And I: 'Master, in such a crew as this
I ought to recognize at least a few
51   who were befouled with these offenses.'

And he to me: 'You muster an empty thought.
The undiscerning life that made them foul
54   now makes them hard to recognize.

'The two groups will collide forever.
These will rise from the grave
57   with fists tight, these with hair cropped.

Mal dare e mal tener lo mondo pulcro
ha tolto loro, e posti a questa zuffa:
60 qual ella sia, parole non ci appulcro.

Or puoi, figliuol, veder la corta buffa
d'i ben che son commessi a la fortuna,
63 per che l'umana gente si rabuffa;

ché tutto l'oro ch'è sotto la luna
e che già fu, di quest' anime stanche
66 non poterebbe farne posare una."

"Maestro mio," diss' io, "or mi dì anche:
questa fortuna di che tu mi tocche,
69 che è, che i ben del mondo ha sì tra branche?"

E quelli a me: "Oh creature sciocche,
quanta ignoranza è quella che v'offende!
72 Or vo' che tu mia sentenza ne 'mbocche.

Colui lo cui saver tutto trascende,
fece li cieli e diè lor chi conduce
75 sì, ch'ogne parte ad ogne parte splende,

distribuendo igualmente la luce.
Similemente a li splendor mondani
78 ordinò general ministra e duce

che permutasse a tempo li ben vani
di gente in gente e d'uno in altro sangue,
81 oltre la difension d'i senni umani;

per ch'una gente impera e l'altra langue,
seguendo lo giudicio di costei,
84 che è occulto come in erba l'angue.

Vostro saver non ha contasto a lei:
questa provede, giudica, e persègue
87 suo regno come il loro li altri dèi.

'Ill-giving and ill-keeping have stolen
the fair world from them and set them to this scuffle.
60   As for that, I prettify no words for it.

'Now you see, my son, what brief mockery
Fortune makes of goods we trust her with,
63   for which the race of men embroil themselves.

'All the gold that lies beneath the moon,
or ever did, could never give a moment's rest
66   to any of these wearied souls.'

'Master,' I said, 'tell me more: this Fortune
whom you mention, who is she that holds
69   the world's possessions tightly in her clutches?'

And he to me: 'O foolish creatures,
what great ignorance besets you!
72   I'll have you feed upon my judgment of her:

'He whose wisdom transcends all
made the heavens and gave them guides,
75   so that all parts reflect on every part

'in equal distribution of the light. Just so,
He ordained for worldly splendors
78   a general minister and guide

'who shifts those worthless goods, from time to time,
from race to race, from one blood to another
81   beyond the intervention of human wit.

'One people comes to rule, another languishes,
in keeping with her judgment,
84   as secret as a serpent hidden in the grass.

'Your wisdom cannot stand against her.
She foresees, she judges, she maintains her reign,
87   as do the other heavenly powers.

Le sue permutazion non hanno triegue:
necessità la fa esser veloce;
90 sì spesso vien chi vicenda consegue.

Quest' è colei ch'è tanto posta in croce
pur da color che le dovrien dar lode,
93 dandole biasmo a torto e mala voce;

ma ella s'è beata e ciò non ode:
con l'altre prime creature lieta
96 volve sua spera e beata si gode.

Or discendiamo omai a maggior pieta;
già ogne stella cade che saliva
99 quand' io mi mossi, e 'l troppo star si vieta."

Noi ricidemmo il cerchio a l'altra riva
sovr' una fonte che bolle e riversa
102 per un fossato che da lei deriva.

L'acqua era buia assai più che persa;
e noi, in compagnia de l'onde bige,
105 intrammo giù per una via diversa.

In la palude va c'ha nome Stige
questo tristo ruscel, quand' è disceso
108 al piè de le maligne piagge grige.

E io, che di mirare stava inteso,
vidi genti fangose in quel pantano,
111 ignude tutte, con sembiante offeso.

Queste si percotean non pur con mano,
ma con la testa e col petto e coi piedi,
114 troncandosi co' denti a brano a brano.

Lo buon maestro disse: "Figlio, or vedi
l'anime di color cui vinse l'ira;
117 e anche vo' che tu per certo credi

'Her mutability admits no rest.
Necessity compels her to be swift,
90   and frequent are the changes in men's state.

'She is reviled by the very ones
who most should praise her,
93   blaming and defaming her unjustly.

'But she is blessed and does not hear them.
Happy with the other primal creatures,
96   she turns her sphere, rejoicing in her bliss.

'Now we must descend to greater anguish.
For every star that rose when I set out
99   is sinking now, and we must not linger here.'

We crossed the circle to the other bank,
beside a spring that bubbles up and flows
102   into a channel it has hewn itself.

The water was darker than the deepest purple.
Accompanied by its murky waves
105   we began our strange descent.

This dreary stream, once it has reached
these malignant, ashen slopes,
108   drains out into the swamp called Styx.

And I, my gaze transfixed, could see
people with angry faces in that bog,
111   naked, their bodies smeared with mud.

They struck each other with their hands,
their heads, their chests and feet,
114   and tore each other with their teeth.

The good master said: 'Son, now you see
the souls of those whom anger overcame.
117   And I would have you know for certain

che sotto l'acqua è gente che sospira,
e fanno pullular quest' acqua al summo,
120   come l'occhio ti dice, u' che s'aggira.

Fitti nel limo dicon: 'Tristi fummo
ne l'aere dolce che dal sol s'allegra,
123   portando dentro accidïoso fummo:

or ci attristiam ne la belletta negra.'
Quest' inno si gorgoglian ne la strozza,
126   ché dir nol posson con parola integra."

Così girammo de la lorda pozza
grand' arco, tra la ripa secca e 'l mézzo,
con li occhi vòlti a chi del fango ingozza.
130   Venimmo al piè d'una torre al da sezzo.

'that plunged beneath these waters,
as your eyes will tell you, are souls whose sighs
120   with bubbles make the water's surface seethe.

'Fixed in the slime they say: "We were sullen
in the sweet air that in the sun rejoices,
123   filled as we were with slothful fumes.

' "Now we are sullen in black mire."
This hymn they gurgle in their gullets,
126   for they cannot get a word out whole.'

Thus we made our circle round that filthy bog,
keeping between the bank and swamp,
fixing our gaze on those who swallow mud.
130   And we came to the foot of a tower at last.

1. Plutus, the god of wealth in classical myth, wishes to prevent the passage of this living soul through Satan's kingdom. That, at least, is what we must surmise from Virgil's reaction, vv. 4–6, which assuages Dante's fear. There is a program of demonic resistance that makes Dante fearful throughout *Inferno*: Charon (*Inf.* III.91–93), Minos (V.19–20), Cerberus (VI.22–24), Phlegyas (VIII.18), the Furies (IX.52–54), the Minotaur (XII.14–15), Geryon (XVII.25–27), Malacoda and the Malebranche (XXI.23–XXIII.57), Nimrod (XXXI.67), Satan (XXXIV.22–27). In almost all of these scenes it is Virgil's task to quell the resistance of the infernal guardians and to reassure his charge.

Pape Satàn, Pape Satàn, aleppe. The third verse suggests that Virgil understands these words spoken by Plutus. If that is correct, he is perhaps the only one to have done so. Over the centuries a continuing debate addresses, rather confusedly, the precise nature of these five words: whether they are part of a recognizable language or not; whether they are totally meaningless or have some meaning; whether they are an invocation of the power of Satan against invading Dante or an oath giving expression to the monster's surprise at the presence of a living soul in hell. For a review of the question see Hollander (Holl.1992.1), who sees this and Nimrod's similarly nonsensical five words (*Inf.* XXXI.67) as parodic inversions of the five words of clear speech called for by St. Paul, concerned about the overreliance of the faithful on speaking in tongues (I Cor. 14:19). Plutus's oath may be garbled speech, but it does contain "pseudo-words" that have meaning: *Pape* represents either a Latin interjection *(papae)* of admiration, as many ancient commentators think, or/and a debased form of the Italian and Latin for "pope" *(papa*—see v. 47: *papi)*; *Satàn* would fairly clearly seem to be a form of the Italian "Satana" or of the Latin "Sathanas" and thus "Satan"; *aleppe,* as some of the first commentators noticed, is the Italian form of the Hebrew word for the first letter of the alphabet, "aleph," as in the Latin expression "alpha ed omega" (the first and last letters of the Greek alphabet, signifying "the beginning and the end"), as God defines Himself in the Bible (Rev. 1:8, repeated at 21:6 and 22:13). If one had to render these nonsense words in English one might say something like "O Pope Satan, my god." Fortunately, one does not have to. For the connection of these words in mixed language to those in the first verses of the seventh canto of *Paradiso* (there, naturally, totally positive in tone and meaning)—the parallelism is certainly striking—see Sarolli (Saro.1971.1), pp. 289–90.

8.   That Virgil refers to Plutus as a wolf ties him to the vice of avarice, since in this poem wolves are often symbols of that vice (e.g., *Purg.* XX.10; *Par.* IX.132; XXVII.55).

10–12.   In justifying Dante's status as visitor to the infernal regions, Virgil refers to the war in heaven (see Rev. 12:7–9), where the archangel Michael is specifically mentioned as a warrior in the battle that sent Satan down into hell with his minions, the fallen angels. Dante's treatment makes it seem that Plutus felt his kinship with these creatures, whom the travelers will encounter at *Inferno* VIII.82–84.

13–15.   Virgil's words, telling exactly how things are with respect to demonic rebellion, are enough to crumple the irascible spirit of Plutus (vv. 13–15).

19.   The author's apostrophe of God's justice reminds us of the centrality of this concern to the entire *Comedy*. See note to *Inferno* III.4.

22–23.   Dante's *locus classicus* for the description of the tumultuous meeting of the Ionian and Mediterranean seas between Sicily and the Italian mainland is found in *Aeneid* III.420–433.

24.   Dante's Italian makes it clear that this dance is the *ridda*, a popular dance in which the linked participants reverse the direction of their circling movement with the playing and singing of each new strophe.

25–30.   For the relatively greater number of condemned souls devoted to avarice see *Aeneid* VI.608–611, the Sibyl's description of Tartarus, which includes a description of the punishment of (unnamed) Sisyphus, eternally rolling his stone (v. 616). Dante appropriates these two details to build the details of his fourth Circle. Virgil's brief description of those who loved riches to excess is without reference to those of the precisely opposite inclination. In Dante's formulation, prodigality is the opposite form of the same vice. This is one of the few examples in the code of ethics found in this poem in which an Aristotelian measure seems to be at work, in which a "golden mean" locates the correct or permissible amount of affection or desire. (See v. 42 for confirmation that there is a proper measure in such things.)

31–35.   It has not often been noted, but, seen from above, the avaricious and prodigal perform a perfect circle in their movement. Their activities in hell (as was true in the world above) mount up to exactly zero. This nullity is reflected in their nameless and unidentifiable condition here; and their circling is to be compared to that performed by Fortune's wheel (see n. to v. 90, below).

36.   Dante's sympathetic responses to various of the damned usually indicate a sense of identity with them. On this occasion, it would rather seem to reveal his horror at the nature of this punishment.

38–39.   Dante allows himself a fairly traditional anticlerical thrust. Christ had led his followers in embracing poverty and, much later, the mendicant orders took vows of poverty, some in remembrance of St. Francis's imitation of Christ in this respect. Thus, while avarice in any person respected for a higher calling would be disgraceful, it is particularly so in a member of the clergy and becomes an easy (and popular) target. It is notable that the clergy are noticed only here—and in number—among the avaricious; none of them is pointed out among the prodigal.

46–48.   The insistence on the large number of clerics among the avaricious (and no other social orders are identified as being avaricious, not even bankers or moneylenders) continues, now including a plurality of popes.

The anonymous plurality of popes mentioned in v. 47 leaves the reader free to supply any number of such pontiffs. The essential impression left by the poem as a whole is that more popes are damned than saved. This is probably true, but Dante does insist that a number of popes are in fact saved. The first and foremost is of course St. Peter, considered by Dante and medieval writers in general as being the first pope. He is seen in paradise by Dante in the heaven of the Fixed Stars, where he has a major role as speaker, but he is referred to from the beginning of the poem to its end (*Inf.* II.24; *Par.* XXXII.133). And Peter himself is the one who tells of the salvations of six other early popes: his two immediate successors Linus and Cletus, both martyred in the first century (*Par.* XXVII.41), as well as four other popes martyred, according to a tradition that Dante followed, in the second and third centuries: Sixtus I, Pius I, Calixtus I, and Urban I

(*Par.* XXVII.44). Also mentioned as being saved are Agapetus I (*Par.* VI.16) and Gregory I (*Par.* XXVIII.133–135). We see Pope Adrian V purging his lethargy on the road to heaven (*Purg.* XIX.99) and Pope Martin IV repenting his zest for eating eels also on his way to paradise (*Purg.* XXIV.22). And there is Pope John XXI, seen as present in the heaven of the Sun and hence among the blessed (*Par.* XII.134). Thus, twelve popes are indicated as being among God's chosen.

Several other popes are referred to, but without having their eventual destinations under God's justice made plain. Such is the case with respect to Sylvester I (*Inf.* XXVII.94), Clement IV (*Purg.* III.125), Innocent III (*Par.* XI.92), and Honorius III (*Par.* XI.98).

The case of the popes who are damned is more complex. Here is an attempt to list the fallen pontiffs referred to in the poem. If the one "who made the great refusal" (*Inf.* III.60) is, as many believe, Pope Celestine V, he would be the first damned pope whom we see. He is followed by the unnamed pontiffs of Canto VII and then by Anastasius II (*Inf.* XI.8). Many believe that Innocent IV is the most certain presence in the unnamed line of precursors alluded to by Nicholas III (*Inf.* XIX.73)—a second instance of a plurality of damned popes, while the saved ones are never referred to in this way. Those that are confirmed as damned are Nicholas himself (*Inf.* XIX.70), Boniface VIII (*Inf.* XIX.53), Clement V (*Inf.* XIX.83), and, a last for good measure, John XXII (*Par.* XXVII.58). Thus at least five popes are definitively damned. In two cases, as we have seen, Dante opens the door to other possibilities. As a result, the absolute possible low is nine (five plus the plural "papi" at *Inf.* VII.47 and "altri" at *Inf.* XIX.73—there must be at least two in each case to account for the plural). Celestine would bring the total to ten. In short, Dante probably did mean to encourage his readers to believe exactly what most of them seem to believe—that more popes were damned than were saved.

57.   That is, the avaricious will have their fists clamped in remembrance of their grasping behaviors, while the prodigal will have their hair shorn to remind them of their lack of care for their possessions (and themselves). Sinclair, in his note to this verse (Sinc.1939.1, p. 105), cites an old Italian proverb: a prodigal spends "even to the hair of his head."

62–96.   Virgil's discourse on the nature and effect of Fortune on mortal lives is notable for its sunniness and equability. The usual and necessary citation among commentators is of Boethius, whose *Consolation of Philosophy* is the standard medieval text on the subject and was well known to Dante. The Lady Philosophy explains to complaining Boethius that humans who suffer like to blame their misfortune on bad luck, expressed by the fortune that turns its back on them. What philosophy makes plain is that the fault lies in ourselves, in that we pitch our hopes on things we should recognize as fallible, fleeting, and of ultimately little importance. What Dante adds to this stern message is a sense of calmness about and even positive acceptance of these facts of human existence. Fortune may be understood as, in the happy formulation of Charles Grandgent (in his proem to this canto), "the Angel of Earth." Nothing that she does should be unexpected; everything that she does is "right." Exactly such an understanding may be found in Dante's own words in his *Monarchia* (II.ix.8), where he says that the force that distributes the goods of the world, victory or defeat in battle, which the pagans attributed to their gods, "we call . . . by the more appropriate and accurate name 'divine providence.' " Particularly helpful discussions of Dante's understanding of fortune may be found in Cioffari's book (Ciof.1940.1), Toja'a article (Toja.1965.1), and Padoan's various remarks on this passage in his commentary.

   The distance that Dante has traveled from the position he took in his *Convivio* (IV.xi.6–8), where the unequal distribution of goods among humans is seen as a defect of Fortune's agency, is manifest. In that passage Fortune is seen as acting randomly; here she is provident (v. 86)—and we should remember that she was traditionally portrayed as blindfolded, unseeing as she acts. In this passage, as one of the angelic hierarchy, she turns her famous "wheel" in knowledge and in bliss. God's in His heaven, Fortune turns her wheel, all's right with the world, which is only and absolutely as it should be.

70–72.   Virgil's desire to "feed" his confused "offspring" so that he may give over his foolish view of Fortune will mark a turning point in the protagonist's understanding of her.

84.   Dante's "serpent hidden in the grass" has been seen, at least from the sixteenth century on, as being a translation of Virgil's third *Eclogue*, verse 93: "latet anguis in herba."

87.   The *altri dèi*, literally "other gods," translated as "other heavenly powers," are the other nine orders of angels.

90.   The rapid tranformations of human states are summarized by the Casini/Barbi commentary to v. 96 as follows: a given human being may

typically move, along eight points on Fortune's wheel, from humility, to patience, to peace, to riches, to pride, to impatience, to war, to poverty. This is a typical "ride" of anyone tied to Fortune's wheel, ending back at the starting point. See note to vv. 31–35, above.

98–99. Virgil's indication of the time reveals that it is now after midnight, some six hours after the travelers set out at 6 PM on Friday evening.

106. The river Styx has a classical history, most notably in the *Aeneid* (VI.323).

109–114. Clearly the protagonist, gazing upon the inhabitants of the fifth Circle, is looking at the wrathful. The problem for interpreters is that wrath, or anger, is a sin of violence, not one of incontinence; yet the poem has not yet left the realm of incontinence behind. Without reviewing the fairly vast literature upon this problem, one can offer some uncomplicated solutions, based on the thirteenth chapter of St. Thomas's commentary on Aristotle's *Ethics* (IV.5). Aristotle, in Thomas's paraphrase, distinguishes three kinds of anger: choleric (which comes upon one quickly and quickly departs), bitter (which lasts long in the heart of the afflicted person, and is not released easily), difficult (which is more hostile, longer-lasting, and directed against those it should not be, and which is not released until the one experiencing this kind of wrath inflicts injury upon an enemy). It seems clear that Dante here shows the punishment of the first sort of wrath in the choleric, who are not guilty of sins of violence, but of intemperance. (For the second set of sinners punished here, see the next note.) In this interpretation, the third form of anger, which has as its intention physical harm to another, is punished only in the realm of the violent against others, in Canto XII—where it should be, and not as a sin of intemperance, which these first two are.

118–126. Those who are punished under the surface of the Styx are, in this formulation (see n. to vv. 109–114), what St. Thomas characterizes as Aristotle's second set of the wrathful, the *amari*, or "bitter." These people kept their anger in, suffering gravely within themselves (as opposed to the choleric, quick to vent their anger in insults and blows). Dante's inventive representation of this kind of wrath shows its exemplars as experiencing the "muddy" or "smoky" sensation of stifled anger.

INFERNO VIII

Io dico, seguitando, ch'assai prima
che noi fossimo al piè de l'alta torre,
li occhi nostri n'andar suso a la cima

per due fiammette che i vedemmo porre,
e un'altra da lungi render cenno,
tanto ch'a pena il potea l'occhio tòrre.

E io mi volsi al mar di tutto 'l senno;
dissi: "Questo che dice? e che risponde
quell'altro foco? e chi son quei che 'l fenno?"

Ed elli a me: "Su per le sucide onde
già scorgere puoi quello che s'aspetta,
se 'l fummo del pantan nol ti nasconde."

Corda non pinse mai da sé saetta
che sì corresse via per l'aere snella,
com'io vidi una nave piccioletta

venir per l'acqua verso noi in quella,
sotto 'l governo d'un sol galeoto,
che gridava: "Or se' giunta, anima fella!"

"Flegïàs, Flegïàs, tu gridi a vòto,"
disse lo mio segnore, "a questa volta:
più non ci avrai che sol passando il loto."

Qual è colui che grande inganno ascolta
che li sia fatto, e poi se ne rammarca,
fecesi Flegïàs ne l'ira accolta.

Lo duca mio discese ne la barca,
e poi mi fece intrare appresso lui;
e sol quand'io fui dentro parve carca.

To continue, let me say that long before
we reached the foot of that high tower
3   our eyes had noted at its top

two flaming lights displayed up there
to which another, so far off the eye
6   could hardly make it out, sent back a signal.

And turning to that sea of wisdom, I asked:
'What does this mean? And that other fire,
9   what does it answer? And who made it?'

And he to me: 'Over the filthy waves
you may already glimpse what is to come,
12   if the marsh-fumes do not hide it from you.'

Never did a bowstring loose an arrow
that whipped away more swiftly through the air
15   than, even as I watched, a skiff came skimming

toward us on the water,
under the guidance of a single helmsman,
18   crying: 'Now you are caught, damned spirit!'

'Phlegyas, Phlegyas, this time you shout in vain,'
replied my lord. 'You will have us no longer
21   than it takes to cross this bog.'

Like one who learns of a deceitful plot
hatched against him and begins to fret,
24   Phlegyas became in his stifled wrath.

My leader stepped into the boat,
and had me follow after.
27   And only then did it seem laden.

Tosto che 'l duca e io nel legno fui,
segando se ne va l'antica prora
30   de l'acqua più che non suol con altrui.

Mentre noi corravam la morta gora,
dinanzi mi si fece un pien di fango,
33   e disse: "Chi se' tu che vieni anzi ora?"

E io a lui: "S'i' vegno, non rimango;
ma tu chi se', che sì se' fatto brutto?"
36   Rispuose: "Vedi che son un che piango."

E io a lui: "Con piangere e con lutto,
spirito maladetto, ti rimani;
39   ch'i' ti conosco, ancor sie lordo tutto."

Allor distese al legno ambo le mani;
per che 'l maestro accorto lo sospinse,
42   dicendo: "Via costà con li altri cani!"

Lo collo poi con le braccia mi cinse;
basciommi 'l volto e disse: "Alma sdegnosa,
45   benedetta colei che 'n te s'incinse!

Quei fu al mondo persona orgogliosa;
bontà non è che sua memoria fregi:
48   così s'è l'ombra sua qui furïosa.

Quanti si tegnon or là sù gran regi
che qui staranno come porci in brago,
51   di sé lasciando orribili dispregi!"

E io: "Maestro, molto sarei vago
di vederlo attuffare in questa broda
54   prima che noi uscissimo del lago."

Ed elli a me: "Avante che la proda
ti si lasci veder, tu sarai sazio:
57   di tal disïo convien che tu goda."

As soon as he and I were in the bark
the ancient prow moves off, cutting deeper
30   through the water than when it carries souls.

While we crossed the stagnant swamp
one cloaked in mud rose up to say:
33   'Who are you that come before your time?'

And I to him: 'If I come, I do not stay.
But you, who are you, now become so foul?'
36   He answered: 'As you can see, I am one who weeps.'

And I to him: 'In weeping and in misery,
accursèd spirit, may you stay.
39   I know you, for all your filth.'

When he stretched both his hands toward the boat,
the wary master thrust him off, saying:
42   'Away there with the other dogs!'

Then my master put his arms around my neck,
kissed my face and said: 'Indignant soul,
45   blessed is she that bore you in her womb!

'In the world this man was full of arrogance.
Not one good deed adorns his memory.
48   That is why his shade is so enraged.

'How many now above who think themselves
great kings will lie here in the mud, like swine,
51   leaving behind nothing but ill repute!"

And I: 'Master, I would be most eager
to see him pushed deep down into this soup
54   before we leave the lake.'

And he to me: 'Before the shore
comes into view you'll have your satisfaction.
57   Your wish deserves to be fulfilled.'

Dopo ciò poco vid'io quello strazio
far di costui a le fangose genti,
60 che Dio ancor ne lodo e ne ringrazio.

Tutti gridavano: "A Filippo Argenti!"
e 'l fiorentino spirito bizzarro
63 in sé medesmo si volvea co' denti.

Quivi il lasciammo, che più non ne narro;
ma ne l'orecchie mi percosse un duolo,
66 per ch'io avante l'occhio intento sbarro.

Lo buon maestro disse: "Omai, figliuolo,
s'appressa la città c'ha nome Dite,
69 coi gravi cittadin, col grande stuolo."

E io: "Maestro, già le sue meschite
là entro certe ne la valle cerno,
72 vermiglie come se di foco uscite

fossero." Ed ei mi disse: "Il foco etterno
ch'entro l'affoca le dimostra rosse,
75 come tu vedi in questo basso inferno."

Noi pur giugnemmo dentro a l'alte fosse
che vallan quella terra sconsolata:
78 le mura mi parean che ferro fosse.

Non sanza prima far grande aggirata,
venimmo in parte dove il nocchier forte
81 "Usciteci," gridò: "qui è l'intrata."

Io vidi più di mille in su le porte
da ciel piovuti, che stizzosamente
84 dicean: "Chi è costui che sanza morte

va per lo regno de la morta gente?"
E 'l savio mio maestro fece segno
87 di voler lor parlar segretamente.

Soon I watched him get so torn to pieces
by the muddy crew, I still give praise
60   and thanks to God for it.

All cried: 'Get Filippo Argenti!'
And that spiteful Florentine spirit
63   gnawed at himself with his own teeth.

Of him I say no more. Then we moved on,
when such a sound of mourning struck my ears
66   I opened my eyes wide to look ahead.

The good master said: 'Now, my son,
we approach the city known as Dis,
69   with its vast army and its burdened citizens.'

And I: 'Master, I can clearly see its mosques
within the ramparts, glowing red
72   as if they'd just been taken from the fire.'

And he to me: 'The eternal fire
that burns inside them here in nether Hell
75   makes them show red, as you can see.'

At last we reached the moats
dug deep around the dismal city.
78   Its walls seemed made of iron.

Not until we'd made a wide approach
did we come to a place where the boatman bellowed:
81   'Out with you here, this is the entrance.'

At the threshold I saw more than a thousand angels
fallen from Heaven. Angrily they shouted:
84   'Who is this, who is not dead,

'yet passes through the kingdom of the dead?'
At this my prudent master made a sign
87   that he would speak with them apart.

Allor chiusero un poco il gran disdegno
e disser: "Vien tu solo, e quei sen vada
90   che sì ardito intrò per questo regno.

Sol si ritorni per la folle strada:
pruovi, se sa; ché tu qui rimarrai,
93   che li ha' iscorta sì buia contrada."

Pensa, lettor, se io mi sconfortai
nel suon de le parole maladette,
96   ché non credetti ritornarci mai.

"O caro duca mio, che più di sette
volte m'hai sicurtà renduta e tratto
99   d'alto periglio che 'ncontra mi stette,

non mi lasciar," diss' io, "così disfatto;
e se 'l passar più oltre ci è negato,
102   ritroviam l'orme nostre insieme ratto."

E quel segnor che lì m'avea menato,
mi disse: "Non temer; ché 'l nostro passo
105   non ci può tòrre alcun: da tal n'è dato.

Ma qui m'attendi, e lo spirito lasso
conforta e ciba di speranza buona,
108   ch'i' non ti lascerò nel mondo basso."

Così sen va, e quivi m'abbandona
lo dolce padre, e io rimagno in forse,
111   che sì e no nel capo mi tenciona.

Udir non potti quello ch'a lor porse;
ma ei non stette là con essi guari,
114   che ciascun dentro a pruova si ricorse.

Chiuser le porte que' nostri avversari
nel petto al mio segnor, che fuor rimase
117   e rivolsesi a me con passi rari.

Then they reined in their great disdain
enough to say: 'You come—alone. Let him be gone,
90   who has so boldly made his way into this kingdom.

'Let him retrace his reckless path alone—
let him see if he can, for you shall stay,
93   you who have led him through this gloomy realm.'

Reader, how could I not lose heart
at the sound of these accursèd words,
96   for I thought I would never make it back.

'O my dear leader, who seven times and more
have braced my confidence and saved me
99   from the dangers that assailed me,

'do not leave me,' I cried, 'helpless now!
If going farther is denied us,
102   let us at once retrace our steps.'

But the mentor who had brought me there replied:
'Have no fear. None can prevent our passage,
105   so great a power granted it to us.

'Wait for me here. Comfort your weary spirit
and feed it with good hope.
108   I will not forsake you in the nether world.'

He goes away and leaves me there,
my gentle father, and I remain in doubt,
111   'yes' and 'no' at war within my mind.

I could not hear what he proposed,
but it was not long he stayed with them
114   before they pushed and scrambled back inside.

Then our adversaries slammed shut the gates
against my master, who, left outside,
117   came back to me with halting steps.

Li occhi a la terra e le ciglia avea rase
d'ogne baldanza, e dicea ne' sospiri:
120 "Chi m'ha negate le dolenti case!"

E a me disse: "Tu, perch' io m'adiri,
non sbigottir, ch'io vincerò la prova,
123 qual ch'a la difension dentro s'aggiri.

Questa lor tracotanza non è nova;
ché già l'usaro a men segreta porta,
126 la qual sanza serrame ancor si trova.

Sovr' essa vedestù la scritta morta:
e già di qua da lei discende l'erta,
passando per li cerchi sanza scorta,
130 tal che per lui ne fia la terra aperta."

He had his eyes upon the ground, his brows
shorn of all confidence. Sighing, he muttered:
120 'Who dares deny me access to the realm of pain?'

To me he said: 'Be not dismayed
at my vexation. In this contest I'll prevail,
123 whatever they contrive to keep us out.

'This insolence of theirs is nothing new:
they showed it once before, at another gate.
126 It still stands open without lock or bolt.

'Over it you saw the deadly writing.
Even now, making his unescorted way
down through the circles, one descends
130 by whom the city shall be opened.'

1.   For the first time the poet interrupts the chronological flow of his narrative, interpolating events that occurred before the situation described in the very last verse of the preceding canto (for a briefer but similar interpolation see the first tercet of the thirteenth canto). The first 81 lines of Canto VIII relate what occurred between the travelers' first experience of the wrathful sinners in the Styx (VII.129) and their arrival at the foot of a tower of the walled city of Dis (VII.130). The self-conscious interruption of the narrative may be enough to account for the self-conscious opening verse: "To continue, let me say . . ." However, Boccaccio, in his commentary to this canto, was the first to sponsor the idea that in fact Dante only now, in Lunigiana in 1306, took up again the composition of his poem, begun in Florence before his exile and left behind when he could not return to the city. According to Boccaccio, a friend brought him the text of the first seven cantos, which had lain fallow for some six or seven years. While most do not credit this version of the history of composition of the *Comedy*, it has some support. See Ferretti (Ferr.1935.1) and Padoan (Pado.1993.1). The latter's book is devoted to a reassessment of the problem of the compositional history of the entire poem. In his view, *Inferno* was composed between 1306 and 1315, while most students of the problem argue for a completion of the first *cantica* around 1310.

4–6.   This mysterious signaling almost certainly refers to the defensive maneuvers of the demonic guardians of hell. Perhaps the fires of the defenders of Dis atop this tower are a warning to those farther along the wall—or at least some think so. Thus the two flames set out here would warn against a force of two enemies, and the answering flame would seem to acknowledge that warning. Yet the primary purpose of the two flames would seem to be to summon Phlegyas (see n. to v. 19) to capture and deliver a soul into bondage. (In this second interpretation, the twin flames do not necessarily indicate the number of interlopers.) Such a view encourages some to believe that Minos hurls the wrathful into the Styx, whence they are retrieved and given proper station by Phlegyas, whose business in the muddy river is not to ferry souls across and into Dis, but to place them in the river, as Caretti (Care.1951.2), p. 6, believes. That solution, however, would imply that the signals from the tower would be deployed each time a wrathful soul is sent down, and that seems improbable. A possible way out is offered by the hypothesis that Phlegyas's function is to round up escaping wrathful souls should they attempt to flee the mud. In such a case, the demons of Dis would assist a fellow demon to wreak pain upon the damned. But then why do the demons signal other demons along the wall? Or are the fires answered by still other demons at Phlegyas's "boathouse"? The details are sparse enough to make a final resolution next to impossible.

7–12.   Dante's three questions are not really answered by Virgil, who does not say exactly what the twinned flame signifies, does not say at all what the second means in answer, and similarly ignores the question of agency with respect to the second flame. He does imply that Phlegyas's skiff is what the custodians of the first flame summoned.

15.   Padoan, in his commentary, points out that Phlegyas's skiff is not large, like Charon's, but small, an infernal speedboat, as it were, meant for the pursuit of individuals and not intended for ferrying crowds of souls across a river.

18.   Phlegyas, who is not in the least interested in Virgil, would seem to believe that Dante is a condemned soul who is trying to escape. As Padoan points out in his commentary to this verse, Dante elsewhere several times uses the adjective *fello* (here translated as "damned") so as to associate it with wrath (see *Inf.* XVII.132; XXI.72; *Par.* IV.15).

19.   "Son of Mars and King of Orchomenos in Boeotia, father of Ixion and Coronis; the latter having been violated by Apollo, by whom she became the mother of Aesculapius, Phlegyas in fury set fire to the temple of Apollo at Delphi, for which sacrilege he was slain by the god and condemned to eternal punishment in the lower world" **(T)**. In the *Aeneid* (VI.618–620) he is mentioned by the Sibyl as now, in Tartarus, warning against such temerity against the gods.

20–21.   Virgil's mocking response makes it seem likely that Phlegyas does at times intervene in the capture and punishment of damned souls, if not under what precise conditions he does so.

22–24.   The brief simile establishes the fact that Phlegyas feels he has been tricked into thinking that he had been summoned to do his usual task. As we have seen, exactly what that is remains something of a mystery. Yet why would other demons have chosen to trick him? Or is the reader to infer a divine plan behind his summons? This last detail, like so many in this part of the narrative (vv. 3–24), raises more questions than it answers.

25–30.   For the relation of this moment, so clearly modeled on Aeneas's stepping into Charon's skiff in *Aeneid* VI.413–414, to Dante's version of that scene at the close of *Inferno* III, see the note to v. 136 of that canto.

31–39.   This is the first time in the poem that we hear an angry debate between the protagonist and one of the sinners. These are often, as here, couched in a form reminiscent of *tenzoni*, poems in the low language of streetwise insult, that were a popular pastime of thirteenth-century Italian poets, including Dante. "Pure" *tenzoni* were usually sonnets. The second participant usually responded to the insults of the first with the same rhyme scheme (and often the identical rhyme words) deployed by the original attacker. Dante's adaptation of the technique in *Inferno* reveals its roots in this form.

32.   This is Filippo Argenti. See n. to v. 61, below.

37.   Casagrande (Casa.1978.1), p. 249, cites a passage in Hugh of St. Victor to explain Dante's curse and Filippo's weeping: "It is a misery to him who, bitter of mind because he cannot exact revenge upon his superior, must take satisfaction in his own tears."

40–45.   After Virgil thrusts Filippo Argenti (see n. to v. 61) back into the Styx, fending off his attempted wrathful assault, he congratulates Dante for his harsh words to this sinner (vv. 37–39). His words are reminiscent of those spoken of Christ in Luke 11:27: "Blessed is the womb that bore you." Sinclair (Sinc.1939.1, p. 119) cites a biblical text as being in concert with the spirit of the protagonist's righteous indignation here: "Do not I hate them, O Lord, that hate you . . . I hate them with perfect hatred: I count them my enemies" (Psalms 139:21–22). In his commentary to *Inferno* XX.28–30 Guido da Pisa put this thought in the following terms: "The suffering of the damned should move no one to compassion, as the Bible attests. And the reason for this is that the time for mercy is here in this world, while in the world to come it is time only for justice."

46.   Some read Filippo's pridefulness as being his "real" sin, and not wrath. Wrath is his besetting vice, but many others may come into play in him or in any sinner. The notion that our disposition to sin must be uni-

tary has no base either in medieval ethical treatises or in ordinary human experience.

61.   From the cries of others the reader finally learns the name of this sinner (Dante has known exactly who he is—see v. 39). Filippo Argenti was a Black Guelph from a powerful Florentine family. His real name was Filippo Adimari de' Cavicciuoli, but he supposedly was known as Filippo Argenti because he had his horse's hooves shod in silver (*argento*). A number of early commentators relate that his brother, Boccaccino, got hold of Dante's possessions when the poet was exiled. If that is true, we have here a pretty clear case of authorial revenge upon a particularly hated enemy. See Francesco Forti, "Filippo Argenti," *ED,* vol. 2, 1970, pp. 873–76.

62.   The word *bizzarro*, explains Boccaccio's comment to this passage, in Florentine vernacular is used of people who "suddenly and for any reason at all lose their tempers." See note to *Inferno* VII.109–114.

63.   Benvenuto da Imola's commentary to this verse: Filippo gnaws himself "just as a proud man will do, unable to avenge the injury done him by someone more powerful."

68.   Dis *(Dite)*, for the Romans another name for Pluto, god of the underworld, for Dante is thereby another name for Lucifer or Satan.

70.   The most visible buildings of this city, seen from afar, are mosques *(meschite)*, thus associating them with what was for Dante and his era a most hostile religious and military force, the Mohammedans.

78.   The iron walls of the City of Dis are emblematic of the fact that from here on down all sins punished are the result of the hardened will, not the whims of appetite. Virgil's Tartarus, into which Aeneas does not penetrate (the Sibyl describes to him its contents) has an iron tower (*Aen.* VI.554: *ferrea turris*) that may be remembered here.

81.   Only here and now do we arrive at the place we left in the final verse of the last canto, under a tower of the City of Dis.

82–85.   The first "citizens" of Dis whom we see are the rebel angels who were defeated, along with Satan, by Michael and his angels. For the first time Virgil will have to deal with adversaries who are not easily swayed.

94–96.   Dante's addresses to the reader are a noteworthy feature of the poem. Perhaps no other literary text contains as many cases of direct address to its readership. The net effect is to forge a relationship between us and the author that makes us partners in his enterprise. His most usual tactic is to ask us to share in the strong emotions he experienced at any given moment; on other occasions he invites us to interpret things difficult to understand. In all cases we feel drawn into the poem, as though we were witnessing what the poet describes ourselves or being asked to share with him the difficulty of interpreting his materials. See discussions in Gmelin (Gmel.1951.1), Auerbach (Auer.1954.1), and Spitzer (Spit.1955.1). And see the article of Vittorio Russo, "appello al lettore," *ED*, vol. 1, 1970, pp. 324–26, for a listing: *Inf.* VIII.94–96; IX.61–63; XVI.127–132; XX.19–24; XXII.118; XXV.46–48; XXXIV.22–27; *Purg.* VIII.19–21; IX.70–72; X.106–111; XVII.1–9; XXIX.97–105; XXXI.124–126; XXXIII.136–138; *Par.* II.1–18; V.109–114; X.7–27; XIII.1–21; XXII.106–111. Thus there are seven in each of the first two *cantiche* and at least five in *Paradiso*. However, and as Russo points out, there may be seven in the third *cantica* as well, since the passage at IX.10–12 may also be included and that at X.7–27 perhaps should be seen as two separate addresses (7–15 and 22–27).

The addresses are a subgroup of the classical rhetorical figure of apostrophe (direct address), which is amply used by this poet. For discussion see the article "apostrofe" by Francesco Tateo, *ED,* vol. 1, 1970, pp. 319–21. Another subdivision of apostrophe in addition to addressing one's reader is found in the invocations of the *Comedy*. See note to *Inferno* II.7–9. There are nine of these in the poem.

97–99.   In their commentary Casini/Barbi insist that, on the model of several biblical passages (e.g., the just man who falls seven times, rising again each time, of Prov. 24:16), the "seven times" is to be taken as indeterminate. They go on to list eight times that Virgil has come to Dante's aid: *Inferno* I.49, II.130, III.94, V.21, VI.22, VII.8, VIII.19, VIII.41.

104–105.   Virgil's reassurance of an understandably shaken Dante, given the strength of opposition from the fallen angels, relies on the promise of divine support made to him, apparently, by Beatrice in the scene reported in *Inferno* II.

106–111.   For the first time since he began his guidance, Virgil feels able to leave Dante to his own devices. The next time that he does so (*Inf.* XVI.37–39) his pupil will even be allowed to visit a group of sinners unguided. Both these moments, in ascending order, reveal the protagonist's growing capacity to deal with sin.

115–117.   For the first time in his role as guide, Virgil suffers defeat in an attempt to gain Dante access to the next stage of the journey. Once again the reader understands that the forces of Dis, schooled in guile and strong of will, are far more stubborn adversaries than those encountered before.

121–126.   Virgil joins his frustration to what hopes he can muster in order to encourage Dante. His main evidence for believing that he will be able to continue is drawn from his witness of the harrowing of hell, of which he gave notice in *Inferno* IV.52–63. J. S. Carroll, in his comment to *Inferno* III.1–9, looks ahead to these verses and cites the apocryphal Gospel of Nicodemus, chapters 13–19, in which the hosts of hell attempted to block Christ's harrowing as source for the attempt of these new rebels to keep Virgil out of their kingdom.

127.   The "deadly writing" over the gate of hell (*Inf.* III.1–9) is so, in the words of Casini/Barbi on this verse, because it tells the damned where they are headed—into eternal death. Thus the writing itself is very much "alive," but it speaks of death.

128–130.   The nature of this descending messenger will be discussed in the note to *Inferno* IX.85. Musa (Musa.1974.1), p. 150, argues that this descent should put us in mind of the descent of the prophesied *nova progenies* (new race) of Virgil's fourth *Eclogue*, v. 7.

How does Virgil know that such aid is coming? Some argue that he "sees" it in his mind; others that Beatrice had promised exactly such help if ever it were needed when she spoke to Virgil in Limbo (*Inf.* II). The text offers confirmation of neither notion, if the latter seems the more probable.

INFERNO IX

Quel color che viltà di fuor mi pinse
veggendo il duca mio tornare in volta,
3   più tosto dentro il suo novo ristrinse.

Attento si fermò com' uom ch'ascolta;
ché l'occhio nol potea menare a lunga
6   per l'aere nero e per la nebbia folta.

"Pur a noi converrà vincer la punga,"
cominciò el, "se non . . . Tal ne s'offerse.
9   Oh quanto tarda a me ch'altri qui giunga!"

I' vidi ben sì com' ei ricoperse
lo cominciar con l'altro che poi venne,
12   che fur parole a le prime diverse;

ma nondimen paura il suo dir dienne,
perch' io traeva la parola tronca
15   forse a peggior sentenzia che non tenne.

"In questo fondo de la trista conca
discende mai alcun del primo grado,
18   che sol per pena ha la speranza cionca?"

Questa question fec' io; e quei "Di rado
incontra," mi rispuose, "che di noi
21   faccia il cammino alcun per qual io vado.

Ver è ch'altra fïata qua giù fui,
congiurato da quella Eritón cruda
24   che richiamava l'ombre a' corpi sui.

Di poco era di me la carne nuda,
ch'ella mi fece intrar dentr' a quel muro,
27   per trarne un spirto del cerchio di Giuda.

The pallor cowardice painted on my face
when I saw my leader turning back
made him hasten to compose his features.

He stopped, like a man intent on listening,
for the eye could not probe far
through that dim air and murky fog.

'Yet we must win this fight,' he began,
'or else.... Such help was promised us.
How long it seems to me till someone comes!'

I clearly saw that he had covered up
his first words with the others that came after,
words so different in meaning.

Still, I was filled with fear by what he said.
Perhaps I understood his broken phrase
to hold worse meaning than it did.

'Does ever anyone from the first circle,
where the only penalty is hope cut off,
descend so deep into this dismal pit?'

I put this question and he answered:
'It seldom happens that a soul from Limbo
undertakes the journey I am on.

'It is true I came here once before,
conjured by pitiless Erichtho,
who could call shades back into their bodies.

'I had not long been naked of my flesh
when she compelled me to go inside this wall
to fetch a spirit from the circle of Judas.

3

6

9

12

15

18

21

24

27

Quell' è 'l più basso loco e 'l più oscuro,
e 'l più lontan dal ciel che tutto gira:
30   ben so 'l cammin; però ti fa sicuro.

Questa palude che 'l gran puzzo spira
cigne dintorno la città dolente,
33   u' non potemo intrare omai sanz' ira."

E altro disse, ma non l'ho a mente;
però che l'occhio m'avea tutto tratto
36   ver' l'alta torre a la cima rovente,

dove in un punto furon dritte ratto
tre furïe infernal di sangue tinte,
39   che membra feminine avieno e atto,

e con idre verdissime eran cinte;
serpentelli e ceraste avien per crine,
42   onde le fiere tempie erano avvinte.

E quei, che ben conobbe le meschine
de la regina de l'etterno pianto,
45   "Guarda," mi disse, "le feroci Erine.

Quest' è Megera dal sinistro canto;
quella che piange dal destro è Aletto;
48   Tesifón è nel mezzo"; e tacque a tanto.

Con l'unghie si fendea ciascuna il petto;
battiensi a palme e gridavan sì alto,
51   ch'i' mi strinsi al poeta per sospetto.

"Vegna Medusa: sì 'l farem di smalto,"
dicevan tutte riguardando in giuso;
54   "mal non vengiammo in Tesëo l'assalto."

"Volgiti 'n dietro e tien lo viso chiuso;
ché se 'l Gorgón si mostra e tu 'l vedessi,
57   nulla sarebbe di tornar mai suso."

'That is the lowest place, the darkest,
and farthest from the heaven that encircles all.
30   Well do I know the way—so have no fear.

'This swamp, which belches forth such noxious stench,
hems in the woeful city, circles it.
33   Now we cannot enter without wrath.'

And he said more, but I do not remember,
for my eyes and thoughts were drawn
36   to the high tower's blazing peak

where all at once, erect, had risen
three hellish, blood-stained Furies:
39   they had the limbs and shape of women,

their waists encircled by green hydras.
Thin serpents and horned snakes entwined,
42   in place of hair, their savage brows.

And he, who knew full well the handmaids
to the queen of endless lamentation,
45   said to me: 'See the fierce Erinyes.

'That is Megaera on the left. On the right
Alecto wails. In the middle
48   is Tisiphone.' And with that he fell silent.

Each rent her breast with her own nails.
And with their palms they struck themselves, shrieking.
51   In fear I pressed close to the poet.

'Let Medusa come and we'll turn him to stone,'
they cried, looking down. 'To our cost,
54   we failed to avenge the assault of Theseus.'

'Turn your back and keep your eyes shut,
for if the Gorgon head appears and should you see it,
57   all chance for your return above is lost.'

Così disse 'l maestro; ed elli stessi
mi volse, e non si tenne a le mie mani,
60   che con le sue ancor non mi chiudessi.

O voi ch'avete li 'ntelletti sani,
mirate la dottrina che s'asconde
63   sotto 'l velame de li versi strani.

E già venìa su per le torbide onde
un fracasso d'un suon, pien di spavento,
66   per cui tremavano amendue le sponde,

non altrimenti fatto che d'un vento
impetüoso per li avversi ardori,
69   che fier la selva e sanz' alcun rattento

li rami schianta, abbatte e porta fori;
dinanzi polveroso va superbo,
72   e fa fuggir le fiere e li pastori.

Li occhi mi sciolse e disse: "Or drizza il nerbo
del viso su per quella schiuma antica
75   per indi ove quel fummo è più acerbo."

Come le rane innanzi a la nimica
biscia per l'acqua si dileguan tutte,
78   fin ch'a la terra ciascuna s'abbica,

vid' io più di mille anime distrutte
fuggir così dinanzi ad un ch'al passo
81   passava Stige con le piante asciutte.

Dal volto rimovea quell' aere grasso,
menando la sinistra innanzi spesso;
84   e sol di quell' angoscia parea lasso.

Ben m'accorsi ch'elli era da ciel messo,
e volsimi al maestro; e quei fé segno
87   ch'i' stessi queto ed inchinassi ad esso.

While my master spoke he turned me round
and, still not trusting to my hands,
60   covered my face with his hands also.

O you who have sound intellects,
consider the teaching that is hidden
63   behind the veil of these strange verses.

And now there came, over the turbid waves,
a dreadful, crashing sound
66   that set both shores to trembling.

It sounded like a mighty wind,
made violent by waves of heat,
69   that strikes the forest and with unchecked force

shatters the branches, hurls them away, and,
magnificent in its roiling cloud of dust, drives on,
72   putting beast and shepherd to flight.

He freed my eyes and said: 'Now look
across the scum of that primeval swamp
75   to where the vapor is most dense and harsh.'

As frogs, before their enemy the snake,
all scatter through the water
78   till each sits huddled on the bank,

I saw more than a thousand lost souls flee
before one who so lightly passed across the Styx
81   he did not touch the water with his feet.

He cleared the thick air from his face,
his left hand moving it away,
84   as if that murky air alone had wearied him.

It was clear that he was sent from Heaven,
and I turned to the master, who signaled me
87   to keep silent and bow down before him.

Ahi quanto mi parea pien di disdegno!
Venne a la porta e con una verghetta
90   l'aperse, che non v'ebbe alcun ritegno.

"O cacciati del ciel, gente dispetta,"
cominciò elli in su l'orribil soglia,
93   "ond' esta oltracotanza in voi s'alletta?

Perché recalcitrate a quella voglia
a cui non puote il fin mai esser mozzo,
96   e che più volte v'ha cresciuta doglia?

Che giova ne le fata dar di cozzo?
Cerbero vostro, se ben vi ricorda,
99   ne porta ancor pelato il mento e 'l gozzo."

Poi si rivolse per la strada lorda,
e non fé motto a noi, ma fé sembiante
102   d'omo cui altra cura stringa e morda

che quella di colui che li è davante;
e noi movemmo i piedi inver' la terra,
105   sicuri appresso le parole sante.

Dentro li 'ntrammo sanz' alcuna guerra;
e io, ch'avea di riguardar disio
108   la condizion che tal fortezza serra,

com' io fui dentro, l'occhio intorno invio:
e veggio ad ogne man grande campagna,
111   piena di duolo e di tormento rio.

Sì come ad Arli, ove Rodano stagna,
sì com' a Pola, presso del Carnaro
114   ch'Italia chiude e suoi termini bagna,

fanno i sepulcri tutt' il loco varo,
così facevan quivi d'ogne parte,
117   salvo che 'l modo v'era più amaro;

Ah, how full of high disdain he seemed to me!
He came up to the gate and with a wand
90   opened it, and there was no resistance.

'O outcasts of Heaven, race despised,'
he began on the terrible threshold, 'whence
93   comes this insolence you harbor in your souls?

'Why do you kick against that will
which never can be severed from its purpose,
96   and has so many times increased your pain?

'What profits it to fight against the fates?
Remember your own Cerberus still bears
99   the wounds of that around his chin and neck.'

Then he turned back along the wretched way
without a word for us, and he seemed pressed,
102   spurred on by greater cares

than those of the man who stands before him.
We turned our steps toward the city,
105   emboldened by his holy words.

We entered without further struggle.
And I, in my great need to see
108   what such a guarded fortress holds,

as soon as I had entered eagerly surveyed
the wide plain stretching on all sides,
111   so filled with bitter torment and despair.

Just as at Arles where the Rhone goes shallow,
just as at Pola, near Quarnero's gulf,
114   which hems in Italy and bathes her borders,

the sepulchers make the land uneven,
so all around me in this landscape
117   the many tombs held even greater sorrow.

ché tra li avelli fiamme erano sparte,
per le quali eran sì del tutto accesi,
120   che ferro più non chiede verun' arte.

Tutti li lor coperchi eran sospesi,
e fuor n'uscivan sì duri lamenti,
123   che ben parean di miseri e d'offesi.

E io: "Maestro, quai son quelle genti
che, seppellite dentro da quell' arche,
126   si fan sentir coi sospiri dolenti?"

E quelli a me: "Qui son li eresïarche
con lor seguaci, d'ogne setta, e molto
129   più che non credi son le tombe carche.

Simile qui con simile è sepolto,
e i monimenti son più e men caldi."
E poi ch'a la man destra si fu vòlto,
133   passammo tra i martìri e li alti spaldi.

For here the graves were strewn with flames
that made them glow with heat
120   hotter than iron is before it's worked.

All their covers were propped open and from them
issued such dire lamentation it was clear
123   it came from wretches in despair and pain.

And I: 'Master, who are these souls
entombed within these chests and who make known
126   their plight with sighs of sorrow?'

And he: 'Here, with all their followers,
are the arch-heretics of every sect.
129   The tombs are far more laden than you think.

'Like is buried here with like,
though the graves burn with an unlike heat.'
Then, after he turned to the right,
133   we passed between the torments and the lofty ramparts.

1–3.   Dante has gone white with cowardice. Seeing this, Virgil tries to compose his own features. In Canto VIII.121 Virgil was angry, and this fact leads many commentators to believe that the color in his face now is still the red flush of anger. On the other hand, others believe (and over the centuries there are roughly as many of one opinion as of the other) that Virgil's *new* color just now is the pallor of frustration and shame. Either reading is possible, but red is probably the better choice, especially since we then have the dramatic contrast between white-cheeked Dante and red-faced Virgil.

7–9.   Virgil's doubt and ensuing confirmation has caused considerable difficulty. The overall sense of the tercet is, however, probably clear enough: "we must win this fight unless (I did not understand what Beatrice told me) . . . No, what she said must be true; but I wish the promised help from heaven would get here." Musa's remark on the passage bears repeating (Musa.1974.1, p. 73): "because during his lifetime [Virgil] could not believe in the coming of Christ, so now he can not believe in the coming of the angel—in spite of his having learned from Beatrice that the Pilgrim's journey is willed in Heaven." In other words, Virgil, condemned to hell for not having had faith, repeats that error even now.

10–15.   A fairly rare example of an interpretive exercise embedded in the poetic text itself, Dante as glossator of Virgil's words and presenter of his own understanding as he heard them. What he thought, then, was perhaps that Virgil was afraid that they would be left in hell, in which case Dante would perish.

17.   The "first circle" is Limbo, where Virgil and the other virtuous heathens have their eternal resting place, and where, in his own words, "without hope we live in longing" (*Inf.* IV.42).

19–27.   Erichtho's conjuration of Virgil may be the single most outrageous example of the utter liberty Dante at times employs in his treatment of classical literature. No such tale exists in any other text before Dante's, nor anything like it. While many point to the similar statement made by the Sibyl, hoping to reassure Aeneas that she has been shown by Hecate (Proserpina) the places of the underworld (*Aen.* VI.562–565), no one has come close to finding a source for a Virgilian journey to the depths of hell under the spell of Erichtho. This Thessalian witch appears in a crucial role in Lucan's *Pharsalia*, the later poet's rather nasty version of Virgil's more benign Sibyl. In a lengthy episode in the sixth book (vv. 507–830) of Lucan's poem, a book with evident parallels to the descent to the underworld in the *Aeneid*, replete with Sibyl-like guide in the person of Erichtho, the witch holds center stage. Serving the curiosity of Sextus Pompeius, son of the great Pompey, one of the major republican opponents of Caesar in the civil war, she agrees to foretell the outcome of the war by practicing her necromantic art on the corpse of a recently slain soldier. What the soldier tells is hardly pleasant news, but is hardly complete, either. He does make plain to Sextus that the ghost of his father will come to him in Sicily (VI.812–813) in order to reveal still more (but Lucan committed suicide by Nero's order before finishing the poem, and the scene was not written). It is out of these materials that Dante has concocted his idiosyncratic tale.

And what is it that Erichtho wanted? In Lucan's poem (VI.586–587) we learn that her greatest desire is to be able to mangle the corpses of Julius Caesar (the poem is set before the murder of Caesar—44 B.C.) and of Pompey. Virgil died in 19 B.C. As he says in this narrative, Erichtho called him (like the young soldier in Lucan's poem, only recently dead) back into his body shortly after he died and sent him down to the ninth Circle, Judecca. Why? Those who have written on this problem have not developed any hypothesis to account for her motive. Yet Dante surely would have given her one in the myth that he was constructing. Or Virgil is simply making up a tall story in order to give himself authority—a dubious hypothesis embraced by some.

We know from Lucan that Erichtho had an unfulfilled ambition, to ravage the corpses of Caesar and Pompey. Where are these located in Dante? Caesar is in Limbo; of Pompey we hear little, and nothing about his station in the afterlife. However, it is at least possible that Dante is playing a game with his reader here. As a co-conspirator of Brutus and Cassius, would Pompey not naturally have been punished along with them? That seems possible. Whatever justification we seek for this strange tale of Virgil's first visit to the realm of the damned, we probably should try to find it in the pages of Lucan. (See Holl.1980.1, pp. 178–80.)

Boccaccio was the first and perhaps lone discussant (in his commentary to *Inf.* IX.25–27) to think of the only biblical tale that contains similar elements (and was surely familiar to Dante), the story of Saul's visit to the witch of Endor, who calls up the spirit of Samuel for Saul; the latter—in a scene more powerful than even anything in Lucan—foretells Saul's death and the defeat of the Israelites at the hands of the Philistines (I Samuel 28:3–25).

27. Judecca, the ninth Circle, named for Judas, betrayer, like all those punished there with him, of a rightful lord and master.

28–30. His tale told, Virgil's point is clear: "I have been all the way down to the bottom of the pit; you can trust in my guidance." The "heaven that encircles all" is almost certainly the Crystalline Sphere, or *primum mobile*.

33. There is debate among commentators as to what exactly this sentence means. It seems more likely that the *ira* ("wrath") referred to is the righteous anger of the forces of God (namely, the angel who is now approaching) rather than the wrath the travelers will encounter in the forces defending the City of Dis, as Boccaccio believes, or the "wrath" they must employ in order to enter the city (the view of most of the early commentators).

38–48. "The three Erinyes or Furies, Alecto, Megaera, and Tisiphone, who dwelt in the depths of Hell and punished men both in this world and after death" (T). See *Aeneid* VI.570–575. In Virgil, as in Greek myth, these three sisters are punishers of crimes of blood. Dante sees them as the handmaids of Proserpina (or Hecate), the queen of hell.

52. "Gorgon Medusa; she alone of the three Gorgons was mortal, and was at first a beautiful maiden, but, in consequence of her having given birth to two children by Poseidon in one of Athena's temples, the latter changed her hair into serpents, which gave her head such a fearful appearance that every one who looked upon it was turned into stone" (T). See Ovid, *Metamorphoses* IV.606–V.249. The Furies' threat to bring out their biggest defensive weapon remains unfulfilled only, we may assume, because of the rapid deployment of God's own siege-weapon, the angelic intercessor.

54. The Furies lament that, when Theseus came to the nether regions with Perithous in order to rescue Proserpina (see *Aen.* VI.392–397), they only imprisoned him, rather than putting him to death, since that left him alive to be rescued by Hercules.

58–63.   Vv. 61–63 contain the second address to the reader in the poem
(see note to *Inf.* VIII.94–96). This one has caused more difficulty than any
other, and "solutions" are so abundant that it is fair to say that none has
won general consent, from the first commentators' exertions until today.
Opinions are divided, first of all, on whether the passage points back in
the text, either primarily to Medusa (seen as despair, heresy, the hardened
will, etc.) or to the Furies (seen as sin itself, or the three main categories of
sin punished in hell [incontinence, violence, fraud], or remorse, etc.), or to
a combination of these. Those who believe that the passage invites the
reader rather to look *forward* than back are in accord that it refers to the
avenging intruder who is about to appear in order to open the locked
gates of Dis; but there is great debate over exactly what the one "sent from
heaven" (v. 85) signifies (see discussion, below). Surely it seems more natu-
ral for the reference to point backwards to something already said. And
indeed something noteworthy and perhaps puzzling has just occurred:
Virgil has covered Dante's eye-covering hands with his own hands as well.
If *this* passage (vv. 58–60) is the one that contains a hidden doctrine (and
few commentators believe it is, but see Hollander [Holl.1969.1], pp. 239–46),
perhaps what it suggests is that stoic restraint is not enough to keep a sin-
ner safe from dangerous temptation (i.e., Dante, had she appeared, *would
have* looked upon Medusa and been turned to stone, just as Ulysses *would
have* listened to the Sirens and been destroyed by them had he not been
restrained by other forces).

64–72.   This splendidly energetic simile is perhaps built out of elements
found in two similes in the *Aeneid* (II.416–419; XII.451–455). In the first of
these the Trojan forces mount an impetuous counterattack upon the
Greek invaders of their city; in the second the forces of Aeneas begin the
eventually victorious final attack upon the armies of Turnus. The celestial
messenger, though only one in number, has the force of a great army; vic-
tory is seconds away.

73.   Now Virgil can allow Dante to use his eyes once more: Medusa is
apparently no longer a threat.

76–78.   A number of commentators and translators have the frogs in this
simile going to the bottom of the pond; they go to land (*a la terra*), as Dante
says they do, and as any intelligent frog will do when a snake enters the
water. This simile probably derives from Ovid, *Metamorphoses* VI.370–381.

81. The angel walks upon the water in imitation of Christ (Matth. 14:25).

82–83. The angel resembles Mercury, as he is described by Statius, *Thebaid* II. 1–11, coming back up from the foul air of the underworld with his caduceus in hand.

85. That this agent of good is "sent from heaven" indicates clearly enough that he is an angel, although debate over his identity still continues. See Silvio Pasquazi, "Messo celeste," *ED*, vol. 3, 1971, making a strong case for his angelic status and giving a summary of the debate. Pasquazi also argues for one traditional further identification, making the *messo* specifically the archangel Michael, who led the forces of the good angels against the rebellious ones in the war in heaven (Rev. 12: 7–9)—see n. to *Inferno* VII. 10–12—exactly the forces he now must combat once more in the netherworld. Over the centuries there has been a continuing argument between those who believe that the *messo* is Mercury and those who believe that he is an angel, and, in some cases, specifically Michael. It seems highly likely that Dante here gives us an archangel Michael "dressed up" as Mercury, a fused identity that is not problematic in any way, given Dante's practice of combining pagan and Christian materials.

86–87. Virgil's command that Dante bow down before the angel removes just about any doubt about the *messo*'s divine status.

89–90. The angel's opening of the barred gates with his *verghetta* ("wand") is almost surely modeled on Mercury's similar opening of the gates of Herse's chamber with his *verga*, i.e., his caduceus (Ovid, *Metam.* II.819).

91. The "outcasts of heaven" are undoubtedly the rebellious angels referred to in *Inferno* VIII.82–83, "more than a thousand angels fallen from Heaven." See also the reference, a few lines earlier in this canto (v. 79), to "a thousand lost souls" who guard the City of Dis, that is, these very angels.

93–99. The angel makes clear, in his address to his fallen brethren, that resistance to the will of God is utterly useless. His reference to the chaining of Cerberus by Hercules reflects *Aeneid* VI.392–396. Dante has now been associated with two classical heroes, Theseus (v. 54) and Hercules. His powers, however, reside not in himself but in his heaven-ordained mission.

100–103. The angel's impassive attitude tells us something about the nature of the inhabitants of hell that we sometimes forget: from God's perspective there is nothing worthy of attention in their plight. The angel only wants to get out of this place as quickly as he can in order to return to eternal bliss, so much so that he has not even a word of greeting or support for the two travelers.

106. This whole passage, from *Inferno* VII.130 to now, the moment of successful entry of the walled City of Dis, narrates a military campaign: Virgil and Dante approach by sea in Phlegyas's military transport ship; the forces ranged against them signal their coming and prepare to do battle, closing the gates and assuming defensive positions on the battlements; they wheel up their main weapons, the Furies, who prepare to unleash their secret weapon, Medusa; the invading forces then deploy *their* secret weapon, the heavenly battering-ram that opens the gates and, in a trice, wins the battle.

112–115. Dante's references to two famous ancient Roman cemeteries, at Arles in France and Pola in Istria, build the scene for us: these grave sites are not mounds in the ground but sarchophagi, raised monuments of stone that contain the remains of the dead.

127–131. Virgil explains to Dante that this sixth Circle of hell encloses many different heretical sects, each of which is punished in a separate sepulchre, and some of which are punished with more, others with less, severity.

Why is heresy punished within the walls of Dis, where all the sins punished are sins of will, not those of appetite? It is interesting to see how often early commentators associate heresy with obstinacy or obduracy; their word is the Latin *pertinax*. Some of them may be reflecting St. Thomas's definition (*S. T.* II–II, q. 5, a. 3): if a man "is not *pertinacious* in his disbelief, he is in that case no heretic, but only a man in error." See, among others, the commentaries of Boccaccio (*Inf.* IX.127; IX.110–133), Benvenuto (*Inf.* IX.112–116; IX.127–129), Francesco da Buti (*Inf.* IX.106–123; X.31–39), John of Serravalle (*Inf.* X.13–15); Daniello (*Inf.* IX.133 [citing Thomas]) and, among the moderns, Poletto (*Inf.* X.28–30), Carroll (*Inf.* IX.132).

132. The turnings to the right here and at *Inferno* XVII.32 have caused puzzlement and some ingenuity. In hell, whenever the direction of their

movement is mentioned, Dante and Virgil elsewhere always head to the left. Only on these two occasions do they move rightward. These two rightward turnings occur just before the entrance to the sixth Circle, in which heresy is punished, and before the exit from the realm of Violence, the seventh Circle. This is another instance in which the commentary tradition has not resolved Dante's plan, if indeed there was one.

INFERNO X

OUTLINE

Ora sen va per un secreto calle,
tra 'l muro de la terra e li martìri,
3   lo mio maestro, e io dopo le spalle.

"O virtù somma, che per li empi giri
mi volvi," cominciai, "com' a te piace,
6   parlami, e sodisfammi a' miei disiri.

La gente che per li sepolcri giace
potrebbesi veder? già son levati
9   tutt' i coperchi, e nessun guardia face."

E quelli a me: "Tutti saran serrati
quando di Iosafàt qui torneranno
12   coi corpi che là sù hanno lasciati.

Suo cimitero da questa parte hanno
con Epicuro tutti suoi seguaci,
15   che l'anima col corpo morta fanno.

Però a la dimanda che mi faci
quinc' entro satisfatto sarà tosto,
18   e al disio ancor che tu mi taci."

E io: "Buon duca, non tegno riposto
a te mio cuor se non per dicer poco,
21   e tu m'hai non pur mo a ciò disposto."

"O Tosco che per la città del foco
vivo ten vai così parlando onesto,
24   piacciati di restare in questo loco.

La tua loquela ti fa manifesto
di quella nobil patrïa natio,
27   a la qual forse fui troppo molesto."

Now my master takes a hidden path
between the city's ramparts and the torments,

3   and I come close behind him.

'O lofty virtue,' I began, 'who lead me
as you will around these impious circles,
6   speak to me and satisfy my wishes.

'The souls that lie within the sepulchres,
may they be seen? For all the lids are raised
9   and there is no one standing guard.'

And he to me: 'All will be shut and sealed
when the souls return from Jehosaphat
12   with the bodies they have left above.

'Here Epicurus and all his followers,
who hold the soul dies with the body,
15   have their sepulchres.

'But soon your need to have an answer
will be satisfied right here,
18   as will the wish you hide from me.'

And I: 'Good leader, from you I do not keep
my heart concealed except to speak few words—
21   as you've from time to time advised.'

'O Tuscan, passing through the city of fire,
alive, and with such courtesy of speech,
24   if it would please you, stay your steps awhile.

'Your way of speaking makes it clear
that you are native to that noble city
27   to which I was perhaps too cruel.'

Subitamente questo suono uscìo
d'una de l'arche; però m'accostai,
30   temendo, un poco più al duca mio.

Ed el mi disse: "Volgiti! Che fai?
Vedi là Farinata che s'è dritto:
33   da la cintola in sù tutto 'l vedrai."

Io avea già il mio viso nel suo fitto;
ed el s'ergea col petto e con la fronte
36   com' avesse l'inferno a gran dispitto.

E l'animose man del duca e pronte
mi pinser tra le sepulture a lui,
39   dicendo: "Le parole tue sien conte."

Com' io al piè de la sua tomba fui,
guardommi un poco, e poi, quasi sdegnoso,
42   mi dimandò: "Chi fuor li maggior tui?"

Io ch'era d'ubidir disideroso,
non gliel celai, ma tutto gliel' apersi;
45   ond' ei levò le ciglia un poco in suso;

poi disse: "Fieramente furo avversi
a me e a miei primi e a mia parte,
48   sì che per due fïate li dispersi."

"S'ei fur cacciati, ei tornar d'ogne parte,"
rispuos' io lui, "l'una e l'altra fïata;
51   ma i vostri non appreser ben quell' arte."

Allor surse a la vista scoperchiata
un'ombra, lungo questa, infino al mento:
54   credo che s'era in ginocchie levata.

Dintorno mi guardò, come talento
avesse di veder s'altri era meco;
57   e poi che 'l sospecciar fu tutto spento,

This voice came suddenly
from one sarcophagus, so that, startled,
30   I drew closer to my leader.

And he to me: 'Turn back! What are you doing?
Look, there Farinata stands erect—
33   you can see all of him from the waist up.'

Already I had fixed my gaze on his.
And he was rising, lifting chest and brow
36   as though he held all Hell in utter scorn.

At which my leader: 'Choose your words with care,'
and his hands, ready, encouraging,
39   thrust me toward him among the tombs.

When I stood at the foot of his tomb
he looked at me a moment. Then he asked,
42   almost in disdain: 'Who were your ancestors?'

And I, eager to obey, held nothing back,
but told him who they were,
45   at which he barely raised his eyebrows

and said: 'They were most bitter enemies
to me, my forebears, and my party—
48   not once, but twice, I had to drive them out.'

'If they were banished,' I responded, 'they returned
from every quarter both the first and second time,
51   a skill that Yours have failed to learn as well.'

Then, beside him, in the open tomb, up came
a shade, visible to the chin: I think
54   he had raised himself upon his knees.

He looked around me as though he wished to see
if someone else were with me,
57   and when his hesitant hopes were crushed,

piangendo disse: "Se per questo cieco
carcere vai per altezza d'ingegno,
60   mio figlio ov' è? e perché non è teco?"

E io a lui: "Da me stesso non vegno:
colui ch'attende là per qui mi mena
63   forse cui Guido vostro ebbe a disdegno."

Le sue parole e 'l modo de la pena
m'avean di costui già letto il nome;
66   però fu la risposta così piena.

Di sùbito drizzato gridò: "Come?
dicesti 'elli ebbe'? non viv' elli ancora?
69   non fiere li occhi suoi lo dolce lume?"

Quando s'accorse d'alcuna dimora
ch'io facëa dinanzi a la risposta,
72   supin ricadde e più non parve fora.

Ma quell' altro magnanimo, a cui posta
restato m'era, non mutò aspetto,
75   né mosse collo, né piegò sua costa;

e sé continüando al primo detto,
"S'elli han quell' arte," disse, "male appresa,
78   ciò mi tormenta più che questo letto.

Ma non cinquanta volte fia raccesa
la faccia de la donna che qui regge,
81   che tu saprai quanto quell' arte pesa.

E se tu mai nel dolce mondo regge,
dimmi: perché quel popolo è sì empio
84   incontr' a' miei in ciascuna sua legge?"

Ond' io a lui: "Lo strazio e 'l grande scempio
che fece l'Arbia colorata in rosso,
87   tal orazion fa far nel nostro tempio."

weeping, he said: 'If you pass through this dark
prison by virtue of your lofty genius,
60   where is my son and why is he not with you?'

And I to him: 'I come not on my own:
he who stands there waiting leads me through,
63   perhaps to one Your Guido held in scorn.'

His words and the manner of his punishment
already had revealed his name to me,
66   and thus was my reply so to the point.

Suddenly erect, he cried: 'What?
Did you say "he held"? Lives he not still?
69   Does not the sweet light strike upon his eyes?'

When he perceived that I made some delay
before I answered, he fell backward
72   and showed himself no more.

But the other, that great soul at whose wish
I had stopped, did not change countenance,
75   nor bend his neck, nor move his chest.

And he, continuing from where he'd paused:
'That they have badly learned this skill
78   torments me more than does this bed.

'But the face of the lady reigning here
will be rekindled not fifty times before you too
81   shall know how difficult a skill that is to learn.

'And, so may you return to the sweet world,
tell me, why are your people,
84   in every edict, so pitiless against my kin?'

Then I to him: 'The havoc and great slaughter
that dyed the Arbia red caused them to raise
87   such prayers in our temple.'

Poi ch'ebbe sospirando il capo mosso,
"A ciò non fu' io sol," disse, "né certo
90   sanza cagion con li altri sarei mosso.

Ma fu' io solo, là dove sofferto
fu per ciascun di tòrre via Fiorenza,
93   colui che la difesi a viso aperto."

"Deh, se riposi mai vostra semenza,"
prega' io lui, "solvetemi quel nodo
96   che qui ha 'nviluppata mia sentenza.

El par che voi veggiate, se ben odo,
dinanzi quel che 'l tempo seco adduce,
99   e nel presente tenete altro modo."

"Noi veggiam, come quei c'ha mala luce,
le cose," disse, "che ne son lontano;
102   cotanto ancor ne splende il sommo duce.

Quando s'appressano o son, tutto è vano
nostro intelletto; e s'altri non ci apporta,
105   nulla sapem di vostro stato umano.

Però comprender puoi che tutta morta
fia nostra conoscenza da quel punto
108   che del futuro fia chiusa la porta."

Allor, come di mia colpa compunto,
dissi: "Or direte dunque a quel caduto
111   che 'l suo nato è co' vivi ancor congiunto;

e s'i' fui, dianzi, a la risposta muto,
fate i saper che 'l fei perché pensava
114   già ne l'error che m'avete soluto."

E già 'l maestro mio mi richiamava;
per ch'i' pregai lo spirto più avaccio
117   che mi dicesse chi con lu' istava.

He sighed and shook his head, then spoke:
'I was not alone, nor surely without cause
90   would I have acted with the rest.

'But it was I alone, when all agreed
to make an end of Florence, I alone
93   who dared speak out in her defense.'

'So may Your seed sometime find peace,
pray untie for me this knot,' I begged him,
96   'which has entangled and confused my judgment.

'From what I hear, it seems
you see beforehand that which time will bring,
99   but cannot know what happens in the present.'

'We see, like those with faulty vision,
things at a distance,' he replied. 'That much,
102   for us, the mighty Ruler's light still shines.

'When things draw near or happen now,
our minds are useless. Without the words of others
105   we can know nothing of your human state.

'Thus it follows that all our knowledge
will perish at the very moment
108   the portals of the future close.'

Then, remorseful for my fault, I said:
'Will You tell him who fell back down
111   his son is still among the living?

'And let him know, if I was slow to answer,
it was because I was preoccupied
114   with doubts You have resolved for me.'

And now my master summoned me,
so that I begged the spirit to reveal,
117   at once, who else was down there with him.

Dissemi: "Qui con più di mille giaccio:
qua dentro è 'l secondo Federico

120   e 'l Cardinale; e de li altri mi taccio."

Indi s'ascose; e io inver' l'antico
poeta volsi i passi, ripensando

123   a quel parlar che mi parea nemico.

Elli si mosse; e poi, così andando,
mi disse: "Perché se' tu sì smarrito?"

126   E io li sodisfeci al suo dimando.

"La mente tua conservi quel ch'udito
hai contra te," mi comandò quel saggio;

129   "e ora attendi qui," e drizzò 'l dito:

"quando sarai dinanzi al dolce raggio
di quella il cui bell' occhio tutto vede,

132   da lei saprai di tua vita il vïaggio."

Appresso mosse a man sinistra il piede:
lasciammo il muro e gimmo inver' lo mezzo
per un sentier ch'a una valle fiede,

136   che 'nfin là sù facea spiacer suo lezzo.

His answer was: 'More than a thousand lie
here with me: both the second Frederick
120   and the Cardinal. Of the rest I do not speak.'

With that he dropped from sight. I turned my steps
to the venerable poet, mulling
123   those words that seemed to augur ill.

He started out, and then, as we were going,
asked: 'Why are you so bewildered?'
126   And I answered fully what he asked.

'Keep in mind what you have heard against you,
but also now give heed to this,'
129   the sage insisted—and he raised one finger.

'When you shall stand before the radiance
of her whose fair eyes see and understand,
132   from her you'll learn the journey of your life.'

Then he turned his footsteps to the left.
Leaving the wall, we headed toward the center
along a path that leads into a pit.
136   Its stench offended even at that height.

1–2.   The path is "hidden" because it lies between the walls of Dis and the sepulchres. See *Aen*. VI.443, the "secreti calles" that lead into the *Lugentes Campi* (Fields of Mourning) where Aeneas encounters the mournful spirit of Dido.

5.   Dante is apparently alluding to the new direction, to the right, in which Virgil now is leading him.

8–9.   The image of the uncovered tombs and the reference to "guards," as Durling and Martinez point out in their commentary (Durl.1996.1), suggest details of the scene surrounding the death and resurrection of Jesus. The actual position of the covering slabs of these funeral monuments is not clear. The passage in *Inf*. XI.6 would make it appear that they may be propped against the sides of the tombs, as Durling and Martinez suggest.

11.   Jehosaphat is the valley in Palestine in which, according to Joel (3:2), all will gather for the Last Judgment.

14–15.   "Epicurus, celebrated Greek philosopher, B.C. 342–270; he started at Athens the philosophic school called after him, which taught that the *summum bonum*, or highest good, is happiness—not sensual enjoyment, but peace of mind, as the result of the cultivation of the virtues. He held that virtue was to be practiced because it led to happiness, whereas the Stoics held that virtue should be cultivated for its own sake" **(T)**. While in the *Convivio* (IV.vi.11–12) Dante defines Epicureanism as the pleasure principle without speaking of it as specifically heretical, here he falls in with a more stringent Christian view, perhaps echoing St. Paul who, in I Cor. 15:32, cites the standard tag for Epicureanism, "Eat, drink, and be merry, for tomorrow we die," as the unworthy countering view to the Resurrection. It is in keeping with this attitude that Dante presents "Epicureans" as those who deny the immortality of the soul.

18.   See the wish expressed by Dante in vv. 6–8, above, which Virgil realizes hides Dante's real desire: he hopes to see, now that he is among "the blacker souls" where Ciacco had said he would find Farinata and four

other Florentines (*Inf.* VI.85), some or one of these, and perhaps the first he there named, Farinata.

22–24. The speaker is Farinata degli Uberti, born in Florence at the turn of the thirteenth century, and by mid-century the head of the Ghibelline faction. Having expelled the Guelphs from the city in 1248, the Ghibellines were themselves expelled in 1258, but, led by Farinata, took revenge quickly at the battle of Montaperti in 1260, at which they utterly routed the Florentine Guelphs and their allies. Subsequently the Ghibellines gathered in council at Empoli, where it was proposed that Florence should be destroyed, to general acclaim. Farinata was the unyielding force of opposition and eventually won the day, saying that he would fight alone with sword in hand to prevent this outcome. The Florentines did not show great appreciation of his acts and never made any exception for his family in their dealings with the various eventual Ghibelline exiles. Farinata died in Florence in 1264. For bibliography on his significance to Dante see Cassell (Cass.1984.1), p. 117.

25. Ever since Guido da Pisa (1328?) commentators have, from time to time, noted the echo here of the words of the bystanders who heard Peter deny his knowledge of Christ a second time; surely, they say, you are one of his followers from Galilee, for your speech makes you plainly so ("loquela tua manifestum te facit"—Matth. 26:73).

27. Against the more usual understanding, that Farinata's "forse" (perhaps) reveals regret at his harshness against his fellow citizens at the battle of Montaperti, consider the judgment of Cassell (Cass.1984.1), p. 19: Farinata displays "the false modesty of gloating understatement."

32. Farinata, who did not believe in Christ's resurrection, here replays it, as it were, rising from his tomb, at this instant making his punishment clearly fit his crime. See *Convivio* II.viii.8 for Dante's own outcry against such failure of belief: "I say that of all the follies the most foolish, the basest, and the most pernicious is the belief that beyond this life there is no other" (tr. Lansing).

33. As Durling (Durl.1981.2, pp. 11–14) and Cassell (Cass.1984.1, pp. 24–26) independently discovered, Farinata rises from his tomb in imitation of the "Man of Sorrows" (see Isaiah 53:3: *virum dolorum*), that image

(the so-called *imago pietatis*) of Jesus rising from the tomb, naked, showing the signs of his torture, not yet having taken on majesty.

35.   That the features of Farinata upon which Dante fastens are his chest and brow underlines his prideful nature. And pride, which we have seen behind the sinful actions of such as Filippo Argenti in Canto VIII, the "root sin" that stands behind so much human failure in the eyes of Dante's Church, is easily understood as a root of heresy, the stiff-necked refusal to believe what has been given as manifest by Christ and his Church.

42.   Farinata's words reveal his pride in familial background. He is an Uberti and a Ghibelline; let all others tremble before him.

45.   Dante's self-identification as minor nobility and a Guelph does not much impress Farinata, who raises his eyebrows—another sign of his pridefulness. See *Inf.* XXXIV.35, where Satan is described as having raised his brows against God.

46–48.   Farinata now wins the second round of his little battle with Dante: yes, he knows Dante's people, and twice over has sent them into exile (1248 and 1260). This canto's scenes play out against a series of dates spread over the second half of the thirteenth century in Florence: 1248, expulsion of the Guelphs; 1258, expulsion of the Ghibellines; 1260, Montaperti and the second expulsion of the Guelphs; 1264, death of Farinata; 1266, defeat of Manfred and the imperial forces at the battle of Benevento and banishment of the Uberti family; 1280, death of Cavalcante the elder; 1289, battle of Campaldino, another Guelph triumph (in which Dante took part); 1290, death of Beatrice; 1300, death of Guido Cavalcanti; 1302, exile of Dante Alighieri.

49–51.   But now the belittled Guelph bites back: our family was twice exiled and came back home twice; yours has not done quite so well (since the Uberti have remained in exile since the aftermath of the battle of Benevento in 1266).

     The reader may note that the adjective "Yours" in v. 51 is capitalized. We have followed the practice of capitalizing the English translation of the respectful plural form of words for the singular "you," so as to alert the reader to their use in Dante's Italian. Three Florentines are the only ones to receive this treatment in hell: Farinata and Cavalcante here, and

Brunetto Latini in Canto XV, the last of these the father of a poet and a poet, respectively.

52–54.   The interruption of the discourse between Dante and Farinata will last for seven tercets, until Farinata, "on hold" while this other drama is played out, will continue the conversation as though there had been no interruption to it.

The far less imposing figure who rises out of the same tomb along-side Farinata, Cavalcante de' Cavalcanti (died ca. 1280), was a wealthy Florentine Guelph and the father of Dante's former "first friend" (see *VN* III.14, XXIV.6, XXX.3), Guido Cavalcanti. Since Guido was alive at the imagined date of Dante's journey, he cannot be found in the afterworld. However, his reputation as a "materialist" makes it seem at least likely that Dante was certain that this aristocratic and independent-minded poet and thinker was coming right here to join his father. It is not accidental that the entire conversation between the father and his son's former friend concerns that son. If Farinata believes in family and party, Cavalcante is the archetypal doting father. Their portraits, showing them in such different lights, are perhaps the finest example we have of such close, contrastive "portraiture" in verse since the classical era. See the study of Erich Auerbach (Auer.1957.1).

One of the finest lyric poets of his time, Guido Cavalcanti was from six to ten years older than Dante. He was married by his family to a woman named Beatrice, in fact the daughter of Farinata. In other words, these two heretical Florentines, Guido's father, Cavalcante, and Farinata, are in-laws; it is notable that, divided by party loyalty as they are, they do not speak to one another. Guido was an ardent Guelph, siding with the Whites (Dante's party also) when the Guelphs divided into two factions. He had a street brawl with the leader of the Black Guelphs, Corso Donati, who had once tried to kill him. "In the summer of 1300, during Dante's priorate (June 15–Aug. 15), it was decided (June 24), in order to put an end to the disturbances caused by the continued hostilities between the two factions, to banish the leaders of both sides, . . . among those who approved this decision being Dante, in his capacity as Prior. It thus came about that Dante was instrumental in sending his own friend into exile, and, as it proved, to his death; for though the exiles were recalled very shortly after the expiry of Dante's term of office (Aug. 15), so that Guido only spent a few weeks at Sarzana, he never recovered from the effects of the malarious climate of the place, and died in Florence at the end of

August in that same year; he was buried in the cemetery of Santa Reparata on Aug. 29 . . ." **(T)**. One might wish to consider the fact that Farinata the Ghibelline and Guido the Guelph had been banished by the priors of Florence, Farinata in 1258, Cavalcanti in 1300. And mindful of the afterlives of these two exiles is the exiled Dante Alighieri, former prior, now himself exiled by the priors of the city.

58. Dante's phrase, "cieco carcere" (dark prison), has long been considered an echo of the same words in Virgil's Latin, *carcere caeco,* at *Aen.* VI.734.

59. The phrase "per altezza d'ingegno" (by virtue of your lofty genius) is clearly meant to remind us of the similar phrase we heard in Dante's first invocation: "O Muse, o alto ingegno" (O Muses, O lofty genius—*Inf.* II.7). However, how we are to interpret the resemblance is not easily resolved. Those who believe that in the first passage Dante was invoking his own poetic powers see in Cavalcanti's doting father's reaction a simple sense of rivalry: which of these two poets is more gifted? If, on the other hand, we believe that Dante, in the invocation, calls for aid from a Higher Power (see note to *Inf.* II.7–9), then the father's question indicates that he doesn't understand, materialist that he is, the nature of true Christian poetic inspiration. His son's genius and that inspiring Dante are not commensurable.

60. Cavalcanti's mournful question about his son's whereabouts has put some commentators (perhaps the first was Daniello, in 1568) in mind of Andromache's equally mournful question about the whereabouts of her husband Hector, "Hector ubi est?" (Where is Hector?—*Aen.* IV.312). But see Durling (Durl.1981.2), p. 25n., arguing for the resonance of Genesis 4:9: "Ubi est Abel frater tuus?" (Where is Abel your brother?) Durling points out that both these "fratricidal" stories culminate in an exile, Cain sent forth from the land a fugitive (Gen. 4:12–16), while Guido was literally sent into exile by the action of Dante and the five other priors of Florence.

61. Dante's words may reflect the Gospel of John (8:28) when Jesus says "a meipso facio nihil" (I do nothing of myself), but only through the Father.

62–63. One of the most debated passages in the poem. For a recent review, with bibliography, see Hollander (Holl.1992.2), pp. 204–6, 222–23. It should be noted that our translation is interpretive; the Italian can mean either what we have said it does or else "whom perhaps your Guido held in scorn." The text thus either indicates that Guido at a certain point perhaps scorned the work of Virgil or else withdrew his approval of Dante's love of Beatrice, to whom perhaps Dante is being led, as Virgil has promised him (*Inf.* I.122–123).

67–69.   The father's premature lament for his living son (but he *will* be dead in four months) in this searing tercet obviously collects the difficult thoughts and feelings of the poet as well. There has been a great deal written about the use of the past definite ("elli ebbe" [he had]) and its possible consequences. Why did Dante say that (v. 63)? Had Guido scorned someone habitually, the use of the imperfect would have been more likely. Those who believe that his scorn was for Virgil (roughly half of those who involve themselves in this quarrel) are right to be puzzled, for such a scornful view of the Latin poet would not seem to have been a sudden shift of attitude (and, in fact, there is no Virgilian element in any of Guido's poems). An attractive alternative explanation is given by Siro Chimenz in his commentary: at a certain point in his relations with Dante, and at least after Beatrice's death, when Dante continued to write of her, Guido *did* come to have disdain for Dante's loyalty to Beatrice. In short, Dante the protagonist is thinking of Guido's climactic "rejection" of Beatrice as a definite past event, one perhaps precisely reflected in a sonnet Guido wrote to Dante expressing his disgust with his former friend.

70–72.   Cavalcante's sudden disappearance rounds out his version of "resurrection," one that fails. In his first line he came up *(surse)* but in his last he falls back *(ricadde)* into his eternal tomb.

73–75.   Farinata's stoic restraint is evident once again; he has been waiting for Dante's attention to return to him in order to continue their difficult conversation about Florentine politics. Unmoved and unmoving, he is the exemplification of the "stone man" admired by Stoic philosophers. He is "great-souled" *(magnanimo)*, a quality of the highest kind in Aristotle's formulation in the *Ethics*, but connected, even in classical times, with a fear that such a man may also be prideful. See Scott (Scot.1977.1), pp. 13–45, for the double valence of the term, which becomes still less even potentially positive in the works of Christian writers.

76–78.   Farinata, more human in his second conversation, admits his sense of frustration in his family's political misfortune; it is, he says, worse torment even than damnation. We may reflect that, in the universe of this poem, there is no worse torment than damnation. Nonetheless, Farinata exudes a certain selfless concern for his family.

79–81.   Bested by Dante's last *riposte*, Farinata now gets even with a prophecy: within fifty months (fifty moons; Proserpina, the moon, is traditionally referred to as queen of hell) Dante himself will know the pain of exile. There surely seems to be fellow-feeling joined to the bleak promise. By July 1304—roughly fifty months from March 1300—the last efforts of the Whites to reenter the city were over and done with (Dante had already given up on their efforts), and Dante knew his exile was, for all intents and purposes, limitless.

82–84.   Having characterized Dante as a fellow-sufferer at the hands of their fellow citizens, Farinata wants to know why his Ghibelline family seems singled out by the actions of the priors.

85–87.   Dante's answer offers the perhaps sole *locus* in this canto that directly relates heresy and politics—and surely the reader has wondered what the connection must be. The "prayers" in the church that he refers to are words uttered in vituperative political councils, thus creating an image of political intrigue, even if of Guelph against Ghibelline, as a form of deformed "religious" activity. Florence seems a city in which politics has become the state religion.

The Arbia is a river near the site of the battle of Montaperti.

89–93.   Farinata's last words on the subject of the Florentine past remind his auditor that he was no more guilty than the rest of the Ghibellines (and many of them have been allowed to return) and that, further, at the council of Empoli (see note to vv. 22–24), he was alone in defending the city from destruction. There is no question but that Dante's view of Farinata is complex. As hard as he is on him, there is also great admiration for some of his qualities as leader, and for his having stood alone, and successfully, in defense of the city. The drama of Ghibellinism for Dante is a central one; what these people want to accomplish politically is not in itself anathema to him—far from it; that they wish to achieve their aims without God is what destroys their credentials as politicians and as human beings.

94–99.   Having realized that Cavalcanti does not know that his son is alive, while Farinata seems to know the future, Dante asks for clarification.

100–108.   Farinata explains that the present and the near future are not known by the sinners, only the time to come. Most believe that what he says applies to all the damned, e.g., Singleton in his commentary to this passage. On the other hand, for the view that this condition pertains only to the heretics see Cassell (Cass.1984.1), pp. 29–31. But see Alberigo, his soul already in hell yet not knowing how or what its body is doing in the world above (*Inf.* XXXIII.122–123). And see note to *Inf.* XIX.54.

The "portals of the future close" at Judgment Day, after which there shall be "no more time" (Rev. 10:6).

109–114.   Dante excuses his "fault": until Farinata explained things, he assumed the damned were aware of present events. Given the historical situation between the poet and Cavalcanti, it is not surprising that the author stages the drama of his understandable guilt at his role in Guido's death in this somewhat strained way.

119.   Frederick II (1194–1250), king of Sicily and Naples (1197–50), known in his own day as *stupor mundi* (the wonder of the world) for his extraordinary verve and accomplishments, presided over one of the most glorious courts in Europe. His political battles with the papacy marked nearly the full extent of his reign (he was the victorious leader of the Sixth Crusade [1228–29], "won" by treaty, while he was under interdict of excommunication).

120.   "Cardinal Ottaviano degli Ubaldini, member of a powerful Tuscan Ghibelline family, known to his contemporaries as 'the Cardinal' *par excellence*, was brother of Ubaldino della Pila (*Purg.* xxiv.29) and uncle of the Archbishop Ruggieri (*Inf.* xxxiii.14); he was made Bishop of Bologna in 1240, when he was under thirty, by special dispensation of Pope Gregory IX, and in 1244 he was created Cardinal by Innocent IV at the Council of Lyons; he was papal legate in Lombardy, and died in 1272. [He] was suspected of favouring the imperial party, and is credited with a saying: 'If I have a soul, I have lost it a thousand times for the Ghibellines' " **(T)**.

123.   Dante is considering the dire event, his exile, that Farinata has predicted, vv. 79–81.

125.   The word used by Virgil to describe Dante's difficulty is *smarrito*, a word that has been associated with the protagonist's initial lost and perilous condition (*Inf.* I.3) and then occurs again (*Inf.* XV.50) with specific

reference to his lostness at the outset of the journey for the last time in the poem. It is also used in such a way as to remind us of his initial situation in *Inf.* II.64, V.72, and XIII.24; in the last two of these scenes the protagonist is feeling pity for sinners, emotion that the poet fairly clearly considers inappropriate.

130–132. Virgil's promise that Beatrice (it can only be she) will lay bare to him the story of his life to come is not fulfilled, even though it is referred to again at *Inf.* XV.88–90. That role, so clearly reserved for Beatrice, is eventually given to Cacciaguida in *Par.* XVII.46–75. The apparent contradiction has caused much consternation. An ingenious solution has been proposed by Marguerite Mills Chiarenza (Chia.1985.1): just as in the *Aeneid* Helenus promises Aeneas that the Sibyl will reveal his future to him (*Aen.* III.458–460) only to have her instead lead him to Anchises, who performs that promised task (VI.756–886), so in the *Comedy* also the promised female "prophet" is replaced by a male. In Chiarenza's view, the "contradiction" is deliberate.

133–136. Virgil now returns to his accustomed leftward direction in his guidance of Dante. See note to *Inf.* IX.132.

INFERNO XI

In su l'estremità d'un'alta ripa
che facevan gran pietre rotte in cerchio,
venimmo sopra più crudele stipa;

e quivi, per l'orribile soperchio
del puzzo che 'l profondo abisso gitta,
ci raccostammo, in dietro, ad un coperchio

d'un grand' avello, ov' io vidi una scritta
che dicea: "Anastasio papa guardo,
lo qual trasse Fotin de la via dritta."

"Lo nostro scender conviene esser tardo,
sì che s'ausi un poco in prima il senso
al tristo fiato; e poi no i fia riguardo."

Così 'l maestro; e io "Alcun compenso,"
dissi lui, "trova che 'l tempo non passi
perduto." Ed elli: "Vedi ch'a ciò penso."

"Figliuol mio, dentro da cotesti sassi,"
cominciò poi a dir, "son tre cerchietti
di grado in grado, come que' che lassi.

Tutti son pien di spirti maladetti;
ma perché poi ti basti pur la vista,
intendi come e perché son costretti.

D'ogne malizia, ch'odio in cielo acquista,
ingiuria è 'l fine, ed ogne fin cotale
o con forza o con frode altrui contrista.

Ma perché frode è de l'uom proprio male,
più spiace a Dio; e però stan di sotto
li frodolenti, e più dolor li assale.

At the brink of a high bank formed
by broken boulders in a circle
3   we stopped above a still more grievous throng.

Here, the unbearable foul stench
belched from that bottomless abyss
6   made us draw back behind the slab

of an imposing tomb, on which I saw inscribed
the words: 'I hold Pope Anastasius:
9   Photinus drew him from the right and proper path.'

'We must delay descending so our sense,
inured to that vile stench,
12   no longer heeds it.'

So spoke the master. I replied: 'I know
you'll find a useful way to pass this time.'
15   And he: 'You'll see that is my plan.'

'My son,' he then began, 'beneath these rocks
there are three circles, smaller, one below the other,
18   but otherwise like those you leave behind.

'All these are filled with souls condemned.
So that the sight alone may later be enough,
21   know how and why they are confined this way.

'Every evil deed despised in Heaven
has as its end injustice. Each such end
24   harms someone else through either force or fraud.

'But since the vice of fraud is man's alone,
it more displeases God, and thus the fraudulent
27   are lower down, assailed by greater pain.

Di vïolenti il primo cerchio è tutto;
ma perché si fa forza a tre persone,
30   in tre gironi è distinto e costrutto.

A Dio, a sé, al prossimo si pòne
far forza, dico in loro e in lor cose,
33   come udirai con aperta ragione.

Morte per forza e ferute dogliose
nel prossimo si danno, e nel suo avere
36   ruine, incendi e tollette dannose;

onde omicide e ciascun che mal fiere,
guastatori e predon, tutti tormenta
39   lo giron primo per diverse schiere.

Puote omo avere in sé man vïolenta
e ne' suoi beni; e però nel secondo
42   giron convien che sanza pro si penta

qualunque priva sé del vostro mondo,
biscazza e fonde la sua facultade,
45   e piange là dov' esser de' giocondo.

Puossi far forza ne la deïtade,
col cor negando e bestemmiando quella,
48   e spregiando natura e sua bontade;

e però lo minor giron suggella
del segno suo e Soddoma e Caorsa
51   e chi, spregiando Dio col cor, favella.

La frode, ond' ogne coscïenza è morsa,
può l'omo usare in colui che 'n lui fida
54   e in quel che fidanza non imborsa.

Questo modo di retro par ch'incida
pur lo vinco d'amor che fa natura;
57   onde nel cerchio secondo s'annida

'The first circle holds the violent
but is divided and constructed in three rings,
30   since violence takes three different forms.

'Violence may be aimed at God, oneself,
or at one's neighbor—thus against all three
33   or their possessions—as I shall now explain.

'Violent death and grievous wounds may be inflicted
upon a neighbor or, upon his goods,
36   pillage, arson, and violent theft.

'And so murderers and everyone who wounds
unjustly, spoilers and plunderers—the first ring
39   punishes all these in separate groups.

'A man may lay injurious hands upon himself
or on his goods, and for that reason
42   in the second ring must he repent in vain

'who robs himself of the world above
or gambles away and wastes his substance,
45   lamenting when he should rejoice.

'Violence may be committed against God
when we deny and curse Him in our hearts,
48   or when we scorn nature and her bounty.

'And so the smallest ring stamps with its seal
both Sodom and Cahors and those
51   who scorn Him with their tongues and hearts.

'Fraud gnaws at every conscience,
whether used on him who trusted
54   or on one who lacked such faith.

'Fraud against the latter only severs
the bond of love that nature makes.
57   Thus in the second circle nest

ipocresia, lusinghe e chi affattura,
falsità, ladroneccio e simonia,
60 ruffian, baratti e simile lordura.

Per l'altro modo quell' amor s'oblia
che fa natura, e quel ch'è poi aggiunto,
63 di che la fede spezïal si cria;

onde nel cerchio minore, ov' è 'l punto
de l'universo in su che Dite siede,
66 qualunque trade in etterno è consunto."

E io: "Maestro, assai chiara procede
la tua ragione, e assai ben distingue
69 questo barátro e 'l popol ch'e' possiede.

Ma dimmi: quei de la palude pingue,
che mena il vento, e che batte la pioggia,
72 e che s'incontran con sì aspre lingue,

perché non dentro da la città roggia
sono ei puniti, se Dio li ha in ira?
75 e se non li ha, perché sono a tal foggia?"

Ed elli a me "Perché tanto delira,"
disse, "lo 'ngegno tuo da quel che sòle?
78 o ver la mente dove altrove mira?

Non ti rimembra di quelle parole
con le quai la tua Etica pertratta
81 le tre disposizion che 'l ciel non vole,

incontenenza, malizia e la matta
bestialitade? e come incontenenza
84 men Dio offende e men biasimo accatta?

Se tu riguardi ben questa sentenza,
e rechiti a la mente chi son quelli
87 che sù di fuor sostegnon penitenza,

'hypocrisy, flatteries, and sorcerers;
lies, theft, and simony;
60   panders, barrators, and all such filth.

'Fraud against the trusting fails to heed
not only natural love but the added bond
63   of faith, which forms a special kind of trust.

'Therefore, in the tightest circle,
the center of the universe and seat of Dis,
66   all traitors are consumed eternally.'

And I: 'Master, your account is clear
and clearly designates the nature
69   of this abyss and its inhabitants.

'But tell me, those spirits in the viscous marsh,
those the wind drives, those the rain beats down on,
72   those clashing with such bitter tongues,

'why are they not punished inside the fiery city
if God's anger is upon them?
75   And if not, why are they so afflicted?'

And he: 'Not often do your wits stray
far afield, as they do now—or is your mind
78   bent on pursuing other thoughts?

'Do you not recall the words
your *Ethics* uses to expound
81   the three dispositions Heaven opposes,

'incontinence, malice, and mad brutishness,
and how incontinence offends God less
84   and incurs a lesser blame?

'If you consider well this judgment
and consider who they are
87   that suffer punishment above, outside the wall,

tu vedrai ben perché da questi felli
sien dipartiti, e perché men crucciata
90   la divina vendetta li martelli."

"O sol che sani ogne vista turbata,
tu mi contenti sì quando tu solvi,
93   che, non men che saver, dubbiar m'aggrata.

Ancora in dietro un poco ti rivolvi,"
diss' io, "là dove di' ch'usura offende
96   la divina bontade, e 'l groppo solvi."

"Filosofia," mi disse, "a chi la 'ntende,
nota, non pure in una sola parte,
99   come natura lo suo corso prende

dal divino 'ntelletto e da sua arte;
e se tu ben la tua Fisica note,
102   tu troverai, non dopo molte carte,

che l'arte vostra quella, quanto pote,
segue, come 'l maestro fa 'l discente;
105   sì che vostr' arte a Dio quasi è nepote.

Da queste due, se tu ti rechi a mente
lo Genesì dal principio, convene
108   prender sua vita e avanzar la gente;

e perché l'usuriere altra via tene,
per sé natura e per la sua seguace
111   dispregia, poi ch'in altro pon la spene.

Ma seguimi oramai che 'l gir mi piace;
ché i Pesci guizzan su per l'orizzonta,
e 'l Carro tutto sovra 'l Coro giace,
115   e 'l balzo via là oltra si dismonta."

'you'll understand why they are set apart
from these wicked spirits and why God's vengeance
90   smites them with a lesser wrath.'

'O sun that heals all troubled sight,
you so content me by resolving doubts
93   it pleases me no less to question than to know.

'But go back a little way,' I said,
'to where you told me usury offends
96   God's goodness, and untie that knot for me.'

'Philosophy, for one who understands her,
observes,' he said, 'and not in one place only,
99   how nature takes her course

'from heavenly intellect and its operation.
And, if you study well your *Physics*,
102   you will find, after not too many pages,

'that human toil, as far as it is able,
follows nature, as the pupil does his master,
105   so that it is God's grandchild, as it were.

'By toil and nature, if you remember Genesis,
near the beginning, it is man's lot
108   to earn his bread and prosper.

'The usurer, who takes another path,
scorns nature in herself and in her follower,
111   and elsewhere sets his hopes.

'But follow me now, for it is time to go.
The Fishes are flickering at the horizon
and all the Wain lies over Caurus. And here,
115   a short way off, is the descent.'

3. The word *stipa* ("throng"—from the verb *stipare* or *stivare*) in Dante (see *Inf.* VII.19; XXIV.82) seems to refer to animals or people crowded together as in a pen or in the hold of a ship (cf. the English "steerage"). Here the term refers to those crowded together in the more restricted area of the narrowing lower three circles of hell, i.e., the subject of Virgil's discourse throughout this canto, the shortest (along with *Inf.* VI, which also has but 115 lines) of the poem.

6. This lid of a second funerary monument is similarly not fully described. Are these lids suspended in air or do they rest on the ground, tilted against the sides of the tombs? See note to *Inferno* X.8–9.

8–9. Dante may have confused Pope Anastasius II (496–98) with the emperor Anastasius I (491–518). In the commentaries there is also a question as to whether Dante's Photinus was a deacon of Thessalonica or the bishop of Sirmium. Further, the grammatical structure of the passage would allow us to understand either that Photinus misled Anastasius into heresy or was himself thus misled by the pope. A passage in Isidore of Seville, if it happens to be Dante's direct or indirect source, resolves two of these three issues. Isidore is speaking of the various kinds of heresy (*Etymologiae* VIII.v.37). According to him, the Photinians are named after Photinus the bishop of Sirmium, who followed the Ebionite heresy (see *Etym.* VIII.v.36) in promulgating the notion that Jesus was born from the natural union of Joseph and Mary. And thus it was Photinus who misled the pope, since this very heresy is named after him. The more usual view in the commentaries is that the Photinus in question was the deacon of Thessalonica, a follower of Acacius, but this is probably not the better interpretation.

10–15. Dante, as though speaking through Virgil to his reader, would seem to be admitting that this canto is not nearly as exciting as those that have gone before (and those that will come after), since it involves nothing but pedantic lecturing. In his little joke the excuse for his reader-unfriendly behavior is that the protagonist's olfactory powers required a rest so that they might become accustomed to the stench of lower hell. No experiential learning being possible, the class had to retire to the schoolroom. Virgil's discourse is thus presented as little more than filler—

even if the reader realizes that the canto has no lesser purpose than that of establishing a system for the organization of the sins of humankind.

22–27. Perhaps the key passage for our understanding of the organization of lower hell. All sins punished therein are sins of *malizia*, malice, in the sense that these sinners all willfully desire to do harm (the incontinent may indeed end up doing harm to others or to themselves, but their desire is for another kind of gratification altogether). Heresy, because it lies within the iron walls of Dis, and is thus also punished as a sin of the will rather than of the appetite (surely it seems closer to malice than to appetite), is perhaps less readily considered a desire to harm others (even though it assuredly, to Dante's mind, does so). *Ingiuria* has thus both its Latin meaning, injustice, acting in opposition to the law *(iniuria)*, and its other meaning, the doing of harm. As Mazzoni (Mazz.1985.1, p. 14) points out, Daniello was the first commentator explicitly to link this passage with its almost certain source in Cicero *(De officiis* I.xiii.41), a passage that defines *iniuria* as having two modes, force or fraud, with fraud meriting the greater hatred.

Here malice is divided into two subgroups, force (violence) and fraud. Fraud itself will shortly be divided into two subgroups (see note to vv. 61–66); but for now Dante has only divided the sins of violence (Cantos XII–XVII) and fraud (Cantos XVIII–XXXIV) into these two large groups. On *malizia* see Mazzoni, pp. 10–14; he demonstrates that for Dante, following St. Thomas, malice reflects *voluntas nocendi*, the will to do harm. For a revisionist view of the entire question see Cogan (Coga.1999.1).

28–33. Virgil divides the sins of violence (synonymous with those of force) into three subsidiary "rings" *(gironi)*. These are, in order of their gravity, violence against God (Cantos XIV–XVII), against one's self (Canto XIII), and against one's neighbor (Canto XII).

34–39. Now, in the order in which we witness them, Virgil describes the three categories of the sin of violence more fully, here violence against others, whether directed against their persons or their property (Canto XII).

40–45. Those violent against themselves or their own property are in the second ring (Canto XIII).

46–51. The third ring encloses those who are violent against God by blaspheming him (Canto XIV); "violent" against nature in the commission of unnatural sexual acts (sodomy, identified by the reference to Sodom, punished in Canto XV—see the confirmation at *Purg.* XXVI.79, where the penitent homosexuals cry out "Soddoma" against their past sins); violent against "art," exemplified in the reference to Cahors, the town in southern France which, in the Middle Ages, had become synonymous with usury (see Virgil's further explanation at vv. 97–111).

52–60.   Turning at last to fraud, Virgil now divides it into two kinds, depending on whether or not it is practiced against those who trust in one or not. He first describes the second and lesser kind, "simple fraud," as it were, committed by those who are punished in the eighth Circle, which we shall learn (*Inf.* XVIII.1) is called "Malebolge" after the ten "evil pockets" that contain them (Cantos XVIII–XXX). Here the poet for whatever reason (to keep his readers on their toes?) allows Virgil to name the sins in no discernible order, while also omitting two of them: (6) hypocrisy, (2) flattery, (4) divination, (10) counterfeiting, (7) thievery, (3) simony, (1) pandering [and seducing, not mentioned here], (5) barratry (the purchase or sale of political office); totally omitted from mention are (8) false counsel and (9) schismatic acts.

61–66.   The second form of fraud, that which severs not only the tie of affection that is natural to humans but that even more sacred one which binds human beings in special relationships of trust, is referred to as treachery (v. 66). Such sinners occupy the ninth Circle (Cantos XXXI–XXXIV).

67–75.   Having told Virgil that his discourse has been clear and convincing, the protagonist nonetheless reveals that he has not quite got it; why, he asks, are not the angry and sullen (Canto VIII), the lustful (Canto V), the gluttonous (Canto VI), and the avaricious and prodigal (Canto VII) punished inside the City of Dis if God holds them in his righteous anger? And if He doesn't, why are they in the state of affliction they are in? Dante has set up his reader with this inattentive question. The protagonist thinks that Virgil's analysis of God's wrath at v. 22 makes God hate only *malizia*, and does not understand the relationship between that form of sin and incontinence.

76–90.   After chastising Dante for his foolishness, Virgil clarifies the situation. Aristotle, he says, in the seventh book of the *Ethics* treats the three dispositions of the soul that Heaven opposes. These are incontinence, malice (the *malizia* of v. 22), and "mad brutishness" *(matta bestialitade)*. The clarity of this statement should not have left so much vexation in its wake, but it has. (For a thorough review of the debate and a solution of the problems that caused it see Francesco Mazzoni's lengthy gloss to these verses, Mazz.1985.1, pp. 25–45.) "Malice," just as it did when it was first used, identifies violence and simple fraud; "mad brutishness" refers to treachery. As Mazzoni demonstrates, both in Aristotle and in Thomas's commentary on the *Ethics* (and elsewhere in his work), "bestiality" is one step beyond malice, just as it is here in Dante; in Thomas's words it is a "magnum augmentum Malitiae," i.e., a similar but worse kind of sin. Nonetheless, there are those who argue that, since *malizia* eventually comes to encompass *both* kinds of fraud (those punished in *both* the eighth and ninth Circles), *matta bestialitade* cannot refer to treachery. Nonetheless, if they were to consider the way in which Dante has handled his various definitions they might realize that he has done here just what he has done at vv. 22–24: he identifies "malice" with violence and fraud and then (at vv. 61–66) adds a third category (and second category of fraud), treachery, just as he does here. For a strong and helpful summary (in English) of the debate, with arguments similar to and conclusions identical with Mazzoni's, see Triolo (Trio.1998.1), whose own initial work on the subject dates to 1968 (see his bibliographical note).

91–96.   Now fully cognizant of the grand design of hell, Dante (like some of his readers?) admits he is having difficulty with one particular: usury. How does it "offend God's goodness" (v. 48)?

97–111.   Weaving strands of Aristotle and St. Thomas, Virgil demonstrates that nature takes her course from the divine mind, and that "art" then follows nature. Humankind, fallen into sin, as is recorded in Genesis (3:17), must earn its bread in the sweat of its brow, precisely by following the rules of nature and whatever craft it practices. And for this reason usurers are understood as sinning against nature, God's child, and *her* child, "art" (in the sense of "craft"), thus the "grandchild" of God and all the more vulnerable to human transgression.

112–115.   Telling time by the stars he cannot see but remembers (here the constellation Pisces ["the Fishes"] in the east and the Big Dipper ["the Wain"], lying to the northwest [Caurus, the northwest wind]), Virgil tells Dante it is time to continue the journey, since it is already ca. 4 AM in Italy. They have been descending for ten hours, and have only fourteen left to them, since the entire trip down will take exactly twenty-four hours, 6 PM Friday evening until 6 PM Saturday (Jerusalem time).

INFERNO XII

OUTLINE

Era lo loco ov' a scender la riva
venimmo, alpestro e, per quel che v'er' anco,
3   tal, ch'ogne vista ne sarebbe schiva.

Qual è quella ruina che nel fianco
di qua da Trento l'Adice percosse,
6   o per tremoto o per sostegno manco,

che da cima del monte, onde si mosse,
al piano è sì la roccia discoscesa,
9   ch'alcuna via darebbe a chi sù fosse:

cotal di quel burrato era la scesa;
e 'n su la punta de la rotta lacca
12   l'infamïa di Creti era distesa

che fu concetta ne la falsa vacca;
e quando vide noi, sé stesso morse,
15   sì come quei cui l'ira dentro fiacca.

Lo savio mio inver' lui gridò: "Forse
tu credi che qui sia 'l duca d'Atene,
18   che sù nel mondo la morte ti porse?

Pàrtiti, bestia, ché questi non vene
ammaestrato da la tua sorella,
21   ma vassi per veder le vostre pene."

Qual è quel toro che si slaccia in quella
c'ha ricevuto già 'l colpo mortale,
24   che gir non sa, ma qua e là saltella,

vid' io lo Minotauro far cotale;
e quello accorto gridò: "Corri al varco;
27   mentre ch'e' 'nfuria, è buon che tu ti cale."

Steep was the cliff we had to clamber down,
rocky and steep, but—even worse—it held
a sight that every eye would shun.

As on the rockslide that still marks the flank
of the Àdige, this side of Trent,
whether by earthquake or erosion at the base,

from the mountain-top they slid away from,
the shattered boulders strew the precipice
and thus give footing to one coming down—

just so was the descent down that ravine.
And at the chasm's jagged edge
was sprawled the infamy of Crete,

conceived in that false cow.
When he caught sight of us, he gnawed himself
like someone ruled by wrath.

My sage cried out to him: 'You think,
perhaps, this is the Duke of Athens,
who in the world above put you to death.

'Get away, you beast, for this man
does not come tutored by your sister,
he comes to view your punishments.'

Like the bull that breaks its tether
just as it receives the mortal blow
and cannot run, but lunges here and there,

so raged the Minotaur. My artful guide
called out: 'Run to the passage:
hurry down while he is in his fury.'

Così prendemmo via giù per lo scarco
di quelle pietre, che spesso moviensi
30   sotto i miei piedi per lo novo carco.

Io gia pensando; e quei disse: "Tu pensi
forse a questa ruina, ch'è guardata
33   da quell'ira bestial ch'i' ora spensi.

Or vo' che sappi che l'altra fïata
ch'i' discesi qua giù nel basso inferno,
36   questa roccia non era ancor cascata.

Ma certo poco pria, se ben discerno,
che venisse colui che la gran preda
39   levò a Dite del cerchio superno,

da tutte parti l'alta valle feda
tremò sì, ch'i' pensai che l'universo
42   sentisse amor, per lo qual è chi creda

più volte il mondo in caòsso converso;
e in quel punto questa vecchia roccia,
45   qui e altrove, tal fece riverso.

Ma ficca li occhi a valle, ché s'approccia
la riviera del sangue in la qual bolle
48   qual che per vïolenza in altrui noccia."

Oh cieca cupidigia e ira folle,
che sì ci sproni ne la vita corta,
51   e ne l'etterna poi sì mal c'immolle!

Io vidi un'ampia fossa in arco torta,
come quella che tutto 'l piano abbraccia,
54   secondo ch'avea detto la mia scorta;

e tra 'l piè de la ripa ed essa, in traccia
corrien centauri, armati di saette,
57   come solien nel mondo andare a caccia.

And so we made our way down the steep landslide
on scree that often shifted
30   under my feet with unexpected weight.

I went on lost in thought. And he said:
'Perhaps you're wondering about this rockslide
33   guarded by that bestial rage I quelled just now.

'I want you to know, the other time
I came down into nether Hell
36   this rock had not yet fallen.

'But surely, if memory does not fail,
it was just before He came who carried off
39   from Dis the great spoil of the highest circle

'when the deep and foul abyss shook on every side,
so that I thought the universe felt love,
42   by which, as some believe,

'the world has many times been turned to chaos.
And at that moment this ancient rock,
45   here and elsewhere, fell broken into pieces.

'But fix your eyes below, for we draw near
the river of blood that scalds
48   those who by violence do injury to others.'

O blind covetousness, insensate wrath,
which in this brief life goad us on and then,
51   in the eternal, steep us in such misery!

I saw a broad moat curving in its arc
that seemed to circle all the plain,
54   just as my guide had said.

Between the edge of moat and precipice
ran centaurs in a file and armed with arrows,
57   as when they went off hunting in our world.

Veggendoci calar, ciascun ristette,
e de la schiera tre si dipartiro
60   con archi e asticciuole prima elette;

e l'un gridò da lungi: "A qual martiro
venite voi che scendete la costa?
63   Ditel costinci; se non, l'arco tiro."

Lo mio maestro disse: "La risposta
farem noi a Chirón costà di presso:
66   mal fu la voglia tua sempre sì tosta."

Poi mi tentò, e disse: "Quelli è Nesso,
che morì per la bella Deianira,
69   e fé di sé la vendetta elli stesso.

E quel di mezzo, ch'al petto si mira,
è il gran Chirón, il qual nodrì Achille;
72   quell' altro è Folo, che fu sì pien d'ira.

Dintorno al fosso vanno a mille a mille,
saettando qual anima si svelle
75   del sangue più che sua colpa sortille."

Noi ci appressammo a quelle fiere isnelle:
Chirón prese uno strale, e con la cocca
78   fece la barba in dietro a le mascelle.

Quando s'ebbe scoperta la gran bocca,
disse a' compagni: "Siete voi accorti
81   che quel di retro move ciò ch'el tocca?

Così non soglion far li piè d'i morti."
E 'l mio buon duca, che già li er' al petto,
84   dove le due nature son consorti,

rispuose: "Ben è vivo, e sì soletto
mostrar li mi convien la valle buia;
87   necessità 'l ci 'nduce, e non diletto.

They saw us coming, stopped, and three
departed from the troop with bows
60   and shafts they had selected with great care.

One cried from afar: 'To what torment
do you come, you two approaching down the slope?
63   Tell us from there. If not, I draw my bow.'

My master said: 'We will give our answer
to Chiron once we have come closer.
66   Your will was always hasty, to your hurt.'

Then he nudged me, saying: 'That is Nessus,
who died for lovely Deianira
69   and fashioned of himself his own revenge.

'The middle one, his gaze fixed on his chest,
is the great Chiron, he who raised Achilles.
72   The other one is Pholus, who was so filled with wrath.

'Around the moat they go in thousands,
shooting arrows at any soul that rises
75   higher from the blood than guilt allows.'

As we drew near those swift wild beasts,
Chiron took an arrow and with its nock
78   pulled back his beard along his jaw.

When he had uncovered his enormous mouth
he said to his companions: 'Have you observed
81   the one behind dislodges what he touches?

'That is not what the feet of dead men do.'
And my good leader, now at Chiron's breast
84   where his two natures join, replied:

'He is indeed alive, and so alone,
it is my task to show him this dark valley.
87   Necessity compels us, not delight.

Tal si partì da cantare alleluia
che mi commise quest' officio novo:
90   non è ladron, né io anima fuia.

Ma per quella virtù per cu' io movo
li passi miei per sì selvaggia strada,
93   danne un de' tuoi, a cui noi siamo a provo,

e che ne mostri là dove si guada,
e che porti costui in su la groppa,
96   ché non è spirto che per l'aere vada."

Chirón si volse in su la destra poppa,
e disse a Nesso: "Torna, e sì li guida,
99   e fa cansar s'altra schiera v'intoppa."

Or ci movemmo con la scorta fida
lungo la proda del bollor vermiglio,
102   dove i bolliti facieno alte strida.

Io vidi gente sotto infino al ciglio;
e 'l gran centauro disse: "E' son tiranni
105   che dier nel sangue e ne l'aver di piglio.

Quivi si piangon li spietati danni;
quivi è Alessandro, e Dïonisio fero
108   che fé Cicilia aver dolorosi anni.

E quella fronte c'ha 'l pel così nero,
è Azzolino; e quell' altro ch'è biondo,
111   è Opizzo da Esti, il qual per vero

fu spento dal figliastro sù nel mondo."
Allor mi volsi al poeta, e quei disse:
114   "Questi ti sia or primo, e io secondo."

Poco più oltre il centauro s'affisse
sovr' una gente che 'nfino a la gola
117   parea che di quel bulicame uscisse.

'One briefly left her song of hallelujah
and came to charge me with this novel task.
90   He is no robber, nor am I a thief.

'But, by that power by which I move my steps
on this wild road, lend us a guide,
93   one of your band to whom we may stay close,

'one who will show us to the ford
and carry this man over on his back,
96   for he is not a spirit that can fly through air.'

Chiron bent his torso to the right, then said
to Nessus: 'Go back and guide them.
99   If you meet another troop, have it give way.'

And with this trusty escort we went on,
skirting the edge of the vermilion boil
102   from which the boiled cried out with piercing shrieks.

There I saw some sunken to the eyebrows,
and the great centaur said: 'They are tyrants
105   who took to blood and plunder.

'Here they lament their ruthless crimes.
Here is Alexander, here cruel Dionysius,
108   who gave to Sicily its years of woe.

'And that brow with such jet-black hair
is Ezzelino, while the other blond one there
111   is Obizzo d'Este, who was indeed

'slain by his stepson in the world above.'
Then I turned to the poet, and he said:
114   'Now let Nessus be your guide and I will follow.'

A little farther on the centaur stopped
above a crowd whose heads, down to their necks,
117   seemed to issue from that boiling stream.

Mostrocci un'ombra da l'un canto sola,
dicendo: "Colui fesse in grembo a Dio
120 lo cor che 'n su Tamisi ancor si cola."

Poi vidi gente che di fuor del rio
tenean la testa e ancor tutto 'l casso;
123 e di costoro assai riconobb' io.

Così a più a più si facea basso
quel sangue, sì che cocea pur li piedi;
126 e quindi fu del fosso il nostro passo.

"Sì come tu da questa parte vedi
lo bulicame che sempre si scema,"
129 disse 'l centauro, "voglio che tu credi

che da quest' altra a più a più giù prema
lo fondo suo, infin ch'el si raggiunge
132 ove la tirannia convien che gema.

La divina giustizia di qua punge
quell' Attila che fu flagello in terra,
135 e Pirro e Sesto; e in etterno munge

le lagrime, che col bollor diserra,
a Rinier da Corneto, a Rinier Pazzo,
che fecero a le strade tanta guerra."
139 Poi si rivolse e ripassossi 'l guazzo.

He pointed out a shade apart, alone:
'In God's bosom that one clove in two
120   the heart that on the Thames still drips with blood.'

Then I saw some who had their heads,
even their whole chests, out of the river,
123   and of these I recognized a number,

as the blood became even more shallow
until it cooked nothing but their feet.
126   And here was our place to cross the moat.

'Just as on this side you can see
the boiling stream always diminishing,'
129   said the centaur, 'so, I'll have you know,

'on the other side the bottom falls away
until it plumbs the depths
132   where tyranny must groan.

'There divine justice stings Attila,
who was a scourge on earth, and Pyrrhus,
135   and Sextus, and eternally wrings

'tears, loosed by the boiling,
from Rinier of Corneto and Rinier Pazzo,
who on the highways made such strife.'
139   Then he turned back and crossed the ford again.

4–10. For the landslide near Trent (in northern Italy, carrying down into the river Adige) and discussion of it in Albertus Magnus, *De meteoris,* see Singleton's comment to these verses: Benvenuto da Imola was the first to identify the landslide as that at Slavini di Marco and to mention Albert's reference to it. Opinion is divided as to whether Dante actually visited this landmark or had merely read about it in Albert's treatise, which was well known to him.

12–13. "The infamy of Crete" is the Minotaur (only identified by name at v. 25), half man and half bull, conceived by the sexually venturesome Pasiphaë (wife of Minos, king of Crete) with a bull, when she placed herself in a wooden replica of a cow in order to enjoy a bovine embrace. See *Purg.* XXVI.87 for another reference to her on the Terrace of the purgation of lust. Most modern commentators, but not all, believe that Dante, in a reversal of the classical tradition, gave the Minotaur a man's head upon a bull's body.

16–21. The Minotaur had his labyrinthine home on Crete, where his violence was kept under some control by feeding to him a yearly tribute from Athens of seven maids and seven youths. Virgil taunts and thus distracts him, reminding him that he was killed by Theseus, instructed by the monster's "sister" Ariadne and guided by her thread back through the labyrinth.

Since the Minotaur is the first infernal guardian whom we meet within the walls of Dis (the rebel angels, the Furies, and the unseen Medusa were located on the city's ramparts in Canto IX), we might want to consider in what way he is different from those we have met in the Circles of Incontinence—Minos (the "step-father" of the Minotaur, as it were—Canto V), Cerberus (Canto VI), and Plutus (Canto VII). Like Charon (Canto III) and Phlegyas (Canto VIII), Minos has a general function, "judging" all the damned souls who confess their besetting sins to him (Charon ferries all across Acheron, Phlegyas seems to be employed in replacing temporarily escaped sinners in the Styx). Thus only Cerberus (gluttony) and Plutus (avarice) would seem to represent a particular sin of incontinence. The Minotaur (and the matter is much debated) seems to represent the entire zone of Violence, as Geryon (Canto XVI) will represent Fraud and the Giants (Canto XXXI), Treachery. If this hypothesis is correct, then the Minotaur's function is precisely similar to that of Geryon and of the Giants, and he is the gatekeeper for the entire seventh Circle (see *Inf.* XII.32). For his connection to violence see Boccaccio's commentary: "When he had grown up and become a most ferocious animal, and of incredible strength, they tell that Minos had him shut up in a prison called the labyrinth, and that he had sent to him there all those whom he wanted to die a cruel death." Rossetti's commentary sees the Minotaur as being associated with all three sins of violence punished in this Circle: "The Minotaur, who is situated at the rim of this tripartite circle, fed, according to myth, on human limbs (violence against one's neighbor); according to the poem [v. 14] was biting himself (violence against oneself) and was conceived in the 'false cow' (violence against nature, daughter of God)."

Surely he is wrathful (this canto has more uses of the word *ira* [wrath] than any other: XII.15, XII.33, XII.49, XII.72). As was pointed out in the note to *Inf.* VII.109–114, the wrath punished in Styx was intemperate wrath, a sin of passion and not of hardened will, while the sin punished here is Aquinas's third sort of anger, that which is kept alive for cold-blooded revenge. For a similar opinion, which insists on the distinction between the incontinence of Filippo Argenti and the intentional, willful behavior that we witness here, see Beck.1984.1, p. 228.

22–25.   The possible Virgilian source (*Aen.* II.223–224) of Dante's simile was perhaps first noted in Tommaseo's commentary: Laocoön, dying beneath the assault of the twin serpents, bellows like a stricken bull that has momentarily escaped death and is now fleeing from the altar because the axe of his executioner has been slightly off target, allowing him a few more minutes of life.

28–30.   Dante's corporality is again brought to our attention; only *he* moves physical objects, as Chiron will duly note at v. 81 (see note to vv. 76–82).

32.   The *ruina* (rockslide), just now referred to in the fourth verse of this canto, is clearly meant to be understood as having been caused by the earthquake at the Crucifixion (see Matth. 27:51).

33.   Wrath, punished in the Styx (the fifth Circle) is here distinguished from "bestial" wrath that is the sign of a hardened will to do violence. As was the case in *Inf.* XI.83 (see note to *Inf.* XI.76–90) Dante uses the word "bestial" to increase the heinousness of a kind of sin. Wrath is a sin of

Incontinence; "bestial wrath," a sin of Violence. Fraud is a sin of malice, "mad brutishness" (treachery) a sin of greater malice.

34–36.   See *Inf.* IX.22–27 where Virgil tells of his previous journey down through the underworld, when he was sent to the ninth Circle by the witch Erichtho (see note to *Inf.* IX.19–27).

39.   "Dis" here is a name for Lucifer: see *Inf.* XXXIV.20.

40–45.   Virgil's explanation of what happened in the immediate after-math of the Crucifixion shows a correct temporal and physical under-standing (he, after all, actually witnessed these phenomena fifty-three years after he arrived in Limbo [see *Inf.* IV.52–63]). However, his use of the Greek poet and philosopher Empedocles (ca. 492–430 B.C.) as authority shows his ingrained pagan way of accounting for one of Christianity's greatest miracles, Christ's ransoming of souls committed to hell. Accord-ing to Empedocles (first referred to at *Inf.* IV.138), in addition to the four elements (earth, water, air, fire) there were two others, and these governed the universe in alternating movements of love (concord) and hatred (chaos). As chaos moves toward concord, crowned by love, that very order, momentarily established, at once recedes and moves back toward chaos. This "circular" theory of history is intrinsically opposed to the Christian view, in which Christ's establishment of love as a universal principle redeemed history once and for all. In Virgil's apparent understanding, the climactic event in Christian history marked only the beginning of a (final?) stage of chaos. For an appreciation of the importance of Vir-gil's misunderstanding of the meaning of the Crucifixion see Baldassaro (Bald.1978.1), p. 101. (For Dante's knowledge of Empedocles's theories through Aristotle, Albertus Magnus, and St. Thomas see G. Stabile, "Empedocle," *ED* [vol. 2, 1970], p. 667.)

48.   The sinners against their neighbors and/or their property are clearly identified as being guilty of the sin of violence, *forza* (force), the first area of *malizia*, according to *Inferno* XI.22–24.

49–51.   The poet's apostrophe (see the similar ones at *Inf.* VII.19–21, XIV.16–18) would seem to identify two of the most immediate causes of violent acts, cupidity and wrath. See Guido da Pisa's commentary on this passage: "the violence that is inflicted on a neighbor arises either from cupidity or wrath."

56–57.   Patrolling the river of blood (identified only later [*Inf.* XIV.116] as "Phlegethon") from its bank are the Centaurs. Some early commentators saw in them a portrait of the bands of mercenary cavalrymen who were such an important feature of the horrendous wars of Dante's divided Italy. As Dante presents them they are seen as replicating their cruel habits as hunters in the world above. The original centaurs, half man and half horse, in Greek myths that came to Dante through various Latin poets, were the "sons" of Ixion and a cloud made to resemble Juno, whom Ixion desired to ravish when Jupiter allowed him entrance to Olympus. His sperm, falling to earth, created one hundred centaurs (their name reflects their number, "centum," and their airy beginning, "aura," or so believed some early commentators, e.g., Guido da Pisa, Pietro di Dante, and John of Serravalle). Their career on earth involved attempted rape at the wedding feast of Pirithous and Hippodamia, where it was necessary for Hercules to intercede in order to disperse them. The centaurs represent the particular sin of violence to others, turned to God's use in punishing those mortals who also sinned in this way.

58–63   The centaurs take Virgil and Dante for wandering damned souls and one of them (we learn that this is Nessus at v. 67) challenges them. His words, "Tell us from there. If not, I draw my bow" *(Ditel costinci; se non, l'arco tiro)* are probably modeled on Charon's to the armed figure of Aeneas (*Aen.* VI.389): "fare age, quid venias, iam istinc, et comprime gressum" (tell me, even from there, why you come here, and hold your steps).

64–66.   Virgil accords greater authority to Chiron than to the other centaurs. Dante's view of him reflects the fact that he was not sired by Ixion's lust, but by the former Olympian-in-chief: "Saturn, enamored of Philyra and fearing the jealousy of his wife, Rhea, changed himself into a horse and in this shape begat Chiron, who took the form of a centaur. Chiron educated Achilles, Aesculapius, Hercules, and many other famous Greeks, and Virgil knows at once that, because he is the wisest, he must be the leader of the band" (Singleton's commentary).

67–69.   Nessus, on the other hand, is one of the Ixion-begotten centaurs. When he tried to rape Hercules' wife, Deianira, according to the ninth book of Ovid's *Metamorphoses*, the great hero shot him with a poisoned arrow as Nessus was crossing a stream with Deianira on his back. Dying, the centaur dipped a tunic into his own poisoned blood (thus explaining exactly what Dante means when he says "fashioned of himself his own revenge") and gave it to Hercules' wife, telling her that whoever put on that tunic would become enamored of her. Years later, when Hercules fell in love with Iole, Deianira gave him the tunic. He put it on, experienced excruciating pain, and committed suicide to end his agony. Vengeful, Nessus displays his connection to violence against others, and precisely that "difficult" anger described by St. Thomas (see note to *Inf.* VII. 109–114).

70–71.   "Chiron's bowed head may be intended to suggest wisdom or an attitude of meditation, as most commentators believe, since he was considered to be the wisest of all the centaurs; but it also serves to direct the reader's gaze to the creature's breast, where its two natures, human and bestial, are joined" (Singleton's commentary). For Chiron as teacher of Achilles see at least Statius, *Achilleid* I.118.

72.   Pholus, like Nessus, and unlike Chiron, whose violence is tempered (and thus made more effective?) by reason, has no better nature to recommend him. He, begotten by Ixion like Nessus, like Nessus died at the hands of Hercules in most of the various Latin versions of the tale that Dante knew, but as the result of an accident: he himself dropped one of Hercules' poisoned arrows on his foot and died.

75.   Degrees of sinfulness control the depth of immersion: sinners are variously swathed in blood up to their eyebrows (v. 103: murderous tyrants); throats (116: murderers); waists (121: plunderers); feet (125: unspecified).

     Some commentators believe that Dante's conception of this river of blood was influenced by his experience as a cavalryman at the battle of Campaldino in 1289, when the slaughter made the rivulets crossing the terrain run with blood. For a description and analysis of that battle see Oert.1968.1.

76–82.   Chiron's remarks are put to the service of reminding the reader of the uniqueness of this fleshly visitor to hell. The "realism" of the detail (when he is described as moving the bristles of his beard with an arrow) has understandably pleased many; it perhaps also forces us to wonder whether the demons of hell have a fleshly or only a spirit presence, for if Dante can move things with his body, apparently Chiron can also— his own beard with the nock of an arrow. This question is never confronted by Dante, who leaves the ontological status of the demons of hell unresolved.

88–89. One of the few references to Beatrice heard in hell. An appeal to such authority is perhaps made to Chiron in view of his unusual rational powers.

93–96. Virgil's request that one of the centaurs bear Dante on his back to cross over the river of blood will be answered indirectly, between vv. 114 and 115.

97–99. The "tour" of the river of blood is only now ready to begin, under the guidance of Nessus, perhaps because Ovid had said of him that he was "membrisque valens scitusque vadorum" (strong of limb and schooled in fording streams—*Metam.* IX.108).

104. Dante's negative view of tyrants, seen as serving themselves rather than the state they govern, is also found in *Monarchia* (III.iv.10).

106–111. The first (and worst) group of the violent against others are the tyrants, including Alexander the Great and Dionysius the Elder of Syracuse. Both these identities are disputed, some modern commentators arguing for Alexander of Pherae, some for Dionysius the Younger, the son of the Elder. Singleton's notes to the passage offer convincing support for both traditional identifications. On Dante's view of tyrants see Carp.1998.1.

Ezzelino III da Romano (1194–1259), Ghibelline strongman in the March of Treviso in northern Italy, was, in Guelph eyes, a monster of cruelty. (See Giovanni Villani's account of his misdeeds, cited by Singleton.) He is coupled with a Guelph, Òpizzo II d'Este (1247–93), lord of Ferrara and a supporter of the French forces in Italy and of the pope. His violence was rewarded in life by his murder at the hands of either his own and "denatured" son or his illegitimate ("natural") offspring (the commentators are divided).

114–115. In handing Dante over to Nessus, Virgil does not tell him to "mount up." Yet this is what we should almost certainly understand is happening. The rest of the canto, up to its final two lines, takes place with Dante looking down from Nessus's back (see note to v. 126). This is almost clear when we consider the next verse: "A little farther on the centaur stopped." Up to now the movements of Dante and Virgil have been noted as they made their way along; now it is the centaur's movement which is recorded. Why? Because Dante is sitting on his back. Why did Dante handle this part of the journey so delicately? Perhaps because he was aware that the scene would have been "outrageous," a Dante on horseback in hell, too much for a reader to accept if merely told. In this formulation the poet once again invites the reader to become his accomplice in making his fiction. (For discussion see Holl.1984.1.)

116–120.   This slightly less bloodied crew contains "mere" murderers, only one of whom is indicated (by periphrasis): Guy de Montfort (1243–98), of royal English blood, in order to avenge his father Simon's murder killed his cousin, Henry of Cornwall in a church at Viterbo in 1271, supposedly while Henry was praying during the elevation of the Host. Henry's heart, returned to England, "still drips with blood" because his murder was not avenged.

121–123.   Those who rise higher from the blood are generally understood to be the non-murderous violent. It seems likely that their counterpart group, perhaps 180 degrees across the river, is the final one referred to before the end of the canto (vv. 134–137). Dante recognizes many of the present group, thus perhaps asking us to understand that they are local Tuscan ruffians.

124–125.   Although those who merely stand in blood are not further identified in any way, we may assume that they were the least destructive of those violent against the property of others, perhaps pickpockets and others of that ilk.

126.   Not every reader notices that at this point Dante (astride Nessus's back, we may want to remember) crosses over the river of blood.

127–132.   As he crosses toward the far side of the river (the one nearer to the center of hell) Nessus looks back over the area they have traversed (to their right), where the river grew increasingly shallow, and then looks left, where, he knows, the riverbed gradually deepens until it reaches its lowest point, which coincides with the first place Dante saw, that in which the tyrants are punished. This information suggests that Dante and Virgil have traversed a semicircle in order to reach this shallowest point, where they have forded the river. The unexplored run of the river thus also occupies 180 degrees of the circle.

133–138.   The only group referred to in that unexplored bend of the river includes those whose violence was limited to property, the group parallel in placement to the third group seen by Dante in his journey along Phlegethon. This new group is situated roughly halfway along the untraversed semicircle. The five identified personages that he has already seen in the one he has traveled are in parallel with the five he will only hear described: Attila the Hun (ca. 406–53), Pyrrhus of Epirus (ca. 318–272 B.C.), and Sextus Pompeius Magnus (d. 35 B.C.), the son of Pompey the Great, who, according to Lucan, disgraced the family name when he turned pirate (*Pharsalia* VI.119–122). The identities of the last two are sometimes disputed; one reason to think that they are as given here is that the resulting group of exemplary plunderers has in common its depredations of Rome. For a brief and clear representation of the various confusions among potential identities for Pyrrhus and Sextus see Botterill (Bott.1990.1), p. 156.

136–138.   The "moderns" are represented by two highwaymen named Rinier, both contemporaries of Dante. Rinier da Corneto worked the wild country around Rome, the Maremma, while Rinier Pazzo, dead by 1280, had his turf in the roads south of Florence and toward Arezzo.

139.   His task accomplished, Nessus crosses back over the river of blood without a word. It seems clear that he would not have crossed over had he not been carrying Dante on his back.

INFERNO XIII

Non era ancor di là Nesso arrivato,
quando noi ci mettemmo per un bosco
3   che da neun sentiero era segnato.

Non fronda verde, ma di color fosco;
non rami schietti, ma nodosi e 'nvolti;
6   non pomi v'eran, ma stecchi con tòsco.

Non han sì aspri sterpi né sì folti
quelle fiere selvagge che 'n odio hanno
9   tra Cecina e Corneto i luoghi cólti.

Quivi le brutte Arpie lor nidi fanno,
che cacciar de le Strofade i Troiani
12   con tristo annunzio di futuro danno.

Ali hanno late, e colli e visi umani,
piè con artigli, e pennuto 'l gran ventre;
15   fanno lamenti in su li alberi strani.

E 'l buon maestro "Prima che più entre,
sappi che se' nel secondo girone,"
18   mi cominciò a dire, "e sarai mentre

che tu verrai ne l'orribil sabbione.
Però riguarda ben; sì vederai
21   cose che torrien fede al mio sermone."

Io sentia d'ogne parte trarre guai
e non vedea persona che 'l facesse;
24   per ch'io tutto smarrito m'arrestai.

Cred'ïo ch'ei credette ch'io credesse
che tante voci uscisser, tra quei bronchi,
27   da gente che per noi si nascondesse.

Nessus had not yet reached the other side
when we made our way into a forest
3   not marked by any path.

No green leaves, but those of dusky hue—
not a straight branch, but knotted and contorted—
6   no fruit of any kind, but poisonous thorns.

No rougher, denser thickets make a refuge
for the wild beasts that hate tilled lands
9   between the Cècina and Corneto.

Here the filthy Harpies nest,
who drove the Trojans from the Strophades
12   with doleful prophecies of woe to come.

They have broad wings, human necks and faces,
taloned feet, and feathers on their bulging bellies.
15   Their wailing fills the eerie trees.

And my good master then began to speak:
'Before you go in deeper you should know,
18   you are, and will be, in the second ring

'until you reach the dreadful sand. Look well—
you will see things that, in my telling,
21   would seem to strip my words of truth.'

Lamentations I heard on every side
but I saw no one who might be crying out
24   so that, confused, I stopped.

I think he thought that I thought
all these voices in among the branches
27   came from people hiding there.

Però disse 'l maestro: "Se tu tronchi
qualche fraschetta d'una d'este piante,
30   li pensier c'hai si faran tutti monchi."

Allor porsi la mano un poco avante
e colsi un ramicel da un gran pruno;
33   e 'l tronco suo gridò: "Perché mi schiante?"

Da che fatto fu poi di sangue bruno,
ricominciò a dir: "Perché mi scerpi?
36   non hai tu spirto di pietade alcuno?

Uomini fummo, e or siam fatti sterpi:
ben dovrebb' esser la tua man più pia,
39   se state fossimo anime di serpi."

Come d'un stizzo verde ch'arso sia
da l'un de' capi, che da l'altro geme
42   e cigola per vento che va via,

sì de la scheggia rotta usciva insieme
parole e sangue; ond' io lasciai la cima
45   cadere, e stetti come l'uom che teme.

"S'elli avesse potuto creder prima,"
rispuose 'l savio mio, "anima lesa,
48   ciò c'ha veduto pur con la mia rima,

non averebbe in te la man distesa;
ma la cosa incredibile mi fece
51   indurlo ad ovra ch'a me stesso pesa.

Ma dilli chi tu fosti, si che 'n vece
d'alcun' ammenda tua fama rinfreschi
54   nel mondo sù, dove tornar li lece."

E 'l tronco: "Si col dolce dir m'adeschi,
ch'i' non posso tacere; e voi non gravi
57   perch' ïo un poco a ragionar m'inveschi.

And so the master said: 'If you break off
a twig among these brambles,
30   your present thoughts will be cut short.'

Then I stretched out my hand
and plucked a twig from a tall thorn-bush,
33   and its stem cried out: 'Why do you break me?'

When it ran dark with blood
it cried again: 'Why do you tear me?
36   Have you no pity in you?

'We once were men that now are turned to thorns.
Your hand might well have been more merciful
39   had we been souls of snakes.'

As from a green log, burning at one end,
that blisters and hisses at the other
42   with the rush of sap and air,

so from the broken splinter oozed
blood and words together, and I let drop
45   the twig and stood like one afraid.

'Could he have believed it otherwise,
O wounded soul,' my sage spoke up,
48   'what he had seen only in my verses,

'he would not have raised his hand against you.
But your plight, being incredible, made me
51   goad him to this deed that weighs on me.

'Now tell him who you were, so that, by way
of recompense, he may revive your fame
54   up in the world, where he's permitted to return.'

And the stem said: 'With your pleasing words
you so allure me I cannot keep silent.
57   May it not offend if I am now enticed to speak.

Io son colui che tenni ambo le chiavi
del cor di Federigo, e che le volsi,
60   serrando e diserrando, sì soavi,

che dal secreto suo quasi ogn' uom tolsi;
fede portai al glorïoso offizio,
63   tanto ch'i' ne perde' li sonni e 'polsi.

La meretrice che mai da l'ospizio
di Cesare non torse li occhi putti,
66   morte comune e de le corti vizio,

infiammò contra me li animi tutti;
e li 'nfiammati infiammar sì Augusto,
69   che 'lieti onor tornaro in tristi lutti.

L'animo mio, per disdegnoso gusto,
credendo col morir fuggir disdegno,
72   ingiusto fece me contra me giusto.

Per le nove radici d'esto legno
vi giuro che già mai non ruppi fede
75   al mio segnor, che fu d'onor sì degno.

E se di voi alcun nel mondo riede,
conforti la memoria mia, che giace
78   ancor del colpo che 'nvidia le diede."

Un poco attese, e poi "Da ch'el si tace,"
disse 'l poeta a me, "non perder l'ora;
81   ma parla, e chiedi a lui, se più ti piace."

Ond' ïo a lui: "Domandal tu ancora
di quel che credi ch'a me satisfaccia;
84   ch'i' non potrei, tanta pietà m'accora."

Perciò ricominciò: "Se l'om ti faccia
liberamente ciò che 'l tuo dir priega,
87   spirito incarcerato, ancor ti piaccia

'I am the one who held both keys
to Frederick's heart, and I could turn them,
60   locking and unlocking, so discreetly

'I kept his secrets safe from almost everyone.
So faithful was I to that glorious office
63   that first I lost my sleep and then my life.

'The slut who never took her whoring eyes
from Caesar's household, the common bane
66   and special vice of courts,

'inflamed all minds against me.
And they, inflamed, did so inflame Augustus
69   that welcome honors turned to dismal woe.

'My mind, in scornful temper,
hoping by dying to escape from scorn,
72   made me, though just, against myself unjust.

'By this tree's new-sprung roots I give my oath:
not once did I break faith
75   with my true lord, a man so worthy of honor.

'If one of you goes back into the world,
let him restore my memory, which still lies helpless
78   beneath the blow that envy dealt it.'

The poet waited, then he said to me:
'Since he is silent now do not waste time
81   but speak if you would ask him more.'

And I replied: 'Please question him
about the things you think I need to know.
84   For I cannot, such pity fills my heart.'

Thus he began again: 'So that this man may,
with ready will, do as your words entreat,
87   may it please you, imprisoned spirit,

di dirne come l'anima si lega
in questi nocchi; e dinne, se tu puoi,
90   s'alcuna mai di tai membra si spiega."

Allor soffiò il tronco forte, e poi
si convertì quel vento in cotal voce:
93   "Brievemente sarà risposto a voi.

Quando si parte l'anima feroce
dal corpo ond' ella stessa s'è disvelta,
96   Minòs la manda a la settima foce.

Cade in la selva, e non l'è parte scelta;
ma là dove fortuna la balestra,
99   quivi germoglia come gran di spelta.

Surge in vermena e in pianta silvestra:
l'Arpie, pascendo poi de le sue foglie,
102   fanno dolore, e al dolor fenestra.

Come l'altre verrem per nostre spoglie,
ma non però ch'alcuna sen rivesta,
105   ché non è giusto aver ciò ch'om si toglie.

Qui le strascineremo, e per la mesta
selva saranno i nostri corpi appesi,
108   ciascuno al prun de l'ombra sua molesta."

Noi eravamo ancora al tronco attesi,
credendo ch'altro ne volesse dire,
111   quando noi fummo d'un romor sorpresi,

similemente a colui che venire
sente 'l porco e la caccia a la sua posta,
114   ch'ode le bestie, e le frasche stormire.

Ed ecco due da la sinistra costa,
nudi e graffiati, fuggendo sì forte,
117   che de la selva rompieno ogne rosta.

'to tell us further how the souls are bound
inside such gnarled wood, and tell us, if you can,
90   if from such limbs one ever is set free.'

Then the tree forced out harsh breath, and soon
that wind was turned into a voice:
93   'My answer shall be brief.

'When the ferocious soul deserts the body
after it has wrenched up its own roots,
96   Minos condemns it to the seventh gulch.

'It falls into the forest, in a spot not chosen,
but flung by fortune, helter-skelter,
99   it fastens like a seed.

'It spreads into a shoot, then a wild thicket.
The Harpies, feeding on its leaves,
102   give pain and to that pain a mouth.

'We will come to claim our cast-off bodies
like the others. But it would not be just if we again
105   put on the flesh we robbed from our own souls.

'Here shall we drag it, and in this dismal wood
our bodies will be hung, each one
108   upon the thorn-bush of its painful shade.'

Our attention was still fixed upon the tree,
thinking it had more to tell us,
111   when we were startled by a noise,

as a man, when he hears
the dogs, and branches snapping,
114   knows the boar and hunters near.

Now, from the left, two souls came running,
naked and torn, and so intent on flight
117   they broke straight through the tangled thicket.

Quel dinanzi: "Or accorri, accorri, morte!"
E l'altro, cui pareva tardar troppo,
120   gridava: "Lano, sì non furo accorte

le gambe tue a le giostre dal Toppo!"
E poi che forse li fallia la lena,
123   di sé e d'un cespuglio fece un groppo.

Di rietro a loro era la selva piena
di nere cagne, bramose e correnti
126   come veltri ch'uscisser di catena.

In quel che s'appiattò miser li denti,
e quel dilaceraro a brano a brano;
129   poi sen portar quelle membra dolenti.

Presemi allor la mia scorta per mano,
e menommi al cespuglio che piangea
132   per le rotture sanguinenti in vano.

"O Iacopo," dicea, "da Santo Andrea,
che t'è giovato di me fare schermo?
135   che colpa ho io de la tua vita rea?"

Quando 'l maestro fu sovr' esso fermo,
disse: "Chi fosti, che per tante punte
138   soffi con sangue doloroso sermo?"

Ed elli a noi: "O anime che giunte
siete a veder lo strazio disonesto
141   c'ha le mie fronde sì da me disgiunte,

raccoglietele al piè del tristo cesto.
I' fui de la città che nel Batista
144   mutò 'l primo padrone; ond' ei per questo

sempre con l'arte sua la farà trista;
e se non fosse che 'n sul passo d'Arno
147   rimane ancor di lui alcuna vista,

The one in front cried: 'Come, come quickly, death!'
And the other, who thought his own pace slow:
120 'Lano, your legs were not so nimble

'at the tournament near the Toppo.'
Then, almost out of breath, he pressed himself
123 into a single tangle with a bush.

Behind them now the woods were thick
with bitches, black and ravenous and swift
126 as hounds loosed from the leash.

On him who had hidden in the tangle
they set their teeth, tore him to pieces,
129 and carried off those miserable limbs.

And then my leader took me by the hand.
He led me to the bush,
132 which wept in vain lament from bleeding wounds.

'O Jacopo da Sant' Andrea,' it said,
'what use was it to make a screen of me?
135 Why must I suffer for your guilty life?'

When the master stopped beside it, he said:
'Who were you, that through so many wounds
138 pour out with blood your doleful words?'

And he to us: 'O souls who have arrived
to see the shameless carnage
141 that has torn from me my leaves,

'gather them here at the foot of this wretched bush.
I was of the city that traded patrons—
144 Mars for John the Baptist. On that account

'Mars with his craft will make her grieve forever.
And were it not that at the crossing of the Arno
147 some vestige of him still remains,

que' cittadin che poi la rifondarno
sovra 'l cener che d'Attila rimase,
avrebber fatto lavorare indarno.

151   Io fei gibetto a me de le mie case."

'those citizens who afterwards rebuilt it
upon the ashes that Attila left behind
would have done their work in vain.
151   I made my house into my gallows.'

1–3.   Ettore Paratore (Para.1965.1, pp. 281–82) has studied the phenomenon of the "connected canti" of the *Comedy*, those, like XII and XIII, in which the action flows from one into the other, in which a canto is not "end-stopped." He counts 16 such in *Inferno*; 10 in *Purgatorio*; 8 in *Paradiso*. That one third of the borders of Dante's cantos are so fluid helps us to understand that he has a strong sense of delineation of the units of the whole and, at the same time, a desire not to be restrained by these borders.

4–9.   Dante refers to the wilds of the Maremma, here between the river Cecina to the north and the town of Corneto to the south, a wild part of Tuscany.

10–15.   The Harpies, heavy birds with the faces of women and clawed hands, the demonic monsters who preside over this canto (once again, like the Minotaur and the Centaurs, part human, part beast), derive from Virgil (*Aen*. III.210–212; 216–217; 253–257). Having twice befouled the food of the Trojan refugees, one of them (Celaeno) then attempts to convince Aeneas and his followers that they, in their voyage to Italy, are doomed to starvation and failure.

20–21.   Virgil's words offer the occasion for a certain ingenuity on the part of some commentators, who believe that Virgil here refers to the text of the *Aeneid*. Literally, what they mean is clear enough: "were I only to tell you what you are about to see, you would not believe me" (i.e., Dante has to hear the vegetation speak in order to accept its ability to do so). But see note to vv. 46–51.

24.   Dante, lost in a dark wood, as he was at the beginning of the poem, is *smarrito* (bewildered), as his path was lost *(smarrita)* in that wood. The repetition of the word here seems deliberate, and perhaps invites us to consider the possibility that the lost soul whom we met in *Inferno* I was in some way himself suicidal.

25.   This is perhaps the most self-consciously "literary" line in a canto filled with "literariness." See the elegant essay by Leo Spitzer (Spit.1942.1) for a close analysis of *Inferno* XIII.

31–39. Dante's hesitant gesture and the sinner's horrified response reflect closely a scene in the *Aeneid* in which Aeneas similarly tears pieces of vegetation from the grave of murdered Polydorus, who finally cries out in words that are echoed in this sinner's complaints (*Aen.* III.22–48). Just before the Greeks overran Troy, Priam sent his son Polydorus to be raised by the Thracian king Polymnestor, and with him the treasure of Troy. Once the city fell, Polymnestor killed Polydorus, stole the treasure, and had the youth's body cast into the sea.

The speaker, we will later learn from the historical details to which he refers (he is never named), is Pier delle Vigne, the chancellor of Frederick II of Sicily and Naples (see note to vv. 58–61). Here he is represented as a "gran pruno" (tall thorn-bush), and while the modifying adjective grants him a certain dignity, it also reduces him to the least pleasant of plants. The forest of the suicides resembles a dense thicket of briar, the only "vegetation" found in hell after the green meadow of Limbo (*Inf.* IV.111).

40–44. Dante's simile, which sounds like the sounds it describes, reduces Pier's natural dignity by giving him so distorted a voice.

46–51. Virgil's apology to Pier for encouraging Dante to pluck a piece of him now clearly evokes the text of the *Aeneid*, thus adding a dimension to the words he had uttered at vv. 20–21.

52–54. Virgil's invitation to Pier to speak so that Dante may "revive his fame" in the world above has a positive result. As we move down through hell, we will find that some sinners look upon their "interview" with this "reporter" as a wonderful opportunity to attempt to clear their name, while others shun any "publicity" at all.

55–57. The beginning of Pier's speech is an Italian version of Pier's noted "chancery style" of Latin oratory turned to document-writing. Pier was known not only for his Latin writings on behalf of Frederick's exercise of imperial power, but for his vernacular poems, which are similarly florid.

His speech to Dante, in its entirety, forms an Italian version of a classical oration, with its parts measured as follows: (1) capturing of the goodwill of the audience (55–57); (2) narrative of events at issue (58–72); (3) peroration, making the climactic point (73–75); (4) petition, seeking the consent of the audience (76–78). (For a more detailed consideration of the rhetorical construction of the speech see Higgins [Higg.1975.1], pp. 63–64.)

58–61.   The speaker identifies himself, if by circumlocution, as Pier della Vigna (or "delle Vigne"): "Petrus de Vinea, minister of the Emperor Frederick II, born at Capua ca. 1190; after studying at Bologna, he received an appointment at the court of Frederick II as notary, and thenceforward he rapidly rose to distinction. He was made judge and protonotary, and for more than twenty years he was the trusted minister and confidant of the Emperor. He was at the height of his power in 1247, but two years later he was accused of treachery, and was thrown into prison and blinded; and soon after he committed suicide (April, 1249)" (T). For the Emperor Frederick II see note to *Inferno* X.119.

Holding the keys to the emperor's heart, the "promised land" of any self-seeking courtier, this Peter is a parodic version of St. Peter, who, in the Christian tradition, holds the keys (one for mercy, one for judgment) that unlock or lock the kingdom of heaven. For the original biblical image of the two keys see Isaiah 22:22.

64.   This "slut" is commonly recognized as envy, the sin of hoping that one's happy neighbor will be made unhappy.

Pier is trying to establish his innocence of the charges that he betrayed his lord by stealing from his treasury. We now know that he was in fact guilty of that fault; however, it is far from clear that Dante knew what we know. See Cassell's gathering of evidence for the case against Pier's barratry (Cass.1984.1, pp. 38–42).

68.   "Augustus," the emperor *par excellence*, is Pier's title for his emperor, Frederick.

70.   Pier's *disdegnoso gusto*, whether pleasure in self-hatred (see Vazzana [Vazz.1998.1] for this reading) or pleasure in imagining his vengeance upon his enemies (see Higgins [Higg.1975.1], p. 72), is presented as the motive for his suicide.

73–75.   How are we to respond to this unquestionably imposing figure? Here is Attilio Momigliano, in his commentary to this passage: "[Pier's] way of speaking, with its lofty sense of fidelity, with its steady clear-sightedness, with its manly rebellion against the injustice of fate, with that indestructible sense of his honor and the desire to redeem it, even in death—all of these dressed in the folds of an austerely embellished eloquence—dwells in our memory like a solemn portrait of a courtier and makes us forget the fault of the suicide, as the words of Francesca, Brunetto, or Ugolino make us forget adultery, sodomy, betrayal. These virtues or passions that redeem, even in hell, a great sin are among the most noble and suggestive inventions of the *Comedy*." Such a view of the "great sinners" of the *Inferno* is attractive, no doubt, in part because it makes Dante a much less "judgmental" poet than in fact he is. However, it is probably better to see that, in the case of Pier (as well as in that of the others mentioned by Momigliano), the sinner speaks of himself in such a way as to condemn himself in his own words, at least if we learn to read him from the ironic angle of vision that the split between the consciousness of the slowly evolving protagonist and that of the knowledgeable poet surely seems to call for.

It was centuries ago that a reader first thought of Judas when he read of Pier. Pietro di Dante, in the second redaction of his commentary to vv. 16–51 of this canto, cites St. Jerome's comment on Psalm 8: "Judas offended God more greatly by hanging himself than by betraying Him." Dante's son, however, never developed the importance of Judas as the quintessential suicide in the controlling image of this canto. In our own time perhaps the first to do so was Giovanni Resta (Rest.1977.1); a fuller expression of this insight was developed by Anthony Cassell (Cass.1984.1, pp. 46–56). While Cassell's reading mainly involves Pier's betrayal of Frederick, the perhaps better understanding is to allow Pier his proclaimed fealty to his emperor, but to realize that his very words reveal that, if his temporal allegiances were respected, they had displaced his only truly significant loyalty, that owed to his only meaningful Lord, Jesus Christ (see Loon.1992.1, p. 39). Like Judas, he did betray his Lord, as Stephany has shown, precisely in his loyalty to the emperor, whom he treats, in his eulogy of Frederick, as in his own kingly person being all the Christ one needed. And thus, in imitation of Judas, he will have his body hanging on a tree for eternity. (For two articles about Frederick, Pier, and the court life that they shaped and shared, see Feng.1981.1 and Step.1982.1).

Pier, as many have noted, has important attributes in common with Dante. Both were political figures who ended up losing the goals of their highly energized activity; both were poets. Yet it seems clear that, for all the fellow-feeling that Dante must have felt for the ruined chancellor, he is more interested in the crucial errors he made in directing his political life to the sharing and taking of power and to that alone. For Dante, the political life can only be lived justly under the sign of the true "emperor," God.

82–84.   The protagonist, like many readers, has been won over by Pier's oratory. As was the case in his meeting with Farinata and Cavalcante in *Inferno* X, he began in fear, then turned to pity. Neither is an attitude recommended by the moral setting of the poem that contains this currently piteous protagonist.

109–126.   This self-contained unit of twenty-seven verses is devoted to a second class of those violent against themselves. These wastrels were "prodigal" in so thoroughly intentional a way that they did not casually toss away their possessions, but willfully destroyed them in a sort of "material suicide." Once again we note the line that Dante has drawn between the incontinent form of a sin (prodigality, punished in *Inferno* VII) and its "malicious" version.

Paget Toynbee describes the two sinners found here as follows: "Lano [Arcolano Maconi], gentleman of Siena, placed by Dante, together with Jacomo da sant' Andrea, among those who have squandered their substance . . . Lano is said to have been a member of the 'Spendthrift Brigade' of Siena, and to have squandered all his property in riotous living. He took part in an expedition of the Florentines and Sienese against Arezzo in 1288, which ended in the Sienese force falling into an ambush and being cut to pieces by the Aretines under Buonconte da Montefeltro at . . . Pieve al Toppo. Lano, being ruined and desperate, chose to fight and be killed, rather than run away and make his escape; hence the allusion of Jacomo in the text . . . Jacomo [and not Dante's "Jacopo"] della Cappella di sant' Andrea of Padua, the son of Odorico Fontana da Monselice and Speronella Delesmanini, a very wealthy lady, whose fortune Jacomo inherited, and squandered in the most senseless acts of prodigality. He is supposed to have been put to death by order of Ezzolino da Romano [see *Inf.* XII.102] in 1239" (T).

130–135.   The relatively minor figure we now encounter, a *cespuglio* (bush) and not the *gran pruno* (tall thorn-bush—v. 32) that holds the soul of Pier delle Vigne, complains against the unintentional despoiling of his leaves by the exhausted Jacomo, who had huddled up against him in order to escape the pursuing hounds. Various of the early commentators identify him as either Lotto degli Agli or Rocco de' Mozzi, yet some of these commentators also suggest that Dante left the name "open" because so many Florentines committed suicide by hanging themselves that he wanted to suggest the frequency of the phenomenon in his native city.

139–151.   The nameless suicide, now more careful of his "body" than he had been when he took his own life, asks to have his torn-off leaves returned to him. He identifies himself as Florentine by referring to the city's first patron, Mars, the god of war, whose replacement by John the Baptist in Christian times had weakened her, according to his not very reliable view. (Dante's sources seem to have confused Attila with Totila, who had in fact besieged the city in 542.)

INFERNO XIV

Poi che la carità del natio loco
mi strinse, raunai le fronde sparte
3   e rende'le a colui, ch'era già fioco.

Indi venimmo al fine ove si parte
lo secondo giron dal terzo, e dove
6   si vede di giustizia orribil arte.

A ben manifestar le cose nove,
dico che arrivammo ad una landa
9   che dal suo letto ogne pianta rimove.

La dolorosa selva l'è ghirlanda
intorno, come 'l fosso tristo ad essa;
12   quivi fermammo i passi a randa a randa.

Lo spazzo era una rena arida e spessa,
non d'altra foggia fatta che colei
15   che fu da' piè di Caton già soppressa.

O vendetta di Dio, quanto tu dei
esser temuta da ciascun che legge
18   ciò che fu manifesto a li occhi mei!

D'anime nude vidi molte gregge
che piangean tutte assai miseramente,
21   e parea posta lor diversa legge.

Supin giacea in terra alcuna gente,
alcuna si sedea tutta raccolta,
24   e altra andava continüamente.

Quella che giva 'ntorno era più molta,
e quella men che giacëa al tormento,
27   ma più al duolo avea la lingua sciolta.

Urged by the love I bore my place of birth,
I gathered up the scattered leaves and gave them back
to him, who had by this time spent his breath.

Then we came to the boundary that divides
the second circling from the third.
And here the dreadful work of justice is revealed.

To tell how strange the new place was,
I say we reached a barren plain
that lets no plant set root into its soil.

The gloomy forest rings it like a garland
and is in turn encircled by the moat.
Here, at the very edge, we stayed our steps

at an expanse of deep and arid sand,
much like the sand pressed long ago
beneath the feet of Cato.

O vengeance of God, how much
should you be feared by all who read
what now I saw revealed before my eyes!

I saw many a herd of naked souls,
all crying out in equal misery,
though each seemed subject to a different law:

some lay face up upon the ground,
some sat, their bodies hunched,
and others roamed about in constant motion.

Most numerous were those who roamed about,
those lying there in torment fewer,
though theirs the tongues crying out the most.

Sovra tutto 'l sabbion, d'un cader lento,
piovean di foco dilatate falde,
30   come di neve in alpe sanza vento.

Quali Alessandro in quelle parti calde
d'Indïa vide sopra 'l süo stuolo
33   fiamme cadere infino a terra salde,

per ch'ei provide a scalpitar lo suolo
con le sue schiere, acciò che lo vapore
36   mei si stingueva mentre ch'era solo:

tale scendeva l'etternale ardore;
onde la rena s'accendea, com' esca
39   sotto focile, a doppiar lo dolore.

Sanza riposo mai era la tresca
de le misere mani, or quindi or quinci
42   escotendo da sé l'arsura fresca.

I' cominciai: "Maestro, tu che vinci
tutte le cose, fuor che ' demon duri
45   ch'a l'intrar de la porta incontra uscinci,

chi è quel grande che non par che curi
lo 'ncendio e giace dispettoso e torto,
48   sì che la pioggia non par che 'l marturi?"

E quel medesmo, che si fu accorto
ch'io domandava il mio duca di lui,
51   gridò: "Qual io fui vivo, tal son morto.

Se Giove stanchi 'l suo fabbro da cui
crucciato prese la folgore aguta
54   onde l'ultimo dì percosso fui;

o s'elli stanchi li altri a muta a muta
in Mongibello a la focina negra,
57   chiamando 'Buon Vulcano, aiuta, aiuta!'

Above the stretching sand, in slow descent,
broad flakes of fire showered down
30   as snow falls in the hills on windless days.

If Alexander, on India's torrid plains,
seeing undiminished flakes of fire fall
33   upon the ground and on his troops,

ordered his men to trample down the soil
so that the flaming shower was put out
36   before the fire caught and spread,

here untrammeled the eternal flames
came down, and the sand took fire
39   like tinder under flint, doubling the torment.

Ever without repose was the rude dance
of wretched hands, now here, now there,
42   slapping at each new scorching cinder.

I began: 'Master, you who overcome all things—
all but the obstinate fiends who sallied forth
45   against us at the threshold of the gate,

'who is that hero who seems to scorn the fire
and lies there grim and scowling
48   so that the rain seems not to torture him?'

And he himself, who had discerned
that I had asked my guide about him,
51   cried: 'What I was alive, I am in death.

'Let Jove wear out his blacksmith
from whom in rage he seized the shining bolt
54   he struck me with on that my final day.

'And though he weary all the others, one by one,
at their black forge in Mongibello,
57   shouting "Help, good Vulcan, help!"

sì com' el fece a la pugna di Flegra,
e me saetti con tutta sua forza:
60   non ne potrebbe aver vendetta allegra."

Allora il duca mio parlò di forza
tanto, ch'i' non l'avea sì forte udito:
63   "O Capaneo, in ciò che non s'ammorza

la tua superbia, se' tu più punito;
nullo martiro, fuor che la tua rabbia,
66   sarebbe al tuo furor dolor compito."

Poi si rivolse a me con miglior labbia,
dicendo: "Quei fu l'un d'i sette regi
69   ch'assiser Tebe; ed ebbe e par ch'elli abbia

Dio in disdegno, e poco par che 'l pregi;
ma, com' io dissi lui, li suoi dispetti
72   sono al suo petto assai debiti fregi.

Or mi vien dietro, e guarda che non metti,
ancor, li piedi ne la rena arsiccia;
75   ma sempre al bosco tien li piedi stretti."

Tacendo divenimmo là 've spiccia
fuor de la selva un picciol fiumicello,
78   lo cui rossore ancor mi raccapriccia.

Quale del Bulicame esce ruscello
che parton poi tra lor le peccatrici,
81   tal per la rena giù sen giva quello.

Lo fondo suo e ambo le pendici
fatt' era 'n pietra, e ' margini da lato;
84   per ch'io m'accorsi che 'l passo era lici.

"Tra tutto l'altro ch'i' t'ho dimostrato,
poscia che noi intrammo per la porta
87   lo cui sogliare a nessuno è negato,

'as once he did on the battlefield of Phlegra,
and though he hurl his shafts at me with all his might,
60   he still would have no joy in his revenge.'

Then my leader spoke with a vehemence
I had not heard him use before: 'O, Capaneus,
63   because your pride remains unquenched

'you suffer greater punishment.
In your own anger lies your agony,
66   a fitting torment for your rage.'

Then, with a calmer look, he said to me:
'He was among the seven kings who once laid siege
69   to Thebes and held—and he still seems to hold—

'God in disdain and to esteem Him lightly.
But his own spiteful ranting, as I made clear,
72   most fittingly adorns his breast.

'Now come along behind me, and be sure
you do not set your feet upon the burning sand
75   but keep your steps close to the forest's edge.'

In silence we went on until we came
to where a little stream spurts from the wood.
78   The redness of it makes me shudder still.

As from the Bulicame flows out a rivulet
the sinful women then divide among them,
81   so this ran down across the sand.

Its bed and both its banks were made of stone,
as was the boundary on either side:
84   I saw our passage lay that way.

'In all else I have shown you
since we entered through the gate
87   whose threshold is denied to none,

cosa non fu da li tuoi occhi scorta
notabile com'è 'l presente rio,
90   che sovra sé tutte fiammelle ammorta."

Queste parole fuor del duca mio;
per ch'io 'l pregai che mi largisse 'l pasto
93   di cui largito m'avëa il disio.

"In mezzo mar siede un paese guasto,"
diss' elli allora, "che s'appella Creta,
96   sotto 'l cui rege fu già 'l mondo casto.

Una montagna v'è che già fu lieta
d'acqua e di fronde, che si chiamò Ida;
99   or è diserta come cosa vieta.

Rëa la scelse già per cuna fida
del suo figliuolo, e per celarlo meglio,
102   quando piangea, vi facea far le grida.

Dentro dal monte sta dritto un gran veglio,
che tien volte le spalle inver' Dammiata
105   e Roma guarda come süo speglio.

La sua testa è di fin oro formata,
e puro argento son le braccia e 'l petto,
108   poi è di rame infino a la forcata;

da indi in giuso è tutto ferro eletto,
salvo che 'l destro piede è terra cotta;
111   e sta 'n su quel, più che 'n su l'altro, eretto.

Ciascuna parte, fuor che l'oro, è rotta
d'una fessura che lagrime goccia,
114   le quali, accolte, fóran quella grotta.

Lor corso in questa valle si diroccia;
fanno Acheronte, Stige e Flegetonta;
117   poi sen van giù per questa stretta doccia,

'your eyes have yet seen nothing of such note
as is this stream before us:
90   its vapor quenches every flame above it.'

These were my leader's words. Hearing them,
I asked him to supply the food
93   for which he had provoked the appetite.

'In the middle of the sea there lies a land,'
he said, 'a wasteland known as Crete.
96   Under its king the world was innocent.

'A mountain rises there, once glad
with leaves and streams, called Ida.
99   Now it is barren like a thing outworn.

'Once Rhea chose it as the trusted cradle
for her child, and there, the better to conceal him
102   when he cried, she had her people raise an uproar.

'Within the mountain stands a huge old man.
He keeps his back turned on Damietta,
105   gazing on Rome as in his mirror.

'His head is fashioned of fine gold,
his breast and arms of purest silver,
108   then to the fork he's made of brass,

'and from there down he is all iron,
but for his right foot of baked clay,
111   and he rests more on this than on the other.

'Every part except the gold is rent
by a crack that drips with tears, which, running down,
114   collect to force a passage through that cavern,

'taking their course from rock to rock into this depth,
where they form Acheron, Styx, and Phlegethon,
117   then, going down this narrow channel,

infin, là ove più non si dismonta,
fanno Cocito; e qual sia quello stagno
120   tu lo vedrai, però qui non si conta."

E io a lui: "Se 'l presente rigagno
si diriva così dal nostro mondo,
123   perché ci appar pur a questo vivagno?"

Ed elli a me: "Tu sai che 'l loco è tondo;
e tutto che tu sie venuto molto,
126   pur a sinistra, giù calando al fondo,

non se' ancor per tutto 'l cerchio vòlto;
per che, se cosa n'apparisce nova,
129   non de' addur maraviglia al tuo volto."

E io ancor: "Maestro, ove si trova
Flegetonta e Letè? ché de l'un taci,
132   e l'altro di' che si fa d'esta piova."

"In tutte tue question certo mi piaci,"
rispuose, "ma 'l bollor de l'acqua rossa
135   dovea ben solver l'una che tu faci.

Letè vedrai, ma fuor di questa fossa,
là dove vanno l'anime a lavarsi
138   quando la colpa pentuta è rimossa."

Poi disse: "Omai è tempo da scostarsi
dal bosco; fa che di retro a me vegne:
li margini fan via, che non son arsi,
142   e sopra loro ogne vapor si spegne."

'down to where there is no more descent,
they form Cocytus: what kind of pond that is
120   you shall see in time—here I say no more.'

Then I asked: 'If that stream flows
down from our world, why do we see it
123   only at this boundary?'

And he answered: 'You know this place is round,
and though you have come far,
126   descending toward the bottom on the left,

'you have not come full circle.
Should some new thing confront us,
129   it need not bring such wonder to your face.'

And I again: 'Master, where are Phlegethon and Lethe?
About the one you're silent, and you say the other
132   is made into a river by this rain.'

'In all your questions you do please me,'
he replied, 'but the red and seething water
135   might well have answered one of those you ask.

'Lethe you shall see: not in this abyss
but where the spirits go to cleanse themselves
138   once their repented guilt has been removed.'

And then: 'Now it is time to leave this forest.
See you stay close behind me.
The borders, which are not on fire, form a path
142   and over both of them all flames are quenched.'

1–3.   The first tercet concludes the action of the preceding canto. This is a particularly egregious example of the way in which Dante deliberately avoids keeping his canto borders "neat" (see note to *Inf.* XIII.1–3).

4–6.   These verses, on the other hand, would have made a "proper" beginning to the fourteenth canto, marking, as they do, the border between the second ring of the seventh Circle (violence against selves) and the third (violence against God). Here we shall witness (as indeed we have done before) the dreadful "art" of God in carrying out His just revenge upon sinners, in this case those who sinned directly against Him.

7–13.   The hellscape, featuring impoverished "vegetation" in the last canto, now is as barren as it can possibly be: nothing can take root in this sand. The retrospective glance reminds us of where we have been in this Circle: Phlegethon, circling the wood, the wood in turn circling the sand (violence against others, against selves, and now against God).

The translation of verse 7, which uses the adjective *nove* either to mean "new" or "strange," or perhaps both at once, attempts to represent this ambiguity.

14–15.   That Dante should refer here to Cato the Younger, who committed suicide at Utica (when further opposition by the republican forces led by him against Julius Caesar's army seemed futile), seems to invite a negative judgment on him. Cato, however, will be presented in *Purgatorio* I and II, in an authorial decision that still baffles commentators, as one of the saved. To refer to him here, a few verses from the wood of the suicides— where Christian readers would normally assume that Cato might be punished—given Dante's plan eventually to reveal his salvation, was a chancy choice for him to have made.

The poet is translating a line from Lucan's *Pharsalia* describing Cato's heroic decision to lead the remnant of dead Pompey's republican forces across the barren sands of Libya in an attempt to escape from Caesar, and to do so, not carried by slaves, as Roman generals were wont to be transported, but on foot himself: "primusque gradus in pulvere ponam" (and I, first among them, shall set my feet upon the sand [*Phars.* IX.395—the citation was perhaps first noted by Daniello in 1568]). (For a treatment of Cato in the context of Canto XIV see Mazzotta [Mazz.1979.1], pp. 47–65.)

Dante thus reads Cato's suicide as something other, an act resembling Christ's sacrifice of Himself so that others may be free (for discussion see Hollander [Holl. 1969.1], pp. 123–31). Such a view may seem blasphemous; it has caused extraordinary exertion on the part of commentators to "allegorize" the saved Cato we find in *Purgatorio* by turning him into an abstract quality rather than treating him as historical. Dante's text will not permit us such luxury of avoidance. His Cato, a Christian through a process that hardly anyone has understood, is saved.

19–27.   This passage is opaque to a first-time reader. Only in retrospect are we able with precision to realize which sinners are alluded to by which postures: those lying supine, the fewest in number, are the blasphemers (and they, because they cursed God, now cry out the loudest); the most numerous class of sinners, moving about incessantly, are the homosexuals, who sinned against nature (Canto XV); the sinners hunched up are the usurers, who sinned againt God's "grandchild," art, or industry (Canto XVI).

28.   The flakes of fire showering down on all those who were violent against God seem most directly derived from the brimstone and fire rained down upon the inhabitants of Sodom and Gomorrah for their allowance of the practice of homosexuality (Genesis 19:24), as was perhaps first observed by Vellutello in his commentary (1544) to this passage.

30.   A clear reference to a line in a sonnet by Guido Cavalcanti, "Biltà di donna" ("A lady's loveliness"), in which, describing things beautiful to behold, he refers to "white snow falling on a windless day" *(e bianca neve scender senza venti)*.

31–36.   The reference is to an incident related in a letter (falsely) attributed to Alexander the Great, writing to his tutor, Aristotle, from his campaign in India. Dante found the text in the *De Meteoris* (I.iv.8) of Albertus Magnus, a work to which he adverts fairly frequently (see, e.g., note to *Inf.* XII.4–10).

40.   Benvenuto da Imola's commentary explains that the "tresca" is a Neapolitan dance in which a leader touches one part of his or her body with a hand, a gesture imitated by all the other dancers; then, rapidly, the leader touches another part, then another, sometimes using one, sometimes two, hands, each gesture, acclerated in time, being similarly imitated by the rest.

43–45.   Dante's preface to his question about the identity of the note-worthy personage before them might be compared to the unnecessarily flippant question posed by a student to a teacher who had been caught out in an earlier mistake. There seems to be no other reason for Dante to remind Virgil of his failure to enter the walls of Dis (*Inf.* VIII.115–117).

46–48.   Like Farinata, Capaneus (we learn his name from Virgil at v. 63) is a figure of some greatness (see *Inf.* X.73, where Farinata is *magnanimo* [great of soul]—and see Statius, *Thebaid* XI.1, where Capaneus is referred to as *magnanimus*); like Farinata, he seems not to be bothered by the pains of hell (*Inf.* X.36).

    The last verb in the tercet is a matter of debate. As always, in our translation we follow Petrocchi, even when we disagree with him. His reading is *marturi*, or "torture"; others prefer the traditional reading, *maturi*, "ripen" or "soften," a view with which we concur.

49–50.   Capaneus, though undergoing the pain inflicted by the burning flakes, is alert enough to overhear the two strangers discussing him. Surely his stoic reserve creates an initial positive impression on the reader.

51–60.   Capaneus was one of the seven kings who besieged Thebes in aid of Polynices, the son of Oedipus whose twin brother, Eteocles, refused to allow him his turn at ruling. The narrative of the death of Capaneus on the walls of Thebes and his boast against Jupiter are drawn from Statius, *Thebaid* X.883–939.

    As Capaneus's oratorical flourish begins, the listener tends to admire the courage of his speech. As it continues, it more and more resembles vainglorious boasting. Capaneus may play the role of a stock character in Roman comedy, the *miles gloriosus*, or braggart soldier. When we study his words we find some disquieting elements in them: alive he was a defamer of the gods, as he is now; he says that Jupiter will not have his revenge against him even if he sends Vulcan in his forge in Mount Etna into mass production of lightning bolts (as was necessary to quell the insurrection of the giants at the battle of Phlegra [see the further reference at *Inf.* XXXI.95]). We may reflect that, in the first place, Jupiter (or indeed the true God he would have blasphemed had he known Him) already *has* his vengeance (one look at supine Capaneus confirms this); in the second, when Jupiter took his revenge at Thebes, it took him but a single bolt to dispatch Capaneus (and Statius says that he was lucky not to live long enough for the second). In short, Capaneus, in his egregious overconfidence, makes something of a fool of himself (and see *Inf.* XXV.15 for confirmation of his prideful opposition to God).

61–66.   The vehemence of Virgil's outburst against Capaneus, underlined as being his most heated condemnation of a sinner yet (and no other will exceed it), is difficult to explain. A student, Edward Sherline (Princeton '82), some years ago suggested that Virgil, already angered by Dante's wry reminder of his previous insufficiency before the walls of Dis (vv. 43–45), is now having *his* revenge on Capaneus, a revenge especially pleasing when Virgil considered what Capaneus was quite effective doing and what he himself had utterly failed to do: besting the defenders of the walls of a hostile city (mere victory of that kind was not enough for Capaneus, who challenged Jupiter himself to combat).

69–70.   Some readers have objected that blasphemy against Jupiter should be welcomed in a Christian dispensation, not punished. Dante's point is clearly that Capaneus meant to oppose the very principle of divine power, no matter what its name.

76–84.   The little stream that the travelers now see is the second (and last) body of water that moves across their usual circular path and downward (see *Inf.* VII.100–108, where the descent from the fourth to the fifth Circle is made alongside a little stream that seems to connect Acheron to Styx). All other gatherings of water have been circles that they had eventually to cross in order to descend. We will soon be able to understand (vv. 115–117) that this particular stream contains waters from Phlegethon that will eventually fall into the frozen Cocytus (heard tumbling down to the eighth Circle at XVI.1–2). Dante and Virgil apparently do not happen to see the stream that connects Styx to Phlegethon because, as Virgil suggests (vv. 128–129), their path does not describe a full circle in every zone (e.g., their passage along Phlegethon, which covers exactly a semicircle, in *Inf.* XII).

The Bulicame is a hot spring near Viterbo from which prostitutes, perhaps not allowed to frequent the public baths, made conduits from the source to service their own dwellings.

The passage to the next and deeper zone of the burning sand now lies right before them (it is a necessary expedient, we want to remember, to get Dante across the burning sand); before they can follow it, Virgil will take up the subject of the waters of hell.

94–111. Virgil, in his presentation of the rivers of hell, pauses first to cre-
ate an etiological myth that explains their source. It has two parts, a history
of Crete and a description of the statue of an old man that stands inside
Mount Ida.

94–102. Virgil's first words rely on the passage in the *Aeneid* (III.104–106)
describing Crete, similarly located "in the middle of the sea" *(medio . . .
ponto)*. It was once "chaste" when it enjoyed a "golden age" under Saturn
(see Iann.1992.2, for Dante's almost entirely positive treatment of Saturn).
But now its mountain, Ida, the site of a sort of classical "Eden," rich in
water and vegetation, is a wasteland; like Eden, it, too, is deserted. Rhea,
Saturn's wife, chose it as the cradle for her son, Jupiter. But now "original
sin" seems to have crept into the Golden Age: the crying child needs to be
protected (in the original myth, of course, from Saturn himself, who had
the unpleasant habit of eating his children so as to be sure not to be
dethroned by one of them).

   That is all we are told. On Crete there was once a Golden Age, but
something went awry. Many commentators refer to the parallel with the
similar narrative found in Ovid (*Metam.* I.89–150), the descent from an age
of gold, to one of silver, to one of bronze, and finally to one of iron, when
Astraea, justice, is the last of the gods to leave the earth. (See note to *Inf.*
XXXIV.121–126.)

103–111. Dante's second myth is more of his own devising. While the
statue of the old man is closely modeled on that found in Nebuchadnezzar's
dream (Daniel 2: 31–35), the poet's enclosure of the statue in Ida seems to
be essentially his own invention. But there are "hydraulic" reasons for
putting him and his tears (these are not found in Daniel) there: Dante
needs to account for the origin of the rivers of hell. The *gran veglio*, within
the mountain, turns his back on Egypt (Damietta, a city in the Nile delta)
and gazes on Rome as though it were his mirror. Interpretations of this
detail vary, but it would seem that the movement of temporal rule from
the East to Rome would account for this representative of the original
political order looking toward its new home. What does he see there?
Probably, in Dante's view, his mirror image, since the empire is totally inef-
fective. He is putting more weight upon his right foot, formed of baked
clay, which most of the early commentators thought represented the cor-
rupt Church; yet an argument can be made that, since the *veglio* is a figura-
tion of pagan man, the Church would be inappropriately a part of his
"physique." In Nebuchadnezzar's dream a rock destroys the feet of the

statue; for Christian exegetes this rock represents Christ, destroying the Old Man and making the new life possible for mankind.

112–114.   The waters that collect from all the non-golden and riven parts of the statue gather somewhere beneath it under Mount Ida and force their way into the underworld. For the root of the image of the rivers of hell as tears from the *veglio*'s eyes in the redeeming blood of Christ on the Cross, flowing into Limbo to redeem Adam, see Silverstein (Silv.1931.1) and Cassell (Cass.1984.1), pp. 58–60. The Old Man is, in this reading, the parodic anticipation of the New Man, the Son of God.

115–129.   And now Virgil can get to his putative main point, the disposition of the rivers of hell. Dante's question in response seems to reveal that he has forgotten what he has seen at the border of Avarice and Wrath (*Inf.* VII.100–108). See note to vv. 76–84, above. On the other hand, Virgil does not make that plain to him. As a result, whether that stream is supposed to be from the same source as this one—the most attractive hypothesis— becomes, at best, moot.

130–138.   Dante's two questions are meant as an aid to the reader, who may not have realized that the river of blood and what has just now been called "Phlegethon" for the first time (at v. 116) are one and the same. As for Lethe, since it is thought of as being a major fluvial appurtenance of the afterworld, the poet wants to reassure his reader that it has not been forgotten in the watery arrangement of hell but awaits discovery in purgatory.

139–142.   The coda ties the action back to where it stopped, at v. 84. The next canto, in fact, will pick up precisely from there (and not here), as though it were the last verse of the canto. For a similar phenomenon earlier on, see note to *Inferno* VIII.1.

INFERNO XV

Ora cen porta l'un de' duri margini;
e 'l fummo del ruscel di sopra aduggia,
3   sì che dal foco salva l'acqua e li argini.

Quali Fiamminghi tra Guizzante e Bruggia,
temendo 'l fiotto che 'nver' lor s'avventa;
6   fanno lo schermo perché 'l mar si fuggia;

e quali Padoan lungo la Brenta,
per difender lor ville e lor castelli,
9   anzi che Carentana il caldo senta:

a tale imagine eran fatti quelli,
tutto che né sì alti né sì grossi,
12   qual che si fosse, lo maestro félli.

Già eravam da la selva rimossi
tanto, ch'i' non avrei visto dov' era,
15   perch' io in dietro rivolto mi fossi,

quando incontrammo d'anime una schiera
che venian lungo l'argine, e ciascuna
18   ci riguardava come suol da sera

guardare uno altro sotto nuova luna;
e sì ver' noi aguzzavan le ciglia
21   come 'l vecchio sartor fa ne la cruna.

Così adocchiato da cotal famiglia,
fui conosciuto da un, che mi prese
24   per lo lembo e gridò: "Qual maraviglia!"

E io, quando 'l suo braccio a me distese,
ficcaï li occhi per lo cotto aspetto,
27   sì che 'l viso abbrusciato non difese

Now one of the stony borders bears us on
and vapor from the stream arose as mist
3   protecting banks and water from the flames.

As the Flemings between Wissant and Bruges,
fearing the tide that rushes in upon them,
6   erect a bulwark to repel the sea,

and as the Paduans build dikes along the Brenta,
to protect their towns and castles
9   before the heat brings floods to Carentana—

in just that way these banks were formed,
except the architect, whoever he was,
12   had made them not as lofty nor as thick.

By now we were so distant from the wood
that I could not have made it out,
15   even had I turned in its direction.

Here we met a troop of souls
coming up along the bank, and each
18   gazed at us as men at dusk will sometimes do,

eyeing one another under the new moon.
They peered at us with knitted brows
21   like an old tailor at his needle's eye.

Thus scrutinized by such a company,
I was known to one of them who caught me
24   by the hem and then cried out, 'What a wonder!'

And while he held his arm outstretched to me,
I fixed my eyes on his scorched face
27   until beneath the charred disfigurement

la conoscenza süa al mio 'ntelletto;
e chinando la mano a la sua faccia,
30   rispuosi: "Siete voi qui, ser Brunetto?"

E quelli: "O figliuol mio, non ti dispiaccia
se Brunetto Latino un poco teco
33   ritorna 'n dietro e lascia andar la traccia."

I' dissi lui: "Quanto posso, ven preco;
e se volete che con voi m'asseggia,
36   faròl, se piace a costui che vo seco."

"O figliuol," disse, "qual di questa greggia
s'arresta punto, giace poi cent' anni
39   sanz' arrostarsi quando 'l foco il feggia.

Però va oltre: i' ti verrò a' panni;
e poi rigiugnerò la mia masnada,
42   che va piangendo i suoi etterni danni."

Io non osava scender de la strada
per andar par di lui; ma 'l capo chino
45   tenea com' uom che reverente vada.

El cominciò: "Qual fortuna o destino
anzi l'ultimo dì qua giù ti mena?
48   e chi è questi che mostra 'l cammino?"

"Là sù di sopra, in la vita serena,"
rispuos' io lui, "mi smarri' in una valle,
51   avanti che l'età mia fosse piena.

Pur ier mattina le volsi le spalle:
questi m'apparve, tornand'ïo in quella,
54   e reducemi a ca per questo calle."

Ed elli a me: "Se tu segui tua stella,
non puoi fallire a glorïoso porto,
57   se ben m'accorsi ne la vita bella;

I could discern the features that I knew
and, lowering my hand toward his face,
30   asked: 'Are You here, Ser Brunetto?'

And he: 'O my son, let it not displease you
if Brunetto Latini for a while turns back
33   with you and lets the troop go on.'

I said to him: 'With all my heart, I pray You,
and if You would have me sit with You, I will,
36   if he who leads me through allows.'

'O son,' he said, 'whoever of this flock stops
even for an instant has to lie a hundred years,
39   unable to fend off the fire when it strikes.

'Therefore, go on. I shall follow at your hem
and later will rejoin my band,
42   who go lamenting their eternal pain.'

I did not dare to leave the higher path
to walk the lower with him, but I kept
45   my head bowed, like one who walks in reverence.

He began: 'What chance or fate is it
that brings you here before your final hour,
48   and who is this that shows the way?'

'In the sunlit life above,' I answered,
'in a valley there, I lost my way
51   before I reached the zenith of my days.

'Only yesterday morning did I leave it,
but had turned back when he appeared,
54   and now along this road he leads me home.'

And he to me: 'By following your star
you cannot fail to reach a glorious port,
57   if I saw clearly in the happy life.

e s'io non fossi sì per tempo morto,
veggendo il cielo a te così benigno,
60 dato t'avrei a l'opera conforto.

Ma quello ingrato popolo maligno
che discese di Fiesole *ab antico*,
63 e tiene ancor del monte e del macigno,

ti si farà, per tuo ben far, nimico;
ed è ragion, ché tra li lazzi sorbi
66 si disconvien fruttare al dolce fico.

Vecchia fama nel mondo li chiama orbi;
gent'è avara, invidiosa e superba:
69 dai lor costumi fa che tu ti forbi.

La tua fortuna tanto onor ti serba,
che l'una parte e l'altra avranno fame
72 di te; ma lungi fia dal becco l'erba.

Faccian le bestie fiesolane strame
di lor medesme, e non tocchin la pianta,
75 s'alcuna surge ancora in lor letame,

in cui riviva la sementa santa
di que' Roman che vi rimaser quando
78 fu fatto il nido di malizia tanta."

"Se fosse tutto pieno il mio dimando,"
rispuos' io lui, "voi non sareste ancora
81 de l'umana natura posto in bando;

ché 'n la mente m'è fitta, e or m'accora,
la cara e buona imagine paterna
84 di voi quando nel mondo ad ora ad ora

m'insegnavate come l'uom s'etterna:
e quant' io l'abbia in grado, mentr' io vivo
87 convien che ne la mia lingua si scerna.

'Had I not died too soon,
seeing that Heaven so favors you,
60   I would have lent you comfort in your work.

'But that malignant, thankless rabble
that came down from Fiesole long ago
63   and still smacks of the mountain and the rock

'rightly shall become, because of your good deeds,
your enemy: among the bitter sorbs
66   it is not fit the sweet fig come to fruit.

'The world has long believed them to be blind,
a people greedy, envious and proud.
69   Be sure you stay untainted by their habits.

'Your destiny reserves for you such honor
both parties shall be hungry to devour you,
72   but the grass shall be far from the goat.

'Let the Fiesolan beasts make forage
of themselves but spare the plant,
75   if on their dung-heap any still springs up,

'the plant in which lives on the holy seed
of those few Romans who remained
78   when it became the home of so much malice.'

'If all my prayers were answered,'
I said to him, 'You would not yet
81   be banished from mankind.

'For I remember well and now lament
the cherished, kind, paternal image of You
84   when, there in the world, from time to time,

'You taught me how man makes himself immortal.
And how much gratitude I owe for that
87   my tongue, while I still live, must give report.

Ciò che narrate di mio corso scrivo,
e serbolo a chiosar con altro testo
90   a donna che saprà, s'a lei arrivo.

Tanto vogl' io che vi sia manifesto,
pur che mia coscïenza non mi garra,
93   ch'a la Fortuna, come vuol, son presto.

Non è nuova a li orecchi miei tal arra:
però giri Fortuna la sua rota
96   come le piace, e 'l villan la sua marra."

Lo mio maestro allora in su la gota
destra si volse in dietro e riguardommi;
99   poi disse: "Bene ascolta chi la nota."

Né per tanto di men parlando vommi
con ser Brunetto, e dimando chi sono
102   li suoi compagni più noti e più sommi.

Ed elli a me: "Saper d'alcuno è buono;
de li altri fia laudabile tacerci,
105   ché 'l tempo saria corto a tanto suono.

In somma sappi che tutti fur cherci
e litterati grandi e di gran fama,
108   d'un peccato medesmo al mondo lerci.

Priscian sen va con quella turba grama,
e Francesco d'Accorso anche; e vedervi,
111   s'avessi avuto di tal tigna brama,

colui potei che dal servo de' servi
fu trasmutato d'Arno in Bacchiglione,
114   dove lasciò li mal protesi nervi.

Di più direi; ma 'l venire e 'l sermone
più lungo esser non può, però ch'i' veggio
117   là surger nuovo fummo del sabbione.

'What You tell of my future I record
and keep for glossing, along with other texts,
90   by a lady of discernment, should I reach her.

'This much I would have You know:
as long as conscience does not chide,
93   I am prepared for Fortune as she wills.

'Such prophecy is not unknown to me.
Let Fortune spin her wheel just as she pleases,
96   and let the loutish peasant ply his hoe.'

At that I saw the right side of my master's face
turned back in my direction. And he said:
99   'He listens well who takes in what he hears.'

Nonetheless, I go on speaking
with ser Brunetto, asking who, of his companions,
102   are most eminent, most worthy to be known.

And he: "Some of them it is good to know.
Others it is better not to mention,
105   for the time would be too short for so much talk.

'In sum, note that all of them were clerics
or great and famous scholars, befouled
108   in the world above by a single sin.

'Priscian goes with that wretched crowd,
and Francesco d'Accorso too. And, had you had
111   a hankering for such filth, you might have seen

the one transferred by the Servant of Servants
from the Arno to the Bacchiglione,
114   where he left his sin-stretched sinews.

'I would say more, but I cannot stay,
cannot continue talking, for over there I see
117   new smoke rising from the sand.

Gente vien con la quale esser non deggio.
Sieti raccomandato il mio Tesoro,
120   nel qual io vivo ancora, e più non cheggio."

Poi si rivolse e parve di coloro
che corrono a Verona il drappo verde
per la campagna; e parve di costoro
124   quelli che vince, non colui che perde.

'People are coming with whom I must not be.
Let my *Treasure*, in which I still live on,
120   be in your mind—I ask for nothing more.'

After he turned back he seemed like one
who races for the green cloth on the plain
beyond Verona. And he looked more the winner
124   than the one who trails the field.

1–3. Both the words *margini* (borders) and *ruscello* (stream) appear in the passage at which the forward motion of the journey was arrested in the previous canto (XIV.79–84). The action, interrupted by Virgil's discourse about Crete and the *gran veglio*, now continues. The poets walk along one of the two "banks" that rise above the barren plain of sand and border the red stream as it heads for the lower regions. Thus we know that all their movement until they reach the edge of the next boundary (XVI.103) is on a downward gradient, headed toward the center of the pit. This revision in their usual procedure (a leftward, circling movement) is necessitated by the topography of the ring of violence against God, the sand where flakes of fire fall and which admits no mortal traversal.

4–12. The double simile compares the construction made by God to carry the "water" of hell toward its final destination to the huge earthworks engineered in Flanders and in northern Italy to protect farmland and human habitations from flood. "Carentana" probably refers (the exact reference is debated in the commentaries) to the mountains north of Padua from which in spring the snows release their torrents.

13–21. Another double comparison. As the poets move away from the wood of the suicides and down across the sand along their dyke, they approach a group of the damned. Its members examine them as men look at one another under a new moon and as an aging tailor concentrates upon threading his needle. The first comparison may suggest the image of homosexual "cruising" in the darkest of moonlit nights (it is difficult for modern readers to imagine how dark the nighttime streets of medieval cities were); the second conveys the intensity of such gazing. For this way of reading many of the words and images of the canto see Pequigney (Pequ.1991.1). And see the endnote after Canto XVI.

23–24. The sinner, standing below Dante, must reach up to touch the hem of his garment. His words of recognition capture the tone of an elderly teacher recognizing his former star pupil and, some would argue, of his effeminacy.

28–30. Dante recognizes his old "teacher," Brunetto Latini (ca. 1220–94). He probably taught Dante by the example of his works rather than in any classroom, but the entire scene is staged as a reunion between teacher and former student.

Brunetto, whose life has a number of similarities to Dante's, was a Florentine Guelph, a man of letters who was much involved in politics, and, not least in importance, he wrote narrative verse in the vernacular; he was also a notary, which accounts for his title, *ser*. He became a *de facto* exile when he learned about the battle of Montaperti (1260) and the triumph of the Ghibellines while he was in France. He stayed there for six years and, in exile, wrote both his French encyclopedic treatise, the *Livre dou Tresor*, or *Treasure*, and his narrative poem in rhymed couplets, referred to as the *Tesoretto (Little Treasure)*, at that point, even though incomplete, the longest narrative poem composed in Italian. Returning to Florence after the "restoration" of 1266 in the wake of the battle of Benevento, he took up his political and notarial chores, and died in the city, much honored, in 1294. (For a careful presentation of the importance of Brunetto for Dante, see Francesco Mazzoni, "Latini, Brunetto," *ED*, vol. 3, 1971, pp. 579–88. See also Mazzoni's essential study of Dante's borrowings from Brunetto [Mazz.1967.3]; and Charles Davis's article [Davi.1967.1].)

The poet's honorific feelings toward Brunetto are perhaps mirrored in the word his name rhymes with: "intelletto." And his answering gesture, to move his face down toward his "teacher," certainly does so as well. (The Petrocchi text here offers what is surely an implausible reading: "la *mano* alla sua faccia" (which we have translated as it stands). It seems nearly certain that the text should read, as it does in many manuscripts, "la *mia* alla sua faccia," i.e., Dante bent his face toward Brunetto's in an act of homage. This better reading is confirmed by the later verse (v. 44) that has Dante walking with his head still bent down in reverence (see note to v. 50).

48.　A number of commentaries on this passage cite *Aeneid* VI.531–534, Deiphobus's similar questions to Aeneas.

It is striking that Brunetto never discovers the identity of Dante's leader (nor did Cavalcante in *Inf.* X). Like Cavalcante's son Guido's, Brunetto's body of work is notably unmarked by Virgil's influence. The omission, in other words, may be entirely intentional.

50.　Dante's reflection upon his own lostness at the outset (*Inf.* I.3, I.14) picks up, as a few commentators have sensed (Pietrobono perhaps the first), a similar passage in Brunetto's *Tesoretto*, vv. 186–90:

e io, in tal corrotto
pensando a capo chino,
perdei il gran cammino,
e tenni a la traversa
d'una selva diversa.

(And I, in such great vexation, my head bowed down, lost the main road and came upon a path that crossed a strange wood.)

The phrase *a capo chino* (my head bowed down) has perhaps been borrowed to describe Dante's reverence before Brunetto (v. 44—see note to vv. 28–30).

54.   Dante had criticized Brunetto's (along with other Tuscan poets') Italian poetry for its low dialectism in *De vulgari eloquentia* (I.xiii.1); now he himself uses a Tuscan dialectical form (*ca,* for *casa,* "house" or "home") as though in apology; and he uses it to express the high and ultimate purpose of his journey, his return to the God who made him. It is a moment of stunning force.

55.   Dante's "star" is probably his natal sign, Gemini. Brunetto here and elsewhere sees Dante's special status as related to the influence of the heavens rather than to the election of Heaven.

58–60.   Brunetto's desire to aid Dante in his current and future plight, given the context of the discussion that follows, would seem rather to refer to his political life than to his literary one, though it is difficult to separate the two.

61–78.   Brunetto, like Farinata (*Inf.* X.79–81), prophesies Dante's exile. His sense of the history of Florence (perhaps reflecting his own treatment of this subject in the first book of his *Tresor*) puts forward the legend that Florence was populated by the Romans after they destroyed neighboring Fiesole in order to put an end to Catiline's conspiracy. Unfortunately, their descendants, the Florentine nobility, allowed the surviving Fiesolans to emigrate and mix their base population with the Roman stock. For Dante, all the city's (and his own) troubles stem from this original mistake.

83–85.   Dante pays his debt to Brunetto. But what was it that Brunetto (or, more likely, his writings) taught Dante about immortality? Brunetto himself (*Tresor* II.cxx.1) says that fame for good works gives one a second life on earth. Surely that is not enough for the Christian Dante, who knows the true meaning of immortality. The only *seconde vie* that matters is in the afterlife. Is Dante saying that Brunetto taught him this? That seems impossible. But he did learn from him how his earthly fame might be established by writing a narrative poem in Italian. And his heavenly reward might be combined with that one if his poem were, unlike Brunetto's work, dedicated to a higher purpose. Perhaps one of the earliest commentators said this best: Brunetto gave Dante "the knowledge that does not allow him to die either in his essential being in the other world, nor with respect to fame in this one" (Jacopo della Lana). For the work of Brunetto that had such effect on Dante see the note to v. 119.

88–90.   The protagonist, responding to Brunetto's warning that his good deeds will not go unpunished (vv. 61–64), adverts to Farinata's similar prophecy and Virgil's promise of Beatrice's eventual explanation of it. See note to *Inf.* X.130–132.

91–94.   Dante claims that he is ready for Fortune's adversity. See the similar but stronger utterance at *Paradiso* XVII.22–24.

95–96.   For a reading of the "peasant" that is based in the representation of Saturn as an old and tired farmer, carrying a spade or mattock, and thus keyed to the allegorical understanding of Saturn as time, see Iannucci (Iann.1982.1). The phrase would then mean: "let Fortune turn her wheel as she pleases and let time continue its relentless course" (p. 6).

99.   This is Virgil's only utterance in the canto. (Walking ahead of Dante, accompanied by Brunetto, who is moving close to the bank, along the sand, Virgil is not "in the frame" for most of the scene.) How we should read the remark is no longer as clear as it once seemed. Is it congratulatory or monitory? All the early commentators who deal with it think it is the latter, i.e., Dante has just uttered a truthful wish (vv. 91–96), but one difficult to live up to. And that seems the most likely reading.

106–114.   Brunetto indicates that all his companions were men of letters, identifying Priscian (the great Latin grammarian of the early sixth century); Francesco d'Accorso (1225–93), a renowned jurist of Bologna; and Andrea de' Mozzi (died 1296). A Florentine, he was made bishop of Florence (on the Arno) in 1287 until he was transferred to Vicenza (on the

Bacchiglione) by Pope Boniface VIII (here ironically referred to with the papal formula "servant of servants") in 1295 for his riotous habits. None of these (neither is Brunetto) is recorded by other writers as having been homosexual. The last verse, indicating Andrea's "sin-stretched sinews" would, however, seem to indicate his sexual activity (and the meaning of this line is thus hotly contested by those who deny that homosexuality is punished in this ring—see the endnote to the next canto).

118.   What is the division that separates these two groups of homosexuals? We should note that Brunetto, accompanying Dante, has gone lower down the sloping sand than he generally does; his group apparently remains higher up. The only clue given us by the text is that his fellows are all men of letters, while the next group will be made up of politicians (but then Brunetto must be considered, at least to some degree, a "politician" himself). Is that what keeps them separate? It does not seem likely. It would rather seem that the two groups are kept separate by their particular form of sexual deviance, as Boccaccio appears to suggest.

119.   It has long been assumed that Brunetto asks Dante's affectionate remembrance of his *Tresor*. In the opinion of some, however, it is far better to understand that the work in question is the *Tesoretto*. To suggest as much is not to deny the importance of the French encyclopedic treatise for Dante, who knew it well and whose memory is suffused by it. However, given his predilection for poetry, it seems likely that for him the pivotal work was the *Tesoretto* because it was his first Italian model for the *Comedy*. It is fairly clear why nearly all the commentators think that Dante is referring to the *Tresor*: It is a major work, at least by comparison to the unfinished *Tesoretto*, and people do not especially appeciate the poetry of Brunetto (perhaps with good reason). But why would Dante not be giving credit to the work which made a difference to *him* as poet? That seems a sensible view of the matter. However, it was only in the eighteenth century that a commentator (Lombardi) would suggest this possibility, and only in the nineteenth that one would seize upon it (Gregorio Di Siena). An as yet unpublished book on Dante and Brunetto by Frank Ordiway extends the evidence offered by Mazzoni (Mazz.1967.3) of Dante's considerable citation of the *Tesoretto* into a strong argument for the reference to the Italian work in this line. For bibliography of those who have argued for the *Tesoretto* see Holl.1992.2, n. 82.

   The text of the *Tesoretto* itself offers evidence that it is the work we should think of here:

Io, Burnetto Latino,
che vostro in ogni guisa
mi son sanza divisa,
a voi mi *racomando*.
Poi vi presento e mando
questo ricco *Tesoro*,
che vale argento ed oro: . . .
(vv. 70–76; italics added)

(I, Brunetto Latini, who am yours in every way,
without any reservation commend myself to you.
Then I present and send to you this rich
Treasure, which is worth silver and gold.)

Within the text of what *we* call the *Tesoretto* we find that its own title for itself is *Tesoro* (and this will occur twice more in the work). And we can hear, in Dante's verse 119, another echo of the Italian work, the verb *raccomandare*. It seems difficult to go on believing that the *Tresor* is on our poet's mind at this crucial juncture of his presentation of his literary "father," his final words in Dante's poem.

121–124. The canto concludes with a simile that perfectly expresses Dante's ambivalent feelings about Brunetto. He looks every bit the winner—but he is in last place. In the actual race run outside Verona, the runners ran naked, according to the early commentators; the winner received a piece of green cloth, while the one who finished last was given a rooster, which he had to carry back into the city with him as a sign of his disgrace and a cause of derisive taunts on the part of his townsmen. The case can be made that Dante treats Brunetto in exactly both these ways.

Two biblical texts are of interest here: "The race is not to the swift, nor the battle to the strong" (Eccles. 9:11); "Know ye not that they which run in a race run all, but one receives the prize?" (I Cor. 9:24).

INFERNO XVI

Già era in loco onde s'udia 'l rimbombo
de l'acqua che cadea ne l'altro giro,
3   simile a quel che l'arnie fanno rombo,

quando tre ombre insieme si partiro,
correndo, d'una torma che passava
6   sotto la pioggia de l'aspro martiro.

Venian ver' noi, e ciascuna gridava:
"Sòstati tu ch'a l'abito ne sembri
9   essere alcun di nostra terra prava."

Ahimè, che piaghe vidi ne' lor membri,
ricenti e vecchie, da le fiamme incese!
12   Ancor men duol pur ch'i' me ne rimembri.

A le lor grida il mio dottor s'attese;
volse 'l viso ver' me, e "Or aspetta,"
15   disse, "a costor si vuole esser cortese.

E se non fosse il foco che saetta
la natura del loco, i' dicerei
18   che meglio stesse a te che a lor la fretta."

Ricominciar, come noi restammo, ei
l'antico verso; e quando a noi fuor giunti,
21   fenno una rota di sé tutti e trei.

Qual sogliono i campion far nudi e unti,
avvisando lor presa e lor vantaggio,
24   prima che sien tra lor battuti e punti,

così rotando, ciascuno il visaggio
drizzava a me, sì che 'n contraro il collo
27   faceva ai piè continüo vïaggio.

I had arrived where we could hear the distant roar
of water falling to the lower circle,
3   like the rumbling hum of bees around a hive,

when three shades at a run
broke from a passing crowd
6   under that rain of bitter torment.

Together they came toward us, each calling:
'Stop, you, who by your garb appear to be
9   a man from our degenerate city.'

Oh, what sores I noticed on their limbs,
both old and new ones, branded by the flames!
12   It pains me still, when I remember them.

My teacher was attentive to their cries,
then turned his face to me and said:
15   'Now wait: to these one must show courtesy.

'And were it not for the fire that the nature
of this place draws down, I would say
18   haste befits you more than it does them.'

When we stopped, they took up again
their old refrain, but once they reached us
21   all three had joined into a single wheel.

As combatants, oiled and naked, are wont to do,
watching for their hold and their advantage,
24   before the exchange of thrusts and blows,

wheeling, each fixed his eyes on me,
so that their feet moved forward
27   while their necks were straining back.

E "Se miseria d'esto loco sollo
rende in dispetto noi e nostri prieghi,"
30   cominciò l'uno, "e 'l tinto aspetto e brollo,

la fama nostra il tuo animo pieghi
a dirne chi tu se', che i vivi piedi
33   così sicuro per lo 'nferno freghi.

Questi, l'orme di cui pestar mi vedi,
tutto che nudo e dipelato vada,
36   fu di grado maggior che tu non credi:

nepote fu de la buona Gualdrada;
Guido Guerra ebbe nome, e in sua vita
39   fece col senno assai e con la spada.

L'altro, ch'appresso me la rena trita,
è Tegghiaio Aldobrandi, la cui voce
42   nel mondo sù dovria esser gradita.

E io, che posto son con loro in croce,
Iacopo Rusticucci fui, e certo
45   la fiera moglie più ch'altro mi nuoce."

S'i' fossi stato dal foco coperto,
gittato mi sarei tra lor di sotto,
48   e credo che 'l dottor l'avria sofferto;

ma perch'io mi sarei brusciato e cotto,
vinse paura la mia buona voglia
51   che di loro abbracciar mi facea ghiotto.

Poi cominciai: "Non dispetto, ma doglia
la vostra condizion dentro mi fisse,
54   tanta che tardi tutta si dispoglia,

tosto che questo mio segnor mi disse
parole per le quali i' mi pensai
57   che qual voi siete, tal gente venisse.

One began: 'If the squalor of this shifting sand
and our blackened, hairless faces
30   put us and our petitions in contempt,

'let our fame prevail on you
to tell us who you are, who fearless
33   move on living feet through Hell.

'He in whose steps you see me tread,
though he go naked, peeled hairless by the fire,
36   was of a higher rank than you imagine.

'He was grandson of the good Gualdrada.
Guido Guerra was his name. In his life
39   he did much with good sense, much with the sword.

'This other, squinching sand behind me,
is Tegghiaio Aldobrandi, whose voice
42   deserved a better welcome in the world.

'And I, who am put to torment with them,
was Jacopo Rusticucci. It was my bestial wife,
45   more than all else, who brought me to this pass.'

Had I been sheltered from the fire
I would have thrown myself among them,
48   and I believe my teacher would have let me.

But because I would have burned and baked,
fright overcame the good intentions
51   that made me hunger to embrace them.

Then I began: 'Not contempt, but sadness,
fixed your condition in my heart so deep—
54   it will be long before it leaves me—

'the moment that my master's words
made me consider that such worthy men
57   as you were coming near.

Di vostra terra sono, e sempre mai
l'ovra di voi e li onorati nomi
60   con affezion ritrassi e ascoltai.

Lascio lo fele e vo per dolci pomi
promessi a me per lo verace duca;
63   ma 'nfino al centro pria convien ch'i' tomi."

"Se lungamente l'anima conduca
le membra tue," rispuose quelli ancora,
66   "e se la fama tua dopo te luca,

cortesia e valor dì se dimora
ne la nostra città sì come suole,
69   o se del tutto se n'è gita fora;

ché Guiglielmo Borsiere, il qual si duole
con noi per poco e va là coi compagni,
72   assai ne cruccia con le sue parole."

"La gente nuova e i sùbiti guadagni
orgoglio e dismisura han generata,
75   Fiorenza, in te, sì che tu già ten piagni."

Così gridai con la faccia levata;
e i tre, che ciò inteser per risposta,
78   guardar l'un l'altro com' al ver si guata.

"Se l'altre volte sì poco ti costa,"
rispuoser tutti, "il satisfare altrui,
81   felice te se sì parli a tua posta!

Però, se campi d'esti luoghi bui
e torni a riveder le belle stelle,
84   quando ti gioverà dicere 'I' fui,'

fa che di noi a la gente favelle."
Indi rupper la rota, e a fuggirsi
87   ali sembiar le gambe loro isnelle.

'I am of your city. How many times
I've heard your deeds, your honored names resound!
60   And I, too, named you with affection.

'I leave bitterness behind for the sweet fruits
promised by my truthful leader.
63   But first I must go down into the very core.'

'That your spirit may long quicken
your limbs,' he replied once more,
66   'and your renown shine after you,

'tell us if valor and courtesy still live
there in our city, as once they used to do,
69   or have they utterly forsaken her?

'Guglielmo Borsiere, grieving with us here
so short a time, goes yonder with our company
72   and makes us worry with his words.'

'The new crowd with their sudden profits
have begot in you, Florence, such excess
75   and arrogance that you already weep.'

This, my face uplifted, I cried out. And the three,
taking it for answer, looked at one another
78   as men do when they face the truth.

'If at other times it costs so little
for you to give clear answers,' they replied in turn,
81   'happy are you to speak so free.

'Therefore, so may you escape from these dark regions
to see again the beauty of the stars,
84   when you shall rejoice in saying "I was there,"

'see that you speak of us to others.'
Then they broke their circle and as they fled
87   their nimble legs seemed wings.

Un amen non saria possuto dirsi
tosto così com' e' fuoro spariti;
90   per ch'al maestro parve di partirsi.

Io lo seguiva, e poco eravam iti,
che 'l suon de l'acqua n'era sì vicino,
93   che per parlar saremmo a pena uditi.

Come quel fiume c'ha proprio cammino
prima dal Monte Viso 'nver' levante,
96   da la sinistra costa d'Apennino,

che si chiama Acquacheta suso, avante
che si divalli giù nel basso letto,
99   e a Forlì di quel nome è vacante,

rimbomba là sovra San Benedetto
de l'Alpe per cadere ad una scesa
102   ove dovea per mille esser recetto;

così, giù d'una ripa discoscesa,
trovammo risonar quell' acqua tinta,
105   sì che 'n poc' ora avria l'orecchia offesa.

Io avea una corda intorno cinta,
e con essa pensai alcuna volta
108   prender la lonza a la pelle dipinta.

Poscia ch'io l'ebbi tutta da me sciolta,
sì come 'l duca m'avea comandato,
111   porsila a lui aggroppata e ravvolta.

Ond' ei si volse inver' lo destro lato,
e alquanto di lunge da la sponda
114   la gittò giuso in quell' alto burrato.

"E' pur convien che novità risponda,"
dicea fra me medesmo, "al novo cenno
117   che 'l maestro con l'occhio sì seconda."

'Amen' could not have been said as quickly
as they vanished. And then my master
90   thought it time to leave.

I followed him, and we had not gone far
before the roar of water was so close
93   we hardly could have heard each other speak.

As the river that is the first to hold
its course from Monte Viso eastward
96   on the left slope of the Apennines,

and up there is called the Acquacheta,
before it pours into its lower bed
99   and, having lost that name at Forlì,

reverberates above San Benedetto
dell'Alpe, falling in one cataract
102   where there might well have been a thousand,

so, down from a precipitous bank, the flood
of that dark water coming down resounded
105   in our ears and almost stunned us.

I had a cord around my waist
with which I once had meant to take
108   the leopard with the painted pelt.

After I had undone it,
as my leader had commanded,
111   I gave it to him coiled and knotted.

Then, swinging round on his right side,
he flung it out some distance from the edge,
114   down into the depth of that abyss.

'Surely,' I said to myself, 'something new
and strange will answer this strange signal
117   the master follows with his eye.'

Ahi quanto cauti li uomini esser dienno
presso a color che non veggion pur l'ovra,
120   ma per entro i pensier miran col senno!

El disse a me: "Tosto verrà di sovra
ciò ch'io attendo e che il tuo pensier sogna;
123   tosto convien ch'al tuo viso si scovra."

Sempre a quel ver c'ha faccia di menzogna
de' l'uom chiuder le labbra fin ch'el puote,
126   però che sanza colpa fa vergogna;

ma qui tacer nol posso; e per le note
di questa comedìa, lettor, ti giuro,
129   s'elle non sien di lunga grazia vòte,

ch'i' vidi per quell' aere grosso e scuro
venir notando una figura in suso,
132   maravigliosa ad ogne cor sicuro,

sì come torna colui che va giuso
talora a solver l'àncora ch'aggrappa
o scoglio o altro che nel mare è chiuso,
136   che 'n sù si stende e da piè si rattrappa.

Ah, how cautious we should be with those
who do not see our actions only,
120   but with their wisdom peer into our thoughts!

He said to me: 'Soon what I expect
and your mind only dreams of will appear.
123   Soon it shall appear before your eyes.'

To a truth that bears the face of falsehood
a man should seal his lips if he is able,
126   for it might shame him, through no fault of his,

but here I can't be silent. And by the strains
of this Comedy—so may they soon succeed
129   in finding favor—I swear to you, reader,

that I saw come swimming up
through that dense and murky air a shape
132   to cause amazement in the stoutest heart,

a shape most like a man's who, having plunged
to loose the anchor caught fast in a reef
or something other hidden in the sea, now rises,
136   reaching upward and drawing in his feet.

1–3.   The opening allusion to the noise of falling water is repeated, once the encounter with the three Florentines is complete, at vv. 92–93.

15–18.   Everything that we learn about these sinners seconds Virgil's positive opinion of them. And in *Inferno* VI.79–82 we read that Dante was particularly interested in meeting Iacopo and Tegghiaio (along with Farinata, Mosca, and the mysterious Arrigo), Florentines who had labored to do good for the city. Again we face a situation in which the sinner seems, apart from his sin, a thoroughly admirable person, and indeed capable of performing good deeds. See also Ciacco in *Inferno* VI.

19–27.   The three sinners who have recognized Dante as Florentine from his clothing continue their lamentation, but now form themselves into a wheeling circle so that they may remain in motion (in accord with their penalty) while also staying in one place, like joggers at a stoplight. Thus while their feet move in one direction, their heads move in an opposite one, so that their glances may stay fixed on Dante.

There is some discussion in the commentaries as to whether Dante refers to classical wrestling, as presented in Latin epics such as Virgil's and Lucan's, or to a contemporary version of the sport, or, indeed, to both.

28–42.   The first-named of three Florentines is Guido Guerra (a member of the family of the Conti Guidi, one of the most powerful in northern Italy); born ca. 1220, grandson of Guido Guerra IV and Gualdrada de' Ravignani, he was a notably successful Guelph political leader, leading them back from exile after the battle of Montaperti (1260) to their crushing defeat of the Ghibellines at Benevento (1266) and their restoration to power in the city; he died in 1272. The second is Tegghiaio Aldobrandi, of the noble Adimari family, contemporary and ally of Guido Guerra in the Guelph cause; along with Guido he counseled the Florentines not to engage in the expedition against Siena that ended in the disastrous defeat at Montaperti. The speaker is Iacopo Rusticucci, also a Guelph, but not, like the two he names, of noble rank (at least according to the Anonimo Fiorentino's commentary to this passage). His house and that of his neighbor, Tegghiaio, were destroyed in the aftermath of Montaperti. In the eyes of most readers, Iacopo blames his unwilling wife for his turning to homosexuality. But now see Chiamenti (Chia.1998.1), who argues that the adjective *fiera* (bestial) used of her rather suggests her bestial pleasure in having anal intercourse with her husband, a form of sexual practice indeed considered sodomitic.

46–51.   Dante's journey through hell produces no scene in which he is as cordial to a group of sinners as this one (see Holl.1996.1). That his affection is directed toward homosexuals is noteworthy, but does not necessarily involve him in anything more than what a modern reader must consider a remarkable lack of the typical Christian heterosexual scorn for homosexuals. The conversation here, like that with Ciacco, is devoted not to the sin of which these men were guilty, but to their political concerns for Florence, which Dante shares enthusiastically. These men are "good Guelphs," as Farinata was a "good Ghibelline," leaders who put true concerns for the city over those of party, as Dante surely believed he himself did.

58–63.   Dante identifies himself, out of modesty we presume, as a fellow Florentine, but not by name. His heavenly destination is enough by way of reward to let him wish to remain modestly anonymous. His reference to the good "deeds" (*ovra*) of these souls joins, in a series of moments with positive things to say about some of Florence's citizens, with Brunetto's reference (*Inf.* XV.60) to Dante's own political work (*opera*) on behalf of Florence, and to the passage that initiated these concerns, with specific reference to Guido Guerra and Iacopo Rusticucci (*Inf.* VI. 79–81), when Dante spoke with Ciacco of the good deeds of some of Florence's citizens.

64–72.   Iacopo's question offers Dante an opportunity to stage one of his frequent invectives against human depravity, especially of the Florentine sort. Guglielmo Borsiere, only recently arrived at this station, has been telling his fellows that the "good old days" are so no longer (while we have a secure date of death only for Guido Guerra [1272], we imagine that his other two companions also have been in hell for a quarter century or so: Florence is much changed). Guglielmo, of whom we know little, was, as his last name informs us, probably a pursemaker. Courtesy (in the sense of decency toward one's fellows but more in the wider sense of a whole courtly code of living) and valor (in the sense of showing attention to the worth of things by one's own conduct) are thus societal values reflected in individual behavior. Find them in Florence today? Dante's answer will be firmly negative.

73–75. The "new rich," having moved in from the surrounding country-side, are without any valor and courtesy, and already the civic price is being paid. Dante's brief but strongly phrased remark is filled with personal—and bitter—experience. We should probably remember the earlier denunciation of the original Fiesolan "barbarian" incursions into pure "Roman" Florence (*Inf.* XV.61–78). This moment of rhetorical elevation marks the only place that the name of the city about which the canto is so largely concerned is allowed to appear.

76. Dante approximates the gesture of an Old Testament prophet, calling for divine retribution, raising his eyes and voice rather to heaven than, as some commentators propose, to Florence.

82–85. Like Ciacco (*Inf.* VI.88) and few others in hell, these men have the confidence in the force of the good that they did on earth to want to be remembered above, even though they are condemned to eternal punishment.

This is the only time in hell that several sinners speak harmoniously as one. And what is also notable is their reference to the stars that shine over earth now, the last reference to them until we come to the concluding line of the *cantica* (*Inf.* XXXIV.139), when Dante and Virgil see them once again.

Beginning with Daniello (who borrowed the notice from his teacher, Trifon Gabriele [Gabr.1993.1]), commentators have remarked on the similarity of the sentiments expressed in their words "when you shall rejoice in saying 'I was there' " to Aeneas's words to his storm-tossed men (*Aen.* I.203): "forsan et haec olim meminisse iuvabit" (perhaps one day it will be a joy to recall even such events as these).

88–89. When this group hurries off to rejoin their fellows (as did Brunetto his), the poet describes their flight as taking no more time than it takes to say "Amen." The detail also probably implies, as it were, an illicit prayer for them on Dante's part, as though the protagonist, in response to their kind words, accepted their prayer for his return to the world, and would like to offer one for them in return. In a sense, the poet's positive treatment of them in this canto is the fulfillment of that wish.

91–93. The sound of water heard in the opening lines of the canto (1–3) is now, since Dante and Virgil have descended the sloping sand toward the center of hell, much louder.

94–105.   Dante, fond of the rivers of Italy as sources for poetic "digres-
sions," describes the Acquacheta (its name means "quiet water") as being
joined by the Riodestro near its source in the Apennines, and then chang-
ing name (to "Montone") at Forlì, before it flows into the Adriatic Sea just
south of Ravenna without pouring first into the Po, the major river of the
region. At its source at San Benedetto dell'Alpe, the meaning seems to be
(and Petrocchi's text is much debated here), when the river was not in
flood, forming the cascade referred to, it might have consisted in only a
thousand rivulets. Phlegethon, descending into Cocytus, is here a waterfall
resembling the Acquacheta in flood.

Perhaps mirroring the length of the river it describes, the simile here
is the longest yet found in *Inferno* (the two closest challengers occur at *Inf.*
III.112–120 and *Inf.* XV.4–12; but the thirteen cantos of Malebolge will at
first equal and finally outdo any other area of the poem for length of sim-
ile: *Inf.* XXI.7–18; *Inf* XXII.1–12; *Inf.* XXIV.1–18; *Inf.* XXVIII.7–21; and
the "champion," *Inf.* XXX. 1–27).

106–108.   Dante's cord is now retrospectively added to the details of the
scene in *Inferno* I (as the full moon will be added to that scene in *Inf.*
XX.127–129). The cord has the function of holding his robes together,
but symbolically may also reflect the cincture of one who attempts to
"gird his loins" and live right. (For bibliography of various interpretations
of the cord's significance see Mercuri [Merc. 1984.1], pp. 14n.–17n.)

Over the years, some commentators have tried to make the case that
the cord is that of a Franciscan garment, and that Dante was a member of
the (lay) Third Order of Franciscans. This may be true (most doubt it),
but the *corda* would offer no proof at all, since Dante knew the technical
name for the cord that bound the garment of a Franciscan: the *capestro*
(*Inf.* XXVII.92).

This passage is linked to the question of the identity of the three
beasts encountered by Dante in *Inferno* I (see note to I.32–54).

109–114.   Virgil pitches Dante's coiled-up cord into the abyss apparently
as a challenge to a creature somewhere down there. The poet builds sus-
pense for the advent of that creature, whose appearance is delayed until
the beginning of the next canto.

115–123.   Does Virgil read Dante's thoughts or is he simply so sensitive to
Dante's way of reacting to events that he can understand what his pupil
must be thinking? For a convincing statement in support of the second

thesis, with review of the various other passages in *Inferno* in which Virgil might seem to be claiming for himself the sort of intellective powers that Beatrice will possess (she *does* read the pilgrim's mind), see Musa.1977.1.

124–132.   Rhetorical energy increases as Dante swears to each of us, his readers, that he actually saw the creature he is about to describe. It is Geryon (only named at *Inf.* XVII.97, but see note at XVII.1–3), as mythical a monster as one can find and, as Castelvetro complained in his commentary, in Dante's handling not even resemblant of any of the descriptions of him found in classical literature. In other words, Dante has put the veracity of the entire *Comedy* (here named for the first of only two times [the second occurs at *Inf.* XXI.2]) upon the reality of Geryon. Where such as Ferrucci (Ferr.1971.1) use the passage to argue that Dante here obviously admits that his poem is no "historical" record of an "actual" journey, Hollander (Holl.1976.1), pp. 111–12; 132–33, bases his countering argument in his perception that the ground for Dante's choice of the "allegory of the theologians" for the *Comedy* lay in his battle with St. Thomas over the literal untruth of poetry; thus, according to him, Dante "claims that his poem is literally true while tacitly admitting that he has made it all up" (p. 133). The difference between these two positions may seem slight, but is major, for one reads the poem differently according as one admits or denies the applicability of theological allegory to its making and to its understanding.

For Dante's distinctions between tragedy and comedy see the concluding discussion in the note to *Inferno* XX.106–114.

133–136.   The concluding simile asks the reader to imagine a detail that cannot be seen: "something other hidden in the sea"; one might argue that precisely this inability to describe what cannot be seen marks the guarantee of Dante's "realistic" descriptive narrative. Makers of "mere fictions" operate under no such limit.

For Geryon as *palombaro*, that is, a man who releases anchors from the objects they attach to and then pulls himself back up to the surface by a cord thrown into the water with him, see Baldelli (Bald.1993.1).

Endnote. The debate concerning homosexuality in these cantos. There has been much recent debate about whether or not the sin punished here is in fact homosexuality. The principal negative findings are those advanced by André Pézard (Peza.1950.1), Richard Kay (Kay.1978.1), and Peter Armour (Armo.1983.1; Armo.1991.1). (Pézard's solution is that these sinners were guilty of blasphemy in deriding the mother tongue; Kay's, that they were guilty of denying the political supremacy of the empire; Armour's, that Brunetto was guilty of a Manichaean heresy. For bibliography of other recent discussions see Contrada [Cont.1995.1].) One of the principal issues facing those who oppose these interesting arguments is that in purgatory homosexuality is regarded a sin of lust and thus of incontinence. If it is punished here, in Violence, it would be in a different category than it occupies there. Had Dante thought of homosexuality as the sin against nature when he composed *Inferno*, with its basic organization taken from Aristotle and Cicero, and as a sin of lust when he composed the second *cantica*, organized by the seven capital sins? If he did so, perhaps he should not have. Despite the significant contradiction that results, most students of the problem remain convinced that the sin punished in Cantos XV and XVI is in fact homosexuality, and are supported by the text itself. The sin punished here is surely what is referred to by the name of the city "Soddoma" (Sodom) at *Inferno* XI.50; in *Purgatorio* XXVI.40 the penitent homosexuals call out that word in self-identification and penitence (and report that they do so at XXVI.79). If Dante had wanted us to separate the two sins, he made it awfully difficult for us to follow his logic in so doing. (For an attempt to rationalize the discrepancy see Pequigney [Pequ.1991.1], pp. 31–39.)

INFERNO XVII

"Ecco la fiera con la coda aguzza,
che passa i monti e rompe i muri e l'armi!
3   Ecco colei che tutto 'l mondo appuzza!"

Sì cominciò lo mio duca a parlarmi;
e accennolle che venisse a proda,
6   vicino al fin d'i passeggiati marmi.

E quella sozza imagine di froda
sen venne, e arrivò la testa e 'l busto,
9   ma 'n su la riva non trasse la coda.

La faccia sua era faccia d'uom giusto,
tanto benigna avea di fuor la pelle,
12   e d'un serpente tutto l'altro fusto;

due branche avea pilose insin l'ascelle;
lo dosso e 'l petto e ambedue le coste
15   dipinti avea di nodi e di rotelle.

Con più color, sommesse e sovraposte
non fer mai drappi Tartari né Turchi,
18   né fuor tai tele per Aragne imposte.

Come talvolta stanno a riva i burchi,
che parte sono in acqua e parte in terra,
21   e come là tra li Tedeschi lurchi

lo bivero s'assetta a far sua guerra,
così la fiera pessima si stava
24   su l'orlo ch'è di pietra e 'l sabbion serra.

Nel vano tutta sua coda guizzava,
torcendo in sù la venenosa forca
27   ch'a guisa di scorpion la punta armava.

'Behold the beast with pointed tail, that leaps
past mountains, shatters walls and weapons!
Behold the one whose stench afflicts the world!'

3

was how my guide began.
Then he signaled to the beast to come ashore
close to the border of our stony pathway.

6

And that foul effigy of fraud came forward,
beached its head and chest
but did not draw its tail up on the bank.

9

It had the features of a righteous man,
benevolent in countenance,
but all the rest of it was serpent.

12

It had forepaws, hairy to the armpits,
and back and chest and both its flanks
were painted and inscribed with rings and curlicues.

15

So many vivid colors Turk or Tartar never wove
in warp and woof or in embroidery on top,
nor were such colors patterned on Arachne's loom.

18

As sometimes barges lie ashore,
partly in water, partly on the land,
and as among the guzzling Germans

21

the beaver sets itself to catch its prey,
so lay this worst of brutes upon the stony rim
that makes a boundary for the sandy soil.

24

Its length of tail lashed in the void,
twisting up its forked, envenomed tip,
armed like a scorpion's tail.

27

Lo duca disse: "Or convien che si torca
la nostra via un poco insino a quella
30   bestia malvagia che colà si corca."

Però scendemmo a la destra mammella,
e diece passi femmo in su lo stremo,
33   per ben cessar la rena e la fiammella.

E quando noi a lei venuti semo,
poco più oltre veggio in su la rena
36   gente seder propinqua al loco scemo.

Quivi 'l maestro "Acciò che tutta piena
esperïenza d'esto giron porti,"
39   mi disse, "va, e vedi la lor mena.

Li tuoi ragionamenti sian là corti;
mentre che torni, parlerò con questa,
42   che ne conceda i suoi omeri forti."

Così ancor su per la strema testa
di quel settimo cerchio tutto solo
45   andai, dove sedea la gente mesta.

Per li occhi fora scoppiava lor duolo;
di qua, di là soccorrien con le mani
48   quando a' vapori, e quando al caldo suolo:

non altrimenti fan di state i cani
or col ceffo or col piè, quando son morsi
51   o da pulci o da mosche o da tafani.

Poi che nel viso a certi li occhi porsi,
ne' quali 'l doloroso foco casca,
54   non ne conobbi alcun; ma io m'accorsi

che dal collo a ciascun pendea una tasca
ch'avea certo colore e certo segno,
57   e quindi par che 'l loro occhio si pasca.

My leader said: 'Now we must change
direction for a moment till we reach
30   that evil beast stretched out down there.'

We descended, therefore, to our right,
and took ten steps along the edge to keep
33   our distance from the sand and flames.

And, when we reached the beast,
I see some people sitting on the sand
36   a short way off, near where it falls away.

Then the master said to me: 'So that nothing
in this circle escape your understanding,
39   go over and examine their condition.

'Let your talk be brief.
While you are gone, I'll ask the beast
42   to lend us its strong shoulders.'

Thus, on the seventh circle's edge,
still farther out, I went alone
45   to where the downcast souls were seated.

Their grief came bursting from their eyes.
With restless hands they sought relief,
48   now from the flame and now from burning sand.

Not otherwise do dogs in summer gnaw and scratch,
now with muzzle, now with paw,
51   when flies or fleas or horseflies bite them.

Although I searched some of the faces
of those on whom the painful fire descends,
54   I knew not one, but I could see

the pouches hanging from their necks
were different colors, each with its coat of arms.
57   On these they seemed to feast their eyes.

E com' io riguardando tra lor vegno,
in una borsa gialla vidi azzurro
60   che d'un leone avea faccia e contegno.

Poi, procedendo di mio sguardo il curro,
vidine un'altra come sangue rossa,
63   mostrando un'oca bianca più che burro.

E un che d'una scrofa azzurra e grossa
segnato avea lo suo sacchetto bianco,
66   mi disse: "Che fai tu in questa fossa?

Or te ne va; e perché se' vivo anco,
sappi che 'l mio vicin Vitalïano
69   sederà qui dal mio sinistro fianco.

Con questi Fiorentin son padoano:
spesse f ïate mi 'ntronan li orecchi
72   gridando: 'Vegna 'l cavalier sovrano,

che recherà la tasca con tre becchi!' "
Qui distorse la bocca e di fuor trasse
75   la lingua, come bue che 'l naso lecchi.

E io, temendo no'l più star crucciasse
lui che di poco star m'avea 'mmonito,
78   torna'mi in dietro da l'anime lasse.

Trova' il duca mio ch'era salito
già su la groppa del fiero animale,
81   e disse a me: "Or sie forte e ardito.

Omai si scende per sì fatte scale;
monta dinanzi, ch'i' voglio esser mezzo,
84   sì che la coda non possa far male."

Qual è colui che sì presso ha 'l riprezzo
de la quartana, c'ha già l'unghie smorte,
87   e triema tutto pur guardando 'l rezzo,

And when I came among them and looked closer,
on a yellow purse I could make out
60   a lion's countenance and form in blue.

Then, farther on, my wandering gaze
made out another crest, blood-red,
63   marked by a goose more white than butter.

And one, who had a pregnant sow, in azure,
embossed on his white wallet, said to me:
66   'What are you doing in this ditch?

'Get out of here. Wait, since you're still alive,
know that my neighbor Vitaliano
69   shall soon be seated to my left.

'Among these Florentines, I come from Padua.
Many a time they deafen me with shouting:
72   "May the sovereign knight come soon,

' "who brings the pouch with three goats on it!" '
Then he twisted his mouth and stuck out his tongue
75   like an ox that licks its nose.

And I, fearing my delay might anger him
who had warned me to keep my stay brief,
78   turned back and left those weary souls.

I found my leader mounted
on the shoulders of the savage beast.
81   He said to me: 'Now be strong and resolute.

'From here on we descend such stairs as these.
You mount in front and I will take the middle
84   so that the tail may do no harm.'

As a man in a shivering-fit of quartan fever,
so ill his nails have lost all color,
87   trembles all over at the sight of shade,

tal divenn' io a le parole porte;
ma vergogna mi fé le sue minacce,
90   che innanzi a buon segnor fa servo forte.

I' m'assettai in su quelle spallacce;
sì volli dir, ma la voce non venne
93   com' io credetti: "Fa che tu m'abbracce."

Ma esso, ch'altra volta mi sovvenne
ad altro forse, tosto ch'i' montai
96   con le braccia m'avvinse e mi sostenne;

e disse: "Gerïon, moviti omai:
le rote larghe, e lo scender sia poco;
99   pensa la nova soma che tu hai."

Come la navicella esce di loco
in dietro in dietro, sì quindi si tolse;
102   e poi ch'al tutto si sentì a gioco,

là 'v' era 'l petto, la coda rivolse,
e quella tesa, come anguilla, mosse,
105   e con le branche l'aere a sé raccolse.

Maggior paura non credo che fosse
quando Fetonte abbandonò li freni,
108   per che 'l ciel, come pare ancor, si cosse;

né quando Icaro misero le reni
sentì spennar per la scaldata cera,
111   gridando il padre a lui "Mala via tieni!"

che fu la mia, quando vidi ch'i' era
ne l'aere d'ogne parte, e vidi spenta
114   ogne veduta fuor che de la fera.

Ella sen va notando lenta lenta;
rota e discende, ma non me n'accorgo
117   se non che al viso e di sotto mi venta.

so was I stricken at his words.
Rebuked by shame, which, in the presence
90   of a worthy master, makes a servant bold,

I mounted on those huge and ugly shoulders.
I wanted to say—though my voice did not come out
93   as I intended—'Make sure you hold me fast!'

But he who had helped me many times before,
in other perils, clasped me in his arms
96   and steadied me as soon as I was mounted,

then said: 'Geryon, move on now. Let your circles
be wide and your descending slow.
99   Keep in mind your unaccustomed burden.'

As a bark backs slowly from its mooring,
so the beast backed off the ledge,
102   and when it felt itself adrift,

turned its tail to where its chest had been and,
extending it, made it wriggle like an eel's,
105   while with its paws it gathered in the air.

Phaeton, I think, felt no greater fear
when he released the reins and the whole sky
108   was scorched, as we still see,

nor wretched Icarus when he felt the melting wax
unfeathering the wings along his back
111   and heard his father shout: 'Not that way!'

than was my terror when I saw
air everywhere around
114   and all things gone from sight except the beast.

On it goes, swimming slowly, slowly
wheeling, descending, but I feel only
117   the wind in my face and blowing from below.

Io sentia già da la man destra il gorgo
far sotto noi un orribile scroscio,
120   per che con li occhi 'n giù la testa sporgo.

Allor fu' io più timido a lo stoscio,
però ch'i' vidi fuochi e senti' pianti;
123   ond' io tremando tutto mi raccoscio.

E vidi poi, ché nol vedea davanti,
lo scendere e 'l girar per li gran mali
126   che s'appressavan da diversi canti.

Come 'l falcon ch'è stato assai su l'ali,
che sanza veder logoro o uccello
129   fa dire al falconiere "Omè, tu cali!"

discende lasso onde si move isnello,
per cento rote, e da lunge si pone
132   dal suo maestro, disdegnoso e fello;

così ne puose al fondo Gerïone
al piè al piè de la stagliata rocca,
e, discarcate le nostre persone,
136   si dileguò come da corda cocca.

Now on our right I heard the torrent's hideous roar
below us, so that I thrust my head forward
120 and dared to look down the abyss.

Then I was even more afraid of being dropped,
for I saw fire and heard wailing,
123 and so, trembling, I hold on tighter with my legs.

And for the first time I became aware
of our descent and wheeling when I saw
126 the torments drawing closer all around me.

As the falcon that has long been on the wing—
and, without sight of lure or bird
129 makes the falconer cry out: 'Oh, you're coming down!'—

descends, weary, with many a wheeling,
to where it set out swiftly, and alights,
132 angry and sullen, far from its master,

so Geryon set us down at the bottom,
at the very foot of the jagged cliff,
and, disburdened of our persons,
136 vanished like an arrow from the string.

1–3.   Virgil's description of Geryon (not identified by name until v. 97) reflects his triple nature in classical literature. In the tradition known to Dante, he enticed strangers to be his guests, only to kill and eat them. He was eventually killed by Hercules. In the *Aeneid* he is twice identified with the number three: he is described as *forma tricorporis umbrae* (the form of the three-bodied shade—VI.289) and again as *tergemini . . . Geryonae* (triple Geryon—VIII.202). Ovid (*Heroides* IX.92) says that "in tribus unus erat" (he was one in three). In classical literature he is sometimes referred to as the king of three Iberian islands—which may account for his tripleness. "Dante's image was profoundly modified, however, by Pliny's description— followed by Solinus—of a strange beast called Mantichora (*Historia Naturalis,* VIII, 30) which has the face of a man, the body of a lion, and a tail ending in a sting like a scorpion's" (Grandgent's introductory note to this canto). All these threes find an answer in the three destructive action verbs describing him in this first tercet. This embodiment of fraud (he is the "foul effigy of fraud" at v. 7) is thus presented as the counterfeit of Christ, three-in-one rather than one-in-three. The very words that introduce this numerically central canto of *Inferno,* "Ecco la fiera" (Behold the beast), would seem to echo the familiar tag for Christ, *Ecce homo* (Behold the man [John 19:5]), as a student at Dartmouth College (Sarah LaBudde, '84) suggested some years ago.

10–11.   The positive words that accompany this description, invoking justice and benignity, remind us of the absence of such qualities in hell. Now they appear, but only as the masks for Fraud. The realm of Violence here will show us its last set of sinners, the usurers, men identified by bestial devices hanging from their throats; this first tip of the iceberg of Fraud is in the form of a huge beast, his bestial and reptilian parts at first mainly hidden in the void, with the fair face of a man. The last book in the Christian scripture tells of similar creatures, the locusts of destruction that will be loosed upon the world who have faces like men and tails like scorpions, with stingers in them (Rev. 9:7; 9:10).

14–18.   The "tattooed" body of Geryon looms in eerie beauty until the resemblance to the similarly "painted" leopard of Canto I.42 (referred to again at XVI.108) suggests that we can understand both these creatures as embodiments of the sins of fraud (see Durling and Martinez on these verses [Durl.1996.1]). And the concluding reference to Arachne (Ovid, *Metam.* VI.5–145), that world-class weaver turned into a spider, whose metamorphosed beguiling art has a purpose: the entrapment of flies. Chiavacci Leonardi (Chia.1991.1) calls attention to Rossetti's commentary to vv. 7–12, in which he interprets the shape of the serpent as a sort of history of the process of fraud: "Fraud begins its work by inspiring trust (the face of a just man); then weaves its deceit (the serpentine trunk); and at last strikes its final blow (the pointed tail)."

19–24. The two similes identify the posture of Geryon in terms of homely images, a boat drawn up to shore, a beaver fishing with its tail. (Beavers were reputed to use their tails as bait, eventually grasping the thereby attracted fish with their paws.) Tommaseo's commentary to this passage pointed out that hyperactive Teutonic appetite was a matter of note as far back as the histories of Tacitus.

28–33. Their descent to the right causes some commentators to think that the travelers have changed direction, as they did in the Circle of heresy; what they have done is merely what they have done before, all across the ring of the violent against nature; that is, they are moving downward toward the center. They have not changed their essential leftward course on this occasion, either.

37–39. For only the second time in the poem Virgil leaves Dante alone (see *Inf.* VIII.106–111). And now, for the first time, he is allowed to visit a group of sinners unguided. Virgil's decision to let him do so probably tells us that he believes the protagonist already proof against the danger or attraction of usury. Further, on both occasions we have come to the end of a large area of hell, first Incontinence and now Violence. For the idea that the infernal voyage is divided into five segments, in each of which the protagonist moves through cycles of unworthy fear and improper sympathy until he reaches firmness against an entire category of sin, see Hollander (Holl.1969.1), pp. 301–7, with addendum in Holl.1980.1, pp. 168–69.

45–48. Having learned that the homosexuals were punished by continual movement, reflective of their agitated lives, the reader now finds the third set of the violent against God sitting in place (and thereby undergoing precisely the punishment that the violent against nature dreaded). Usurers, we may understand, have caused money to race from hand to hand, but were themselves stationary, unmoved movers hunched over their desks in the pursuit of gain. We are in the third and final zone of the third ring of the seventh Circle. Like the first, it is located at a margin of that Circle (see *Inf.* XIV.12).

55–57.   The usurers, rendered unrecognizable by the burning (and by the degrading nature of their sin, which is a sin against God's "grandchild," industry, yet is also a sin against His child, nature, because it makes money "copulate"), have their only identity in the coats-of-arms hanging from their necks, fastened loose enough so that they themselves can see them. Their identities are made known to an observer by these devices, but they would rather seem to be gazing on their "real" selves, the money that used to fill their purses, than on their escutcheons.

59–60.   This device indicates the Gianfigliazzi family of Florence, Black Guelphs. Exactly which member of the family is not known, but perhaps Dante was happy to leave the door open to the widest possible speculation.

62–63.   The arms of the Obriachi family, Florentine Ghibellines. Once again commentators have proposed various individuals, but without a victorious candidate emerging.

64–66.   The "star" among the usurers, the only one with a speaking part, is, most commentators believe, Reginaldo degli Scrovegni, the only non-Florentine in the little group of identified sinners. He was from Padua and was a usurer on a major scale. A penitential desire to make up for paternal usurious practice reputedly moved his son, Arrigo, to endow the construction of the Scrovegni Chapel, its walls devoted to Giotto's frescoes, one of the most beautiful interior spaces in the Western world.

67–69.   Reginaldo's discourtesy to Dante is matched by his envious report that his fellow Paduan (and fellow usurer, still alive as late as 1307), Vitaliano del Dente (there is some disagreement as to his exact identity among the commentators) will join him here one of these days.

72–73.   Mocking his Florentine companions in usury, Reginaldo reports that they, too, are awaiting a townsman, the "king of the usurers" of Dante's day (and alive until 1310), Giovanni Buiamonte, a Ghibelline.

74–78. Reginaldo's animalistic, sub-verbal facial gesture in response to the reported conversations of his companions conveys some of the self-enclosed antisocial nature of these sinners. They really did not care for anything but money. Dante, having been warned by Virgil to return quickly (and the whole scene has a rushed urgency about it), heads back toward Virgil—and Geryon.

This little narrative (vv. 43–78) of Dante's first (and last) "solo" adventure in the *Inferno* is carried out with a striking mixture of brief understatement and the only vivid colors we find in the *cantica* (as Chiavacci Leonardi points out in her commentary to v. 63). The quick spareness of the narration allows the poet to give us five personages in this brief space. And for all the brightness of the color on the devices that we see, the net effect is of an enervated attachment, not so much to wealth as to the lonely pursuit of infinite gathering.

82. The "stairs" to which Virgil refers are monstrous creatures, as he looks ahead to their means of conveyance over the great gaps in walkable terrain that they will face at Cocytus (Canto XXXI, Antaeus will be their "stairs" then) and at the center of the Earth (Canto XXXIV, where Satan's legs will be the ladder Virgil climbs to begin to draw Dante up from hell).

97–99. Virgil's commands to Geryon, coupled with the monster's instantaneous disappearance once his tour of duty is ended, make the reader realize that Virgil has used extraordinarily persuasive arguments to tame this beast. His having sent Dante away also reminds us of the time he left his charge alone but in sight of his temporary yet crushing defeat at the hands of the demons at the walls of Dis. This time he first gets his pupil out of viewing range and then, we do not know how, manages to control a most difficult demon and turn him into the first helicopter. If Dante is the main learner in *Inferno*, Virgil learns a few things himself.

106–108. The extraordinary journey put fear into our hero, which he now may compare to that felt by classical precursors who failed on similar flights. As Brownlee points out, Phaeton (his story is found in Ovid, *Metam.* II.47–324) dropped the reins of his heavenly chariot as a result of his terror upon looking at the constellation Scorpio, while Dante mounts on the scorpion-tailed Geryon in order to accomplish his flight (Brow.1984.1), p. 136.

The "scorching" of the sky, the path of Phaeton's fall, is the Milky Way.

109–111.   Icarus (Ovid, *Metam*. VIII.183–235), on a second extraordinary flight that failed, did not obey the instructions of his father, Daedalus, trying instead to turn a voyage home into a trip through the galaxy. If the protagonist then thought of these two precursors, he must have thought that he, too, might die for his temerity; the poet, however, making the analogies now, sees the comic resolution of a voyage that might have turned tragic except for the fact that this voyager had God on his side.

115–126.   This, perhaps the single most melodramatic and implausible narrative passage in the *Comedy*, is accomplished with considerable art. Dante, his face at first pushed up against the body of the beast, sees nothing. He feels the wind on his face, hears the torrent below, finally gets his eyes into play and sees the flames of lower hell, hears the cries of the damned, and finally, now that he is able to look, realizes the pattern of his descending flight from the "approach" of the circling and rising hellscape.

127–136.   The simile re-introduces falconry to the poem; references to this sport of hunting with birds will reappear several times. The similetic falcon, like Geryon an unwilling worker, has come down before finishing his mission (to catch a bird or be summoned home by the falconer's lure); to compound his bad birdmanship, he does not even land on his master's arm, but far afield. Geryon, on the other hand, while equally rebellious, does complete his flight as his master (Virgil) had ordered. The simile, now that the fearsome flight is over, has a way of making Geryon less terrifying than he was, comparing him to a small bird of prey. At this midpoint of the *Comedy* we have a provisional comic ending, with Dante safe and sound exactly halfway there. (For Dante's distinctions between tragedy and comedy see the note to *Inferno* XX.106–114.) The last two verses of the canto, however, give Geryon a last moment of terrifying will and power.

INFERNO XVIII

Luogo è in inferno detto Malebolge,
tutto di pietra di color ferrigno,
3   come la cerchia che dintorno il volge.

Nel dritto mezzo del campo maligno
vaneggia un pozzo assai largo e profondo,
6   di cui *suo loco* dicerò l'ordigno.

Quel cinghio che rimane adunque è tondo
tra 'l pozzo e 'l piè de l'alta ripa dura,
9   e ha distinto in dieci valli il fondo.

Quale, dove per guardia de le mura
più e più fossi cingon li castelli,
12   la parte dove son rende figura,

tale imagine quivi facean quelli;
e come a tai fortezze da' lor sogli
15   a la ripa di fuor son ponticelli,

così da imo de la roccia scogli
movien che ricidien li argini e ' fossi
18   infino al pozzo che i tronca e raccogli.

In questo luogo, de la schiena scossi
di Gerïon, trovammoci; e 'l poeta
21   tenne a sinistra, e io dietro mi mossi.

A la man destra vidi nova pieta,
novo tormento e novi frustatori,
24   di che la prima bolgia era repleta.

Nel fondo erano ignudi i peccatori;
dal mezzo in qua ci venien verso 'l volto,
27   di là con noi, ma con passi maggiori,

There is a place in Hell called Malebolge,
fashioned entirely of iron-colored rock,
3   as is the escarpment that encircles it.

At the very center of this malignant space
there yawns a pit, extremely wide and deep.
6   I will describe its plan all in due time.

A path that circles like a belt around the base
of that high rock runs round the pit,
9   its sides descending in ten ditches.

As where concentric moats surround a castle
to guard its walls, their patterns clear
12   and governed by a meaningful design,

in such a pattern were these ditches shaped.
And, just as narrow bridges issue from the gates
15   of fortresses to reach the farthest bank,

so ridges stretched from the escarpment
down across the banks and ditches
18   into the pit at which they end and join.

Dropped from Geryon's back, this was the place
in which we found ourselves. The poet kept
21   to the left and I came on behind him.

To our right I saw a suffering new to me,
new torments, and new scourgers,
24   with whom the first ditch was replete.

The sinners in its depth were naked,
those on our side of the center coming toward us,
27   the others moving with us, but with longer strides,

come i Roman per l'essercito molto,
l'anno del giubileo, su per lo ponte
30   hanno a passar la gente modo colto,

che da l'un lato tutti hanno la fronte
verso 'l castello e vanno a Santo Pietro,
33   da l'altra sponda vanno verso 'l monte.

Di qua, di là, su per lo sasso tetro
vidi demon cornuti con gran ferze,
36   che li battien crudelmente di retro.

Ahi come facean lor levar le berze
a le prime percosse! già nessuno
39   le seconde aspettava né le terze.

Mentr' io andava, li occhi miei in uno
furo scontrati; e io sì tosto dissi:
42   "Già di veder costui non son digiuno."

Per ch'ïo a figurarlo i piedi affissi;
e 'l dolce duca meco si ristette,
45   e assentio ch'alquanto in dietro gissi.

E quel frustato celar si credette
bassando 'l viso; ma poco li valse,
48   ch'io dissi: "O tu che l'occhio a terra gette,

se le fazion che porti non son false,
Venedico se' tu Caccianemico.
51   Ma che ti mena a sì pungenti salse?"

Ed elli a me: "Mal volontier lo dico;
ma sforzami la tua chiara favella,
54   che mi fa sovvenir del mondo antico.

I' fui colui che la Ghisolabella
condussi a far la voglia del marchese,
57   come che suoni la sconcia novella.

just as, because the throngs were vast the year
of Jubilee, the Romans had to find a way
30   to let the people pass across the bridge,

so that all those on one side face the castle,
heading over to Saint Peter's,
33   these, on the other, heading toward the mount.

Here and there on the dark rock above them
I watched horned demons armed with heavy scourges
36   lashing them cruelly from behind.

Ah, how they made them pick their heels up
at the first stroke! You may be certain
39   no one waited for a second or a third.

While I went on my eye was caught
by one of them, and quickly I brought out:
42   'It seems to me I've seen that man before.'

And so I paused to make him out.
My gentle leader stopped with me,
45   and then allowed me to retrace my steps.

The scourged soul thought that he could hide
by lowering his face—to no avail.
48   I said: 'You there, with your eyes cast down,

'if I'm not mistaken in your features,
you're Venèdico Caccianemico.
51   What has brought you to such stinging torture?'

And he replied: 'Unwillingly I tell it,
moved only by the truth of what you've said,
54   which brings to mind the world that once I knew.

'It was I who urged Ghisolabella
to do the will of that marquis,
57   no matter how the foul tale goes around.

E non pur io qui piango bolognese;
anzi n'è questo loco tanto pieno,
60   che tante lingue non son ora apprese

a dicer 'sipa' tra Sàvena e Reno;
e se di ciò vuoi fede o testimonio,
63   rècati a mente il nostro avaro seno."

Così parlando il percosse un demonio
de la sua scurïada, e disse: "Via,
66   ruffian! qui non son femmine da conio."

I' mi raggiunsi con la scorta mia;
poscia con pochi passi divenimmo
69   là 'v' uno scoglio de la ripa uscia.

Assai leggeramente quel salimmo;
e vòlti a destra su per la sua scheggia,
72   da quelle cerchie etterne ci partimmo.

Quando noi fummo là dov' el vaneggia
di sotto per dar passo a li sferzati,
75   lo duca disse: "Attienti, e fa che feggia

lo viso in te di quest' altri mal nati,
ai quali ancor non vedesti la faccia
78   però che son con noi insieme andati."

Del vecchio ponte guardavam la traccia
che venìa verso noi da l'altra banda,
81   e che la ferza similmente scaccia.

E 'l buon maestro, sanza mia dimanda,
mi disse: "Guarda quel grande che vene,
84   e per dolor non par lagrime spanda:

quanto aspetto reale ancor ritene!
Quelli è Iasón, che per cuore e per senno
87   li Colchi del monton privati féne.

'I'm not the only Bolognese here lamenting.
This place is so crammed with them
60   that not so many tongues have learned to say

' "sipa" between the Sàvena and the Reno.
And if you'd like some confirmation,
63   bring our greedy dispositions back to mind.'

While he was speaking a demon struck him
with his lash and said: 'Away, pimp!
66   there are no women here to trick.'

Then I rejoined my escort. A few steps farther
and we came upon a place
69   where a ridge jutted from the bank.

This we ascended easily and,
turning to the right upon its jagged ledge,
72   we left behind their endless circling.

When we came to the point above the hollow
that makes a passage for the scourged,
75   my leader said: 'Stop, let them look at you,

'those other ill-born souls whose faces
you have not yet seen, since we have all
78   been moving in the same direction.'

From the ancient bridge we eyed the band
advancing toward us on the other side,
81   driven with whips just like the first.

And the good master, without my asking, said:
'See that imposing figure drawing near.
84   He seems to shed no tears despite his pain.

'What regal aspect he still bears!
He is Jason, who by courage and by craft
87   deprived the men of Colchis of the ram.

Ello passò per l'isola di Lenno
poi che l'ardite femmine spietate
90   tutti li maschi loro a morte dienno.

Ivi con segni e con parole ornate
Isifile ingannò, la giovinetta
93   che prima avea tutte l'altre ingannate.

Lasciolla quivi, gravida, soletta;
tal colpa a tal martiro lui condanna;
96   e anche di Medea si fa vendetta.

Con lui sen va chi da tal parte inganna;
e questo basti de la prima valle
99   sapere e di color che 'n sé assanna."

Già eravam là 've lo stretto calle
con l'argine secondo s'incrocicchia,
102   e fa di quello ad un altr' arco spalle.

Quindi sentimmo gente che si nicchia
ne l'altra bolgia e che col muso scuffa,
105   e sé medesma con le palme picchia.

Le ripe eran grommate d'una muffa,
per l'alito di giù che vi s'appasta,
108   che con li occhi e col naso facea zuffa.

Lo fondo è cupo sì, che non ci basta
loco a veder sanza montare al dosso
111   de l'arco, ove lo scoglio più sovrasta.

Quivi venimmo; e quindi giù nel fosso
vidi gente attuffata in uno sterco
114   che da li uman privadi parea mosso.

E mentre ch'io là giù con l'occhio cerco,
vidi un col capo sì di merda lordo,
117   che non parëa s'era laico o cherco.

'Then he ventured to the isle of Lemnos,
after those pitiless, bold women
90   put all the males among them to their death.

'There with signs of love and polished words
he deceived the young Hypsipyle,
93   who had herself deceived the other women.

'There he left her, pregnant and forlorn.
Such guilt condemns him to this torment,
96   and Medea too is thus avenged.

'With him go all who practice such deceit.
Let that be all we know of this first ditch
99   and of the ones it clenches in its jaws.'

Now we had come to where the narrow causeway
intersects the second ridge to form
102   a buttress for another arch.

From here we heard the whimpering of people
one ditch away, snuffling with their snouts
105   and beating on themselves with their own palms.

The banks, made slimy by a sticky vapor
from below, were coated with a mould
108   offending eyes and nose.

The bottom is so deep we could see nothing
unless we climbed to the crown of the arch,
111   just where the ridge is highest.

We went up, and from there I could see,
in a ditch below, people plunged in excrement
114   that could have come from human privies.

Searching the bottom with my eyes I saw
a man, his head so smeared with shit
117   one could not tell if he were priest or layman.

Quei mi sgridò: "Perché se' tu sì gordo
di riguardar più me che li altri brutti?"
120 E io a lui: "Perché, se ben ricordo,

già t'ho veduto coi capelli asciutti,
e se' Alessio Interminei da Lucca:
123 però t'adocchio più che li altri tutti."

Ed elli allor, battendosi la zucca:
"Qua giù m'hanno sommerso le lusinghe
126 ond' io non ebbi mai la lingua stucca."

Appresso ciò lo duca "Fa che pinghe,"
mi disse, "il viso un poco più avante,
129 sì che la faccia ben con l'occhio attinghe

di quella sozza e scapigliata fante
che là si graffia con l'unghie merdose,
132 e or s'accoscia e ora è in piedi stante.

Taïde è, la puttana che rispuose
al drudo suo quando disse 'Ho io grazie
grandi apo te?': 'Anzi maravigliose!'
136 E quinci sian le nostre viste sazie."

He railed: 'What whets your appetite to stare at me
more than all the others in their filth?'
120   And I answered: 'The fact, if I remember right,

'that once I saw you when your hair was dry—
and you are Alessio Interminei of Lucca.
123   That's why I eye you more than all the rest.'

Then he, beating on his pate:
'I am immersed down here for the flattery
126   with which my tongue was never cloyed.'

And then my leader said to me: 'Try to thrust
your face a little farther forward,
129   to get a better picture of the features

'of that foul, disheveled wench down there,
scratching herself with her filthy nails.
132   Now she squats and now she's standing up.

'She is Thaïs, the whore who, when her lover asked:
"Have I found favor with you?"
answered, "Oh, beyond all measure!"
136   And let our eyes be satisfied with that.'

1–18. The extended introductory passage interrupts the narrative in order to set the new scene: Malebolge, the eighth Circle, with its ten varieties of fraudulent behaviors. Only in *Inferno* does an equal number of cantos (17 and 17) create a precise center for a *cantica* in the space between two cantos, and we have just passed it. The last canto ended with a sort of "comic" conclusion to Dante's dangerous voyage on Geryon. He has now traversed precisely half of the literary space devoted to the underworld. Thus, fully half of the *cantica*, Cantos XVIII to XXXIV, is dedicated to the sins of Fraud. That division tells us something about the poet's view of human behavior, namely that it is better typified by the worst of sins than by the lesser ones.

The poetry of Malebolge, studied by Sanguineti (Sang.1962.1), is strikingly self-confident. One has the feeling that Dante, having finished his apprenticeship, now has achieved a level of aesthetic performance that may have surprised even him. In the seventh canto he had conjoined two kinds of sinners, the avaricious and the prodigal; but these are two sides of the same sin. Here for the first time, as something of a *tour de force*, he includes two entirely separate categories of sin in a single canto, one of them itself subdivided into two groups, as in Canto VII—all of this in 115 lines. The precision of the operation is noteworthy, and may be represented as follows:

(1) *panders & seducers*	(2) *flatterers*
disposition of both (22–39)	disposition (100–114)
modern exemplar (52–66)	modern exemplar (115–126)
classical exemplar (82–99)	classical exemplar (127–136)

The hellscape offers a gray stone circular wall surrounding a stone "field," which in turn surrounds a pit (the "keep" of this "castle"); the field is divided into ten valleys, which resemble moats set around a castle. The analogy is complete, but works in reverse, since a castle rises above its surroundings, while this "castle" is a hole leading into hell. Our first view of Malebolge (the name is a Dantean coinage made up of words meaning "evil" and "pouches") makes it seem like a vast, emptied stadium, e.g., the Colosseum, which Dante might have seen in 1301 if he indeed visited Rome then, or the arena of Verona, which he probably saw at least by

1304. The former hypothesis is attractive in that the second image of the canto is also modeled on Roman architecture: the bridge over the Tiber between the Vatican and the city.

19–21. The narrative is now joined to the action concluding the last canto and the poets resume their leftward circling movement.

22–27. The panders, moving from left to right as Dante views them, are moving in a direction contrary to his; the seducers, moving from his right to his left, and thus moving in parallel with him, are going faster than he; but then he has no demons lashing him with whips.

28–33. The simile, reflecting the Roman invention of two-way traffic in 1300 for the crowds thronging to the holy places, on the bridge across the Tiber, from the city (to St. Peter's, after they pass Castel Sant'Angelo) and back again (to the area of Monte Giordano, just off the Tiber), has caused some to argue that Dante had been in Rome during the Jubilee. It is more likely that he was in fact there in 1301 and heard tell of this modern wonder of crowd control. That the first city that Malebolge calls to mind is Rome in the Jubilee Year is not without its ironic thrust, especially since it had been Pope Boniface VIII, so hated by Dante, who proclaimed this great event (the first in the Church's history).

35. In his commentary to the passage Benvenuto da Imola suggests that the panders are punished by horned devils because their actions resulted in the cuckoldry of others.

50. Venedico was an important political figure of Bologna in the second half of the thirteenth century. His sin was in selling his own sister to Opizzo of Este (see *Inf.* XII.111). He actually died in 1302, although Dante obviously believed he had died before 1300.

58–61. Venedico's pleasantry insists that there are more Bolognesi in this zone of hell than currently populate the city itself. "Sipa" is ancient dialectical Bolognese for "yes," and thus the phrase means "have grown up speaking Bolognese dialect" between the rivers that mark the eastern and western confines of the city.

66. The demon's rough remark is variously understood: either "there are no women here to defraud" (as Venedico did his sister), or "there are no

women here for sale" (to offer to Dante). And there may also be a hint of slang words for female genitalia. In our translation we have tried to keep both of the first meanings possible.

72.   The circlings of the whipped sinners, not of the ditches themselves, are almost certainly what is referred to, just as Francesco da Buti, in his commentary to this passage, said centuries ago. However, it was only some eighty years ago that Enrico Bianchi (Bian.1921.1) brought such a comprehension back to the verse, thereby increasing its power: the reference is to the Florentine custom of whipping a condemned man along the route to his execution. Most contemporary commentators accept this reading.

73–78.   At the high point of the bridge over the ditch on their way toward the next *bolgia* the travelers stop to observe the second set of sinners in this one, whom they have not been able to examine because these were going along in the same direction as were they, and at a faster clip.

83–85.   Like Capaneus (*Inf.* XIV.46–48), the heroic Jason is allowed to keep some of his dignity and his stoical strength.

86–96.   Jason, who will be remembered in *Paradiso* in a far more positive light, as the precursor of Dante in his having taken a great voyage and returned with the golden fleece (*Par.* II.16–18; XXV.7; XXXIII.94–96), is here presented as the classical exemplar of the vile seducer. Dante has Virgil condense the lengthy narrative of Jason's exploits found in Ovid (*Metam.* VII.1–424) into two details, the seductions of Hypsipyle (daughter of the king of Lemnos) and of Medea (daughter of the king of Colchis).

      For the resonance at v. 91 of Beatrice's description of Virgilian utterance as "parola ornata" see the note to *Inf.* II.67. As for Jason's *segni* (signs of love), Dante may be thinking of his ability to move Medea by tears as well as words (see *Metam.* VII.169).

100–114.   The second ditch is filled with supernatural excrement (it only *seems* to have come from the toilets of humans). What do flatterers do? It is unnecessary to repeat the slang phrases that are used in nearly all languages to characterize their utterance. What they did above, they do below, wallowing in excrement, their faces ingesting it as animals guzzle food from their troughs (see v. 104).

122.   Alessio Interminei is the first Lucchese whom we encounter, but there will be others, below. Dante seems systematically to include in hell representatives of all the major Tuscan cities.

133–135.   Thaïs is a courtesan in Terence's comic play *Eunuchus*, and had a reputation even into the Middle Ages as a flatterer. Whether Dante is citing Terence directly (most currently dispute this) or through Cicero (*De amicitia* XXVI.98—a text that Dante assuredly did know and which explicitly associates Thaïs with flattery, though there and in Terence she is the one flattered, not the flatterer) is a matter that still excites argument. For the most recent claims for Dante's knowledge of Terence see Villa (Vill.1984.1); but see also the countering arguments of Barański (Bara.1993.1), pp. 230–38.

INFERNO XIX

O Simon mago, o miseri seguaci
che le cose di Dio, che di bontate
3   deon essere spose, e voi rapaci

per oro e per argento avolterate,
or convien che per voi suoni la tromba,
6   però che ne la terza bolgia state.

Già eravamo, a la seguente tomba,
montati de lo scoglio in quella parte
9   ch'a punto sovra mezzo 'l fosso piomba.

O somma sapïenza, quanta è l'arte
che mostri in cielo, in terra e nel mal mondo,
12   e quanto giusto tua virtù comparte!

Io vidi per le coste e per lo fondo
piena la pietra livida di fóri,
15   d'un largo tutti e ciascun era tondo.

Non mi parean men ampi né maggiori
che que' che son nel mio bel San Giovanni,
18   fatti per loco d'i battezzatori;

l'un de li quali, ancor non è molt' anni,
rupp' io per un che dentro v'annegava:
21   e questo sia suggel ch'ogn' omo sganni.

Fuor de la bocca a ciascun soperchiava
d'un peccator li piedi e de le gambe
24   infino al grosso, e l'altro dentro stava.

Le piante erano a tutti accese intrambe;
per che sì forte guizzavan le giunte,
27   che spezzate averien ritorte e strambe.

O Simon Magus! O wretches of his kind,
greedy for gold and silver,
who prostitute the things of God

that should be brides of goodness!
Now must the trumpet sound for you,
because your place is there in that third ditch.

We had come to where the next tomb lay,
having climbed to the point upon the ridge
that overlooks the middle of the trench.

O Supreme Wisdom, what great art you show
in Heaven, on earth, and in the evil world,
and what true justice does your power dispense!

Along the sides and bottom I could see
the livid stone was pierced with holes,
all round and of a single size.

They seemed to me as wide and deep
as those in my beautiful Saint John
made for the priests to baptize in,

one of which, not many years ago,
I broke to save one nearly drowned in it—
and let this be my seal, to undeceive all men.

From the mouth of each stuck out
a sinner's feet and legs up to the thighs
while all the rest stayed in the hole.

They all had both their soles on fire.
It made their knee-joints writhe so hard
they would have severed twisted vines or ropes.

Qual suole il fiammeggiar de le cose unte
muoversi pur su per la strema buccia,
30   tal era lì dai calcagni a le punte.

"Chi è colui, maestro, che si cruccia
guizzando più che li altri suoi consorti,"
33   diss' io, "e cui più roggia fiamma succia?"

Ed elli a me: "Se tu vuo' ch'i' ti porti
là giù per quella ripa che più giace,
36   da lui saprai di sé e de' suoi torti."

E io: "Tanto m'è bel, quanto a te piace:
tu se' segnore, e sai ch'i' non mi parto
39   dal tuo volere, e sai quel che si tace."

Allor venimmo in su l'argine quarto;
volgemmo e discendemmo a mano stanca
42   là giù nel fondo foracchiato e arto.

Lo buon maestro ancor de la sua anca
non mi dipuose, sì mi giunse al rotto
45   di quel che si piangeva con la zanca.

"O qual che se' che 'l di sù tien di sotto,
anima trista come pal commessa,"
48   comincia' io a dir, "se puoi, fa motto."

Io stava come 'l frate che confessa
lo perfido assessin, che, poi ch'è fitto,
51   richiama lui per che la morte cessa.

Ed el gridò: "Se' tu già costì ritto,
se' tu già costì ritto, Bonifazio?
54   Di parecchi anni mi mentì lo scritto.

Se' tu sì tosto di quell' aver sazio
per lo qual non temesti tòrre a 'nganno
57   la bella donna, e poi di farne strazio?"

As flames move only on the surface
of oily matter caught on fire,
30   so these flames flickered heel to toe.

'Who is that, master, who in his torment
wriggles more than any of his fellows
33   and is licked by redder flames?'

And he: 'If you like, I'll take you down
along the lower bank and you will learn,
36   from him, his life and his misdeeds.'

And I: 'Whatever pleases you is my desire.
You are my lord and know I do your will.
39   You know, too, what I leave unsaid.'

Then we came to the fourth embankment,
turned and descended on our left
42   into a narrow bottom pierced with holes.

The good master clasped me to his side
and did not set me down until we came
45   to the pit of one lamenting with his shanks.

'Whoever you are, with your upper parts below,
planted like a post, you wretched soul,'
48   said I, 'come out with something, if you can.'

I stood there like a friar who confesses
a treacherous assassin. Once done,
51   he calls the friar back to stay his death.

And he cried out: 'Is that you already,
are you here already, Boniface?
54   By several years the writing lied to me.

'Are you so swiftly sated with those profits
for which you did not fear to take by guile
57   the beautiful Lady and to do her outrage?'

Tal mi fec' io, quai son color che stanno,
per non intender ciò ch'è lor risposto,
60   quasi scornati, e risponder non sanno.

Allor Virgilio disse: "Dilli tosto:
'Non son colui, non son colui che credi' ";
63   e io rispuosi come a me fu imposto.

Per che lo spirto tutti storse i piedi;
poi, sospirando e con voce di pianto,
66   mi disse: "Dunque che a me richiedi?

Se di saper ch'i' sia ti cal cotanto,
che tu abbi però la ripa corsa,
69   sappi ch'i' fui vestito del gran manto;

e veramente fui figliuol de l'orsa,
cupido sì per avanzar li orsatti,
72   che sù l'avere e qui me misi in borsa.

Di sotto al capo mio son li altri tratti
che precedetter me simoneggiando,
75   per le fessure de la pietra piatti.

Là giù cascherò io altresì quando
verrà colui ch'i' credea che tu fossi,
78   allor ch'i' feci 'l sùbito dimando.

Ma più è 'l tempo già che i piè mi cossi
e ch'i' son stato così sottosopra,
81   ch'el non starà piantato coi piè rossi:

ché dopo lui verrà di più laida opra,
di ver' ponente, un pastor sanza legge,
84   tal che convien che lui e me ricuopra.

Nuovo Iasón sarà, di cui si legge
ne' Maccabei; e come a quel fu molle
87   suo re, così fia lui chi Francia regge."

I became like those who stand there mocked,
not comprehending what is said to them,
60   and thus not knowing what to say in turn.

Then Virgil said: 'Tell him right away,
"I'm not the one, I'm not the one you think." '
63   I gave the answer I was told to give.

At that the spirit's feet began to writhe.
Then, sighing, with a plaintive voice, he said:
66   'What is it then you want from me?

'If you are so keen to learn my name
that you descended from the bank for it,
69   know that I was cloaked in the great mantle.

'But in truth I was a son of the she-bear
and so avid was I to advance my cubs
72   I filled my purse as now I fill this hole.

'Beneath my head are crushed the others
who practiced simony before me,
75   now flattened into fissures in the rock.

'In turn I, too, shall be thrust lower down
as soon as he arrives whom I mistook you for
78   when I called out my hasty question.

'But the time I have already roasted my feet,
standing here upside down, is already longer
81   than he'll be planted with his feet on fire.

'For after him shall come a lawless shepherd
from the west, one even fouler in his deeds,
84   fit to be the cover over him and me.

'A new Jason shall he be, the one of whom
we read in Maccabees, and even as the king indulged
87   Jason, so the king of France shall deal with him.'

Io non so s'i' mi fui qui troppo folle,
ch'i' pur rispuosi lui a questo metro:
90 "Deh, or mi dì: quanto tesoro volle

Nostro Segnore in prima da san Pietro
ch'ei ponesse le chiavi in sua balìa?
93 Certo non chiese se non 'Viemmi retro.'

Né Pier né li altri tolsero a Matia
oro od argento, quando fu sortito
96 al loco che perdé l'anima ria.

Però ti sta, ché tu se' ben punito;
e guarda ben la mal tolta moneta
99 ch'esser ti fece contra Carlo ardito.

E se non fosse ch'ancor lo mi vieta
la reverenza de le somme chiavi
102 che tu tenesti ne la vita lieta,

io userei parole ancor più gravi;
ché la vostra avarizia il mondo attrista,
105 calcando i buoni e sollevando i pravi.

Di voi pastor s'accorse il Vangelista,
quando colei che siede sopra l'acque
108 puttaneggiar coi regi a lui fu vista;

quella che con le sette teste nacque,
e da le diece corna ebbe argomento,
111 fin che virtute al suo marito piacque.

Fatto v'avete dio d'oro e d'argento;
e che altro è da voi a l'idolatre,
114 se non ch'elli uno, e voi ne orate cento?

Ahi, Costantin, di quanto mal fu matre,
non la tua conversion, ma quella dote
117 che da te prese il primo ricco patre!"

I do not know if then I was too bold
when I answered him in just this strain:
90   'Please tell me, how much treasure

'did our Lord insist on from Saint Peter
before He gave the keys into his keeping?
93   Surely He asked no more than "Follow me,"

'nor did Peter, or the others, take gold or silver
from Matthias when he was picked by lot
96   to fill the place lost by the guilty soul.

'Stay there then, for you are justly punished,
guarding well those gains, ill-gotten,
99   that made you boldly take your stand against King Charles.

'And were it not that I am still restrained
by the reverence I owe the keys supreme,
102   which once you held in the happy life above,

'I would resort to even harsher words
because your avarice afflicts the world,
105   trampling down the good and raising up the wicked.

'Shepherds like you the Evangelist had in mind
when he saw the one that sits upon the waters
108   committing fornication with the kings,

'she that was born with seven heads
and from ten horns derived her strength
111   so long as virtue pleased her bridegroom.

'You have wrought yourselves a god of gold and silver.
How then do you differ from those who worship idols
114   except they worship one and you a hundred?

'Ah, Constantine, to what evil you gave birth,
not by your conversion, but by the dowry
117   that the first rich Father had from you!'

E mentr' io li cantava cotai note,
o ira o coscïenza che 'l mordesse,
120   forte spingava con ambo le piote.

I' credo ben ch'al mio duca piacesse,
con sì contenta labbia sempre attese
123   lo suon de le parole vere espresse.

Però con ambo le braccia mi prese;
e poi che tutto su mi s'ebbe al petto,
126   rimontò per la via onde discese.

Né si stancò d'avermi a sé distretto,
sì men portò sovra 'l colmo de l'arco
129   che dal quarto al quinto argine è tragetto.

Quivi soavemente spuose il carco,
soave per lo scoglio sconcio ed erto
che sarebbe a le capre duro varco.
133   Indi un altro vallon mi fu scoperto.

And while I sang such notes to him,
whether gnawed by anger or by conscience,
120   he kicked out hard with both his feet.

Truly I believe this pleased my leader,
he listened with a look of such contentment
123   to the sound of the truthful words I spoke.

Therefore, he caught me in his arms
and, when he had me all upon his breast,
126   remounted by the path he had descended,

nor did he tire of holding me so close
but bore me to the summit of the arch
129   that crosses from the fourth dike to the fifth.

Here gently he set down his burden,
gently on account of the steep, rough ridge
that would have made hard going for a goat.
133   And there, before me, another valley opened.

1–6.   "In the Bible, Simon Magus was a sorcerer of Samaria who was converted by the preaching of Philip the evangelist (see Acts 8:9–13). When he subsequently attempted to buy the power of conferring the Holy Ghost, he was severely rebuked by the apostle Peter for thinking that the gift of God might be purchased with money (see Acts 8:14–24). From the name Simon is derived the word 'simony,' which is applied to all traffic in sacred things, especially the buying or selling of ecclesiastical offices" (Singleton's comment).

For the intrinsic and striking distinction between the man named Simon, who was a *magus* (Acts 8:9), and the apostle Peter, also named Simon (*Simon Petrus*—John 20:2, 20:6), see Singleton (Sing.1965.1) as well as Herzman and Stephany (Herz.1978.1), pp. 40, 46. Nicholas is seen as the follower of Simon Magus, while Dante presents himself as the follower of Simon Peter.

For studies of the canto as a whole see Fost.1969.1 and the third chapter of Musa.1974.1.

16–21.   Some have argued that this passage is not credible if taken literally and, therefore, must be understood as metaphorical. See Spitzer (Spit.1943.1) and, more recently, Noakes (Noak.1968.1), who argues that the public vow of adherence to the French king taken, in the baptistry and thus in proximity to the font, before Charles of Valois entered Florence in 1302, is what Dante now confesses he "broke." The language of the passage is so concrete that it seems difficult to credit such an ingenious solution.

Mazzoni (Mazz.1981.1) affirms the literal meaning of the passage, while leaving in doubt the nature of the act that Dante claims to have performed. Reviewing the commentary tradition, he supports the view of most of the early commentators that the noun *battezzatori* refers to the priests who performed baptismal rites. Mirko Tavoni (Tavo.1992.1) gives reasons for believing that it refers to the fonts themselves. That question is probably not resolvable, as the noun can have either meaning.

All the early commentators take the incident referred to here as actually having occurred, when a child, playing with other children, became lodged in one of the smaller baptismal fonts of the Florentine baptistry. Castelvetro has perhaps the most believable explanation; in his view the baptismal font and its several little *pozzetti* were protected by a thin wooden covering in order to protect the holy water from sight (and desacralizing droppings?). It is *this* and not the marble of the font (which Benvenuto da Imola has Dante breaking with an axe brought to him by a bystander) that the poet broke, thus saving the near-drowned child. His solemn oath, reminiscent of the language describing papal bulls and their seals, now stakes his authority as Florentine and poet on the charitable nature of his act, which others had apparently characterized as sacrilegious. Whatever explanation we find most acceptable, it seems clear that Dante is referring to an actual event that his former fellow-citizens would remember.

22–24.   We shall later learn that Dante here comes face to feet with a pope, Nicholas III (vv. 69–72). The inverted figure, like Judas in the central mouth of Lucifer (*Inf.* XXXIV.63), has his head within, his legs without. Dante's use of *bocca* (mouth) for the opening of the hole into which he descends suggests that eventually Nicholas will be eaten and digested by hell itself once the next simoniac pope comes to his eternal station.

25.   For the parodic inversion of Pentecostal fire in the punishment of sins that involve the perversion of the gift of the Holy Spirit, in particular as manifest in the misuse of extraordinary gifts of persuasion found among those punished as heresiarchs, sodomites, simoniacs, and false counselors, see Reginald French (Fren.1964.1), pp. 8–10.

28–30.   For the oil referred to here as indicative, parodically, of the anointing unction that priests offer those who suffer, see Herzman and Stephany (Herz.1978.1), pp. 49–51. Unction is usually associated with the head, not the feet; the ironic point is clear.

35.   The further bank of the *bolgia* is not as high as the nearer one because the slope of the Malebolge cuts away the topmost part of each successive pouch. For this reason Virgil will lead Dante over the third *bolgia* to the fourth embankment only to climb down into the third from this vantage point.

37–39.   Dante's submissiveness to his lord, acknowledging Virgil's awareness of his wishes, is surely meant to contrast with Nicholas's rebellious offense to his.

46–47.   The pope's situation is reminiscent of St. Peter's upside-down crucifixion (see Herzman and Stephany [Herz.1978.1, p. 44]), but also refers to the Florentine mode of dispatching convicted assassins, "planting" them upside down in a hole and then suffocating them when the hole is filled back up with earth: "Let the assassin be planted upside down, so that he may be put to death."

49–51.   Dante now assumes the role of confessing friar. The last verse of the tercet has caused controversy. While *cessare*, used transitively, ordinarily in Dante means "to avoid," most agree that here it means "delay." In our translation we have tried to hedge, using "stay" in such a way as to allow it to be interpreted either as "put off (for a while)" or "put a stop to."

52–53.   The first naming of Pope Boniface VIII (Benedetto Caetani) in the poem. Succeeding Celestine V in January 1295 and dying in October 1303, he greatly strengthened the power of the papacy, while also asserting its temporal power in the realm Dante allowed to empire alone. His support of the Black Guelphs and the French forces in Florence earned him Dante's unflagging enmity. Nicholas's taking Dante for Boniface is grimly yet hilariously amusing.

54.   Some have suggested that the condition of future knowledge alluded to by Farinata (*Inf.* X.100–108) pertains only to the heretics; this passage would seem to indicate clearly that others, as well, and perhaps all those in hell, have some sense of the future but none of the present. Nicholas had "read" in the "book of the future" that Boniface would be on his way to hell as of 1303, and is thus now confused, as he expects no one else to pile in on top of him but Boniface.

57.   The beautiful Lady is, resolved from metaphor, the Church, Christ's "bride."

69–72.   Pope Nicholas III (Giovanni Gaetano Orsini) served from 1277–80, openly practicing nepotism in favor of his relations. His references to the "she-bear" and her "cubs" reflect his family name, Orsini (*orsa* means "bear" in Italian), one of the most powerful of Roman families.

79–87.   Clement is compared to Jason, brother of the high priest Onias. From the king of Syria, Antiochus IV Epiphanes, he bought his brother's position and then brought pagan practices to Jerusalem (see II Mach. 4:7–26). In short, to Dante he seemed a Jewish "simoniac pope," prefiguring the corrupt practices of Clement. Dante condemns, as Durling points out (Durl.1996.1, p. 300), a number of Clement's actions, including "his role in Philip's destruction of the Templars, *Purg*. XX.91–93; the removal of the papal see to Avignon, *Purg*. XXXII.157–160; his simony, *Par*. XVII.82; and his betrayal of Henry VII, *Par*. XXX.142–148."

This is perhaps the crucial passage for those who debate the internal dating of the composition of the poem. First, one should explain its literal meaning. Nicholas has now been "cooking" for twenty years (1280–1300). The Frenchman Bertrand de Got, who served as Pope Clement V from 1305–1314 and who supervised the papacy's removal to Avignon in 1309, an act that caused much Italian outrage (and notably Dante's [see *Purg*. XXXII.157–160; *Epist*. XI.21–26]), will replace Boniface as topmost simoniac pope before Boniface spends twenty years in that position of punishment, i.e., before 1323. If the first *cantica* was composed, as many, but not all, propose, between 1306–07 and 1309–10, Dante here is either making a rough (and chancy) prediction that Clement, who suffered from ill health, would die sometime before 1323, or he is knowingly referring to the death of Clement in 1314. However, most, observing Dante's general practice in "predicting" only things actually known to him, argue that this is a prophecy *post eventum*, i.e., that the passage was written after April of 1314, when Clement died. If that is true, then either the traditional dating of the poem's composition is incorrect, and it was written later (and much more quickly) than is generally believed (ca. 1313–1321), or Dante inserted this passage while he was revising *Inferno* in 1315 before circulating it. This is Petrocchi's solution (Petr.1969.1), and many follow it. For an opposing view, see Padoan (Pado.1993.1). And for a summary of the question and bibliography see A. E. Quaglio, "Commedia, Composizione," *ED* (vol. 2, 1970), pp. 81–82.

That this is the only reference to Clement before well into *Purgatorio* lends support to the idea that this passage is a later interpolation. In a paper written in 1999 Stefano Giannini (Gian.1999.1), a graduate student at Johns Hopkins University, examined all the references to events occurring after 1300 in *Inferno*. His provisional results are as follows: 22 references to events occurring between 1300 and 1304; 4 references to events occurring between 1306 and 1309 (all between Cantos XXVI and XXIX); this sole reference to an event occurring in 1314. These results would certainly seem to support those who maintain that this passage is a later interpolation and that *Inferno* was essentially completed during the first decade of the fourteenth century

88–89.   Dante's coyness here is palpable: of course he is not being "too bold" *(troppo folle)* in the eyes of any just observer. At the same time he is clearly aware of the enormity of his "singing" such a "tune" to a pope.

90–117.   Dante's great outburst of invective against Nicholas (and all simoniac popes) is based on the history of the Church, beginning with Christ's calling of Peter, moving to Peter's and the other apostles' choosing Matthias by lot to take the place of Judas. After Dante alludes to Nicholas's vile maneuvering against the Angevin king, Charles I of Sicily, he returns to the Bible, now to Rev. 17, interpreted positively as the presentation of the Roman Church as keeper of the seven gifts of the Holy Spirit and the Ten Commandments. (For the relationship between the woman here [Rome as honest wife of the Caesars, free of papal constraint] and the whore of *Purgatorio* XXXII [Rome as the corrupted Church after the Donation of Constantine] see Davis [Davi.1998.1], p. 271.) Dante's oration ends with a final slam at papal worship of "the golden calf," joining the final apostrophe of the canto in rebuke of Constantine as the source of most of Christianity's troubles when he granted the papacy temporal authority.

115–117.   The author's apostrophe of the emperor Constantine (reigned 306–337) holds him responsible for the so-called "Donation of Constantine," by which he granted temporal sovereignty to Pope Sylvester I (314–335)—and his successors—over Italy and the rest of the western empire. This document was considered genuine until Lorenzo Valla, in the fifteenth century, demonstrated that it was a forgery. For Dante it was genuine and a cause for excited concern. (His views on the subject are exposited forcefully in the later *Monarchia* [III.x.1–9]). In his view the emperor was not empowered to give over his authority; thus the document was truthful, but its legitimacy compromised.

We are perhaps meant to understand by these lines that Sylvester, who cured Constantine of leprosy and was, as a result, rewarded by him with authority over the Roman Empire, is the bottom-most pope in this hole, the "first rich Father," a condition that was to his immediate benefit but to the eventual loss of all Christians.

124–126.   Virgil's pleasure in Dante is indeed so great that he embraces him and carries him back out of the *bolgia.*

128–130.   Virgil sets Dante down upon the bridge that overlooks the fourth *bolgia,* in which, in the next canto, Dante will observe the diviners.

INFERNO XX

Di nova pena mi conven far versi
e dar matera al ventesimo canto
3   de la prima canzon, ch'è d'i sommersi.

Io era già disposto tutto quanto
a riguardar ne lo scoperto fondo,
6   che si bagnava d'angoscioso pianto;

e vidi gente per lo vallon tondo
venir, tacendo e lagrimando, al passo
9   che fanno le letane in questo mondo.

Come 'l viso mi scese in lor più basso,
mirabilmente apparve esser travolto
12   ciascun tra 'l mento e 'l principio del casso,

ché da le reni era tornato 'l volto,
e in dietro venir li convenia,
15   perché 'l veder dinanzi era lor tolto.

Forse per forza già di parlasia
si travolse così alcun del tutto;
18   ma io nol vidi, né credo che sia.

Se Dio ti lasci, lettor, prender frutto
di tua lezione, or pensa per te stesso
21   com' io potea tener lo viso asciutto,

quando la nostra imagine di presso
vidi sì torta, che 'l pianto de li occhi
24   le natiche bagnava per lo fesso.

Certo io piangea, poggiato a un de' rocchi
del duro scoglio, sì che la mia scorta
27   mi disse: "Ancor se' tu de li altri sciocchi?

Of strange new pain I now must make my verse,
giving matter to the canto numbered twenty
of this first *canzone*, which tells of those submerged.

By now I was all eagerness to see
what sights the chasm, bathed in tears
of anguish, would disclose.

I saw people come along that curving canyon
in silence, weeping, their pace the pace of slow
processions chanting litanies in the world.

As my gaze moved down along their shapes,
I saw into what strange contortions
their chins and chests were twisted.

Their faces were reversed upon their shoulders
so that they came on walking backward,
since seeing forward was denied them.

Perhaps some time by stroke of palsy
a person could be twisted in that way,
but I've not seen it nor do I think it likely.

Reader, so may God let you gather fruit
from reading this, imagine, if you can,
how I could have kept from weeping

when I saw, up close, our human likeness
so contorted that tears from their eyes
ran down their buttocks, down into the cleft.

Yes, I wept, leaning against a spur
of the rough crag, so that my escort said:
'Are you still witless as the rest?

3

6

9

12

15

18

21

24

27

Qui vive la pietà quand' è ben morta;
chi è più scellerato che colui
30   che al giudicio divin passion comporta?

Drizza la testa, drizza, e vedi a cui
s'aperse a li occhi d'i Teban la terra;
33   per ch'ei gridavan tutti: 'Dove rui,

Anfïarao? perché lasci la guerra?'
E non restò di ruinare a valle
36   fino a Minòs che ciascheduno afferra.

Mira c'ha fatto petto de le spalle;
perché volse veder troppo davante,
39   di retro guarda e fa retroso calle.

Vedi Tiresia, che mutò sembiante
quando di maschio femmina divenne,
42   cangiandosi le membra tutte quante;

e prima, poi, ribatter li convenne
li duo serpenti avvolti, con la verga,
45   che rïavesse le maschili penne.

Aronta è quel ch'al ventre li s'atterga,
che ne' monti di Luni, dove ronca
48   lo Carrarese che di sotto alberga,

ebbe tra ' bianchi marmi la spelonca
per sua dimora; onde a guardar le stelle
51   e 'l mar non li era la veduta tronca.

E quella che ricuopre le mammelle,
che tu non vedi, con le trecce sciolte,
54   e ha di là ogne pilosa pelle,

Manto fu, che cercò per terre molte;
poscia si puose là dove nacqu' io;
57   onde un poco mi piace che m'ascolte.

'Here piety lives when pity is quite dead.
Who is more impious than one who thinks
30   that God shows passion in His judgment?

'Raise your head! Raise it and look on him
under whose feet the earth gaped open
33   in sight of all the shouting Thebans:

' "Where are you rushing, Amphiaraus? Why
do you leave the war?" Nor did he stop his plunge
36   until he fell to Minos, who lays hold on all.

'See how his shoulder-blades are now his chest.
Because he aspired to see too far ahead
39   he looks behind and treads a backward path.

'See Tiresias, who changed his likeness
when he was turned from male to female,
42   transformed in every member.

'Later on he had to touch once more
the two twined serpents with his rod
45   before he could regain his manly plumes.

'He who puts his back to that one's belly is Aruns.
In the hills of Luni—where the Carraresi,
48   who shelter in the valley, work the earth—

'he lived inside a cave in that white marble,
from which he could observe the sea and stars
51   in a wide and boundless prospect.

'And that female whose backward-flowing tresses
fall upon her breasts so they are hidden,
54   and has her hairy parts on that same side,

'was Manto, who searched through many lands
before she settled in the place where I was born—
57   for just a moment hear me out on this.

Poscia che 'l padre suo di vita uscìo
e venne serva la città di Baco,
60   questa gran tempo per lo mondo gio.

Suso in Italia bella giace un laco,
a piè de l'Alpe che serra Lamagna
63   sovra Tiralli, c'ha nome Benaco.

Per mille fonti, credo, e più si bagna
tra Garda e Val Camonica e Pennino
66   de l'acqua che nel detto laco stagna.

Loco è nel mezzo là dove 'l trentino
pastore e quel di Brescia e 'l veronese
69   segnar poria, s'e' fesse quel cammino.

Siede Peschiera, bello e forte arnese
da fronteggiar Bresciani e Bergamaschi,
72   ove la riva 'ntorno più discese.

Ivi convien che tutto quanto caschi
ciò che 'n grembo a Benaco star non può,
75   e fassi fiume giù per verdi paschi.

Tosto che l'acqua a correr mette co,
non più Benaco, ma Mencio si chiama
78   fino a Govèrnol, dove cade in Po.

Non molto ha corso, ch'el trova una lama,
ne la qual si distende e la 'mpaluda;
81   e suol di state talor esser grama.

Quindi passando la vergine cruda
vide terra, nel mezzo del pantano,
84   sanza coltura e d'abitanti nuda.

Lì, per fuggire ogne consorzio umano,
ristette con suoi servi a far sue arti,
87   e visse, e vi lasciò suo corpo vano.

'After her father had parted from this life
and the city of Bacchus was enslaved,
60   she wandered for a time about the world.

'High in fair Italy, at the foot of the alps
that form a border with Germany near Tyrol,
63   lies a lake they call Benàco.

'By a thousand springs and more, I think,
the region between Garda, Val Camonica, and Pennino
66   is bathed by waters settling in that lake.

'There is an island in its middle
that the pastors of Trent, Brescia, and Verona,
69   should they pass that way, would bless.

'Peschiera, a strong and splendid fortress
against the Brescians and the Bergamese,
72   sits on the lowest point of land around.

'There all the water Benàco's bosom cannot hold
flows over and descends into a river
75   running through green pastures.

'This river, as it leaves the lake
and all the way to Govérnolo, is called
78   the Mincio until it falls into the Po.

'Before that, after but the briefest run,
it levels off and spreads to make a swamp
81   sometimes scarce of water in the summer.

'When she passed that way, the cruel virgin
saw dry land in the middle of the marsh
84   where no one lived and no one tilled the soil.

'There, to avoid all company, she stopped,
with only servants, to ply her magic arts.
87   There she lived and left her empty body.

Li uomini poi che 'ntorno erano sparti
s'accolsero a quel loco, ch'era forte
90 per lo pantan ch'avea da tutte parti.

Fer la città sovra quell' ossa morte;
e per colei che 'l loco prima elesse,
93 Mantüa l'appellar sanz' altra sorte.

Già fuor le genti sue dentro più spesse,
prima che la mattia da Casalodi
96 da Pinamonte inganno ricevesse.

Però t'assenno che, se tu mai odi
originar la mia terra altrimenti,
99 la verità nulla menzogna frodi."

E io: "Maestro, i tuoi ragionamenti
mi son sì certi e prendon sì mia fede,
102 che li altri mi sarien carboni spenti.

Ma dimmi, de la gente che procede,
se tu ne vedi alcun degno di nota;
105 ché solo a ciò la mia mente rifiede."

Allor mi disse: "Quel che da la gota
porge la barba in su le spalle brune,
108 fu—quando Grecia fu di maschi vòta,

sì ch'a pena rimaser per le cune—
augure, e diede 'l punto con Calcanta
111 in Aulide a tagliar la prima fune.

Euripilo ebbe nome, e così 'l canta
l'alta mia tragedìa in alcun loco:
114 ben lo sai tu che la sai tutta quanta.

Quell' altro che ne' fianchi è così poco,
Michele Scotto fu, che veramente
117 de le magiche frode seppe 'l gioco.

'Later on, the people scattered round about
collected there because it was protected
90   by the marsh on every side.

'They built the city over those dead bones
and, after her who first had claimed the spot,
93   named it Mantua, with no spells or incantations.

'Once, its population was more plentiful,
before the foolishness of Casalodi
96   bore the brunt of Pinamonte's guile.

'I charge you, therefore, should you ever hear
my city's origin described another way,
99   allow no lie to falsify the truth.'

And I: 'Master, to me your explanation
is so convincing and so takes my trust
102   that any other tale would seem spent embers.

'But tell me, among these people who are passing,
if you see any worthy of my notice,
105   for my thoughts keep going back to them alone.'

Then he replied: 'The one whose beard
falls from his jowls onto his swarthy shoulders
108   was—when Greece was so deprived of males

'that the only ones still there were in their cradles—
a soothsayer. At Aulis, along with Calchas,
111   he told the favoring time for setting sail.

'Eurypylus was his name, and thus he is sung
in certain verses of my lofty tragedy,
114   as you know very well, who know it all.

'That other, with the skinny shanks,
was Michael Scot, who truly understood
117   the way to play the game of magic tricks.

Vedi Guido Bonatti; vedi Asdente,
ch'avere inteso al cuoio e a lo spago
120   ora vorrebbe, ma tardi si pente.

Vedi le triste che lasciaron l'ago,
la spuola e 'l fuso, e fecersi 'ndivine;
123   fecer malie con erbe e con imago.

Ma vienne omai, ché già tiene 'l confine
d'amendue li emisperi e tocca l'onda
126   sotto Sobilia Caino e le spine;

e già iernotte fu la luna tonda:
ben ten de' ricordar, ché non ti nocque
alcuna volta per la selva fonda."
130   Sì mi parlava, e andavamo introcque.

'See Guido Bonatti. See Asdente, who now regrets
not having worked his leather and his thread—
120   but he repents too late.

'See the wretched women who gave up needle,
spool, and spindle to take up fortune-telling,
123   casting spells with images and herbs.

'But come now, for Cain, with his thorns,
already stands above the border of both hemispheres
126   and touches the waves below Seville,

'and last night was the moon already round.
Surely you recall it did not harm you
at any time in the deep wood.'
130   These were his words while we were moving on.

1–3.   The uniquely self-conscious opening of this canto, featuring the only explicit numeration of a canto in the poem, has caused a certain puzzlement and even consternation. One discussant, H. D. Austin, has argued that its prosaic superfluity recommends that future editors either excise it from the poem, as an addition by an overenthusiastic scribe, or at least print it in square brackets (Aust.1932.1, pp. 39–40). Its self-consciousness and difficulty, one might argue in rejoinder, are precisely signs of Dantean authorship.

The opening line portrays a poet who only unwillingly commits himself to the difficult task he now must assume. Many of the words of this first tercet have received close critical attention. *Nova* has either the sense (or both senses, as our translation would indicate) of "new" or "strange" (see D'Ovidio [Dovi.1926.1], p. 318). *Matera* is, as Chiavacci Leonardi says (Chia.1991.1), p. 599, a "technical term," one used to denote the subject that a writer chooses to treat. *Canto* is here used for the first time (it will be used again only at *Inf.* XXXIII.90, *Par.* V.16 and V.139) to indicate a part of the poem; as Barański (Bara.1995.3, pp. 3–4) has pointed out, the early commentators found this term strange, rendering it with Latin or Italian words for "chapter" or "book." *Canzone* is a still more troubling choice of word (it is used twice more, *Purg.* XXXI.134, XXXII.90); in *De vulgari eloquentia* (e.g., *Dve* II.viii.2–9) it is the word (*cantio* in Dante's Latin) that describes the lofty vernacular ode that Dante presents (with himself as most successful practitioner of the form) as the height of poetic eloquence in the mother tongue, and thus "tragic" in tone, because it is like the lofty style of the classical poets. Is Dante suggesting that *Inferno* is tragic? (For some thoughts along this line see Hollander [Holl.1980.1], pp. 137–40.) It is only in *Purg.* XXXIII.140 that he will finally give a part of the poem the name it now enjoys: *cantica,* with its religious (resonance of Solomon's Canticle of Canticles [see Pert.1991.1, pp. 107–8]) and "comic" overtones. And finally there is the apparently strikingly inexact word *sommersi,* which has seemed to many commentators wrong, since the damned are not submerged in water but buried under earth. Marino Barchiesi (Barc.1973.2), p. 85, resolved this problem by finding a probable source in the *Aeneid* (VI.267), where Virgil asks the gods for permission "pandere res alta terra et caligine mersas" (to reveal things immersed deep in earth and darkness).

If the opening tercet causes this much difficulty, what follows will

often be at least as challenging. One of the most interesting and provoca-
tive studies of the canto remains Parodi's essay (Paro.1908.1). It is a canto
that is still today renowned for its problematic nature.

4–9.   The first description of the diviners insists upon their silence and
their misery, expressed by tears, the only form of expression allowed them,
given the fact that their necks are twisted, thus cutting off the possibility
of speech. We are probably meant to reflect on the fact that their voices,
announcing their false prescriptions, were the instruments of their decep-
tion of their clients/victims.

10–12.   Hollander has suggested (Holl.1980.1, p. 141) that the image of
the twisted necks of the diviners, with the resultant loss of the capacity
of speech, may have been suggested by a text in Lucan (*Phars.* V.197),
in which Apollo closes off the throat of a prophetess (Phemonoe) before
she can reveal the rest of a dire prophecy, thus depriving her Roman
listener of news of his unhappy destiny: "Cetera suppressit faucesque
obstruxit Apollo" (Apollo closed her throat and suppressed the rest of her
speech).

13–15.   The backward-looking diviners suffer this *contrapasso* for having
looked, with wrongful intent, into the future. Biblical references have
seemed apt to an occasional commentator. Pietro di Dante adduces Isaiah
44:25: "[I am the Lord] That frustrates the tokens of the liars, and makes
diviners mad; that turns wise men backward, and makes their knowledge
foolish."

19–24.   The first tercet of this fourth address to the reader in this *cantica*
(see note to *Inf.* VIII.94–96) is generally understood as indicating that,
given the sad sight he must behold, Dante is excusing himself from blame
for weeping. Benvenuto da Imola, however, has a differing view (and says
that "this subtle fiction is poorly understood by many others"). According
to him, Dante's tears reveal his guilty feelings about his own involvement
in astrological prediction and that "as a result he presents himself as weep-
ing out of compassion for others, and for himself because of his own
errors." It is possible to read the passage in an even harsher light. If the
reader is to "gather fruit" from reading this passage, is it not likely that its
point is that Dante was wrong to weep for these creatures? What he feels is
sadness at the human figure rendered so contorted, forgetting the reason
for the (entirely just) punishment.

25–27.   Dante weeps and thereby earns Virgil's rebuke (which commentators since Tommaseo have related to the words that Jesus directed to Peter and the other apostles, slow to take his meaning, found in Matthew 15:16: "Adhuc et vos sine intellectu estis?" (Are you also even yet without understanding?) A question that has exercised many readers is whether the protagonist already knows that those punished here are the diviners. While some, like Ettore Caccia (Cacc.1967.1, p. 695) and Antonino Pagliaro (Pagl.1967.1, p. 611), argue that Dante weeps only at the piteous condition of the contorted human body, and not for the lot of the diviners, others, like Marino Barchiesi (Barc.1973.1, p. 62) reply that such distinction-making is oversubtle. Indeed, the whole context of the canto would make it seem necessary that Virgil's rebuke is not aimed at so wide a target, but rather at Dante's failure to react adversely to the diviners.

28–30.   Perhaps the tercet in the canto that has caused the most debate. Where is "here" (qui)? Who is indicated by the first "who" (chi)? And what does the last verse of the tercet mean? In response to the first two questions, Hollander has made the following observations (Holl.1980.1, p. 147), dividing the most plausible series of answers into two groups: "(1) If Dante weeps for lost humanity in general, qui refers to hell in general and chi almost certainly refers to Dante. (2) If Dante weeps for the diviners in particular, qui refers to this bolgia and chi almost certainly applies to the diviners." Carlo Steiner, in his commentary to this passage, argues that it seems logically inconsistent for Virgil to call Dante "witless" at v. 27 and "impious" at v. 29, as stupidity and impiety are some stages distant one from another.

As for the complicated philological problem regarding the exact reading of verse 30, this writer, along with many another, accepts the arguments of Petrocchi (Petr.1966.1, pp. 181–82) for the reading "passion comporta" (and not "compassion porta" or "passïon porta"). For a fuller exposition, based on texts in Statius and St. Augustine, see Holl.1980.1, pp. 147–57, citing, for Augustine, the earlier discussions of Filomusi Guelfi (Filo.1911.1), pp. 192–95; and now see Puccetti (Pucc.1994.1), pp. 199–206. For brief descriptions of a good half-dozen competing interpretations of the sin of the diviners see Caccia (Cacc.1967.1), pp. 688–90.

31–39.   In Canto XI Virgil has two continuous speeches of some length, vv. 15–66 and vv. 76–115. We are here involved in Virgil's longest single speech in the poem, vv. 27–99. Having warned Dante against the sin of divination, he now proceeds to identify its exemplars, beginning with five classical diviners. The first of these derives from Statius. "Amphiaraus . . . was one of the seven kings who joined in the expedition against Thebes (*Inf.* XIV.68); foreseeing that the issue would be fatal to himself, he concealed himself to avoid going to the war, but his hiding-place was revealed by his wife Eriphyle, who had been bribed by Polynices with the necklace of Harmonia (*Purg.* XII.50–51). Amphiaraus, as had been foreseen, met his death at Thebes, being swallowed up by the earth, but before he died he enjoined his son Alcmaeon to put Eriphyle to death on his return from Thebes, in punishment of her betrayal of him (*Par.* IV.103–105)" **(T)**. The incidents referred to here are a somewhat reinvented version of the narrative found in Statius (*Thebaid* VII.690–823; VIII.1–210). For Dante's willful distortions of the story of this augur, who is portrayed with great sympathy by Statius, see Holl.1980.1, pp. 170–73.

40–45.   "Tiresias, famous soothsayer of Thebes. According to the story he once separated with his staff two serpents which he found coupled in a wood, whereupon he was changed into a woman for seven years; at the expiration of this period he found the same two serpents and struck them again, whereupon he was changed back into a man. Subsequently, Jupiter and Juno having differed as to which of the two sexes experienced the greater [sexual] pleasure, the question was referred to Tiresias, as having belonged to both sexes, and he decided in favour of woman, which coincided with the opinion of Jupiter; Juno thereupon in anger struck him with blindness, but Jupiter, by way of compensation, endowed him with the gift of prophecy (Ovid, *Metam.* III.316–38)" **(T)**. For a study of Dante's recasting of Ovid's essentially positive presentation of Tiresias, making him a repulsive figure rather than the truthful and blameless seer he is in Ovid, with particular attention to the *verga*, or magic wand, that Dante contrives for him, thus associating him with Circe and Mercury, see Holl.1980.1, pp. 173–84.

46–51.   "Aruns, Etruscan soothsayer, who, according to Lucan (*Phars.* I.584–638) foretold the civil war, which was to end in the death of Pompey and the triumph of Caesar. Dante . . . describes him as having dwelt in a cave . . . in the Carrara hills" **(T)**. Castelvetro, in his comment on this passage, points out that, in Lucan's text, Aruns does not dwell in a cave but within the walls of Luni and that, furthermore, he was not an astrologer (as Dante implies) but used other means to develop his soothsaying (e.g., studying the flight of birds, the innards of animals, the course of the thunderbolt).

52–56. "Manto, daughter of Tiresias, Theban prophetess . . . ; Dante here puts into Virgil's mouth an account of the founding of Mantua by Manto . . . which is totally inconsistent with Virgil's own account as given in the *Aeneid* (X.198–200). By an oversight Dante also includes *la figlia di Tiresia*, who can be none other than Manto, among the persons mentioned by Statius who Virgil says are together with himself in Limbo (*Purg.* XXII.113)" **(T)**. Compared with the violence done to classical texts in the preceding three examples (Amphiaraus, Tiresias, and Aruns), that done to Virgil's tale of Manto is even more remarkable. Even her hair seems to belong to another, whether the uncombed locks of frenetic Erichtho ("inpexis . . . comis"—*Phars.* VI.518), as Benvenuto da Imola suggested, or those of the Sibyl (perhaps the "source" for Lucan's witch's hair), "non comptae . . . comes" (*Aeneid* VI.48), as noted by Grabher. Since the Roman poet, as surely Dante realized, had deliberately associated his birthplace (Pietola, then probably known as Andes, near Mantua) with Manto, so as to make himself, like her, a *vates*, or prophet (see the study by Marie Desport [Desp.1952.1]), Dante now makes his *maestro ed autore* recant the fiction that he himself had devised. (Virgil's commentators themselves had wondered how the Greek Manto could have come to Italy in order to found her city, since Virgil's poem is the only text to contain this claim.)

One of the lasting problems left by this canto is its eventual contradiction of Dante's placement of Manto in Limbo in *Purgatorio* XXII.113, where Virgil tells Statius that various of the characters of whom the later poet wrote are found in that zone of the afterworld. Previous writers had resorted to various hypotheses, none particularly satisfying, in order to explain how Dante could have forgotten what he had said about Manto here when he wrote the later passage, or that, with equal failure to satisfy, "the daughter of Tiresias" of *Purgatorio* XXII was someone other than Manto, or even that the original text read something other than "la figlia di Tiresia." Two Americans have argued independently that the apparent contradiction is intentional, and is based on Dante's willful insistence that the Manto portrayed by Virgil was indeed a diviner, while the same character portrayed by Statius was not (she is rather the dutiful daughter of Tiresias, helping with the chores, as it were). See Richard Kay (Kay.1978.2) and Robert Hollander (Holl.1980.1), pp. 205–13. Kay also argues, less convincingly, that Dante thought of Virgil's Manto as historical and of Statius's character as fictive, thus further excusing the bilocation.

57–60. With risible understatement, the poet has Virgil ask for a little of the protagonist's time (his digression will continue until verse 99, occupying fully fourteen *terzine*). This passage begins by tacitly acknowledging the utter fictiveness of this account, since we have no source for what happened to Manto after Tiresias's death (and the conquest of Thebes by Creon). Dante puts, into the mouth of Virgil, an account of her voyage into Italy. As is the case for that undertaken by Ulysses in Canto XXVI, there is no known source for this one, either.

61–63.   We turn our attention from the story of Manto in order to examine the landscape of Italy, to which she will repair in her wanderings. Benaco is now known as Lake Garda.

64–69.   The fresh waters of northern Italy, entering into Garda, with its island that might serve for Christian services if the various bishops of its neighboring dioceses were to gather there, since a chapel on the island was subject to the jurisdiction of all three of them, will be seen to contrast with the muddy waters surrounding Manto's adoptive homeland once we arrive there. For discussion of the meaning of these geographical references see Caccia (Cacc.1966.1).

70–72.   The fortress at Peschiera, under the control of the Scaliger family of Verona, with whom Dante was on good terms by the time he was writing the *Comedy*, is seen as strong enough to hold off attacks from the cities of Brescia or Bergamo.

73–78.   Leaving Benaco (Garda), the waters that began in the mountains to the north now head south (in the Mincio) and finally, after reaching Governolo, east (in the Po—in which they finally reach the [Adriatic] sea).

79–81.   Here the attention of Dante turns back to a spot that the waters reach *before* they attain Governolo, the untilled, swampy land that will become the site of Mantua.

85–93.   Finally here is Manto. She is described as "vergine cruda" (cruel virgin [in the sense that she does not like the company of men]), a phrase that may reflect Statius's description of her (*Thebaid* IV.463) as "innuba Manto" and/or Dante's description of that other diviner, Erichtho, who is "Eritón cruda" at *Inf.* IX.23. Here she practiced her divinatory arts with her servants and died. Those who had fled her fearsome presence returned after her death and built Virgil's city upon her bones, giving it her name, but not her divinatory capacity. What is at first shocking about this account is that it contradicts what we find in the *Aeneid*, where (X.198–203) we learn that the city was founded by Ocnus, the son of Manto. In other words, Dante has excised (indeed, has forced Virgil himself to excise) Ocnus. For if Manto had had progeny, as she did according to Virgil, then her mantic ability might have been passed on to others—the claim that Virgil was evidently himself bent upon making in his poem, only to be forced to recant it here in Dante's. It is an extraordinary moment.

94–96. Dante's reference to a late-thirteenth-century political disaster in Mantua probably seems gratuitous to the modern reader. Given the poet's concern with the condition of his own Florence, however, we can appreciate his interest in the dramatic events resulting from when the Guelph leader of Mantua, the Count of Casalodi, allowed himself to be tricked by the Ghibelline Pinamonte Bonacolsi, who apparently convinced him to expel many of the nobles in order to mollify the populace, angered by his having come from Brescia to rule in 1272. Foolishly exiling even members of his own party, he was in time bereft of supporters; in 1291, Pinamonte led a popular revolt that sent the count into exile and killed the remaining noble families. The tercet offered Dante a moment's bitter reflection upon his own condition as exiled Guelph, brought about by the similar folly of his fellow citizens.

97–102. Capping his (to us absurd yet amusing) contradiction of the details of the founding of Mantua published in his own poem, Virgil now gets Dante to swear that he will regard only the current version of that history as truthful, and that he will consider any other version, i.e., the Roman poet's own, as nothing other than a lie. The protagonist dutifully assents. Thus is Virgil made to remove the stain of divination from his poem and from himself. The result is eventually quite different from what the tactic might have been intended to secure, i.e., Virgil's poem is seen precisely as associated with this fault. See Barolini (Baro.1998.1), pp. 283–84.

106–114. "Eurypylus, augur sent by the Greeks to consult the oracle of Apollo as to their departure from Troy; he brought back the reply that, as their departure from Greece had cost them a bloody sacrifice in the death of Iphigenia, so by blood must they purchase their return (*Aen.* II.114–119). Dante, who describes Eurypylus as having a long beard, . . . makes Virgil say (vv. 110–113) that Eurypylus was associated with Calchas in foretelling the time of the sailing of the Greek fleet from Aulis; but there is no mention of this fact in the *Aeneid*" (**T**). Toynbee's version is not exactly correct. Not even in Sinon's lying account of these events, to which the text refers, is Eurypylus said to be an augur: the message that he brings back from Apollo's shrine is then interpreted by Calchas, the "true" augur in the *Aeneid*, to mean that Sinon must be sacrificed. We should reflect that Dante must have realized that none of what Sinon says is truthful. Yet he nonetheless uses this material in order to concoct his own still more inauthentic version of events. See Holl.1980.1, pp. 200–3.

The phrase with which Virgil indicates the *Aeneid*, "l'alta mia tragedìa," has caused only some debate, as most commentators believe that, for Dante, with regard to its plot, Virgil's epic was a "comedy" because it begins in difficulty (the shipwreck that initiates the action) and ends in happiness (the impending marriage of Aeneas and Lavinia; the impending foundation of Rome). Its style, on the other hand, is generally seen as lofty, and thus, in Dante's understanding of such things, "tragic" (see, for example, *Inf.* XXVI.82, where Virgil also refers to epic writing as being in the high, or tragic style: "quando nel mondo gli alti versi scrissi" [when, in the world, I wrote my lofty verses]). For an attack on the usual understanding, beginning with the view that Virgil's phrase would then be pleonastic ("l'alta mia tragedìa" would need to be understood as having the sense of "my lofty high poem," twice referring to the stylistic level of the work), and arguing that both for a few early commentators and in Dante's own views the plot of the *Aeneid* is indeed tragic, see Holl.1980.1, pp. 214–18; Holl.1983.1, pp. 130–34; Holl.1993.2, pp. 19, 62–66. According to this reading, the meaning of Virgil's phrase is that his poem is lofty in style and unhappy at its conclusion, the death of Turnus at the hands of Aeneas, who gives over the ideal of clemency when he kills his enemy.

115–117.   "Michael Scot, who perhaps belonged to the family of the Scots of Balwearie in Fifeshire, was born ca. 1175; after studying at Oxford and Paris, he spent some time at Toledo, where he acquired a knowledge of Arabic, and thus gained access to the Arabic versions of Aristotle, some of which he translated into Latin at the instigation of the Emperor Frederick II, at whose court at Palermo he resided for several years; he died before 1235. His own works, which deal almost exclusively with astrology, alchemy, and the occult sciences in general, are doubtless responsible for his popular reputation as a wizard. Many of his alleged prophecies are recorded by the commentators, and by Villani, Salimbene, and others" (**T**). For a description of his *Liber astronomicus* see Lynn Thorndike (Thor.1923.1), vol. 2, pp. 826–35.

118.   "Bonatti, who was a tiler by trade, seems to have acted as domestic astrologer to Guido da Montefeltro; it is said to have been by his aid that the latter won his decisive victory over the French papal forces at Forlì, May 1, 1282. Bonatti wrote (ca. 1270) a work on astrology *(Decem tractatus Astrologiae)*, which was printed at Augsburg in 1491" **(T)**.

118–120.   "Maestro Benvenuto, nicknamed Asdente (i.e., toothless), a shoe-maker of Parma who was famed as a prophet and soothsayer during the latter half of Cent. XIII . . . ; referred to, as 'il calzolaio di Parma,' as an instance of an individual who would be noble, if notoriety constituted nobility *(Conv.* IV.xvi.6)" **(T)**.

121–123.   Dante's eight astrologers have moved from classical through thirteenth-century exemplars, the recent ones in descending nobility and literacy. His list now declines to an anonymous plurality of commonfolk, women who practice witchcraft through brewing magic potions and mak-ing images of their clients' enemies.

124–126.   The moon is setting over the point that demarcates the border of the hemisphere of land (with its center, in the medieval and moralized cartographical conception, at Jerusalem) and that of water. The moon is setting in the ocean west of Seville and the sun is about to rise, from the perspective of one watching at Jerusalem. Medieval legend has it that what is often referred to in our time as "the man in the moon" was the image of Cain carrying a bundle of thorns. For a study of this tradition see Prato's book (Prat.1881.1). For the astronomical and cartographical ramifications of the passage see Gizzi (Gizz.1974.1), vol. 2, pp. 113–36.

127–129.   Once again (see, for example, *Inf.* XVI.106–108) Dante adds a detail to an earlier scene in the poem, the prologue, the action of which takes place on this earth. There is no mention of the moon in the first canto. It is also not possible that Virgil means *yesterday* night, as some pro-pose, for Dante and Virgil were then already in hell, having begun their descent on Friday evening after Dante spent his night in the wood on Thursday: " 'yesternight,' i.e. the night before last, it being now early morning" is the explanation offered in Tozer's gloss on this verse.

130.   Having proscribed the word *introcque* from the illustrious vernacular in *De vulgari eloquentia (Dve* I.xiii.2), Dante here employs it. It is a latinism (derived from *inter hoc*) and means, roughly, "meanwhile." That is how

Dante uses it as an example of crude Florentine "municipal" speech in *De vulgari*: "Since we ain't got nuthin' else to do, let's eat" would be a colloquial American equivalent of the example he gives. If writers of the illustrious vernacular are to avoid such expressions, we are perhaps forced to reflect that Dante's Comedy, unlike Virgil's lofty Tragedy, is written in the low style (and has a "happy ending"). For discussions in this vein see Barberi Squarotti (Barb. 1972.1), p. 281, and Hollander (Holl. 1980.1), pp. 214–18.

INFERNO XXI

Così di ponte in ponte, altro parlando
che la mia comedìa cantar non cura,
3 venimmo; e tenavamo 'l colmo, quando

restammo per veder l'altra fessura
di Malebolge e li altri pianti vani;
6 e vidila mirabilmente oscura.

Quale ne l'arzanà de' Viniziani
bolle l'inverno la tenace pece
9 a rimpalmare i legni lor non sani,

ché navicar non ponno—in quella vece
chi fa suo legno novo e chi ristoppa
12 le coste a quel che più vïaggi fece;

chi ribatte da proda e chi da poppa;
altri fa remi e altri volge sarte;
15 chi terzeruolo e artimon rintoppa—:

tal, non per foco ma per divin' arte,
bollia là giuso una pegola spessa,
18 che 'nviscava la ripa d'ogne parte.

I' vedea lei, ma non vedëa in essa
mai che le bolle che 'l bollor levava,
21 e gonfiar tutta, e riseder compressa.

Mentr' io là giù fisamente mirava,
lo duca mio, dicendo "Guarda, guarda!"
24 mi trasse a sé del loco dov' io stava.

Allor mi volsi come l'uom cui tarda
di veder quel che li convien fuggire
27 e cui paura sùbita sgagliarda,

Thus from one bridge to the next we came
until we reached its highest point, speaking
3   of things my Comedy does not care to sing.

We stopped to look into the next crevasse
of Malebolge and heard more useless weeping.
6   All I could see was an astounding darkness.

As in the arsenal of the Venetians
in wintertime they boil the viscous pitch
9   to caulk their unsound ships

because they cannot sail—one rebuilds
his ship, while still another plugs
12   the seams of his, weathered by many a voyage:

one hammers at the stem, another at the stern,
this one makes the oars, that one twists the ropes
15   for rigging, another patches jib and mainsail—

so, not with fire, but by the art of God,
a thick pitch boiled there,
18   sticking to the banks on either side.

I saw the pitch but still saw nothing in it
except the bubbles raised up by the boiling,
21   the whole mass swelling and then settling back.

While I stared fixedly upon the seething pitch,
my leader cried: 'Look out, look out!'
24   and drew me to him, away from where I stood.

Then I turned like a man, intent
on making out what he must run from,
27   undone by sudden fear,

che, per veder, non indugia 'l partire:
e vidi dietro a noi un diavol nero
30   correndo su per lo scoglio venire.

Ahi quant' elli era ne l'aspetto fero!
e quanto mi parea ne l'atto acerbo,
·33   con l'ali aperte e sovra i piè leggero!

L'omero suo, ch'era aguto e superbo,
carcava un peccator con ambo l'anche,
36   e quei tenea de' piè ghermito 'l nerbo.

Del nostro ponte disse: "O Malebranche,
ecco un de li anzïan di Santa Zita!
39   Mettetel sotto, ch'i' torno per anche

a quella terra, che n'è ben fornita:
ogn' uom v'è barattier, fuor che Bonturo;
42   del no, per li denar, vi si fa *ita*."

Là giù 'l buttò, e per lo scoglio duro
si volse; e mai non fu mastino sciolto
45   con tanta fretta a seguitar lo furo.

Quel s'attuffò, e tornò sù convolto;
ma i demon che del ponte avean coperchio,
48   gridar: "Qui non ha loco il Santo Volto!

qui si nuota altrimenti che nel Serchio!
Però, se tu non vuo' di nostri graffi,
51   non far sopra la pegola soverchio."

Poi l'addentar con più di cento raffi,
disser: "Coverto convien che qui balli,
54   sì che, se puoi, nascosamente accaffi."

Non altrimenti i cuoci a' lor vassalli
fanno attuffare in mezzo la caldaia
57   la carne con li uncin, perché non galli.

who does not slow his flight for all his looking back:
just so I caught a glimpse of some dark devil
30   running toward us up the ledge.

Ah, how ferocious were his looks
and fierce his gesturing,
33   with wings spread wide and nimble feet!

One of his shoulders, which were high and pointed,
was laden with the haunches of a sinner
36   he held hooked by the tendons of his heels.

From our bridge he said: 'O Malebranche,
here is one of Santa Zita's Elders.
39   Thrust him under, while I head back for more

'to that city, where there's such a fine supply.
Every man there—except Bonturo—is a swindler.
42   There money turns a No into an Ay.'

He flung him down and turned back up
the stony ridge. Never did a mastiff
45   set loose to chase a thief make greater haste.

The sinner sank, then rose again, his face all pitch.
The demons, under cover of the bridge, cried out:
48   'This is no place for the Holy Visage!

'Here you swim a different stroke than in the Serchio!
Unless you'd like to feel our hooks,
51   don't let yourself stick out above the pitch.'

Then, with a hundred hooks and more,
they ripped him, crying: 'Here you must do your dance
54   in secret and pilfer—can you?—in the dark.'

In just the same way cooks command their scullions
to take their skewers and prod the meat down
57   in the cauldron, lest it float back up.

Lo buon maestro "Acciò che non si paia
che tu ci sia," mi disse, "giù t'acquatta
60   dopo uno scheggio, ch'alcun schermo t'aia;

e per nulla offension che mi sia fatta,
non temer tu, ch'i' ho le cose conte,
63   per ch'altra volta fui a tal baratta."

Poscia passò di là dal co del ponte;
e com' el giunse in su la ripa sesta,
66   mestier li fu d'aver sicura fronte.

Con quel furore e con quella tempesta
ch'escono i cani a dosso al poverello
69   che di sùbito chiede ove s'arresta,

usciron quei di sotto al ponticello,
e volser contra lui tutt'i runcigli;
72   ma el gridò: "Nessun di voi sia fello!

Innanzi che l'uncin vostro mi pigli,
traggasi avante l'un di voi che m'oda,
75   e poi d'arruncigliarmi si consigli."

Tutti gridaron: "Vada Malacoda!";
per ch'un si mosse—e li altri stetter fermi—
78   e venne a lui dicendo: "Che li approda?"

"Credi tu, Malacoda, qui vedermi
esser venuto," disse 'l mio maestro,
81   "sicuro già da tutti vostri schermi,

sanza voler divino e fato destro?
Lascian' andar, ché nel cielo è voluto
84   ch'i' mostri altrui questo cammin silvestro."

Allor li fu l'orgoglio sì caduto,
ch'e' si lasciò cascar l'uncino a' piedi,
87   e disse a li altri: "Omai non sia feruto."

Then my good master said: 'Squat down
behind that rock and find some cover
60   so that they do not see that you are here.

'As for any outrage they may do me,
have no fear. I know this place and had
63   exactly such a scuffle here before.'

After he had crossed the bridge
and reached the other bank,
66   he had to show how resolute he was:

With all the rage and uproar
of dogs that rush upon a beggar—
69   who quickly starts to beg where he has stopped—

they swarmed on him from underneath the bridge
with threatening hooks. But he cried out:
72   'Wait! Let none of you do harm!

'Before you grapple at me with your hooks
let one of you come forth to hear me out.
75   Then take counsel, whether to use your claws.'

All cried: 'Let Malacoda go.' One moved—
the rest stood still—and he came forward,
78   grumbling: 'This won't do him any good.'

'Consider, Malacoda,' said my master,
'whether you would see me come this far
81   unstopped by all your hindering

'without the will of God and favoring fate?
Let us proceed, for it is willed in Heaven
84   that I guide another down this savage way.'

Then his pride was so abashed that he let drop
the billhook to his feet, saying to the others:
87   'Enough, let no one touch him.'

E 'l duca mio a me: "O tu che siedi
tra li scheggion del ponte quatto quatto,
90   sicuramente omai a me ti riedi."

Per ch'io mi mossi e a lui venni ratto;
e i diavoli si fecer tutti avanti,
93   sì ch'io temetti ch'ei tenesser patto;

così vid'ïo già temer li fanti
ch'uscivan patteggiati di Caprona,
96   veggendo sé tra nemici cotanti.

I' m'accostai con tutta la persona
lungo 'l mio duca, e non torceva li occhi
99   da la sembianza lor ch'era non buona.

Ei chinavan li raffi e "Vuo' che 'l tocchi,"
diceva l'un con l'altro, "in sul groppone?"
102   E rispondien: "Si, fa che gliel' accocchi."

Ma quel demonio che tenea sermone
col duca mio, si volse tutto presto
105   e disse: "Posa, posa, Scarmiglione!"

Poi disse a noi: "Più oltre andar per questo
iscoglio non si può, però che giace
108   tutto spezzato al fondo l'arco sesto.

E se l'andare avante pur vi piace,
andatevene su per questa grotta;
111   presso è un altro scoglio che via face.

Ier, più oltre cinqu' ore che quest' otta,
mille dugento con sessanta sei
114   anni compié che qui la via fu rotta.

Io mando verso là di questi miei
a riguardar s'alcun se ne sciorina;
117   gite con lor, che non saranno rei."

And my leader said to me: 'You there, cowering
among the broken boulders of the bridge,
90   now you may come back to me in safety.'

At that I stirred and hastened to him.
Then the devils all came surging forward
93   so that I feared they might not keep the truce.

Just so do I recall the troops
afraid to leave Caprona with safe-conduct,
96   finding themselves among so many enemies.

I drew my body up against my leader
but kept my eyes fixed on their faces,
99   which were far from friendly.

They aimed their hooks, and one said to another:
'How about I nick him on the rump?'
102   And the other answered: 'Sure, let him have one.'

But the demon who was speaking with my leader
turned round at once and said:
105   'Easy does it, Scarmiglione!'

And then to us: 'You can't continue farther
down this ridge, for the sixth arch
108   lies broken into pieces at the bottom.

'If you desire to continue on,
then make your way along this rocky ledge.
111   Nearby's another crag that yields a passage.

'Yesterday, at a time five hours from now,
it was a thousand two hundred sixty-six years
114   since the road down here was broken.

'I'm sending some men of mine along that way
to see if anyone is out to take the air.
117   Go with them—they won't hurt you.'

"Tra'ti avante, Alichino, e Calcabrina,"
cominciò elli a dire, "e tu, Cagnazzo;
120   e Barbariccia guidi la decina.

Libicocco vegn' oltre e Draghignazzo,
Cirïatto sannuto e Graffiacane
123   e Farfarello e Rubicante pazzo.

Cercate 'ntorno le boglienti pane;
costor sian salvi infino a l'altro scheggio
126   che tutto intero va sovra le tane."

"Omè, maestro, che è quel ch'i' veggio?"
diss' io, "deh, sanza scorta andianci soli,
129   se tu sa' ir; ch'i' per me non la cheggio.

Se tu se' sì accorto come suoli,
non vedi tu ch'e' digrignan li denti
132   e con le ciglia ne minaccian duoli?"

Ed elli a me: "Non vo' che tu paventi;
lasciali digrignar pur a lor senno,
135   ch'e' fanno ciò per li lessi dolenti."

Per l'argine sinistro volta dienno;
ma prima avea ciascun la lingua stretta
coi denti, verso lor duca, per cenno;
139   ed elli avea del cul fatto trombetta.

'Step forward, Alichino, Calcabrina,'
he continued, 'and you Cagnazzo,
120   and let Barbariccia lead the squad.

'Let Libicocco come too, and Draghignazzo,
Ciriatto with his tusks, and Graffiacane,
123   Farfarello, and madcap Rubicante.

'Have a good look around the boiling glue.
Keep these two safe as far as the next crag
126   that runs all of a piece above the dens.'

'Oh, master,' I said, 'I don't like what I see.
Please, let us find our way without an escort,
129   if you know how. As for me, I do not want one.

'If you are as vigilant as ever,
don't you see they grind their teeth
132   while with their furrowed brows they threaten harm?'

And he to me: 'Don't be afraid.
Let them grind on to their hearts' content—
135   they do it for the stewing wretches.'

Off they set along the left-hand bank,
but first each pressed his tongue between his teeth
to blow a signal to their leader,
139   and he had made a trumpet of his asshole.

1–3.   What is the subject under discussion as the travelers leave the fourth bridge and reach the midpoint of the fifth? Most commentators simply avoid the issue, which probably must remain moot, as Conrieri argues (Conr.1981.1, pp. 1–2).

Dante's choice of title for his work caused some early commentators difficulty, but not all of them. Guido da Pisa, for instance, nearly certainly echoing the epistle to Cangrande, says that this work is a comedy because, like other comedies, it begins in misery and adversity and ends in prosperity and happiness (incipiunt a miseria et adversitate et finiunt in prosperitatem et felicitatem). Others see only the stylistic reference of the term, as in the case of Benvenuto, for whom the title simply means "my book in the vernacular" (meus liber vulgaris). But others, like Francesco da Buti, allow that they are puzzled, wondering whether or not Dante should so have entitled it, but then allowing that it was his right to do whatever he chose. For a brief consideration of Dante's sense of tragedy and comedy see the concluding discussion in the note to *Inferno* XX.106–114.

7–21.   Castelvetro objects that Dante's wonderfully energetic simile is almost entirely made up of extraneous elements, i.e., he needed only to say that the pitch in the *bolgia* was as black as that in the arsenal at Venice. Of course, that is the beauty of it, as Dante paints his scene as though he had seen the pictures of Brueghel before they were painted. Trucchi's gloss points out that the "honest mercantilism" of the Venetians, with all its vitality, stands against the sordid conniving of barrators. The pitch, the punishing agent of this *bolgia*, is the apt sign of the nature of barrators (whom we today call "grafters"), working in secret and leaving such practitioners enlimed with its sticky sign, attaching to all who practice this kind of fraud. "Barratry, the buying and selling of public office, is the civil equivalent of simony, the buying and selling of church office, the sin punished in the third *bolgia*" (Singleton's comment).

Verse 11, "chi fa suo legno novo," is understood by nearly all the commentators to refer to the construction of new ships. However, the entire context here involves the rebuilding of existent vessels; thus our translation has it that this phrase refers to making an old ship new.

29.   This figure introduces the "traditional medieval" devils of plays and festivals to the poem. No other scenes in *Inferno* are as closely linked to the popular culture of the period as these in the cantos devoted to barratry.

34–36.   Benvenuto suggests that this figure, laden with what resembles a slaughtered corpse, reminds us of a butcher taking a carcass to be skinned and sold. Christopher Kleinhenz has indicated another (and parodic) likely source: Christ as the Good Shepherd (the *pastor bonus* of the Bible and of medieval illustrations), holding a saved lamb on his shoulder (Klei.1982.1, pp. 129–31).

37.   The name of this class of devils, Malebranche, fits well the place, Malebolge, and means "Evil Claws," referring to their hooked hands, and perhaps to their forked prongs.

38.   The elders of Lucca were the city's magistrates, similar in their governance to the priors of Florence. Zita was a young servant woman of the city, dead in the 1270s, to whom were reputed great kindness and numerous miracles. While she was not canonized until 1690, she was reputed a saint shortly after her death, and her cult flourished around her tomb in the church of San Frediano in Lucca.

As for the identity of this nameless Lucchese, Guido da Pisa seems to have been the first commentator to say that he was Martino Bottario (or Bottai). He seems to have shared political (and thus grafting) power with Bonturo Dati, mentioned in v. 41. There is another fact about him that is striking: he apparently died, according to Guido, on 26 March 1300, that is, at least in certain calculations, on the very day that is now unfolding in Dante's poem. Francesco da Buti confirms his name and also registers the date of his death, now given as the Friday night before Holy Saturday (but only referring to the month of March, strangely, since Good Friday fell on 9 April in 1300). Later commentators, if they refer to this material, all have the death date as occurring on 9 April, even though this is not authorized by the first commentators to claim that Martino is the Lucchese here present. For particulars see Pietro Mazzamuto, *ED,* vol. 1, 1970, pp. 313–14.

39.   The notion that barrators come straight from earth to this point in hell, carried off by a devil, seems to violate the rule that all must cross Acheron with Charon (*Inf.* III.122–123) and then go before Minos to be judged (*Inf.* V.7–12). Even the black Cherub who carries off the soul of

Guido da Montefeltro is said (by Guido himself) to have carried him only as far as Minos (*Inf.* XXVII.124). Thus Singleton reasons that the devil at least stops briefly at Minos's place of judgment in order to allow the formal sentencing to take place. (Must we also imagine that he accompanies barrators from Lucca aboard Charon's skiff?) It is surely true that Dante is generally precise in honoring the ground rules that he establishes; it is also true that he has written a poem, one that allows him to please his fancy when he chooses.

41–42. Bonturo Dati, who did not die until 1325, was famed for his barratry. A popular tale has it that when Boniface VIII, embracing him at an encounter when Bonturo visited him on an embassy, shook him, Bonturo said, in return, "You have just shaken half of Lucca" (meaning to indicate Martino as the other half). Dante's devil's exclusion of him from among the Lucchesi who, suborned by money, will turn an elder's "no" into a "yes" is indubitably ironic and sarcastic: no one in Lucca is a greater grafter than he.

46–48. The ironic edge of the devils' remark is variously interpreted, depending on the meaning of *convolto*. Does this sinner return to the surface with his face now covered with pitch (in which case he resembles the ebony face of Christ on the much-venerated image of the Crucifixion in San Martino, in Lucca)? or is he bent in two, emerging with his backside from the pitch (in which case he looks like a citizen of Lucca kneeling to prostrate himself before the image)? Strong arguments are made for each interpretation, and each is supported by a further text (*Inf.* XXII.25–28, 19–24), in which the sinners in this *bolgia* are compared, second to frogs with only their snouts out of water, first to dolphins showing their backs as they move through water. Either meaning is completely possible, but most contemporary commentators prefer the latter, perhaps because it is the more burlesque.

49. The Serchio is the river near Lucca in which citizens swam for refreshment in the days of summer. That the devils address Martino would tend to support the notion that it is his head that has surfaced rather than his rump, i.e., they would seem to be saying "Man, that's no way to do your imitation of the Holy Visage!"

58–62. Virgil's self-assurance will shortly prove to be ill-founded. Here begins the longest episode in the *Inferno*; it will run through Canto XXIII.57, some 290 verses. See Hollander (Holl.1984.3), pp. 85–86.

63. Some Renaissance commentators (e.g., Vellutello and Daniello) insist on the proximity of the word *baratta* to barratry, which would indicate that the word is likely to indicate a previous scuffle with these very demons—who certainly seem the types to have bothered Virgil on his descent to Cocytus when Erichtho sent him on his mission down there (*Inf.* IX.22–27). The first commentator in the DDP to try a different tack is Singleton, who argues that the primary reference is to Virgil's difficulties with the devils at the walls of Dis (see *Inf.* VIII, 82–130) or to some skirmish that he had with these devils on his previous journey to lower hell (*Inf.* IX, 22–30). The fact that Virgil is shortly to be found out of his depth in his struggle with the Malebranche, again after exhibiting self-confidence in the face of hostile demons, supports this reading.

67–72. Virgil's calm assurance is shredded by the attack of the "dogs" who rush out upon him, a poor beggar. The simile is hard on Virgil, who only barely manages to regain control of the situation, which, we remember, is being observed by Dante, squatting in hiding on the bridge.

76–78. The entry on the scene of Malacoda ("Eviltail"), the lead devil of the Malebranche of Malebolge, is perfectly in character, as we shall see. He pretends to be servile, but mutters under his breath about his sense of Virgil's futility.

79–84. Virgil's aplomb, his "high style" contrasting with demonic "vernacular," serves at once to set him apart from the "low-life" devils and their leader, Malacoda, but also to make him seem slightly ridiculous, since Malacoda, not he, is eventually in control of the situation, as Virgil will only finally realize, to his considerable chagrin, in Canto XXIII.140–141. Virgil's reference in v. 83 to the fact that he is not alone ("Let *us* proceed") for the first time alerts Malacoda and his cohort to Dante's hidden presence.

85–87. Malacoda's fearful gesture, letting fall his billhook, is a masterful ploy that succeeds in getting Virgil to lower his guard. See Guyler (Guyl.1972.1), p. 34.

88–93. Virgil, tricked, orders Dante to leave his hiding-place. The devils, sensing fresh meat, crowd forward. Dante's fear is a more realistic response to the situation than is Virgil's self-assurance.

95.   Dante was present at the successful siege of Caprona in 1289, a caval-
ryman observing the success of the mission of his Tuscan Guelphs against
this Pisan stronghold. It is to his lasting credit that what he remembers for
us is how the victims must have felt when they came out under a pact of
safe conduct. Dante, exiled on the charge of barratry by his fellow citizens,
here perhaps means to remind them that he had borne arms on behalf of
the republic in its victories, the siege of Caprona in August 1289 and the
previous great victory at Campaldino that June, referred to later in this
scene (XXII.4–5). He was not a grafter, scheming in the dark, but a
cavalryman who did his deeds in the fearsome clarity of war. There have
been several attempts in the last two centuries to relate the scenes and
personages of these cantos of barratry to Dante's own experiences as
accused barrator perfidiously sent into exile on this pretext (and thus pre-
sented as attacked by the twelve priors of Florence, the Malebranche), and
to his military experiences, offered as vindication against such malicious
and untrue charges. For cautionary remarks, urging restraint in such inter-
pretation, see Conrieri (Conr.1981.1), pp. 38–39.

100–105.   Dante's fears are justified; only Malacoda's intervention prevents
the bullying devils from assaulting him with their hooks. Malacoda holds
back Scarmiglione, encouraging him to await a more propitious moment
for his attack. Scarmiglione is the first of the twelve devils to be named.
He is apparently not included in the squad of ten put under Barbariccia's
control—see note to vv. 118–123.

106–111.   Malacoda's partial truth (the sixth bridge, over the *bolgia* of
hypocrisy, is in ruins) is quickly joined to a total fabrication (the next
bridge along their route is intact). *All* the bridges are down, as Virgil will
be told by Fra Catalano in Canto XXIII.133–138.

112–114.   This extraordinarily precise time reference is the most certain
text in the poem for establishing an external date for the journey. It is 7 AM
of Holy Saturday, since Christ, according to Dante (*Conv*. IV.xxiii.10), died
at noon. In fact, Dante here is modifying the facts, if on the authority of
Luke 23:44, who gives the time of the preternatural darkness as noon.
Even Luke, however, is clear that Jesus died at 3 PM. Dante is willing to
rewrite any text to suit his purpose.

From this passage we learn that the events narrated in this poem
occurred in Easter week of 1300. However, and as we have seen, Dante
seems to be conflating two dates for the start of the journey, each of

which is propitious, 25 March and 8 April (the actual date of Good Friday in 1300) in order to gain the maximum significant referentiality. See note to *Inf.* I.1.

115–117.   Malacoda lies yet again, promising safe conduct. Once again Virgil is trusting, Dante not.

118–123.   Dante's pleasure in developing *nomi parlanti* (names that bespeak the quality of their possessors) is evident here. His playful naming is based on the aggressive bestial characteristics of these creatures.

   Dante's thoroughness and care in his handling of the demons' names is underlined by the fact that each of the ten members of the *decina* (from *decuria*, the Latin military term for a "squad" of ten troopers) is named exactly once in the following canto, as follows (with Sinclair's [Sinc.1939.1, p. 279] English approximations of some of these names in parentheses): Barbariccia (Curlybeard—XXII.29), Graffiacane (Scratchdog—34), Rubicante (Redface—40), Ciriatto (Swineface—55), Libicocco (70), Draghignazzo (Vile Dragon—73), Farfarello (94), Cagnazzo (Low Hound—106), Alichino (112), and Calcabrina (133).

125–126.   Malacoda lies again: the devils understand that they are to take Dante and Virgil by surprise, attacking Dante later on.

127–132.   Dante's pleas to Virgil will fall on deaf ears, but we sense already (and will shortly have confirmed) that he, not his guide, understands what the devils are up to.

133–135.   Virgil's response to Dante's question, based on correct observation and resultant correct interpretation of the devils' true motives, marks yet another moment in this canto in which the reader is nearly forced to observe how harshly the guide is being treated by the author. In recent years there has been an increasing acknowledgment of what should have been clear to any reader who is willing to give over the notion that the *Comedy* is essentially an "allegorical" poem in which the character Virgil represents "Reason." See, among others, Bacchelli (Bacc.1954.1), Ryan.1982.2, Holl.1984.3.

136–139.   The devils either prepare to make or have already made a farting sound with their tongues stuck through their teeth in answer to Malacoda's prior "war-signal" of a fart. See Sarolli's appreciation of this low-mimetic scene as part of the tradition of *musica diaboli*, the hellish music that stands in total contrast with the heavenly music we shall hear in *Paradiso* (Saro.1971.1, pp. 5n., 363–80). The perverse devils turn their mouths into anuses in preparing to answer Malacoda's (and he is surely aptly named in light of this sound) turning his anus into a bugle, the gestures constituting a sign of "understanding among the malefactors and a sign of their derision for Virgil's self-confident misreading of their intentions" (Holl.1984.3, p. 90).

INFERNO XXII

Io vidi già cavalier muover campo,
e cominciare stormo e far lor mostra,
3   e talvolta partir per loro scampo;

corridor vidi per la terra vostra,
o Aretini, e vidi gir gualdane,
6   fedir torneamenti e correr giostra;

quando con trombe, e quando con campane,
con tamburi e con cenni di castella,
9   e con cose nostrali e con istrane;

né già con sì diversa cennamella
cavalier vidi muover né pedoni,
12   né nave a segno di terra o di stella.

Noi andavam con li diece demoni.
Ahi fiera compagnia! ma ne la chiesa
15   coi santi, e in taverna coi ghiottoni.

Pur a la pegola era la mia 'ntesa,
per veder de la bolgia ogne contegno
18   e de la gente ch'entro v'era incesa.

Come i dalfini, quando fanno segno
a' marinar con l'arco de la schiena
21   che s'argomentin di campar lor legno,

talor così, ad alleggiar la pena,
mostrav' alcun de' peccatori 'l dosso
24   e nascondea in men che non balena.

E come a l'orlo de l'acqua d'un fosso
stanno i ranocchi pur col muso fuori,
27   sì che celano i piedi e l'altro grosso,

I have seen the cavalry break camp,
prepare for an attack, make their muster
3 and at times fall back to save themselves.

I have seen outriders in your land,
O Aretines. I have seen raiding-parties,
6 tournaments of teams, hand-to-hand jousts

begun with bells, trumpets, or drums,
with signals from the castle,
9 with summons of our own and those from foreign lands.

But truly never to such outlandish fanfare
have I seen horsemen move, or infantry,
12 or ship set sail at sign from land or star.

On we went, escorted by ten demons.
What savage company! But, as they say,
15 'in church with saints, with guzzlers in the tavern.'

My attention was fixed upon the pitch
to note each detail of this gulch
18 and of the people poaching in it.

Like dolphins, when they arch their backs
above the water, giving sailors warning
21 to prepare to save their ship,

so from time to time, to ease his pain,
one of the sinners would show his back
24 and, quick as lightning, hide it once again.

And just as in a ditch at water's edge
frogs squat with but their snouts in sight,
27 their bodies and their legs all hidden,

sì stavan d'ogne parte i peccatori;
ma come s'appressava Barbariccia,
30   così si ritraén sotto i bollori.

I' vidi, e anco il cor me n'accapriccia,
uno aspettar così, com' elli 'ncontra
33   ch'una rana rimane e l'altra spiccia;

e Graffiacan, che li era più di contra,
li arruncigliò le 'mpegolate chiome
36   e trassel sù, che mi parve una lontra.

I' sapea già di tutti quanti 'l nome,
sì li notai quando fuorono eletti,
39   e poi ch'e' si chiamaro, attesi come.

"O Rubicante, fa che tu li metti
li unghioni a dosso, sì che tu lo scuoi!"
42   gridavan tutti insieme i maladetti.

E io: "Maestro mio, fa, se tu puoi,
che tu sappi chi è lo sciagurato
45   venuto a man de li avversari suoi."

Lo duca mio li s'accostò allato;
domandollo ond' ei fosse, e quei rispuose:
48   "I' fui del regno di Navarra nato.

Mia madre a servo d'un segnor mi puose,
che m'avea generato d'un ribaldo,
51   distruggitor di sé e di sue cose.

Poi fui famiglia del buon re Tebaldo;
quivi mi misi a far baratteria,
54   di ch'io rendo ragione in questo caldo."

E Cirïatto, a cui di bocca uscia
d'ogne parte una sanna come a porco,
57   li fé sentir come l'una sdruscia.

so were the sinners scattered everywhere.
But they, at the approach of Barbariccia,

30   withdrew back down beneath the boiling.

There I saw—and my heart still shudders at it—
one who lingered, as it can happen

33   that one frog stays while yet another plunges,

and Graffiacane, who was nearest him,
caught a billhook in his pitchy locks

36   and hauled him out, looking like an otter.

By now I knew their names,
since I had noted these when they were chosen

39   and when they called to one another.

'Set your claws to work, Rubicante,
see you rip his skin off,'

42   shouted all the accursèd crew together.

And I: 'Master, if you can do it,
find out the name of this poor wretch

45   caught in the clutches of his enemies.'

My leader got up close beside him
and asked him where he came from. He replied:

48   'I was born in the kingdom of Navarre.

'My mother, who had conceived me by a wastrel—
destroyer of himself and all his goods—

51   put me in service with a man of rank.

'Then I joined the retinue of worthy Thibaut:
there first I set myself to taking bribes,

54   for which I pay the reckoning in this heat.'

And Ciriatto, from whose jaw curved up
on either side a tusk, like the wild boar's,

57   made him feel how one of these could rip.

Tra male gatte era venuto 'l sorco;
ma Barbariccia il chiuse con le braccia
60   e disse: "State in là, mentr' io lo 'nforco."

E al maestro mio volse la faccia;
"Domanda," disse, "ancor, se più disii
63   saper da lui, prima ch'altri 'l disfaccia."

Lo duca dunque: "Or dì: de li altri rii
conosci tu alcun che sia latino
66   sotto la pece?" E quelli: "I' mi partii,

poco è, da un che fu di là vicino.
Così foss' io ancor con lui coperto,
69   ch'i' non temerei unghia né uncino!"

E Libicocco "Troppo avem sofferto,"
disse; e preseli 'l braccio col runciglio,
72   sì che, stracciando, ne portò un lacerto.

Draghignazzo anco i volle dar di piglio
giuso a le gambe; onde 'l decurio loro
75   si volse intorno intorno con mal piglio.

Quand' elli un poco rappaciati fuoro,
a lui, ch'ancor mirava sua ferita,
78   domandò 'l duca mio sanza dimoro:

"Chi fu colui da cui mala partita
di' che facesti per venire a proda?"
81   Ed ei rispuose: "Fu frate Gomita,

quel di Gallura, vasel d'ogne froda,
ch'ebbe i nemici di suo donno in mano,
84   e fé sì lor, che ciascun se ne loda.

Danar si tolse e lasciolli di piano,
sì com' e' dice; e ne li altri offici anche
87   barattier fu non picciol, ma sovrano.

The mouse had fallen in with wicked cats.
But Barbariccia blocked them with his arms
60   and said: 'Stand back and let me jab him,'

then turned to face my master:
'Speak up, if you are eager to learn more,
63   before I let him have a mangling.'

And my leader: 'Of the other sinners in the pitch,
tell me, is anyone Italian?'
66   And he: 'I just now came from one

'who hailed from near those parts. I wish
I still were with him in the pitch—
69   then I'd have no fear of hook or claw!'

Then Libicocco said: 'This is just too much,'
caught him with his grapple by the arm
72   and, ripping, gouged out a hunk of flesh.

Draghignazzo, too, wanted to catch him up,
by the legs, at which their captain
75   wheeled round on them with an ugly look.

After their fury had subsided,
my leader seized this chance to ask
78   the one still staring at his wound:

'Who is the one you spoke of, from whom
you parted so unwisely when you came ashore?'
81   And he replied: 'It was Fra Gomìta

'of Gallura, a vessel full of fraud,
who had his master's enemies in hand
84   but dealt with them so each one sings his praises.

'He took their money and discreetly let them off,
as he himself admits. And in his other actions
87   he was no small-time swindler but a king.

Usa con esso donno Michel Zanche
di Logodoro; e a dir di Sardigna
90   le lingue lor non si sentono stanche.

Omè, vedete l'altro che digrigna;
i' direi anche, ma i' temo ch'ello
93   non s'apparecchi a grattarmi la tigna."

E 'l gran proposto, vòlto a Farfarello
che stralunava li occhi per fedire,
96   disse: "Fatti 'n costà, malvagio uccello!"

"Se voi volete vedere o udire,"
ricominciò lo spaürato appresso,
99   "Toschi o Lombardi, io ne farò venire;

ma stieno i Malebranche un poco in cesso,
sì ch'ei non teman de le lor vendette;
102   e io, seggendo in questo loco stesso,

per un ch'io son, ne farò venir sette
quand' io suffolerò, com' è nostro uso
105   di fare allor che fori alcun si mette."

Cagnazzo a cotal motto levò 'l muso,
crollando 'l capo, e disse: "Odi malizia
108   ch'elli ha pensata per gittarsi giuso!"

Ond' ei, ch'avea lacciuoli a gran divizia,
rispuose: "Malizioso son io troppo,
111   quand' io procuro a' mia maggior trestizia."

Alichin non si tenne e, di rintoppo
a li altri, disse a lui: "Se tu ti cali,
114   io non ti verrò dietro di gualoppo,

ma batterò sovra la pece l'ali.
Lascisi 'l collo, e sia la ripa scudo,
117   a veder se tu sol più di noi vali."

'Don Michel Zanche of Logudoro
keeps company with him and, when speaking
90   of Sardegna, their tongues are never weary.

'Oh, look at that one there, gnashing his teeth!—
I would say more, but I'm afraid that demon's
93   getting set to give my mange a scratching.'

And the great marshal, turning to Farfarello,
who was rolling his eyes, ready to strike,
96   said: 'Back off, you filthy bird!'

'If you would care to see or hear,'
the frightened spirit then began again,
99   'Tuscans or Lombards, I can make some come.

'But let the Malebranche stand away
so that the sinners have no fear of vengeance,
102   and, keeping to my place right here,

'for one of me, I will make seven come
if I whistle, as is our custom
105   when one of us pulls free out of the pitch.'

At this Cagnazzo lifted up his snout and said,
shaking his head: 'Hear the cunning stunt
108   he has contrived to throw himself back in!'

And he, with artifice in store, replied:
'I must indeed be cunning if I procure
111   still greater anguish for my friends.'

Alichino couldn't stand this any more and said,
in opposition to the others: 'If you dive
114   back in I won't pursue you on the run—

'oh no! I'll beat my wings above the pitch.
Let's leave the ridge and hide behind the bank.
117   We'll see if you alone can take us on.'

O tu che leggi, udirai nuovo ludo:
ciascun da l'altra costa li occhi volse,
120 quel prima, ch'a ciò fare era più crudo.

Lo Navarrese ben suo tempo colse;
fermò le piante a terra, e in un punto
123 saltò e dal proposto lor si sciolse.

Di che ciascun di colpa fu compunto,
ma quei più che cagion fu del difetto;
126 però si mosse e gridò: "Tu se' giunto!"

Ma poco i valse: ché l'ali al sospetto
non potero avanzar; quelli andò sotto,
129 e quei drizzò volando suso il petto:

non altrimenti l'anitra di botto,
quando 'l falcon s'appressa, giù s'attuffa,
132 ed ei ritorna sù crucciato e rotto.

Irato Calcabrina de la buffa,
volando dietro li tenne, invaghito
135 che quei campasse per aver la zuffa;

e come 'l barattier fu disparito,
così volse li artigli al suo compagno,
138 e fu con lui sopra 'l fosso ghermito.

Ma l'altro fu bene sparvier grifagno
ad artigliar ben lui, e amendue
141 cadder nel mezzo del bogliente stagno.

Lo caldo sghermitor sùbito fue;
ma però di levarsi era neente,
144 sì avieno inviscate l'ali sue.

Barbariccia, con li altri suoi dolente,
quattro ne fé volar da l'altra costa
147 con tutt' i raffi, e assai prestamente

Now, reader, you shall hear strange sport.
All turned their backs to where the sinner stood,
120   he first who'd most opposed the plan.

The Navarrese chose his moment well,
planted his feet and in a second
123   leaped and escaped from their designs.

At this they all were angry at their blunder,
but most of all the one whose fault it was,
126   so that he darted up and cried: 'Now you are caught!'

It did him little good, for even wings
could not catch up with terror: the sinner dove
129   and the devil turned up his breast in flight,

just as the wild duck, when the falcon nears,
dives for the bottom, and the bird of prey
132   must fly back up, angry and outsmarted.

Calcabrina, furious at this trick,
was winging close behind him, eager for the sinner
135   to break away as an excuse to scuffle,

and, since the barrator had vanished,
he turned his claws against his fellow
138   and came to grips with him above the ditch.

But the other was indeed a full-fledged hawk,
fierce with his talons, and the pair of them
141   went tumbling down into the scalding pond.

The heat unclutched them in a moment,
but they had so beglued their wings
144   there was no way to rise above the pitch.

Barbariccia, lamenting with the rest,
had four of them fly to the other bank,
147   each with his hook in hand, and in no time

di qua, di là discesero a la posta;
porser li uncini verso li 'mpaniati,
ch'eran già cotti dentro da la crosta.

151   E noi lasciammo lor così 'mpacciati.

on this side and on that they clambered down
to their posts, reaching out their grapples
to the pitch-trapped pair, already cooked to a crust.

151   And that is how we left them in that broil.

1–12.   The similetic array of signals for troop movements in battle or for the start of a sporting event, a small catalogue of things and techniques domestic and foreign, is, we remember, the poet's way of responding to the demonic fart that concluded the last canto and ushered Dante off on his journey under the guidance of the *decuria*, Malacoda's squad, now under the control of Barbariccia. Vv. 4–5 are generally taken to refer to the battle of Campaldino in 1289.

This, even if it is not a "true simile," is the first of eleven canto-opening similes in the poem. See *Inferno* XXIV.1–18; XXX.1–27; XXXI.1–6; *Purgatorio* VI.1–12; XVII.1–12; *Paradiso* IV.1–9; XVII.1–6; XXIII.1–12; XXIX.1–9; XXXI.1–15.

13–15.   Professor Kevin Brownlee, in a seminar at Dartmouth College in 1985, suggested that these verses and the atmosphere of the entire scene in XXI and XXII reflect some earmarks of the French *fabliau*: physical violence, proverbial remarks, animalistic traits, physically stronger characters being bested by cleverer weak ones. For the farcical elements in these cantos see Spitzer (Spit.1942.1 and Spit.1944.1).

19–30.   The two similes describe the actions of the barrators in motion and at rest. They only move to relieve their pain for a moment or to duck under the pitch (thus increasing their pain) in order to avoid a hooking by the devils—a pain still more disturbing, as well as embarrassing.

It was apparently a current belief that dolphins approached ships when they sensed that a storm at sea was brewing.

37–39.   Dante claims to remember the names as they were called out by Malacoda (*Inf.* XXI.118–123) and then repeated by various of the demons in the course of the action.

48–54.   "Ciampolo, name given by the commentators to a native of Navarre, who . . . describes himself as a retainer of King Thibault II of Navarre [1253–70], in whose service he practiced [barratry]" **(T)**. About Ciampolo (for "Gian Paolo," pronounced "Giampolo") we know nothing except what is furnished by the early commentators.

59–60.   Barbariccia, as leader of the troupe, intervenes to allow Virgil the opportunity for further questions. Ciriatto had gored Ciampolo as he dangled from the end of Graffiacane's hook (vv. 55–57). Now Barbariccia extends his long arms around the place where the pitchy sinner stands to ward the others off: he wants Ciampolo for himself. (This view and our translation respect the readings of the details of this passage and of v. 123 in the Bosco/Reggio commentary.)

64–66.   Virgil wants to know, on behalf of Dante, whether there are other Italians in the pitch. The word *latino*, while it may of course mean "Latin," more frequently in Dante means "Italian," as in *Conv.* IV.xxviii.8, where Guido da Montefeltro is referred to as "lo nobilissimo nostro latino" (the most noble of us Italians). See also *Purg.* XI.58 and *Purg.* XIII.92.

67.   Ciampolo says that he has come from one who hails from a place near Italy; as we shall learn (v. 82), he speaks of Sardinia.

70–75.   Two devils can barely be restrained; indeed, before Barbariccia once again asserts his authority, allowing Virgil yet another question, Libicocco succeeds in giving Ciampolo a second wound (see vv. 55–57 for Ciriatto's earlier thrust into his flesh).

81–87.   "Frate Gomita, Sardinian friar who, having been appointed [ca. 1294] chancellor or deputy of Nino Visconti of Pisa, judge of Gallura, abused his position to traffic in the sale of public offices. Nino turned a deaf ear to all complaints against him until he discovered that the friar had connived at the escape of certain prisoners who were in his keeping, whereupon Nino had him hanged forthwith" (T). For Nino see note to *Inf.* XXXIII.1–3.

88.   "Michael Zanche, Governor of Logodoro in Sardinia; he seems to have acted as intendant for Enzio, natural son of the Emperor Frederick II, who received the title of King of Sardinia on his marriage with Adelasia di Torres, heiress of Logodoro and Gallura; after Adelasia's divorce from Enzio, Michael married her, and assumed the government of the Sardinian provinces, which he retained until c. 1290, when he was murdered by Branca d'Oria of Genoa (*Inf.* XXXII.137)" (T). Toynbee's data, based on indications found in the early commentators, is currently treated with some caution.

91–96.   Once again the conversation between Ciampolo and Virgil is interrupted by the devils' vicious sport, with order being maintained only by Barbariccia's firm insistence. De Robertis has noted the parallels between Ciampolo and the protagonist as objects of the devils' attention (DeRo.1981.1, p. 3).

97–99.   As crafty as his keepers, Ciampolo uses Dante and Virgil to set up his countermeasures, offering to bring to the surface barrators who will speak their language, Tuscans and Lombards (he has evidently caught the linguistic marks of their birthplaces in their accents). Dante, of course, is variously recognized as a Tuscan from his speech, but it comes as something of a surprise when we discover Virgil actually speaking in Lombard dialect (*Inf*. XXVII.20–21).

100–123.   The game Ciampolo devises involves the following ploys on his part and reactions by the Malebranche: (1) Ciampolo's cleverly indirect invitation to the devils to withdraw so as not to frighten off (putative) emergent Tuscans and Lombards whom he, sitting down to show his own apparent good faith, will whistle up if there are no devils visible; (2) Cagnazzo's understanding that this is a ruse; (3) Ciampolo's countermove: "But you must give them room. Do you think *I* would cause my fellow-sufferers still greater suffering?" (of course he would!); (4) Alichino's being won over by Ciampolo's wiles, mainly because he is so eager for a fight, whether Ciampolo is tricking them or not; he gets all his mates, even the suspicious Cagnazzo (and Barbariccia, we must surmise), to move down behind the ridge so as not to be visible from the pitch and challenges Ciampolo to try to escape him, if he dare; (5) Ciampolo's dive from the ridge as he makes good his escape. The rhythm of this central action in Canto XXII parallels that in the previous canto, in which two observers have entirely different interpretations of the same phenomena. Cagnazzo and Alichino here respectively play the parts of Dante and Virgil in the previous scene: Cagnazzo and Dante discern the motives of Ciampolo and the devils, respectively, while Alichino and Virgil do not.

   At v. 123 we have translated the noun *proposto* as "designs," i.e., "intention," as Bosco/Reggio argue in their comment to this verse.

124–144.   The postlude to Ciampolo's escape also is filled with action: (1) Alichino speeds after the Navarrese but cannot catch up with him; (2) Calcabrina takes out his rage on Alichino, whose gullibility led to the loss of their plaything; (3) they both fall into the pitch.

145–150.   Barbariccia directs four of his band to fly across to the other side of the ditch as part of a rescue mission, while he and the remaining three extend their hooks from the top of the bank, which the ten had hidden behind, in a mutual effort to pull their fallen comrades from the gluey pitch.

151.   Virgil and Dante seize the occasion to escape.

INFERNO XXIII

Taciti, soli, sanza compagnia
n'andavam l'un dinanzi e l'altro dopo,
3   come frati minor vanno per via.

Vòlt' era in su la favola d'Isopo
lo mio pensier per la presente rissa,
6   dov' el parlò de la rana e del topo;

ché più non si pareggia "mo" e "issa"
che l'un con l'altro fa, se ben s'accoppia
9   principio e fine con la mente fissa.

E come l'un pensier de l'altro scoppia,
così nacque di quello un altro poi,
12   che la prima paura mi fé doppia.

Io pensava così: "Questi per noi
sono scherniti con danno e con beffa
15   sì fatta, ch' assai credo che lor nòi.

Se l'ira sovra 'l mal voler s'aggueffa,
ei ne verranno dietro più crudeli
18   che 'l cane a quella lievre ch'elli acceffa."

Già mi sentia tutti arricciar li peli
de la paura e stava in dietro intento,
21   quand' io dissi: "Maestro, se non celi

te e me tostamente, i' ho pavento
d'i Malebranche. Noi li avem già dietro;
24   io li 'magino sì, che già li sento."

E quei: "S'i' fossi di piombato vetro,
l'imagine di fuor tua non trarrei
27   più tosto a me, che quella dentro 'mpetro.

Silent, alone, and unescorted
we went on, one in front, the other following,
as Friars Minor walk along the roads.

The brawl played out before our eyes
put me in mind of Aesop's fable
in which he told the tale of frog and mouse,

for 'issa' and 'mo' are not more like in meaning
than one case and the other, if we compare
with circumspection their beginnings and their ends.

Just as one thought issues from another,
so, from the first, another now was born
that made me twice as fearful as before.

I thought, 'It's our fault they have been cheated,
and with such hurt and shame
I'm sure it must enrage them.

'If rage is added to their malice,
they will pursue us still more cruelly
than the hound that sets his fangs into a hare.'

I could feel my scalp go taut with fear
and kept my thoughts fixed just behind me
as I spoke: 'Master, can't you quickly

'hide yourself and me? I am in terror
of the Malebranche; I sense them there behind us,
imagine them so clear I almost hear them.'

And he: 'If I were made of leaded glass
I could not reflect your outward likeness
in less time than I grasp the one inside you.

3
6
9
12
15
18
21
24
27

Pur mo venieno i tuo' pensier tra 'miei,
con simile atto e con simile faccia,
30   sì che d'intrambi un sol consiglio fei.

S'elli è che sì la destra costa giaccia,
che noi possiam ne l'altra bolgia scendere,
33   noi fuggirem l'imaginata caccia."

Già non compié di tal consiglio rendere,
ch'io li vidi venir con l'ali tese
36   non molto lungi, per volerne prendere.

Lo duca mio di sùbito mi prese,
come la madre ch'al romore è desta
39   e vede presso a sé le fiamme accese,

che prende il figlio e fugge e non s'arresta,
avendo più di lui che di sé cura,
42   tanto che solo una camiscia vesta;

e giù dal collo de la ripa dura
supin si diede a la pendente roccia,
45   che l'un de' lati a l'altra bolgia tura.

Non corse mai sì tosto acqua per doccia
a volger ruota di molin terragno,
48   quand' ella più verso le pale approccia,

come 'l maestro mio per quel vivagno,
portandosene me sovra 'l suo petto,
51   come suo figlio, non come compagno.

A pena fuoro i piè suoi giunti al letto
del fondo giù, ch'e' furon in sul colle
54   sovresso noi; ma non lì era sospetto:

ché l'alta provedenza che lor volle
porre ministri de la fossa quinta,
57   poder di partirs' indi a tutti tolle.

'Just now your thought commingled with my own,
alike in attitude and aspect,
30   so that of both I've formed a single plan.

'If the slope there to the right allows us
to make our way into the other ditch,
33   we shall escape the chase we both envision.'

Before he finished telling me his plan
I saw them coming, wings outspread,
36   closing in to catch us.

My leader in a moment snatched me up,
like a mother who, awakened by the hubbub
39   before she sees the flames that burn right near her,

snatches up her child and flees,
and, more concerned for him than for herself,
42   does not delay to put a shift on.

Down from the rim of that stony bank,
supine, he slid along the sloping rock
45   that forms one border of the next crevasse.

Never did water, as it nears the paddles,
rush down along the sluices
48   cut through earth to turn a millwheel

more swiftly than my master down that bank,
bearing me along clasped to his breast
51   as if I were his child, not his companion.

No sooner had he touched the bottom with his feet
than the devils were above us on the ridge.
54   Yet now we had no cause for feeling fear,

for high Providence, which made them
wardens of the fifth crevasse,
57   deprives them of the power to leave it.

Là giù trovammo una gente dipinta
che giva intorno assai con lenti passi,
60   piangendo e nel sembiante stanca e vinta.

Elli avean cappe con cappucci bassi
dinanzi a li occhi, fatte de la taglia
63   che in Clugnì per li monaci fassi.

Di fuor dorate son, sì ch'elli abbaglia;
ma dentro tutte piombo, e gravi tanto,
66   che Federigo le mettea di paglia.

Oh in etterno faticoso manto!
Noi ci volgemmo ancor pur a man manca
69   con loro insieme, intenti al tristo pianto;

ma per lo peso quella gente stanca
venìa sì pian, che noi eravam nuovi
72   di compagnia ad ogne mover d'anca.

Per ch'io al duca mio: "Fa che tu trovi
alcun ch'al fatto o al nome si conosca,
75   e li occhi, sì andando, intorno movi."

E un che 'ntese la parola tosca,
di retro a noi gridò: "Tenete i piedi,
78   voi che correte sì per l'aura fosca!

Forse ch'avrai da me quel che tu chiedi."
Onde 'l duca si volse e disse: "Aspetta,
81   e poi secondo il suo passo procedi."

Ristetti, e vidi due mostrar gran fretta
de l'animo, col viso, d'esser meco;
84   ma tardavali 'l carco e la via stretta.

Quando fuor giunti, assai con l'occhio bieco
mi rimiraron sanza far parola;
87   poi si volsero in sé, e dicean seco:

Down there we came upon a lacquered people
who made their round, in tears, with listless steps.
60   They seemed both weary and defeated.

The cloaks they wore had cowls that fell
over their eyes, cut like the capes
63   made for the monks at Cluny.

Gilded and dazzling on the outside,
within they are of lead, so ponderous
66   that those imposed by Frederick would seem but straw.

Oh what a toilsome cloak to wear forever!
Once more we turned to the left, then went along
69   beside them, intent upon their wretched wailing.

Their burden made that weary people
move so slowly we had new companions
72   each time we put one foot before the other.

And I said to my leader: 'Cast your eyes
this way and that as we walk on.
75   See if you know the names or deeds of any.'

And one of them, hearing my Tuscan speech,
cried out behind us: 'Stay your feet,
78   you who race through this sullen air.

'I perhaps can answer what you asked.'
At that my leader turned around to say:
81   'Wait a moment, then continue at his pace.'

I stopped and noticed two whose looks
showed haste of mind to reach me,
84   but their load and the narrow way detained them.

When they came near they looked at me askance
for a while, without a word,
87   until they turned to one another, saying:

"Costui par vivo a l'atto de la gola;
e s'e' son morti, per qual privilegio
90   vanno scoperti de la grave stola?"

Poi disser me: "O Tosco, ch'al collegio
de l'ipocriti tristi se' venuto,
93   dir chi tu se' non avere in dispregio."

E io a loro: "I' fui nato e cresciuto
sovra 'l bel fiume d'Arno a la gran villa,
96   e son col corpo ch'i' ho sempre avuto.

Ma voi chi siete, a cui tanto distilla
quant' i' veggio dolor giù per le guance?
99   e che pena è in voi che sì sfavilla?"

E l'un rispuose a me: "Le cappe rance
son di piombo sì grosse, che li pesi
102   fan così cigolar le lor bilance.

Frati godenti fummo, e bolognesi;
io Catalano e questi Loderingo
105   nomati, e da tua terra insieme presi

come suole esser tolto un uom solingo,
per conservar sua pace; e fummo tali,
108   ch'ancor si pare intorno dal Gardingo."

Io cominciai: "O frati, i vostri mali …";
ma più non dissi, ch'a l'occhio mi corse
111   un, crucifisso in terra con tre pali.

Quando mi vide, tutto si distorse,
soffiando ne la barba con sospiri;
114   e 'l frate Catalan, ch'a ciò s'accorse,

mi disse: "Quel confitto che tu miri,
consigliò i Farisei che convenia
117   porre un uom per lo popolo a' martìri.

'The way his throat moves, this one must be alive.
And if they are dead, what gives them the right
90   to go uncovered by the heavy stole?'

and then to me: 'O Tuscan, who have come
to this assembly of sad hypocrites,
93   do not disdain to tell us who you are.'

'In the great city, by the fair river Arno,'
I said to them, 'I was born and raised,
96   and I am here in the body that was always mine.

'But who are you in whom I see distilled
the misery running down your cheeks in tears?
99   And what is the grief you bear that glitters so?'

And one of them answered: 'Our golden cloaks
are made of lead, and they're so dense,
102   like scales we creak beneath their weight.

'We were Jovial Friars, born in Bologna.
My name was Catalano, his, Loderingo.
105   Your city made the two of us a pair,

'where usually a single man was chosen,
to keep the peace within, and we were such
108   that all around Gardingo the ruins can be seen.'

I began: 'O Friars, your evil deeds . . .'
but said no more, for one there caught my eye,
111   fixed cross-wise to the ground by three short stakes.

Seeing me, he writhed all over,
blowing sighs into his beard,
114   and Fra Catalano, observing this, said:

'That man you see nailed down
advised the Pharisees it was the better course
117   that one man should be martyred for the people.

Attraversato è, nudo, ne la via,
come tu vedi, ed è mestier ch'el senta
120   qualunque passa, come pesa, pria.

E a tal modo il socero si stenta
in questa fossa, e li altri dal concilio
123   che fu per li Giudei mala sementa."

Allor vid' io maravigliar Virgilio
sovra colui ch'era disteso in croce
126   tanto vilmente ne l'etterno essilio.

Poscia drizzò al frate cotal voce:
"Non vi dispiaccia, se vi lece, dirci
129   s'a la man destra giace alcuna foce

onde noi amendue possiamo uscirci,
sanza costrigner de li angeli neri
132   che vegnan d'esto fondo a dipartirci."

Rispuose adunque: "Più che tu non speri
s'appressa un sasso che da la gran cerchia
135   si move e varca tutt' i vallon feri,

salvo che 'n questo è rotto e nol coperchia;
montar potrete su per la ruina,
138   che giace in costa e nel fondo soperchia."

Lo duca stette un poco a testa china;
poi disse: "Mal contava la bisogna
141   colui che i peccator di qua uncina."

E 'l frate: "Io udi' già dire a Bologna
del diavol vizi assai, tra ' quali udi'
144   ch'elli è bugiardo e padre di menzogna."

Appresso il duca a gran passi sen gì,
turbato un poco d'ira nel sembiante;
ond' io da li 'ncarcati mi parti'
148   dietro a le poste de le care piante.

'He is stretched out naked, as you see,
across the path and he must feel
120   the weight of each who passes.

'Just so his father-in-law is racked with us
down here and with the others of the council
123   that was a seed of evil for the Jews.'

I saw that Virgil marveled at the sight
of this shape stretched as on a cross,
126   so ignoble in his eternal exile.

Then he addressed the friar with these words:
'May it please you, if it is permitted,
129   to say if on our right there is a passage

'by which we two might leave this place
without requiring help from some black angels
132   to pluck us from these depths.'

And he replied: 'Nearer than you hope there lies
a rocky ridge that crosses all the savage valleys
135   from the farthest circle inward.

'It has fallen only here and fails to reach across.
You can clamber up the sloping rubble
138   that lies upon the bottom and piles up along the side.'

My leader stood a while, his head bent down, then said:
'He who rips the sinners in the other ditch
141   misled us in his picture of this place.'

And the friar: 'At one time in Bologna I heard tell
of the Devil's many vices, and I heard
144   he is a liar and the father of all lies.'

At that my leader stalked off with long strides,
a moment's look of anger on his face.
And so I left those overburdened souls
148   to follow in the imprints of his cherished feet.

1–3. The quiet opening of the canto compares the two travelers to pairs of Franciscan mendicants. As John of Serravalle reminds us in his comment to this passage, the more authoritative of the two traditionally went before. Thus, when we consider the considerable time spent in exploring Virgil's difficulties in the preceding two cantos, we probably ought to perceive the delicate irony inherent in these verses.

4–18. The fable runs roughly as follows: a mouse, wishing to cross a river, is advised by an apparently friendly frog to allow himself to be attached to that frog by a string, to which project he consents. Once the frog, mouse in tow, reaches midstream, he dives in an attempt to drown the mouse. An overflying kite, or hawk, seeing the struggling mouse atop the waters, dives down, captures and kills the mouse—and the attached frog, a bonus. It seems sensible to believe that, as the protagonist reviews the events of the prior canto, he thinks of two things: the aptness of the fable to the situation of Ciampolo (mouse), Alichino (frog), and Calcabrina (kite), as well as to his own: Dante (mouse), Virgil (frog), and the Malebranche (kite). Thus the beginning and the end of the fable are particularly apt to his situation: in order to reach the next *bolgia* he has tied himself to Virgil, and now the kite must be on its way. That Virgil should be cast in the role of the double-dealing frog seemed so unlikely that apparently no one, before Guyler, pp. 35–40, suggested as much. While this writer agrees with him, the complexity of the passage, it should be noted, guarantees that its meaning will continue to be debated.

The words "mo" and "issa" are both dialectical forms, meaning "right now," derived from the Latin *modo* (used again in this canto at v. 28 and a total of twenty-five times in the poem) and *ipsa hora* (see *Purg.* XXIV.55). Hollander (Holl.1984.3), p. 93, suggests that the choice of words for "now" accentuates the imminent and immediate danger in which Dante finds himself.

The absolute source of this fable of "Aesop" is not known, but it seems that Dante may have been acquainted with both the collection circulated under the name *Romulus*, which McKenzie (McKe.1900.1) says is the (Carolingian) collection adverted to by the various fourteenth-century commentators who discuss the passage, and the later one (12th century) assembled by Waltherius Anglicus. Clara Kraus ("Esopo," *ED*, vol. 2, 1970, pp. 729–30) points out, following McKenzie, that this particular fable derives from an unknown non-Aesopic source, even if the poet presents it as being by him. (Dante had referred to Aesop once previously: *Conv.* IV.xxx.4. For the question of sources see also Mandruzzato (Mand.1955.1) and Guyler (Guyl.1972.1), pp. 29–31, the latter reviewing the discussions of McKenzie, Larkin (Lark.1962.1 and Lark.1966.1), and Padoan (Pado.1964.1) and eventually favoring Waltherius as source text.

19.   For Dante's hair, curling tight with fear, Pietro di Dante adduces *Aeneid* II.774: "steteruntque comae" (and my hair stood on end). The setting for the scene is the night of the destruction of Troy. A few lines earlier (v. 733), Aeneas is warned by his father, Anchises, to flee: "nate, ... fuge, nate; propinquant" (my son, my son, flee—they are coming closer). Moments later, Aeneas realizes that he has lost Creusa, and turns back to the flaming city to find her. His wife's ghost appears to him in a vision that is the cause of his hair standing on end. If Dante was thinking of this scene, as Pietro believed, he has perhaps put Anchises' warning about the fast-approaching Greek marauders into his own mouth, the advice he might have expected to have heard from Virgil, *his* "father," and the author of that scene. For these observations see Hollander (Holl.1984.3), p. 94.

25–30.   As Mark Musa (Musa.1977.1) has pointed out, Virgil, here and elsewhere (*Inf.* IV.51; X.17–18; XVI.119–120; XIX.39; XXVI.73–74), is either accorded by the protagonist or confers upon himself the power of "reading Dante's mind." Musa shows that, rather than the power actually to read the protagonist's thoughts, Virgil's capacity is one of heightened rationality, not the kind of supernatural power enjoyed by Beatrice, who, like all beatified souls, has precisely the ability to read the unvoiced thoughts of others; in other words, Virgil is able to fathom what Dante is thinking from the context of the experiences that they share, and nothing more than that.

Dante refers to mirrors being made by backing clear glass with lead in *Convivio* III.ix.8.

34–36.   The Malebranche are back, the "kite" of the fable, about to pounce on "mouse" and "frog."

37–45.   This simile, classical in form, seems to have no classical counterpart (although the fires of dying Troy may come to mind), whether in image or in language; rather, it seems to be among those that Dante draws from contemporary experience, ruinous fires being a pronounced feature of medieval town life. Virgil's customary paternal role here is resolved into a maternal one. That we should take this surprising change as meant positively is guaranteed by a later scene, just as Virgil has left the poem and returned to Limbo. At this moment of greatest pathos involving Dante's love for his guide and teacher, Dante turns back to him as a frightened child runs to his mother (*Purg.* XXX.44), only to find him gone forever.

46–48.   The second simile is also without classical origin. Commentators point out that land mills were powered by water, diverted from other sources along sluices, while water mills were situated in the rivers or streams that powered them.

52–57.   At the border of their domain the Malebranche, so swift on their own turf, are now frozen into immobility by the laws of God's governance of hell, as Dante and Virgil look back at them. The victims of earthly barrators are not similarly protected.

58–60.   The new set of sinners is characterized, in a total change of pace, by slowness and quiet, in stark contrast with the extraordinarily energetic, even frenetic, pace of the cantos of barratry.

They are "lacquered" in that they are covered by gilded mantles (v. 64).

61–63.   The hypocrites, "dressed" as monks, are in fact represented by only two personages, Catalano and Loderingo, both friars (see n. to vv. 104–108). The hypocrisy of the clergy—and especially of the mendicant orders—was a medieval commonplace, one most effectively exploited by such writers as Boccaccio and Chaucer.

While many early commentators believed that the monastery referred to was located in Köln (Cologne), in Germany, the predominant modern view is that this is the great Benedictine monastery in France, at Cluny.

64.   "Ypocresia . . . dicitur ab 'epi' quod est 'supra' et 'crisis' quod est 'aurum' " (Hypocrisy is so called from "epi," that is, "above," and "crisis," that is, "gold"). This familiar gloss, deriving from Uguccione of Pisa, is found in the third redaction of Pietro di Dante's commentary.

66.   Almost all the early commentators relate the tale that Frederick II (see *Inf.* X.119) put those who had particularly offended him to the fol-

lowing torture and death: he would have them covered with a thick "cape" of lead and placed in a large crucible, under which a fire was set, causing the lead to melt and the victim to suffer greatly before dying. While there is no evidence to connect Frederick with this practice, it seems clear that many of his contemporaries believed that he indeed did dispatch his enemies in this way.

76. Once again Dante's Tuscan speech serves to find him damned souls whose lives will be of interest. See *Inf.* X.22; XXII.99.

92. For Dante's word "hypocrites" commentators frequently cite Matthew 6:16: "Moreover when you fast, be not, as the hypocrites, of a sad countenance: for they disfigure their faces, that they may appear to men to fast."

102. The friars are like creaking scales (literally, "balances" in Dante's Italian) because the weight they support on their lurching shoulders is so tremendous that they "creak" beneath it.

103. "Frati gaudenti, 'Jovial Friars,' popular name of the knights of a military and conventual order, called the Knights of Our Lady . . . , which was [re-]founded in 1261 by certain citizens of Bologna under the sanction of [Pope] Urban IV. The object of the order was to make peace between the contending factions in the different cities of Italy, and to reconcile family feuds, and to protect the weak against their oppressors. The nickname 'Frati Gaudenti' is supposed to have been bestowed upon the knights on account of the laxity of their rules, which permitted them to marry and to live in their own homes, and merely required them to abstain from the use of gold and silver trappings, from attending at secular banquets, and from encouraging actors; while they bound themselves not to take up arms, save in defence of widows and orphans, and of the Catholic faith, or for the purpose of making peace between man and man" **(T)**. For Dante's relationship to Bologna see Raimondi (Raim.1967.1).

104–108. Catalano (ca. 1210–85) was a Bolognese Guelph of the Catalani family; Loderingo degli Andalò (ca. 1210–93) belonged to a Ghibelline family of the city. Loderingo was one of the founders of the Bolognese order of the Frati Gaudenti, and Catalano was also involved in it. While their allegiances to opposing parties made them seem to be an ideal "couple" to serve as *podestà* (an office usually taken on by a single non-citizen, chosen in the hope of guaranteeing fairness) of a faction-riddled city, their vows to the pope meant that, once they were chosen to serve in Florence in 1266, they in fact sided with the forces of the pope (Clement IV) against the Florentine Ghibellines, with the result that the area known as the Gardingo, where some of the most powerful Ghibelline families lived (including Farinata's Uberti—see *Inf.* X), was razed by the populace with at least the tacit consent of these two.

109. There is dispute as to whether Dante's broken apostrophe of the two friars (or, as some believe, of friars in general) was going to be one of rebuke (e.g., Benvenuto da Imola) or commiseration (e.g., Francesco da Buti). The context and the similar moment in *Inferno* XIX.90–117, when Dante upbraids Pope Nicholas III, both would seem to support the harsher reading.

110–117. Dante's attention is drawn by the figure crucified upon the ground, attached through his hands and his conjoined feet. From Catalano's description it will become clear that this is Caiaphas, the high priest who urged the Pharisees "that one man should be martyred for the people" and bears that burden of responsibility for the death of Jesus (see John 11:50). As Chiavacci Leonardi points out (Chia.1991.1, p. 696), Caiaphas masks his own vicious motives for wanting to give over Jesus as a desire for the public weal (i.e., saving the rest of the Hebrews from Roman repression), thus justifying his presence among the hypocrites.

118–120. The punishment of Caiaphas (and of his fellows in this act of hypocrisy, referred to in the next tercet) is a refinement upon that of the rest of the hypocrites. They are cloaked in lead, he is naked (his Christ-centered hypocrisy deserves to be revealed); yet he, too, feels the weight of hypocrisy on his own body when each of the others, in turn, slowly walks over his outstretched form.

121–123. Catalano refers to Annas, the father-in-law of Caiaphas, who presided over the council of the Pharisees (the "others" of the text) by which Jesus was condemned. It was this action, in Dante's mind, which was punished in the destruction of the second Temple by the forces of the Roman emperor Vespasian, led by his son Titus, in 70 A.D. and in the resultant diaspora of the Hebrew people.

124–126.   The high priest, unlike Jesus, is crucified upon the ground and trodden upon (thus seeming so "ignoble"). There has been much discussion of the possible reasons for Virgil's "marveling" over the crucified shape of Caiaphas. Castelvetro, in error, says that Virgil would have seen Caiaphas on an earlier visit to the depths; Lombardi gets this right: when Virgil was sent down by Erichtho, Christ had not yet been crucified and Caiaphas not yet been damned. Further, and as Margherita Frankel has argued (Fran.1984.1, p. 87), Virgil has already seen Christ and his Cross (*Inf*. IV.53–54). Nonetheless, and as others have pointed out, Virgil does not marvel at others who were not here before his first visit. Rossetti further remarks that nowhere else in *Inferno* does Virgil marvel at *any* other sinner, the text thus conferring a specialness upon this scene. Benvenuto da Imola and Vellutello both offered an interesting hypothesis, which has since made its way into some modern commentaries: the verse at line 117, "one man should be martyred for the people," seems to echo a verse from the *Aeneid* (V.815): "per multis dabitur caput" (one life shall be given for many). (In that passage Neptune speaks of the coming "sacrifice" of Palinurus.) Vellutello sees that "prophecy" as an unwitting Virgilian prophecy of Christ, and suggests that Virgil now wonders at how close he had come. If that seems perhaps a forced reading, a similar effect is gained by the phrase that Dante uses to indicate Caiaphas's punishment in his "eternal exile" *(etterno essilio)*. That phrase will only be used once again in the poem, precisely by Virgil himself to indicate *his own* punishment in Limbo (*Purg.* XXI.18), as Castelvetro observed. The Anonimo Fiorentino, perhaps better than many later commentators, caught the flavor of this passage, which he reads as indicating Virgil's grief for himself because he had not lived in a time when he could have known Christ. In this reader's view, Virgil wonders at Caiaphas because the high priest had actually known Christ in the world and yet turned against Him. Had Virgil had that opportunity, he thinks, his life (and afterlife) would have been very different.

131.   The "black angels" are obviously the winged devils of the last *bolgia*. Are they actually fallen angels, or does Virgil merely speak ironically, employing the figure antiphrasis, indicating devils by their opposites? Most of the commentators seem to believe that these really are fallen angels. This may be a questionable interpretation, since Dante seems clear about the kinds of fallen angels found in hell: neutral (Canto III.37–42) and rebellious (Canto VIII.82–83). If this were the only other place in hell in

which we found evil creatures referred to as "angels," it would seem likely that the term would be merely a figure of speech on Virgil's part. However, we also have the black Cherub referred to by Guido da Montefeltro (*Inf.* XXVII.113). See the note to that passage.

133–138. Virgil's question to Catalano (and Loderingo) receives this devastating answer: he has been fooled by Malacoda; all the bridges connecting the fifth and sixth "valleys" are down.

142–144. Catalano's bit of "university wit" is the last straw for Virgil, pilloried with understated sarcasm for trusting in the words of devils. Catalano cites Scripture (John 8:44): "Diabolus est mendax et pater eius" (The devil is a liar and the father of lies).

145–148. Virgil, angered (as well he might be), strides away, followed by the protagonist. We reflect that it is Dante who has contrived this whole elaborate scene to the discomfiture of Virgil, but who now, as a character in the poem, follows humbly and caringly in his dear leader's footsteps. Hollander (Holl. 1984.4), pp. 115–17, has suggested that this last verse is modelled on the concluding verses of Statius's *Thebaid* (XII.816–817): ". . . nec tu divinam Aeneida tempta, / sed longe sequere et vestigia semper adora" (do not attempt to rival the divine *Aeneid*, but follow at a distance, always worshiping its footsteps). With this gesture Statius tries to reassure his reader (and perhaps himself) that he feels no envy toward Virgil's greatness; Dante's gesture has a different task to perform, to reassure himself (and his reader) that, for all that the poet has put Virgil through in these cantos of barratry, he nonetheless reveres his great pagan guide.

INFERNO XXIV

In quella parte del giovanetto anno
che 'l sole i crin sotto l'Aquario tempra
3   e già le notti al mezzo dì sen vanno,

quando la brina in su la terra assempra
l'imagine di sua sorella bianca,
6   ma poco dura a la sua penna tempra,

lo villanello a cui la roba manca,
si leva, e guarda, e vede la campagna
9   biancheggiar tutta; ond' ei si batte l'anca,

ritorna in casa, e qua e là si lagna,
come 'l tapin che non sa che si faccia;
12   poi riede, e la speranza ringavagna,

veggendo 'l mondo aver cangiata faccia
in poco d'ora, e prende suo vincastro
15   e fuor le pecorelle a pascer caccia.

Così mi fece sbigottir lo mastro
quand' io li vidi sì turbar la fronte,
18   e così tosto al mal giunse lo 'mpiastro;

ché, come noi venimmo al guasto ponte,
lo duca a me si volse con quel piglio
21   dolce ch'io vidi prima a piè del monte.

Le braccia aperse, dopo alcun consiglio
eletto seco riguardando prima
24   ben la ruina, e diedemi di piglio.

E come quei ch'adopera ed estima,
che sempre par che 'nnanzi si proveggia,
27   così, levando me sù ver' la cima

In that season of the youthful year
when the sun cools his locks beneath Aquarius
and the dark already nears but half the day,

and when the hoarfrost copies out upon the fields
the very image of her snowy sister—
although her pen-point is not sharp for long—

the peasant, short of fodder, rises,
looks out, and sees the countryside
turned white, at which he slaps his thigh,

goes back indoors, grumbling here and there
like a wretch who knows not what to do,
then goes outside again and is restored to hope,

seeing that the world has changed its face
in that brief time, and now picks up his crook
and drives his sheep to pasture.

Thus the master caused me to lose heart
when I saw how troubled was his brow
and just as quickly came the poultice to the wound,

for no sooner had we reached the broken bridge
than he turned to me with that gentle glance
I first saw at the mountain's foot.

He looked with care upon the ruin,
took thought, chose a plan of action,
then opened out his arms and took me in them.

And like one who reckons as he works,
always planning before-hand what comes next,
thus, while raising me to a boulder's top,

d'un ronchione, avvisava un'altra scheggia
dicendo: "Sovra quella poi t'aggrappa;
30   ma tenta pria s'è tal ch'ella ti reggia."

Non era via da vestito di cappa,
ché noi a pena, ei lieve e io sospinto,
33   potavam sù montar di chiappa in chiappa.

E se non fosse che da quel precinto
più che da l'altro era la costa corta,
36   non so di lui, ma io sarei ben vinto.

Ma perché Malebolge inver' la porta
del bassissimo pozzo tutta pende,
39   lo sito di ciascuna valle porta

che l'una costa surge e l'altra scende;
noi pur venimmo al fine in su la punta
42   onde l'ultima pietra si scoscende.

La lena m'era del polmon sì munta
quand'io fui sù, ch'i' non potea più oltre,
45   anzi m'assisi ne la prima giunta.

"Omai convien che tu così ti spoltre,"
disse 'l maestro; "ché, seggendo in piuma,
48   in fama non si vien, né sotto coltre;

sanza la qual chi sua vita consuma,
cotal vestigio in terra di sé lascia,
51   qual fummo in aere e in acqua la schiuma.

E però leva sù; vinci l'ambascia
con l'animo che vince ogne battaglia,
54   se col suo grave corpo non s'accascia.

Più lunga scala convien che si saglia;
non basta da costoro esser partito.
57   Se tu mi 'ntendi, or fa sì che ti vaglia."

he searched for yet another crag
and said: 'Take hold of that one next
30   but test to see if it will bear your weight.'

This was no climb for people wearing leaden cloaks.
Though he was weightless and I was being pushed,
33   how hard a climb it was from one crag to the other!

Were it not that on this side of the dike
the slope was shorter—I cannot speak for him—
36   I would have given up.

But since all Malebolge inclines
down to the mouth of the lowest pit,
39   it follows that each valley is constructed

with one side higher than the other.
At last we made it to the point
42   where the outermost stone had broken off.

And there I felt my lungs so sucked of breath
that I could go no farther,
45   but sat down as quickly as I could.

'Now must you cast off sloth,' my master said.
'Sitting on feather cushions or stretched out
48   under comforters, no one comes to fame.

'Without fame, he who spends his time on earth
leaves only such a mark upon the world
51   as smoke does on the air or foam on water.

'Get to your feet! Conquer this laboring breath
with strength of mind, which wins the battle
54   if not dragged down by body's weight.

'There is a longer stair that must be climbed.
It's not enough to leave these souls behind.
57   If you take my meaning, let it be of use.'

Leva'mi allor, mostrandomi fornito
meglio di lena ch'i' non mi sentia,
60   e dissi: "Va, ch'i' son forte e ardito."

Su per lo scoglio prendemmo la via,
ch'era ronchioso, stretto e malagevole,
63   ed erto più assai che quel di pria.

Parlando andava per non parer fievole;
onde una voce uscì de l'altro fosso,
66   a parole formar disconvenevole.

Non so che disse, ancor che sovra 'l dosso
fossi de l'arco già che varca quivi;
69   ma chi parlava ad ire parea mosso.

Io era vòlto in giù, ma li occhi vivi
non poteano ire al fondo per lo scuro;
72   per ch'io: "Maestro, fa che tu arrivi

da l'altro cinghio e dismontiam lo muro;
ché, com' i' odo quinci e non intendo,
75   così giù veggio e neente affiguro."

"Altra risposta," disse, "non ti rendo
se non lo far; ché la dimanda onesta
78   si de' seguir con l'opera tacendo."

Noi discendemmo il ponte de la testa
dove s'aggiugne con l'ottava ripa,
81   e poi mi fu la bolgia manifesta:

e vidivi entro terribile stipa
di serpenti, e di sì diversa mena
84   che la memoria il sangue ancor mi scipa.

Più non si vanti Libia con sua rena;
ché se chelidri, iaculi e faree
87   produce, e cencri con anfisibena,

At that I rose, pretending to more breath
than I had in me, and said:
60   'Go on then, for I am strong and resolute.'

We labored up a ridge,
rugged, narrow, difficult,
63   and steeper far than was the last.

Not to seem so spent, I talked as I climbed up.
Then, from the next ditch, came a voice
66   that seemed unfit for forming words.

I could not make out what it said,
though I was at the crown that arches over,
69   but he who spoke seemed to be moving.

Hard as I strained to see, it was too dark
for living eyes to plumb the depths.
72   And so I said: 'Master, take your way

'to the next ledge where we can leave this bridge.
From here I make out nothing with my ears
75   nor with my eyes see anything down there.'

'I give no other answer than to take you,'
he said, 'for a just request
78   should be followed by the act, in silence.'

We left the bridge at the abutment
where it comes to rest on that eighth bank.
81   From there the contents of the ditch came into view.

In it I saw a dreadful swarm of serpents,
of so strange a kind that even now
84   when I remember them it chills my blood.

Let Libya with all her sands no longer boast,
for though she fosters chelydri, jaculi,
87   phareae, cenchres, and amphisbaena,

né tante pestilenzie né sì ree
mostrò già mai con tutta l'Etïopia
90 né con ciò che di sopra al Mar Rosso èe.

Tra questa cruda e tristissima copia
corrëan genti nude e spaventate,
93 sanza sperar pertugio o elitropia:

con serpi le man dietro avean legate;
quelle ficcavan per le ren la coda
96 e 'l capo, ed eran dinanzi aggroppate.

Ed ecco a un ch'era da nostra proda,
s'avventò un serpente che 'l trafisse
99 là dove 'l collo a le spalle s'annoda.

Né O sì tosto mai né I si scrisse,
com' el s'accese e arse, e cener tutto
102 convenne che cascando divenisse;

e poi che fu a terra sì distrutto,
la polver si raccolse per sé stessa
105 e 'n quel medesmo ritornò di butto.

Così per li gran savi si confessa
che la fenice more e poi rinasce,
108 quando al cinquecentesimo anno appressa;

erba né biado in sua vita non pasce,
ma sol d'incenso lagrime e d'amomo,
111 e nardo e mirra son l'ultime fasce.

E qual è quel che cade, e non sa como,
per forza di demon ch'a terra il tira,
114 o d'altra oppilazion che lega l'omo,

quando si leva, che 'ntorno si mira
tutto smarrito de la grande angoscia
117 ch'elli ha sofferta, e guardando sospira:

she never reared so many venomous pests,
nor so appalling—not with all of Ethiopia
90   and the lands that lie along the Red Sea coast.

Amid this fearsome and most awful plenty,
people, naked and in terror, were running
93   without hope of refuge or of heliotrope.

Their hands were tied behind their backs with snakes
that thrust their heads and tails between the legs
96   and joined, knotting themselves in front.

And behold, one of these souls was near our ridge
when a serpent launched and pierced him through
99   right where the neck and shoulders join.

Never has 'o' nor even 'i' been writ so quick
as he caught fire and burned, turned,
102   in the very act of falling, into ashes.

And as he lay unmade upon the ground,
the dust gathered itself of its own accord
105   and suddenly he was himself again.

Just, as is attested by great sages,
the phoenix perishes and is reborn
108   when it approaches its five-hundredth year—

lifelong it feeds on neither grain nor grasses,
but thrives on drops of frankincense and cardamom,
111   while nard and myrrh make up its winding sheet—

and just as one who faints, and knows not why—
whether possessed by devils that pull him down
114   or seized by the sickness that causes men to fall—

rises to his feet, and gazes round,
wholly bewildered by the breathless anguish
117   he has undergone, and as he looks, he sighs,

tal era 'l peccator levato poscia.
Oh potenza di Dio, quant' è severa,
120   che cotai colpi per vendetta croscia!

Lo duca il domandò poi chi ello era;
per ch'ei rispuose: "Io piovvi di Toscana,
123   poco tempo è, in questa gola fiera.

Vita bestial mi piacque e non umana,
sì come a mul ch'i' fui; son Vanni Fucci
126   bestia, e Pistoia mi fu degna tana."

E ïo al duca: "Dilli che non mucci,
e domanda che colpa qua giù 'l pinse;
129   ch'io 'l vidi omo di sangue e di crucci."

E 'l peccator, che 'ntese, non s'infinse,
ma drizzò verso me l'animo e 'l volto,
132   e di trista vergogna si dipinse;

poi disse: "Più mi duol che tu m'hai colto
ne la miseria dove tu mi vedi,
135   che quando fui de l'altra vita tolto.

Io non posso negar quel che tu chiedi;
in giù son messo tanto perch'io fui
138   ladro a la sagrestia d'i belli arredi,

e falsamente già fu apposto altrui.
Ma perché di tal vista tu non godi,
141   se mai sarai di fuor da' luoghi bui,

apri li orecchi al mio annunzio, e odi.
Pistoia in pria d'i Neri si dimagra;
144   poi Fiorenza rinova gente e modi.

Tragge Marte vapor di Val di Magra
ch'è di torbidi nuvoli involuto;
147   e con tempesta impetüosa e agra

such did that sinner seem when he had risen.
O how stern it is, the power of God,
120   hurling such blows as it takes vengeance!

When my leader asked him who he was:
'From Tuscany I rained down,' was his answer,
123   'not long ago, into this savage gorge.

'I loved the life of beasts and not of men,
just like the mule I was. I am Vanni Fucci,
126   animal. Pistoia was my fitting den.'

And I to my leader: 'Tell him not to slip away,
then ask what sin has thrust him to this depth,
129   for I knew him as a man of blood and rages.'

And the sinner, listening, did not dissemble,
but set his mind and eyes on me,
132   then colored with a wrathful shame

and said: 'For you to catch me
in this misery pains me more
135   than when I was taken from the other life.

'I can't refuse to answer what you ask.
I am thrust so far below because I stole
138   its lovely ornaments from the sacristy

'and the blame was wrongly laid upon another.
But, so you take no joy in seeing me this low,
141   if ever you escape from these dark regions,

'open your ears to my prophecy and hear:
First, Pistoia strips herself of Blacks,
144   then Florence changes families and fashions.

'Next Mars draws up a bolt from Val di Magra,
engulfed by torn and threatening clouds,
147   and, with violent and stinging storms,

sovra Campo Picen fia combattuto;
ond'ei repente spezzerà la nebbia,
sì ch'ogne Bianco ne sarà feruto.
151   E detto l'ho perché doler ti debbia!"

'on Campo Piceno the battle shall be joined.
The headlong bolt shall rend the clouds,
striking and wounding every White.

151   And this I have told that it may make you grieve.'

1–21.   This elaborate canto-opening simile (see note to *Inf.* XXII.1–12) and its aftermath knit the narrative back together: Virgil had walked away from Catalano (and from Dante) at the end of the last canto; now, getting his anger under control, he turns back to reassure Dante and continue his leadership. That is a fair summary of how the simile works as a reflection of what is happening between the two characters. However, this simile (like the Aesopic material in Canto XXIII) can be read for more than one set of equivalences: (1) Virgil's frown (hoarfrost) melts and he once again encourages Dante (the humble wretch), who eventually will, having completed the journey, feed us (his sheep) with the pages of the poem; (2) the devils' deception (hoarfrost), in the form of an incorrect presentation of the terrain, discourages Virgil (the wretch), who finally reads the signs right and will lead Dante (his sheep) to pasture. A form of this second simultaneous reading was proposed by Lansing (Lans.1977.1), pp. 77–80.

As Frankel has noted (Fran.1984.1), pp. 82–83, the simile itself is divided into two rather different stylistic zones; the first six verses are "classicizing" and rather high-flown, while the final nine are in the low style. Hollander (Holl.1984.4) suggests that the first tercet of the "classical" part derives from Virgil's third *Georgic* (vv. 303–304), a citation also found in the second and third redactions of the commentary of Pietro di Dante, and also noted by Tommaseo. For other studies in English of this much studied simile see Bake.1974.1, Econ.1976.1, and Lans.1977.1 (pp. 74–80); for Dante's knowledge of the *Georgics* see Marigo (Mari.1909.1).

The reference to Aquarius sets the time within the simile as winter, since the sun is in that constellation from 21 January to 21 February. And so the sun cools his "locks" (its rays) in this season.

22–24.   The sight of the *ruina*, the scree fallen at the Crucifixion, now gives Virgil hope: it is a way up and out of the *bolgia*. Catalano, unlike Malacoda, has given him valuable advice.

31.   The phrase "people wearing leaden cloaks" obviously refers to the hypocrites whom we saw in the last canto.

32–36.   The protagonist's physical difficulty, since unlike Virgil he must move his flesh and bones against the pull of gravity, is insisted on. The interplay between Virgil and Dante, now with roles reversed from Cantos XXI–XXIII (when Virgil was the one at a disadvantage) goes on for some time, through verse 60. It is in no way meant to make the reader believe, as did John Ruskin, in *Modern Painters*, that "Dante was a notably bad climber."

37–40.   Once again (see *Inf.* XIX.35 and note) the poet insists that the far sides, or banks, of each *bolgia* are not as high as the ones encountered first, since the sloping floor of the Malebolge cuts *down* across each ditch.

49–51.   The commentators are almost unanimous in taking Virgil's words at face value and as sound advice. See, for example, Chiavacci Leonardi (Chia.1991.1), pp. 712–13, who argues for earthly fame's "double valence" in the poem; she claims that it is sometimes an excusable aim (as here), sometimes a culpable one. Certainly the net effect of Virgil's appeal here is to get Dante moving upward in order to continue to the top of the ridge, whence he will be able to see into the next ditch as he continues his journey. Yet is it not strange that the motivation offered by Virgil is not the need to struggle onward toward the presence of God so much as it is the reward of earthly fame? Rossetti, in his commentary, was perhaps the first to observe the resonance of what has now become a standard citation for these verses, the entirely similar similes found in the book of Wisdom (5:15): "like the insubstantial foam that is dispersed by the storm, like the smoke that is dissipated by the wind." In Wisdom the comparisons are to the hopes of the impious man (as opposed to those of the just, whose thoughts are set on God [5:16]). Narrowly construed, Virgil's words are those of the impious man who lodges his hopes in the most transitory of things—exactly what the poem will later establish as the true and fleeting nature of earthly fame (*Purg.* XI.91–93). If we were to imagine St. Thomas as guide here, we would expect his words to have been quite different. Beginning with Gregorio Di Siena, commentators also cite another apposite text for these lines, *Aeneid* V.740, "tenuis fugit ceu fumus in auras": it is the vision of Anchises that vanishes from Aeneas's sight "like thin smoke into the air."

Cantos XXI–XXIV thus include Virgil's most difficult moments as guide to the Christian underworld. The rest of the *cantica* is mainly without such unsettling behavior toward his master and author on the poet's part. But this will start up again in a series of moments that are difficult for Virgil in the early cantos of *Purgatorio*.

58–64.   In a moment that will strike anyone who is in fact a "notably bad climber" with its aptness, the passage insists on Dante's effort to convince his guide that he is better furnished with breath than in fact he is.

65–66.   These lines introduce a problem (who is speaking?) that will weave itself through the text until perhaps the eighteenth verse of the next canto.

67–78.   These twelve verses have no other point than to underline the intensity of Dante's curiosity about the identity of the speaker whose unintelligible voice he has just heard. It would be unlikely for him to have left his riddle unanswered. See note to vv. 17–18 of the next canto.

Verse 69 has been the cause of much debate. Is the word in the text *ire* (as in Petrocchi's edition, meaning "to go") or *ira* (wrath)? For a treatment of the problem see Hollander (Holl.1983.2), offering a listing of the history of the commentary tradition (pp. 29–31) and concluding that the text originally read *ira*, as almost all the early commentators believed, with the major exception of Pietro di Dante. For a countering view see Stef.1993.1, p. 85.

Once again, while not in agreement with it, we have preserved the letter of Petrocchi's text in our translation. Berthier, who opts for *ira*, cites St. Thomas to the effect that one of the five effects of wrath is precisely to cause in the furious sinner "clamor irrationabilis" (irrational cries), perhaps exactly what Dante has made out. It also remains difficult to explain how one can hear, from a distance and in darkness, how a being is "moved" to getting into motion, while it is not at all difficult to hear, in precisely these circumstances, that a voice is moved by wrath.

79–81.   The new prospect before Dante's eyes, once he is over the seventh *bolgia*, having descended from the bridge that connects to the eighth, completely absorbs his attention. The identity of the speaker, which he has been so eager to learn, is now forgotten—for a while.

82–84.   Now begins the drama of the marvelous, what Milton might have called "things unattempted yet in prose or rhyme." Many have commented upon the exuberance of Dante's treatment of the scene of the thieves. On the question of the perhaps problematic virtuosity of this and the next canto see Terd.1973.1; for a reply see Hawk.1980.1.

85–87. The serpents derive, as almost all commentators duly note, from the ninth book of Lucan's *Pharsalia* with its description of the Libyan desert, replete with them. They are all beyond the pale of any known zoology. For Dante's knowledge of Lucan in general see Para. 1965.2.

88–90. Dante adapts Lucan's somewhat unusual term for "serpent" (*pestis*—which generally means "plague") and now imagines as many deserts as he knows of containing still other improbable serpentine creatures.

91–96. The scene, with its principal actors naked, afraid, and trying to hide, evokes, as Hollander has argued (Holl. 1983.2), p. 34, the description of Adam and Eve hiding from God in the Garden of Eden after they have sinned (Gen. 3:9–10): "Vocavitque Dominus Deus Adam, et dixit ei: 'Ubi es?' Qui ait, 'Vocem tuam audivi in paradiso et timui, eo quod nudus essem, et abscondi me' " (And the Lord God called Adam and asked, "Where are you?" And Adam said, "I heard your voice in the garden and I grew afraid, because I was naked, and I hid myself"). Hollander goes on to examine nine more moments in this scene that reflect the "primal scene" of thievery in Eden, including the parodic version of the fig leaves with which Adam and Eve covered their loins in Gen. 3:7 found here in vv. 95–96. See also Beal. 1983.1, pp. 103–5, for resonances of the Edenic scene in this passage.

The heliotrope was a stone that supposedly had the power to render its possessor invisible, as Boccaccio's Calandrino was urged to believe by his trickster friends (*Decameron* VIII.3). On the heliotrope's properties see Ciof. 1937.1.

97. This figure, so rudely attacked, will turn out to be Vanni Fucci (v. 125).

98–99. For this and the two other forms of punishment found in this *bolgia* see the "Table of Metamorphoses," the endnote to Canto XXV.

100. Since the so-called Ottimo Commento (1333), commentators have agreed that these two letters are written most quickly because they are written in a single stroke. But do these two letters signify anything? For instance, are they a code for Dante's vaunt against Ovid (i.e., "I [*io*] can portray metamorphosis even better than you")? Or do they represent

the negation of Vanni's self (i.e., "io" spelled backwards)? For an inge-
nious argument, extending this second hypothesis, see Darby Chapin
(Darb.1971.1), suggesting an Ovidian source. She argues that, when Io was
transformed into a cow (*Metam.* I.646–650), medieval commentators rep-
resented her new hoofprint as made of the two letters of her name, the
"I" written inside the "O" so as to represent the cleft in her newly formed
hooves (**Ꙩ**).

107–111. The reference to the phoenix is also Ovidian (*Metam.*
XV.392–402). That rare bird was reputed to live five hundred years and
then be reborn out of the ashes of its own perfumed funeral pyre. Chris-
tian exegetes thus easily took the phoenix as a symbol of Christ (see
Beal.1983.1, pp. 105–7). Vanni, seen in this light, thus parodically enacts the
death and resurrection of Christ.

119–120. The poet's exclamation is part of his presentation of himself
not as a merely ingenious teller of fantastic tales, but as the scribe of God,
only recording what he actually saw of God's just retaliation for sins per-
formed against Him. See Romans 12:19, where Paul offers the words of
God, "Vengeance is mine; I shall repay."

122–126. Vanni Fucci's laconic self-identification tells us that he was an
illegitimate son (of the Lazzari family of Pistoia) and insists upon his bes-
tiality (some early commentators report that his nickname was "Vanni the
Beast"). He died sometime after 1295, when he apparently left Pistoia, and
before 1300—although this is not certain.

127–129. Dante's response indicates that he had once known Vanni and
thought of him as guilty of sins of violence, not necessarily those of
fraud.

132–139. Vanni's shame and honest self-description give him a certain
moral advantage over many of the dissembling sinners whom we meet.
At the same time his wrathful character extends not only to self-hatred,
but to hatred of others, as his ensuing harsh words for Dante will reveal
(vv. 140–151). His character, so briefly etched, is that of a familiar enough
figure, the embittered destroyer of any human bond.

The theft of sacred objects from the sacristy of the chapel of St. James
in Pistoia—which caused an uproar when it occurred, ca. 1293–95—was
first not laid to his door and he indeed had left the city before his complic-

ity was revealed by one of his confederates, soon afterwards put to death for his part in the crime. There is speculation that the eventual truth of Vanni's involvement was only discovered after 1300, yet in time for Dante to present it as "news" here in his poem.

140–142.   Vanni's prophecy is the last of these "personal prophecies" found in *Inferno*. There are nine of these in the *Comedy*. (See note to *Inf.* VI.64–66.) He offers it as a form of revenge on Dante for having seen him in such distress.

143–150.   The riddling expression of the language of prophecy is, at least for a contemporary of Vanni's and Dante's, for the most part not difficult to unravel. Pistoia's White Guelphs will drive out the Black party in 1301; Florence's Blacks will do the same in the same year to the Whites in that city (with one consequence being Dante's exile). In 1302 the Blacks of Pistoia, allied with Moroello Malaspina ("the headlong bolt"), will have their revenge upon the Whites, taking their stronghold at Serravalle. Some understand that Vanni also (or only) refers to the eventual Black victory over the Whites in Pistoia itself in 1306.

151.   Vanni's acerbic ending, personalizing the prophecy as a way of making Dante grieve, is his tit-for-tat response for the grief that Dante has caused him by seeing him. He may be damned for thievery, but his party will be victorious, while Dante's will be roundly defeated.

INFERNO XXV

Al fine de le sue parole il ladro
le mani alzò con amendue le fiche,
3   gridando: "Togli, Dio, ch'a te le squadro!"

Da indi in qua mi fuor le serpi amiche,
perch' una li s'avvolse allora al collo,
6   come dicesse "Non vo' che più diche";

e un'altra a le braccia, e rilegollo,
ribadendo sé stessa sì dinanzi,
9   che non potea con esse dare un crollo.

Ahi Pistoia, Pistoia, ché non stanzi
d'incenerarti sì che più non duri,
12   poi che 'n mal fare il seme tuo avanzi?

Per tutt' i cerchi de lo 'nferno scuri
non vidi spirto in Dio tanto superbo,
15   non quel che cadde a Tebe giù da' muri.

El si fuggì che non parlò più verbo;
e io vidi un centauro pien di rabbia
18   venir chiamando: "Ov' è, ov' è l'acerbo?"

Maremma non cred' io che tante n'abbia,
quante bisce elli avea su per la groppa
21   infin ove comincia nostra labbia.

Sovra le spalle, dietro da la coppa,
con l'ali aperte li giacea un draco;
24   e quello affuoca qualunque s'intoppa.

Lo mio maestro disse: "Questi è Caco,
che, sotto 'l sasso di monte Aventino,
27   di sangue fece spesse volte laco.

Then, making the figs with both his thumbs,
the thief raised up his fists and cried:
'Take that, God! It's aimed at you!'

3

From that time on the serpents were my friends,
for one of them coiled itself around his neck
as if to say, 'Now you shall speak no more,'

6

while another enmeshed his arms and held him fast,
knotting itself so tight around his front
he could not even twitch his arms.

9

Ah, Pistoia, Pistoia, why won't you resolve
to burn yourself to ashes, cease to be,
since you exceed your ancestors in evil?

12

Through all the gloomy rounds of Hell
I saw no soul so prideful against God,
not even him who toppled from the walls at Thebes.

15

He ran away without another word.
And then I saw a centaur full of rage
come shouting: 'Where, where is that unripe soul?'

18

Maremma does not have as many snakes,
I think, as he had on his back,
from where the human part begins down to the rump.

21

On his shoulders, just at the nape of the neck,
crouched a dragon with its wings spread wide
that sets on fire whatever it encounters.

24

My master said: 'That is Cacus,
who in the cave beneath the Aventine
many times over has made a lake of blood.

27

Non va co' suoi fratei per un cammino,
per lo furto che frodolente fece
30   del grande armento ch'elli ebbe a vicino;

onde cessar le sue opere biece
sotto la mazza d'Ercule, che forse
33   gliene diè cento, e non sentì le diece."

Mentre che sì parlava, ed el trascorse,
e tre spiriti venner sotto noi,
36   de' quai né io né 'l duca mio s'accorse,

se non quando gridar: "Chi siete voi?"
per che nostra novella si ristette,
39   e intendemmo pur ad essi poi.

Io non li conoscea; ma ei seguette,
come suol seguitar per alcun caso,
42   che l'un nomar un altro convenette,

dicendo: "Cianfa dove fia rimaso?"
per ch'io, acciò che 'l duca stesse attento,
45   mi puosi 'l dito su dal mento al naso.

Se tu se' or, lettore, a creder lento
ciò ch'io dirò, non sarà maraviglia,
48   ché io che 'l vidi, a pena il mi consento.

Com' io tenea levate in lor le ciglia,
e un serpente con sei piè si lancia
51   dinanzi a l'uno, e tutto a lui s'appiglia.

Co' piè di mezzo li avvinse la pancia
e con li anterïor le braccia prese;
54   poi li addentò e l'una e l'altra guancia;

li diretani a le cosce distese,
e miseli la coda tra 'mbedue
57   e dietro per le ren sù la ritese.

'His road is different from his brothers'
because he stole, with wicked cunning,
30   the herd of cattle he found near at hand.

'For that his wily ways were ended
beneath the club of Hercules, who struck perhaps
33   a hundred blows, though he felt not the tenth.'

While my master spoke the centaur had run past.
Below where we were standing, three new souls
36   had neared, although we did not see them

until we heard their shouts: 'You,
who are you?' At that he stopped his tale
39   and we gave heed to them alone.

I knew none of them, and yet it happened—
as often happens by some chance—
42   that one had cause to speak another's name,

asking: 'What's become of Cianfa?'
And then, to catch my guide's attention,
45   I held my finger up from chin to nose.

If, reader, you are slow to credit
what I'm about to tell you, it's no wonder:
48   I saw it, and I myself can scarce believe it.

While I stood staring, with raised brows,
a reptile with six legs propelled itself
51   at one of them, and fastened itself to him.

It grabbed his belly with its middle claws,
then with its forepaws held his arms
54   and bit him on both cheeks.

It stretched its hind feet down the other's thighs,
thrusting its tail between them
57   and curled it up behind, above the buttocks.

Ellera abbarbicata mai non fue
ad alber sì, come l'orribil fiera
60   per l'altrui membra avviticchiò le sue.

Poi s'appiccar, come di calda cera
fossero stati, e mischiar lor colore,
63   né l'un né l'altro già parea quel ch'era:

come procede innanzi da l'ardore,
per lo papiro suso, un color bruno
66   che non è nero ancora e 'l bianco more.

Li altri due 'l riguardavano, e ciascuno
gridava: "Omè, Agnel, come ti muti!
69   Vedi che già non se' né due né uno."

Già eran li due capi un divenuti,
quando n'apparver due figure miste
72   in una faccia, ov' eran due perduti.

Fersi le braccia due di quattro liste;
le cosce con le gambe e 'l ventre e 'l casso
75   divenner membra che non fuor mai viste.

Ogne primaio aspetto ivi era casso:
due e nessun l'imagine perversa
78   parea; e tal sen gio con lento passo.

Come 'l ramarro sotto la gran fersa
dei dì canicular, cangiando sepe,
81   folgore par se la via attraversa,

sì pareva, venendo verso l'epe
de li altri due, un serpentello acceso,
84   livido e nero come gran di pepe;

e quella parte onde prima è preso
nostro alimento, a l'un di lor trafisse;
87   poi cadde giuso innanzi lui disteso.

Never did clinging ivy fix itself
so tight upon a tree as did that fearsome beast
60   entwine itself around the other's limbs.

Then they fused together, as if made
of molten wax, mixing their colors
63   so that neither seemed what it had been before,

as over the surface of a scrap of parchment,
before the flame, a brownish color comes
66   that is not black, yet makes the white die out.

The other two were looking on and each
was shouting: 'Oh my, Agnello, how you change!
69   Look, now you are neither two nor one!'

Already the two heads had been united,
two sets of features blending,
72   both lost in a single face.

Four separate limbs combined to form two arms.
The thighs and calves, the stomach and the chest
75   turned into members never seen before.

All trace of their first aspect was erased
and the unnatural figure seemed both two
78   and none and lumbered off at its slow pace.

As the green lizard beneath the scorching lash
of dog-day heat, between one hedge and the next,
81   seems lightning as it streaks across the road,

just so appeared—darting toward the bellies
of the other two—a little fiery reptile,
84   black and livid as a peppercorn.

That part where first we are nourished
it transfixed in one of them
87   and then fell prone before him.

Lo trafitto 'l mirò, ma nulla disse;
anzi, co' piè fermati, sbadigliava
90   pur come sonno o febbre l'assalisse.

Elli 'l serpente e quei lui riguardava;
l'un per la piaga e l'altro per la bocca
93   fummavan forte, e 'l fummo si scontrava.

Taccia Lucano omai là dov' e' tocca
del misero Sabello e di Nasidio,
96   e attenda a udir quel ch'or si scocca.

Taccia di Cadmo e d'Aretusa Ovidio,
ché se quello in serpente e quella in fonte
99   converte poetando, io non lo 'nvidio;

ché due nature mai a fronte a fronte
non trasmutò sì ch'amendue le forme
102   a cambiar lor matera fosser pronte.

Insieme si rispuosero a tai norme,
che 'l serpente la coda in forca fesse,
105   e 'l feruto ristrinse insieme l'orme.

Le gambe con le cosce seco stesse
s'appiccar sì, che 'n poco la giuntura
108   non facea segno alcun che si paresse.

Togliea la coda fessa la figura
che si perdeva là, e la sua pelle
111   si facea molle, e quella di là dura.

Io vidi intrar le braccia per l'ascelle,
e i due piè de la fiera, ch'eran corti,
114   tanto allungar quanto accorciavan quelle.

Poscia li piè di rietro, insieme attorti,
diventaron lo membro che l'uom cela,
117   e 'l misero del suo n'avea due porti.

The one transfixed just stared, said nothing.
Indeed, with his feet stock-still, he yawned,
90   as if deep sleep or fever had assailed him.

He and the reptile stared at one another.
Both gave out dense smoke, one from its wound,
93   the other from its mouth. Then their smoke merged.

Let Lucan now fall silent where he tells
of poor Sabellus and Nasidius,
96   and let him wait to hear what comes forth now!

Let Ovid not speak of Cadmus or Arethusa,
for if his poem turns him into a serpent
99   and her into a fountain, I grudge it not,

for never did he change two natures, face to face,
in such a way that both their forms
102   were quite so quick exchanging substance.

Their corresponding changes went like this:
the reptile split its tail into a fork
105   and he that was wounded drew his feet together.

First his calves and then his thighs began
to knit so that in but a moment
108   no sign of a division could be seen.

The cloven tail assumed the shapes
the other one was losing, and his skin
111   was turning soft while the other's hardened.

I saw the man's arms shrinking toward the armpits
and the brute's forepaws, which had been short,
114   lengthen, precisely as the other's dwindled.

Then the hind-paws, twisting together,
became the member that a man conceals,
117   and from his own the wretch had grown two paws.

Mentre che 'l fummo l'uno e l'altro vela
di color novo, e genera 'l pel suso
120   per l'una parte e da l'altra il dipela,

l'un si levò e l'altro cadde giuso,
non torcendo però le lucerne empie,
123   sotto le quai ciascun cambiava muso.

Quel ch'era dritto, il trasse ver' le tempie,
e di troppa matera ch'in là venne
126   uscir li orecchi de le gote scempie;

ciò che non corse in dietro e si ritenne
di quel soverchio, fé naso a la faccia
129   e le labbra ingrossò quanto convenne.

Quel che giacëa, il muso innanzi caccia,
e li orecchi ritira per la testa
132   come face le corna la lumaccia;

e la lingua, ch'avëa unita e presta
prima a parlar, si fende, e la forcuta
135   ne l'altro si richiude; e 'l fummo resta.

L'anima ch'era fiera divenuta,
suffolando si fugge per la valle,
138   e l'altro dietro a lui parlando sputa.

Poscia li volse le novelle spalle,
e disse a l'altro: "I' vo' che Buoso corra,
141   com' ho fatt' io, carpon per questo calle."

Così vid' io la settima zavorra
mutare e trasmutare; e qui mi scusi
144   la novità se fior la penna abborra.

E avvegna che li occhi miei confusi
fossero alquanto e l'animo smagato,
147   non poter quei fuggirsi tanto chiusi,

While the smoke veils one and now the other
with new color and grows hair here
120   and elsewhere strips it off,

one of them rose to his feet, the other fell,
but neither turned aside his baleful glare
123   under which each muzzle changed its shape.

In the one erect it shrank in to the temples,
and, from the excess flesh absorbed,
126   two ears extruded from smooth cheeks.

Whatever did not recede, left over
from that excess, made a nose for the face
129   and gave the lips a proper thickness.

The one prone on the ground shoves out his snout
and draws his ears into his head
132   as a snail draws in its horns,

and his tongue, till now a single thing
and fit for speech, divides, and the other's
135   forked tongue joins, and the smoke stops.

The soul just now become a brute takes flight,
hissing through the hollow, and the other,
138   by way of speaking, spits after him.

Then he turned his new-made shoulders and he said
to the third: 'I want Buoso to run, as I have done,
141   down on all fours along this road.'

Thus I saw the seventh rabble change
and change again, and let the newness of it
144   be my excuse if my pen has gone astray.

And though my eyes were dazed
and my mind somewhat bewildered,
147   these sinners could not flee so stealthily

ch'i' non scorgessi ben Puccio Sciancato;
ed era quel che sol, di tre compagni
che venner prima, non era mutato;

151   l'altr' era quel che tu, Gaville, piagni.

but I with ease discerned that Puccio Lameshanks,
and he alone, of the three companions
in that group, remained unchanged.

151   The other, Gaville, was the one whom you lament.

1–3. Emphasizing the close relationship between the two cantos, this one begins in absolute continuation of the action of the last, as though there were no formal divide between them.

Vanni's obscene gesture to God is variously understood. Francesco da Buti, in his gloss, says that the gesture is made by extending two fingers on each hand (apparently the same gesture as giving the sign of the horns, for cuckoldry, but the commentator does not say so), and in this case, four fingers in all, thus accounting for the verb *squadrare* ("to square"), with its resonance of fourness. Beginning with Pompeo Venturi in the 1730s, most commentators say that the gesture is made by placing the thumb between the index and middle fingers. Ignazio Baldelli, however, has recently argued that the gesture involves making the image of the female pudenda with thumb and index finger (Bald.1997.1). Whatever the precise gesture Vanni made, it was not a polite one.

4. The serpents, according to Guido da Pisa, become Dante's "friends" because they undo the reason for the curse laid on the serpent in the Garden (Gen. 3:15); these serpents are doing something praiseworthy despite their unappealing ancestry.

5–9. The serpents attaching themselves to Vanni reminded Tommaseo of the serpents that kill the sons of Laocoön and eventually capture the priest himself in their coils and strangle him (*Aeneid* II.201–224). Other commentators have not followed his lead.

10–12. The poet apostrophizes Pistoia as he nears the end of the section of these cantos devoted to Vanni Fucci. The next thieves whom we will see will all be Florentines.

13–15. Vanni's pride is unfavorably compared even to that displayed by Capaneus (*Inf.* XIV.49–60). We are reminded once more that sins, in any given sinner (living or dead) are often several; Capaneus, a blasphemer, and Vanni Fucci, a thief, are both portrayed as being motivated by pride against God.

17–18. It is here, at last, that we find the answer to the question the text left us with in the last canto—or so Hollander (Holl.1983.2), pp. 36–37, has claimed. Verses 65–78 of the previous canto had Dante eager to discover the identity of the speaker of those unformed words and Virgil getting him closer to their source so that he could have his answer. The descent, however, allows him to see still other (very distracting) things: the serpents and then Vanni Fucci. The moment Vanni disappears we finally hear that voice and have our question answered. All commentators who have dealt with the issue have argued either that the voice was Vanni's or that its identity was intentionally and totally masked by the author. It seems, on the other hand, that the voice is that of Cacus, the thieving centaur, who will be named at v. 25. What do we discover? He is angry ("pien di rabbia"), as was that voice (*ad ira mosso,* and not *ad ire mosso*); he cries out in perverse imitation of God's voice in the Garden in the Bible (Gen. 3:9) asking hiding Adam, "Where are you?" (See note to *Inf.* XXIV.91–96.) Cacus is in pursuit of Vanni Fucci, "unripe" *(acerbo)* because of his sin. Later in the poem Satan is also portrayed as having fallen from heaven "unripe" *(acerbo)* in his sinfulness (*Par.* XIX.48), while Adam, beginning his life innocent, without sin, is referred to as having been created by God "ripe" *(maturo)* in the Garden (*Par.* XXVI.91). Thus, in this "replay" of the primal scene of theft in the Garden, Vanni takes on the role of Adam after the Fall, having moved from ripeness to unripeness, hiding from his just maker, while Cacus plays the unlikely role of the vengeful God in pursuit of his fallen child.

19–33.   Cacus was strictly speaking not a centaur, but the tradition that he was one extends at least until the prologue of Cervantes' *Don Quixote*. Virgil does refer to him as "semihominis Caci" (half-human Cacus) at *Aeneid* VIII.194, but his context is clear: Cacus is the son of Vulcan, not of Ixion, father of the Centaurs. And so Dante's decision to make him a centaur, a "brother" of the keepers of the first ring of violence in *Inferno* XII, is either completely his own or reflects a tradition about which we know nothing. (See G. Padoan, "Caco," *ED,* vol. 1, 1970, pp. 741–42.) On the other hand, many details of this passage clearly reflect those found in the lengthy passage describing Hercules' killing of Cacus for his theft of cattle in Virgil's poem (VIII.184–275), dragging them into his cave backwards so that their hoofprints would lead away from the guilty party's lair. It seems clear that Dante here had Virgil's poem in mind as his prime source and that he knowingly distorts Virgilian text: in Virgil, Cacus is not a centaur; in Virgil his mouth gives forth smoke and fire (vv. 198–199; 252–255; 259) while in Dante he has a dragon on his back to do that for him; in Virgil, Hercules strangles Cacus (vv. 260–261) while in Dante he clubs him over the head (see Holl. 1983.2, pp. 40–41). We have seen such willful rearrangement of Virgilian material before, notably in *Inferno* XX, and will see it again (see *Inf.* XXXI.103–105), when the unseen Briareus will be described in very un-Virgilian terms (see note to *Inf.* XXXI.97–105). As Beal points out (Beal. 1983.1), pp. 108–10, Cacus was often seen as related to Satan, since Hercules was frequently understood to represent Christ.

The Maremma is a boggy region of Tuscany, the Aventine one of the seven hills of Rome.

34–36. The frenetic action described in this canto is so amply described that less than 15 percent of its verses are spoken by its characters, the lowest figure for any canto in the *Inferno*.

The three sinners will turn out to be Agnello (named at v. 68), Buoso (v. 140), Puccio (v. 148); Cianfa literally joins Agnello (named at v. 43); Francesco will be added, referred to indirectly (v. 151). Thus there are five Florentine thieves seen here in this *bolgia*.

43. The first of the five Florentines referred to in the canto, Cianfa, according to early commentators, was a member of the Donati family; he apparently died in 1289.

44–45. Dante's digital gesture hushes Virgil. When we consider the enormous liberties the poet has just taken with the text of the *Aeneid*, we may not be surprised, within the fiction, at his rather peremptory treatment of his leader.

49–51. As we will eventually be able to puzzle out, Cianfa is the serpent attaching itself, in a parody of sexual embrace, to Agnello. See endnote to this canto for some details.

64–66. The third of these three rapid comparisons has caused difficulty: does the poet refer to a flame moving across a piece of parchment, turning the nearer material brown before it blackens? or to the wick of a candle, which similarly turns brown before turning black? The strongest case for the former is that, in the case of the candlewick, the brown color moves *down* the wick, while Dante says the brown moves *suso* ("up," "along"). See Chia. 1991.1, p. 746.

68. Agnello (or Agnolo) dei Brunelleschi, a Ghibelline family, of whom the commentators have little to say that can be relied upon as coming

from history rather than from Dante's placement of him among the thieves.

69–72.   For the "mating" of the two thieves, twentieth-century commentators, beginning perhaps with Grandgent, point to the conjunction in a single bisexual body of Ovid's nymph Salmacis and Hermaphroditus (*Metam.* IV.373–379).

79–81.   The final coupling of the canto conjoins Buoso and Francesco in yet a third version of punishment seen in this *bolgia* (see the endnote to the canto). The "dog days" are the hottest part of summer in late July and early August.

82–90.   A new figure (Francesco) assaults one of the remaining two (Agnello and Cianfa have moved off), known as Buoso, as we shall learn near the canto's end.

94–102.   The three rhetorically balanced tercets perform a task slightly different from the one they are traditionally accorded, i.e., the modern poet's victorious boast over his creaky classical forebears. But that is what the first two both seem to do: let Lucan be silent with his horrible tales of soldiers slain by serpents in the Libyan desert in Book IX of the *Pharsalia*; let Ovid be silent with his tales of Cadmus, transmogrified into a serpent (*Metam.* IV.563–603), and of Arethusa, transformed into a spring (*Metam.* V.572–641). The third puts forward the modern poet's superiority: Buoso and Francesco do not sustain individual transformations, but exchange their very natures, one becoming the other. Is the radical difference between Lucan/Ovid and Dante the poetic novelty of the latter, as would seem to be the case? Or is it rather the result of this poet's *not* inventing his marvels, but merely describing them? We all realize that the first explanation is in fact correct, Dante *does* (and means to) outdo his classical precursors. But then we may reflect that his claim is that he is not making this up, but merely observing "reality," God's vengeance on the floor of the seventh *bolgia*. Let fictive poets yield to this new Christian teller of truths revealed, the humble scribe of God. We do not have to believe this claim, but we can sense that it is being lodged.

103–138.   This, the most fully described of the various metamorphoses found in these two cantos, is broken by Castelvetro into seven stages of mutual transformation, Francesco into a man and Buoso into a serpent.

The former becomes a man as follows: (1) his tail becomes legs, (2) his front paws become arms, (3) his rear legs become a penis, (4) his hide becomes skin, (5) his posture changes from prone to erect, (6) his snout becomes a face, (7) his serpentine hiss becomes a voice. Buoso, naturally, goes through exactly the obverse process.

139–141.　Francesco, not identified until the last verse of the canto, turns momentarily away from Buoso, having regained his power of speech, only to use it to express his desire to punish him, addressing Puccio (see v. 148). As for Buoso, his identity is much debated. Michele Barbi (Barb.1934.1), pp. 305–22, suggests that he is probably Buoso di Forese Donati (died ca. 1285).

144.　Campi points to Landino's and Vellutello's understanding of this Florentine verb, *abborracciare,* as meaning to make something of a botch of things as a result of working too quickly. Thus Dante's worries that his pen, following these never-before-observed and rapid transformations, may have blotted his page a bit when he attempted to set them down.

148.　Puccio Galigai, nicknamed "Lameshanks," of a Ghibelline family. As for the reason for his not undergoing transformation, as do the four other Florentines in this canto, Fallani, in his commentary, follows Filomusi Guelfi (Filo.1911.1), suggesting that Puccio Sciancato, the only sinner in this *bolgia* who is not changed in form, perhaps represents simple fraud, also treated by Aquinas in the passage referred to in the endnote that follows.

151.　Francesco de' Cavalcanti (the identification is not certain) who, murdered by inhabitants of the town of Gaville, in the upper Arno valley, was avenged by his relations.

ENDNOTE: TABLE OF METAMORPHOSES, *INFERNO* XXIV & XXV

Vanni Fucci	Agnello & Cianfa	Buoso & Francesco
(XXIV.97–120)	(XXV.49–78)	(XXV.79–141)
serpent bites neck and shoulders from rear	six-footed serpent bites head from in front	four-footed serpent bites belly from front
burns to ashes and returns in same nature immediately	turn into a new creature of shared nature	exchange their natures
resurrection	mutation	transmutation
three comparisons: o/i phoenix epileptic	three comparisons: ivy on tree hot waxes blending burning parchment	three comparisons: lizard in path man in sleep/fever snail's horns

Thomas Aquinas, Summa Theol. II, II, q. 66, a. 6: on aggravated theft, cited by Filomusi Guelfi (Filo. 1911.1), pp. 199–206:

Sacrilegio: theft of church property	Peculato: theft of goods commonly held	Plagio: theft from fellow men

INFERNO XXVI

OUTLINE

INFERNO XXVI

Godi, Fiorenza, poi che se' sì grande
che per mare e per terra batti l'ali,
e per lo 'nferno tuo nome si spande!

Tra li ladron trovai cinque cotali
tuoi cittadini onde mi ven vergogna,
e tu in grande orranza non ne sali.

Ma se presso al mattin del ver si sogna,
tu sentirai, di qua da picciol tempo,
di quel che Prato, non ch'altri, t'agogna.

E se già fosse, non saria per tempo.
Così foss' ei, da che pur esser dee!
ché più mi graverà, com' più m'attempo.

Noi ci partimmo, e su per le scalee
che n'avea fatto iborni a scender pria,
rimontò 'l duca mio e trasse mee;

e proseguendo la solinga via,
tra le schegge e tra ' rocchi de lo scoglio
lo piè sanza la man non si spedia.

Allor mi dolsi, e ora mi ridoglio
quando drizzo la mente a ciò ch'io vidi,
e più lo 'ngegno affreno ch'i' non soglio,

perché non corra che virtù nol guidi;
sì che, se stella bona o miglior cosa
m'ha dato 'l ben, ch'io stessi nol m'invidi.

Quante 'l villan ch'al poggio si riposa,
nel tempo che colui che 'l mondo schiara
la faccia sua a noi tien meno ascosa,

Take joy, oh Florence, for you are so great
your wings beat over land and sea,
3   your fame resounds through Hell!

Among the thieves, I found five citizens of yours
who make me feel ashamed, and you
6   are raised by them to no great praise.

But if as morning nears we dream the truth,
it won't be long before you feel the pain
9   that Prato, to name but one, desires for you.

Were it already come, it would not be too soon.
But let it come, since come indeed it must,
12   and it will weigh the more on me the more I age.

We left that place and, on those stairs
that turned us pale when we came down,
15   my leader now climbed back and drew me up.

As we took our solitary way
among the juts and crags of the escarpment,
18   our feet could not advance without our hands.

I grieved then and now I grieve again
as my thoughts turn to what I saw,
21   and more than is my way, I curb my powers

lest they run on where virtue fails to guide them,
so that, if friendly star or something better still
24   has granted me its boon, I don't misuse the gift.

As when a peasant, resting on a hillside—
in the season when he who lights the world
27   least hides his face from us,

come la mosca cede a la zanzara,
vede lucciole giù per la vallea,
30   forse colà dov' e' vendemmia e ara:

di tante fiamme tutta risplendea
'l'ottava bolgia, sì com' io m'accorsi
33   tosto che fui là 've 'l fondo parea.

E qual colui che si vengiò con li orsi
vide 'l carro d'Elia al dipartire,
36   quando i cavalli al cielo erti levorsi,

che nol potea sì con li occhi seguire,
ch'el vedesse altro che la fiamma sola,
39   sì come nuvoletta, in sù salire:

tal si move ciascuna per la gola
del fosso, ché nessuna mostra 'l furto,
42   e ogne fiamma un peccatore invola.

Io stava sovra 'l ponte a veder surto,
sì che s'io non avessi un ronchion preso,
45   caduto sarei giù sanz' esser urto.

E 'l duca, che mi vide tanto atteso,
disse: "Dentro dai fuochi son li spirti;
48   catun si fascia di quel ch'elli è inceso."

"Maestro mio," rispuos' io, "per udirti
son io più certo; ma già m'era avviso
51   che così fosse, e già voleva dirti:

chi è 'n quel foco che vien sì diviso
di sopra, che par surger de la pira
54   dov' Eteòcle col fratel fu miso?"

Rispuose a me: "Là dentro si martira
Ulisse e Dïomede, e così insieme
57   a la vendetta vanno come a l'ira;

at the hour when the fly gives way to the mosquito—
sees fireflies that glimmer in the valley
30   where perhaps he harvests grapes and ploughs his fields,

with just so many flames the eighth crevasse
was everywhere aglow, as I became aware
33   once I arrived where I could see the bottom.

And as the one who was avenged by bears
could see Elijah's chariot taking flight,
36   when the horses reared and rose to Heaven,

but made out nothing with his eyes
except the flame alone
39   ascending like a cloud into the sky,

so each flame moves along the gullet
of the trench and—though none reveals the theft—
42   each flame conceals a sinner.

Rising to my feet to look, I stood up
on the bridge. Had I not grasped a jutting crag,
45   I would have fallen in without a shove.

My leader, when he saw me so intent, said:
'These spirits stand within the flames.
48   Each one is wrapped in that in which he burns.'

'Master,' I replied, 'I am the more convinced
to hear you say it. That is what I thought,
51   and had it in my mind to ask you this:

'Who is in the flame so riven at the tip
it could be rising from the pyre
54   on which Etèocles was laid out with his brother?'

He replied: 'Within this flame find torment
Ulysses and Diomed. They are paired
57   in God's revenge as once they earned his wrath.

e dentro da la lor fiamma si geme
l'agguato del caval che fé la porta
60   onde uscì de' Romani il gentil seme.

Piangevisi entro l'arte per che, morta,
Deïdamìa ancor si duol d'Achille,
63   e del Palladio pena vi si porta."

"S'ei posson dentro da quelle faville
parlar," diss' io, "maestro, assai ten priego
66   e ripriego, che 'l priego vaglia mille,

che non mi facci de l'attender niego
fin che la fiamma cornuta qua vegna;
69   vedi che del disio ver' lei mi piego!"

Ed elli a me: "La tua preghiera è degna
di molta loda, e io però l'accetto;
72   ma fa che la tua lingua si sostegna.

Lascia parlare a me, ch'i' ho concetto
ciò che tu vuoi; ch'ei sarebbero schivi,
75   perch' e' fuor greci, forse del tuo detto."

Poi che la fiamma fu venuta quivi
dove parve al mio duca tempo e loco,
78   in questa forma lui parlare audivi:

"O voi che siete due dentro ad un foco,
s'io meritai di voi mentre ch'io vissi,
81   s'io meritai di voi assai o poco

quando nel mondo li alti versi scrissi,
non vi movete; ma l'un di voi dica
84   dove, per lui, perduto a morir gissi."

Lo maggior corno de la fiamma antica
cominciò a crollarsi mormorando,
87   pur come quella cui vento affatica;

'In their flame they mourn the stratagem
of the horse that made a gateway
60   through which the noble seed of Rome came forth.

'There they lament the wiles for which, in death,
Deidamìa mourns Achilles still,
63   and there they make amends for the Palladium.'

'If they can speak within those flames,'
I said, 'I pray you, master, and I pray again—
66   and may my prayer be a thousand strong—

'do not forbid my lingering awhile
until the twin-forked flame arrives.
69   You see how eagerly I lean in its direction.'

And he to me: 'Your prayer deserves
much praise. Therefore, I grant it,
72   but on condition that you hold your tongue.

'Leave speech to me, for I have understood
just what you want. And, since they were Greeks,
75   they might disdain your words.'

Once the flame had neared, when he thought
the time and moment right,
78   I heard my leader speaking in this way:

'O you who are twinned within a single fire,
if I have earned your favor while I lived,
81   if I have earned your favor—in whatever measure—

'when, in the world, I wrote my lofty verses,
then do not move away. Let one of you relate
84   just where, having lost his way, he went to die.'

And the larger horn of that ancient flame
began to murmur and to tremble,
87   like a flame that is worried by the wind.

indi la cima qua e là menando,
come fosse la lingua che parlasse,
90   gittò voce di fuori e disse: "Quando

mi diparti' da Circe, che sottrasse
me più d'un anno là presso a Gaeta,
93   prima che sì Enëa la nomasse,

né dolcezza di figlio, né la pieta
del vecchio padre, né 'l debito amore
96   lo qual dovea Penelopè far lieta,

vincer potero dentro a me l'ardore
ch'i' ebbi a divenir del mondo esperto
99   e de li vizi umani e del valore;

ma misi me per l'alto mare aperto
sol con un legno e con quella compagna
102   picciola da la qual non fui diserto.

L'un lito e l'altro vidi infin la Spagna,
fin nel Morrocco, e l'isola d'i Sardi,
105   e l'altre che quel mare intorno bagna.

Io e ' compagni eravam vecchi e tardi
quando venimmo a quella foce stretta
108   dov' Ercule segnò li suoi riguardi

acció che l'uom più oltre non si metta;
da la man destra mi lasciai Sibilia,
111   da l'altra già m'avea lasciata Setta.

'O frati,' dissi, 'che per cento milia
perigli siete giunti a l'occidente,
114   a questa tanto picciola vigilia

d'i nostri sensi ch'è del rimanente
non vogliate negar l'esperïenza,
117   di retro al sol, del mondo sanza gente.

Then, brandishing its tip this way and that,
as if it were the tongue of fire that spoke,
90   it brought forth a voice and said: 'When I

'took leave of Circe, who for a year and more
beguiled me there, not far from Gaëta,
93   before Aeneas gave that name to it,

'not tenderness for a son, nor filial duty
toward my agèd father, nor the love I owed
96   Penelope that would have made her glad,

'could overcome the fervor that was mine
to gain experience of the world
99   and learn about man's vices, and his worth.

'And so I set forth on the open deep
with but a single ship and that handful
102   of shipmates who had not deserted me.

'One shore and the other I saw as far as Spain,
Morocco—the island of Sardegna,
105   and other islands set into that sea.

'I and my shipmates had grown old and slow
by the time we reached the narrow strait
108   where Hercules marked off the limits,

'warning all men to go no farther.
On the right-hand side I left Seville behind,
111   on the other I had left Ceüta.

' "O brothers," I said, "who, in the course
of a hundred thousand perils, at last
114   have reached the west, to such brief wakefulness

' "of our senses as remains to us,
do not deny yourselves the chance to know—
117   following the sun—the world where no one lives.

Considerate la vostra semenza:
fatti non foste a viver come bruti,
120   ma per seguir virtute e canoscenza.'

Li miei compagni fec' io sì aguti,
con questa orazion picciola, al cammino,
123   che a pena poscia li avrei ritenuti;

e volta nostra poppa nel mattino,
de' remi facemmo ali al folle volo,
126   sempre acquistando dal lato mancino.

Tutte le stelle già de l'altro polo
vedea la notte, e 'l nostro tanto basso,
129   che non surgëa fuor del marin suolo.

Cinque volte racceso e tante casso
lo lume era di sotto da la luna,
132   poi che 'ntrati eravam ne l'alto passo,

quando n'apparve una montagna, bruna
per la distanza, e parvemi alta tanto
135   quanto veduta non avëa alcuna.

Noi ci allegrammo, e tosto tornò in pianto;
ché de la nova terra un turbo nacque
138   e percosse del legno il primo canto.

Tre volte il fé girar con tutte l'acque;
a la quarta levar la poppa in suso
e la prora ire in giù, com' altrui piacque,
142   infin che 'l mar fu sovra noi richiuso."

' "Consider how your souls were sown:
you were not made to live like brutes or beasts,
120   but to pursue virtue and knowledge."

'With this brief speech I had my companions
so ardent for the journey
123   I could scarce have held them back.

'And, having set our stern to sunrise,
in our mad flight we turned our oars to wings,
126   always gaining on the left.

'Now night was gazing on the stars that light
the other pole, the stars of our own so low
129   they did not rise above the ocean floor.

'Five times the light beneath the moon
had been rekindled and as often been put out
132   since we began our voyage on the deep,

'when we could see a mountain, distant,
dark and dim. In my sight it seemed
135   higher than any I had ever seen.

'We rejoiced, but joy soon turned to grief:
for from that unknown land there came
138   a whirlwind that struck the ship head-on.

'Three times it turned her and all the waters
with her. At the fourth our stern reared up,
the prow went down—as pleased Another—
142   until the sea closed over us.'

1–3.   Matching the ironic apostrophe of Pistoia that follows the departure of Vanni Fucci in the last canto, vv. 10–12, this one of Florence comes in the wake of the poem's departure from the five Florentine thieves. The image of Florence as winged has caused some puzzlement. While commentators, beginning perhaps with Scartazzini/Vandelli, point out that Dante's words most probably echo the Latin inscription, dating to 1255, on the façade of the Florentine Palazzo del Podestà, proclaiming that Florence is in possession of the sea, the land, indeed the entire world, we are still left to speculate on Dante's reasons for presenting her as winged. Whatever his reason, we might want to reflect that he thought of himself as the "wingèd one" because of the easy pun available from his surname, Alighieri, in Latin "aliger" (wingèd). See Shan.1975.1 and Shan.1977.1. In this canto the apostrophized city and the seafaring Ulysses are both associated with "wings" ("in our mad flight we turned our oars to wings" [v. 125]); at least intrinsically, the protagonist is also. He is on a better-purposed "flight." For these motifs and another related one see Corti (Cort.1990.1).

7.   The text alludes to the classical and medieval belief that morning dreams were more truthful in their content than any others. Guido da Pisa is the first (but hardly the last) to refer to a text in Ovid to this effect (*Heroides* XIX.195–196). On the subject see Speroni's article (Sper.1948.1). And see, for the same view of morning dreams, *Purgatorio* IX.16–18.

8–12.   The passage about Prato has caused two interpretive problems: (1) Does it refer to the anger felt by Cardinal Niccolò da Prato when he failed to bring peace between the warring Florentine factions in 1304, or to the rebellion of the town of Prato in 1309, when Florence's small neighbor cast out its Black Guelphs? (2) Is Dante heartened or heartsick as he contemplates this "future" event?

It was only in the eighteenth century that a commentator suggested a reference to the cardinal (Venturi). Further, since the second event was probably roughly contemporaneous to the writing of this canto, it seems likely that Dante would have enjoyed having so recent a piece of news as confirmation of his "prophecy." As to his emotions, it seems more reasonable to reflect that Dante is admitting that he will only be happy once the power of the Black Guelphs of Florence is destroyed; he is in pain as he awaits that liberation. In other words, this is not an expression of sadness

for the city's coming tribulation, but a desire to see them come to pass—
and that is the common view of the early commentators.

14.   While we do not believe that Dante says here what Petrocchi says he
does, we have, as always, followed his text, which reads *iborni* (pallid, the
color and coolness of ivory) and not, as the text had previously stood,
i borni (the outcroppings of the rocks). In our opinion the "old" reading is
the superior one. Instead of "on those stairs that turned us pale when we
came down" we would say "on the stairs the jutting rocks had made for
our descent."

19–24.   According to Pertile (Pert.1979.1), those who propose a negative
view of Ulysses fail to acknowledge the importance of these verses, which
reveal the poet's sympathy for the Greek hero even now as he writes of
him. He cites (p. 37) Ovid (*Metam.* XIII.135–139) in support of his argu-
ment. However, that text offers Ulysses' vaunt of his own worthiness to
receive the arms of Achilles (denying the claims of Ajax), and the entire
passage gives us the portrait of a figure full of pride and self-love. See Hol-
lander (Holl.1969.1), pp. 115–16, arguing that Dante, in this passage, is fully
conscious of his previous "Ulyssean" efforts, undertaken by his venture-
some and prideful intellect, and now hopes to keep them under control.
Castelvetro's reading of the passage is in this vein; according to him the
poet grieves "for having improperly put to use my genius." Dante hopes, in
other words, to be exactly *unlike* Ulysses.

25–30.   The first of two elaborate similes in prologue to the appearance
of Ulysses deals with the number of false counselors: they are as numer-
ous as fireflies. Dante, as peasant *(il villano)* resting on his hillside *(poggio*—
Frankel [Fran.1986.1, pp. 102–5], contrasts his "humble" hillock with
Ulysses' "prideful" mountain [v. 133]), looks out upon this valley full of
fireflies. This peaceful scene lulls many readers into a sort of moral exemp-
tion for Ulysses; if he looks so pleasant, how can he be seen as sinful? In
fact, the distancing effect of the simile makes Ulysses seem small and rela-
tively insignificant. We can imagine how he might feel, told that he had
been compared to a firefly.

Many readers are rightly reminded of the previous simile involving a
rustic *(lo villanello)* at *Inferno* XXIV.7–15.

31.   For the flames as reminiscent of the Epistle of James (3:4–6) see
Bates and Rendall (Bate.1989.1) and Cornish (Corn.1989.1): "Behold also

the ships, which though they be so great, and are driven by fierce winds, yet are turned about with a very small helm, wherever the steersman pleases. Even so the tongue is a little member, and boasts many things. Behold how great a matter a little fire kindles! And the tongue is a fire, a world of iniquity: so is the tongue among our members, that it defiles the whole body, and sets on fire the course of nature, and it is set on fire of hell." Pietro di Dante was the first to cite this passage in connection with Dante's description of the flames here.

34–42. The second Ulyssean simile describes the flame-wrapped appearance of Ulysses in terms of Elijah's fiery ascent to heaven. Perhaps the first extended discussion of the biblical text behind the passage was offered by Frankel (Fran. 1986.1), pp. 110–16, who argues that, while Elijah is seen as antithetical to Ulysses (see Cass.1984.1, pp. 88–93), Dante is also seen as related to the negative aspect of Elisha (his pride in taking on the prophet's mantle)—see II Kings 2:9–12. She is answered by Ferretti Cuomo (Ferr. 1995.1), who sees Elisha as only a positive figure of Dante, similarly accepting his role as successor prophet. For the same view see Hollander (Holl. 1969.1), p. 117.

Elisha was avenged by the bears in that the forty-two children who mocked his prophetic calling, addressing him as "Baldy" *(calve)*, were attacked and lacerated by two bears (II Kings 2:23–24). Dante refers to this incident in *Epistle* VI.16.

43–45. The protagonist's excitement at the prospect of seeing Ulysses is evident (Ulysses has not been identified yet, but the poet seems to be taking a liberty in allowing his character to fathom who is about to appear). In his reckless abandon to gain experience of this great sinner, he resembles Ulysses himself.

48. Virgil's point seems to be that each of the flame-enclosed sinners is covered by the external sign of their inner ardor, their longing to captivate the minds of those upon whom they practiced their fraudulent work.

52–54. Almost all commentators point to the passage in Statius's *Thebaid* (XII. 429–432) that describes the immolation of the corpses of the two warring brothers, Eteocles and Polynices, whose enmity was the root of the civil war in Thebes and is manifest now even in their death, as the smoke from their burning bodies will not join. Among the early commentators only Pietro di Dante noticed that the same scene is reported in similar ways in Lucan as well (*Phars.* I.551–552).

55–57.   Ulysses and Diomedes are clearly indicated as suffering the punishment of God for their fraudulent acts; yet this indictment has not kept readers from admiring them—or at least Ulysses. Perhaps the central problem in the large debate that has surrounded Dante's version of the Greek hero in the last century-and-a-half is how sympathetically we are meant to respond to him. To put that another way, what is the nature of Ulysses' sin, and how urgently is it meant to govern the reader's sense of his worth? And a further complication is of more recent vintage: what should we make of the at least apparent similarity between Ulysses and Dante himself? Chiavacci Leonardi has made a useful distinction between the two essential attitudes that distinguish divergent readings of the undoubtedly heroic figure (Chia.1991.1, p. 762): (1) Ulysses is marked by greatness; he is unfortunate but guiltless; (2) he is characterized by the sin of pride, like Adam. For an example of the first view see Francesco De Sanctis in 1870: Dante "erects a statue to this precursor of Christopher Columbus, a pyramid set in the mud of hell" (DeSa.1949.1), pp. 201–2. For similar views see Croce (Croc.1921.1), p. 98, and Fubini (Fubi.1966.1). Attilio Momigliano, in his comment to vv. 64–69, throws all caution to the wind. He complains that the first sixty-three verses of the canto are too dry and erudite. Now that Ulysses is on the scene, we breathe the air of true and enthusiastic poetry. "Appearances notwithstanding," he says, "Dante not only does not condemn the fraudulent acts of Ulysses and Diomedes, he exalts them." The negative view in modern discussions was enunciated clearly by Bruno Nardi (Nard.1942.1). See also Wilhelm (Wilh.1960.1); Padoan (Pado.1977.1); Hollander (Holl.1969.1), pp. 114–23; Scott (Scot.1971.1); Iannucci (Iann.1976.1). Recently a third "school" has opened its doors, one that finds Ulysses less than totally admirable and yet associated with Dante, who presents himself, just beneath the lines of his text, as a trespassing voyager himself. See Mazzotta (Mazz.1975.1), p. 41; Stierle (Stie.1988.1); Barolini (Baro.1992.1), *passim;* Bloom (Bloo.1994.1), pp. 85–89. For a rejoinder to the position of these critics see Stull and Hollander (Stul.1991.1 [1997]), pp. 43–52.

58–63.   Virgil lists the sins of the two heroes: the stratagem of the troop-hiding Trojan horse (with which Ulysses, if not Diomedes, is associated in Virgil, *Aen.* II); Ulysses' trickery in getting Achilles to join the war against

Troy, thus abandoning, on the isle of Scyros, his beloved Deidamia (as recounted in Statius's unfinished *Achilleid*), who subsequently died of grief at the news of his death in Troy; the joint adventure in which they stole the Palladium, image of Athena, a large wooden statue, in return for which the horse served as a fraudulent peace-offering (*Aen.* II.163–169). Those who, like Momigliano, believe that the fraudulent acts of Ulysses and Diomedes are exalted by Dante, should be reminded that Virgil, in the *Aeneid*, is pretty hard on them. Diomedes, for his part in the theft of the Palladium, is impious (*impius—Aen.* II.163) while Ulysses is called an "inventor of crimes" (*scelerum . . . inventor—Aen.* II.164). It seems more than likely that Dante would have shared Virgil's views of these matters. For the recovery of the notion, widespread in the ancient commentators, that Ulysses is best described as "astutus" (in the sense of possessing low cunning) see Kay.1980.1; Aher.1982.1.

Sources for Dante's Ulysses are found nearly everywhere, so much so that one has a feeling that more are called than should be chosen: Virgil (Loga.1964.1; Pado.1977.1; Thom.1967.1, pp. 44–46; Thom.1974.1, pp. 52–61); Ovid (Pico.1991.2); Persius (Chie.1998.1); Statius's *Achilleid* (Pado.1977.1, pp. 173–76; Hage.1997.1); Lucan (Stul.1991.1); Tacitus (VonR.1986.2); the Alexander cycle (Aval.1966.1; VonR.1986.1); as built on negative correspondences with Moses (Porc.1997.1, pp. 20–25). There are of course many more. For three Latin passages (from Cicero, Horace, and Seneca) that may have helped shape Dante's conception of Ulysses see Singleton's comment to vv. 90–120.

For the vast bibliography of work devoted to Dante's Ulysses see Cass.1981.1 and Seri.1994.1, pp. 155–91.

64–69.   Now that Dante knows that the flame contains Ulysses, his ardor to hear him speak is nearly overwhelming.

70–75.   See Donno (Donn.1973.1) for the notion that here Virgil actually speaks Greek (if not assuming the role of Homer, as some have argued) because of a fable, which Dante might have known, that had it that Diomedes, forced back into wandering when his homecoming is ruined by news of his wife's infidelity, went off to Daunia (Apulia?) and eventually died thereabouts. Some of the birds that dwelled there became known as "Diomedian birds." Their main trait was to be hostile to all barbarians and friendly to all Greeks (pp. 30–31). On the basis of this fable, Donno argues, Virgil chooses to address Diomedes and Ulysses in Greek. The argument may be forced, but it is interesting. The passage is puzzling and its difficulty is compounded by what is found at *Inferno* XXVII.20, when Guido da Montefeltro says that he has heard Virgil speaking Lombard dialect to Ulysses.

79–84. Virgil identifies himself as Ulysses' (and Diomedes') "author." Now this is strictly true, since both of them appear (if rather unfavorably) in the *Aeneid*. Nonetheless, one can understand why some commentators have imagined that Virgil is pretending to be Homer as he addresses Ulysses and Diomedes. However, that he refers to his work as *li alti versi* ("my lofty verses") probably connects with his earlier description of his *Aeneid*, "l'alta mia tragedìa" (my lofty tragedy), at *Inferno* XX.113. It seems most sensible to believe that Virgil is speaking whatever language he usually speaks.

90–93. Ulysses' speech begins, like classical epic, *in medias res* (in the midst of the action, i.e., not at its beginning). Dante would seem to be portraying him as the author of his own self-celebrating song, a "mini-epic," as it were. He makes it sound as though staying with Circe, the enchantress, were less culpable than it probably was, in Dante's eyes. His next gesture is to boast that *he* had come to Gaeta before Aeneas did, which city Aeneas names after his dead nurse, who died and was buried there (*Aen.* VII.2). Thus does Ulysses put himself forward as a rivalrous competitor of Virgil's hero.

94–99. Ulysses' aim, to discover the truth about the world and about mankind, sounds acceptable or even heroic to many contemporary readers. When we examine the prologue to this thought, in which he denies his family feeling for Telemachus, Laertes, and Penelope in order to make his voyage, we may begin to see the inverted parallelism to the hero whom he would emulate and best, Aeneas, loyal to Ascanius, Anchises, and Creusa. If Ulysses is venturesome, Aeneas is, as Virgil hardly tires of calling him, *pius*, a "family man" if ever there was one.

100–111. He and his crew of aging, tired sailors head out across the Mediterranean from Italy and reach the gates of Hercules, the very sign, even as Ulysses reports it, of the end of the known world. While Dante does not refer to it (nor to the previous voyages of Marco Polo), a number of recent commentators speculate that he was aware of the voyage of the

Vivaldi brothers in 1291. They, in search of India, sailed out through the Strait of Gibraltar, having passed Spain and Africa, and were never heard from again.

112–113.   It is a commonplace in the commentaries to believe that the opening words of Ulysses' speech to his men reflect the first words of Aeneas to *his* men (*Aen.* I.198). Several, however, also refer to the similar passage in Lucan (*Phars.* I.299), but without making any further case for Lucan's greater appositeness here. Stull and Hollander (Stul.1991.1), pp. 8–12, argue that Caesar's infamous words to his men, urging them to march on Rome, are cited far more precisely: the phrase "che per cento milia / perigli" (through a hundred thousand perils) mirrors nearly exactly Lucan's "qui mille pericula" (through a thousand perils) except for the added touch that Ulysses is even more grandiloquent than Lucan's florid Julius. The result seems fairly devastating to all those who argue for a positive valence for Dante's Ulysses, which is close to impossible to assert if the essential model for the hero is Julius Caesar, portrayed in Lucan as the worst of rabble-rousing, self-admiring leaders, here at the moment that begins the civil war that will destroy the republic. For Lucan, and for Dante, this is one of the most terrible moments in Roman history. Stull and Hollander explore a series of resonances of Lucan's text in this canto.

118–120.   Ulysses' final flourish not only won over his flagging shipmates, it has become a rallying cry of Romantic readers of this scene, from Tennyson to Primo Levi. What can be wrong with such desires, so fully human? Alessandra Colangeli, a student at the University of Rome, suggested, after she heard a lecture on this canto on 10 March 1997, that Ulysses' words seemed to echo those of the serpent in the Garden to Adam and Eve, promising that, if they were to eat the forbidden fruit, they would become like gods, knowing good and evil (Gen. 3:5). For a similar if more general view of Ulysses as the tempter see Cassell (Cass.1984.1), p. 86. Since Adam's later words to Dante (*Par.* XXVI.115–117) rehearse both the scene in the Garden and Ulysses' transgression, the eating from the tree and the trespass of an established limit, the association has some grounding in Dante's text. Baldelli (Bald.1998.1) is the latest to argue that the speech is the *locus* of Ulysses' fraudulent counsel, since he, anticipating the reckless adventure of the Vivaldi brothers, urges his men to go beyond the known limits in search of experience.

Gustavo Vinay (Vina.1960.1), pp. 5–6, points out that these verses echo the opening of the *Convivio* ("All men naturally desire knowledge"). His insight gives support to those who have argued that Ulysses is staged as a precursor, as it were, of the venturesome younger Dante, in whose more mature view a number of positions put forward in *Convivio* have become something of an embarrassment. For such opinions see, among others, Valli (Vall.1935.1), Hollander (Holl.1969.1), pp. 114–18, and Holl.1975.1; Freccero (Frec.1986.1 [1973]), pp. 188–90; Gagliardi (Gagl.1994.1), pp. 330–32, resuscitating Valli's views (his title derives from Valli's).

121–123.   Ulysses' summary of the result of his speech is a masterpiece of false modesty. Once he has uttered his words, his exhausted companions are ready for anything. We now perhaps notice that one of his key words is "little," one mark of a speaker who masks his pride in false humility: his reduced company of shipmates is *picciola* (v. 102); so is the time left his men on earth (*picciola*, v. 114); and now his oration is also but a little thing (v. 122), *picciola* used one more time, a total of three times in twenty-one verses. Ulysses is, in modern parlance, a con artist, and a good one, too. He has surely fooled a lot of people.

124–126.   His men, his "brothers," now show their real relationship to Ulysses: it is an instrumental one. They are his oars. As Carroll suggests in his commentary, "Is it not possible that this wild adventure is narrated as the last piece of evil counsel of which Ulysses was guilty?"

127–135.   The five-month voyage, the ship's stern to the east (the site of sunrise, perhaps the most familiar medieval image for Christ), occupies three tercets. Ulysses, abetted by his rowers, has stormed Olympus. They are the first mortals to see the mount of purgatory since Adam and Eve left it. God's punishment does not wait long to overcome them.

136.   For a possible source of this verse in the Bible (John 16:20), see Chiappelli (Chia.1989.1), p. 123: "You shall weep and lament, but the world shall rejoice; and you shall be sorrowful, but your sorrow shall be changed to joy." For another, perhaps more apt, see Durling (Durl.1996.1), p. 414, citing James 4:9: "Be afflicted, and mourn, and weep: let your laughter be turned to mourning, your joy to heaviness."

137–138.   The whirlwind is frequently associated with God's power used in punishment. See, among others, Cassell (Cass.1984.1), pp. 90–92.

139–141.   The final image of Ulysses' narrative is based, as a commentator as early in the tradition as Guido da Pisa realized, on *Aeneid* I.116–117, where Virgil describes the only ship in Aeneas's flotilla to be destroyed in the storm at sea: ". . . but a wave whirls the ship, driving it three times around in the same place, and then a sudden eddy swallows it up in the sea." The echo is probably not without consequence for our view of the would-be hero Ulysses: "The ship in point is that which carried the Lycians and faithful Orontes and which goes down within sight of the land that would have saved its sailors, as does Ulysses' ship. It is a ship of the damned. Aeneas, in his piety, is the hero; Ulysses, in his heroicness, is the failure" (Holl.1969.1, p. 121).

142.   The final verse of the canto seems also to have a classical antecedent (one not previously noted), the final verses of the seventh book of Statius's *Thebaid*. There, the seer Amphiaraus, the first of the "seven against Thebes" to die in that civil war, plunges into a chasm in the earth only to have the land then close back in above him (*Theb*. VII.821–823): "and as he sank he looked back at the heavens and groaned to see the plain meet above him, until a fainter shock joined once more the parted fields and shut out the daylight from Avernus" (trans. Mozley). Dante has referred to Amphiaraus's descent into hell at *Inferno* XX.31–36. If he is thinking of it here, it would call to mind still another pagan hero who may serve as a model for Ulysses' rash voyage and entombment.

INFERNO XXVII

Già era dritta in sù la fiamma e queta
per non dir più, e già da noi sen gia
3   con la licenza del dolce poeta,

quand' un'altra, che dietro a lei venìa,
ne fece volger li occhi a la sua cima
6   per un confuso suon che fuor n'uscia.

Come 'l bue cicilian che mugghiò prima
col pianto di colui, e ciò fu dritto,
9   che l'avea temperato con sua lima,

mugghiava con la voce de l'afflitto,
sì che, con tutto che fosse di rame,
12   pur el pareva dal dolor trafitto;

così, per non aver via né forame
dal principio nel foco, in suo linguaggio
15   si convertïan le parole grame.

Ma poscia ch'ebber colto lor vïaggio
su per la punta, dandole quel guizzo
18   che dato avea la lingua in lor passaggio,

udimmo dire: "O tu a cu' io drizzo
la voce e che parlavi mo lombardo,
21   dicendo 'Istra ten va, più non t'adizzo,'

perch' io sia giunto forse alquanto tardo,
non t'incresca restare a parlar meco;
24   vedi che non incresce a me, e ardo!

Se tu pur mo in questo mondo cieco
caduto se' di quella dolce terra
27   latina ond' io mia colpa tutta reco,

The flame now stood erect and still,
meaning to speak no more, and was departing
with the gentle poet's leave,

when another flame, coming close behind,
caused our eyes to fix upon its tip,
drawn by the gibberish that came from it.

As the Sicilian bull that bellowed first
with the cries of him whose instrument
had fashioned it—and that was only just—

used to bellow with the victim's voice
so that, although the bull was made of brass,
it seemed transfixed by pain,

thus, having first no course or outlet
through the flame, the mournful words
were changed into a language all their own.

But once the words had made their way
up to the tip, making it flicker
as the voice had done when it had formed them,

we heard it say: 'O you at whom I aim my voice
and who, just now, said in the Lombard tongue:
"Now go your way, I ask you nothing more,"

'though I've arrived, perhaps, a little late,
let it not trouble you to stay and speak with me.
Though I am in the flame, as you can see, it irks me not.

'If you are only a short while fallen
into this blind world from that sweet land
of Italy, from which I bring down all my sins,

3

6

9

12

15

18

21

24

27

dimmi se Romagnuoli han pace o guerra;
ch'io fui d'i monti là intra Orbino
e 'l giogo di che Tever si diserra."

Io era in giuso ancora attento e chino,
quando il mio duca mi tentò di costa,
dicendo: "Parla tu; questi è latino."

E io, ch'avea già pronta la risposta,
sanza indugio a parlare incominciai:
"O anima che se' là giù nascosta,

Romagna tua non è, e non fu mai,
sanza guerra ne' cuor de' suoi tiranni;
ma 'n palese nessuna or vi lasciai.

Ravenna sta come stata è molt' anni:
l'aguglia da Polenta la si cova,
sì che Cervia ricuopre co' suoi vanni.

La terra che fé già la lunga prova
e di Franceschi sanguinoso mucchio,
sotto le branche verdi si ritrova.

E 'l mastin vecchio e 'l nuovo da Verrucchio,
che fecer di Montagna il mal governo,
là dove soglion fan d'i denti succhio.

Le città di Lamone e di Santerno
conduce il lïoncel dal nido bianco,
che muta parte da la state al verno.

E quella cu' il Savio bagna il fianco,
così com' ella sie' tra 'l piano e 'l monte,
tra tirannia si vive e stato franco.

Ora chi se', ti priego che ne conte;
non esser duro più ch'altri sia stato,
se 'l nome tuo nel mondo tegna fronte."

'tell me if Romagna lives in peace or war.
I came from where the mountains stand between
30   Urbino and the ridge from which the Tiber springs.'

I still stood bending down to hear,
when my leader nudged my side and said:
33   'It's up to you to speak—this one is Italian.'

And I, who had my answer ready,
without delay began to speak:
36   'O soul that is hidden from my sight down there,

'your Romagna is not, and never was,
free of warfare in her rulers' hearts.
39   Still, no open warfare have I left behind.

'Ravenna remains as it has been for years.
The eagle of Polenta broods over it
42   so that he covers Cervia with his wings.

'The town that once withstood the lengthy siege,
making of the French a bloody heap,
45   is now again beneath the green claws of the lion.

'The elder mastiff of Verrucchio and the younger,
who between them had harsh dealing with Montagna,
48   sharpen their teeth to augers in the customary place.

'The young lion on a field of white,
who rules Lamone's and Santerno's cities,
51   changes sides between the summer and the snows.

'And the city whose flank the Savio bathes:
as she lives between tyranny and freedom,
54   so she lies between the mountain and the plain.

'But now, I beg you, tell us who you are.
Be no more grudging than another's been to you,
57   so may your name continue in the world.'

Poscia che 'l foco alquanto ebbe rugghiato
al modo suo, l'aguta punta mosse
60   di qua, di là, e poi diè cotal fiato:

"S'i' credesse che mia risposta fosse
a persona che mai tornasse al mondo,
63   questa fiamma staria sanza più scosse;

ma però che già mai di questo fondo
non tornò vivo alcun, s'i' odo il vero,
66   sanza tema d'infamia ti rispondo.

Io fui uom d'arme, e poi fui cordigliero,
credendomi, sì cinto, fare ammenda;
69   e certo il creder mio venìa intero,

se non fosse il gran prete, a cui mal prenda!,
che mi rimise ne le prime colpe;
72   e come e *quare*, voglio che m'intenda.

Mentre ch'io forma fui d'ossa e di polpe
che la madre mi diè, l'opere mie
75   non furon leonine, ma di volpe.

Li accorgimenti e le coperte vie
io seppi tutte, e sì menai lor arte,
78   ch'al fine de la terra il suono uscie.

Quando mi vidi giunto in quella parte
di mia etade ove ciascun dovrebbe
81   calar le vele e raccoglier le sarte,

ciò che pria mi piacëa, allor m'increbbe,
e pentuto e confesso mi rendei;
84   ahi miser lasso! e giovato sarebbe.

Lo principe d'i novi Farisei,
avendo guerra presso a Laterano,
87   e non con Saracin né con Giudei,

When the fire had done its roaring for a while,
after its fashion, the point began to quiver
60   this way and that, and then gave breath to this:

'If I but thought that my response were made
to one perhaps returning to the world,
63   this tongue of flame would cease to flicker.

'But since, up from these depths, no one has yet
returned alive, if what I hear is true,
66   I answer without fear of being shamed.

'A warrior was I, and then a corded friar,
thinking, cinctured so, to make amends.
69   And surely would my hopes have come to pass

'but for the Great Priest—the devil take him!—
who drew me back to my old ways.
72   And I would like to tell you how and why.

'While I still kept the form in flesh and bones
my mother gave me, my deeds were not
75   a lion's but the actions of a fox.

'Cunning stratagems and covert schemes,
I knew them all, and was so skilled in them
78   my fame rang out to the far confines of the earth.

'When I saw I had reached that stage of life
when all men ought to think
81   of lowering sail and coiling up the ropes,

'I grew displeased with what had pleased before.
Repentant and shriven, I became a friar.
84   And woe is me! it would have served.

'But he, Prince of the latter-day Pharisees,
engaged in battle near the Lateran
87   and not with either Saracen or Jew,

ché ciascun suo nimico era Cristiano,
e nessun era stato a vincer Acri
90   né mercatante in terra di Soldano,

né sommo officio né ordini sacri
guardò in sé, né in me quel capestro
93   che solea fare i suoi cinti più macri.

Ma come Costantin chiese Silvestro
d'entro Siratti a guerir de la lebbre,
96   così mi chiese questi per maestro

a guerir de la sua superba febbre;
domandommi consiglio, e io tacetti
99   perché le sue parole parver ebbre.

E' poi ridisse: 'Tuo cuor non sospetti;
finor t'assolvo, e tu m'insegna fare
102   sì come Penestrino in terra getti.

Lo ciel poss' io serrare e diserrare,
come tu sai; però son due le chiavi
105   che 'l mio antecessor non ebbe care.'

Allor mi pinser li argomenti gravi
là 've 'l tacer mi fu avviso 'l peggio,
108   e dissi: 'Padre, da che tu mi lavi

di quel peccato ov' io mo cader deggio,
lunga promessa con l'attender corto
111   ti farà trïunfar ne l'alto seggio.'

Francesco venne poi, com' io fu' morto,
per me; ma un d'i neri cherubini
114   li disse: 'Non portar; non mi far torto.

Venir se ne dee giù tra ' miei meschini
perché diede 'l consiglio frodolente,
117   dal quale in qua stato li sono a' crini;

'for all his enemies were Christian—
not one of them had gone to conquer Acre
90   or traffic in the Sultan's lands—

'paid no heed, for his part, to the highest office
or his holy orders, nor, for mine,
93   to the cord that used to keep its wearers lean.

'As Constantine once had Sylvester summoned
from Soracte to cure his leprous sores,
96   so this man called on me to be his doctor

'and cure him of the fever of his pride.
He asked me for advice, but I kept silent
99   because his words were like a drunkard's words.

'And then he spoke again: "Let not your heart mistrust:
I absolve you here and now if you will teach me
102   how I can bring Praeneste to the ground.

' "I have the power, as well you know, to lock
and unlock Heaven, because the keys are two
105   for which the pope before me had no care."

'His threatening tactics brought me to the point
at which the worse course seemed the one of silence.
108   And so I said: "Father, since you cleanse me

' "of the sin that I must even now commit:
Promising much with scant observance
111   will seal your triumph on the lofty throne."

'The moment I was dead, Francis came for me.
But one of the dark Cherubim cried out:
114   "No, wrong me not by bearing that one off.

' "He must come down to serve among my minions
because he gave that fraudulent advice.
117   From then till now I've dogged his footsteps.

ch'assolver non si può chi non si pente,
né pentere e volere insieme puossi
120   per la contradizion che nol consente.'

Oh me dolente! come mi riscossi
quando mi prese dicendomi: 'Forse
123   tu non pensavi ch'io löico fossi!'

A Minòs mi portò; e quelli attorse
otto volte la coda al dosso duro;
126   e poi che per gran rabbia la si morse,

disse: 'Questi è d'i rei del foco furo';
per ch'io là dove vedi son perduto,
129   e sì vestito, andando, mi rancuro."

Quand' elli ebbe 'l suo dir così compiuto,
la fiamma dolorando si partio,
132   torcendo e dibattendo 'l corno aguto.

Noi passamm' oltre, e io e 'l duca mio,
su per lo scoglio infino in su l'altr' arco
che cuopre 'l fosso in che si paga il fio
136   a quei che scommettendo acquistan carco.

      ' "One may not be absolved without repentance,
      nor repent and wish to sin concurrently—
120   a simple contradiction not allowed."

      'Oh, wretch that I am, how I shuddered
      when he seized me and said: "Perhaps
123   you didn't reckon I'd be versed in logic."

      'He carried me to Minos, who coiled his tail
      eight times around his scaly back
126   and, having gnawed it in his awful rage,

      'said: "Here comes a sinner for the thieving fire."
      And so, just as you see me, I am damned,
129   cloaked as I am. And as I go, I grieve.'

      Once he had brought his words to this conclusion,
      the weeping flame departed,
132   twisting and tossing its pointed horn.

      We continued on our way, my guide and I,
      over the ridge and up the arch that spans
      the ditch where those are paid their due
136   who, for disjoining, gather up their load.

1–2. Ulysses' speech ends, his tongue of fire erect (i.e., not waving about [see *Inf.* XXVI.85–89]) and stilled.

3. This innocent detail—Virgil's dismissal of Ulysses—will resurface at v. 21 with the addition of rather striking information about the language of Virgil's last words to Ulysses, uttered but not recorded here.

4–6. The next flame-enclosed shade, who will turn out to be a modern-day Ulysses, Guido da Montefeltro, was well known enough that he never has to be identified in more than indirect ways (vv. 67–78). Born ca. 1220, Guido was one of the great Ghibelline captains of the last third of the thirteenth century, winning a number of important victories for the nonetheless eventually unsuccessful Ghibelline cause. He was reconciled to the Church in 1286, but then took up his soldiering against the Guelphs once again, finally desisting only in 1294. In 1296 he joined the Franciscan order (v. 67). However, in the following year Pope Boniface VIII cajoled him into reentering the world of military affairs, this time working against the Ghibellines (the Colonna family, which held the fortress of Palestrina, Roman Praeneste, as detailed in the text [vv. 85–111]). Guido died in 1298 in the Franciscan monastery at Assisi.

While other pairs of preceding cantos contain those who had committed the same sin (VII–VIII [the wrathful]; X–XI [heretics]; XV–XVI [sodomites]; XXIV–XXV [thieves]), only XXVI and XXVII treat two major figures guilty of the same sin, perhaps suggesting how closely Guido and Ulysses are related in Dante's imagination.

7–15. This simile is derived either from various histories (Pietro di Dante mentions Orosius and Valerius Maximus) or from Ovid, *Ars amatoria* I.653–656. The ancient tyrant of Agrigento (in Sicily), Phalaris, had the Athenian Perillus construct for him a brazen bull in which he could roast his victims alive. Their screams were transformed into what resembled the bellowings of a bull. Once the instrument of torture was finished, Phalaris ordered that Perillus be its first victim, thus testing his handicraft. It worked. Ovid's moral to the story (*Ars* I.655–656) seems to be echoed in Dante's verse 8: "there is no law more just than that the craftsman of death should die by his own handicraft."

16–18.   These verses make clear for the first time how the mechanics of speech of the fraudulent counselors work; their words are formed by their tongues, within their fires, and then produced by the tips of their flames. When Guido first appeared (v. 6) he was apparently only mumbling about his pain within his flame.

19–21.   Guido's address to Virgil not only insists that the Roman poet was speaking his (native—see *Inf.* I.68) Lombard, i.e., north Italian, dialect, but then offers in evidence his exact words. What are we to understand about the language in which Virgil first addressed Ulysses (*Inf.* XXVI.72–75)? Was it the same as this? Or is this, as seems more likely, the colloquial manner in which he sends him away? The entire problem has vexed many a commentator, and no simple resolution has as yet emerged.

25–27.   Perhaps because he cannot see clearly from within his flame, Guido cannot tell whether Virgil (or Dante, for that matter) is a living soul or a dead fellow-sinner, just now come down from Italy to spend eternity here. The reason for Dante's insistence on this detail will be made plain when Guido reveals himself only because he does not believe that Dante will ever resurface to tell his miserable story.

28.   When Guido died (1298), the peace in Romagna had not yet been confirmed, as it was the following year. The region of Romagna is situated in the eastern north-central part of Italy.

33.   Not only is Guido an Italian *(latino)*, he is that Italian whom Dante had designated as most noble *(lo nobilissimo nostro latino)* in *Convivio* IV.xxviii.8. Commentators have been concerned about this apparent contradiction (for an attempt to mitigate it see Pertile [Pert.1982.1], pp. 171–75). If, however, Dante had changed his mind about a number of his positions in *Convivio*, as others believe, there is no reason to find the contradiction anything less than intentional. Further, he may not have known of Guido's involvement with Boniface when he wrote the passage praising him in *Convivio*. See note to vv. 106–111.

Virgil's passing the questioning of Guido (a modern) over to Dante reminds us of his insisting on it for Ulysses (an ancient) in the previous canto.

37–39.   Dante's reference to Romagna answers Guido's first question: there is peace—of a sort—there now.

40–54. Dante now enlightens Guido (and only an expert in the political and geographical lore of the region would understand his elliptical speech) about the condition of eight cities and fortified towns of Romagna, governed by various tyrants: Ravenna, Cervia, Forlì, Verrucchio, Rimini, Faenza, Imola, and Cesena. Guido had been in military action in many of them, with mixed results.

55–57. Having answered some of the concerns of Guido (whom he as yet does not recognize), Dante asks for a similar favor, offering fame in the world as a reward.

61–66. Guido's response, made familiar to English readers by T. S. Eliot as the epigraph to *The Love Song of J. Alfred Prufrock*, makes it clear that, for him, report among the living would bring infamy, not fame. Since he believes that Dante is a damned soul, and thus unable to regain the world of the living, he will speak.

67. Guido sums up his life in a single line: he went from bad to good. In fact, he went from bad to good to bad again. Dante may have reflected that his own life was exactly the opposite in its movements, from good to bad, but then from bad to good. Guido did not have a Beatrice to lead him back to the true path, only a Boniface.

70–72. Boniface VIII, according to Guido, led him from his life of religious retreat back into political machinations. Like Francesca da Rimini, Guido da Montefeltro blames his fall upon another; like her, he will tell Dante the reasons for it. See *Inf.* V.119, where Dante asks Francesca to tell "a che e come" (how and by what signs) she came into Love's power; Guido will tell Dante "e come e *quare*" (Latin "why," more precisely "in what respect" [how and why]) the reasons for his fall into perdition.

75. According to contemporary documents, Guido was actually referred to as "the fox." His quality of *astutia*, or "cunning," further identifies him with Ulysses (see note to *Inf.* XXVI.58–63).

79–81. Guido's nautical metaphors clearly relate him, perhaps more plainly than before, to Ulysses. For the curious notice on the part of Filippo Villani (in his life of Guido Bonatti) that Guido da Montefeltro was "full of all cunning [*astutia*]" and that he was known among the Italians as "the new Ulysses" see Hollander (Holl. 1980. 1), p. 142. This would suggest either that, in Dante's day, Guido was actually referred to in this way, or that Filippo, a great reader of Dante, is freely interpreting the reason for the juxtaposition of these two great figures in *Inferno*.

82–84.   Guido speaks of his contrition, confession, and satisfaction as though they were the merest of conveniences to attain an end. Do we believe, on the strength of this account, that he had actually fooled God?

85–93.   Guido's vicious slam of Boniface, with its concomitant enthusiasm for the abandoned devotion to crusading, is not in any respect at odds with Dante's own thoughts. Boniface is attacking Palestrina and its Christian inhabitants, none of whom had joined the Saracens in their retaking of Acre in 1291, until then the only remaining Christian possession in the Holy Land, or gone there only to do business with the enemy. Instead of attacking the infidel (or backsliding Christians) he moves against his coreligionists.

Boniface cares nothing for Christians, according to Guido (and Dante). Not only does he not oppose the heathen in order to make war on his own, he does not honor his own holy orders, nor those of Guido the friar. The use of the term *capestro* (cord) here has implications for those who believe that the *corda* at *Inferno* XVI. 106 is a reference to Dante's status as a Franciscan. (See note to *Inf.* XVI. 106–108.)

94–97.   In the fourth century, Constantine, suffering from leprosy, had Pope Sylvester I brought to him from his cave on Soracte (where he was in hiding because of Constantine's persecution of Christians) to cure him. When the pontiff did so, Constantine converted to Christianity (and ended up in paradise, according to Dante [*Par.* XX. 55–60]); but he also out of gratitude was reputed to have given Sylvester authority over the western empire, centered in the city of Rome. (See note to *Inf.* XIX. 115–117.)

102.   Penestrino is modern Palestrina, not far from Rome, and was ancient Praeneste. The Colonna family were in rebellion against Boniface's authority and had defended themselves in this fortress.

103–105.   Boniface's claim is utterly false, as Guido will learn. His reference to Celestine V here makes it seem all the more likely that it is he who is referred to in *Inferno* III. 59–60.

106–111.   Silence as a defensive weapon against this pope was probably the only way out; but his imposing insistence was too much for Guido, and he makes his bargain.

A continuing debate follows verse 110. Did Dante read these words in chroniclers who preceded him (e.g., Riccobaldo of Ferrara, Francesco Pipino of Bologna, both of whom wrote before 1313, if we are not sure exactly when), or did they get them from Dante? Some contemporary commentators (e.g., Bosco/Reggio) favor the precedence of Riccobaldo's chronicle, perhaps written between 1308 and 1313, and believe that Dante's account (and revision of his former positive view of Guido) derive from it.

112–114.   Markulin (Mark.1982.1) considers the possibility that Guido has invented the battle between St. Francis and the black Cherub (a member of the second highest rank of angels, associated with knowledge). Discomfort with the scene has been abroad for a while. Castelvetro did not hide his annoyance, seeing that Dante had portrayed the soul of Francis as having made an error in thinking that Guido was to be saved and thus could not possibly have been sent from heaven by God (and was consequently wasting his time), for which reasons he criticizes Dante for not speaking with greater reverence.

Guido's son Buonconte will be caught up in a similar struggle between devil and angel, with the angel winning (*Purg.* V.104–105). Such a scene may find justification in medieval popularizing art, but Castelvetro is right to complain about its theological absurdities. On the other hand, Dante is writing a poem and not a treatise. That he repeats the motif would seem to indicate that we are meant to take it "seriously." See note to *Inferno* XXIII.131.

116.   Perhaps the most discussed issue in these cantos is developed from this verse. What is "fraudulent advice" *(consiglio frodolente)* precisely? Is it the sin that condemns Guido? Is Ulysses condemned for the same sin? Fraudulent counsel is giving someone evil advice (whether or not it is effective advice) or acting in such fraudulent ways as to lead others into harming themselves. Since Virgil, in Canto XI.52–60, leaves the sins of the eighth and ninth *bolgia* unnamed, this is the only indication we have for a clear determination of the sin punished in these two cantos. Any other solution seems less satisfactory, if there have been many who have been eager to try to find one.

118–120.   While Dante, in *Convivio* III.xiii.2, clearly states that fallen angels cannot philosophize, since love is a basic requirement of true philosophizing and they are without love, it is clear that they can use logic, one of the tools of philosophy.

124.   This fallen angel does the "right thing" and stops his descent with his victim at Minos. See note to *Inferno* XXI.39.

128–132.   Unlike Ulysses, who ends his speech with a certain majesty, Guido insists upon his bitterness, realizing eternally his foolishness in his having given over his chance for love and salvation when he did the bidding of Boniface. The canto opens with Ulysses' flame calm and steady (vv. 1–2) and ends with that of Guido writhing.

INFERNO XXVIII

Chi poria mai pur con parole sciolte
dicer del sangue e de le piaghe a pieno
3   ch'i' ora vidi, per narrar più volte?

Ogne lingua per certo verria meno
per lo nostro sermone e per la mente
6   c'hanno a tanto comprender poco seno.

S'el s'aunasse ancor tutta la gente
che già, in su la fortunata terra
9   di Puglia, fu del suo sangue dolente

per li Troiani e per la lunga guerra
che de l'anella fé sì alte spoglie,
12   come Livïo scrive, che non erra,

con quella che sentio di colpi doglie
per contastare a Ruberto Guiscardo;
15   e l'altra il cui ossame ancor s'accoglie

a Ceperan, là dove fu bugiardo
ciascun Pugliese, e là da Tagliacozzo,
18   dove sanz' arme vinse il vecchio Alardo;

e qual forato suo membro e qual mozzo
mostrasse, d'aequar sarebbe nulla
21   il modo de la nona bolgia sozzo.

Già veggia, per mezzul perdere o lulla,
com' io vidi un, così non si pertugia,
24   rotto dal mento infin dove si trulla.

Tra le gambe pendevan le minugia;
la corata pareva e 'l tristo sacco
27   che merda fa di quel che si trangugia.

Who, even in words not bound by meter,
and having told the tale many times over,
3   could tell the blood and wounds that I saw now?

Surely every tongue would fail,
for neither thought nor speech
6   has the capacity to hold so much.

Could all the wounded troops again assemble:
first from Apulia, land laid low by war,
9   who grieved for their lost blood

shed by the Trojans, then all those
of the long war, whose corpses were despoiled
12   of piles of rings—as Livy writes, who does not err—

together with the ones who felt the agony of blows
fighting in the fields against Guiscard,
15   and those whose bones still lie in heaps

at Ceperano, where each Apulian played it false,
and those near Tagliacozzo,
18   where old Alardo conquered without force of arms:

and should one show his limb pierced through,
another his, where it has been cut off,
21   it would be nothing to the ninth pit's filth.

No cask ever gapes so wide for loss
of mid- or side-stave as the soul I saw
24   cleft from the chin right down to where men fart.

Between the legs the entrails dangled. I saw
the innards and the loathsome sack
27   that turns what one has swallowed into shit.

Mentre che tutto in lui veder m'attacco,
guardommi e con le man s'aperse il petto,
30   dicendo: "Or vedi com' io mi dilacco!

vedi come storpiato è Mäometto!
Dinanzi a me sen va piangendo Alì,
33   fesso nel volto dal mento al ciuffetto.

E tutti li altri che tu vedi qui,
seminator di scandalo e di scisma
36   fuor vivi, e però son fessi così.

Un diavolo è qua dietro che n'accisma
sì crudelmente, al taglio de la spada
39   rimettendo ciascun di questa risma,

quand' avem volta la dolente strada;
però che le ferite son richiuse
42   prima ch'altri dinanzi li rivada.

Ma tu chi se' che 'n su lo scoglio muse,
forse per indugiar d'ire a la pena
45   ch'è giudicata in su le tue accuse?"

"Né morte 'l giunse ancor, né colpa 'l mena,"
rispuose 'l mio maestro, "a tormentarlo;
48   ma per dar lui esperïenza piena,

a me, che morto son, convien menarlo
per lo 'nferno qua giù di giro in giro;
51   e quest' è ver così com' io ti parlo."

Più fuor di cento che, quando l'udiro,
s'arrestaron nel fosso a riguardarmi
54   per maraviglia, oblïando il martiro.

"Or dì a fra Dolcin dunque che s'armi,
tu che forse vedra' il sole in breve,
57   s'ello non vuol qui tosto seguitarmi,

While I was caught up in the sight of him,
he looked at me and, with his hands, ripped open
30   his chest, saying: 'See how I rend myself,

'see how mangled is Mohammed!
Ahead of me proceeds Alì, in tears,
33   his face split open from his chin to forelock.

'And all the others whom you see
sowed scandal and schism while they lived,
36   and that is why they here are hacked asunder.

'A devil's posted there behind us
who dresses us so cruelly,
39   putting each of this crew again to the sword

'as soon as we have done our doleful round.
For all our wounds have closed
42   when we appear again before him.

'But who are you to linger on the ridge?—
perhaps you put off going to the torment
45   pronounced on your own accusation.'

'Death does not have him yet nor does his guilt
lead him to torment,' replied my master,
48   'but to give him greater knowledge

'I, who am dead indeed, must shepherd him
from circle to circle, through this Hell down here.
51   And this is as true as that I speak to you.'

On hearing this, more than a hundred souls
halted in the ditch to stare at me
54   in wonder, each forgetful of his pain.

'You, who perhaps will shortly see the sun,
warn Fra Dolcino to provide himself—
57   unless he'd like to join me here quite soon—

sì di vivanda, che stretta di neve
non rechi la vittoria al Noarese,
60   ch'altrimenti acquistar non saria leve."

Poi che l'un piè per girsene sospese,
Mäometto mi disse esta parola;
63   indi a partirsi in terra lo distese.

Un altro, che forata avea la gola
e tronco 'l naso infin sotto le ciglia,
66   e non avea mai ch'una orecchia sola,

ristato a riguardar per maraviglia
con li altri, innanzi a li altri aprì la canna,
69   ch'era di fuor d'ogne parte vermiglia,

e disse: "O tu cui colpa non condanna
e cu' io vidi in su terra latina,
72   se troppa simiglianza non m'inganna,

rimembriti di Pier da Medicina,
se mai torni a veder lo dolce piano
75   che da Vercelli a Marcabò dichina.

E fa sapere a' due miglior da Fano,
a messer Guido e anco ad Angiolello,
78   che, se l'antiveder qui non è vano,

gittati saran fuor di lor vasello
e mazzerati presso a la Cattolica
81   per tradimento d'un tiranno fello.

Tra l'isola di Cipri e di Maiolica
non vide mai sì gran fallo Nettuno,
84   non da pirate, non da gente argolica.

Quel traditor che vede pur con l'uno,
e tien la terra che tale qui meco
87   vorrebbe di vedere esser digiuno,

'with stocks of victuals, lest the siege of snow
hand the Novarese the victory
60   not otherwise so easy to attain.'

One foot raised, halted in mid-stride,
Mohammed spoke these words,
63   then setting down that foot, went on his way.

Another, with his throat pierced through
and nose hacked off just where the brows begin,
66   and only one ear left upon his head,

stopped with the rest of them to gape in wonder
and, before the others did, opened his windpipe,
69   scarlet on the skin side as it was,

to say: 'O you whom guilt does not condemn
and whom I saw above in Italy,
72   if in your likeness I am not deceived,

'should you ever see that gentle plain again
that slopes from Vercelli down to Marcabò,
75   for Pier da Medicina spare a thought.

'And let the two chief men of Fano know,
both messer Guido and Angiolello,
78   that, unless our foresight here is vain,

'through a brutal tyrant's treachery
near La Cattolica they shall be heaved
81   out of their ship with weights to sink them down.

'Between the islands of Cyprus and Majorca
Neptune never witnessed so terrible a crime,
84   whether one committed by pirates or by Greeks.

'That traitor, who sees through one eye only
and rules the city that another down here with me
87   would take delight in never having seen,

farà venirli a parlamento seco;
poi farà sì, ch'al vento di Focara
90   non sarà lor mestier voto né preco."

E io a lui: "Dimostrami e dichiara,
se vuo' ch'i' porti sù di te novella,
93   chi è colui da la veduta amara."

Allor puose la mano a la mascella
d'un suo compagno e la bocca li aperse,
96   gridando: "Questi è desso, e non favella.

Questi, scacciato, il dubitar sommerse
in Cesare, affermando che 'l fornito
99   sempre con danno l'attender sofferse."

Oh quanto mi pareva sbigottito
con la lingua tagliata ne la strozza
102   Curïo, ch'a dir fu così ardito!

E un ch'avea l'una e l'altra man mozza,
levando i moncherin per l'aura fosca,
105   sì che 'l sangue facea la faccia sozza,

gridò: "Ricordera'ti anche del Mosca,
che disse, lasso! 'Capo ha cosa fatta,'
108   che fu mal seme per la gente tosca."

E io li aggiunsi: "E morte di tua schiatta";
per ch'elli, accumulando duol con duolo,
111   sen gio come persona trista e matta.

Ma io rimasi a riguardar lo stuolo,
e vidi cosa ch'io avrei paura,
114   sanza più prova, di contarla solo;

se non che coscïenza m'assicura,
la buona compagnia che l'uom francheggia
117   sotto l'asbergo del sentirsi pura.

'will have the men of Fano come to parley
and he will so deal with them that, to control
90   Focara's wind, they'll need no vows or prayers.'

And I: 'Point out to me and make him known,
if you would have me carry news of you above,
93   the one to whom that city's sight was bitter.'

Then he laid his hand upon the jaw
of one of his companions, pried his lips apart,
96   and cried: 'This is he, but he does not speak.

'Banished, he quenched the doubt in Caesar,
affirming that, to a man prepared,
99   delay was always harmful.'

Ah, how distressed he seemed to me,
his tongue sliced off deep in his throat,
102   Curio, who'd been so bold in speech!

And then another whose hands had been chopped off,
raising his stumps up in the murky air
105   so that the blood from them befouled his face,

cried out: 'Surely you'll remember Mosca also,
who said, alas: "A done deed finds its purpose."
108   For Tuscany, that was an evil seed.'

'And death to your own stock,' I added then.
At that, one sorrow piled upon another,
111   he made off, like a man berserk with grief.

But I stayed on to watch the troop
and saw a thing I would be loath
114   to mention without further proof,

were I not comforted by conscience,
the bosom friend that fortifies a man
117   beneath the armor of an honest heart.

Io vidi certo, e ancor par ch'io 'l veggia,
un busto sanza capo andar sì come
120   andavan li altri de la trista greggia;

e 'l capo tronco tenea per le chiome,
pesol con mano a guisa di lanterna:
123   e quel mirava noi e dicea: "Oh me!"

Di sé facea a sé stesso lucerna,
ed eran due in uno e uno in due;
126   com' esser può, quei sa che sì governa.

Quando diritto al piè del ponte fue,
levò 'l braccio alto con tutta la testa
129   per appressarne le parole sue,

che fuoro: "Or vedi la pena molesta,
tu che, spirando, vai veggendo i morti:
132   vedi s'alcuna è grande come questa.

E perché tu di me novella porti,
sappi ch'i' son Bertram dal Bornio, quelli
135   che diedi al re giovane i ma' conforti.

Io feci il padre e 'l figlio in sé ribelli;
Achitofèl non fé più d'Absalone
138   e di Davìd coi malvagi punzelli.

Perch' io parti' così giunte persone,
partito porto il mio cerebro, lasso!,
dal suo principio ch'è in questo troncone.
142   Così s'osserva in me lo contrapasso."

I truly saw, and seem to see it still,
a headless body make its way
120   like all the others in that dismal flock.

And by its hair he held his severed head
swinging in his hand as if it were a lantern.
123   The head stared at us and said: 'Oh, woe!'

Of himself he made himself a lamp,
and they were two in one and one in two.
126   How this can be He knows who so ordains it.

When he was just at the foot of the bridge
he raised his arm high and, with it, that head,
129   so as to make his words sound more distinct:

'You, who view the dead with breath yet in your body,
look upon my grievous punishment.
132   Is any other terrible as this?

'So you may carry back the news of me,
know I am Bertran de Born, the one
135   who urged the young king on with bad advice.

'Father and son I set to enmity.
Ahithophel stirred no worse ill between
138   Absalom and David with his wicked goading.

'Because I severed persons thus conjoined,
severed, alas, I carry my own brain
from its starting-point here in my body.
142   In me you may observe fit punishment.'

1–6. For Dante's disclaimer of the ability to describe the blood and wounds that surpass both words and memory (even were he to revert to prose to do so), see Virgil's similar disclaimer in *Aeneid* VI.625–627: "And if I had a hundred tongues and as many mouths, along with a voice of iron, I could not put together all the shapes of crime nor run through all the catalogue of torments." The passage was first cited by Pietro di Dante and is now a commonplace in the commentaries.

7–21. This elliptical version of a simile, so rich in its catalog of the horrors of war, involves four battles (or series of battles), two of them ancient, two modern, roughly as follows:

1150 B.C. ca.	Aeneas's Trojans triumph in south and central Italy;
216 B.C.	Romans are defeated by the Carthaginians at Cannae;
1070 ca.	Robert Guiscard's Normans defeat the Saracens;
1266 & 1268	Manfred, then Conradin, defeated by Charles of Anjou.

In this series of military actions the Roman and/or imperial side first wins, then loses disastrously. The intrinsic view of history here is more chaotic than directed. Absent is Dante's more optimistic view of history unfolding as a Roman and Christian manifestation of the spirit moving through time to its appointed goal. And we might further reflect that winning and losing battles has little to do with one's final destination in God's plan: Aeneas wins, but is in Limbo (*Inf.* IV.122), Robert Guiscard wins and is in heaven (*Par.* XVIII.48), Manfred loses and is on his way to heaven (*Purg.* III.112).

For Dante's relation to martial epic, a genre surely drawn to our attention by these scenes of war, see Hollander (Holl.1989.1). While Dante's position here would also seem to look down on "mere" martial epic, with all its pointless slaughter, he nonetheless reveals an aptitude for the genre.

9–11. Puglia (Apulia) here, most commentators agree, is meant in its wider sense, i.e., not only the southeast portion of the Italian peninsula, but the region including Lazio. The Trojans are then Aeneas and his men (some believe the reference is to the later Romans). The "long war" is the second Punic War (218–201 B.C.), during which the Romans suffered a terrible defeat at the hands of Hannibal's Carthaginian forces at Cannae (216 B.C.) in Apulia. Historians relate that after the battle a Carthaginian envoy showed the Roman senate the vast number of gold rings taken from the fingers of noble Romans killed in the battle.

12. The problem of the extent of Dante's knowledge of Livy remains a vexed one. Commentators point out that Dante here would rather seem to be following Orosius (or Augustine) than Livy, but still appeals to Livy as the most authoritative historian of Rome. His vast compendium, *Ab urbe condita,* did not come through the ages intact; precisely which parts of it were known to Dante is not known to us.

13–14. Robert Guiscard, a Norman, won many victories in Puglia ca. 1060–80 to consolidate his power as duke of the region, including what for Dante was the most important one, that over the Saracens, which apparently helped to gain him his place in *Paradiso* (XVIII.48).

15–16. The text alludes to Manfred's disastrous loss, occasioned, in Dante's view, by the betrayal of his Apulian allies, at the battle near Ceperano that was prologue to his final defeat and death at the hands of the forces of the French king Charles of Valois at the battle of Benevento (1266). Manfred is the first saved soul found once Dante begins his ascent of the mount of purgatory (*Purg.* III.112).

17–18. Two years after the defeat at Benevento, the Ghibelline forces, now under Conradin, the grandson of the emperor Frederick II, suffered their final defeat near Tagliacozzo, in the Abruzzi, again at the hands of the forces of Charles of Anjou, who, after the battle, had Conradin put to death, thus ending the Hohenstaufen succession in Italy. Alardo was the French knight Érard de Valéry, who gave Charles the strategic advice that gained him military advantage on the field.

19–21. This image, suggesting layers of excavated battlefields, each containing vast areas of wounded soldiers holding out their mutilated limbs, gives us some sense of Dante's view of the end result of war, sheer human butchery. Bosco/Reggio suggest that this *bolgia* brings into mind the image of a huge slaughterhouse.

For the Virgilian resonance (*Aen.* II.361–362) of these lines, see Tommaseo's comment: this is Aeneas's response when he must tell the terrible carnage during the night of the fall of Troy.

22–31. This disgusting image of Mohammed derives from Dante's conviction that the prophet was in fact a Christian whose schismatic behavior took the form of founding (in 630) what Dante considered a rival sect rather than a new religion, Islam. Thus Mohammed reveals himself as divided in two.

32–33. Alì, disciple, cousin, and son-in-law of Mohammed, became the fourth leader of the Muslims. But the issues surrounding his succession in 656 divided them into two factions, Sunni and Shiite, that continue to this day.

35. All punished here are described by this verse. "Scandal," in this sense, means a promulgated doctrine that leads others to stumble and lose their way to the truth. See Thomas Aquinas, *Summa theologica* II–II, q. 43, a. 1, resp., on the Greek word σκάνδαλον, or "stumbling block." Thus all here either caused schism in others or themselves lead schismatic groups, the first three religious (Mohammed, Alì, Fra Dolcino), the last five political (Pier da Medicina, Malatestino, Curio, Mosca, Bertran de Born).

37–40. The unseen devil of this ditch joins the cast of devils of the Malebolge, the whippers of the first *bolgia* and the hookers of the fifth. In this case there seems to be one devil alone, perhaps intended to remind the reader of the solitary Cherub, with flaming sword, sent to guard the Garden after Adam and Eve had been ejected from it (Gen. 3:24). (See *Purgatorio* VIII.25–27, where this passage is more clearly alluded to.) It is only in Malebolge that we find such creatures.

43–45. Mohammed evidently believes that Dante is one of the dead sinners. But how or why he thinks that such as they can loiter in hell, doing a bit of sightseeing before they go to judgment, is not easily explained. Virgil's response (v. 49) makes it clear that only he, in this pair of visitors, is a dead soul.

55–60. Disabused of his erring view, Mohammed uses the occasion to send a message to his fellow in religious schism, Fra Dolcino. A northerner, from Novara (balancing the southern setting of the opening of the canto), Dolcino Tornielli was the head, from ca. 1300, of a group known as the Apostolic Brethren (*gli Apostolici*). This "order" had as its aim the restoration of the simplicity of apostolic times to the Christian religion. Its enemies accused Dolcino of holding heretical ideas, such as the community of goods and women. It did not help Dolcino's case that he was accompanied by a beautiful woman, Margaret of Trent, reputed to be his mistress. Pope Clement V preached a crusade against the Brethren in 1305. In 1307, starved out by their enemies in the high country to which they had retreated, the Brethren were captured. Margaret and Dolcino were burned at the stake.

61–63.   Mohammed's placement of his suspended foot is read by some as a mere "realistic detail." Rasha Al-Sabah (Alsa.1977.1) argues for an iconographic reading, based in a passage in St. Thomas on Proverbs 6:12–19, in which "a wicked man with lying mouth, sowing discord," has "feet that are swift in running to mischief." His posture, one foot suspended, may also refer to the Greek term "σκάνδαλον," for "stumbling block," found at v. 35.

65.   This bloodied figure, thus sliced by the sword-wielding devil, will be revealed as Pier da Medicina at v. 73. For the reminiscence of Virgil's description of the disfigured visage of Deiphobus (*Aen.* VI.494–497), similarly deprived of his nose, see Scartazzini's commentary and many later ones as well.

68.   Pier opens his windpipe to speak, since the devil's cut had wounded him there, thus preventing his breath from reaching his mouth.

70–75.   The early commentators are not sure exactly who Pier of Medicina (a town between Bologna and Imola) was, but Dante and he apparently knew one another. While the nature of his schismatic behavior thus lies in shadow, the fact that his ensuing remarks refer to political intrigue would seem to mark him also as a political, rather than a religious, schismatic.

76–81.   Pier refers, in his prophecy, which parallels that given by Mohammed, initially to two victims of "schism," Guido del Cassero and Angiolello di Carignano, first identified by Guiniforto in 1440, and then to the victimizer, Malatestino Malatesta, lord of Rimini. (He is referred to as "the younger mastiff" in the last canto at v. 46.) The details are not known to any commentators, but apparently Dante knew that these two leaders of the city of Fano were tricked by Malatestino into coming to confer with him at the town of La Cattolica. His men caught them in their ship on their way (or after they left) and drowned them.

82–84.   Unriddled, the passage means that the entire Mediterranean Sea never witnessed so great a crime. For the phrase "gente argolica," meaning "Greeks," a synecdoche based on the part (the denizens of Argos) for the whole (Greece), see *Aeneid* II.78, as was noted in Torraca's commentary (1905).

85–87.   Malatestino, one-eyed, holds Rimini, the city that Curio (v. 102) wishes he had never seen (because it was there that he offered the advice that condemns him to this punishment).

89–90.   The two men of Fano (v. 76) will have no need of prayer for help against the tricky winds off Focara's point because they will be dead.

91–93.   Dante, his appetite whetted by Pier's elliptical phrasing at v. 87, wants him to expand.

96–102.   Pier opens the tongueless mouth of Curio, seen as a schismatic for his advice to Caesar to march on Rome, thus destroying the republic and causing the civil wars. For Curio in Lucan and Dante see Stul.1991.1, pp. 27–28.

103–108.   The description of Mosca dei Lamberti is one of the most affecting in this canto filled with affective moments. Mosca was among those Florentine citizens mentioned by Dante (*Inf.* VI.80) as having attempted to do good in the divided city; for his crime, of those mentioned he is the farthest down in hell. A fervent Ghibelline, in 1216 he urged the murder of Buondelmonte dei Buondelmonti, who, engaged to a girl of the Amidei family, married a Donati instead. The result of this killing was the origin of the bitter rivalry between the Amidei and the Donati, Ghibellines and Guelphs respectively, and of the civil discord that tore Florence apart. Mosca is thus seen as a modern-day Curio, urging the powerful to do what in their hearts they must have known was not to be done.

His words, "a done deed finds its purpose," so mercilessly laconic, now cause him enough by way of regret that we can sense some justification in Dante's original characterization of him.

109–111.   Dante is nonetheless stern in his criticism of Mosca, not accepting his gesture of penitence, and Mosca is left with his deserved heartbreak.

115–117. The poet's self-assurance, playful though it certainly is, may offend some readers. He can narrate what is to follow because he knows he actually saw the next scene, a shade carrying his severed head.

130–138. Bertran de Born, one of the great poets of war of his or any time (and thus greatly admired by Ezra Pound in the last century) loved to see destruction of towns and men. One thinks of Robert Duvall's character in Francis Ford Coppola's film *Apocalypse Now*, who loved the smell of napalm in the morning. It is often pointed out that v. 132 is a reprise of a passage in the Lamentations of Jeremiah (Lament. 1:12), already cited by Dante in the opening verses of an "exploded" sonnet in his *Vita nuova* (VII.1–3) to express his own solitary sadness in love. In a sense, they are part of Bertran's punishment, the "tough guy" portrayed as self-pitying.

Bertran was a Gascon nobleman of the second half of the twelfth century. His poetry, written in Provençal, which is reflected in several passages in this canto, is not the subject of his discourse. Rather, he condemns himself for his implacable schismatic actions at the English court, where he supported and encouraged the rebellious plotting of Prince Henry against his own father, Henry II, king of the realm. For a text that encapsulates the problem presented in Bertran and all the other political schismatics, see Luke 11:17: "Every kingdom divided against itself is brought to desolation" (cited by Marianne Shapiro [Shap.1974.1], p. 114).

For the reference to Ahitophel's similar support and encouragement of Absalom's rebellion against *his* father, King David, see II Samuel 15:7–18:15.

142. The word *contrapasso* is generally understood to be based on an Aristotelian term in its Latin translation, *contrapassum*, used in the same sense that the biblical concept of retribution, expressed in the Latin *lex talionis* (the taking of an eye for an eye, etc.), is understood to have. That is, one does something wrong and receives the appropriate punishment for doing it. Out of the Hebrew and Aristotelian concept (the latter refined by Thomas's commentary on Aristotle), Dante supposedly developed this idea, which is given a name here, but has been operative since we saw the first sinners in hell, the neutrals, in Canto III. For a lengthy and helpful gloss, see Singleton on this verse. Valerio Lucchesi (Lucc.1991.1) has mounted a complex argument attempting to deny this positive understanding of the term by Dante on the basis of its instability as a concept that St. Thomas actually embraces.

INFERNO XXIX

La molta gente e le diverse piaghe
avean le luci mie sì inebrïate,
3   che de lo stare a piangere eran vaghe.

Ma Virgilio mi disse: "Che pur guate?
perché la vista tua pur si soffolge
6   là giù tra l'ombre triste smozzicate?

Tu non hai fatto sì a l'altre bolge;
pensa, se tu annoverar le credi,
9   che miglia ventidue la valle volge.

E già la luna è sotto i nostri piedi;
lo tempo è poco omai che n'è concesso,
12   e altro è da veder che tu non vedi."

"Se tu avessi," rispuos' io appresso,
"atteso a la cagion per ch'io guardava,
15   forse m'avresti ancor lo star dimesso."

Parte sen giva, e io retro li andava,
lo duca, già faccendo la risposta,
18   e soggiugnendo: "Dentro a quella cava

dov' io tenea or li occhi sì a posta,
credo ch'un spirto del mio sangue pianga
21   la colpa che là giù cotanto costa."

Allor disse 'l maestro: "Non si franga
lo tuo pensier da qui innanzi sovr' ello.
24   Attendi ad altro, ed ei là si rimanga;

ch'io vidi lui a piè del ponticello
mostrarti e minacciar forte col dito,
27   e udi' 'l nominar Geri del Bello.

The many people and their ghastly wounds
did so intoxicate my eyes
3   that I was moved to linger there and weep.

But Virgil said: 'What are you staring at?
Why is your gaze so fixed upon the depths
6   that hold those mournful, mutilated shades?

'You have not done so at the other pits.
In case you plan to count the sinners one by one,
9   think: this hollow circles twenty-two miles round.

'The moon already lies beneath our feet.
The time we are allotted soon expires
12   and there is more to see than you see here.'

'Had you understood,' I was quick to answer,
'the reason for my close inspection,
15   perhaps you would have let me stay there longer.'

All the while my guide was moving on,
with me, intent on my reply, behind him.
18   And then I added: 'Within that hole

'where I had fixed my gaze, I do believe
someone of my own blood lament
21   the sin that costs so dear down there.'

Then the master said: 'Trouble your mind
no more because of him.
24   Turn it to other things and let him be,

'for I saw him there below the bridge,
pointing his finger at you, fierce with threats,
27   and I heard him called Geri del Bello.

Tu eri allor sì del tutto impedito
sovra colui che già tenne Altaforte,
30   che non guardasti in là, sì fu partito."

"O duca mio, la vïolenta morte
che non li è vendicata ancor," diss' io,
33   "per alcun che de l'onta sia consorte,

fece lui disdegnoso; ond' el sen gio
sanza parlarmi, sì com' ïo estimo:
36   e in ciò m'ha el fatto a sé più pio."

Così parlammo infino al loco primo
che de lo scoglio l'altra valle mostra,
39   se più lume vi fosse, tutto ad imo.

Quando noi fummo sor l'ultima chiostra
di Malebolge, sì che i suoi conversi
42   potean parere a la veduta nostra,

lamenti saettaron me diversi,
che di pietà ferrati avean li strali;
45   ond' io li orecchi con le man copersi.

Qual dolor fora, se de li spedali
di Valdichiana tra 'l luglio e 'l settembre
48   e di Maremma e di Sardigna i mali

fossero in una fossa tutti 'nsembre,
tal era quivi, e tal puzzo n'usciva
51   qual suol venir de le marcite membre.

Noi discendemmo in su l'ultima riva
del lungo scoglio, pur da man sinistra;
54   e allor fu la mia vista più viva

giù ver' lo fondo, là 've la ministra
de l'alto Sire infallibil giustizia
57   punisce i falsador che qui registra.

'Just then you were so thoroughly engrossed
in him who once was lord of Hautefort
30   you didn't glance that way before your kinsman left.'

'O my leader, the violent death he died,
for which no vengeance has been taken yet,'
33   I said, 'by any person partner to his shame,

'made him indignant. That is why he went away
without addressing me—or so I think—
36   and why he has made me pity him the more.'

Thus we continued talking till we reached
the first point on the ridge that could have shown
39   the next pit's bottom, had there been more light.

When we stood above the final cloister
of Malebolge and all of its lay brothers
42   became discernible to us,

strange arrows of lament, their shafts,
with pity at their tips, pierced me,
45   so that I pressed my hands against my ears.

If the contagion of every hospital
in Valdichiana, from July until September,
48   and in the Maremma and Sardegna, were amassed

in one malarial ditch, such suffering
was in that place. And from it rose
51   the stench of festering limbs.

We came down, always to our left, and reached
the last bank of the lengthy crag.
54   And then my eyes could have a better view

into the pit, there where the minister
of God on high, unerring justice, punishes
57   the counterfeiters whom she here records.

Non credo ch'a veder maggior tristizia
fosse in Egina il popol tutto infermo,
60   quando fu l'aere sì pien di malizia,

che li animali, infino al picciol vermo,
cascaron tutti, e poi le genti antiche,
63   secondo che i poeti hanno per fermo,

si ristorar di seme di formiche;
ch'era a veder per quella oscura valle
66   languir li spirti per diverse biche.

Qual sovra 'l ventre e qual sovra le spalle
l'un de l'altro giacea, e qual carpone
69   si trasmutava per lo tristo calle.

Passo passo andavam sanza sermone,
guardando e ascoltando li ammalati,
72   che non potean levar le lor persone.

Io vidi due sedere a sé poggiati,
com' a scaldar si poggia tegghia a tegghia,
75   dal capo al piè di schianze macolati;

e non vidi già mai menare stregghia
a ragazzo aspettato dal segnorso,
78   né a colui che mal volontier vegghia,

come ciascun menava spesso il morso
de l'unghie sopra sé per la gran rabbia
81   del pizzicor, che non ha più soccorso;

e sì traevan giù l'unghie la scabbia,
come coltel di scardova le scaglie
84   o d'altro pesce che più larghe l'abbia.

"O tu che con le dita ti dismaglie,"
cominciò 'l duca mio a l'un di loro,
87   "e che fai d'esse tal volta tanaglie,

I think it could have been no greater sorrow
to see the people of Aegina stricken,
60   with such corruption in the very air

that every animal, even the smallest worm,
perished, and, later, as the poets hold for certain,
63   these ancient people were restored to life,

hatched from the eggs of ants—
no greater sorrow, than in that somber valley
66   to see those spirits, heaped on one another, languishing.

Some lay upon the bellies or the backs
of others, still others dragged themselves
69   on hands and knees along that gloomy path.

Step by step we went ahead in silence,
looking and listening to the stricken spirits,
72   who could not raise their bodies from the ground.

Two I saw seated, propped against each other
as pans are propped to warm before the fire,
75   each of them blotched with scabs from head to foot.

And never did I see a stable-boy,
with his master waiting, nor youth whose chore
78   keeps him from sleep, ply his curry-comb

more hurriedly than each one clawed his nails
across his skin because of that mad itch,
81   which knows no other remedy,

and their nails tore off scabs
as a knife strips scales from bream
84   or other fish with even larger scales.

'You there, stripping off your coat of mail,'
began my leader, addressing one of them,
87   'and sometimes making pincers of your fingers,

dinne s'alcun Latino è tra costoro
che son quinc' entro, se l'unghia ti basti
90   etternalmente a cotesto lavoro."

"Latin siam noi, che tu vedi sì guasti
qui ambedue," rispuose l'un piangendo;
93   "ma tu chi se' che di noi dimandasti?"

E 'l duca disse: "I' son un che discendo
con questo vivo giù di balzo in balzo,
96   e di mostrar lo 'nferno a lui intendo."

Allor si ruppe lo comun rincalzo;
e tremando ciascuno a me si volse
99   con altri che l'udiron di rimbalzo.

Lo buon maestro a me tutto s'accolse,
dicendo: "Dì a lor ciò che tu vuoli";
102   e io incominciai, poscia ch'ei volse:

"Se la vostra memoria non s'imboli
nel primo mondo da l'umane menti,
105   ma s'ella viva sotto molti soli,

ditemi chi voi siete e di che genti;
la vostra sconcia e fastidiosa pena
108   di palesarvi a me non vi spaventi."

"Io fui d'Arezzo, e Albero da Siena,"
rispuose l'un, "mi fé mettere al foco;
111   ma quel per ch'io mori' qui non mi mena.

Vero è ch'i' dissi lui, parlando a gioco:
'I' mi saprei levar per l'aere a volo';
114   e quei, ch'avea vaghezza e senno poco,

volle ch'i' li mostrassi l'arte; e solo
perch' io nol feci Dedalo, mi fece
117   ardere a tal che l'avea per figliuolo.

'tell us whether, among those gathered here,
any are Italian, so may your nails
90   last you in this task for all eternity.'

'We whom you see so blasted are Italian,'
answered one of them, through his tears,
93   'but who are you, that you inquire of us?'

And my leader: 'I am one who makes his way
down with this living man from ledge to ledge.
96   And my intention is to show him Hell.'

They stopped propping one another up
and each one, trembling, turned in my direction,
99   as others did who'd overheard those words.

The good master drew up close to me,
saying, 'Ask them what you will.'
102   And I began, since this had been his wish:

'So that your memory may not fade away
from minds of men in the world above
105   but live on yet for many suns to come,

'tell me who you are, and where you hail from.
Do not let your foul and sickening torment
108   keep you from telling me your names.'

And one of them replied: 'I was of Arezzo.
Albero of Siena had me burned alive.
111   But what I died for does not bring me here.

'It is true I said to him in jest:
"I do know how to rise into the air and fly!"
114   And he, who had the will but not the wit,

'asked me to show him how. And just because
I failed to make him Daedalus, he had me set
117   on fire by one who took him as his son.

Ma ne l'ultima bolgia de le diece
me per l'alchìmia che nel mondo usai
120   dannò Minòs, a cui fallar non lece."

E io dissi al poeta: "Or fu già mai
gente sì vana come la sanese?
123   Certo non la francesca sì d'assai!"

Onde l'altro lebbroso, che m'intese,
rispuose al detto mio: "Tra'mene Stricca
126   che seppe far le temperate spese,

e Niccolò che la costuma ricca
del garofano prima discoverse
129   ne l'orto dove tal seme s'appicca;

e tra'ne la brigata in che disperse
Caccia d'Ascian la vigna e la gran fonda,
132   e l'Abbagliato suo senno proferse.

Ma perché sappi chi sì ti seconda
contra i Sanesi, aguzza ver' me l'occhio,
135   sì che la faccia mia ben ti risponda:

sì vedrai ch'io son l'ombra di Capocchio,
che falsai li metalli con l'alchìmia;
e te dee ricordar, se ben t'adocchio,
139   com' io fui di natura buona scimia."

'But Minos, incapable of error,
damned me to the last of these ten ditches
120   for the alchemy I practiced in the world.'

And I said to the poet: 'Was ever a people
quite so fatuous as the Sienese?
123   Why, not even the French can match them!'

Whereupon the other leper, hearing me,
replied: 'Except, of course for Stricca—
126   he knew how to moderate his spending—

'and for Niccolò—the first one to devise
a costly use for cloves,
129   there in the garden where such seeds take root—

'and for that band in whose company
Caccia d'Asciano squandered his vineyards
132   and his fields, and Abbagliato showed his wit.

'But, to let you know who's in your camp
against the Sienese, look close at me
135   so that my face itself may answer you.

'You will see I am the shade of Capocchio,
who altered metal by means of alchemy.
And, if you are the man I take you for,
139   you will recall how good an ape I was of nature.'

1–3.   Dante's weeping eyes have reminded commentators, beginning with
Tommaseo, of biblical sources, particularly Isaiah 16:9 and 34:7, as well as
Ezekiel 23:33. Durling (Durl.1996.1), p. 458, suggests an echo of a passage
in St. Augustine's *Confessions* (VI.8), when Alypius is described as becom-
ing drunk at the sight of the blood spilled at the Roman games.

4–7.   Virgil's rebuke, reminiscent of that found in Canto XX (vv. 27–30),
is particularly stern, as though Dante were guilty of the sort of appalling
human ghoulishness that makes people today gather at the scenes of fatal
accidents.

8–9.   Virgil's sarcastic thrust for the first time in the poem offers us a
measurement of the size of one of the areas of hell: this *bolgia* is twenty-
two miles in circumference. (We will discover, at *Inf.* XXX.86, that the
next *bolgia*'s circumference is exactly half this one's.) These two measure-
ments were the cause of an orgy of calculating in the Renaissance, involv-
ing no less a figure than Galileo in absurd plottings of an implausibly huge
Inferno. For an account of these see John Kleiner (Klei.1994.1), pp. 23–56.

10.   Castelvetro hears the echo here of the Sibyl's words in *Aeneid* VI.539:
"nox ruit, Aenea; nos flendo ducimus horas" (Night is coming, Aeneas; we
waste the time in weeping). He goes on to add that Servius, in his com-
mentary to *Aeneid* VI.255, pointed out that only a single day was granted
by the gods for Aeneas's journey to the underworld. We understand that
the same is true for Dante, whose voyage in hell takes exactly twenty-four
hours.

11–12.   Virgil's lunar time-telling suggests that, since *Inferno* XXI.112,
some six hours have passed, making it ca. 1:30 PM now and leaving less
than five hours for the completion of the journey.

13–21.   Defending himself against the charge of idle curiosity, Dante
informs Virgil that he was looking for the shade of a relative among the
schismatics. The exchange shows that Virgil cannot in fact "read" Dante's
thoughts. See note to *Inferno* XXIII.25–30.

22–27.   Virgil now adds some details to Canto XXVIII: he had seen Geri del Bello menace Dante while the protagonist was so preoccupied by Bertran de Born. This family drama runs as follows. Geri del Bello, Dante's father's cousin, was evidently something of a troublemaker (he was once cited for attacking a man in Prato in 1280). He was murdered, perhaps at about this time, by a member of the Sacchetti family, and revenge was only achieved by another member of the Alighieri clan ca. 1310 (perhaps just as Dante was finishing *Inferno*). The details are far from clear, and the accounts in the early commentators diverge. See Simonetta Saffiotti Bernardi and Renato Piattoli, "Alighieri, Geri," *ED*, vol. 1, 1970.

31–36.   For the delicate interplay between Dante's aristocratic sense of the necessity of acting on behalf of his family's honor and his Christian knowledge that vengeance is the province of God alone, see Pertile (Pert.1998.1), pp. 378–84. Pertile also argues that Dante and Geri play out the roles of Aeneas and Dido in the underworld, when the guilty former lover fails to communicate with the shade of his offended dead paramour and leaves with his guilt unresolved (*Aen.* VI.450–476). Dante's feeling *pio*— piteous toward Geri—would seem to connect him with Virgil's *pius Aeneas*, who also honored his familiars.

37–39.   The change in setting, from one *bolgia* to the other, is more abrupt than usual. The first thirty-six verses of the canto have been a sort of personal addendum to the last canto; the rest of it will combine with the next one to present the final ditch of the Malebolge, devoted to the punishment of forgery, in various forms: of metals (all in Canto XXIX), of persons, of coins, of words (all in Canto XXX). For the "fraudulent" blending of metals by alchemists, those punished in the rest of this canto, see Meye.1969.1.

40–45.   These "lay brothers" of the "monastery" of the forgers are piteous in their aspect and in their groans; the protagonist, now of sterner stuff than he had been under the influence of his relative's unavenged murder, covers his ears (where he had feasted his drunken eyes at the beginning of the canto).

46–51.   The Valdichiana and Maremma, in Tuscany, and Sardinia were all characterized by malarial outbreaks in the summer. Commentators speak of the special hospitals set up in the Valdichiana to deal with outbreaks of the disease.

52–53.   They cross the last bridge, now seen as an entity, the long span (interrupted over the sixth *bolgia*) that traverses the extent of Malebolge.

54–57.   God's unerring justice is portrayed as the punishing agent of the counterfeiters. But what does it mean that she records or "registers" them? And where is "here"? Most early commentators argued that "here" referred to the *bolgia*. Beginning in the Renaissance, the majority believe that it refers to this world. But what sense does it make to say that justice "registers" sinners in this world? The image is of writing down a person's name in a book. For a review of the debate over the line (57) see Hollander (Holl.1982.1), proposing that "here" means "this book," i.e., Dante's *Inferno*, a solution put forth (although never discussed by later commentators) by John of Serravalle in the fifteenth century. Dante will once again (and only once again) use the verb *registrare*: see *Purgatorio* XXX.63, when his name, "Dante," is "registered here," i.e., in his text.

58–66.   Details from Ovid's lengthy account of the plague, sent by Juno, on the island of Aegina (*Metam.* VII.523–657) is here used in simile to describe the falsifiers, who have become plague-blasted shades of humans because of their counterfeiting, in which that which is worth less is made to seem worth more. That their affliction is an infernal version of leprosy (some commentators believe it is scabies [see v. 82]) is attested by Bosco/Reggio (commentary to this verse) on the basis of medieval medical treatises, some of which report that scabies is a secondary symptom of leprosy. Capocchio, the second of the two sinners revealed here, is described as "leprous" (v. 124).

In verse 63 Dante takes mere poetic fictiveness to task (in *Conv.* IV.xxvii.17 he had referred to this story as a *favola* [fable]). His "real" sinners may resemble the plague-victims in Ovid's fanciful tale; unlike them, however, they are not present in a fable, but in a truthful narrative. Here Dante's insistence on the veracity of what he relates is so challenging that we can see the wink in his eye.

73–84.   The three rapid comparisons are the very stuff of homely poetry: pans on a stove, stable boys currying horses, cooks' helpers cleaning fish. We have seen precisely this stylistic range before, paired similetic passages describing the same thing in two very different registers, that of classical myth deployed alongside that of "scenes from everyday life." Among other things, this second register, with its ordinary, even ugly, names of things in the real world, helps us "believe" that Dante's poetry is in fact "true," while

Ovid's is not—even as we acknowledge that Dante is as much a fabulist as was Ovid.

85–90.   Even Virgil's ironic *captatio*, his attempt to win Griffolino's goodwill, reflects the low style of things in this scene.

109–120.   Griffolino d'Arezzo was in fact burned at the stake for a charge of heresy brought by Albero di Siena, perhaps the natural son of the bishop of Siena, ca. 1270. Thus he was put to death for a sin he did not commit, but condemned by God for the one he did: falsifying metals. Dante obviously enjoyed telling this tale of buffoonish credulity, in which Griffolino failed in his role of Daedalus to Albero's Icarus, and which would have fit a *novella* of Boccaccio, even though it is irrelevant to the sin punished here.

121–123.   Florentines love to belittle the Sienese; Italians love to belittle the French. Dante gets two for one.

124–135.   Capocchio was burned alive as an alchemist in 1293. As was the case when we listened to Griffolino, what we first hear about from him does not concern falsification, but another topic altogether—the luxurious living of the Sienese, down to their overindulgence in the use of cloves to season their food. This is exemplified in Stricca the spendthrift; Niccolò the gourmet; and Caccia d'Asciano who, with Abbagliato, was part of the notorious *brigata spendereccia* (Spendthrift Brigade) of Siena, which liked to gather to eat and drink and then destroy the plates and service while they were at it.

136–139.   Capocchio was, according to some early commentators, known to Dante in their early days as students. He was supposedly a particularly adept imitator of the words and gestures of others, a talent which he later extended to "alchemical" malfeasance, to his cost. For the concept of the ape as mimic, see Curtius (Curt.1948.1), pp. 538–40.

INFERNO XXX

Nel tempo che Iunone era crucciata
per Semelè contra 'l sangue tebano,
come mostrò una e altra f ïata,

Atamante divenne tanto insano,
che veggendo la moglie con due figli
andar carcata da ciascuna mano,

gridò: "Tendiam le reti, sì ch'io pigli
la leonessa e 'leoncini al varco";
e poi distese i dispietati artigli,

prendendo l'un ch'avea nome Learco,
e rotollo e percosselo ad un sasso;
e quella s'annegò con l'altro carco.

E quando la fortuna volse in basso
l'altezza de' Troian che tutto ardiva,
sì che 'nsieme col regno il re fu casso,

Ecuba trista, misera e cattiva,
poscia che vide Polissena morta,
e del suo Polidoro in su la riva

del mar si fu la dolorosa accorta,
forsennata latrò sì come cane;
tanto il dolor le fé la mente torta.

Ma né di Tebe furie né troiane
si vider mäi in alcun tanto crude,
non punger bestie, nonché membra umane,

quant'io vidi in due ombre smorte e nude,
che mordendo correvan di quel modo
che 'l porco quando del porcil si schiude.

Once when Juno, furious with Semele,
vented her rage against the house of Thebes,
as she had done on more than one occasion,

Athamas went so raving mad that when he saw
his wife come near with both their children,
holding one on this arm, one on that,

he shouted: "Let's spread the nets so I can trap
the lioness with her cubs as they go past!"
Then he reached out and with pitiless claws

he seized the one who was called Learchus,
whirled him round and dashed him on a rock.
At that she drowned herself with her other burden.

And when Fortune had subdued the haughty,
all-daring spirit of the Trojans,
so that both king and kingdom were brought down,

Hecuba—wretched, sorrowing, a captive—
when she saw Polyxena slaughtered and,
grieving woman, when she saw

Polydorus lying dead upon the shore,
went mad and started barking like a dog,
so greatly had her grief deranged her mind.

But no Theban crazed with rage—
or Trojan—did ever seem as cruel
in rending beasts, much less human parts,

as did two pallid, naked shades I saw,
snapping their jaws as they rushed up
like swine charging from an opened sty.

L'una giunse a Capocchio, e in sul nodo
del collo l'assannò, sì che, tirando,
30   grattar li fece il ventre al fondo sodo.

E l'Aretin che rimase, tremando
mi disse: "Quel folletto è Gianni Schicchi,
33   e va rabbioso altrui così conciando."

"Oh," diss' io lui, "se l'altro non ti ficchi
li denti a dosso, non ti sia fatica
36   a dir chi è, pria che di qui si spicchi."

Ed elli a me: "Quell' è l'anima antica
di Mirra scellerata, che divenne
39   al padre, fuor del dritto amore, amica.

Questa a peccar con esso così venne,
falsificando sé in altrui forma,
42   come l'altro che là sen va, sostenne,

per guadagnar la donna de la torma,
falsificare in sé Buoso Donati,
45   testando e dando al testamento norma."

E poi che i due rabbiosi fuor passati
sovra cu' io avea l'occhio tenuto,
48   rivolsilo a guardar li altri mal nati.

Io vidi un, fatto a guisa di lëuto,
pur ch'elli avesse avuta l'anguinaia
51   tronca da l'altro che l'uomo ha forcuto.

La grave idropesì, che sì dispaia
le membra con l'omor che mal converte,
54   che 'l viso non risponde a la ventraia,

faceva lui tener le labbra aperte
come l'etico fa, che per la sete
57   l'un verso 'l mento e l'altro in sù rinverte.

The one came at Capocchio, set its tusks
into his neck, then dragged him
30   so his belly scraped the rock-hard ground.

And the Aretine, who stood there, trembling,
said to me: 'That demon's Gianni Schicchi,
33   and in his rabid rage he mauls the others.'

'Oh,' I said to him, 'so may that other not fix
its teeth in you, be kind enough to tell me
36   just who it is before it runs away.'

And he answered: 'That is the ancient soul
of wicked Myrrha, who became enamored
39   of her father with more than lawful love.

'She contrived to sin with him
by taking on another person's shape,
42   as did that other, eager to decamp,

'to gain the queen mule of the herd,
take on the shape of Buoso Donati,
45   drawing up a will and giving it due form.'

When those two frenzied shades, on whom
I'd fixed my eyes, had hurried off,
48   I turned to look at others born for sorrow.

One I saw, fashioned like a lute—
had he been sundered at the groin
51   from the joining where a man goes forked.

The heavy dropsy, which afflicts the body
with its ill-digesting humor
54   so that the face and belly do not match,

forced his lips to draw apart
as a person parched with hectic fever curls
57   one lip to his chin and twists the other up.

"O voi che sanz' alcuna pena siete,
e non so io perché, nel mondo gramo,"
60   diss' elli a noi, "guardate e attendete

a la miseria del maestro Adamo;
io ebbi, vivo, assai di quel ch'i' volli,
63   e ora, lasso!, un gocciol d'acqua bramo.

Li ruscelletti che d'i verdi colli
del Casentin discendon giuso in Arno,
66   faccendo i lor canali freddi e molli,

sempre mi stanno innanzi, e non indarno,
ché l'imagine lor vie più m'asciuga
69   che 'l male ond' io nel volto mi discarno.

La rigida giustizia che mi fruga
tragge cagion del loco ov' io peccai
72   a metter più li miei sospiri in fuga.

Ivi è Romena, là dov' io falsai
la lega suggellata del Batista;
75   per ch'io il corpo sù arso lasciai.

Ma s'io vedessi qui l'anima trista
di Guido o d'Alessandro o di lor frate,
78   per Fonte Branda non darei la vista.

Dentro c'è l'una già, se l'arrabbiate
ombre che vanno intorno dicon vero;
81   ma che mi val, c'ho le membra legate?

S'io fossi pur di tanto ancor leggero
ch'i' potessi in cent' anni andare un'oncia,
84   io sarei messo già per lo sentiero,

cercando lui tra questa gente sconcia,
con tutto ch'ella volge undici miglia,
87   e men d'un mezzo di traverso non ci ha.

'O you who go unpunished here—I know not why—
through this world of misery,'
60   he said, 'behold and then consider

'the suffering of Master Adam.
Alive, I had in plenty all I wanted.
63   And now I crave a single drop of water!

'The streams that, in the Casentino,
run down along green hillsides to the Arno,
66   keeping their channels cool and moist,

'flow before my eyes forever, and not in vain,
because their image makes me thirst still more
69   than does the malady that wastes my features.

'The rigid justice that torments me
employs the landscape where I sinned
72   to make my sighs come faster.

'In those parts lies Romena, where I forged
the coinage stamped with John the Baptist.
75   For that I left my body burned above.

'If I could only see down here the wretched souls
of Guido, Alessandro, or their brother,
78   I'd not give up that sight for Fonte Branda.

'One of them is here with us already,
if the furious shades who move about don't lie.
81   What good is that to me whose limbs are bound?

'If I were only light enough to budge
a single inch each hundred years,
84   I would by now have started on my way

'to seek him out in this pit's bloated shapes,
even though it runs eleven miles around
87   and spreads not less than half a mile across.

Io son per lor tra sì fatta famiglia;
e’ m’indussero a batter li fiorini
90   ch’avevan tre carati di mondiglia.”

E io a lui: “Chi son li due tapini
che fumman come man bagnate ’l verno,
93   giacendo stretti a’ tuoi destri confini?”

“Qui li trovai—e poi volta non dierno—,”
rispuose, “quando piovvi in questo greppo,
96   e non credo che dieno in sempiterno.

L’una è la falsa ch’accusò Gioseppo;
l’altr’ è ’l falso Sinon greco di Troia:
99   per febbre aguta gittan tanto leppo.”

E l’un di lor, che si recò a noia
forse d’esser nomato sì oscuro,
102   col pugno li percosse l’epa croia.

Quella sonò come fosse un tamburo;
e mastro Adamo li percosse il volto
105   col braccio suo, che non parve men duro,

dicendo a lui: “Ancor che mi sia tolto
lo muover per le membra che son gravi,
108   ho io il braccio a tal mestiere sciolto.”

Ond’ ei rispuose: “Quando tu andavi
al fuoco, non l’avei tu così presto;
111   ma sì e più l’avei quando coniavi.”

E l’idropico: “Tu di’ ver di questo:
ma tu non fosti sì ver testimonio
114   là ’ve del ver fosti a Troia richesto.”

“S’io dissi falso, e tu falsasti il conio,”
disse Sinon; “e son qui per un fallo,
117   e tu per più ch’alcun altro demonio!”

'It is their fault that I have such companions,
for it was they who made me strike the florins
90   that held three carats' worth of dross.'

And I to him: 'Who are these two wretches
who steam as wet hands do in winter
93   and lie so very near you on your right?'

'I found them when I rained into this trough,'
he said, 'and even then they did not move about,
96   nor do I think they will for all eternity.

'One is the woman who lied accusing Joseph,
the other is false Sinon, the lying Greek from Troy.
99   Putrid fever makes them reek with such a stench.'

And one of them, who took offense, perhaps
at being named so vilely, hit him
102   with a fist right on his rigid paunch.

It boomed out like a drum. Then Master Adam,
whose arm seemed just as sturdy,
105   used it, striking Sinon in the face,

saying: 'Although I cannot move about
because my legs are heavy,
108   my arm is loose enough for such a task.'

To which the other answered: 'When they put you
to the fire, your arm was not so nimble,
111   though it was quick enough when you were coining.'

And the dropsied one: 'Well, that is true,
but you were hardly such a truthful witness
114   when you were asked to tell the truth at Troy.'

'If I spoke falsely, you falsified the coin,'
said Sinon, 'and I am here for one offense alone,
117   but you for more than any other devil!'

"Ricorditi, spergiuro, del cavallo,"
rispuose quel ch'avëa infiata l'epa;
120 "e sieti reo che tutto il mondo sallo!"

"E te sia rea la sete onde ti crepa,"
disse 'l Greco, "la lingua, e l'acqua marcia
123 che 'l ventre innanzi a li occhi sì t'assiepa!"

Allora il monetier: "Così si squarcia
la bocca tua per tuo mal come suole;
126 ché s'i' ho sete e omor mi rinfarcia,

tu hai l'arsura e 'l capo che ti duole,
e per leccar lo specchio di Narcisso,
129 non vorresti a 'nvitar molte parole."

Ad ascoltarli er' io del tutto fisso,
quando 'l maestro mi disse: "Or pur mira,
132 che per poco che teco non mi risso!"

Quand' io 'l senti' a me parlar con ira,
volsimi verso lui con tal vergogna,
135 ch'ancor per la memoria mi si gira.

Qual è colui che suo dannaggio sogna,
che sognando desidera sognare,
138 sì che quel ch'è, come non fosse, agogna,

tal mi fec' io, non possendo parlare,
che disïava scusarmi, e scusava
141 me tuttavia, e nol mi credea fare.

"Maggior difetto men vergogna lava,"
disse 'l maestro, "che 'l tuo non è stato;
144 però d'ogne trestizia ti disgrava.

E fa ragion ch'io ti sia sempre allato,
se più avvien che fortuna t'accoglia
dove sien genti in simigliante piato:
148 ché voler ciò udire è bassa voglia."

'You perjurer, keep the horse in mind,'
replied the sinner with the swollen paunch,
120   'and may it pain you that the whole world knows.'

'And may you suffer from the thirst,' the Greek replied,
'that cracks your tongue, and from the fetid humor
123   that turns your belly to a hedge before your eyes!'

Then the forger: 'And so, as usual,
your mouth gapes open from your fever.
126   If I am thirsty, and swollen by this humor,

'you have your hot spells and your aching head.
For you to lick the mirror of Narcissus
129   would not take much by way of invitation.'

I was all intent in listening to them,
when the master said: 'Go right on looking
132   and it is I who'll quarrel with you.'

When I heard him speak to me in anger
I turned and faced him with a shame
135   that circles in my memory even now.

As a man who dreams that he is being harmed
and, even as he dreams, hopes he is dreaming,
138   longing for what is, as though it weren't—

so it was with me, deprived of speech:
I longed to seek his pardon—and all the while
141   I did so without knowing that I did.

'Less shame would cleanse a greater fault than yours,'
my master said, 'and that is why
144   you may set down the load of such remorse.

'Do not forget I'm always at your side
should it fall out again that fortune take you
where people are in wrangles such as this.
148   For the wish to hear such things is base.'

1–12.   This is the first of two lengthy classical opening similes derived from the third, fourth, and thirteenth books of Ovid's *Metamorphoses*. Dante's classical material in this first sally involves the matter of Thebes, his favorite example of the "city of destruction" in ancient times. Juno, jealous of Semele, daughter of Cadmus, founder of Thebes, takes out her wrath on the city by destroying Semele herself (only referred to indirectly here in v. 3) and her sister, Ino, the consort of Athamas, king of Orchomenus. Juno's revenge in this second instance is achieved by making Athamas go mad. In his distemper he kills his son Learchus, thus causing Ino to leap with the other (Melicertes) into the sea (see *Metam.* IV.512–530).

13–21.   The second tale is related to Troy, that other classical "city of destruction." After the fall of the city, the widowed queen, Hecuba, was, according to Ovid's account in his thirteenth book, carried off by the Greeks. When they stopped in Thrace, she witnessed the sacrifice of her daugher Polyxena on the tomb of Achilles and then, when she had gone to the sea for water to prepare the corpse for burial, found the body of her son Polydorus, murdered by the Thracian king, Polymnestor, washed up on the shore beside her. At this she went mad, and began barking like a dog (*Metam.* XIII.404–406). Finally, she killed Polymnestor, according to Ovid, by tearing out his eyes.

22–27.   The completion of each opening similetic comparison is only now put forward. Reduced to madness, Athamas kills his own child, Hecuba, the king who had killed her son (*Metam.* XIII.558–564). Nonetheless, they are less savage than the two bestial forms that now appear.

28–33.   One of these two sinners attacks and bears off Capocchio, who had held our attention at the end of the last canto. This new shade is thus associated with Athamas, acting out his maddened rage, and is identified by Griffolino, the other sinner we met in Canto XXIX, as Gianni Schicchi. Where Capocchio had been scratching himself, he now gets his scabrous belly scraped by the ground as he is dragged off.

Gianni Schicchi was a member of the Florentine Cavalcanti family and was renowned for his ability to impersonate others. He was dead by 1280. Commentators speculate that Dante would have heard tell of his impersonations while he was still a boy. One particular case is detailed a few lines farther on (vv. 42–45).

37–41. Griffolino explains to Dante that the other furious shade is that of Ovid's Myrrha (*Metam.* X.298–502). She, daughter of Cinyras, king of Cyprus, disguised herself, abetted by her nurse, as a willing young woman (her mother being absent) in order to sleep with her father. In the development of the canto, she is at least formally in parallel with Hecuba (since Gianni plays the part of Athamas), but beyond their common feminine savagery there is little to associate them.

We may speculate that all the Ovidian material of this canto has marginalized Virgil. Indeed, he does not speak a word until v. 131. This is the longest silence on his part since he entered the poem in its first canto; it is 169 lines since he last spoke at XXIX.101. For preceding long Virgilian silences see *Inferno* V.112–VI.93; XV.1–99; XVI.18–121. In two cantos he speaks only a single verse: *Inferno* XV.99 and XXVII.33. However, the longest Virgilian silences in the poem await us. *Inferno* XXXII is the first canto in the poem in which he does not speak a word (and he is silent between XXXI.134 and XXXIII.106, a total of 255 verses); *Purgatorio* XXIV is the second and the longest (with Virgil silent between XXIII.15 and XXV.17, a total of 288 verses).

42–45. The story of Gianni Schicchi's impersonation of the dead and testamentless Buoso Donati in order to help the surviving Schicchi family members get an inheritance they feared they would otherwise lose delighted the early commentators, who take pleasure in repeating it. Gianni's payment for himself was to will himself the best animal—the lead mule—of Buoso's herd. Puccini's opera, bearing his name as its title, continues to purvey Gianni's tale.

46–48. Reading the last canto for the first time, we may have assumed that the tenth *bolgia* was devoted to detailing the punishment of a single form of falsification, alchemical deceptions, punished in a single way, by the scabs that cover the bodies of these leprous sinners (see note to *Inf.* XXIX.58–66). After reading Canto XXX we have learned that there is a total of four species of falsification, each punished by a particular disease. The three species in this canto are as follows: impersonators (hydrophobia), counterfeiters of coin (dropsy), perjurors (fever). Here we come to the second in this group, the counterfeiters.

49–51.   For the musical elements in the description of this sinner (he will find a name, Master Adam, at v. 61), see Iannucci (Iann.1995.1). The lute, which resembles "a pregnant guitar" (as a waggish student of music once insisted) was, in Dante's time, generally regarded as a "serious" instrument, like David's harp, and thus associated with the "right" kind of musical performance. Iannucci points out (p. 114) that this is the only stringed instrument mentioned in hell. Adam, who *looks like* a lute, ends up sounding like a drum (v. 103), an instrument, as Iannucci argues, associated with such lower forms of musical amusement as public spectacles. For the symbolic inversions in the musicality of this scene see Heilbronn (Heil.1983.1).

52–57.   Dropsy, in which a main symptom is the retention of water, which distends parts of the body, was also characterized by terrible thirst.

58–61.   Resentfully noting Dante's lack of punishment, the sinner identifies himself. Master Adam, according to some commentators an Englishman, was in the employ of the Conti Guidi of Romena (in the Casentino, not far from Florence). (We will hear more of this family in vv. 73–87.) They convinced him to falsify the gold florin, stamped with the image of John the Baptist, the patron of Florence, by pouring gold of only 21 (and not 24) carats, a carat being one twenty-fourth of an ounce. On the symbolic importance of money, as it is reflected in this canto, see Shoaf (Shoa.1983.1), pp. 39–48. Adam's crime was discovered and he was burned alive in Florence in 1281.

His name almost inevitably reminds the reader of his namesake, the first sinner. For discussion of the way in which this "new Adam" is in fact a modern version of the first one, see Mussetter (Muss.1978.1).

As many note, the language here again reflects that found in the Lamentations of Jeremiah. See note to *Inferno* XXVIII.130–138.

64–69.   Adam's memories of "the green hills of home" torment him, only increasing his punishment. What for the reader is a moment of pastoral escape from hellish thoughts is for him torment. For a Virgilian source of the image see *Eclogue* X.42, describing "cool streams and gentle meadows."

76–78.   Envy, often marked by the desire to see those who are well off suffering, rules Adam's heart. He would rather see his employers punished than slake his thirst. Fonte Branda, according to the early commentators, is the famous spring in Siena. Later writers have argued for another, of the same name, in the vicinity of Romena. However, that the earliest commentators do not refer to it probably seconds the notion that the more famous one is referred to here.

79–81.   Guido had died in 1281 and news of his location in this *bolgia* has reached Adam through one of the rabid impersonators who range the territory.

82–87.   Adam's "impossible dream" is to be able to move an inch in a hundred years—and even that is beyond him. Were it not, Manfredi Porena did the math and calculated that, at even this speed, it would take him 700,000 years to find Guido.

That this *bolgia* is half the circumference and breadth of the last one has given those who would like to establish the exact size of Dante's hell the two coordinates they think they need. Such calculation is a temptation to be avoided. See the note to *Inferno* XXIX.8–9. Adam undercalculates the diameter, which is 3.5 miles, considerably. We reflect that his dubious measurement is the result of his dropsied bulk and consequent laziness. A half mile is hundreds of thousands of years of (for him impossible) movement.

88–90.   Adam's hatred of the Conti Guidi is understandable; his placing the entire blame on them for his own misdeeds is typical of certain sinners, always finding a cause for their failures in the hearts and minds of others.

97–99.   Adam first identifies Potiphar's wife (Gen. 39:6–20), who, having failed to seduce Joseph, accused *him* before Pharaoh of attempting to seduce *her*. Then he identifies Sinon (as he is known from the second book of the *Aeneid*), whose misrepresentations led to the destruction of Troy. Both suffer from high fever, seen not as a symptom of other ailments, but as a disease in itself; both worked treacherously against a "chosen people," the Hebrews and the Trojans.

100–103.   Angered by the words of Master Adam, Sinon's first gesture is to strike him on his taut paunch, which booms like a drum. This act begins a series of exchanged insults, begun and ended by Adam. Until the last in the series, each one occupies a single tercet (Adam's final flourish will occupy two). As many who have written on this scene have reflected, Dante's technique here is modeled on the exchange of poetic insult found in the genre called *tenzone*. See note to *Inferno* VIII.31–39.

115.   Not only are these exchanges generally reflective of the tradition of the *tenzone*, this particular verse has been seen (e.g., Casini/Barbi's commentary in 1921) as rehearsing a particular *tenzone*, one between Cecco Angiolieri and Dante (whose sonnet, apparently the occasion for Cecco's, is lost). Cecco's ("Dante Alighieri, s'i' so' bon begolardo") begins roughly as follows:

> Dante Alighieri, if I'm a foolish bard,
> I can feel your lance just behind my back;
> If I'm out for dinner, you're there for a snack;
> If I chew the fat, you but suck the lard.

118.   For Virgil's presentation of Sinon's lie see *Aeneid* II.152–159.

126–129.   Adam's last words remind Sinon that, even if the counterfeiter is suffering from dropsy, his accuser has got a case of fever. His last *riposte* jibes at Sinon's thirst, which would lead him to the "mirror of Narcissus," i.e., a pool that would reflect his true, hideous self—which image he would destroy out of thirst, in a sort of grubby version of the original myth. As Brownlee pointed out, this reference begins the "Narcissus program" in the *Commedia*, which includes references to the myth in a number of passages, and in all cantos numbered XXX (Brow.1978.1), pp. 205–6.

131–135.   Virgil's harsh rebuke here seems on the mark, certainly to Dante himself. Dante's emphatic acceptance of it stands in clear contrast to his rejection of the similar rebuke in the last canto (*Inf.* XXIX.4–12), where Virgil had not understood the cause of his staring into the ninth *bolgia*. Here Dante has become an interested bystander (rather than a man with a mission), enjoying the back-and-forth argument between the two sinners (just as do we) because it is both violent and amusing.

136–141.   This is a remarkable simile (or "pseudo-simile" on the grounds that it "compares a thing, person, or emotion with itself"—in the words of Eric Mallin (see Mall.1984.1), p. 15. (Mallin discusses this particular simile, pp. 28–31.) Tozer's prior remark in his commentary (1901) is of interest:

"This is a conspicuous instance of an interesting class of similes—viz. those drawn from mental experiences—of which there are as many as thirty in the *Divine Comedy*." The simile is difficult enough that a prose paraphrase may help to make its point clearer: "As a man dreams of being harmed and of wishing he were only dreaming (which he in fact is), so did I, unable to speak, feel ashamed because I could not excuse myself—while all the while my blushing was doing just that for me."

142–148.   Virgil accepts Dante's unvoiced apology and warns him against future backsliding of this kind. Berthier, in his gloss, cites from St. Bernard, *De ordine vitae,* from a passage, he says, located "before its middle": "audire quod turpe est, pudori maximo est" (it is most shameful to give ear to vile things).

INFERNO XXXI

Una medesma lingua pria mi morse,
sì che mi tinse l'una e l'altra guancia,
3   e poi la medicina mi riporse;

così od' io che solea far la lancia
d'Achille e del suo padre esser cagione
6   prima di trista e poi di buona mancia.

Noi demmo il dosso al misero vallone
su per la ripa che 'l cinge dintorno,
9   attraversando sanza alcun sermone.

Quiv' era men che notte e men che giorno,
sì che 'l viso m'andava innanzi poco;
12   ma io senti' sonare un alto corno,

tanto ch'avrebbe ogne tuon fatto fioco,
che, contra sé la sua via seguitando,
15   dirizzò li occhi miei tutti ad un loco.

Dopo la dolorosa rotta, quando
Carlo Magno perdé la santa gesta,
18   non sonò sì terribilmente Orlando.

Poco portäi in là volta la testa,
che me parve veder molte alte torri;
21   ond' io: "Maestro, dì, che terra è questa?"

Ed elli a me: "Però che tu trascorri
per le tenebre troppo da la lungi,
24   avvien che poi nel maginare abborri.

Tu vedrai ben, se tu là ti congiungi,
quanto 'l senso s'inganna di lontano;
27   però alquanto più te stesso pungi."

The same tongue that had stung me
so that both my cheeks turned red,
3 had also brought my cure,

just as the spear of Achilles and his father—
so I have heard it told—would be the cause
6 first of a painful, then a welcome, gift.

We turned our backs upon that dismal valley,
first climbing up the bank that circles it,
9 then crossing over, while speaking not a word.

Here it was less than night and less than day—
I could not see too far ahead.
12 But I heard a horn-blast that would have made

the loudest thunderclap seem faint.
To find its source I turned my eyes
15 back to the place from which the din had come.

After the woeful rout when Charlemagne
had lost his holy band of knights,
18 Roland did not sound so terrible a blast.

I had not looked that way for long
when I saw what seemed a range of lofty towers,
21 and I said: 'Master, tell me, what city is this?'

And he to me: 'Because you try to pierce
the darkness from too far away,
24 it follows that you err in your perception.

'When you are nearer, you will understand
how much your eyesight is deceived by distance.
27 Therefore, push yourself a little harder.'

Poi caramente mi prese per mano
e disse: "Pria che noi siam più avanti,
30   acciò che 'l fatto men ti paia strano,

sappi che non son torri, ma giganti,
e son nel pozzo intorno da la ripa
33   da l'umbilico in giuso tutti quanti."

Come quando la nebbia si dissipa,
lo sguardo a poco a poco raffigura
36   ciò che cela 'l vapor che l'aere stipa,

così forando l'aura grossa e scura,
più e più appressando ver' la sponda,
39   fuggiemi errore e crescémi paura;

però che, come su la cerchia tonda
Montereggion di torri si corona,
42   così la proda che 'l pozzo circonda

torreggiavan di mezza la persona
li orribili giganti, cui minaccia
45   Giove del cielo ancora quando tuona.

E io scorgeva già d'alcun la faccia,
le spalle e 'l petto e del ventre gran parte,
48   e per le coste giù ambo le braccia.

Natura certo, quando lasciò l'arte
di sì fatti animali, assai fé bene
51   per tòrre tali essecutori a Marte.

E s'ella d'elefanti e di balene
non si pente, chi guarda sottilmente,
54   più giusta e più discreta la ne tene;

ché dove l'argomento de la mente
s'aggiugne al mal volere e a la possa,
57   nessun riparo vi può far la gente.

Then with affection he took me by the hand
and said: 'Before we travel farther,
30   and so the fact may seem to you less strange,

'you should be told: these are not towers,
but giants and, from the navel down,
33   each stands behind the bank that rings the pit.'

As, when the mist is lifting,
little by little we discern things
36   hidden in the air made thick by fog,

so, when my eyes saw through the heavy dark
and I got nearer to the brink,
39   error left me and fear came in its place.

For, as all around her ring of walls
Monteriggioni is crowned with towers,
42   so at the cliff-edge that surrounds the pit

loomed up like towers half the body bulk
of horrifying giants, those whom Jove
45   still threatens from the heavens when he thunders.

Now I could discern the face of one,
his chest and shoulders, a portion of his paunch,
48   and, hanging at his sides, his arms.

Surely nature did well when she renounced
the craft of making creatures such as these,
51   depriving Mars of such practitioners.

If she does not repent her elephants
and whales, when one reviews the matter closely
54   she will be found more cautious and more just.

For when the power of thought
is coupled with ill will and naked force
57   there is no refuge from it for mankind.

La faccia sua mi parea lunga e grossa
come la pina di San Pietro a Roma,
60   e a sua proporzione eran l'altre ossa;

sì che la ripa, ch'era perizoma
dal mezzo in giù, ne mostrava ben tanto
63   di sovra, che di giugnere a la chioma

tre Frison s'averien dato mal vanto;
però ch'i' ne vedea trenta gran palmi
66   dal loco in giù dov' omo affibbia 'l manto.

"Raphèl maì amècche zabì almi,"
cominciò a gridar la fiera bocca,
69   cui non si convenia più dolci salmi.

E 'l duca mio ver' lui: "Anima sciocca,
tienti col corno, e con quel ti disfoga
72   quand' ira o altra passïon ti tocca!

Cércati al collo, e troverai la soga
che 'l tien legato, o anima confusa,
75   e vedi lui che 'l gran petto ti doga."

Poi disse a me: "Elli stessi s'accusa;
questi è Nembrotto per lo cui mal coto
78   pur un linguaggio nel mondo non s'usa.

Lasciànlo stare e non parliamo a vòto;
ché così è a lui ciascun linguaggio
81   come 'l suo ad altrui, ch'a nullo è noto."

Facemmo adunque più lungo vïaggio,
vòlti a sinistra; e al trar d'un balestro
84   trovammo l'altro assai più fero e maggio.

A cigner lui qual che fosse 'l maestro,
non so io dir, ma el tenea soccinto
87   dinanzi l'altro e dietro il braccio destro

His face appeared to me as long and broad
as is, in Rome, the pine cone at St. Peter's,
60   his other parts as large in like degree,

so that the bank, which hid him like an apron
from his middle downwards, still showed
63   so much of him above that quite in vain

three Frieslanders might boast of having reached
his hair. For I saw thirty spans of him
66   beneath the place where men make fast their cloaks.

'Raphèl maì amècche zabì almi,'
the savage mouth, for which no sweeter
69   psalms were fit, began to shout.

And, in response, my leader: 'You muddled soul,
stick to your horn! Vent yourself with that
72   when rage or other passion takes you.

'Search at your neck, you creature of confusion,
and you will find the rope that holds the horn
75   aslant your mammoth chest.'

Then he to me: 'He is his own accuser.
This is Nimrod, because of whose vile plan
78   the world no longer speaks a single tongue.

'Let us leave him and not waste our speech,
for every language is to him as his
81   to others, and his is understood by none.'

Then, turning to our left, we continued
with our journey. A bowshot farther on
84   we found the next one, bigger and more savage.

Now who had plied his craft to bind him so
I cannot say, but his right arm
87   was bound behind him, the other one in front,

d'una catena che 'l tenea avvinto
dal collo in giù, sì che 'n su lo scoperto
90   si ravvolgëa infino al giro quinto.

"Questo superbo volle esser esperto
di sua potenza contra 'l sommo Giove,"
93   disse 'l mio duca, "ond' elli ha cotal merto.

Fïalte ha nome, e fece le gran prove
quando i giganti fer paura a' dèi;
96   le braccia ch'el menò, già mai non move."

E io a lui: "S'esser puote, io vorrei
che de lo smisurato Brïareo
99   esperïenza avesser li occhi mei."

Ond' ei rispuose: "Tu vedrai Anteo
presso di qui che parla ed è disciolto,
102   che ne porrà nel fondo d'ogne reo.

Quel che tu vuo' veder, più là è molto
ed è legato e fatto come questo,
105   salvo che più feroce par nel volto."

Non fu tremoto già tanto rubesto,
che scotesse una torre così forte,
108   come Fïalte a scuotersi fu presto.

Allor temett' io più che mai la morte,
e non v'era mestier più che la dotta,
111   s'io non avessi viste le ritorte.

Noi procedemmo più avante allotta,
e venimmo ad Anteo, che ben cinque alle,
114   sanza la testa, uscia fuor de la grotta.

"O tu che ne la fortunata valle
che fece Scipïon di gloria reda,
117   quand' Anibàl co' suoi diede le spalle,

by chains that from the neck down held him fixed.
They wound five times around his bulk
90   on the part of him that we could see.

'This prideful spirit chose to test his strength
against almighty Jove,' my leader said,
93   'and this is his reward.

'He is Ephialtes. He joined the great assault
when giants put the gods in fear.
96   Those arms he brandished he can move no more.'

And I to him: 'If it is allowed,
I'd like to see with my own eyes
99   Briareus and his immeasurable bulk.'

He replied: 'It is Antaeus you shall see.
He is close by, he speaks, he is not fettered.
102   And he shall set us down into the very depth of sin.

'The one you want to see is farther on,
in fetters also, shaped like this one here,
105   except that from his looks he seems more fierce.'

Never did mighty earthquake shake a tower
with such great speed and force
108   as Ephialtes shook himself at that.

Then more than ever I was afraid of dying:
my fear alone would have sufficed to bring it on,
111   had I not noted how tightly he was bound.

Going farther on, we came upon Antaeus.
Without the added measure of his head,
114   he stood a full five ells above the pit.

'O you, who—in the fateful valley
that made Scipio an heir to glory,
117   when Hannibal with all his men displayed their backs—

recasti già mille leon per preda,
e che, se fossi stato a l'alta guerra
120 de' tuoi fratelli, ancor par che si creda

ch'avrebber vinto i figli de la terra:
mettine giù, e non ten vegna schifo,
123 dove Cocito la freddura serra.

Non ci fare ire a Tizio né a Tifo:
questi può dar di quel che qui si brama;
126 però ti china e non torcer lo grifo.

Ancor ti può nel mondo render fama,
ch'el vive, e lunga vita ancor aspetta
129 se 'nnanzi tempo grazia a sé nol chiama."

Così disse 'l maestro; e quelli in fretta
le man distese, e prese 'l duca mio,
132 ond' Ercule sentì già grande stretta.

Virgilio, quando prender si sentio,
disse a me: "Fatti qua, sì ch'io ti prenda";
135 poi fece sì ch'un fascio era elli e io.

Qual pare a riguardar la Carisenda
sotto 'l chinato, quando un nuvol vada
138 sovr' essa sì, ched ella incontro penda:

tal parve Antëo a me che stava a bada
di vederlo chinare, e fu tal ora
141 ch'i' avrei voluto ir per altra strada.

Ma lievemente al fondo che divora
Lucifero con Giuda, ci sposò;
né, sì chinato, li fece dimora,
145 e come albero in nave si levò.

'you, who took as prey a thousand lions,
and by whose strength, it seems some do believe,
120 had you been at the war on Heaven with your brethren,

'the sons of earth would have prevailed—
pray set us down, do not disdain to do so,
123 upon Cocytus, shackled by the cold.

'Don't make us go to Tityus or Typhon.
This man can give what everyone here longs for.
126 Therefore bend down and do not curl your lip.

'He still can make you famous in the world,
because he lives, and hopes for years of living,
129 if Grace does not recall him sooner than his time.'

Thus spoke the master. The other was quick
to reach out with his hands—the mighty grip
132 once felt by Hercules—and seized my guide.

Virgil, when he felt himself secured, said:
'Here, let me take hold of you!'
135 Then he made a single bundle of himself and me.

As when one sees the tower called Garisenda
from underneath its leaning side, and then a cloud
138 passes over and it seems to lean the more,

thus did Antaeus seem to my fixed gaze
as I watched him bend—that was indeed a time
141 I wished that I had gone another road.

Even so, he set us gently on the bottom
that swallows Lucifer with Judas.
Nor in stooping did he linger
145 but, like a ship's mast rising, so he rose.

1–6.   The reader—at least on a second reading—may admire Dante's insistence on his authorial freedom in not marking the border between Malebolge and the ninth Circle at the canto's edge. Instead, with another classical simile (and Momigliano notes the large numbers of classical allusions sprinkled through Cantos XXVIII–XXXI), he delays the transition until v. 7.

Virgil's rebuke in Canto XXX.130–132 had both caused Dante embarrassment and supplied the antidote: his blush of shame (which reassured Virgil of his charge's moral development). The most likely source for Dante's reference to the lance of Achilles, which had the magical property of curing with a second touch the very wound that it had caused, is Ovid, *Remedia Amoris* I.43–44: "The Pelian spear [in Dante's understanding, the spear of Peleus?] that once had wounded his enemy, the son of Hercules [Telephus], also brought comfort to the wound," a tale presented as being of somewhat dubious provenance, as another one of those pagan yarns ("so I have heard it told"). For some of the problems associated with this text see Singleton's commentary. Ovid in fact refers to the spear given by Chiron, the centaur (see *Inf.* XII.71), who lived on Mt. Pelion, to Achilles himself. At least one other medieval poet before Dante, Bernard de Ventadour, had referred to the weapon as belonging first to Peleus. Dante knew that Peleus was the father of Achilles, from, if nowhere else, Statius's *Achilleid* (I.90).

7–13.   The departure from Malebolge and arrival in the penumbral murk of the last *bolgia* is anything but dramatic. Here nothing is distinct until Dante hears a horn-blast. We shall eventually learn that this is sounded by Nimrod (v. 77).

16–18.   The reference to the *Chanson de Roland*, a text that, Cecchetti reminds us, Dante knew in a form probably most unlike anything we read today (Cecc.1990.1, p. 409), is the reader's first sure sign that we are in the realm of treachery, not mere "simple fraud." As Scott points out (Scot.1985.1), pp. 29–30, for most medieval readers there was perhaps no worse betrayal than that of Ganelon (punished in the next canto, XXXII.122), whose treacherous act, in 778, was directed against Charlemagne, the future emperor (crowned in Rome on Christmas Day in 800) and future saint (canonized in 1165, exactly one hundred years before Dante's birth); he betrayed Charlemagne's rear guard to the Saracen invaders. Roland blew Oliphant, his horn, too late to bring back Charlemagne and his troops, miles distant, in time to save his part of the army, all of whom were slaughtered at Roncesvalles by the Saracens. Reminded of that blast, we know we are among the treacherous.

The parallels set up by the scene are interesting. If Nimrod plays the role of Roland, his horn-blast is timely enough to prevent the entrance of the "invaders," Dante and Virgil, but equally ineffectual. There is an "emperor" in this scene, too, "lo 'mperador del doloroso regno" (the emperor of the woeful kingdom), Satan (XXXIV.28). And Nimrod's blast is meant to warn the Satanic forces of the advent of the enemy, as Roland's was. Who is the Ganelon of the scene? Antaeus, who will "betray" his lord by helping Dante and Virgil descend into Satan's stronghold. If all these inverse parallels work, we have to add another: Dante and Virgil are the Saracens in this series of analogies by contrary.

19–27.   Dante's confusion, as he peers through the mist, causes him to take giants for towers. For the medieval works on optics that lie behind the description of Dante's misperceptions here, see Dronke (Dron.1986.1), p. 36.

28–33.   Virgil, as gently and reassuringly as he can, prepares Dante to behold the giants. As the guardians of this zone of hell, as the most proximate servants of Satan, as it were, the giants are seen to represent the sin of pride. That is how Pietro di Dante saw them centuries ago: "Gigantes figurative pro superbis accipiuntur" (The giants are to be figuratively understood as those who are prideful).

34–39.   The second simile of the canto is without classical decoration. It involves improving sight, whether because a mist gradually lifts or because a walker gets closer to the indistinct object he examines from afar.

40–45.   The third simile compares the looming giants with the towers of the fortified town, Monteriggione, a Sienese outpost situated on the road between Florence and Siena. In the thirteenth century its defensive walls were supplemented by fourteen towers, each over sixty feet in height.

For the attempt of the giants to overthrow the Olympian gods, referred to obliquely here, see note at vv. 94–96.

49–57.   Dante's meditation on the handiwork of Nature, God's child (see *Inf.* XI.99–105), can only be taken seriously, by a modern reader, when one considers that, according to Genesis 6:4, once "giants walked the earth." Nature, as implementer of God's design, is "more cautious and more just" because she now fashions her largest creatures without intelligence, thus better protecting humans.

58–66.   The anatomy of the giants, visible only above their waists, since the bank forms a sort of apron, or "fig leaf" (*perizoma*—see the word in Gen. 3:7) for them, is described from the head down, to their shoulders ("where men make fast their cloaks"), to their waists. The giant's head, which resembles the bronze pinecone Dante might well have seen in Rome in 1301 in the Vatican, is about eleven feet in height. Three Frieslanders, reputed to be among the tallest of men, standing on one another's shoulders, would have reached merely from the bank to the bottom of his locks, some twenty-two feet, if we allow the topmost Frieslander to reach up with an arm toward that hair. This leaves a foot or two of neck unmeasured. Further, Dante himself, measuring by eye, thinks that the distance from the bank to the giant's shoulders is some thirty spans (a span equals the space covered by a hand spread open), also some twenty-two feet. Dante indicates that the giant is about thirty-five feet tall measured from the waist, his midpoint, and thus some seventy feet in all. One senses his amusement at the reader who will do this calculation.

67.   The garbled speech that issues from Nimrod's mouth has caused a veritable orgy of interpretive enthusiasm. (The reader should be aware that we are not at all sure about what these words looked like when they left Dante's pen; as nonsense, they may have caused more scribal confusion than others. Hence, any attempt to "construe" them should be extremely cautious, which has certainly not been the case.) Dante has variously been assumed to have known more Aramaic or Arabic or Hebrew than he likely could have, and to have deployed this arcane knowledge in creating a meaningful phrase. For a review of various attempts to make these words "make sense," with bibliography, see Ettore Caccia, "Raphèl maì amècche zabì almi," *ED,* vol. 4, 1973. And see the note to *Inferno* VII.1, where Plutus also speaks five garbled words. While it is nearly certainly true that we are not meant to be able to understand Nimrod's words (that is the point Virgil makes, after all), it is nonetheless likely that they, like those of Plutus, should be seen as corrupted versions of words that do make sense. "Raphel" can hardly fail to remind us of the name of the archangel

Raphael, "maì" seems a version of the Italian word for "ever" (or "never"), "amècche" could be a series of simple words (*a me che*: "to," "me," "that"), "zabì" sounds like a slide into dialectical speech, and "almi" is perfectly good Italian for "holy," "divine." The point is not that these words make any sense; it is rather that they do not. Like Plutus's outburst, they are meant to be understood as corrupted speech. And, as was true in that case, they are intended to keep these intruders out of the place this guardian has been posted to guard. See Chiari (Chia.1967.1), p. 1107, who argues that Nimrod's cry is the product of anger and menace common to all infernal guardians.

These five words may refer to St. Paul's desire that the Corinthians speak five words with understanding rather than ten thousand in tongues (I Cor. 14:19), as was first noted by Pézard (Peza.1958.1), p. 59; he was supported by one commentator, Giacalone, in 1968, and then by Kleinhenz (Klei.1974.1), p. 283n. Hollander (Holl.1992.1) attempts to take this 'program' into passages in *Purgatorio* and *Paradiso*.

For the importance to Dante of St. Paul, who does not appear as a personage in the *Commedia*, see Angelo Penna and Giovanni Fallani, "Paolo, santo," *ED*, vol. 4, 1973; Giorgio Petrocchi (Petr.1988.1).

69.   That Dante refers to this fallen speech as "psalms" *(salmi)*, even negatively, reminds the reader that Nimrod's words reflect the divine origin of language, if we hear it now in its postlapsarian condition.

70–81.   Virgil's stinging remarks to Nimrod (which are in fact quite amusing) have drawn puzzled responses from some commentators. Why does Virgil address Nimrod, since the giant cannot understand him? Or are his words meant only for Dante? Some complain that it is like speaking to an animal for him to speak to this creature. Precisely so. And we humans do this all the time. It matters not at all that Nimrod cannot understand. The reader can.

Virgil treats Nimrod like a drunk at a New Year's Eve party, telling him to give over attempts at speech and content himself with blowing his horn. Referring to the giant's rage, he underlines the oppositional intent of his outburst; calling him "creature of confusion" *(anima confusa)*, he probably alludes to the "confusion of tongues" that followed in the wake of the building of the Tower of Babel. Before dismissing Nimrod as unworthy of further speech, Virgil makes this association clear. In Genesis, Nimrod was not a giant, but "a mighty hunter before the Lord" (10:9). It is probably to St. Augustine, who mentions him three times in *De civitate Dei*

XVI as a giant, that we owe Dante's decision to do so as well. The building of the tower and the resultant "confusion" of language (Gen. 11:1–9) was, for Dante, one of the defining moments in the history of human language, the "linguistic fall" described there paralleling the fall of Adam and Eve. See Arno Borst (Bors.1957.1), vol. 2, pp. 869–75, for Dante's place in the history of responses to the building of the tower.

Nimrod will be referred to by name twice more in the poem (*Purg.* XII.34; *Par.* XXVI.126), so that he is mentioned once in each *cantica*. For this phenomenon, words that appear a single time in each *cantica*, see Hollander (Holl.1988.3), pp. 108–10.

84–90.   The second of the three giants whom we see in this canto (we shall hear of three others) will be identified shortly (v. 94) as Ephialtes. Unlike Nimrod, too stupid to be dangerous, this one, bigger still and far more fierce, is capable of the harm that the poet feared in vv. 55–57.

91–96.   Ephialtes was one of the giants who attempted, by piling Pelion on Ossa, to scale Olympus and overthrow the gods. He and his fellow rebels were killed by Jove at Phlegra (*Inf.* XIV.58).

97–105.   Dante wants to see Briareus because, we suppose, he has read about him in the *Aeneid* (X.565–567); he has a hundred arms and hands and breathes fire from fifty mouths and breasts. It is important to note that Virgil himself apologizes for this account: *dicunt,* he says, "or so they say," the same tactic that Dante has used when warning us against the excesses of pagan mythmaking when he imports it to his own poem (see *Inf.* XXIX.63; XXXI.4). Dante, however, wants to have some fun at his fellow poet's expense. Briareus, Virgil explains (like a host who does not want to produce a particularly embarrassing guest at a party), is *way* up ahead there, and he looks just like Ephialtes, anyway. What Dante has made his *auctor* do is to apologize for including such unbelievable rot in the divine *Aeneid*, while allowing Virgil to escape the discomfort of actually having to gaze upon the "normal," Dantean version of a proper giant, human in everything but his size. Most commentators do not perceive the humor of this moment. However, for a sense of Dante's playfulness here, see Andreoli in 1856 and Trucchi in 1936.

Not only is Antaeus a "normal" giant (we see what Dante has gotten us to assent to by overruling "excessive" gigantism—an acceptance of "normal" gigantism), but he is a relatively friendly one, unfettered, we assume, because he did not fight against the gods at Phlegra. The son of Neptune and Gea, Earth, Antaeus was invincible in combat so long as he remained in contact with earth. Hercules, discovering this, was able to hold him free from the earth and kill him, crushing him in his hands. On Dante's treatment of Antaeus, see Rabuse (Rabu.1961.1).

108.   Ephialtes is angry, either because he thinks Virgil and Dante will have more success with Antaeus or because Virgil has said that Briareus looks even meaner than he.

113–114.   The size of Antaeus's upper body, not including his head, is seven ells, about twenty-two feet, thus roughly the same as Nimrod's.

115–124.   Virgil begins by referring to the Battle of Zama in 202 B.C., where Scipio Africanus defeated Hannibal (revenge for the Battle of Cannae in 216—see *Inf.* XXVIII.9–11), thus successfully concluding the second Punic War, which had begun so badly. Needless to say, this (for Dante and any Roman-minded reader) great victory is hardly of a comparable magnitude to that of a giant capturing a lot of lions. Thus the reference to Zama offers a backhanded compliment to Antaeus, who killed his lions in the same place that Scipio defeated Hannibal.

   Virgil finds himself in a difficult situation. As was not the case with Ulysses, when Virgil could boast that he had written of his exploits (even if not very favorably, he *had* at least written of the Greek hero—see *Inf.* XXVI.80–82), he has not written about Antaeus at all. To make matters worse, he *did* once mention a certain Antaeus, a soldier in Turnus's ranks, mowed down by Aeneas in his Achilles-like battlefield fury in *Aeneid* X.561. And, still worse, this mention of an Antaeus who is merely a walk-on corpse in Virgil's poem precedes by only four lines Virgil's mention of Briareus (see note to vv. 97–105). And so here is a poet who has, intrinsically at least, insulted the giant whom he now wants to cajole. What is he to do? What he does is borrow from Lucan (of course only *we* know that he is accomplishing this chronologically impossible feat) in order to praise Antaeus. It was Lucan, not Virgil, who told the tale of Antaeus the lion-killer (*Phars.* IV.601–602), and it was Lucan, not Virgil, who explicitly compared Antaeus favorably to Briareus, not to mention Typhon and Tityus (the two other giants of whom we are about to hear at v. 124). See *Pharsalia* IV.595–597. Gea had more reason to boast of this gigantic son, Antaeus, than of the others, Typhon, or Tityus, or fierce Briareus; and she was merciful to the gods when she did not set loose Antaeus on the field at Phlegra. (This detail offers the matter for Virgil's second instance of the greatness of Antaeus.) It can hardly be coincidental that all four of the giants present in Virgil's speech here are also together in Lucan's text. And so Virgil's two gestures toward Antaeus are both taken from Lucan. It is an extraordinarily amusing moment; one can imagine how Dante smiled as he composed it. Nonetheless, many of his commentators vehemently deny that this passage is ironic. It is difficult to see with what justice they do so. For what has Virgil really said to Antaeus? "You killed a lot of lions right near the place where Rome won one of its greatest military victories; you didn't fight at the battle in which your brothers were killed by the gods."

125–132. Virgil's *captatio benevolentiae* has not been successful. Antaeus still needs persuading. Dante, Virgil tells him, can do what he didn't do: make Antaeus famous. Perhaps Antaeus was a better reader of classical texts than some imagine; his lip was still curled with disdain after Virgil's praise had ended. Fame is the spur; Antaeus bends and grasps Virgil, in a benevolent replay of his own death scene, when Hercules held him in *his* hands.

136–141. The fourth and last simile of the canto refers to one of two towers (the shorter one, in fact, but the one that "leans" the most) built in Bologna in 1109 and 1110. Towers and giants have pride in common, and so the comparison is not without its moral reasons. Its visual reasons are indisputably stunning, a tower that seems to be falling because a cloud is passing over it.

142–143. For the tradition of hell as a devouring mouth, reflected in these verses, see Sonia Gentili (Gent.1997.1), pp. 177–82. And for a larger, more speculative, view, one that holds that hell is programmatically modeled on the shape of the human body (with the last Circle as the anus), see Durling (Durl.1981.1)

There has been much debate as to where the giants stand in relation to the floor of Hell. Are their feet on the floor itself or do they stand on a ledge above it? See the next canto, vv. 16–18 and the note thereto.

144–145. No one in hell sticks around after work, neither angelic messenger (*Inf.* IX.100–103) nor cooperative monster (*Inf.* XVII.133–136).

Guiniforto, in his comment to this passage, suggests that Dante must have had a small boat in mind, the mast of which may be raised very quickly.

An entire canto has been devoted to a transition from one circle to the next. We realize, once all the exuberant poetic play has stopped, that we are on the lowest point in Dante's universe, the floor of hell. From here, everywhere is up.

INFERNO XXXII

S'ïo avessi le rime aspre e chiocce,
come si converrebbe al tristo buco
3   sovra 'l qual pontan tutte l'altre rocce,

io premerei di mio concetto il suco
più pienamente; ma perch'io non l'abbo,
6   non sanza tema a dicer mi conduco;

ché non è impresa da pigliare a gabbo
discriver fondo a tutto l'universo,
9   né da lingua che chiami mamma o babbo.

Ma quelle donne aiutino il mio verso
ch'aiutaro Anfïone a chiuder Tebe,
12   sì che dal fatto il dir non sia diverso.

Oh sovra tutte mal creata plebe
che stai nel loco onde parlare è duro,
15   mei foste state qui pecore o zebe!

Come noi fummo giù nel pozzo scuro
sotto i piè del gigante assai più bassi,
18   e io mirava ancora a l'alto muro,

dicere udi'mi: "Guarda come passi:
va sì, che tu non calchi con le piante
21   le teste de' fratei miseri lassi."

Per ch'io mi volsi, e vidimi davante
e sotto i piedi un lago che per gelo
24   avea di vetro e non d'acqua sembiante.

Non fece al corso suo sì grosso velo
di verno la Danoia in Osterlicchi,
27   né Tanaï là sotto 'l freddo cielo,

If I had verses harsh enough and rasping
as would befit this dismal hole
upon which all the other rocks weigh down,

more fully would I press out the juice
of my conception. But, since I lack them,
with misgiving do I bring myself to speak.

It is no enterprise undertaken lightly—
to describe the very bottom of the universe—
nor for a tongue that cries 'mommy' and 'daddy.'

But may those ladies who aided Amphion
to build the walls of Thebes now aid my verse,
that the telling be no different from the fact.

O you misgotten rabble, worse than all the rest,
who fill that place so hard to speak of,
better had you here been sheep or goats!

When we were down in that ditch's darkness,
well below the giant's feet
my gaze still drawn by the wall above us,

I heard a voice say: 'Watch where you walk.
Step so as not to tread upon our heads,
the heads of wretched, weary brothers.'

At that I turned to look about.
Under my feet I saw a lake
so frozen that it seemed more glass than water.

Never in winter did the Austrian Danube
nor the far-off Don, under its frigid sky,
cover their currents with so thick a veil

com' era quivi; che se Tambernicchi
vi fosse sù caduto, o Pietrapana,
30   non avria pur da l'orlo fatto cricchi.

E come a gracidar si sta la rana
col muso fuor de l'acqua, quando sogna
33   di spigolar sovente la villana,

livide, insin là dove appar vergogna
eran l'ombre dolenti ne la ghiaccia,
36   mettendo i denti in nota di cicogna.

Ognuna in giù tenea volta la faccia;
da bocca il freddo, e da li occhi il cor tristo
39   tra lor testimonianza si procaccia.

Quand' io m'ebbi dintorno alquanto visto,
volsimi a' piedi, e vidi due sì stretti,
42   che 'l pel del capo avieno insieme misto.

"Ditemi, voi che sì strignete i petti,"
diss' io, "chi siete?" E quei piegaro i colli;
45   e poi ch'ebber li visi a me eretti,

li occhi lor, ch'eran pria pur dentro molli,
gocciar su per le labbra, e 'l gelo strinse
48   le lagrime tra essi e riserrolli.

Con legno legno spranga mai non cinse
forte così; ond' ei come due becchi
51   cozzaro insieme, tanta ira li vinse.

E un ch'avea perduti ambo li orecchi
per la freddura, pur col viso in giùe,
54   disse: "Perché cotanto in noi ti specchi?

Se vuoi saper chi son cotesti due,
la valle onde Bisenzo si dichina
57   del padre loro Alberto e di lor fue.

as I saw there. For had Tambernic fallen on it,
or Pietrapana, the ice would not
have creaked, not even at the edge.

30

And as frogs squat and croak,
their snouts out of the water, in the season
when peasant women often dream of gleaning,

33

so shades, ashen with cold, were grieving, trapped
in ice up to the place the hue of shame appears,
their teeth a-clatter like the bills of storks.

36

Downturned were all their faces, their mouths
gave witness to the cold, while from their eyes
came testimony of their woeful hearts.

39

I gazed around a while; then I looked down
and saw two shades so shackled to each other
their two heads' hair made but a single skein.

42

'Tell me, you with chests pressed close,' I said,
'who are you?' They strained their necks,
and, when they had raised their faces,

45

their eyes, till then moist only to the rims,
dripped tears down to their lips, and icy air
then froze those tears—and them to one another.

48

Clamp never gripped together board to board
so tight, at which such anger overcame them
they butted at each other like two rams.

51

And one of the other shades, who'd lost both ears
to the cold, and kept his face averted, said:
'Why do you reflect yourself so long in us?

54

'If you would like to know who these two are,
the valley out of which Bisenzio flows
belonged once to their father, Albert, and to them.

57

D'un corpo usciro; e tutta la Caina
potrai cercare, e non troverai ombra
60   degna più d'esser fitta in gelatina:

non quelli a cui fu rotto il petto e l'ombra
con esso un colpo per la man d'Artù;
63   non Focaccia; non questi che m'ingombra

col capo sì, ch'i' non veggio oltre più,
e fu nomato Sassol Mascheroni;
66   se tosco se', ben sai omai chi fu.

E perché non mi metti in più sermoni,
sappi ch'i' fu' il Camiscion de' Pazzi;
69   e aspetto Carlin che mi scagioni."

Poscia vid'io mille visi cagnazzi
fatti per freddo; onde mi vien riprezzo,
72   e verrà sempre, de' gelati guazzi.

E mentre ch'andavamo inver' lo mezzo
al quale ogne gravezza si rauna,
75   e io tremava ne l'etterno rezzo;

se voler fu o destino o fortuna,
non so; ma, passeggiando tra le teste,
78   forte percossi 'l piè nel viso ad una.

Piangendo mi sgridò: "Perché mi peste?
se tu non vieni a crescer la vendetta
81   di Montaperti, perché mi moleste?"

E io: "Maestro mio, or qui m'aspetta,
sì ch'io esca d'un dubbio per costui;
84   poi mi farai, quantunque vorrai, fretta."

Lo duca stette, e io dissi a colui
che bestemmiava duramente ancora:
87   "Qual se' tu che così rampogni altrui?"

'From a single womb they sprang, and though you seek
throughout Caïna, you will find no shade
more fit to be fixed in aspic,

'not him whose breast and shadow were pierced
by a single blow from Arthur's hand,
nor Focaccia, nor the one whose head so blocks

'my view that I cannot see past him
and whose name was Sassol Mascheroni—
if you are Tuscan you know well who he was.

'And, so you coax no further words from me,
know that I was Camiscion de' Pazzi,
and I await Carlino for my exculpation.'

After that I saw a thousand faces purple
with the cold, so that I shudder still—
and always will—when I come to a frozen ford.

Then, while we made our way toward the center,
where all things that have weight converge,
and I was shivering in the eternal chill,

if it was will or fate or chance
I do not know, but, walking among the heads,
I struck my foot hard in the face of one.

Wailing, he cried out: 'Why trample me?
Unless you come to add to the revenge
for Montaperti, why pick on me?'

And I: 'Master, would you wait for just a moment
so that I may resolve a doubt about this person.
And then I'll make what haste you like.'

My leader stopped, and I said to the shade,
who was still shouting bitter curses:
'And who are you, so to reproach another?'

60

63

66

69

72

75

78

81

84

87

"Or tu chi se' che vai per l'Antenora,
percotendo," rispuose, "altrui le gote,
90   sì che, se fossi vivo, troppo fora?"

"Vivo son io, e caro esser ti puote,"
fu mia risposta, "se dimandi fama,
93   ch'io metta il nome tuo tra l'altre note."

Ed elli a me: "Del contrario ho io brama.
Lèvati quinci e non mi dar più lagna,
96   ché mal sai lusingar per questa lama!"

Allor lo presi per la cuticagna
e dissi: "El converrà che tu ti nomi,
99   o che capel qui sù non ti rimagna."

Ond' elli a me: "Perché tu mi dischiomi,
né ti dirò ch'io sia, né mosterrolti
102   se mille fiate in sul capo mi tomi."

Io avea già i capelli in mano avvolti,
e tratti glien' avea più d'una ciocca,
105   latrando lui con li occhi in giù raccolti,

quando un altro gridò: "Che hai tu, Bocca?
non ti basta sonar con le mascelle,
108   se tu non latri? qual diavol ti tocca?"

"Omai," diss' io, "non vo' che più favelle,
malvagio traditor; ch'a la tua onta
111   io porterò di te vere novelle."

"Va via," rispuose, "e ciò che tu vuoi conta;
ma non tacer, se tu di qua entro eschi,
114   di quel ch'ebbe or così la lingua pronta.

El piange qui l'argento de' Franceschi:
'Io vidi,' potrai dir, 'quel da Duera
117   là dove i peccatori stanno freschi.'

'No, who are you to go through Antenora,'
he answered, 'buffeting another's cheeks?
90   Were I alive, this still would be an outrage.'

'Well, I'm alive,' I said, 'and if it's fame you seek,
it might turn out to your advantage
93   if I put your name among the others I have noted.'

And he: 'I long for just the opposite.
Take yourself off and trouble me no more—
96   you ill know how to flatter at this depth.'

Then I grabbed him by the scruff of the neck
and said: 'Either you name yourself
99   or I'll leave you without a single hair.'

And he: 'You can peel me bald and I
won't tell you who I am, nor give a hint,
102   even if you jump upon my head a thousand times.'

I now had his hair twisted in my hand
and had already plucked a tuft or two,
105   while he howled on, keeping his eyes cast down,

when another cried: 'What ails you, Bocca?
Isn't it enough, making noise with your jaws,
108   without that howling too? What devil's at you?'

'Now you no longer need to say a word,
vile traitor,' said I, 'to your shame
111   shall I bring back true news of you.'

'Be off,' he answered, 'and tell what tale you will.
But don't be silent, if you escape from here,
114   about the one whose tongue was now so nimble.

'Here he laments the Frenchmen's silver.
"I saw him of Duera," you can say,
117   "there where they set the sinners out to cool."

Se fossi domandato 'Altri chi v'era?'
tu hai dallato quel di Beccheria
120   di cui segò Fiorenza la gorgiera.

Gianni de' Soldanier credo che sia
più là con Ganellone e Tebaldello,
123   ch'aprì Faenza quando si dormia."

Noi eravam partiti già da ello,
ch'io vidi due ghiacciati in una buca,
126   sì che l'un capo a l'altro era cappello;

e come 'l pan per fame si manduca,
così 'l sovran li denti a l'altro pose
129   là 've 'l cervel s'aggiugne con la nuca:

non altrimenti Tidëo si rose
le tempie a Menalippo per disdegno,
132   che quei faceva il teschio e l'altre cose.

"O tu che mostri per sì bestial segno
odio sovra colui che tu ti mangi,
135   dimmi 'l perché," diss' io, "per tal convegno,

che se tu a ragion di lui ti piangi,
sappiendo chi voi siete e la sua pecca,
nel mondo suso ancora io te ne cangi,
139   se quella con ch'io parlo non si secca."

'And if someone were to ask you: "Who else was there?"
beside you is the one from Beccherìa——
120   Florence sawed his throat in two.

'I think Gianni de' Soldanier is farther on,
with Ganelon and Tebaldello,
123   who opened up Faenza while it slept.'

We had left him behind when I took note
of two souls so frozen in a single hole
126   the head of one served as the other's hat.

As a famished man will bite into his bread,
the one above had set his teeth into the other
129   just where the brain's stem leaves the spinal cord.

Tydeus gnawed the temples of Melanippus
with bitter hatred just as he was doing
132   to the skull and to the other parts.

'O you, who by so bestial a sign
show loathing for the one whom you devour,
135   tell me why,' I said, 'and let the pact be this:

'if you can give just cause for your complaint,
then I, knowing who you are and what his sin is,
may yet requite you in the world above,
139   if that with which I speak does not go dry.'

1–9.   Dante apologizes for not having under his control a language rough enough to be the exact counterpart of what he must describe. For the relationship of the diction of the passage to that found in Dante's *Rime petrose*, see Poletto's commentary (1894), perhaps the first to contain this observation, now become customary. See also Blasucci (Blas.1969.1).

The place he needs to describe is the center of the entire universe (at least it is in the geocentric view). If he had the right words, he would be able to set forth more adequately what he indeed fully understands, i.e., his *conception* does not come short of the nature of these things (see v. 12), but his words may. Dante draws this distinction with some care. To repeat, his "conception" is one matter, his description of it another (it is the "juice" that he must "squeeze" from the "fruit" of his experience). And the setting of that experience into verse is no light task (*impresa*—for the importance of this word, referring variously to Dante's journey and to his poem, see Holl.1969.1, p. 230, citing its other three occurrences in the poem [*Inf.* II.41 and II.47; *Par.* XXXIII.95]), not one for a tongue capable only of "babytalk." For the linguistic program concerning "babytalk" found in the *Commedia* and its oppositional relation to that previously advanced by Dante in *De vulgari eloquentia*, see Holl.1980.2. Here Dante is including two words, "mommy" and "daddy," that he himself had explicitly proscribed from the illustrious vernacular (*Dve* II.vii.4).

10–12.   This is Dante's second invocation. For the program of invocation in the poem as a whole, see note to *Inferno* II.7–9. Here the poet seeks aid only from the Muses and only for his ability to find the right words for his difficult task in rendering such unpleasant matter. His "conception" (see v. 4), we may understand, is already formed (in *Inf.* II.7 he implicitly asked for that, as well).

The reference to the poet Amphion probably derives from the *Ars poetica* of Horace (vv. 394–396), a work well known to Dante. Amphion was able, through the magic of his inspired lyre-playing, to compel the rocks of Mt. Cithaeron to move down the mountain and, of their own accord, create the walls of Thebes. Dante, describing the Infernal "city of destruction," the ninth Circle, home of Lucifer, asks for the help of the Muses in order to build, not the physical city, but his image of it in words that do justice to the conception he has been given.

13–15. The poet's address to all the denizens of Cocytus seems to have been aimed particularly at the arch-sinner punished here, Judas, by its reference, first noted by Pietro di Dante, to Matthew 26:24, Christ's words to Judas, for whom it had been better "not to have been born."

16–18. The narrative of this ultimate part of the first *cantica* has been held in abeyance for nine self-conscious opening lines about the poet's craft, for an invocation, and then for an apostrophe. The visit to the pit of the universe has finally begun. However, Dante's failure to manage these details more clearly has rattled his readers. Do the giants stand on the icy floor of Cocytus? Apparently not. Here Dante asserts that he and Virgil find themselves far below the feet of Antaeus. They do not seem, however, to have themselves descended that distance. Rather, it seems more likely that Antaeus has set them down just about where they find themselves now. Some commentators object, since most humans, and certainly most giants, are probably not limber enough (or long-armed enough) to bend at the waist and deposit a burden well below the level of their feet. Do we learn where the giants stand? No. Is Dante concerned lest their feet become chilled on the ice? No. Might they be standing on some sort of ledge? Yes. Can we be certain that they are? No. Might Antaeus have longer arms than we like to think? Yes. Can we know that he does? No. This is a poem, and, especially when it deals with the marvelous, while it is at times amazingly precise, it is also, at other times, exasperatingly (to certain readers) imprecise. As a result, beginning perhaps with Bianchi (1868), commentators have invented a ledge for Antaeus, and hence all the giants, to stand on. It has become part of the furniture of the poem, even if Dante did not construct it.

19–21. The identity of this voice has long puzzled readers. Torraca, essentially alone in this opinion, opts for Virgil; many for an unnamed sinner; many others for one (or both) of the Alberti brothers, whom we see in vv. 41–51. Benvenuto da Imola, followed only by his student John of Serravalle, makes probably the best surmise: the voice is that of Camicione de' Pazzi, a position that seems sensible, as we shall see as we move through the scene, but has had no success among the commentators.

22–24. Dante had been looking back up in the direction of Antaeus and wondering at the height of the wall he now stood beneath. The voice calls on him to attend to his surroundings, as he now immediately does, realizing that he is standing on a frozen lake.

25–30. A double simile describes the thickness of the ice, greater than even that found on the Danube or the Don, so thick that even had a mountain (whether Tambura or Pania, in the Apuan Alps above Lucca) fallen upon it, it would not have even creaked.

31–36. A second simile reflects the protagonist's new awareness that there are sinners in this ice, looking like frogs in summer (and how they must wish for summer, these shades), with just their snouts out of the water, and their teeth sounding like the clicking bills of storks.

37–39. This first group of sinners (we will learn eventually that there are four groups, each in a somewhat different posture) have their heads facing downwards. Their mouths clatter with the cold, their eyes run with tears (as we shall find out, that is a better condition than that enjoyed by those lower down in the ninth Circle). We are in Caïna, named for Cain, the first murderer (of his brother Abel).

46–51. These two (we will shortly learn that they are brothers) lift up their heads to behold Dante, which causes their tears to spill over their faces and onto their lips (instead of onto the ice), thus gluing them together still more firmly when their tears become gelid. Frozen into a parody of the Christian kiss of peace, they respond by moving the only part of them they can, their foreheads, which they use to butt one another in anger. Once we hear who they are, we will understand the reason for such hatred.

54–69. The speaker is Camicione de' Pazzi. Nothing much is known of him except that he, from near Florence (the Val d'Arno) murdered his relative Ubertino. His is the only voice we hear in this first zone of Cocytus, the prime reason to believe that it was he who spoke at vv. 19–21. Having warned Dante to be careful as he began walking, lest he kick the inseparate heads of the two brothers, he now identifies them for Dante. Alessandro and Napoleone degli Alberti, counts of Mangona, were also "neighbors" of Dante's, living in the countryside near Prato. While little is known of them, they apparently killed one another in the 1280s as the result of a dispute over their inheritance from their father.

Also here, says Camicione, is Mordred (vv. 61–62), who killed King Arthur and was slain by him, as recounted in the Old French *Morte d'Arthur*. The blow of Arthur's lance left a hole clear through Mordred's body so that a ray of sunlight passed through it—and thus through his shadow as well. And Focaccia is here (v. 63). That was the nickname (see Aher.1982.2) of Vanni dei Cancellieri of Pistoia, a White Guelph reputed by various commentators to have murdered various of his relatives, most probably at least his cousin Detto, a member of the Black Guelphs, ca. 1286. Also present is Sassol Mascheroni (vv. 63–66), another Florentine who murdered a relative in a quarrel over an inheritance. After he identifies himself, Camicione says that his relative, Carlino, will commit a still greater sin, betraying a White stronghold in the Val d'Arno to Black forces for money—a sin fit for the next zone, Antenora, where political treachery is punished, thus making (in his own eyes, at least) Camicione's sin seem less offensive.

Carlino's treachery and death took place only in 1302; therefore, Camicione is using the power of the damned to see into the future, of which we were told in *Inferno* X.100–108. The staging of a future damnation just here perhaps has consequence for Francesca's projected damnation of her husband in 1304 to precisely this circle and zone: Gianciotto is headed here, according to her (*Inf.* V.107). Since Dante uses this occasion precisely to predict the later coming of a damned soul currently still alive, we may be reminded of Francesca's similar prediction. And we sense how easy it would have been for Dante to have had Camicione, guilty of the same sin as Gianciotto, tell of his future presence in Caïna, thus "guaranteeing" Francesca's prediction. And he, like Francesca in this, tries to exculpate himself to some degree by insisting that the person he refers to is more guilty than he is, and will be punished still lower down in hell.

70–72.　We have crossed a border without knowing it. The ice of Cocytus is not marked, as were the Malebolge, with clear delineators that separate one sin from another. This difference may result from Dante's sense of the essential commonality of all sins treacherous in nature, so utterly debased (they are referred to as "matta bestialitade" in *Inf.* XI.82–83).

The four areas of Cocytus make concentric circles, each lower in the ice than the last, as we move toward the center. We understand that we have reached a new zone only because the faces of the damned look straight out at us (and are not bent down, as they were in Caïna). This zone is named after Antenor, the Trojan who, a grandson of Priam, in the non-Virgilian versions of the story of the Trojan War, urged that Helen be given back to Menelaus. After Paris refused to give her back, Antenor, in such sources as Dictys Cretensis, is responsible for betraying the city to the Greeks. He escaped from the city and founded Padua (see *Purg.* V.75).

73–78.   The protagonist's footwork has raised questions in many. Did he
kick Bocca on purpose? The language is such that answering is not easy.
Was the blow the result of will (his own) or fate (destiny, as determined by
God) or chance (mere accident, a thing of no consequence to the Divine
Mind)? These three alternatives offer a range of genuine and separate pos-
sibilities, which is not true for all the hypotheses that one may consult in
the commentary tradition. As Bosco/Reggio argue, that Dante kicks the
head *hard* makes it difficult to believe that his will was not involved.

79–81.   The victim of Dante's kick, we will learn at v. 106, is Bocca degli
Abati. Bocca's betrayal occurred on the battlefield at Montaperti (1260)
when he, a member of the Florentine Guelph army, cut off the arm of the
standard-bearer at the height of the battle. The ensuing disastrous defeat of
the Guelphs at the hands of the Ghibellines was sometimes laid at his
door, as it is here by Dante.

82–85.   The protagonist thinks he knows that this might well be Bocca,
and gets Virgil's permission to question him. We recall how stern Virgil
was in his rebuke of Dante for listening to the "tenzone" between Master
Adam and Sinon in Canto XXX.131–132. Here he stands complacently to
one side as Dante gets involved in a fairly violent "tenzone" himself. But
now, one might argue, he is actively engaged in remonstrating with a
wrongdoer and thus has Virgil's full support.

87–112.   This "tenzone" is in five parts. (1) Dante begins it with a rebuke
for Bocca's bad manners (a sinner in the depth of hell should treat mor-
tal special visitors better than he has done); Bocca answers with con-
tinuing complaint. (2) Dante offers fame—for a price; Bocca answers
rudely. (3) Dante moves to a threat of physical assault; Bocca defies him.
(4) Dante begins pulling out Bocca's hair; Bocca "barks," thus moving
another sinner there present to name him (he is answering in Bocca's
place, as it were). (5) Dante rejoices in his victory over Bocca; Bocca
remains sullen.
        The Italian at v. 90 is, in itself, ambivalent. Because of the conjugation
of the imperfect subjunctive, "se fossi vivo" can either mean "were I alive"
or "were you alive." Since Bocca, like Camicione (if he is the speaker of
vv. 19–21), seems to be able to tell that Dante is in the flesh, e.g., from the
sound of his footfall on the ice, from the force of his kick, it would make
no sense for him to doubt Dante's presence as a living being. Further,
Dante's response would seem to follow better if Bocca's words are under-

stood as meaning, "were I alive." Our translation runs accordingly. (There are those who dispute this reading.)

At vv. 103–105 Dante is playfully citing his own vengeful and sexually charged desire to pull the hair of the "stony lady" in one of his *Rime petrose*, "Così nel mio parlar," vv. 66–73. For the most recent discussion see Pasquini (Pasq.1999.1), pp. 31–33, noting as well various other resonances of the "stony rhymes" in this canto. See also the study of Durling and Martinez (Durl.1990.1) for a wider view.

113–123.   Bocca's revenge for his "betrayal" by Buoso da Duera is to reveal the names of others in Antenora so that they may join him in infamy as a result of Dante's eventual report to the living, the first of these, naturally, being Buoso himself (vv. 114–117). Buoso was a Ghibelline (he is "paired" with the Guelph Bocca) who, entrusted by Manfred's high command to hold the high passes near Parma against the invading army of Charles of Anjou in 1265, apparently accepted a bribe in order to let the Guelph forces reach Parma without a fight.

Tesauro de' Beccheria (vv. 119–120), abbot of Vallombrosa, a Ghibelline, was accused of treacherously assisting the Florentine Ghibellines, banned from the city in 1258, to reenter Florence. He was beheaded for betraying the city.

Gianni de' Soldanieri (v. 121), also a Ghibelline, joined the popular uprising against the Ghibelline leaders of Florence just after the defeat and death of the great Ghibelline leader, Manfred, at Benevento in 1266. He thus was seen as betraying his own party.

Ganelon (v. 122) treacherously betrayed Charlemagne's rear guard at Roncesvalles in 778. See *Inferno* XXXI.16–18.

Tebaldello Zambrasi of Faenza (v. 122), also a Ghibelline, betrayed his fellow Ghibellines of Bologna who, having been exiled, had taken refuge in Faenza. In 1280 Tebaldello opened a gate of his city, just before dawn, to a war party of Bolognese Guelphs so that they might avenge themselves upon their fellow citizens. Tebaldello himself died in 1282 in another battle.

124–125.   A sudden change in the protagonist's attention reveals the pair of sinners whom we will shortly know as Ugolino and Ruggieri (vv. 13–14 of the next canto), the one with his head above the other's.

127–132.   Again Dante blends an unadorned "ordinary" scene (a hungry man wolfing down a loaf of bread) with classical material (a passage from

Statius's *Thebaid* VIII.751–762) in a double simile. The moment in Statius describes Tydeus, dying in battle, asking his men to cut off for him the head of Melanippus, whom he had just slain, but who had first given him his own mortal blow. They do so (Capaneus [*Inf.* XIV] is the one who carries the body to him). With savage joy Tydeus, dying, chews upon the head of the man who had killed him.

133.   For the "bestial sign" as reflecting the words of St. Paul, see Freccero's essay, "Bestial Sign and Bread of Angels" (Frec.1986.1), p. 160: "But if you bite one another, take heed or you will be consumed by one another" (Galatians 5:15). The cannibalistic scene before us here introduces the concerns with starvation that will be so prominent in the first half of the next canto.

135–139.   Dante offers to present to the world this sinner's case (so that it may judge whether or not his wrath is justified) if he will but reveal his name and the offense committed by the other sinner. Dante fulfills this promise in the following canto, and the world—or at least the Dantean part of it—has been arguing about that case ever since.

There is also a dispute over the exact meaning of the last line of Dante's oath. A number of understandings have been offered: "as long as I do not die first" (the choice of many of the early commentators); "as long as my tongue does not fail me" (also popular among the early commentators); "if this cold [of Cocytus] does not wither it" (only Torraca and Pietrobono; probably not worth serious consideration); "if my words do not die" (Grabher and Fallani); "if it does not become paralyzed" (Steiner and quite a few modern commentators). It seems clear that Dante, in this vernacular and pithy oath, swears on his life that he will carry out his promise. Tozer (1901) paraphrases adequately: "If I live to recount it." Recently Guglielmo Gorni has tried an entirely new tack: "if my Florentine vernacular survives" (Gorn.1996.1), but this seems more venturesome than necessary.

When we finish reading this canto we may reflect on the singular fact that, for the first time since he entered the poem in its sixty-seventh verse, Virgil has not spoken in an entire canto. See note to *Inferno* XXX.37–41.

INFERNO XXXIII

La bocca sollevò dal fiero pasto
quel peccator, forbendola a' capelli
3   del capo ch'elli avea di retro guasto.

Poi cominciò: "Tu vuo' ch'io rinovelli
disperato dolor che 'l cor mi preme
6   già pur pensando, pria ch'io ne favelli.

Ma se le mie parole esser dien seme
che frutti infamia al traditor ch'i' rodo,
9   parlare e lagrimar vedrai insieme.

Io non so chi tu se' né per che modo
venuto se' qua giù; ma fiorentino
12   mi sembri veramente quand'io t'odo.

Tu dei saper ch'i' fui conte Ugolino,
e questi è l'arcivescovo Ruggieri:
15   or ti dirò perché i son tal vicino.

Che per l'effetto de' suo' mai pensieri,
fidandomi di lui, io fossi preso
18   e poscia morto, dir non è mestieri;

però quel che non puoi avere inteso,
cioè come la morte mia fu cruda,
21   udirai, e saprai s'e' m'ha offeso.

Breve pertugio dentro da la Muda,
la qual per me ha 'l titol de la fame,
24   e che conviene ancor ch'altrui si chiuda,

m'avea mostrato per lo suo forame
più lune già, quand'io feci 'l mal sonno
27   che del futuro mi squarciò 'l velame.

He raised his mouth from his atrocious meal,
that sinner, and wiped it on the hair
3   of the very head he had been ravaging.

Then he began: 'You ask me to revive
the desperate grief that racks my heart
6   even in thought, before I tell it.

'But if my words shall be the seeds that bear
infamous fruit to the traitor I am gnawing,
9   then you will see me speak and weep together.

'I don't know who you are, nor by what means
you have come down here, but when I listen to you speak,
12   it seems to me you are indeed from Florence.

'Take note that I was Count Ugolino,
and he Archbishop Ruggieri. Let me
15   tell you why I'm such a neighbor to him.

'How, as the consummation of his malicious schemes,
after I'd lodged my trust in him, he had me seized
18   and put to death, there is no need to tell.

'But when you learn what you cannot have heard—
that is to say, the cruelty of my death—
21   then you shall know if he has wronged me.

'A little spyhole in the Mew, which now
on my account is called the Tower of Hunger,
24   where others yet shall be imprisoned,

'had through its opening shown me several moons,
when, in a dreadful dream,
27   the veil was rent, and I foresaw the future.

Questi pareva a me maestro e donno,
cacciando il lupo e 'lupicini al monte
30   per che i Pisan veder Lucca non ponno.

Con cagne magre, studïose e conte
Gualandi con Sismondi e con Lanfranchi
33   s'avea messi dinanzi da la fronte.

In picciol corso mi parieno stanchi
lo padre e ' figli, e con l'agute scane
36   mi parea lor veder fender li fianchi.

Quando fui desto innanzi la dimane,
pianger senti' fra 'l sonno i miei figliuoli
39   ch'eran con meco, e dimandar del pane.

Ben se' crudel, se tu già non ti duoli
pensando ciò che 'l mio cor s'annunziava;
42   e se non piangi, di che pianger suoli?

Già eran desti, e l'ora s'appressava
che 'l cibo ne solëa essere addotto,
45   e per suo sogno ciascun dubitava;

e ïo senti' chiavar l'uscio di sotto
a l'orribile torre; ond' io guardai
48   nel viso a' mie' figliuoi sanza far motto.

Io non piangëa, sì dentro impetrai:
piangevan elli; e Anselmuccio mio
51   disse: 'Tu guardi sì, padre! che hai?'

Perciò non lagrimai né rispuos' io
tutto quel giorno né la notte appresso,
54   infin che l'altro sol nel mondo uscìo.

Come un poco di raggio si fu messo
nel doloroso carcere, e io scorsi
57   per quattro visi il mio aspetto stesso,

'This man appeared to be the lord and master,
hunting the wolf and wolfcubs on the mountain
30   that hides Lucca from the sight of Pisans.

'Along with well-trained hounds, lean and eager,
he had ranged in his front rank
33   Gualandi, Sismondi, and Lanfranchi.

'Father and sons, after a brief pursuit,
seemed to be flagging, and it seemed to me I saw
36   the flesh torn from their flanks by sharp incisors.

'When I awoke before the dawn of day
I heard my children, in that prison with me,
39   weep in their sleep and ask for bread.

'You are cruel indeed, thinking what my heart
foretold, if you remain untouched by grief,
42   and if you weep not, what can make you weep?

'Now they were awake, and the hour drew near
at which our food was brought to us.
45   Each of us was troubled by his dream.

'Down below I heard them nailing shut
the entry to the dreadful tower. I looked
48   my children in the face, without a word.

'I was so turned to stone inside I did not weep.
But they were weeping, and my little Anselm
51   said: "You look so strange, father, what's wrong?"

'Even then I shed no tear, and made no answer
all that day, and all the night that followed
54   until the next day's sun came forth upon the world.

'As soon as some few rays had made their way
into the woeful prison, and I discerned
57   four other faces stamped with my expression,

ambo le man per lo dolor mi morsi;
ed ei, pensando ch'io 'l fessi per voglia
60   di manicar, di sùbito levorsi

e disser: 'Padre, assai ci fia men doglia
se tu mangi di noi: tu ne vestisti
63   queste misere carni, e tu le spoglia.'

Queta'mi allor per non farli più tristi;
lo dì e l'altro stemmo tutti muti;
66   ahi dura terra, perché non t'apristi?

Poscia che fummo al quarto dì venuti,
Gaddo mi si gittò disteso a' piedi,
69   dicendo: 'Padre mio, ché non m'aiuti?'

Quivi morì; e come tu mi vedi,
vid' io cascar li tre ad uno ad uno
72   tra 'l quinto dì e 'l sesto; ond' io mi diedi,

già cieco, a brancolar sovra ciascuno,
e due dì li chiamai, poi che fur morti.
75   Poscia, più che 'l dolor, poté 'l digiuno."

Quand' ebbe detto ciò, con li occhi torti
riprese 'l teschio misero co' denti,
78   che furo a l'osso, come d'un can, forti.

Ahi Pisa, vituperio de le genti
del bel paese là dove 'l sì suona,
81   poi che i vicini a te punir son lenti,

muovasi la Capraia e la Gorgona,
e faccian siepe ad Arno in su la foce,
84   sì ch'elli annieghi in te ogne persona!

Che se 'l conte Ugolino aveva voce
d'aver tradita te de le castella,
87   non dovei tu i figliuoi porre a tal croce.

'the sorrow of it made me gnaw my hands.
And they, imagining I was doing this
60   from hunger, rose at once, saying:

' "Father, we would suffer less
if you would feed on us: you clothed us
63   in this wretched flesh—now strip it off."

'Then, not to increase their grief, I calmed myself.
That day and the next we did not speak a word.
66   O hard earth, why did you not engulf us?

'When we had come as far as the fourth day
my Gaddo threw himself on the ground before me,
69   crying, "O father, why won't you help me?"

'There he died; and even as you see me now
I watched the other three die, one by one,
72   on the fifth day and the sixth. And I began,

'already blind, to grope over their bodies,
and for two days called to them, though they were dead.
75   Then fasting had more power than grief.'

Having said this, with maddened eyes he seized
that wretched skull again between his teeth
78   and clenched them on the bone just like a dog.

Ah Pisa, how you shame the people
of that fair land where 'sì' is heard!
81   Since your neighbors are so slow to punish you,

may the islands of Capraia and Gorgona
move in to block the Arno at its mouth
84   and so drown every living soul in you!

Even if Count Ugolino bore the name
of traitor to your castles, you still
87   should not have put his children to such torture.

Innocenti facea l'età novella,
novella Tebe, Uguiccione e 'l Brigata
90   e li altri due che 'l canto suso appella.

Noi passammo oltre, là 've la gelata
ruvidamente un'altra gente fascia,
93   non volta in giù, ma tutta riversata.

Lo pianto stesso lì pianger non lascia,
e 'l duol che truova in su li occhi rintoppo,
96   si volge in entro a far crescer l'ambascia;

ché le lagrime prime fanno groppo,
e sì come visiere di cristallo,
99   rïempion sotto 'l ciglio tutto il coppo.

E avvegna che, sì come d'un callo,
per la freddura ciascun sentimento
102   cessato avesse del mio viso stallo,

già mi parea sentire alquanto vento;
per ch'io: "Maestro mio, questo chi move?
105   non è qua giù ogne vapore spento?"

Ond' elli a me: "Avaccio sarai dove
di ciò ti farà l'occhio la risposta,
108   veggendo la cagion che 'l fiato piove."

E un de' tristi de la fredda crosta
gridò a noi: "O anime crudeli
111   tanto che data v'è l'ultima posta,

levatemi dal viso i duri veli,
sì ch'ïo sfoghi 'l duol che 'l cor m'impregna,
114   un poco, pria che 'l pianto si raggeli."

Per ch'io a lui: "Se vuo' ch'i' ti sovvegna,
dimmi chi se', e s'io non ti disbrigo,
117   al fondo de la ghiaccia ir mi convegna."

Their tender years, you modern Thebes,
declared Uguiccione and Brigata innocent,
90   and the other two this canto names above.

We went on farther, to where the ice-crust
rudely wraps another sort of souls,
93   their faces not turned down but up.

The very weeping there prevents their weeping,
for the grief that meets a barrier at the eyelids
96   turns inward to augment their anguish,

since their first tears become a crust
that like a crystal visor fills
99   the cups beneath the eyebrows.

Although the cold had made
all feeling leave my face
102   as though it were a callus,

I still could feel a breath of wind.
And I said: 'Master, who sets this in motion?
105   Are not all winds banished here below?'

Thus he to me: 'You will come soon enough
to where your eyes will give an answer,
108   seeing the source that puts out such a blast.'

And one of the wretches in the icy crust
cried out: 'O souls, so hard of heart
111   you are assigned the lowest station,

'lift from my face these rigid veils
so I can vent a while the grief that swells
114   my heart, until my tears freeze up again.'

'If you want my help, let me know your name,'
I answered. 'Then, if I do not relieve you,
117   may I have to travel to the bottom of the ice.'

Rispuose adunque: "I' son frate Alberigo;
i' son quel de la frutta del mal orto,
120   che qui riprendo dattero per figo."

"Oh," diss' io lui, "or se' tu ancor morto?"
Ed elli a me: "Come 'l mio corpo stea
123   nel mondo sù, nulla scïenza porto.

Cotal vantaggio ha questa Tolomea,
che spesse volte l'anima ci cade
126   innanzi ch'Atropòs mossa le dea.

E perché tu più volontier mi rade
le 'nvetrïate lagrime dal volto,
129   sappie che, tosto che l'anima trade

com fec' ïo, il corpo suo l'è tolto
da un demonio, che poscia il governa
132   mentre che 'l tempo suo tutto sia vòlto.

Ella ruina in sì fatta cisterna;
e forse pare ancor lo corpo suso
135   de l'ombra che di qua dietro mi verna.

Tu 'l dei saper, se tu vien pur mo giuso;
elli è ser Branca Doria, e son più anni
138   poscia passati ch'el fu sì racchiuso."

"Io credo," diss' io lui, "che tu m'inganni;
ché Branca Doria non morì unquanche,
141   e mangia e bee e dorme e veste panni."

"Nel fosso sù," diss' el, "de' Malebranche,
là dove bolle la tenace pece,
144   non era ancora giunto Michel Zanche,

che questi lasciò il diavolo in sua vece
nel corpo suo, ed un suo prossimano
147   che 'l tradimento insieme con lui fece.

He spoke: 'I am Fra Alberigo. I am he
who harvested the evil orchard,
120   and here, for figs, I am repaid in dates.'

'Oh,' said I to him, 'are you already dead?'
And he to me: 'I have no knowledge
123   how my body fares in the world above.

'Such privilege has this Ptolomea,
that many times a soul may fall down here
126   before Atropos has cut it loose.

'So that you may be all the more inclined
to scrape these tear-drops glazed upon my face,
129   know that the moment a soul betrays

'as I did, its body is taken by a devil,
who has it then in his control
132   until the time allotted it has run.

'The soul falls headlong to this cesspool.
Perhaps the body of this shade, who spends
135   the winter with me here, still walks the earth,

'as you must know, if you've come down just now.
He is Branca d'Oria. Quite some years
138   have passed since he was thus confined.'

'I think,' I said to him, 'you're fooling me.
For Branca d'Oria is not yet dead: he eats
141   and drinks and sleeps and puts on clothes.'

'In the ditch above, of the Malebranche,'
he said, 'where the clingy pitch is at the boil,
144   Michel Zanche had not yet arrived

'when this man left a devil in his stead
to own his body, as did his kinsman,
147   his partner in the treacherous act.

Ma distendi oggimai in qua la mano;
aprimi li occhi." E io non gliel' apersi;
150 e cortesia fu lui esser villano.

Ahi Genovesi, uomini diversi
d'ogne costume e pien d'ogne magagna,
153 perché non siete voi del mondo spersi?

Ché col peggiore spirto di Romagna
trovai di voi un tal, che per sua opra
in anima in Cocito già si bagna,
157 e in corpo par vivo ancor di sopra.

'But now extend your hand and open
my eyes for me.' I did not open them.
150   And to be rude to him was courtesy.

O, men of Genoa, race estranged
from every virtue, crammed with every vice,
153   why have you not been driven from the earth?

With the most heinous spirit of Romagna
I found a son of yours who, for his evil deeds,
even now in Cocytus bathes his soul
157   while yet his body moves among the living.

1–3.   The complications of political intrigue lie behind the story that we are about to hear. For a review, in English, see Singleton's commentary to vv. 17–18. The main particulars are as follows. Count Ugolino della Gherardesca (ca. 1220–89) was of a Ghibelline family of Pisa. In 1275 he joined with the Guelph Visconti family in order to advance his own political ambitions, but failed to do so when his plans became known and he was banished. He returned to Pisa and now joined with the Archbishop, Ruggieri degli Ubaldini (grandson of Ottaviano degli Ubaldini [see *Inf.* X.120]), a Ghibelline, and conspired with him against Judge Nino Visconti, a Guelph, and, in Dante's eyes, a good man (we see him, on his way to salvation, in *Purg.* VIII.53). In 1288, Ugolino and Ruggieri managed to force Nino to leave the city, thus allowing them a free hand. At this point, however, Ruggieri decided to be rid of Ugolino, and had him accused of "betraying" Pisa by giving some of its outlying castles to the Florentines and the Lucchesi (he had in fact been trying to negotiate a political advantage to Pisa in these dealings). With that as an excuse, Ruggieri had Ugolino imprisoned in the summer of 1288, along with two sons and two grandsons (Dante has made the tale more pathetic by making all four of the children young—but Ugolino was in his sixties when the five of them were imprisoned). They were starved to death in February 1289.

Ugolino is found in Antenora, and thus was a betrayer of party or country. In what did his sin consist? Dante refers to the "betrayal" involving the castles in v. 86, but seems to think this was only an accusation. However, his real treacherous behavior, in Dante's eyes, may have involved either his betrayal of his own Ghibelline party, or of the good forces in Pisa itself in his double-dealing with Judge Nino, who also happened to be his grandson.

Almost all admire the horror of this scene, Ugolino lifting his gore-stained mouth from Ruggieri's neck, then wiping it on the hair of his enemy's head. We may reflect that Ugolino is moved to cease his vengeful chewing by his hope for further, greater vengeance: Dante's recounting of his case against Ruggieri in the world above.

4–6.   Ugolino's first words are nearly universally observed to be a citation of the opening of Aeneas's sad speech to Dido in *Aeneid* II.3–8, a passage also nearly universally cited for the beginning of Francesca's second speech to Dante (*Inf.* V.121–123). Why the repetition? Hollander (Holl.1984.5), p. 550, suggests that it represents a sort of test for the reader, who now hears another "sympathetic sinner" trying to capture the goodwill of the protagonist (and, indeed, of the reader) and is supposed to realize that this refrain has been heard before, similarly put to the service of exculpating a sinner by that very sinner.

For a second Virgilian resonance here see *Aeneid* I.209, where Aeneas hides the grief in his heart from his companions ("premit altum corde dolorem"); the echo of these words ("che 'l *cor* mi *preme*") was noted by Tommaseo, who observes the differing contexts.

8. The phrasing of Ugolino's hoped-for fruition of infamy for Ruggieri possibly reflects the language of the parable of the sower (Luke 8:4–11), where Jesus interprets the seed as the word of God. Durling and Martinez (Durl.1996.1), p. 531, suggest the importance, for the images of fruition used both by Ugolino and Alberigo, of Matthew 7:20, "by their fruits you shall know them."

9. Both Francesca (*Inf.* V.126) and Ugolino weep and speak simultaneously, each of them in imitation of Aeneas's imagined hardened soldier, who would have to speak through tears if he had the fall of Troy to narrate (*Aen.* II.6–8). And both Francesca and Ugolino are accompanied by a companion who does not speak in Dante's presence.

11–12. Like Farinata (*Inf.* X.25), Ugolino realizes that Dante is Florentine from his speech.

20–21. The story of Ugolino's imprisonment and death was familiar to all who lived in Tuscany. What Dante could not have known, Ugolino says, was how much he had suffered. The way in which he says this, on the other hand, indicates the sort of egotism that we will experience all through his speech. Here is a man who has experienced death in the company of his children; we do not even hear of them at first, since his attention is fixed entirely on himself. See Holl.1984.5, p. 551.

22–24. The tower (the edifice remains, without its tower, in the Piazza dei Cavalieri in Pisa to this day) would not serve as prison many years into the fourteenth century, but it apparently still did so when Dante wrote these lines.

26–27.   For the supposed greater truth of morning dreams see note to *Inferno* XXVI.7.

28–36.   Ugolino's dream turns out to have been completely accurate: Ruggieri, out hunting on Mount San Giuliano, is after Ugolino (the wolf) and his children (the cubs). He has set, ahead of the chase, the waiting ambushers, the Ghibelline leaders of Pisa, and with his hounds he is driving his victims toward them and to their destruction.

For the canine imagery in Cocytus and especially in this canto, see Brugnoli (Brug.1989.1).

37–39.   Ugolino awakes from the dream to find its reality before his eyes, his children hungry in their sleep and crying for their daily bread, usually brought them in the morning (see vv. 43–44).

40–42.   Ugolino is angered by the fact that Dante is not weeping. The protagonist, unlike most readers, has evidently found a moral vantage point from which there seems something wrong with this narration. Since we have seen him weep for other apparently less sympathetic figures, his lack of compassion might serve as a clue to us about our own reactions.

In this canto, vv. 5–75, words for weeping and grief (*piangere, lagrimare, doglia, dolere, dolore,* and *doloroso*) occur a total of thirteen times (see Holl.1969.1, p. 306). And see Vittorio Russo (Russ.1966.1) for a wider study of this phenomenon.

45.   Apparently the children have had a dream similar to their father's. The process of the starvation of Ugolino and his children roughly coincided with the Lenten season.

46–48.   Ugolino's dream now has a finer point. He understands at once that they are to die, caught by the hunter Ruggieri and his men. His first impulse, which will be repeated, is to keep silent.

49.   Ugolino, who has just criticized Dante for being cruel because he does not weep, now tells the protagonist that he himself did not weep when he perceived the fate of his sons and of himself. Indeed, he turned to stone. For Hollander (Holl.1984.5), pp. 552–55, the key passage that stands behind this scene is found in Luke's Gospel, 11:5–13, Christ's parable of the importunate friend. A man is visited by a friend at midnight and

goes to the house of another friend to seek bread in order to feed his guest. The importuned friend replies, "Trouble me not, the door is now shut, and my children are with me in bed; I cannot rise and give you." Christ comments on the parable, insisting that importuning will eventually work: "If a son shall ask for bread of any of you that is a father, will he give him a stone?" The various details of the parable, in a form that is both parallel and antithetic to the action recounted here, find their place in Ugolino's narrative: the knocking on the door echoed in the hammer blows nailing up the prison, the man in bed with his children behind a locked door, and the father who will not give his son a stone when he asks for bread. Ugolino, however, gives his sons exactly that, a stony silence. When we ask ourselves what we would do in that situation, we probably know. We would speak, not be silent (see Botterill [Bott.1988.2], p. 287); we would weep with our children, not show stoic reserve; and, if we were thirteenth-century Italians, we would pray with them after having sought their forgiveness for having involved them, innocent, in our political machinations. The opening passage of Luke 11 has a prayer for us, should we require one, for it is in that text that Jesus teaches his disciples what we know as "the Lord's prayer."

58–63.   Ugolino, silent, biting his hands from grief, causes the children to think that he is hungry and they offer themselves to him for food. They, like their father, can only think literally about nourishment, forgetting the symbolic eucharistic value of bread. (Freccero [Frec.1986.1], pp. 156–57, believes that their offer *is* eucharistic and spiritually motivated.) This is the last conversation among them.

64–69.   The father, thinking that display of his own sorrow will only increase the pain felt by his sons, teaches them his lesson: stoic silence in the face of death. Had Seneca written this canto, perhaps we would be justified in thinking Ugolino's reserve a valuable example of courage. The silence is only broken once more, on this fourth day, by Gaddo, dying, who asks the question the reader, too, might very well ask: "O father, why won't you help me?" The drama of paternity that we find in this canto is not that proposed, in his beautiful essay, by Francesco De Sanctis (DeSa.1967.1), but that of a terribly failing father.

The total absence of religious concerns in Dante's portrait of Ugolino is in contrast to the tale that circulates in some of the commentaries, first in 1333 in the Ottimo Commento, that Ugolino, realizing they were all to die, asked for a friar to confess them, and was refused. Had Dante included such a detail, his Ugolino would have seemed a much different man.

74. Only now that it is too late does Ugolino break the silence with his cries. It is the last heartbreaking detail of his failure as a father. The tale that he tells to win Dante's sympathy has also failed, as we shall see.

75. Did Ugolino ingest his children? For a history of the centuries-long debate see Hollander (Holl.1985.2). For a strong argument in favor of the notion, see Herzman (Herz.1980.1). To most, the position represented by Herzman and others, mainly (in recent years) Americans, seems a not convincing interpretation. In Singleton's opinion, it is a "curious view," one "hardly worth a serious rebuttal." This writer stands with Geoffrey Chaucer's view of the matter in the *Monk's Tale*, v. 2455: "Hymself, despeired, eek for hunger starf" (and he, despairing, also [i.e., as the children had] died from hunger). One wishes that Chaucer had used a term for starvation, but that might not have rhymed or scanned. "Digiuno" (fasting) is not the same thing as "hunger." And surely Chaucer knew that.

An observation in the commentary of Guido da Pisa also offers evidence that the number of days in the narrative (seven) is significant in this regard. Guido says, "And lest it seem impossible that one could have lived six days without food, heed Macrobius on the *Dream of Scipio*. He says that the life of a man cannot last beyond seven days without food." If Dante, with his so carefully calculated seven days to starvation, is aware of this bit of medical lore, Ugolino died at the limit of human endurance without nourishment. Had he ingested the flesh of his children, he would have lived longer. Further, when the corpses were exhibited outside the tower, after their removal, the scandal of the teeth-torn flesh would have made the rounds. No such story did, with the exception of a variant, somewhat suspect, in the text of the commentary of Jacopo della Lana. See Holl.1985.2, n. 24.

76–78. His tale told, Ugolino resumes his bestial rage against the cause of his woes, the skull of Ruggieri, whose evil plots bested Ugolino's own machinations. For the view that Ugolino hides his own culpability behind that of others, see Barberi Squarotti (Barb.1972.2).

79–90. Romantic readers, who admire Ugolino, do not often read past verse 75 with close attention. Dante's apostrophe of Pisa, "new Thebes," blames the city, not for killing Ugolino, which it had a reason to do (if not perhaps a correct one), but for killing the children. All of Dante's sympathy is lodged with the children, none with Ugolino. And here we are not speaking of the protagonist (who was firm enough himself against Ugolino's entreaties for pity), but of the author.

In *Dve* (I.viii.2–5) Dante had divided Europeans into three large linguistic groups, Provençal, French, and Italian, by their respective ways of saying "yes," *oc, oïl*, and *sì*. He thus, at vv. 79–80, refers to the inhabitants of Italy.

Capraia and Gorgona are islands in the Mediterranean that then belonged to Pisa.

91–93.   The transition to Ptolomea is as abrupt as that to Antenora had been (*Inf.* XXXII.70). And once again the determining detail is the positioning of the faces of those punished in the area. These now have their faces turned upwards (where those in Antenora looked straight ahead and those in Caïna had their faces tilted downward).

Most commentators believe that Ptolomea, where treachery to guests and friends is punished, gets its name from Ptolemy, the captain of Jericho who, as recorded in I Machabees 16:11–17, invited his father-in-law, Simon Maccabeus, and his two sons to a banquet and then, once they had drunk, slew them. (There is dispute about the matter, some proposing Ptolemy XII, king of Egypt, 51–47 B.C., who murdered Pompey as a favor to Julius Caesar [Lucan, *Phars.* VIII.536–712].)

94–99.   Their upturned visages turn the eye sockets into cups in which the tears of the sinners become small basins of ice. Fra Alberigo will three times ask Dante to clear these for him (vv. 112–114, 127–128, 148–150).

100–105.   Despite his frozen facial skin, Dante feels a wind, and asks Virgil how this can be, since the sun, creator of wind, is absent from this place.

106–108.   Pietro di Dante suggests that the wind emanating from Satan, to which Virgil alludes gingerly, not wanting to alarm Dante unduly (cf. his behavior as they approached the giants in *Inf.* XXXI.29–33), is a perverse imitation of the breath of the Holy Spirit referred to in Acts 2:3.

109–114.   The only speaking presence in Ptolomea (identified as Fra Alberigo in v. 118) believes that Dante and Virgil are sinners destined for Judecca, the "lowest station" in Inferno. In Antenora the souls seemed to be able to tell that Dante was alive; here, perhaps because of their greater physical discomfort and icebound blindness, their sensory capacities seem more limited than those of the souls above them.

115–117.   Dante's "agreement" with Alberigo is utterly cynical; he has no intention of helping this sinner in any way, and says what he says only to get the sinner to disclose himself, swearing a misleading oath in order to reassure him (of course he is going to the "bottom of the ice," but not as a sinner for his eternal punishment, but as a very privileged visitor).

118–120.   A member of the Jovial Friars (see note to *Inf.* XXIII.103), Alberigo was a Guelph from Faenza, and, in 1285, invited two of his relatives, with one of whom he had had a dispute, to dinner. When he called out for the fruit course, the prearranged signal, hired assassins rushed into the room and killed his guests. Now, he says, he is having a fruit course of his own, in which he is getting more (and worse) than he gave, date for fig (since, in Dante's day, dates were more expensive than figs).

122–133.   Here, in answer to the protagonist's question, based in his surprise at finding him here, since he had not heard that he had died, Alberigo reveals the poet's extraordinary innovation. Those who have broken the guest laws die in their souls as soon as they do so, so that their souls go to hell, leaving their bodies alive on earth. As early as Pietro di Dante, some commentators have pointed to a possible source in John 13:27, where it is said that, shortly after Judas betrayed Jesus at the Last Supper, Satan entered into Judas.

Atropos (v. 126) is the third of the three Fates (Clotho spins the fabric for the skein of our lives, Lachesis lets it out from her distaff, and Atropos snips it off at our deaths).

134–147.   To prove his point, Alberigo points out someone he believes Dante might know taking his "winter vacation" here in Ptolomea, Branca d'Oria. He was a Ghibelline nobleman of Genoa who, with the help of another family member, treacherously murdered his father-in-law, Michel Zanche (see *Inf.* XXII.88), around 1294. Thus his soul has been down here for six years, while his body is still eating, drinking, sleeping, and putting on clothes, as Dante insists. History contrived to make Dante's fiction all the more amusing. Branca, who was born ca. 1233, lived into his nineties, only dying in 1325, thus outliving his condemner, Dante. Perhaps he had the great pleasure of reading about his "wintering" soul as he enjoyed his life in Genoa.

148–150.   For the third time Alberigo asks Dante to clear the ice from his eyes, and now Dante, having what he wanted from him, simply does not do so. There are those who argue that the protagonist here behaves more like a sinner than a Christian, but by now we should be used to his approved form of righteous indignation. And there is no reproof for such behavior from Virgil here.

151–157.   Matching the apostrophe attacking Pisa that ended the first part of the canto (vv. 79–90), this one of Genoa concludes the visit to Ptolomea, one of the shortest episodes in the *Inferno*.

INFERNO XXXIV

"*Vexilla regis prodeunt inferni*
verso di noi; però dinanzi mira,"
3   disse 'l maestro mio, "se tu 'l discerni."

Come quando una grossa nebbia spira,
o quando l'emisperio nostro annotta,
6   par di lungi un molin che 'l vento gira,

veder mi parve un tal dificio allotta;
poi per lo vento mi ristrinsi retro
9   al duca mio, ché non lì era altra grotta.

Già era, e con paura il metto in metro,
là dove l'ombre tutte eran coperte,
12   e trasparien come festuca in vetro.

Altre sono a giacere; altre stanno erte,
quella col capo e quella con le piante;
15   altra, com' arco, il volto a' piè rinverte.

Quando noi fummo fatti tanto avante,
ch'al mio maestro piacque di mostrarmi
18   la creatura ch'ebbe il bel sembiante,

d'innanzi mi si tolse e fé restarmi,
"Ecco Dite," dicendo, "ed ecco il loco
21   ove convien che di fortezza t'armi."

Com' io divenni allor gelato e fioco,
nol dimandar, lettor, ch'i' non lo scrivo,
24   però ch'ogne parlar sarebbe poco.

Io non mori' e non rimasi vivo;
pensa oggimai per te, s'hai fior d'ingegno,
27   qual io divenni, d'uno e d'altro privo.

'The banners of the King of Hell advance
on us. Look straight before you

3   and see if you can make him out,' my master said.

As when a thick mist rises, or when our hemisphere
darkens to night, one may discern

6   a distant windmill by its turning sails,

it seemed to me I saw such a contrivance.
And, to avoid the wind, I drew in close

9   behind my leader: there was nowhere else to hide.

Now—and I shudder as I write it out in verse—
I was where the shades were wholly covered,

12   showing through like bits of straw in glass.

Some are lying down, still others stand erect:
some with heads, some with footsoles up,

15   some bent like bows, their faces to their toes.

When we had gotten far enough along
that my master was pleased to let me see

18   the creature who was once so fair of face,

he took a step aside, then brought me to a halt:
'Look there at Dis! And see the place

21   where you must arm yourself with fortitude.'

Then how faint and frozen I became,
reader, do not ask, for I do not write it,

24   since any words would fail to be enough.

I did not die, nor did I stay alive.
Imagine, if you have the wit,

27   what I became, deprived of both.

Lo 'mperador del doloroso regno
da mezzo 'l petto uscia fuor de la ghiaccia;
30   e più con un gigante io mi convegno,

che i giganti non fan con le sue braccia:
vedi oggimai quant' esser dee quel tutto
33   ch'a così fatta parte si confaccia.

S'el fu sì bel com' elli è ora brutto,
e contra 'l suo fattore alzò le ciglia,
36   ben dee da lui procedere ogne lutto.

Oh quanto parve a me gran maraviglia
quand' io vidi tre facce a la sua testa!
39   L'una dinanzi, e quella era vermiglia;

l'altr' eran due, che s'aggiugnieno a questa
sovresso 'l mezzo di ciascuna spalla,
42   e sé giugnieno al loco de la cresta:

e la destra parea tra bianca e gialla;
la sinistra a vedere era tal, quali
45   vegnon di là onde 'l Nilo s'avvalla.

Sotto ciascuna uscivan due grand' ali,
quanto si convenia a tanto uccello:
48   vele di mar non vid' io mai cotali.

Non avean penne, ma di vispistrello
era lor modo; e quelle svolazzava,
51   sì che tre venti si movean da ello:

quindi Cocito tutto s'aggelava.
Con sei occhi piangëa, e per tre menti
54   gocciava 'l pianto e sanguinosa bava.

Da ogne bocca dirompea co' denti
un peccatore, a guisa di maciulla,
57   sì che tre ne facea così dolenti.

The emperor of the woeful kingdom
rose from the ice below his breast,
30   and I in size am closer to a giant

than giants are when measured to his arms.
Judge, then, what the whole must be
33   that is proportional to such a part.

If he was fair as he is hideous now,
and raised his brow in scorn of his creator,
36   he is fit to be the source of every sorrow.

Oh, what a wonder it appeared to me
when I perceived three faces on his head.
39   The first, in front, was red in color.

Another two he had, each joined with this,
above the midpoint of each shoulder,
42   and all the three united at the crest.

The one on the right was a whitish yellow,
while the left-hand one was tinted like the people
45   living at the sources of the Nile.

Beneath each face two mighty wings emerged,
such as befit so vast a bird:
48   I never saw such massive sails at sea.

They were featherless and fashioned
like a bat's wings. When he flapped them,
51   he sent forth three separate winds,

the sources of the ice upon Cocytus.
Out of six eyes he wept and his three chins
54   dripped tears and drooled blood-red saliva.

With his teeth, just like a hackle
pounding flax, he champed a sinner
57   in each mouth, tormenting three at once.

A quel dinanzi il mordere era nulla
verso 'l graffiar, che tal volta la schiena
60   rimanea de la pelle tutta brulla.

"Quell' anima là sù c'ha maggior pena,"
disse 'l maestro, "è Giuda Scarïotto,
63   che 'l capo ha dentro e fuor le gambe mena.

De li altri due c'hanno il capo di sotto,
quel che pende dal nero ceffo è Bruto:
66   vedi come si storce, e non fa motto!;

e l'altro è Cassio, che par sì membruto.
Ma la notte risurge, e oramai
69   è da partir, ché tutto avem veduto."

Com' a lui piacque, il collo li avvinghiai;
ed el prese di tempo e loco poste,
72   e quando l'ali fuoro aperte assai,

appigliò sé a le vellute coste;
di vello in vello giù discese poscia
75   tra 'l folto pelo e le gelate croste.

Quando noi fummo là dove la coscia
si volge, a punto in sul grosso de l'anche,
78   lo duca, con fatica e con angoscia,

volse la testa ov' elli avea le zanche,
e aggrappossi al pel com' om che sale,
81   sì che 'n inferno i' credea tornar anche.

"Attienti ben, ché per cotali scale,"
disse 'l maestro, ansando com' uom lasso,
84   "conviensi dipartir da tanto male."

Poi uscì fuor per lo fóro d'un sasso
e puose me in su l'orlo a sedere;
87   appresso porse a me l'accorto passo.

For the one in front the gnawing was a trifle
to the clawing, for from time to time
60   his back was left with not a shred of skin.

'That soul up there who bears the greatest pain,'
said the master, 'is Judas Iscariot, who has
63   his head within and outside flails his legs.

'As for the other two, whose heads are dangling down,
Brutus is hanging from the swarthy snout—
66   see how he writhes and utters not a word!—

'and from the other, Cassius, so large of limb.
But night is rising in the sky. It is time
69   for us to leave, for we have seen it all.'

At his request I clasped him round the neck.
When the wings had opened wide enough
72   he chose the proper time and place

and took a handhold on those hairy flanks.
Then from hank to hank he clambered down
75   between the thick pelt and the crusted ice.

When we had come to where the thighbone
swivels, at the broad part of the hips,
78   my leader, with much strain of limb and breath,

turned his head where Satan had his shanks
and clung to the hair like a man climbing upward,
81   so that I thought we were heading back to Hell.

'Hold on tight, for by such rungs as these,'
said my master, panting like a man exhausted,
84   'must we depart from so much evil.'

Then out through an opening in the rock he went,
setting me down upon its edge to rest.
87   And then, with quick and cautious steps, he joined me.

Io levai li occhi e credetti vedere
Lucifero com' io l'avea lasciato,
90   e vidili le gambe in sù tenere;

e s'io divenni allora travagliato,
la gente grossa il pensi, che non vede
93   qual è quel punto ch'io avea passato.

"Lèvati sù," disse 'l maestro, "in piede:
la via è lunga e 'l cammino è malvagio,
96   e già il sole a mezza terza riede."

Non era camminata di palagio
là 'v' eravam, ma natural burella
99   ch'avea mal suolo e di lume disagio.

"Prima ch'io de l'abisso mi divella,
maestro mio," diss' io quando fui dritto,
102   "a trarmi d'erro un poco mi favella:

ov' è la ghiaccia? e questi com' è fitto
sì sottosopra? e come, in sì poc' ora,
105   da sera a mane ha fatto il sol tragitto?"

Ed elli a me: "Tu imagini ancora
d'esser di là dal centro, ov' io mi presi
108   al pel del vermo reo che 'l mondo fóra.

Di là fosti cotanto quant' io scesi;
quand' io mi volsi, tu passasti 'l punto
111   al qual si traggon d'ogne parte i pesi.

E se' or sotto l'emisperio giunto
ch'è contraposto a quel che la gran secca
114   coverchia, e sotto 'l cui colmo consunto

fu l'uom che nacque e visse sanza pecca;
tu haï i piedi in su picciola spera
117   che l'altra faccia fa de la Giudecca.

I raised my eyes, thinking I would see
Lucifer still the same as I had left him,
90 but saw him with his legs held upward.

And if I became confused, let those dull minds
who fail to see what point I'd passed
93 comprehend what I felt then.

The master said to me: 'Get to your feet,
for the way is long and the road not easy,
96 and the sun returns to middle tierce.'

It was not the great hall of a palace,
where we were, but a natural dungeon,
99 rough underfoot and wanting light.

'Master, before I tear myself from the abyss,'
I said once I had risen,
102 'say a few words to rid me of my doubt.

'Where is the ice? Why is this one fixed now
upside down? And how in so few hours
105 has the sun moved from evening into morning?'

And he to me: 'You imagine you are still
beyond the center, where I grasped the hair
108 of the guilty worm by whom the world is pierced.

'So you were, as long as I descended,
but, when I turned around, you passed the point
111 to which all weights are drawn from every side.

'You are now beneath the hemisphere
opposite the one that canopies the landmass—
114 and underneath its zenith that Man was slain

'who without sin was born and sinless lived.
You have your feet upon a little sphere
117 that forms Judecca's other face.

Qui è da man, quando di là è sera;
e questi, che ne fé scala col pelo,
120   fitto è ancora sì come prim' era.

Da questa parte cadde giù dal cielo;
e la terra, che pria di qua si sporse,
123   per paura di lui fé del mar velo,

e venne a l'emisperio nostro; e forse
per fuggir lui lasciò qui loco vòto
126   quella ch'appar di qua, e sù ricorse."

Luogo è là giù da Belzebù remoto
tanto quanto la tomba si distende,
129   che non per vista, ma per suono è noto

d'un ruscelletto che quivi discende
per la buca d'un sasso, ch'elli ha roso,
132   col corso ch'elli avvolge, e poco pende.

Lo duca e io per quel cammino ascoso
intrammo a ritornar nel chiaro mondo;
135   e sanza cura aver d'alcun riposo,

salimmo sù, el primo e io secondo,
tanto ch'i' vidi de le cose belle
che porta 'l ciel, per un pertugio tondo.
139   E quindi uscimmo a riveder le stelle.

'Here it is morning when it is evening there,
and the one whose hair provided us a ladder
120   is fixed exactly as he was before.

'It was on this side that he fell from Heaven.
And the dry land that used to stand, above,
123   in fear of him immersed itself in water

'and fled into our hemisphere. And perhaps
to escape from him the land we'll find above
126   created this lacuna when it rushed back up.'

As far as one can get from Beelzebub,
in the remotest corner of this cavern,
129   there is a place one cannot find by sight,

but by the sound of a narrow stream that trickles
through a channel it has cut into the rock
132   in its meanderings, making a gentle slope.

Into that hidden passage my guide and I
entered, to find again the world of light,
135   and, without thinking of a moment's rest,

we climbed up, he first and I behind him,
far enough to see, through a round opening,
a few of those fair things the heavens bear.
139   Then we came forth, to see again the stars.

1. The first verse of the last canto of *Inferno* (like the first verse of the last canto of *Purgatorio*) is in Latin. Its first three words are identical to the first verse of a hymn of the True Cross composed by Venantius Fortunatus (sixth century) but the last, obviously, has been added by Dante. Satan, still in the distance, is naturally not "advancing" against Dante and Virgil, but the wind he emits might have made it seem that way as they approach him. Satan, as we shall see, is immobile.

This is the only complete Latin verse in the *cantica*, but see seven earlier Latin words or phrases: *Inferno* I.65; I.70; XV.62; XVI.88; XVIII.6; XXI.42; XXVII.72.

4–7. "The Satanic mills" of William Blake may not reflect this passage, even as much as Blake read Dante, yet Dante's simile immediately presents Satan as a vast contraption doing its necessary work in the architect's plan for this infernal city. We reflect that this was once the fairest of angels, now reduced, despite his awesome size, to mindless iteration of his wings. Joan Ferrante speaks of "Lucifer, who emits no sound but sends forth a silent and freezing wind of hate, a parody perhaps of the love-inspiring tongues of flame brought to the Apostles by the Holy Spirit" (Ferr.1969.1), p. 38.

8–9. Commentators occasionally remark that Dante has here forgotten the fact that insubstantial Virgil, a shade, would give Dante no shelter at all. The "rules" of the poem overrule the "rules" of even his own physics if and when he chooses. For example, Virgil picks Dante up and carries him at *Inferno* XIX.124–125 and XXIII.37. See note to *Inferno* VI.34–36.

10. Since Tommaseo, in 1837, commentators have cited, for this verse, Aeneas's words as he tells the story of Laocoön (*Aen.* II.204): "horresco referens" (I shudder merely to tell it). In the *Aeneid* two serpents are moving toward the priest to kill him; here, the Serpent is being approached by Virgil and Dante. The differing context is eventually reassuring, but the protagonist is, for the last time in this *cantica*, filled with fear.

11–12. For the third time in Cocytus the fact that we have crossed a boundary is made clear only by the fact that sinners are now punished in a different posture. This last realm is named, of course, for Judas, who betrayed his rightful Lord, Jesus Christ.

13–15. The sinners here are frozen inside the ice, as though tossed into it helter-skelter before it froze and now stuck in their various postures eternally, like straw caught in molten glass in the artisan's shop and now fastened in that glass, a lasting imperfection in it. Their postures are horizontal (whether facedown or supine we cannot tell—perhaps both), vertical (both head-up and head-down), or bent in two. We eventually realize that in this zone we will not learn the identity of any of these sinners, a situation that may remind us of the anonymity that was insisted on for the neutrals in *Inferno* III.49–51. All of our attention is saved for Lucifer and the three special betrayers who are punished in his mouth.

20–21. Virgil uses the classical name for the king of hell, as he has once before (*Inf.* XI.65), and as he did in his own poem (e.g., *Aen.* VI.269). This is the last time that we will hear that name, as we are shortly to leave his "kingdom." The phrase "Ecco Dite" here surely echoes the phrase used of Jesus, before he is sentenced to death, "Ecce homo." See note to *Inferno* XVII.1–3.

22–27. The last verse of this seventh and last address to the reader in *Inferno* is treated by most commentators as a triviality, i.e., Dante assures the reader that he was indeed half-dead (as he has already said). See, for example, the comment found in Bosco/Reggio: "The expression simply translates . . . that simple and banal phrase . . . in Italian, *mezzo morto* [half dead]." Does Dante need to ask us to exercise our wits, if we have these, in order to understand *that*? The portentousness of his declaration that he cannot write what he became because words would fail him cannot be squared with such an interpretation, words for which would fail no one. Few, however, have come forward with more vital readings. Gregorio Di Siena, in his commentary, quotes Torricelli, who says that at this moment Dante is passing from the state of death to the state of living in God's forgiveness. Ernesto Trucchi, who bridles at the terribly uninteresting readings put forward by previous commentators, claims that this is the moment in which, in the protagonist, the fear of hell becomes the fear of God. More recently, Durling and Martinez propose (Durl.1996.1, p. 544) the following: "This moment is the culmination of the penitential imitation of Christ in the descent into hell, symbolically the pilgrim's death to sin, that is, the death of the 'old man,' leading to the reversal of direction from descent to ascent." They give credit to Freccero's essay "The Sign of Satan" (Frec.1986.1), pp. 167–79. Whether we accept their interpretation or not, it does seem that they, and very few others, have responded with the kind of attention that the passage obviously calls for.

30–31.   That is, "I am, proportionally, closer in size to a giant than a giant is to Lucifer." For the size of the giants, ca. seventy feet, see the note to *Inferno* XXXI.58–66. Let us, merely for purposes of calculation, agree that Dante was six feet tall. The equation is simple: $6/70 = 70/x; x = 817$. Since a body is roughly 2.5 times an arm's length, Satan is some 2000 feet tall and thus looms, from the waist up, over the ice by some 1000 feet.

35.   Satan, once of the highest order of angels, the Seraphim, has come a long way down. It is worth noting that the only other sinner in hell referred to as raising his brows is prideful Farinata (*Inf.* X.45).

37–38.   The "wonder" that is Satan even now reminds us of his divine origin. As many have noted, he stands before us as a parodic version of Christ crucified, even to his physical resemblance to the scene on Golgotha, in which Christ was upon a cross between two thieves. For a representation of the three-headed Satan known to Dante from the mosaic on the ceiling of the Baptistry in Florence see Bosco/Reggio's commentary.

39–45.   The three colors of Satan's faces have caused much debate. Almost all the early commentators equate them with the opposites of the three attributes of the trinitarian God, Love, Power, and Knowledge. They associate red with anger, thus hatred (or impotence), yellowish white with impotence (or hatred), and black with ignorance. As many note, these are not particularly convincing schemes, if their overall applicability seems acceptable.

46–51.   The six wings of Satan are his six wings as one of the angelic order of Seraphim (Isaiah 6:2); they are now not glorious in color but the wings of a giant bat. Their resemblance to sails on a great ship is parodic, since Satan proceeds nowhere, but connects with images associated with Ulysses (*Inf.* XXVI) and the ship bringing the saved souls to the shore of purgatory (*Purg.* I).

53–57.   Guido da Pisa associates Satan's tears and mastication with a biblical text (Matth. 8:12), Jesus' words to the centurion concerning those who fail to believe: "and there shall be weeping and gnashing of teeth."

61–67.   The three most gravely punished sinners of the poem are Judas Iscariot, who betrayed Jesus (founder of the Church), as well as Brutus and Cassius, who betrayed Julius Caesar (the first ruler of the empire). Judas is tortured more severely, his back flayed (see vv. 58–60) as was Christ's, on the way to Golgotha, bearing the cross. Nonetheless, Brutus and Cassius, those stalwarts of the Roman Republic, which Dante honored so notably (see Holl.1986.1), are not treated a great deal better. When we consider that another "conspirator" against Julius, Cato the Younger, is found saved in the next canto (*Purg.* I), we must surely be puzzled. For Dante, despite his predominant hostility to him as a man (see Stul.1991.1, pp. 33–43), Julius was nonetheless the first emperor of Rome, and thus served a divinely-ordained purpose. For this reason, Brutus and Cassius are seen as betrayers of their rightful lord.

68–69.   It is now nightfall of the Saturday of Easter weekend; the journey to this point has lasted precisely twenty-four hours. We have also reached the border of the midpoint of this canto, verse 69 of 139. The next verse begins the action that will encompass another twenty-four-hour period, seventy verses that will extend through exactly as many hours as have been consumed by the journey up to now.

71–75.   When Satan opens his wings, Virgil, with Dante holding on to him, seizes the moment to grasp the animal-like flank of "the Beast."

76–84.   At the very center of the universe even Virgil, a shade, feels the pull of gravity as he tries to move back up toward the light.

   The locution describing Virgil's changed direction, "ov' elli avea le zanche" (where he had his shanks), has caused debate, some believing that the "he" refers to Virgil himself, i.e., turned his head to where *his* legs had been; others, that he turned his head to where Satan's leg were. Our translation follows Hatcher and Musa, who opt for Satan's legs (Hatc.1964.1 and Hatc.1966.1), pointing out, among other things, that Dante's insertion of the pronoun "elli" before the verb "avea" makes it almost necessary to draw this conclusion, since he never else inserts a pronoun into a sequence of verbs without introducing a new subject of the verb; that is, if the line read "[Virgilio] volse la testa ov' avea le zanche," Virgil would clearly be the implied subject of the second verb. According to Hatcher and Musa, the "elli" all but removes that possibility.

Since Dante doesn't understand (see vv. 90–93) that he has reached the center of the universe and is being moved back upward toward the surface of the earth at the antipodes, he assumes that Virgil is going back up toward the ice of Cocytus.

94–96.   It is now 7:30 AM (midway between 6:00 and 9:00, the first "tierce," or three-hour period, into four of which the solar day was divided (6–9; 9–noon; noon-3; 3–6). Since moments ago (v. 68) we had learned that it was 6 PM in Jerusalem, how can this be? For the first time in the poem Virgil tells time by the sun, and not the moon; and he tells it by the position of the sun in purgatory, twelve hours ahead of Jerusalem (where it is currently 7:30 PM). We are leaving hell behind.

97–120.   Even though the travelers have to traverse an enormous distance in seventy lines, thirty-nine of them (88–126) are devoted to their new situation, Dante's three questions, and Virgil's responses. The setting is a space on the convex side of the ice of Cocytus, i.e., on its far side. The only remaining evidence of the infernal core is offered by the legs of Lucifer, sticking up through the crust of the area that contains the rest of him. We are on the other side of the ice, and there is nothing more by way of constructed space to catch our eye.

Dante wants to know why he no longer sees the ice, why Lucifer is "upside down," and how it can already be morning. Some of Virgil's explanations have already been adverted to. He also explains that they are now under the southern hemisphere of the world above, not the northern, where Christ was put to death and whence they had begun their descent.

121–126.   Virgil's final words in *Inferno* create, as it were, the foundation myth of sin: how it established itself in the world that God had made good. Forti (Fort.1986.1), p. 246, refers to the passage as a "genuine cosmological myth," to the fall of Lucifer as "the first event that occurs in time" (p. 259).

It is worth considering a similar passage in Ovid (*Metam.* I.151–162): Astraea, or justice, has just left the earth. The battle of Phlegra ensues (about which we have heard in Canto XXXI [44–45, 91–96, 119–121]); once the giants are destroyed, mother Earth, Gea, forms man in their image, if smaller, out of their gore. But this new stock, too, is contemptuous of the gods. Soon enough Lycaon (the "wolf-man") will commit the first murder, one that will eventually lead to the murder of Julius Caesar (v. 201).

Here, in the final moments of the final canto, we learn of the first things to occur in terrestrial time: Satan fell from heaven and crashed into our earth (see *Par.* XXIX.55–57). To flee from him, all the land in the southern hemisphere hid beneath the sea and moved to the north of the equator, while the matter that he displaced in his fall rose up behind him to form the mount of purgatory.

Over the years there have been efforts to find contradictions to this view of the earth's "geology" in Dante's later *Questio de aqua et terra* (1320). Bruno Nardi (Nard.1959.1) made a case for the contradiction. Freccero's review (Frec.1961.1) offered strong rebuttals to Nardi's main arguments. The magisterial edition produced by Mazzoni (Mazz.1979.2) convincingly presents the work as Dantean. Pasquazi (Pasq.1985.1) makes a strong case for the absence of any significant contradiction. For a study of the wider question see Stabile (Stab.1983.1).

127–132.   Along a passage in the rock through the space contained between the floor formed by the convex side of Cocytus and the underside of the earth above, the travelers follow the sound of a stream. It, many suggest, is the river Lethe, running down into hell filled with the sins now forgotten by all who have purged themselves of them (*Purg.* XXVIII.127–130).

133–138.   There is no pausing for rest that now seems a waste of time, given the nearness of the light. Looking through a crevice (the word in Italian is *pertugio*, the same word used to describe the opening through which Ugolino could see the moon from his cell [*Inf.* XXXIII.22]) in the earth's surface, whence, we assume, comes the little stream that they are following, Dante is able to see a few stars in the firmament above him.

139.   In a single verse the *cantica* concludes. And in this line both Virgil and Dante actually step out of hell, and now can see the full expanse of the dawn sky, filled with stars. Both *Purgatorio* and *Paradiso* will also end with the word "stars" *(stelle)*, the goals of a human sight that is being drawn to God. There is no doubt as to the fact that even *Inferno*, ending in happiness of this kind, is a comedic part of a comedic whole.

Index of these items (in their English forms, where these exist) in the Italian text of *Inferno*. NB: (1) if a character or place is mentioned more than once in a canto, only the first reference is present; (2) no distinction has been made between direct and indirect references; i.e., one will find "Laertes" instead of "Ulysses, father of."

This index is meant to help the reader find subjects, treated in the notes, that may not be readily remembered as being related to a particular passage.

What follows is precisely that, not an inclusive bibliography of studies relevant to Dante or even to his *Inferno*, which alone would be voluminous. Abbreviated references in the texts of the notes are keyed to this alphabetical listing. For those interested in the general condition of Dantean bibliography, however, a few remarks may be helpful.

Since an extended bibliography for the study of Dante includes tens of thousands of items, those who deal with the subjects that branch out from the works of this writer are condemned to immoderate labor and a sense that they are always missing something important. While even half a century ago it was possible to develop, in a single treatment, a fairly thorough compendium of the most significant items (e.g., S. A. Chimenz, *Dante*, in *Letteratura italiana. I maggiori* [Milan: Marzorati, 1954], pp. 85–109), the situation today would require far more space. Fortunately, the extraordinary scholarly tool represented by the *Enciclopedia dantesca*, dir. U. Bosco, 6 vols. (Rome, Istituto della Enciclopedia Italiana, 1970–78—henceforth *ED*) has given Dante studies its single most important bibliographical resource, leaving only the last quarter century—which happens to be the most active period in the history of Dante studies—uncovered. However, for the years 1965–90 Enzo Esposito has edited a helpful guide, *Dalla bibliografia alla storiografia: la bibliografia dantesca nel mondo dal 1965–1990* (Ravenna: Longo, 1995). A closer analysis of a shorter period is available in "Bibliografia Dantesca 1972–1977," ed. Leonella Coglievina, *Studi Danteschi* 60 (1988): 35–314 (presenting 3121 items for this five-year period). The bibliography in *ED*, vol. 6, pp. 499–618 (a length that gives some sense of the amount of basic information available), contains ca. 5000 items and is of considerable use, breaking its materials into convenient categories. (Its bibliography of bibliographies alone runs six double-column pages, pp. 542–47.) The *ED* also, of course, contains important bibliographical indications in many of its entries. A major new English source for bibliographical information has recently been published: *The Dante Encyclopedia,* ed. Richard Lansing (New York: Garland, 2000).

In the past dozen years, Dante studies, perhaps more than any other post-classical area of literature, has moved into "the computer age." There is a growing online bibliography available, developed from the bibliography of American Dante studies, overseen by Richard Lansing for the Dante Society of America, which includes a growing number of Italian items (http://www.princeton.edu/~dante). Some seventy-one commentaries to the *Commedia* are now available through the Dartmouth Dante Project (opened 1988), still best reached via Telnet (telnet library.dartmouth.edu; at the prompt type "connect dante"), but soon to be available on the Web as well. There is also the new Princeton Dante Project (http://www.princeton.edu/dante), a multimedia edition of the *Commedia* (open to public use since 1999) overseen by Robert Hollander, which also functions as an entry point to most of the many Dante sites on the Web, perhaps most notably that established and maintained by Otfried Lieberknecht in Berlin, which is a source of an enormous amount of information about Dante in electronic form, and, in the autumn of 2000, the site being developed by the Società Dantesca Italiana (www.danteonline.it).

LIST OF WORKS CITED IN THE NOTES

Aher.1982.1
Ahern, John, "Dante's Slyness: The Unnamed Sin of the Eighth Bolgia," *Romanic Review* 73 (1982): 275–91.

Aher.1982.2
Ahern, John, "Apocalyptic Onomastics: Focaccia (*Inferno* XXXII, 63)," *Romance Notes* 23 (1982): 181–84.

Ales.1993.1
Alessio, Gian Carlo, and Claudia Villa, "Per *Inferno* I, 67–87," in *Dante e la "bella scola" della poesia: Autorità e sfida poetica,* ed. A. A. Iannucci (Ravenna: Longo, 1993 [1984]), pp. 41–64.

Alsa.1977.1
Al-Sabah, Rasha, "*Inferno* XXVIII: The Figure of Muhammad," *Yale Italian Studies* 1 (1977): 147–61.

Armo.1983.1
Armour, Peter, "Dante's Brunetto: The Paternal Paterine?" *Italian Studies* 38 (1983): 1–38.

Armo.1991.1
Armour, Peter, "The Love of Two Florentines: Brunetto Latini and Bondie Dietaiuti," *Lectura Dantis [virginiana]* 9 (1991): 60–71.

Auer.1954.1
Auerbach, Erich, "Dante's Addresses to the Reader," *Romance Philology* 7 (1954): 268–78.

Auer.1957.1
Auerbach, Erich, "Farinata and Cavalcante," in *Mimesis: The Representation of Reality in Western Literature*, tr. W. Trask (New York: Doubleday Anchor, 1957 [1946]), pp. 151–77.

Auer.1958.1
Auerbach, Erich, "*Sermo humilis*," in *Literary Language and Its Public in Late Latin Antiquity and in the Middle Ages*, tr. R. Manheim (Princeton: Princeton University Press, 1965 [1958]), pp. 25–66.

Aust.1932.1
Austin, H. D., "The Submerged (*Inf.*, XX, 3)," *Romanic Review* 23 (1932): 38–40.

Aval.1975.1
Avalle d'Arco, Silvio, ". . . de fole amor," in *Modelli semiologici nella "Commedia" di Dante* (Milan: Bompiani, 1975), pp. 97–121; 137–73.

Bacc.1954.1
Bacchelli, Riccardo, "Da Dite a Malebolge: la tragedia delle porte chiuse e la farsa dei ponti rotti," *Giornale storico della letteratura italiana* 131 (1954): 1–32.

Bake.1974.1
Baker, David J., "The Winter Simile in *Inferno* XXIV," *Dante Studies* 92 (1974): 77–91.

Bald.1978.1
Baldassaro, Lawrence, "*Inferno* XII: The Irony of Descent," *Romance Notes* 19 (1978): 98–103.

Bald.1988.1
Baldelli, Ignazio, "Dante, i Guidi e i Malatesta," *Annali della Scuola Normale Superiore di Pisa,* serie 3, 18 (1988): 1067–70.

Bald.1993.1
Baldelli, Ignazio, "Un errore lessicografico: 'palombaro' e Gerione palombaro," in *Omaggio a Gianfranco Folena* (Padua: Editoriale Programma, 1993), pp. 243–49.

Bald.1997.1
Baldelli, Ignazio, "Le 'fiche' di Vanni Fucci," *Giornale storico della letteratura italiana* 174 (1997): 1–38.

Bald.1998.1
Baldelli, Ignazio, "Dante e Ulisse," *Lettere Italiane* 50 (1998): 358–73.

Bara.1981.1
Barański, Zygmunt G., "*Inferno* VI.73: A Controversy Re-examined," *Italian Studies* 36 (1981): 1–26.

Bara.1993.1
Barański, Zygmunt G., "Dante e la tradizione comica latina," in *Dante e la "bella scola" della poesia: Autorità e sfida poetica*, ed. A. A. Iannucci (Ravenna: Longo, 1993), pp. 225–45.

Bara.1995.3
Barański, Zygmunt G., "The Poetics of Meter: *Terza rima,* 'canto,' 'canzon,' 'cantica,' " in *Dante Now: Current Trends in Dante Studies*, ed. Theodore J. Cachey, Jr. (Notre Dame: University of Notre Dame Press, 1995), pp. 3–41.

Bara.1997.1
Barański, Zygmunt G., ed., *Seminario Dantesco Internazionale: Atti del primo convegno tenutosi al Chauncey Conference Center, Princeton, 21–23 ottobre 1994* (Florence: Le Lettere, 1997).

Barb.1934.1
Barbi, Michele, *Problemi di critica dantesca* (Florence: Sansoni, 1934).

Barb.1934.2
Barbi, Michele, "Ancora sul testo della *Divina Commedia*," *Studi Danteschi* 18 (1934): 5–57.

Barb.1972.1
Barberi Squarotti, Giorgio, "*Inferno*, XX" [*Ateneo Veneto* 1965], in *L'artificio dell'eternità* (Verona: Fiorini, 1972), pp. 235–81.

Barb.1972.2
Barberi Squarotti, Giorgio, "L'orazione del conte Ugolino," in *L'artificio dell'eternità* (Verona: Fiorini, 1972), pp. 283–332.

Barc.1973.1
Barchiesi, Marino, "Catarsi classica e 'medicina' dantesca, Dal canto XX dell'*Inferno*," *Letture classensi* 4 (1973): 9–124.

Barc.1973.2
Barchiesi, Marino, "Il Testo e il Tempo," *Il Verri,* ser. V, no. 4 (December 1973): 76–95.

Baro.1984.1
Barolini, Teodolinda, *Dante's Poets* (Princeton: Princeton University Press, 1984).

Baro.1992.1
Barolini, Teodolinda, *The Undivine "Comedy": Detheologizing Dante* (Princeton: Princeton University Press, 1992).

Baro.1997.1
Barolini, Teodolinda, "Guittone's *Ora parrà*, Dante's *Doglia mi reca*, and the *Commedia*'s Anatomy of Desire," in *Seminario Dantesco Internazionale: Atti del primo convegno tenutosi al Chauncey Conference Center, Princeton, 21–23 ottobre 1994*, ed. Z. G. Barański (Florence: Le Lettere, 1997), pp. 3–23.

Baro.1998.1
Barolini, Teodolinda, "Canto XX: True and False See-ers," in *Lectura Dantis: "Inferno"*, ed. A. Mandelbaum, A. Oldcorn, C. Ross (Berkeley: University of California Press, 1998), pp. 275–86.

Bate.1989.1
Bates, Richard, and Thomas Rendall, "Dante's Ulysses and the Epistle of James," *Dante Studies* 107 (1989): 33–44.

Beal.1983.1
Beal, Rebecca, "Dante among Thieves: Allegorical Soteriology in the Seventh *Bolgia* (*Inferno* XXIV and XXV)," *Medievalia* 9 (1983): 101–23.

Beck.1984.1
Becker, Christopher, "Justice among the Centaurs," *Forum Italicum* 18 (1984): 217–29.

Bell.1989.1
Bellomo, Saverio, ed., Filippo Villani, *Expositio seu comentum super "Comedia" Dantis Allegherii* (Florence: Le Lettere, 1989).

Benf.1995.1
Benfell, V. Stanley, "Prophetic Madness: The Bible in *Inferno* XIX," *Modern Language Notes* 110 (1995): 145–63.

Beno.1983.1
Benoit, Raymond, "*Inferno* V," *The Explicator* 41, 3 (1983): 2.

Bian.1921.1
Bianchi, Enrico, "Le 'cerchie eterne,' " *Studi Danteschi* 3 (1921): 137–39.

Blas.1969.1
Blasucci, Luigi, "L'esperienza delle *Petrose* e il linguaggio della *Divina Commedia*," in his *Studi su Dante e Ariosto* (Milan: Ricciardi, 1969), pp. 1–35.

Bloo.1994.1
Bloom, Harold, "The Strangeness of Dante: Ulysses and Beatrice," in his *The Western Canon: The Books and the School of the Ages* (New York: Harcourt Brace, 1994), pp. 76–104.

Bors.1957.1
Borst, Arno, *Der Turmbau von Babel,* 3 vols. (Stuttgart: A. Hiersemann, 1957–60).

Bott.1988.2
Botterill, Steven, "Rereading Lancelot: Dante, Chaucer, and *Le Chevalier de la Charrette,*" *Philological Quarterly* 67 (1988): 279–89.

Bott.1990.1
Botterill, Steven, "*Inferno* XII," in *Dante's "Divine Comedy", Introductory Readings, I: "Inferno"* (Special issue, *Lectura Dantis Virginiana,* vol. I), ed. T. Wlassics (Charlottesville, Va.: University of Virginia, 1990), pp. 149–62.

Boyd.1981.1
Boyde, Patrick, *Dante Philomythes and Philosopher: Man in the Cosmos* (Cambridge: Cambridge University Press, 1981).

Boyd.1993.1
Boyde, Patrick, *Perception and passion in Dante's "Comedy"* (Cambridge: Cambridge University Press, 1993).

Brow.1978.1
Brownlee, Kevin, "Dante and Narcissus (*Purg.* XXX, 76–99)," *Dante Studies* 96 (1978): 201–6.

Brow.1984.1
Brownlee, Kevin, "Phaeton's Fall and Dante's Ascent," *Dante Studies* 102 (1984): 135–44.

Brug.1981.1
Brugnoli, Giorgio, "Chi per lungo silenzio parea fioco," in *Letterature comparate: problemi e metodo. Studi in onore di Ettore Paratore*, vol. 3 (Bologna: Pàtron, 1981).

Brug.1989.1
Brugnoli, Giorgio, "Le 'cagne conte,'" in *Filologia e critica dantesca: studi offerti a Aldo Vallone* (Florence: Olschki, 1989), pp. 95–112.

Brug.1993.1
Brugnoli, Giorgio, "Omero," in *Dante e la "bella scola" della poesia: Autorità e sfida poetica*, ed. A. A. Iannucci (Ravenna: Longo, 1993), pp. 65–85.

Busn.1922.1
Busnelli, Giovanni, "La ruina del secondo cerchio e Francesca da Rimini," *Miscellanea Dantesca pubblicata a cura del Comitato cattolico padovano per il VI centenario della morte del Poeta* (Padua, 1922), pp. 49–60.

Cacc.1966.1
Caccia, Ettore, "L'accenno di Dante a Garda e i versi 67–69 nel canto XX dell'*Inferno*," in *Dante e la cultura veneta*, ed. V. Branca and G. Padoan (Florence: Olschki, 1966), pp. 307–25.

Cacc.1967.1
Caccia, Ettore, "Canto XX," in *"Inferno": Lectura Dantis Scaligera* (Florence: Le Monnier, 1967), pp. 673–724.

Camb.1970.1
Cambon, Glauco, "Synaesthesia in the *Divine Comedy*," *Dante Studies* 88 (1970): 3–5.

Cami.1950.1
Camilli, Amerindo, "La cronologia del viaggio dantesco," *Studi Danteschi* 29 (1950): 61–84.

Care.1951.1
Caretti, Lanfranco, *Il canto di Francesca* (Lucca: Lucentia, 1951).

Care.1951.2
Caretti, Lanfranco, "Una Interpretazione Dantesca," in *Studi e ricerche di letteratura italiana* (Florence: La Nuova Italia, 1951), pp. 4–14.

Caro.1967.1
Carozza, Davy, "Elements of the *roman courtois* in the Episode of Paolo and Francesca (*Inferno* V)," *Papers on Language and Literature* 3 (1967): 291–301.

Carp.1998.1
Carpi, Umberto, "I tiranni (a proposito di *Inf.* XII)," *L'Alighieri* 39 (1998): 7–31.

Casa.1978.1
Casagrande, Gino, "Dante e Filippo Argenti: riscontri patristici e note di critica testuale," *Studi Danteschi* 51 (1978): 221–54.

Casa.1997.1
Casagrande, Gino, "Parole di Dante: il 'lungo silenzio' di *Inferno* I, 63," *Giornale storico della letteratura italiana* 174 (1997): 243–54.

Case.1943.1
Casella, Mario, " 'L'amico mio e non della ventura,' " *Studi Danteschi* 27 (1943): 117–34.

Cass.1971.1
Cassata, Letterio, "Tre *cruces* dantesche: I. La *ruina* dei lussuriosi," *Studi Danteschi* 48 (1971): 5–14.

Cass.1981.1
Cassell, Anthony K. " 'Ulisseana': A Bibliography of Dante's Ulysses to 1981," *Italian Culture* 3 (1981): 23–45.

Cass.1984.1
Cassell, Anthony K., *Dante's Fearful Art of Justice* (Toronto: University of Toronto Press, 1984).

Cass.1989.1
Cassell, Anthony K., "Il silenzio di Virgilio: *Inferno* I, 62–63," *Letture classensi* 18 (1989): 165–76.

Cass.1989.2
Cassell, Anthony K., *Lectura Dantis Americana: "Inferno" I* (Philadelphia: University of Pennsylvania Press, 1989).

Cecc.1990.1
Cecchetti, Giovanni, "*Inferno* XXXI," *Lectura Dantis [virginiana]* 6 ([supplement] 1990): 400–411.

Chia.1967.1
Chiari, Alberto, "Canto XXXI," in *Lectura Dantis Scaligera*, dir. Mario Marcazzan (Florence: Le Monnier, 1967 [1962]), pp. 1091–1121.

Chia.1984.1
Chiavacci Leonardi, Anna Maria, "Questioni di punteggiatura in due celebri attacchi danteschi (*Inf.*, II 76–78 e X 67–69)," *Lettere Italiane* 36 (1984): 3–24.

Chia.1985.1
Chiarenza, Marguerite Mills, "Time and Eternity in the Myths of *Paradiso* XVII," in *Dante, Petrarch, Boccaccio: Studies in the Italian Trecento in Honor of Charles S. Singleton*, ed. A. S. Bernardo and A. L. Pellegrini (Binghamton, N.Y.: Medieval & Renaissance Texts and Studies, 1985), pp. 134–35.

Chia.1989.1
Chiappelli, Fredi, "Il colore della menzogna nell'*Inferno* dantesco," *Letture classensi* 18 (1989): 115–28.

Chia.1991.1
Chiavacci Leonardi, Anna Maria, *Inferno, con il commento di A. M. C. L.* (Milan: Mondadori, 1991).

Chia.1998.1
Chiamenti, Massimiliano, "Due *schedulae* ferine: Dante, *Rime* CIII 71 e *Inf.* XVI 45," *Lingua nostra* 59 (1998): 7–10.

Chie.1998.1
Chierichini, Claudia, "La III *Satira* di Persio 'fra le righe' di *Inferno* XXVI," *L'Alighieri* 11 (1998): 95–103.

Ciof.1937.1
Cioffari, Vincenzo, "A Dantc Note: *Heliotropum*," *Romanic Review* 28 (1937): 59–62.

Ciof.1940.1
Cioffari, Vincenzo, *The Conception of Fortune and Fate in the Works of Dante* (Cambridge, Mass.: Dante Society of Cambridge, Mass., 1940).

Coga.1999.1
Cogan, Marc, *The Design in the Wax: The Structure of the "Divine Comedy" and Its Meaning* (Notre Dame: University of Notre Dame Press, 1999).

Conr.1981.1
Conrieri, Davide, "Letture del canto XXI dell'*Inferno*," *Giornale storico della letteratura italiana* 158 (1981): 1–43.

Cont.1976.1
Contini, Gianfranco, *Un' idea di Dante* (Turin: Einaudi, 1976)

Cont.1995.1
Contrada, Deborah, "Brunetto's Sin: Ten Years of Criticism (1977–1986)," in *Dante: Summa Medievalis*, ed. C. Franco and L. Morgan (Stony Brook, N.Y.: Forum Italicum, 1995), pp. 192–207.

Corn.1989.1
Cornish, Alison, "The Epistle of James in *Inferno* 26," *Traditio* 45 (1989–90): 367–79.

Cort.1990.1
Corti, Maria, "On the Metaphors of Sailing, Flight, and Tongues of Fire in the Episode of Ulysses (*Inf.* 26)," *Stanford Italian Review* 9 (1990): 33–47.

Crim.1993.1
Crimi, Erminia Maria Dispenza, *"Cortesia" e "Valore" dalla tradizione a Dante* (Rovito: Marra, 1993).

Croc.1921.1
Croce, Benedetto, *La poesia di Dante,* 2nd ed. (Bari: Laterza, 1921).

Curt.1948.1
Curtius, Ernst Robert, *European Literature and the Latin Middle Ages,*
tr. W. R. Trask (New York: Harper & Row, 1963 [1948]).

Darb.1971.1
Darby Chapin, D. L., "IO and the Negative Apotheosis of Vanni Fucci,"
Dante Studies 89 (1971): 19–31.

Davi.1957.1
Davis, Charles Till, *Dante and the Idea of Rome* (Oxford: Oxford
University Press, 1957).

Davi.1967.1
Davis, Charles T., "Brunetto Latini and Dante," *Studi medievali* 8 (1967):
421–50.

Davi.1998.1
Davis, Charles T., "Canto XIX: Simoniacs," in *Lectura Dantis: "Inferno,"* ed.
A. Mandelbaum, A. Oldcorn, C. Ross (Berkeley: University of California
Press, 1998), pp. 262–74.

DeAn.1993.1
de Angelis, Violetta, ". . . e l'ultimo Lucano," in *Dante e la "bella scola" della
poesia: Autorità e sfida poetica,* ed. A. A. Iannucci (Ravenna: Longo, 1993),
pp. 145–203.

Delc.1989.1
Delcorno, Carlo, *Exemplum e letteratura tra medioevo e rinascimento* (Bologna:
Il Mulino, 1989).

DeRo.1981.1
De Robertis, Domenico, "In viaggio coi demòni (canto XXII
dell'*Inferno*)," *Studi Danteschi* 53 (1981): 1–29.

DeSa.1949.1
De Sanctis, Francesco, *Storia della letteratura italiana,* 4th ed. (Bari: Laterza,
1949 [1870]).

DeSa.1967.1
De Sanctis, Francesco, "L'Ugolino di Dante," in his *Opere*, vol. 5 (Turin: Einaudi, 1967 [1869]), pp. 681–704.

Desp.1952.1
Desport, Marie, *L'Incantation virgilienne: Virgile et Orphée* (Bordeaux: Delmas, 1952).

DiSc.1995.1
Di Scipio, Giuseppe, *The Presence of Pauline Thought in the Works of Dante* (Lewiston, N.Y.: The Edwin Mellen Press, 1995).

Domb.1970.1
Dombrowski, Robert, "The Grain of Hell: A Note on Retribution in *Inferno* VI," *Dante Studies* 88 (1970): 103–8.

Donn.1973.1
Donno, Daniel J., "Dante's Ulysses and Virgil's Prohibition," *Italica* 50 (1973): 26–37.

Dovi.1926.1
D'Ovidio, Francesco, "Esposizione del canto XX dell'*Inferno*," in his *Nuovo volume di studi danteschi* (Caserta-Rome: A. P. E., 1926), pp. 313–55.

Dozo.1991.1
Dozon, Marthe, *Mythe et symbole dans La divine comédie* (Florence: Olschki, 1991).

Dron.1975.1
Dronke, Peter, "Francesca and Héloise," *Comparative Literature* 27 (1975): 113–35.

Dron.1986.1
Dronke, Peter, "The Giants in Hell," in his *Dante and Medieval Latin Traditions* (Cambridge: Cambridge University Press, 1986), pp. 32–54.

Dron.1989.1
Dronke, Peter, "Symbolism and Structure in *Paradiso* 30," *Romance Philology* 43 (1989): 29–48.

Durl. 1981.1
Durling, Robert, "Deceit and Digestion in the Belly of Hell," in *Allegory and Representation: Selected Papers from the English Institute, 1979–80,* ed. Stephen A. Greenblatt (Baltimore: The Johns Hopkins University Press, 1981), pp. 61–93.

Durl. 1981.2
Durling, Robert M., "Farinata and the Body of Christ," *Stanford Italian Review* 2 (1981): 5–35.

Durl. 1990.1
Durling, Robert M., and Ronald L. Martinez, *Time and the Crystal: Studies in Dante's "Rime petrose"* (Berkeley: University of California Press, 1990).

Durl. 1996.1
Durling, Robert M., *The "Divine Comedy" of Dante Alighieri,* Notes by R. M. Durling and Ronald Martinez (New York and Oxford: Oxford University Press, 1996).

Econ. 1976.1
Economou, George D., "The Pastoral Simile of *Inferno* XXIV and the Unquiet Heart of the Christian Pilgrim," *Speculum* 51 (1976): 637–46.

ED
Enciclopedia dantesca, 6 vols. (Rome: Istituto della Enciclopedia Italiana, 1970–78).

Fabb. 1910.1
Fabbri, Fabio, "Le invocazioni nella *Divina Commedia,*" *Giornale dantesco* 18 (1910): 186–92.

Feng. 1981.1
Fengler, Christie K., and William A. Stephany, "The Capuan Gate and Pier della Vigna," *Dante Studies* 99 (1981): 145–57.

Ferr. 1935.1
Ferretti, Giovanni, *I due tempi della composizione della "Divina Commedia"* (Bari: Laterza, 1935).

Ferr.1969.1
Ferrante, Joan, "The Relation of Speech to Sin in the *Inferno*," *Dante Studies* 87 (1969): 33–46.

Ferr.1971.1
Ferrucci, Franco, "Comedía," *Yearbook of Italian Studies* 1 (1971): 29–52.

Ferr.1984.1
Ferrante, Joan, *The Political Vision of the "Divine Comedy"* (Princeton: Princeton University Press, 1984).

Ferr.1993.1
Ferrante, Joan, "A Poetics of Chaos and Harmony," in *The Cambridge Companion to Dante*, ed. R. Jacoff (Cambridge: Cambridge University Press, 1993), pp. 153–71.

Ferr.1994.1
Ferretti Cuomo, Luisa, *Anatomia di un'immagine ("Inferno" 2 127–132): saggio di lessicologia e di semantica strutturale* (New York: Peter Lang, 1994).

Ferr.1995.1
Ferretti Cuomo, Luisa, "La polisemia delle similitudini nella *Divina Commedia*. Eliseo: un caso esemplare," *Strumenti critici* 10 n.s. (1995): 105–42.

Filo.1911.1
Filomusi Guelfi, Lorenzo, *Nuovi studi su Dante* (Città di Castello: Lapi, 1911), pp. 185–95.

Fort.1961.1
Forti, Fiorenzo, "Il limbo dantesco e i megalopsichoi dell'Etica nicomachea," *Giornale storico della letteratura italiana* 138 (1961): 329–64.

Fort.1986.1
Forti, Carla, "Nascita dell'Inferno o nascita del Purgatorio: nota sulla caduta del Lucifero dantesco," *Rivista di letteratura italiana* 4 (1986): 241–60.

Fost.1969.1
Foster, Kenelm, "The Canto of the Damned Popes: *Inferno* XIX," *Dante Studies* 87 (1969): 47–68.

Fran.1982.1
Frankel, Margherita, "Biblical Figurations in Dante's Reading of the *Aeneid*," *Dante Studies* 100 (1982): 13–23.

Fran.1984.1
Frankel, Margherita, "Dante's Anti-Virgilian *villanello*," *Dante Studies* 102 (1984): 81–109.

Fran.1986.1
Frankel, Margherita, "The Context of Dante's Ulysses: the Similes in *Inferno* XXVI," *Dante Studies* 104 (1986): 25–42.

Frec.1961.1
Freccero, John, "Satan's Fall and the *Quaestio de aqua et terra*," *Italica* 38 (1961): 99–115.

Frec.1986.1
Freccero, John, *Dante: The Poetics of Conversion,* ed. Rachel Jacoff (Cambridge: Harvard University Press, 1986).

Fren.1964.1
French, Reginald, "Simony and Pentecost," *Annual Report of the Dante Society* 82 (1964): 3–17.

Fron.1998.1
Frongia, Eugenio N., "Canto III: The Gate of Hell," in *Lectura Dantis: "Inferno"* (Berkeley, Los Angeles: University of California Press, 1998), pp. 36–49.

Fubi.1966.1
Fubini, Mario, "Il peccato d'Ulisse" and "Il canto XXVI dell'*Inferno*," in his *Il peccato d'Ulisse e altri scritti danteschi* (Milan: Ricciardi, 1966), pp. 1–76.

Fubi.1967.1
Fubini, Mario, "*Inferno*: canto XXVIII," in *Lectura Dantis Scaligera*, dir. Mario Marcazzan (Florence: Le Monnier, 1967 [1962]), pp. 999–1021.

Gabr.1993.1
Gabriele, Trifon, *Annotationi nel Dante fatte con M. Trifon Gabriele in Bassano,* ed. Lino Pertile (Bologna: Commissione per i testi di lingua, 1993 [1525–27]).

Gagl.1994.1
Gagliardi, Antonio, *La tragedia intellettuale di Dante: Il "Convivio"* (Catanzaro: Pullano, 1994).

Gent.1997.1
Gentili, Sonia, " 'Ut canes infernales': Cerbero e le Arpie in Dante," in *I "monstra" nell' "Inferno" dantesco: tradizione e simbologie* (Spoleto: Centro italiano di studi sull'alto medioevo, 1997), pp. 177–203.

Gian.1999.1
Giannini, Stefano, "Post-1300 Time-References in Dante's *Inferno,"* unpublished paper prepared at Johns Hopkins University, 7 June 1999.

Gizz.1974.1
Gizzi, Corrado, *L'astronomia nel poema sacro* (Naples: Loffredo, 1974).

Gmel. 1951.1
Gmelin, Hermann, "Die Anrede an den Leser in der *Göttlichen Komödie,"* *Deutsches Dante-Jahrbuch* 30 (1951): 130–40.

Gmel.1966.1
Gmelin, Hermann, *Kommentar: die Hölle* (Stuttgart: Klett, 1966).

Gorn.1995.1
Gorni, Guglielmo, *Dante nella selva: il primo canto della "Commedia"* (Parma: Pratiche, 1995).

Gorn.1996.1
Gorni, Guglielmo, " 'Se quella con ch'io parlo non si secca' (*Inferno* XXXII 139)," in *Operosa parva per Gianni Antonini,* ed D. De Robertis & F. Gavazzeni (Verona: Valdonega, 1996), pp. 41–46.

Guyl.1972.1
Guyler, Sam, "Virgil the Hypocrite—Almost: A Re-interpretation of *Inferno* XXIII," *Dante Studies* 90 (1972): 25–42.

Hage.1997.1
Hagedorn, Suzanne C., "A Statian Model for Dante's Ulysses," *Dante Studies* 115 (1997): 19–43.

Hami.1921.1
Hamilton, George L., "The Gilded Leaden Cloaks of the Hypocrites (*Inferno,* XXIII, 58–66)," *Romanic Review* 12 (1921): 335–52.

Hart.1995.1
Hart, Thomas, " 'Per misurar lo cerchio' (*Par.* XXXIII 134) and Archimedes' *De mensura circuli:* Some Thoughts on Approximations to the Value of π," in *Dante e la scienza,* ed. P. Boyde and V. Russo (Ravenna: Longo, 1995), pp. 265–335.

Hatc.1964.1
Hatcher, Anna Granville, and Mark Musa, "Lucifer's Legs," *Publications of the Modern Language Association of America* 79 (1964): 191–99.

Hatc.1966.1
Hatcher, Anna Granville, and Mark Musa, "Lucifer's Legs, Again," *Modern Language Notes* 81 (1966): 88–91.

Hawk.1980.1
Hawkins, Peter S., "Virtuosity and Virtue: Poetic Self-Reflection in the *Commedia,*" *Dante Studies* 98 (1980): 1–18.

Heil.1983.1
Heilbronn, Denise, "Master Adam and the Fat-Bellied Lute (*Inf.* XXX)," *Dante Studies* 101 (1983): 51–65.

Herz.1978.1
Herzman, Ronald, and William A. Stephany, " 'O miseri seguaci': Sacramental Inversion in *Inferno* XIX," *Dante Studies* 96 (1978): 39–65.

Herz.1980.1
Herzman, Ronald B., "Cannibalism and Communion in *Inferno* XXXIII," *Dante Studies* 98 (1980): 53–78.

Higg.1975.1
Higgins, David H., "Cicero, Aquinas, and St. Matthew in *Inferno* XIII," *Dante Studies* 93 (1975): 61–94.

Holl.1969.1
Hollander, Robert, *Allegory in Dante's "Commedia"* (Princeton: Princeton University Press, 1969).

Holl.1975.1
Hollander, Robert, "*Purgatorio* II: Cato's Rebuke and Dante's *scoglio*," *Italica* 52 (1975): 348–63.

Holl.1976.1
Hollander, Robert, "Dante *Theologus-Poeta*," *Dante Studies* 94 (1976): 91–136.

Holl.1976.2
Hollander, Robert, "The Invocations of the *Commedia*," *Yearbook of Italian Studies* 3 (1976): 235–40.

Holl.1980.1
Hollander, Robert, "The Tragedy of Divination in *Inferno* XX," in *Studies in Dante* (Ravenna: Longo, 1980), pp. 131–218.

Holl.1980.2
Hollander, Robert, "Babytalk in Dante's *Commedia*," in *Studies in Dante* (Ravenna: Longo, 1980), pp. 115–29.

Holl.1982.1
Hollander, Robert, "Dante's 'Book of the Dead': A Note on *Inferno* XXIX, 57," *Studi Danteschi* 54 (1982): 31–51.

Holl.1983.1
Hollander, Robert, *Il Virgilio dantesco: tragedia nella "Commedia"* (Florence: Olschki, 1983).

Holl.1983.2
Hollander, Robert, "*Ad ira parea mosso*: God's Voice in the Garden," *Dante Studies* 101 (1983): 27–49.

Holl.1984.1
Hollander, Robert, "Dante on Horseback? (*Inferno* XII, 93–126)," *Italica* 61 (1984): 287–96.

Holl.1984.2
Hollander, Robert, "A Note on Dante's Missing Musaeus (*Inferno* IV, 140–141)," *Quaderni d'italianistica* 5 (1984): 217–21.

Holl.1984.3
Hollander, Robert, "Virgil and Dante as Mind-Readers (*Inferno* XXI and XXIII)," *Medioevo romanzo* 9 (1984): 85–100.

Holl.1984.4
Hollander, Robert, "Dante's 'Georgic' (*Inferno* XXIV, 1–18)," *Dante Studies* 102 (1984): 111–21.

Holl.1984.5
Hollander, Robert, "A Note on *Inferno* XXXIII, 37–74: Ugolino's Importunity," *Speculum* 59 (1984): 549–55.

Holl.1985.1
Hollander, Robert, "Dante's Pagan Past," *Stanford Italian Review* 5 (1985): 23–36.

Holl.1985.2
Hollander, Robert, "Ugolino's Supposed Cannibalism: A Bibliographical Note and Discussion," *Quaderni d'italianistica* 6 (1985): 64–81.

Holl.1986.1
Hollander, Robert, and Albert Rossi, "Dante's Republican Treasury," *Dante Studies* 104 (1986): 59–82.

Holl.1988.1
Hollander, Robert, "Dante's *Commedia* and the Classical Tradition: the Case of Virgil," in *The "Divine Comedy" and the Encyclopedia of Arts and Sciences: Acta of the International Dante Symposium, 13–16 November 1983, Hunter College, New York,* ed. G. Di Scipio and A. Scaglione (Amsterdam: John Benjamins, 1988), pp. 15–26.

Holl.1988.3
Hollander, Robert, "An Index of Hapax Legomena in Dante's *Commedia*," *Dante Studies* 106 (1988): 81–110.

Holl.1989.1
Hollander, Robert, "Dante and the Martial Epic," *Mediaevalia* 12 (1989): 62–91.

Holl.1990.2
Hollander, Robert, "The 'Canto of the Word' (*Inferno* 2)," *Lectura Dantis Newberryana*, ed. P. Cherchi and A. C. Mastrobuono, vol. II (Evanston: Northwestern University Press, 1990), pp. 95–119.

Holl.1992.1
Hollander, Robert, *Dante and Paul's "five words with understanding,"* Occasional Papers, No. 1, Center for Medieval and Early Renaissance Texts and Studies (Binghamton, N.Y.: Medieval and Renaissance Texts and Studies, 1992).

Holl.1992.2
Hollander, Robert, "Dante and Cino da Pistoia," *Dante Studies* 110 (1992): 201–31.

Holl.1993.1
Hollander, Robert, "Le opere di Virgilio nella *Commedia* di Dante," in *Dante e la "bella scola" della poesia: Autorità e sfida poetica*, ed. A. A. Iannucci (Ravenna: Longo, 1993), pp. 247–343.

Holl.1993.2
Hollander, Robert, *Dante's Epistle to Cangrande* (Ann Arbor: University of Michigan Press, 1993).

Holl.1993.3
Hollander, Robert, "Dante and his Commentators," in *The Cambridge Companion to Dante*, ed. R. Jacoff (Cambridge: Cambridge University Press, 1993), pp. 226–36.

Holl.1996.1
Hollander, Robert, "Dante's Harmonious Homosexuals (*Inferno* 16.7–90)," *Electronic Bulletin of the Dante Society of America* (June 1996).

Holl.1999.1
Hollander, Robert, "Dante's 'dolce stil novo' and the *Comedy*," in *Dante: mito e poesia. Atti del secondo Seminario dantesco internazionale,* ed. M. Picone and T. Crivelli (Florence: Cesati, 1999), pp. 263–81.

Holl.2000.1
Hollander, Robert, *Dante Alighieri* (Rome: Editalia, 2000).

Iann.1976.1
Iannucci, A. A., "Ulysses' *folle volo*: the Burden of History," *Medioevo romanzo* 3 (1976): 410–45.

Iann.1979.1
Iannucci, Amilcare, "Beatrice in Limbo: a Metaphoric Harrowing of Hell," *Dante Studies* 97 (1979): 23–45.

Iann.1979.2
Iannucci, Amilcare, "Limbo: the Emptiness of Time," *Studi Danteschi* 52 (1979–80): 69–128.

Iann.1980.1
Iannucci, Amilcare, "Forbidden Love: Metaphor and History," *Annali della Facoltà di Lettere e Filosofia, Università di Siena* 11 (1980): 341–58.

Iann.1982.1
Iannucci, Amilcare A., "*Inferno* XV.95–96: Fortune's Wheel and the Villainy of Time," *Quaderni d'italianistica* 3 (1982): 1–11.

Iann.1992.1
Iannucci, Amilcare, "The Gospel of Nicodemus in Medieval Italian Literature," *Quaderni d'italianistica* 14 (1992): 191–220.

Iann.1992.2
Iannucci, Amilcare, "Saturn in Dante," in *Saturn: from Antiquity to the Renaissance*, ed. M. Ciavolella and A. A. Iannucci (University of Toronto: Dovehouse, 1992), pp. 51–67.

Iann.1995.1
Iannucci, Amilcare A., "Musical Imagery in the Mastro Adamo Episode," in *Da una riva e dall'altra: Studi in onore di Antonio D'Andrea*, ed. Dante Della Terza (Florence: Edizioni Cadmo, 1995), pp. 103–18.

Jaco.1982.1
Jacoff, Rachel, "The Tears of Beatrice," *Dante Studies* 100 (1982): 1–12.

Jaco.1989.1
Jacoff, Rachel, and William Stephany, *Lectura Dantis Americana: "Inferno" II* (Philadelphia: University of Pennsylvania Press, 1989).

Jaco.1991.1
Jacoff, Rachel, and Jeffrey T. Schnapp, eds., *The Poetry of Allusion: Virgil and Ovid in Dante's "Commedia"* (Stanford: Stanford University Press, 1991).

Kaul.1968.1
Kaulbach, Ernest N., "*Inferno* XIX, 45: The 'Zanca' of Temporal Power," *Dante Studies* 86 (1968): 127–35.

Kay.1978.1
Kay, Richard, *Dante's Swift and Strong: Essays on "Inferno" XV* (Lawrence: The Regents Press of Kansas, 1978)

Kay.1978.2
Kay, Richard, "Dante's Double Damnation of Manto," *Res publica litterarum* 1 (1978): 113–28.

Kay.1980.1
Kay, Richard, "Two Pairs of Tricks: Ulysses and Guido in Dante's *Inferno* XXVI–XXVII," *Quaderni d'italianistica* 1 (1980): 107–24.

Klei.1974.1
Kleinhenz, Christopher, "Dante's Towering Giants," *Romance Philology* 27 (1974): 269–85.

Klei.1975.1
Kleinhenz, Christopher, "Infernal Guardians Revisited: 'Cerbero, il gran vermo' (*Inferno* VI, 22)," *Dante Studies* 93 (1975): 185–99.

Klei.1982.1
Kleinhenz, Christopher, "Iconographic Parody in *Inferno* XXI," *Res publica litterarum* 5 (1982): 125–37.

Klei.1986.1
Kleinhenz, Christopher, "Notes on Dante's Use of Classical Myths and the Mythographical Tradition," *Romance Quarterly* 33 (1986): 477–84.

Klei.1994.1
Kleiner, John, *Mismapping the Underworld: Daring and Error in Dante's "Comedy"* (Stanford: Stanford University Press, 1994).

Lans.1977.1
Lansing, Richard, *From Image to Idea: A Study of the Simile in Dante's "Commedia"* (Ravenna: Longo, 1977).

Lark.1962.1
Larkin, Neil M., "Another Look at Dante's Frog and Mouse," *Modern Language Notes* 77 (1962): 94–99.

Lark.1966.1
Larkin, Neil M., "*Inferno* XXIII, 4–9, Again," *Modern Language Notes* 81 (1966): 85–88.

Loga.1964.1
Logan, Terence P., "The Characterization of Ulysses in Homer, Virgil and Dante: A Study in Sources and Analogues," *Annual Report of the Dante Society* 82 (1964): 19–46.

Loon.1992.1
Looney, Dennis, "Believing in the Poet: *Inferno* XIII," *Allegorica* 13 (1992): 39–52.

Lucc.1991.1
Lucchesi, Valerio, "Giustizia divina e linguaggio umano: metafore e polisemie del contrapasso dantesco," *Studi Danteschi* 63 (1991 [1997]): 53–126.

Madd.1996.1
Maddox, Donald, "The Arthurian Intertexts of *Inferno* V," *Dante Studies* 114 (1996): 113–27.

Mall.1984.1
Mallin, Eric S., "The False Simile in Dante's *Commedia*," *Dante Studies* 102 (1984): 15–36.

Mand.1955.1
Mandruzzato, Enzo, "L'apologo 'della rana e del topo' e Dante," *Studi Danteschi* 33 (1955–56): 147–65.

Marc.1999.1
Marchesi, Simone, " 'Epicuri de grege porcus': Ciacco, Epicurus and Isidore of Seville," *Dante Studies* 117 (1999): 117–31.

Mari.1909.1
Marigo, Aristide, "Le *Georgiche* di Virgilio fonte di Dante," *Giornale dantesco* 17 (1909): 31–44.

Mark.1982.1
Markulin, Joseph, "Dante's Guido da Montefeltro: A Reconsideration," *Dante Studies* 100 (1982): 25–40.

Mazz.1965.1
Mazzoni, Francesco, "Saggio di un nuovo commento alla *Divina Commedia*: il Canto IV dell'*Inferno*," *Studi Danteschi* 42 (1965): 29–206.

Mazz.1967.1
Mazzoni, Francesco, *Saggio di un nuovo commento alla "Divina Commedia": "Inferno"—Canti I–III* (Florence: Sansoni, 1967).

Mazz.1967.2
Mazzoni, Francesco, *Il canto VI dell' "Inferno"* in *Nuove letture dantesche* (Florence: Le Monnier, 1967).

Mazz.1967.3
Mazzoni, Francesco, "Brunetto in Dante," intr. to *Il Tesoretto. Il Favolello* [of Brunetto Latini] (Alpignano: A. Tallone, 1967), pp. ix–xl.

Mazz.1975.1
Mazzotta, Giuseppe, "Poetics of History: *Inferno* XXVI," *Diacritics* (summer 1975): 37–44.

Mazz.1977.1
Mazzoni, Francesco, "Il canto V dell'*Inferno*" (Lectura Dantis Romana: Letture degli anni 1973–76; Rome: Bonacci, 1977), pp. 97–143.

Mazz.1979.1
Mazzotta, Giuseppe, *Dante, Poet of the Desert* (Princeton: Princeton University Press, 1979).

Mazz.1979.2
Mazzoni, Francesco, ed., Dante Alighieri, *Opere minori*, vol. II (Milan-Naples: Ricciardi, 1979), pp. 691–880.

Mazz.1981.1
Mazzoni, Francesco, "Dante's *battezzatori* (*Inf.* XIX, 16–21)," English outline of an unpublished talk presented to the Dante Society of America on the occasion of the 100th anniversary of the founding of the Society, Istituto Culturale Italiano, New York, 24 June 1981.

Mazz.1985.1
Mazzoni, Francesco, *Canto XI dell' "Inferno" (Lectura Dantis Neapolitana)*, dir. P. Giannantonio (Naples: Loffredo, 1985).

Mazz.1993.1
Mazzotta, Giuseppe, *Dante's Vision and the Circle of Knowledge* (Princeton: Princeton University Press, 1993).

Mazz.1995.1
Mazzoni, Francesco, "Tematiche politiche fra Guittone e Dante," in *Guittone d'Arezzo nel settimo centenario della morte: Atti del Convegno Internazionale di Arezzo (22–24 aprile 1994)*, ed. M. Picone (Florence: Franco Cesati, 1995), pp. 351–83.

McKe.1900.1
McKenzie, Kenneth, "Dante's References to Aesop," *Seventeenth Annual Report of the Dante Society* (1900): 1–14.

Meng.1979.1
Mengaldo, Pier Vincenzo, ed., *De vulgari Eloquentia,* in Dante Alighieri, *Opere minori,* vol. II (Milan and Naples: R. Ricciardi, 1979).

Merc.1984.1
Mercuri, Roberto, *Semantica di Gerione* (Rome: Bulzoni, 1984).

Merc.1998.1
Mercuri, Roberto, "Il canto II dell'*Inferno,*" *L'Alighieri* 11 (1998): 7–22.

Meye.1969.1
Meyer, Sharon E., "Dante's Alchemists," *Italian Quarterly* 12 (1969): 185–200.

Mont.1962.1
Montano, Rocco, *Storia della poesia di Dante,* vol. I (Naples: Quaderni di Delta, 1962).

Moor.1896.1
Moore, Edward, *Studies in Dante,* First Series: *Scripture and Classical Authors in Dante* (Oxford: Clarendon, 1969 [1896]).

Musa.1974.1
Musa, Mark, *Advent at the Gates* (Bloomington: Indiana University Press, 1974).

Musa.1977.1
Musa, Mark, "Virgil Reads the Pilgrim's Mind," *Dante Studies* 95 (1977): 149–52.

Muss.1978.1
Mussetter, Sally, "*Inferno* XXX: Dante's Counterfeit Adam," *Traditio* 34 (1978): 427–35.

Nard.1942.1
Nardi, Bruno, "La tragedia di Ulisse," in his *Dante e la cultura medievale* (Bari: Laterza, 1942), pp. 89–99.

Nard.1959.1
Nardi, Bruno, *La caduta di Lucifero e l'autenticità della "Quaestio de aqua et terra"* (Torino, S.E.I. [Lectura Dantis Romana]: 1959) [now in B. Nardi, *"Lecturae" e altri studi danteschi,* ed. R. Abardo (Firenze: Le Lettere, 1990), pp. 227–65].

Nard.1960.1
Nardi, Bruno, "Dante e Celestino V," in *Dal "Convivio" alla "Commedia"*, con premessa alla ristampa di O. Capitani (Rome: Istituto Storico Italiano per il Medio Evo, 1992 [1960]), pp. 315–30.

Neri.1937.1
Neri, Ferdinando, "La voce *lai* nei testi italiani," *Atti della Reale Accademia delle Scienze di Torino, classe di scienze morali, storiche e filologiche* 72 (1937): 105–19.

Noak.1968.1
Noakes, Susan, "Dino Compagni and the Vow in San Giovanni: *Inferno* XIX, 16–21," *Dante Studies* 86 (1968): 41–63.

Oert.1968.1
Oerter, Herbert L., "Campaldino, 1289," *Speculum* 43 (1968): 429–50.

Pado.1961.1
Padoan, Giorgio, "Colui che fece per viltà il gran rifiuto," *Studi Danteschi* 38 (1961): 75–128.

Pado.1964.1
Padoan, Giorgio, "Il liber *Esopi* e due episodi dell'*Inferno*," *Studi Danteschi* 41 (1964): 75–102.

Pado.1965.1
Padoan, Giorgio, "Dante di fronte all'umanesimo letterario," *Lettere Italiane* 17 (1965): 237–57.

Pado.1969.1
Padoan, Giorgio, "Il Limbo dantesco," *Lettere Italiane* 21 (1969): 369–88.

Pado.1977.1
Padoan, Giorgio, "Ulisse 'fandi fictor' e le vie della sapienza. Momenti di una tradizione (da Virgilio a Dante)," in his *Il pio Enea e l'empio Ulisse: Tradizione classica e intendimento medievale in Dante* (Ravenna: Longo, 1977 [1960]), pp. 170–99.

Pado.1993.1
Padoan, Giorgio, *Il lungo cammino del "Poema sacro": studi danteschi* (Florence: Olschki, 1993).

Pagl.1967.1
Pagliaro, Antonino, *Ulisse: ricerche semantiche sulla "Divina Commedia"* (Messina-Florence: D'Anna, 1967).

Para.1965.1
Paratore, Ettore, "Analisi 'retorica' del canto di Pier della Vigna," *Studi Danteschi* 42 (1965): 281–336.

Para.1965.2
Paratore, Ettore, "Lucano e Dante," in his *Antico e nuovo* (Caltanissetta: Sciascia, 1965), pp. 165–210.

Paro.1908.1
Parodi, E. G., "La critica della poesia classica nel ventesimo canto dell'*Inferno*," *Atene e Roma* 11 (1908): 183–95, 237–50.

Pasq.1985.1
Pasquazi, Silvio, "Sulla cosmogonia di Dante (*Inferno* XXXIV e *Questio de aqua et terra*)," in his *D'Egitto in Ierusalemme* (Rome: Bulzoni, 1985), pp. 121–56.

Pasq.1996.1
Pasquini, Emilio, "Il *Paradiso* e una nuova idea di figuralismo," *Intersezioni* 16 (1996): 417–27.

Pasq.1999.1
Pasquini, Emilio, "Lettura di *Inferno* XXXII," *L'Alighieri* 40 (1999): 29–37.

Pequ.1991.1
Pequigney, Joseph, "Sodomy in Dante's *Inferno* and *Purgatorio*,"
Representations 36 (1991): 22–42.

Pert.1979.1
Pertile, Lino, "Dante e l'ingegno di Ulisse," *Stanford Italian Review* 1 (1979):
35–65.

Pert.1980.1
Pertile, Lino, "Il nobile castello, il paradiso terrestre e l'umanesimo
dantesco," *Filologia e critica* 5 (1980): 1–29.

Pert.1982.1
Pertile, Lino, "*Inferno* XXVII. Il peccato di Guido da Montefeltro," *Atti
dell'Istituto Veneto di Scienze, Lettere ed Arti* 141 (1982–83): 147–78.

Pert.1991.1
Pertile, Lino, "*Canto-cantica-Comedía* e l'Epistola a Cangrande," *Lectura
Dantis [virginiana]* 9 (fall 1991): 103–23.

Pert.1998.1
Pertile, Lino, "Canto XXIX: Such Outlandish Wounds," in *Lectura Dantis:
"Inferno"*, ed. A. Mandelbaum, A. Oldcorn, C. Ross (Berkeley: University
of California Press, 1998), pp. 378–91.

Petr.1957.1
Petrocchi, Giorgio, "Intorno alla pubblicazione dell'*Inferno* e del
Purgatorio," *Convivium* 25 (1957): 652–69.

Petr.1966.1
Petrocchi, Giorgio, *Dante Alighieri: La Commedia secondo l'antica vulgata*,
ed. G. Petrocchi (Florence: Le Lettere, 1994 [1966]), vol. I, Introduzione.

Petr.1966.2
Petrocchi, Giorgio, *Dante Alighieri: La Commedia secondo l'antica vulgata*,
ed. G. Petrocchi (Florence: Le Lettere, 1994 [1966]), vol. II, *Inferno*.

Petr.1969.1
Petrocchi, Giorgio, *Itinerari danteschi*, Premessa a cura di C. Ossola (Milan:
Franco Angeli, 1994² [Bari: Laterza, 1969]).

Petr.1988.1
Petrocchi, Giorgio, "San Paolo in Dante," in *Dante e la Bibbia*,
ed. G. Barblan (Florence: Olschki, 1988), pp. 235–48.

Peza.1950.1
Pézard, André, *Dante sous la pluie de feu* (Paris: Vrin, 1950).

Peza.1958.1
Pézard, André, "Le Chant des géants," *Bulletin de la Société d'études
dantesques du Centre universitaire méditerranéen* 7 (1958): 53–72.

Pico.1989.1
Picone, Michelangelo, "Baratteria e stile comico in Dante," in *Studi
Americani su Dante*, ed. G. C. Alessio e R. Hollander (Milan: Franco
Angeli, 1989): pp. 63–86.

Pico.1991.1
Picone, Michelangelo, "La *lectio Ovidii* nella *Commedia*. la ricezione
dantesca delle *Metamorfosi*," *Le Forme e la Storia* 3 (1991): 35–52.

Pico.1991.2
Picone, Michelangelo, "Dante, Ovidio e il mito di Ulisse," *Lettere Italiane*
43 (1991): 500–16.

Pico.1993.1
Picone, Michelangelo, "L'Ovidio di Dante," in A. Iannucci, ed., *Dante e la
"bella scola" della poesia* (Ravenna: Longo, 1993), pp. 107–44.

Pico.1994.1
Picone, Michelangelo, "Dante argonauta: la ricezione dei miti ovidiani
nella *Commedia*," in M. Picone and B. Zimmermann, eds., *Ovidius
redivivus: von Ovid zu Dante* (Stuttgart: M&P Verlag, 1994), pp. 173–202.

Pico.1995.1
"Guittone e Dante" [three articles, by Guglielmo Gorni, Roberto
Antonelli, and Francesco Mazzoni], in *Guittone d'Arezzo nel settimo
centenario della morte: Atti del Convegno Internazionale di Arezzo (22–24 aprile
1994)*, ed. M. Picone (Florence: Franco Cesati, 1995), pp. 307–83.

Pine.1961.1
Pine-Coffin, R. S., tr., St. Augustine, *Confessions* (Baltimore: Penguin, 1961).

Pogg.1957.1
Poggioli, Renato, "Tragedy or Romance? A Reading of the Paolo and Francesca Episode in Dante's *Inferno*," *Publications of the Modern Language Association* 72 (1957): 313–58.

Porc.1997.1
Porcelli, Bruno, "Peccatum linguae, modello mosaico, climax narrativa nel canto di Ulisse" [1991], in his *Nuovi studi su Dante e Boccaccio con analisi della "Nencia"* (Pisa: Istituti editoriali e poligrafici internazionali, 1997), pp. 9–26.

Porc.1997.2
Porcelli, Bruno, "Beatrice nei commenti danteschi del Landino e del Vellutello" [1994], in his *Nuovi studi su Dante e Boccaccio con analisi della "Nencia"* (Pisa: Istituti editoriali e poligrafici internazionali, 1997), pp. 57–78.

Prat.1881.1
Prato, Stanislao, *Caino e le spine secondo Dante e la tradizione popolare* (Ancona: Garzanti, 1881).

Pucc.1994.1
Puccetti, Valter, "La galleria fisiognomica del canto XX dell'*Inferno*," *Filologia e critica* 19 (1994): 177–210.

Rabu.1961.1
Rabuse, Georg, "Dantes Antäus-Episode, der Höllengrund und das *Somnium Scipionis*," *Archiv für Kulturgeschichte* 43 (1961): 18–51.

Raim.1967.1
Raimondi, Ezio, "I canti bolognesi dell'*Inferno* dantesco," in *Dante e Bologna nei tempi di Dante* (Bologna: Commissione per i Testi di Lingua, 1967), pp. 239–48.

Rest.1977.1
Resta, Gianvito, "Il canto XIII dell'*Inferno*," in *"Inferno": letture degli anni 1973–1976*, ed. S. Zennaro (Rome: Bonacci, 1977), pp. 335–36.

Reyn.1995.1
Reynolds, Suzanne, "*Orazio satiro* (*Inferno* IV, 89): Dante, the Roman satirists, and the Medieval Theory of Satire," in *"Libri poetarum in quattuor species dividuntur": Essays on Dante and "genre,"* ed. Z. G. Barański, *The Italianist,* no. 15 (1995), Supplement[2]: 128–44.

Russ.1966.1
Russo, Vittorio, "Il 'dolore' del conte Ugolino," *Sussidi di esegesi dantesca* (Napoli: Liguori, 1966), pp. 147–81.

Ryan.1982.2
Ryan., C. J., "*Inferno* XXI: Virgil and Dante: A Study in Contrasts," *Italica* 59 (1982): 16–31.

Samu.1944.1
Samuel, Irene, "Semiramis in the Middle Age: The History of a Legend," *Medievalia et Humanistica* 2 (1944): 32–44.

Sang.1958.1
Sanguineti, Edoardo, "Dante, *praesens historicum*," *Lettere Italiane* 10 (1958): 263–87.

Sang.1962.1
Sanguineti, Edoardo, *Interpretazione di Malebolge* (Florence: Olschki, 1962).

Sant.1923.1
Santini, Pietro, "Sui fiorentini 'che fur sì degni,' " *Studi Danteschi* 6 (1923): 25–44.

Saro.1971.1
Sarolli, Gian Roberto, *Prolegomena alla "Divina Commedia"* (Florence: Olschki, 1971).

Scot.1971.1
Scott, John A., "*Inferno* XXVI: Dante's Ulysses," *Lettere Italiane* 23 (1971): 145–86.

Scot.1977.1
Scott, John A., *Dante magnanimo; studi sulla "Commedia"* (Florence: Olschki, 1977).

Scot.1979.1
Scott, John A., "Dante's Francesca and the Poet's Attitude toward Courtly Literature," *Reading Medieval Studies* 5 (1979): 4–20.

Scot.1985.1
Scott, John A., "Treachery in Dante," in *Studies in the Italian Renaissance: Essays in Memory of Arnolfo B. Ferruolo* (Naples: Società Editrice Napoletana, 1985), pp. 27–42.

Seri.1994.1
Seriacopi, Massimo, *All'estremo della "Prudentia": L'Ulisse di Dante* (Rome: Zauli, 1994).

Shan.1975.1
Shankland, Hugh, "Dante 'Aliger,' " *Modern Language Review* 70 (1975): 764–85.

Shan.1977.1
Shankland, Hugh, "Dante 'Aliger' and Ulysses," *Italian Studies* 32 (1977): 21–40.

Shap.1974.1
Shapiro, Marianne, "The Fictionalization of Bertran de Born (*Inf.* XXVIII)," *Dante Studies* 92 (1974): 107–16.

Shap.1975.1
Shapiro, Marianne, "Semiramis in *Inferno* V," *Romance Notes* 16 (1975): 455–56.

Shoa.1975.1
Shoaf, R. A., "Dante's *colombi* and the Figuralism of Hope in the *Divine Comedy*," *Dante Studies* 93 (1975): 27–59.

Shoa.1983.1
Shoaf, R. A., *Dante, Chaucer, and the Currency of the Word* (Norman, Okla.: Pilgrim Books, 1983).

Silv. 1931.1
Silverstein, H. Theodore, "The Weeping Statue and Dante's *Gran Veglio*," *Harvard Studies and Notes in Philology and Literature* 13 (1931): 165–84.

Silv. 1937.1
Silverstein, Theodore, "Did Dante Know the Vision of St. Paul?" *Harvard Studies and Notes in Philology and Literature* 19 (1937): 231–47.

Silv. 1997.1
Silverstein, Theodore, and Anthony Hilhorst, eds., *Apocalypse of Paul: A New Critical Edition of Three Long Latin Versions* (Geneva: Patrick Cramer, 1997).

Simo. 1993.1
Simonelli, Maria Picchio, *Lectura Dantis Americana: "Inferno" III* (Philadelphia: University of Pennsylvania Press, 1993).

Sing. 1965.1
Singleton, Charles S., "*Inferno* XIX: O Simon Mago!" *Modern Language Notes* 80 (1965): 92–99.

Sowe. 1983.1
Sowell, Madison U., "A Bibliography of the Dantean Simile to 1981," *Dante Studies* 101 (1983): 167–80.

Spag. 1997.1
Spaggiari, Barbara, "Antecedenti e modelli tipologici nella letteratura in lingua d'oïl," in *I "monstra" nell' "Inferno" dantesco: tradizione e simbologie* (Spoleto: Centro italiano di studi sull'alto medioevo, 1997), pp. 107–40.

Sper. 1948.1
Speroni, Charles, "Dante's Prophetic Morning-Dreams," *Studies in Philology* 45 (1948): 50–59.

Spit. 1942.1
Spitzer, Leo, "Speech and Language in *Inferno* XIII," *Italica* 19 (1942): 77–104.

Spit.1943.1
Spitzer, Leo, "Two Dante Notes: I. An Autobiographical Incident in *Inferno* XIX; II. Libicocco," *Romanic Review* 34 (1943): 248–62.

Spit.1944.1
Spitzer, Leo, "The Farcical Elements in *Inferno*, Cantos XXI–XXIII," *Modern Language Notes* 59 (1944): 83–88.

Spit.1955.1
Spitzer, Leo, "The Addresses to the Reader in the *Commedia*," *Italica* 32 (1955): 143–66.

Stab.1983.1
Stabile, Giorgio, "Cosmologia e teologia nella *Commedia*: la caduta di Lucifero e il rovesciamento del mondo," *Letture classensi* 12 (1983): 139–73.

Stef. 1993.1
Stefanini, Ruggero, "In nota a un commento," *Lectura Dantis [virginiana]* 13 (1993): 78–89.

Step.1982.1
Stephany, Wm. A., "Pier della Vigna's Self-fulfilling Prophecies: the 'Eulogy' of Frederick II and *Inferno* 13," *Traditio* 38 (1982): 193–212.

Stie.1988.1
Stierle, Karlheinz, "Odysseus und Aeneas: Eine typologische Konfiguration in Dantes *Divina Commedia*," in *Das fremde Wort: Studien zur Interdependenz von Texten, Festschrift für Karl Maurer zum 60. Geburtstag,* ed. Ilse Nolting-Hauff & Joachim Schulze (Amsterdam: B. R. Grüner, 1988), pp. 111–54.

Stul.1991.1
Stull, William, and Robert Hollander, "The Lucanian Source of Dante's Ulysses," *Studi Danteschi* 63 (1991 [1997]): 1–52.

Swin.1962.1
Swing, T. K., *The Fragile Leaves of the Sibyl* (Westminster, Md.: The Newman Press, 1962).

Taaf.1822.1
Taaffe, J., *A Comment on the "Divine Comedy" of Dante Alighieri* (London: John Murray, 1822).

Tavo.1992.1
Tavoni, Mirko, "Effrazione battesimale tra i simoniaci (*Inf.* XIX 13–21)," *Rivista di letteratura italiana* 10 (1992): 457–512.

Terd.1973.1
Terdiman, Richard, "Problematic Virtuosity: Dante's Depiction of the Thieves (*Inferno* XXIV–XXV)," *Dante Studies* 91 (1973): 27–45.

Thom.1967.1
Thompson, David, "Dante's Ulysses and the Allegorical Journey," *Dante Studies* 85 (1967): 33–58.

Thom.1974.1
Thompson, David, *Dante's Epic Journeys* (Baltimore: Johns Hopkins University Press, 1974).

Thor.1923.1
Thorndike, Lynn, *A History of Magic and Experimental Science* (New York: Macmillan, 1923).

Toya.1965.1
Toja, Gianluigi, "La Fortuna," *Studi Danteschi* 42 (1965): 247–60.

Trio.1998.1
Triolo, Alfred A., "Malice and Mad Bestiality," in *Lectura Dantis: "Inferno"*, ed. A. Mandelbaum, A. Oldcorn, C. Ross (Berkeley: University of California Press, 1998), pp. 150–64.

Vall.1935.1
Valli, Luigi, "Ulisse e la tragedia intellettuale di Dante," in his *La struttura morale dell'universo dantesco* (Rome: Ausonia, 1935), pp. 26–40.

Vazz.1998.1
Vazzana, Steno, "Il 'disdegnoso gusto' di Pier de le Vigne," *L'Alighieri* 11 (1998): 91–94.

Vill.1984.1
Villa, Claudia, *La "lectura Terentii"* (Padua: Antenore, 1984), esp. pp. 137–89.

Vill.1993.1
Villa, Claudia, "Dante lettore di Orazio," in *Dante e la "bella scola" della poesia: Autorità e sfida poetica*, ed. A. A. Iannucci (Ravenna: Longo, 1993), pp. 87–106.

Vina.1960.1
Vinay, Gustavo, "Dante e Ulisse," *Nova Historia* 12 (1960): 4–20.

VonR.1986.1
Von Richthofen, Erich, "La dimensión atlántica del Ulises y del Alejandro medievales en el contexto del mito herácleo gaditano," in *Philologica hispaniensia in honorem Manuel Alvar*, Vol. III (Madrid: Gredos, 1986), pp. 423–34.

VonR.1986.2
Von Richthofen, Erich, "¿Deriva de Tácito el episodio atlántico de Ulises (Dante, *Inferno*, XXVI, 83 y ss.)?" in *Studia in honorem prof. M. De Riquer*, Vol. I (Barcelona: Crema, 1986), pp. 579–83.

Wilh.1960.1
Wilhelm, Julius, "Die Gestalt des Odysseus in Dantes *Göttlicher Komödie*," *Deutsches Dante-Jahrbuch* 38 (1960): 75–93.

Wilk.1926.1
Wilkins, E. H., "The Prologue of the *Divine Comedy*," *Annual Report of the Dante Society* 42 (1926): 1–7.